DISORDERS OF
BEHAVIORAL AND EMOTIONAL REGULATION
IN THE FIRST YEARS OF LIFE

*Early risks and intervention in the developing
parent–infant relationship*

Mechthild Papoušek , Michael Schieche, and Harald Wurmser (Eds.)

Translated by Kenneth Kronenberg

ZERO
TO
THREE®

National Center for Infants,
Toddlers, and Families

Washington, DC

Published by

ZERO TO THREE
2000 M St., NW, Suite 200
Washington, DC 20036-3307
(202) 638-1144
Toll-free orders (800) 899-4301
Fax: (202) 638-0851
Web: http://www.zerotothree.org

National Center for Infants,
Toddlers, and Families

The mission of the ZERO TO THREE Press is to publish authoritative research, practical resources, and new ideas for those who work with and care about infants, toddlers, and their families. Books are selected for publication by an independent Editorial Board. The views contained in this book are those of the authors and do not necessarily reflect those of ZERO TO THREE: National Center for Infants, Toddlers and Families, Inc.

These materials are intended for education and training to help promote a high standard of care by professionals. Use of these materials is voluntary and their use does not confer any professional credentials or qualification to take any registration, certification, board or licensure examination, and neither confers nor infers competency to perform any related professional functions.

The user of these materials is solely responsible for compliance with all local, state or federal rules, regulations or licensing requirements. Despite efforts to ensure that these materials are consistent with acceptable practices, they are not intended to be used as a compliance guide and are not intended to supplant or to be used as a substitute for or in contravention of any applicable local, state or federal rules, regulations or licensing requirements. ZERO TO THREE expressly disclaims any liability arising from use of these materials in contravention of such rules, regulations or licensing requirements.

The views expressed in these materials represent the opinions of the respective authors. Publication of these materials does not constitute an endorsement by ZERO TO THREE of any view expressed herein, and ZERO TO THREE expressly disclaims any liability arising from any inaccuracy or misstatement.

Cover and text design and composition: Design Consultants

"Regulationsstörungen der frühen Kindheit. Frühe Risiken und Hilfen im Entwicklungskontext der Eltern-Kind-Beziehungen". Bern: Hans Huber, 2004

Library of Congress Cataloging-in-Publication Data

Regulationsstörungen der frühen Kindheit. English.
   Disorders of behavioral and emotional regulation in the first years of life : early risks and intervention in the developing parent-infant relationship / Mechthild Papoušek, Michael Schieche, and Harald Wurmser (eds.) ; translated by Kenneth Kronenberg.
      p. ; cm.
   Includes bibliographical references and index.
   ISBN 978-1-934019-17-7
   1. Infant psychiatry. 2. Behavior disorders in children. 3. Emotional problems of children. 4. Emotions in infants. 5. Child psychotherapy—Parent participation. 6. Object relations (Psychoanalysis) 7. Parent and infant. I. Papoušek, Mechthild. II. Schieche, Michael. III. Wurmser, Harald. IV. Title.
   [DNLM: 1. Infant Behavior—psychology. 2. Parent-Child Relations. 3. Emotions. 4. Infant. 5. Object Attachment. WS 105.5.F2 R344 2004a]
   RJ502.5.R4413 2008
   618.92'89--dc22
                                    2007039364

For permission for academic photocopying (for course packets, study materials, etc.) by copy centers, educators, or university bookstores or libraries, of this and other ZERO TO THREE materials, please contact Copyright Clearance Center, 222 Rosewood Drive, Danvers, MA 01923; phone, (978) 750-8400; fax, (978) 750-4744; or visit its Web site at www.copyright.com.

10 9 8 7 6 5 4 3 2 1

Printed in the United States of America

Suggested citations:

Book citation: Papoušek, M., Schieche, M., & Wurmser, H. (Eds.). (2008). *Disorders of behavioral and emotional regulation in the first years of life: Early risks and intervention in the developing parent–infant relationship* (K. Kronenberg, Trans.). Washington, DC: ZERO TO THREE. (Original work published 2004).

Chapter citation: Resch, F. (2008). Developmental psychopathology in early childhood: Interdisciplinary challenges. In M. Papoušek, M. Schieche, & H. Wurmser (Eds.). *Disorders of behavioral and emotional regulation in the first years of life: Early risks and intervention in the developing parent–infant relationship* (K. Kronenberg, Trans.), (pp. 13–25). Washington, DC: ZERO TO THREE. (Original work published 2004).

". . . much flows between people, back and forth.
The dramatic persona is always between them.
. . . Each belongs to the other, and the best
lies between them: it is momentary and forever,
and here is room for music."

Hugo von Hofmannsthal, 1911
Unwritten epilogue to the Strauss opera "Der Rosenkavalier"

CONTENTS

FOREWORD

Emotional regulation, the ability to modulate arousal, is at the heart of adaptive development in infancy, with links to disorders of sleeping, feeding, attention, and affect. From a developmental perspective, these individual disorders are closely related in that they reflect an imbalance between reactive and regulatory processes, and a mismatch between the developing infant and parents.

Learning to regulate emotions is a primary task of the infant's first year that continues well into the second and third years of life, through the interplay of ongoing parent–infant interaction in conjunction with the infant's developing biological systems. Although some early regulation difficulties resolve in the course of this process, when parents are able to adapt their behavior to the infant's unique characteristics, others do not, resulting in disordered interactions, maladaptive patterns of development, and family crises. Because the mother–infant system and, often, the broader family system, both influence and are influenced by these regulatory disorders, professionals must treat them as disorders of the system, rather than disorders of the infant or parent alone.

The editors of this volume, Mechthild Papoušek, Michael Schieche, and Harald Wurmser, have drawn on the concepts, methods, and findings of several decades of research on infant emotional regulation to ameliorate problems of regulation and behavior through a transactional, system-based approach. In this volume, they and their contributors describe their clinical interventions and document their effectiveness through detailed case studies and empirical data collected over 15 years. Like the development of emotional regulation, their clinical approach to treating disorders of emotional regulation is transactional, with changes that occur in the interplay of infant and parents in response to intervention prompting changes in the intervention itself. To foster attunement between infant and parents, the clinician needs to be attuned to the system as it is transformed and adapt the intervention to match the new pattern of interaction.

An essential component of the intervention process is establishing goodness of fit, a match between characteristics of infants and parental responses that allows parents to compensate for what their babies are unable to do on their own. In turn, matching requires a precise analysis of parent–infant communication in order for the clinician to identify what needs to change in the system for this compensatory process to operate. Implicit in this approach is recognition of individual variability in what both infant and parent bring to their relationship. On the infant's side, an extreme temperament characterized by intense negative reactions to everyday experiences creates an imbalance by requiring more of the infant's inhibitory processes, and of parents whose task is to help maintain balance. For most parents, accommodating to their infants' negativity is challenging, but it is doable with moderate support in the form of information (that the infant's temperament is not the parents' fault and that it will modulate as the infant develops with the parents' assistance) and regular breaks from caring for their infants to prevent exhaustion and burnout. For others, parenting a negatively reactive infant is overwhelming because of their own history of poor parenting, together with currently stressful life circumstances. In these instances, the intervention must be broader in scope and may include assistance in obtaining the basic necessities of food and housing, as well as therapy to help parents work out strained or abusive partner relationships or to develop the emotional competencies that support intuitive parenting. Consistent with several recent studies of highly negatively reactive infants and their parents, the contributors describe how the confluence of extreme infant temperamental characteristics and disrupted parenting creates high risk of system disruption. By providing parents with resources, intervention helps them to overcome the imbalance that ensues and to foster adaptive development in their infants.

Emotional regulation during infancy sets the stage for future development in the individual and in the system. Although interventions later in childhood may be helpful in ameliorating emotional problems that have their roots in infancy, the cycle of negative reciprocity that develops during infancy may be increasingly difficult to reverse within the parent–child system. Thus, this book is an important resource for psychologists, physicians, nurses, day care staff and teachers, social workers, and psychiatrists who work with parents and infants during the first 3 years of life. It has a great deal also to offer infancy researchers who may be interested in the fruits of their investigations for improving the well-being of parents and children and supporting their development.

Susan C. Crockenberg, PhD
Professor of Psychology
University of Vermont
Burlington, VT
January 19, 2007

PREFACE

What could be more enchanting than to take a crying baby in one's arms and feel him relax, snuggle in, and slowly calm down? And what is more disappointing, discouraging, and perhaps even hurtful than to hold a baby who, for no apparent reason, cries inconsolably, body stiff, and seems to be unreachable despite all of one's best efforts? An infant's crying has two faces: It may elicit tenderness and desire to soothe, or helplessness and rage. It can be a signal that encourages attachment or one that jeopardizes the early relationship by triggering depression and, in some cases, even neglect or abuse.

For every five healthy babies and infants, there is at least one who brings unusual stresses for its parents with behaviors such as inconsolable crying, sleep disorders, refusal to eat, chronic moodiness, incessant demands for attention, fearful clinging, or tantrums. Such children place considerable demands on parents' relational and child-rearing capacities, causing them to question their competence in the parental role. They become afraid to face their difficult baby, this strong-willed little tyrant in their midst. Many of these parents feel alone with their problem, blamed by their families, isolated from their neighbors and surroundings, cut off, and not taken seriously enough by child specialists.

In 1991, we inaugurated the Munich Interdisciplinary Research and Intervention Program for Fussy Babies at the Center for Social Pediatrics in Munich, Germany. The goal, modest at first, was to decode the enigma of infant colic and to offer parents timely support. An additional goal was even more challenging: to gain access as early as possible to disorders of parent–infant communication and the resulting distress in these relationships. We set out to study the conditions that lead to these problems, to identify early signs of trouble and the effects on the parent–infant relationship, and to elaborate on approaches and methods for diagnosis, targeted treatment, and preventive intervention. Building on the concepts and methods of interdisciplinary infancy research, we designed a clinical research paradigm in which disorders of behavioral and emotional regulation could be systematically analyzed at their onset within the developmental context of the parent–child relationships. The interdisciplinary team immediately found itself faced with a number of interesting challenges that had not been anticipated. Among these was the unexpectedly widespread need for help, primarily with regard to older infants and toddlers who, in the context of other symptoms, continued to fuss and cry excessively. Additional challenges arose from the need to provide help for the large number of these parents suffering from multiple psychosocial burdens and psychological disorders.

During the first years, scientific analyses focused on early excessive crying. Later, in 1999, a grant from the Bavarian State Ministry of Labor and Social Affairs, Family, Women, and Health made it possible for us to analyze a comprehensive sample of 701 referred families with children in the age range of birth to 3 years. The results provided the basis for a comprehensive research symposium on early regulation disorders in 2002 and were later published as a professional handbook in German in 2004. It is hoped that this translation of the original book will make this information available to a wider, more international audience.

Over the course of data analysis, the problems of colicky babies were given a new name: *disorders of behavioral and emotional regulation.* Conceptually, this was an important detail, as this diagnosis neither blames parents for early caregiving failures nor prejudiciously labels the baby. Rather, it draws attention to the need for a systems approach that involves the interaction of infant and parents in facing the regulatory developmental tasks of early childhood adaptation. The problems reside in dysfunctional parent–infant interactions to which each partner contributes.

This book summarizes current scientific and clinical evidence of the most frequent disorders of behavioral and emotional regulation typically observed during the first years of life within the developing systems of parent–infant communication, attachment, and early relationships. They comprise a colorful spectrum of behavioral syndromes ranging from early excessive crying, sleep and feeding disorders, failure to thrive, and problems of attentional and emotional regulation, to disturbances in the regulatory balance between attachment and exploration and/or between dependence and autonomy in the second and third years of life. The book combines contributions by internationally well-known authors from a variety of disciplines and current knowledge from the international interdisciplinary literature, as well as clinical results and long-term diagnostic and therapeutic experience from the Munich Program. The authors try to build a bridge from current empirical research and new clinical data to practical applications of this knowledge for diagnostics, counseling, and parent–infant psychotherapy, including detailed case presentations for illustration.

The first section, *Regulation Disorders in an Arena of Interdisciplinary Discourse,* deals with the theoretical conceptualization and classification of disorders of behavioral and emotional regulation, situating them between normal developmental perturbations on the one side and early manifestations of psychopathology on the other.

From the perspective of developmental pediatrics, Remo H. Largo and Caroline Benz-Castellano provide evidence of amazing individual variability among children, based on longitudinal studies in normal populations using as examples the development of sleeping through the night, sleeping in the parents' bed, and bladder control. They argue that early problematic behavior and age-related developmental perturbations such as crying, sleeping, or feeding problems result from a misfit between parental expectations and child-rearing attitudes on the one side and the infant's individual maturational and constitutional dispositions and needs on the other. The authors use this evidence as a basis on which to propose practical applications for early preventive intervention.

From the perspective of developmental psychopathology and child psychiatry, Franz Resch discusses recent trends in child and adolescent psychiatry such as the shift from traditional medical concepts of psychiatric disease to more developmentally oriented transactional conceptualizations of disorders and from an emphasis on categorical diagnostic classifications to more dimensional approaches. He particularly stresses the importance of early disorders of affect regulation and development of self, which may originate and progress as a result of transactions between temperamental characteristics of the child, psychological disturbance or trauma of primary caregivers, and contextual factors.

The chapter by Harald Wurmser and Mechthild Papoušek presents characteristics of the entire sample of 701 infants and toddlers who were examined and treated at the Munich Program between 1994 and 1997. The authors summarize basic sociodemographic characteristics as well as incidence of somatic and psychosocial risk factors in these children and their families. They also report data related to the most frequent clinical syndromes and their age-related distributions, co-occurrences, and common characteristics.

On the basis of the preceding chapters, Mechthild Papoušek introduces the central concept of the book, that of disorders of behavioral and emotional regulation in infancy. Using a dynamic developmental systems approach, she draws connections among disorders involving crying, feeding, sleeping, and other behavioral problems in infancy. She then provides a developmental model that accounts for the unique characteristics of infant development, in particular the close interrelations between development of infant mental health, attachment, and parent–infant relationships. This model integrates basic insights and knowledge from dynamic systems theory and infancy research with clinical and psychodynamic concepts from the field of infant mental health. The diagnosis *disorder of behavioral and emotional regulation* signifies a new kind of patient: the parent–infant system. Residing neither in the infant alone nor in one or both parents alone, the problems originate, become exacerbated, and tend to persist in the developmental context of everyday parent–infant interactions and parent–child relationships.

The four chapters of the second section, *Age-Related Clinical Syndromes*, summarize current empirical knowledge and clinical experience in relation to the main behavioral syndromes observed in the first years of life, such as excessive and inconsolable crying, sleep disorders, feeding disorders, and failure to thrive, and typical age-related syndromes of emotional and behavioral regulation in the second and third years of life, such as excessive clinging, anxiousness and social withdrawal, excessive defiance, and aggressive/oppositional behavior. Each syndrome is illustrated by a detailed case presentation. Building on clinical data from the Munich Program and on the current literature, the authors present the clinical syndrome, its prevalence, developmental origins and etiology, typical interaction patterns, prognosis, and specific diagnostic and therapeutic interventions.

The third section, *Parent–Infant Counseling and Psychotherapy*, emphasizes general aspects of counseling and treatment. Following an introduction to the qualitative criteria of therapeutic evaluation and evidence-based treatment approaches, Klaus Sarimski provides a meta-analysis of relevant therapeutic interventions by summarizing recent critical surveys of behavioral treatment approaches to excessive crying and sleep and feeding disorders.

Renate Barth and Tamara Jacubeit focus on the psychodynamic aspects of sleep and feeding disorders. Barth introduces Selma Fraiberg's concept of "ghosts in the nursery" and describes the overall framework and goals of parent–infant psychotherapy. These are elucidated by vivid case vignettes that illustrate psychodynamic themes, neurotic conflicts, and defense mechanisms that frequently lie hidden behind severe and persistent sleep disorders. Jacubeit tracks Fraiberg's "ghosts" in another context, the family dining table. She provides impressive evidence of unconscious reenactments of relational patterns and unresolved conflict from the parents' past observed in dyadic feeding interactions or family interactions at mealtime. In several case vignettes, she illustrates the procedures of video-supported parent–infant psychotherapy, aiming at expelling the ghost from these problematic feeding interactions.

Ruth Wollwerth de Chuquisengo and Mechthild Papoušek present the integrative communication-centered approach to parent–infant counseling and psychotherapy as developed in the Munich Program. The therapeutic concept is based on the developmental systems approach described in chapter 4. Parent–infant communication serves as the main focus and port of entry into the system, representing the interface between the behavioral and representational levels of parent–infant interactions. The authors describe the basic modules, which include developmental counseling, supportive psychotherapy, video-supported guidance in parent–infant communication, and psychodynamic communication-centered relational therapy.

The authors of the fourth section, *Early Identification of Long-Term Risks and Preventive Intervention*, deal with the long-term outcome and prognosis of regulation disorders and discuss early predictors as well as starting points and opportunities for preventive interventions. Harald Wurmser and coworkers begin their chapter with a critical review of prospective longitudinal studies of community-based and referred clinical samples of infants with early excessive crying. They report on a 30-month follow-up of clinically referred infants with early excessive crying from the Munich Program. The majority of these infants had regulatory problems in more than one domain, and their crying had persisted beyond 3 months of age under conditions of various accumulated risk factors. The data point to a constellation of risk factors that may lead to internalizing and externalizing behavior problems for these children in the third year of life.

Manfred Laucht and coworkers from the Mannheim longitudinal risk study report remarkably similar results. The authors provide impressive evidence that 3-month-old infants with multiple regulatory problems are at increased risk of unfavorable developmental outcomes even as late as the ages of 8 and 11 years. These risks are particularly evident under conditions involving both early dysfunctional mother–infant interactions and significant psychosocial risk factors.

Mechthild Papoušek focuses on a subgroup of infants with multiple regulatory problems who are noteworthy because of their dysphoric restlessness, problems of attention regulation, and disinterest in play. On the basis of clinical observation of an increasing number of individual cases from the Munich Program and recent research on the early development of attention regulation, the author discusses potential developmental links between this syndrome and attention deficit/hyperactivity disorder (ADHD) in school-age children. She indicates starting points for targeted preventive interventions at the level of dysfunctional parent–infant play and problems of sensory integration in the early years.

On behalf of the staff of the Munich Program, we wish to thank Hubertus von Voss, director of the Munich Center for Social Pediatrics and the District Administration of Oberbayern for helping the program to come into being and continue to grow. Meanwhile, the program has become a firmly established source of support and assistance for infants and their families with early regulatory and relational disorders. We particularly wish to thank the Bavarian State Ministry of Labor and Social Affairs, Family, Women, and Health for a generous 2-year research grant in 1999–2000.

We owe much gratitude to our primary mentor, teacher, adviser, and companion over many years, Hanuš Papoušek. We thank Renate Barth, Remo Largo, Manfred Laucht, Franz Resch, and their co-authors, who enriched and complemented the book with their contributions. We also greatly appreciate the work of our former and present staff members, sensory integration therapists, and social workers at the Center for Social Pediatrics for their personal involvement in the elaboration and application of the diagnostic and therapeutic concepts, for their diligent documentation and acquisition of data, and for their contributions as authors and co-authors to the contents of this book. In addition to the authors represented in the book, we are particularly indebted to all of our co-workers whose efforts helped make the Munich Program a success; the valuable study results of many of our graduate and postgraduate students found their way into individual chapters, for which we are very appreciative.

The English translation of our original book has been made possible by ZERO TO THREE Press, with the early support and valuable assistance of Emily Fenichel prior to her untimely death. We extend our deep appreciation to Emily and also to Michelle Martineau Green who continued to see the effort through to completion. To our translator, Kenneth Kronenberg, we express our sincere thanks for his tireless work and stimulating communication with us about appropriate terminology and concepts to be used in the English version. We owe special gratitude to Lynne Sanford Koester for her immediate readiness to help out with the final editing of the translation. The close cooperation and creative exchange of ideas with her helped us to find the most effective ways of articulating our concepts and results for an English audience.

In regard to the editorial style of the book, we have chosen to alternate use of gender-based pronouns with each chapter rather than using the more awkward he/she combinations. It should also be noted that the names and all identifying information related to clinical case examples have been changed to protect the families who participated in the Munich Program.

Early disorders of behavioral and emotional regulation in the context of the developing parent–child relationships represent virgin soil for scientific research. The individual chapters of this book offer valuable answers for many groups of professionals who deal with difficult infants or toddlers and their stressed families. Many questions, however, remain unresolved because research on infant mental health and developmental psychopathology of early childhood is still in its early stages. It is the intent of this book to awaken the curiosity of its readers and to serve as an impetus for scientific engagement in this fascinating area. Only with the combined efforts of scientists, clinical researchers, and therapists will we learn to identify harbingers of later disorders more reliably than is now possible, to understand more precisely the transactional mechanisms and processes in parent–infant communication that contribute to early developmental psychopathology, and to improve and refine our approaches for targeted preventive and therapeutic interventions that can improve the lives of infants and their families in the long-term.

This book is dedicated to all the children and their parents who sought support at our program and—we hope—found help in dealing with their distress and worries. We wish them the best for a future enriched by positive reciprocity and mutual enjoyment in their growing relationship.

March 2007
Mechthild Papoušek

CRITICAL MOMENTS IN CHILDHOOD DEVELOPMENT: THE ZURICH FIT MODEL

Remo H. Largo
Caroline Benz-Castellano

This work was supported by the Schweizerischer Nationalfonds (Project # 3200-064047.00/1).

INTRODUCTION

Every child's development is characterized by progressions and regressions, positive and negative moments, and some phases that are more predictable or satisfying than others. Not even the most competent parents can avoid feeling that they are sometimes on a rollercoaster. Although difficulties of all kinds may be a part of normal development, coping with them is also an expected part of child rearing. Figure 1.1 lists a few—but by no means all—developmental and behavioral problems that are often observed during the first years of life. Each problem tends to occur at a particular age. For example, excessive crying typically occurs during the first 3 months; biting, scratching, or hitting other children is more likely to be seen when a child is between 2 and 5 years old.

Figure 1.1. Typical Developmental Difficulties During the Early Years.

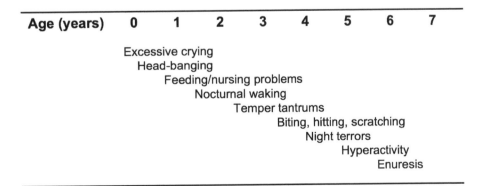

Source: Largo, 1993.

Which behavioral problems a child is likely to develop depends not only on age but also on individual disposition. For example, in a play group small children react differently when they do not feel at ease: One child may wet his pants, another may have trouble sleeping that evening, and a third may develop a stomach ache. Some of these responses to stress can themselves be quite stressful to both the child and the parents.

In their attempts to deal with these behaviors, parents, pediatricians, and educators look first for possible causes. Regressive behavior, for example, might be traced to jealousy of a younger brother or sister. An eating problem in a 3-year-old may be caused by organic disease, but it may also signal a socioemotional problem based in the relationship between the child and his parents. A misfit between the child and the people in his caregiving environment is far more likely than organic causes to result in developmental difficulties. A misfit is said to occur when a child's behavior does not match the expectations and demands made by his social environment. The parents, for example, may firmly—albeit erroneously— insist that a child must eat absolutely everything on his plate. The child may respond by refusing to eat at all, while the parents become even more entrenched in their position. As a result, they may try to force their child to eat, firmly believing this is "for his own good." Misfits, organic disorders, and socioemotional problems are not mutually exclusive and can certainly appear in combination.

If the fit between the child's individual developmental needs and the environment is sufficiently congruent, the child will feel happy, take a healthy interest in his surroundings, and develop a good sense of self-esteem. This fit is shown schematically in Figure 1.2. We have borrowed the term *fit* from Stella Chess and Alexander Thomas (1984). Chess and Thomas introduced the expression "goodness of fit" to indicate that a child develops best when there is congruence among his temperament and motivation and the expectations, demands, and potentialities of the environment. The Zurich fit model

Figure 1.2. Zurich Fit Model.

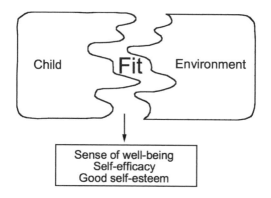

Source: Largo, 1999.

expanded on this concept to include not only temperament and motivation but all major developmental areas such as language, cognition, or social competence (Largo, 1999).

The three most important aspects of fit between child and caregivers are (a) the sense of physical and emotional security the child gets from his primary caregivers, (b) the extent to which he is accepted socially by peers and adults, and (c) the child's perception of his own development and efficacy.

Because children are continually developing, parents need to adapt constantly; the fit is never permanent. Complete congruence between the child and his environment is only possible for short periods of time. Everyday friction, such as when a mother calls her child to dinner and he is so involved in what he is doing that he either doesn't hear or doesn't want to hear, is an expectable part of development and one that can't be avoided. Such temporary conflicts will not lead to more deep-seated behavioral problems or developmental disorders so long as there is generally good enough congruence between the child and his social environment in other respects.

Adjusting the fit is a challenge, in part because parents have to keep up continually with their child's development and adapt their caregiving behaviors accordingly. Children are so different in terms of their specific needs and peculiarities that every child requires individualized responses. Difficulties may arise when parents adhere to particular child-rearing models and expectations of how a child should behave. Such models may be appropriate for some children but not for others. An open-minded attitude toward each child's individuality will help children master developmental challenges more easily than preprogrammed rules of conduct and rigid expectations.

Three examples of developmental turning points during early childhood illustrate how a misfit develops when the caregiving environment is not adapted adequately to the needs of the child. The three turning points are nocturnal waking, sleeping in the parents' bed, and acquiring bladder and bowel control. We will also show how such a misfit can and will be corrected when the parents adapt to the child's individual requirements.

The data used in this chapter to document early childhood development were collected over the course of the Zurich longitudinal studies, in which, over a 50-year period, more than 700 healthy children were followed from birth to adulthood. In these studies, the children's development and growth were tested at birth and then at 1, 3, 6, 9, 12, 18, and 24 months. Testing was conducted annually thereafter until the onset of puberty, and every 6 months after that. Researchers used a semistructured questionnaire to collect data on the frequency of nocturnal waking, sleeping in the parents' bed, and bladder and bowel control, among other aspects of development.

NOCTURNAL WAKING

Waking up is an integral part of normal sleep behavior at all ages. However, during the first few years children may stay awake because they are not able to soothe themselves and go back to sleep. They may seek parental attention, want their pacifier or bottle, or expect to be rocked back to sleep. According to the Zurich studies, between 30% and 50% of infants wake up at night at least once a week (see Figure 1.3), with approximately 15% waking up every night (Bühler & Largo, 1981; Jenni, Zinggeler-Fuhrer, Iglowstein, Molinari, & Largo, 2005).

There are several reasons why children wake up at night (see chapter 6). One frequent—if not the most frequent—reason is that parents tend to overestimate their child's need for sleep, although there seems to be a major disagreement on this point between researchers in the United States and Europe (see Jenni et al., 2005).

Figure 1.4 describes the duration of nocturnal sleep during the first years of life (Iglowstein, Jenni, Molinari, & Largo, 2003). During the 1st month, the average duration of nocturnal sleep is 8 hours. This rises to almost 12 hours by the 12th month and then falls off steadily. As can be seen in Figure 1.4, the duration of sleep differs from child to child at each age. For example, even though the average duration of nocturnal sleep at 1 year is about 12 hours, some children at this age need only 10 hours or less, whereas others may require up to 14 hours.

Most parents are pleased when their child sleeps longer than expected; only occasionally do they worry. Even if parents underestimate their child's sleep requirements, their doing so rarely leads to sleep problems. However, difficulties may arise when a child sleeps less than his parents think he should. When a child who only needs 10 hours of sleep is forced to lie in bed for 12 hours or more, the parents unwittingly pave the way for sleep problems. The child can't fall asleep and wakes up at night or too early in the morning. The child's behavior indicates that this sleep pattern is determined by his individual biological needs.

The picture painted here is that of a classic mismatch between parental expectations and a child's individual sleep needs. This unhappy situation can be corrected if the parents ascertain just how much

Figure 1.3. Frequency of Nocturnal Waking (All Degrees of Severity).

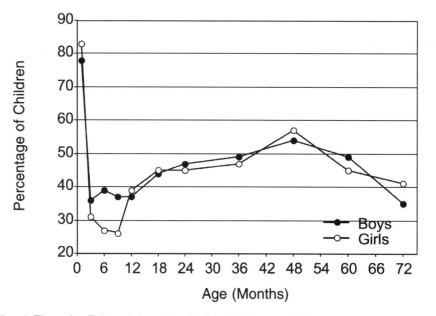

Source: Jenni, Zinggeler-Fuhrer, Iglowstein, Molinari, & Largo, 2005.

sleep their child needs and adapt to it. A sleep log can be a useful observational tool for this purpose. Parents simply record how long their child actually sleeps over 10 to 14 days. If the child stays in bed only as long as he actually sleeps, the chances are good that the sleep disorder will be resolved.

In an intervention study involving 52 preschool children with sleep problems, 38% of the parents were able to adjust their expectations to the actual sleep needs of their child. When they filled out the sleep log, they realized that their expectations did not match the sleep behavior of their child. Additional counseling was provided for 62% of the families. In 47% of these cases, parents became able to adjust bedtime to the individual needs of their children, sufficiently well that the children no longer woke up in the middle of the night. In 15% of the families, additional factors, such as psychosocial ones, resulted in the need for family or individual therapy (Largo & Hunziker, 1984).

Most parents were able to adjust to the individual traits of their children. Not only did they resolve a sleep problem that was annoying to them, but their experience was positive in the following respects as well:

- They realized that they could correctly read their child's behavior and perceive his individual needs.
- As parents, they realized that they understood the individual needs of their child better than any expert.
- Once they were able to adjust to their child's individual needs, the behavioral problems disappeared.

Experiences like this give parents greater confidence in their child-rearing competence because they see that, with a modest amount of guidance from professionals, they can solve a vexing behavior problem on their own. This understanding makes the next critical steps in the child's development easier to face.

Figure 1.4. Duration of Nocturnal Sleep During the First 6 Years.

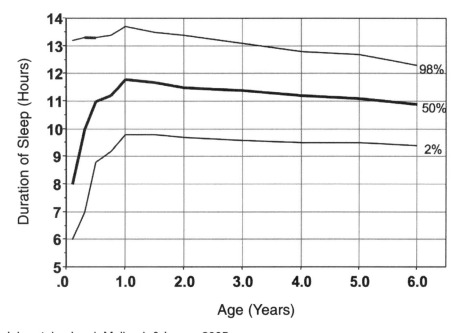

Source: Iglowstein, Jenni, Molinari, & Largo, 2005.

Figure 1.5. Children Sleeping in Their Parents' Bed.

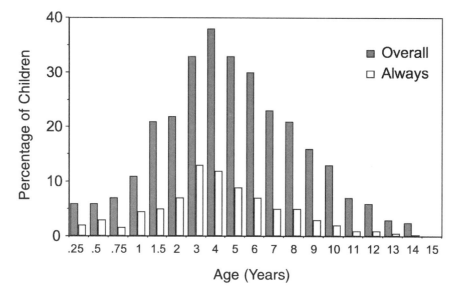

Note. Overall = sporadic to every night; Always = every night; Zurich longitudinal studies; *N* = 472 children
Source: Jenni, Zinggeler-Fuhrer, Iglowstein, Molinari, & Largo, 2005.

CO-SLEEPING

In the Zurich sample, the proportion of children who slept in their parents' bed increased between the first and fourth year from approximately 10% to almost 40% (see Figure 1.5). Up to the fourth year, approximately 15% of children slept with their parents all the time. After the fourth year, that proportion decreased steadily to only a few percent at the onset of puberty.

Why do increasing numbers of children migrate to their parents' bedroom up to the age of 4? There are three primary reasons: (a) the development of self-recognition, (b) the development of autonomy and attachment, and (c) magical thinking.

Self-recognition

Self-recognition begins between 18 and 24 months (Bischof-Köhler, 1989). The child begins to recognize himself as a person, sets boundaries, and shows empathic behavior. Self-recognition is a prerequisite for speech development, enabling the child to use his first name and use the word "I" when speaking (see Figure 1.6).

With the onset of self-recognition toward the end of the second year, the child appears to realize when he wakes up at night that he is alone (as mentioned before, waking up frequently at night is normal sleep behavior). He also becomes conscious of the feeling of having been abandoned and of his need for closeness. At this age, the child's motor skills are such that he can get out of bed. His ability to orient himself spatially is good enough to steer him to his parents' bedroom when he wants closeness and security.

Figure 1.6. Development of Self-Recognition in the Rouge Test and Use of "I" in Language.

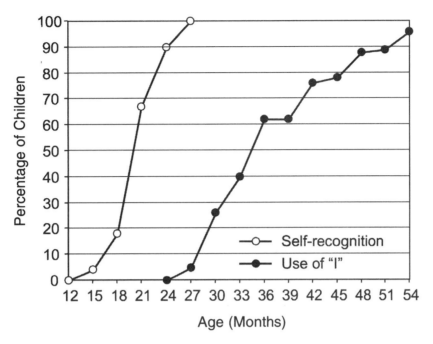

Source: Zurich longitudinal studies.

The development of attachment and autonomy

During the first and second year the child develops an emotional attachment to the people who take care of him—mostly his parents (especially his mother) or other primary caregivers, such as a grandmother or nanny. Two-year-olds begin to detach from their closest caregivers and turn to other familiar adults. Eventually, they turn to other children for comfort and reassurance as well (see Figure 1.7).

Each child goes through these changes in attachment and relational behavior on his own timetable. As a result, the internal capacity to get along without a primary caregiver differs greatly among children at any particular age. Some 2- or 3-year-olds play happily in a group even when their mothers aren't present, whereas other children have a hard time being in a play group without their mothers even at ages 4 or 5.

Children between the ages of 2 and 5 may have very different needs for security and attention. Whether a child seeks closeness with his parents when he wakes up at night depends not only on his individual development, but also on how secure and safe the child feels during the day. Children who get little closeness or attention during the day tend to seek out their parents at night.

Figure 1.7. Development of Attachment Relationships From Infancy Into Early Childhood.

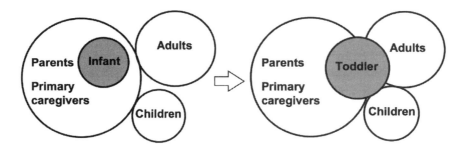

Magical thinking

A child's first detachment from his primary caregivers is associated with ambivalence and anxiety. Magical thinking begins to appear between the ages of 2 and 5 (Fraiberg, 1959), when children are first able to express their feelings symbolically. Children in this age range fill their pretend play with people, and many invent imaginary friends whom they treat like family members. Fantastic and whimsical figures also populate young children's imaginations. As they lie awake at night, some children imagine ghosts emerging from behind cabinets and curtains, or hear threatening voices and strange sounds behind doors and walls. When this occurs, children may naturally feel afraid and abandoned.

Where precisely is the misfit here? A significant percentage of infants and young children express their need for closeness by their behavior: They do not want to be left alone at night. Most parents, however, do not want to have their children in bed with them. They expect their children to sleep alone, even though they themselves do so only under exceptional circumstances. Although they would not leave a child alone during the day, they expect the child to be alone all night.

Over the entire history of humankind, children have slept with other people. Even today, millions of children in numerous cultures do not sleep alone. Yet in Western industrial societies, a misfit between culture and basic human needs has become the norm. For at least some infants and young children, being forced to sleep by themselves constitutes an unduly heavy burden. For these children, adjusting the fit might involve giving them the opportunity to sleep in the same room with siblings or other familiar people.

TOILET TRAINING

Many parents find toilet training a real challenge. To achieve a good fit, parents must find answers to two questions: When should toilet training begin? How should it be carried out? Theoretically, parents have two choices:

- An authoritarian attitude toward child rearing that stresses the importance of success in toilet training. It is the parents' task to get their child clean and dry—and to take credit when he is.

- A child-oriented attitude that stresses the development and initiative of the child. The child determines when he will begin toilet training and how it will proceed; the parents follow his lead and support his efforts.

In the Zurich longitudinal studies, we were able to analyze the effectiveness of both child-rearing approaches (Largo, Molinari, von Siebenthal, & Wolfensberger, 1996). In the first of these longitudinal studies, conducted in the 1950s, a few parents began toilet training when their children were only 1 month old. At 3 months, 13%, and at 6 months, 32% of parents held their children over a piece of cloth, child-sized potty, or a toilet bowl several times per day. At the end of the first year, 96% of the parents had begun toilet training with their children. Parents gave two chief reasons for starting toilet training this early. The first was an educational reason: Parents believed that the earlier toilet training was begun, and the more intensively it was pursued, the earlier the child would stay clean and dry. The second, practical, reason was that washing diapers was time consuming and unpleasant. Understandably, the mothers wanted to be rid of this unpleasant task as quickly as possible.

Attitudes toward toilet training became more relaxed during the 1960s and 1970s. This change was less due to a reevaluation of child-rearing practices than to changes in household technology driving modifications in parenting practices. Washers and dryers made diaper washing easier, and disposable diapers eventually freed parents from this chore completely. Parents who participated in the second Zurich longitudinal study, conducted in the 1980s, began potty training during the 9th month at the earliest. At the end of the first year of life, 20% of girls and 16% of boys had been placed on a toilet (in the first study, this was true of 96% of children!).

In the second study, parents began to toilet train girls 12 months later than in the first study, and boys 14 months later. Whereas more than 90% of the children were placed on the toilet at about 12 months in the first study, only 30% of infants in the second study had been placed on the potty by the time they were a year old (see Figure 1.8).

The intensity with which parents carried out toilet training differed greatly between the two studies. In the first study, 44% of 18-month-olds were placed on the potty by their parents at least five times per day.

Figure 1.8. The Start of Toilet Training in the 1950s and 1980s.

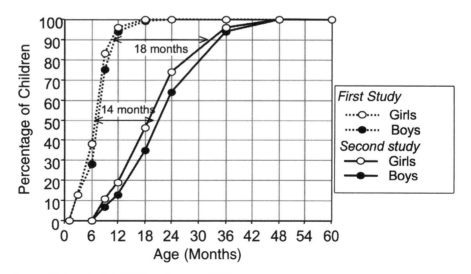

Source: Largo, Molinari, von Siebenthal, & Wolfensberger, 1996.

Figure 1.9. The Development of Daytime and Nighttime Bladder Control.

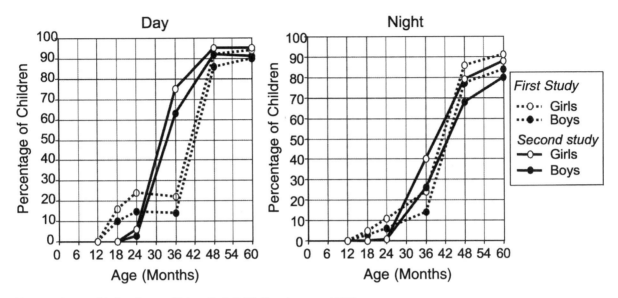

Source: Largo, Molinari, von Siebenthal, & Wolfensberger, 1996.

Very few parents in the second study carried out such intensive toilet training. The data analysis shows that, from the beginning of toilet training until children were consistently dry during both day and night, children in the first study were placed on the toilet on an average of 1,300 more occasions than the children in the second study. How did these different child-rearing styles affect the children's training?

Daytime bladder control developed as follows (see Figure 1.9). Between 12 months and 24 months, more children in the first group were dry during the day than in the second group. However, the success of early and intensive training in the first study was more apparent than real. The dry children wet fewer diapers because their mothers placed them on the potty up to 10 times per day. For children 36 months old, the results were precisely the reverse. At this point, more children in the second study stayed dry than in the first. When children were 4 and 5 years old, approximately the same percentage of children in each study were dry during the day. Nocturnal bladder control showed similar curves in both studies.

The development of bladder control is determined by the level of individual maturity and cannot be accelerated by training. Most children are able to stay dry sometime between 2 and 5 years of age. However, children need models (parents and siblings) and parental support to gain competency in this area (e.g., teaching the child how to take off his pants by himself).

SUMMARY

The concept of fit between young children and their parents translates into a child-oriented approach to child rearing. Parents who practice this approach:

- Adapt to the individual needs of the child by reading the child's behavior, being attuned to his needs, and supporting him in his moves toward independence;
- Allow the child to signal when he is developmentally ready to adopt a particular behavior;
- Allow the child to become independent in areas of his own choosing and on a self-determined schedule;
- Consider carefully how they will guide the child through expectable developmental difficulties; and
- Adapt to their child's needs.

REFERENCES

Bischof-Köhler, D. (1989). *Spiegelbild und Empathie*. Bern, Switzerland: Hans Huber.

Bühler, M., & Largo R. H. (1981). Aspekte des Schlafverhaltens zwischen 2 und 18 Jahren. *Helvetica Paediatrica Acta, 36*, 333–541.

Chess, S., & Thomas, A. (1984). *Origins and evolution of behavior disorders*. New York: Brunner/Mazel.

Fraiberg, S. (1959). *The magic years*. New York: Scribner Library.

Iglowstein, I., Jenni, O., Molinari, L., & Largo, R. H. (2003). Sleep duration from infancy to adolescence: Reference values and generational trends. *Pediatrics, 111*, 302–307.

Jenni, O. G., Zinggeler-Fuhrer, H., Iglowstein, I., Molinari, L., & Largo, R. H. (2005). A longitudinal study of bedsharing and sleep problems among Swiss children in the first 10 years of life. *Pediatrics, 115*, 233–240.

Largo, R. H. (1993). Verhaltens- und Entwicklungsauffälligkeiten: Störungen oder Normvarianten? *Monatsschrift für Kinderheilkunde, 141*, 698–703.

Largo, R. H. (1999). *Kinderjahre*. München, Germany: Piper.

Largo, R. H., & Hunziker, H. A. (1984). A developmental approach in the management of children with sleep disturbances in the first three years of life. *European Journal of Pediatrics, 142*, 170–173.

Largo, R. H., Molinari, L., von Siebenthal, K., & Wolfensberger, U. (1996). Does a profound change in toilet-training affect development of bowel and bladder control? *Developmental Medicine and Child Neurology, 38*, 106–116.

CHAPTER 2

DEVELOPMENTAL PSYCHOPATHOLOGY IN EARLY CHILDHOOD: INTERDISCIPLINARY CHALLENGES

Franz Resch

INTRODUCTION

Debate over whether infant personality is determined more by heredity or more by environmental factors has heated up considerably over the past several years. Some proponents of inherited predisposition have on occasion gone so far as to state that human traits are genetically predetermined and that a child's upbringing and environment are of minimal significance (Rowe, 1997). On the other hand, some attribute the increasing prevalence of psychological problems and crime among children and adolescents to societal changes (for an overview, see Resch et al., 1999).

Child development researchers, however, have reached a consensus: An individual's behavior is not determined solely by genetics but rather by the interplay between genetic tendencies and the social context in which the individual is embedded. Psychiatrists have reached a similarly nuanced perspective. They acknowledge the diagnostic and therapeutic necessity of integrating biological psychiatry and the reconstruction of biographical experience. Science can no longer view infant behavior ahistorically as a mere expression of brain functions. Nor does it make any sense to ignore the neuronal basis of experience when considering a patient's life history (Resch & Möhler, 2001). One may consider the child's mental development as, in large part, embedded in a relational matrix. The development of the self results from reciprocal interactions between the child's internal and external worlds and progresses from intersubjective interactions to intrasubjective constructions, or working models of the child and significant others in her caregiving environment. Every individual is embedded in a framework of interpersonal relationships that represents a significant precondition for the development of sustained physical well-being, an internal image of the world, and a concept of self. By their very nature, human beings need a social context in which to develop.

CLARIFYING TERMINOLOGY

Within the context of psychiatry and psychotherapy, developmental psychopathology offers a distinct perspective. Its mission is to use a dynamic view of adaptation and development to understand psychological disorders. Developmental psychopathologists do not view symptoms only as signs of mental illness within the individual but also as a reflection of the child's problems in coping with her social environment. This perspective leaves open the question of whether a child's mental health disorder stems primarily from constitutional factors or from the child's relationships with adult caregivers. In early childhood in particular, neither child nor caregivers are to blame for the child's difficulties. Usually, the real "patient" is the relationship between the child and her primary caregivers.

Such a perspective breaks away from traditional psychiatric models of mental illness. It encourages hypotheses about the complex genesis of relational problems and seeks to develop a conceptual framework for therapeutic strategies to improve dysfunctional relationships. In the following sections, we present a brief description of the emotional system and then show how impairments in the child's early interactions may crystallize into later psychological disorders.

From the perspective of developmental psychopathology, all psychological disorders more or less mirror impairments of the emotional system. *Emotions* are not only a fundamental means by which human beings express themselves but also represent a significant basis upon which decisions are made. Emotions create an internal climate for thoughts and ideas, and they determine the valence that we ascribe to phenomena, thereby creating meaning. They also influence interpersonal communication via facial expressions and other nonverbal signs; as a result, emotions form the basis for the early relationships that are crucial for the development of the self.

We understand *affects* as the inherited psychobiological basis of emotions. They significantly influence information processing and prepare us to act in particular ways. Humans have an inborn capacity for recognizing and interpreting affective signals, making it possible for us to visualize or empathize with the emotional state of others. Emotions are defined as the totality of affective and associated cognitive processes. Whereas affective reactivity seems to remain constant over the lifespan of the individual, the emotions become increasingly nuanced. For example, both expressive components (e.g., facial) and explanatory and decision-making structures of the cognitive system become more elaborated with time (Resch et al., 1999). Human beings think and feel simultaneously. Personality develops in the light of emotions.

PERSONALITY DEVELOPMENT AND TEMPERAMENT

According to Fiedler (1995), personality is defined by characteristic behaviors and interactional styles employed to adapt culturally and socially and to imbue interpersonal relationships with meaning. The concept of *personality* comprises the entire spectrum of functional levels, while *temperament* describes more the physiological or constitutional foundations of personality. In Allport's (1970) formulation, for example, temperament is a sort of raw material out of which personality is elaborated. According to him, temperament is associated with the internal biochemical climate in which personality develops (Allport, 1970). In summary, temperament traits may be defined as ontogenetically anchored, genetically transmitted interindividual differences based in biology that may, however, be modified by experience and later development (Rothbart & Ahadi, 1994). In other words, temperament encompasses constitutional differences in activity, reactivity, and self-regulation.

Gray's (1982) model, in particular, has become the point of departure for more far-reaching theories (Nigg, 2000). Gray postulated a behavioral activation system (BAS) and an opposing behavioral inhibition system (BIS). The BAS is controlled by reward; its neurophysiological substrate is in the basal ganglia. The BIS reacts to punishment and novel stimuli and expresses itself as anxiety and the tendency to withdraw. Stimulation of the BIS leads to a state of increased physiological arousal and attention. At the cognitive level, the BIS compares a particular situation as it is with the situation as expected and then modifies behavior such that these are brought into congruence. At the neurophysiological level, this function is linked to the septohippocampal system.

Modern temperament research indicates that children's reactivity—especially to unfamiliar people, surroundings, or situations—is, as far as we can tell, a fundamental component of human behavioral disposition. Kagan's series of longitudinal studies has found remarkable stability between 21-month-olds' anxious retreat behavior in response to novel stimuli and the behavior of these children as preschoolers (Kagan, Reznick, & Snidman, 1987). However, Kagan and Snidman (1999) also hypothesized that the manifestation of shy and fearful behavior in a 2-year-old depends on the additional effects of environmental stressors on the child's original temperamental disposition. Rosenbaum and colleagues (1992), studying behaviorally highly reactive children who met criteria for an anxiety disorder, found that one or both of their parents were more likely to have anxiety disorders than parents of children who were free of anxiety disorders. This may indicate that increased reactivity is a vulnerability factor that may later manifest itself as pathological anxiety if influenced by living with an anxious parent. The caregiving environment may modify or even amplify the influence of temperament on behavior over time. Plomin, Coon, Carey, DeFries, and Fulker (1991), by comparing adopted with nonadopted children, concluded that approximately 30% of variation in temperament is determined by environmental influences.

In summary, although temperament is behavioral disposition that is largely genetically determined, it may be modified by environmental factors. Temperament has more to do with the intensity of behavior and feelings than with their actual content (Resch & Möhler, 2001). Temperamental dimensions become effective in the emotional system, characterizing basic propensities to respond affectively in interactional repertoires.

PERSONALITY DEVELOPMENT AND EARLY INTERACTIONS

Empirical studies of infants' and young children's early interactions with primary caregivers describe how personality develops in the context of interactions within the caregiving environment. Numerous researchers have studied and described in detail the significance of early mother–child interaction for later development (for reviews of this research, see Dornes, 1998, and Stern, 1983).

The following constructs are central to this line of research:

• *Intuitive competencies of parents.* Mechthild and Hanuš Papoušek have written about intuitive competencies of parents that make it possible for them to adjust to their infant and her perceptual system and to respond appropriately to the child's emotional needs (H. Papoušek & Papoušek, 1987; M. Papoušek, 1994). As a result of these unconscious behavioral capacities, parents involuntarily change their tone of voice and modulate their intonation when addressing their baby. They intuitively situate their faces an average of 8–9 inches from their infant's eyes. This is apparently the distance at which very young infants, whose ability to focus is limited, see most clearly. Parents' intuitive competencies also include the ability to follow the infant's focus of attention, and to pick up on the infant's actions. By allowing the infant to take the initiative, instead of dominating the interaction, parents intuitively preserve space for development. (For more on the concept of intuitive parental competencies, see chapter 4).

• *Affect attunement.* According to Stern (1985), affect attunement means that the mother picks up on the intensity and dynamics of the infant's expressions of emotion and repeats them, frequently in another sensory modality. Stern described an 8-month-old boy who tries to get hold of a toy out of reach with visible signs of increasing effort. The mother joins in with a vocal expression that echoes the infant's effort. By making a response that is either stronger or weaker than the baby's original expression, the mother can stimulate, modulate, or dampen the infant's expressions of affect. Over time, her accentuations may actually shape these expressions (Dornes, 1993). Picking up on features of the infant's affective expressions, the mother modulates the intensity, rhythm, and temporal contours of her communicated affect. Caregiver and child may thus reach a common affective state.

Affect attunement may have perilous consequences when parental fantasies and fears subtly change the emotional state of the infant. When primary caregivers respond insensitively to a child by repeatedly interrupting her flow of actions, or respond to her signals with unexpected behavior, they may do harm to the child's ability to self-regulate affective arousal (Harris, 1994). Thus, affective hyperreactivity of a child is not necessarily innate but may have developed in escalating vicious circles in interactions with an insensitive caregiver.

• *Social referencing.* Campos and Stenberg (1981) described the tendency of 8-month-old infants, after being confronted with interesting but anxiety-provoking situations or objects, to look to the mother and react to her facial expression and voice. If the mother communicates anxiety, the infant will respond fearfully; if she smiles, the infant will become curious. Social referencing is a means for communicating and sharing affective evaluations; the emotional reactivity of the child is affected in the process. The caregiver has the means by which to alleviate threatening situations as well as to support intentional, goal-directed action via the mechanism of social referencing. An encouraging look from the mother helps the child to overcome insecurity in situations that elicit ambivalence between approach and withdrawal. Repeated critical, rejecting, anxious, or worried looks can—when they inappropriately reflect the parent's state of mind rather than actual danger that may result from the child's activity—turn an ordinary situation into a frightening scenario. Through interaction with a primary caregiver a child learns to ascribe meaning to novel situations and, in the process, to decrease or avoid stress by referencing significant others. However, this process succeeds only if the child can trust the adult's evaluation.

• *Attachment.* Bowlby (1969) and Ainsworth, Blehar, Waters, and Wall (1978) were the first to develop a scientific conceptualization of the specific emotional relationship of the child to her parents and possibly a few other important caregivers in the social environment. They and their students investigated this concept, which they called *attachment,* empirically. Attachment theory has greatly influenced current concepts and research in the field of developmental psychopathology (Cicchetti & Cohen, 1995).

Very few people in a child's social environment become selected attachment figures. The quality of attachment is not an individual characteristic of either the child or the adult in a relationship, but rather an interpersonal quality that both partners maintain and elaborate over the course of numerous interactions. All of the above interactional phenomena are involved in shaping the attachment relationship. Attachment fulfills the child's need for closeness and offers a secure base for curiosity and exploration, while at the same time guaranteeing safety, comfort, and support in the face of danger. Secure attachment represents a young child's fundamental trust in a primary caregiver, who can help her find a balance between behavioral activation and inhibition, differentiate her emotions, and regulate affect appropriately (for an overview of attachment research, see Cassidy & Shaver, 1999).

FIT BETWEEN THE CHILD AND PRIMARY CAREGIVERS

Sameroff's (1993) transactional model of development draws attention to the reciprocal influence of constitutional factors and environmental conditions. Parents and other important caregivers influence a child, but the child is capable as well of creating and modifying her own social environment. For example, a newborn's expression of negative affect, such as emotional unresponsiveness or inconsolable crying, may evoke changes in the mother's intuitive capacity to respond. She may withdraw, ignore the baby's signals, or avoid playful contact (M. Papoušek, 2000; Van den Boom & Hoeksma, 1994). Infant responses that function as negative feedback to the parent's interventions such as back-arching or inconsolability despite a parent's soothing efforts may elicit unfavorable reactions, which, in turn, may have a negative influence on the child's development.

Historically, the transactional model (Sameroff, 1993) developed out of the transition from linear to interactive developmental models and gave impetus at the clinical level to the concept of *fit*, according to which temperamental and environmental variables interact in an additive or multiplicative manner. Thomas and Chess (1977) coined the term *goodness of fit*, which was originally suggested by Henderson (1913), and the associated concepts of *consonance* and *dissonance*. For example, an active, impulsive, and difficult child will presumably fare better in a tolerant family with living space adequate to her needs than with rigid parents living in a cramped city apartment. According to Zentner (1998), in the fit model the qualities of temperament that are inherent to the individuality of the child constitute a point of departure for the reaction of parents and other educators. Whether or not quality of temperament represents a developmental risk factor depends on the demands placed on a child by her particular environment. Psychological disturbances may result when conditions arise during the developmental process that jeopardize optimal emotional regulation. The concept of fit undoubtedly represents progress in the nature–nurture debate. Nevertheless, there is a need for further empirical studies on specific interactional mechanisms; for prospective longitudinal research, such as the Mannheim longitudinal risk study (see chapter 14); and for more studies on disorders of behavioral and emotional regulation, such as those described in this book (chapters 4–8). The concept of fit combines the acting individual with an equally acting environment. The child seeks out and fashions environmental conditions according to her needs; at the same time, these environmental conditions shape the child.

PERSONALITY DEVELOPMENT AND THE CONCEPT OF SELF

According to Fonagy, Gergely, Jurist, and Target (2002), affect regulation and personality develop through a mechanism of "mentalization"—that is, the child's acquisition of self-reflective functions. Mentalization enables the child to distinguish between internal and external worlds and between interpersonal and personal spheres. The primary caregiver uses facial expressions to mirror or respond to the child's affect; at the same time she signals that she is not expressing her own emotional state but rather giving information, intended for the child, about the child's emotional state. Such mirroring, in the context of the attachment relationship, helps the child to develop a sense and representation of her own emotional state. Emotional states become part of the child's experience of self.

A central assumption of developmental psychopathology is that, over the course of maturation, every human being develops an internal model of the world. These models vary according to the individual's experience of interaction with the environment. Children construct models of the world, self, and other people (object images) from both cognitive and affective components of experience. As a complete, integrated, and indivisible system, affective–logical scripts form the basis for the child's psychological structure. The child's images of the world, the self, and of other people all become further differentiated and generalized as development proceeds. The child's affective–logical reference system prepares the child to adapt to the world in a meaningful way (Ciompi, 1997).

A structural model of the self that has both explicit (verbally expressible, conscious) and implicit (nondeclarative, unconscious) experiential components can be thought of as an extension of ideas advanced by Damon and Hart (1982). The subjective self (self as subject) is based on an implicit mental model that has developed from the complexity of neuronal networks starting in the first months of life. The subjective self gives evidence of a thinking, feeling, and acting agent. The subjective self is linked to affective processes and corresponds to the integrated immediate ego experience in the life context. As Resch and colleagues (1999) observed, self-reflective validation of the integrated ego experience leads to a feeling of identity.

In contrast, one may identify an objective self (self as object) that feeds off of autobiographical (i.e., episodic and semantic) memory. Bischof (1996) spoke of a figural ego concept. The *objective self* represents the totality of affective–cognitive information about the self from various domains: a physical self, a social self, a psychological (or spiritual) self, and so on. The objective self becomes the foundation of evaluative reflection, which in the final analysis determines the sense of self-worth (Resch, 2001a).

Although the *core self* of the infant (Stern, 1983) still represents an implicit affective–cognitive mental script, the child at the stage of an intersubjective self has already elaborated representations of interaction in the form of an objective self. From the beginning of the second year onward, the child develops a clear conceptual image of self and others, whom the child eventually learns to name.

From the 18th month onward, the child develops a verbal self-understanding simultaneously with her emerging symbolic capacities (Stern, 1983). At the stage of the *narrative self* (from the 18th to the 36th month), the child is able to distinguish her mental images from those of others. The child is able to symbolize her mental images in concepts and images and to use them. In this phase, the child's self becomes explicit and develops a first form of self-recognition. The child is able to say "I," knows her name, recognizes herself in the mirror, and can describe herself in relationships with others.

In the phase of the *autobiographical self*, which becomes evident during the fourth year, we begin to see metacognition (thinking about thinking). By the age of 4, children have developed social role-playing and can therefore see themselves from the perspective and standpoint of others. In other words, a "theory of mind" (Bischof-Köhler, 1998) has developed. The child is able to refer competently to the subjective state of another and to distinguish her opinions from the points of view of others. At this point, the child is able to consider what a listener knows and to make initial judgments about what is real and what is not. In other words, the child recognizes himself as someone "able to talk about himself." Köhler (1998) has discussed in detail the development of the autobiographical self and its significance in connection with the development of memory functions.

Possibly during elementary school and almost assuredly after the age of 11 or 12, the child develops a self-concept that is analogous to that of adulthood in as much as second-order metacognition becomes possible. The self at this stage may be characterized as *autoreflexive*. The child not only reflects upon herself from the perspective of another person, but also becomes able to achieve a certain autoreflective distance from herself.

Toddlers have a much more strongly implicit system of self than do school-age children and adolescents, whose self-reflection takes on ever more nuanced forms. The objective self typically continues to be developed and differentiated, so that the intercorrelation of the individual domains of the self decreases over the course of development (Evans, Brody, & Noam, 1995). The adult self is characterized by different facets of personality. According to Evans, Brody, and Noam (2001), such developmental processes of the self are helpful in overcoming negative emotions.

DISORDERS OF THE EARLY DEVELOPMENT PROCESS

Affect regulation and mentalization in the context of attachment are subject to an array of disorders that may eventually lead to behavioral problems after the late toddler stage.

Disorders of affective dialogue occur both as unpredictable emotional responses on the part of the child's primary caregivers and as overreactions by the child that overtax the parents. Fonagy et al. (2002) described in detail the mechanism of pathological affect mirroring. For example, in affect mirroring, the caregiver may fail to signal that she is not expressing her own emotional state. A mother's facial reaction to her infant's affective expression then becomes real—without the "as if" quality—and conveys to the infant the feeling that her mother shares that affect as well. This pattern of interaction can be very dangerous in the case of fear, for example, because the child becomes even more fearful when she sees her mother's frightened expression. If the caregiver takes on the infant's affect as her own—that is, if the infant's fear makes the mother fearful or the infant's expressions of rage make her angry—affect mirroring becomes seriously dysfunctional. In such cases, emotional dialogue is interrupted and the overtaxed caregiver ceases to be available as a secure attachment figure.

Another set of problems involving affect mirroring occurs when facial expressions and gestures are conveyed back to the infant as mirroring, but the caregiver has misjudged the infant's emotional state and therefore inadvertently mirrors another emotion. The caregiver's faulty perception results in giving the infant inappropriate feedback, which leads to an incongruence between the infant's internal experience and her reflexive interpretation. According to Fonagy and colleagues (2002), repeated invalidation and reinterpretation of the child's self can lead to the development of a *false self* and narcissistic emptiness, which may eventually lead not only to impairment of affect regulation, but to narcissistic personality problems as well (alternating feelings of emptiness, self-doubt, and delusions of grandeur).

A special attribute of parent–infant relationships is the parents' tendency to interpret their infant's behavior. For example, parents may tend to overestimate the degree of intentionality in their infant's behavior (Hinde, 1976). Along with this tendency, parental fantasies and memories from their own childhood experiences may intrude in the dialogue between parent and child, calling to mind Selma Fraiberg's (1980) notion of "ghosts in the nursery." Not infrequently, parents unwittingly find themselves repeating traumatic relational patterns from their own childhood, so that the baby is confronted with aspects of her parents' unconscious. This process may affect the child's development to the extent that the mother unconsciously distorts the meaning of the infant's behavior (Cramer, 1986). Affects and fantasies of the parent are projected onto the infant, and parents attribute inappropriate intentions to their infant's behavior. Their attribution of meaning plays a decisive role in the formation of the child's concept of self (Dornes, 1998). The more pressing the parents' unconscious fantasies and conflicts are, the greater the probability that their distorted interpretation of the infant's signals will coincide with potentially pathological consequences (Resch & Möhler, 2001).

The projection of repressed negative parts of the parents' self at this early stage is not the only mechanism that transmits relational and attachment disorders onto the next generation. Impaired affect mirroring is another direct mechanism. Particularly in severe relational disorders—for example, if a parent had been abused as a child—this mechanism may have aggravating consequences for parent–child interaction, and therefore also for the development of the child's personality. When a child's boundaries are violated by aggressive parental projections that are related to the parent's trauma, there is a danger of reenacting the experience of abuse with the infant (Möhler & Resch, 2000). This mechanism is illustrated by the following case study (from Resch & Möhler, 2001).

CASE VIGNETTE

A mother brought her 8-week-old daughter to the clinic because of "intolerable hysterical fits," which triggered threatening outbursts and abusive impulses in the mother. Because of distorted perception, the mother incorrectly interpreted her infant's crying as an intentional and willful expression aimed against her. She felt her child to be dangerous at several levels: She experienced her child's movements as physically aggressive toward her, and expressed the fear that in a few years she would be overwhelmed by her child's aggressive potential.

The mother was also frightened by what she experienced as the baby's demandingess and insatiability. The mother seemed to interpret even neutral vocal expressions as manipulative, sadistic, and greedy. She responded by instituting a rigidly regimented set of caregiving rules. She monitored her husband's and mother-in-law's compliance with her regime. Any departure from the rules triggered fears in the mother that the infant would become "spoiled" and eventually overwhelm her with her greediness.

The mother's history was illuminating. As early as she could remember, she had been beaten and kicked by her own mother. But worst of all had been her mother's "hysterical" screaming fits. No one supported her or took her seriously when she was a child, although she repeatedly told her father and a teacher what was happening. Only once did her father, whom she described as an alcoholic, hurry home from work after she telephoned him and reported that she feared for her life. Now, as a new mother, she perceived her 8-week-old daughter as her own mother, who screamed at and abused her. The infant's crying triggered these memories, with the consequence that the mother projected these intrusive aggressive memory traces onto her infant. As a result, the mother perceived her infant as sadistic and manipulative, and responded to all of her baby's emotions with inappropriate aggression. She relived the fear of being at the mercy of an intrusive and violent person—thus her conviction that her baby would soon develop overwhelming powers and that she herself would lose control. In the course of early mother–infant psychotherapy, the mother's distorted perceptions were interpreted and corrected. Offered a corrective emotional experience within a therapeutic relationship, she was able to confront her continuously rekindled memories and overcome her fears.

THE DEVELOPMENT OF PSYCHOLOGICAL DISORDERS

Psychological disorders may develop in early childhood through three basic mechanisms that are often interrelated.

1. Innate disorders—with a high impact of genetic factors on behavioral phenotype—may lead to severe impairment in mother–child interaction. One example is autism (Bartlett, Gharani, Millonig, & Brzustowicz, 2005), which causes disordered nonverbal and, later, verbal communication. The ability to recognize and decode affect is impaired in autistic children; the ability to delimit other subjects as psychological beings in the real world appears difficult. Such genetic diseases of the autistic spectrum like Rett syndrome (Shahbazian & Zoghbi, 2002) are, however, seldom seen in daily practice. The other two mechanisms are much more frequent.

2. Traumatization occurs in dramatic, affect-charged situations in which the child is threatened or made overwhelmingly insecure in some manner, and in which no adult help is immediately forthcoming. The *Diagnostic Classification of Mental Health and Developmental Disorders of Infancy and Early Childhood, Revised Edition* (DC:0–3R; ZERO TO THREE, 2005) gives a detailed description of the symptoms and diagnostic criteria of posttraumatic stress disorder. Not infrequently, a primary caregiver is involved in the traumatization as victim or perpetrator, particularly in cases of violence or sexual abuse. The impact of traumatization on memory, self-development, and affect regulation, as well as the development of dissociative disorders, has been discussed by Brunner and colleagues (2000); Prohl and colleagues (2001), and Resch, Brunner, and Parzer (1998). Cumulative traumatization, that is, multiple traumas at various times in a person's life that impair development, is found in more than 60% of adolescent patients with a history of intentional self-harm (Resch, 2001b).

3. The most frequent way in which emotional impairments develop in early childhood is through parental, infant, and situational factors that compromise parent–infant communication. It is less the dramatic events than failures in affective attunement, small everyday crises, steadily effective misinterpretation of the infant's feelings, and repetitive excessive reactions by the infant or primary caregivers that lead to trouble. The sum total of all the small misunderstandings, errors, moments of inattention, and inability to respond correctly to each other forms the substance from which disorders of behavioral and emotional regulation, early relational disorders, and maladaptation syndromes are made. This book is concerned with this group of children, which constitutes the majority of patients in daily practice.

Ongoing interactional conflict, a constant tendency to ascribe motives inappropriately, repeated affective overreactions—all of these leave their mark on attachment security. Insecure or disordered attachment may lead to an imbalance in coping with temperamental hyperreactivity, and to impairment in emotional differentiation. Parents and children bring to the dialogue their own vulnerabilities, hypersensitivities, and limitations. If dialogue fails, development of the child's self will be jeopardized or disordered. In later life, such children have difficulty dealing with everyday problems. When disorders arise in early childhood, the parent–child relationship is likely to be the patient. After the first 3 years of life, the patient is the child herself.

Children of mothers with schizophrenia have been shown to differ at an early age from children of mothers with affective disorders inasmuch as they exhibit subtle impairments of social referencing (Parnas & Carter, 2002). Children with insecure attachment and severe behavioral inhibition tend to develop emotional disorders at preschool age (see the review by Resch & Möhler, 2001). Children with insecure attachment who grow up in social risk groups frequently exhibit psychological problems at school age and adolescence, such as lack of contact with peers, depression, labile mood, and externalizing aggressive behavior problems (see the review by Greenberg, 1999).

It seems essential to view the psychological and biological consequences of trauma, general stress, and negative interactions over the entire course of development (Cicchetti & Walker, 2001). Multiple converging paths lead to psychopathology. They are associated with neuronal circuits that have been altered by psychological or physical stressors as well as by genetic vulnerabilities, early experiences, and long-term negative life events. Children and adolescents with negative early experiences and impaired self-development, in turn, tend to invite new negative experiences as a result of their own risk-taking behavior (drug abuse, delinquency).

Early diagnosis and intervention to repair dysfunctional relational patterns between infants and their primary caregivers have the potential to yield significant positive long-term consequences and to prevent psychological disorders in later childhood. Normalization of early interactional patterns between caregiver and infant may counteract the escalating vicious cycles of progressive developmental psychopathology. Early intervention in the context of troubled parent–infant relationships provides challenges and chances for interdisciplinary cooperation.

A comprehensive approach to early emotional upbringing should involve more than just physicians and psychotherapists. Educators, early intervention specialists, and child care professionals should be included as well. However, a fundamental change in society's attitude toward children must take place before such an overall approach can be translated into action. Parents need social appreciation as well as material and personal support from competent advisers and other personnel in times of crisis. But they also need support from within a social environment that values the education of children and is tolerant of families with children. A mother who feels supported and a father who does not fear unemployment are more capable of devoting themselves to dialogue with their child than a family that is under economic stress and that receives more criticism than help. The early emotional upbringing of children in our complex postmodern information society should be of concern to us all.

REFERENCES

Ainsworth, M. D. S., Blehar, M. C., Waters, E., & Wall, S. (1978). *Patterns of attachment: A psychological study of the Strange Situation.* Hillsdale, NJ: Erlbaum.

Allport, G. W. (1970). *Gestalt und Wachstum in der Persönlichkeit.* Meisenheim, Germany: Hain.

Bartlett, C. W., Gharani, N., Millonig, J. H., & Brzustowicz, L. M. (2005). Three autism candidate genes: A synthesis of human genetic analysis with other disciplines. *Internaional Journal of Developmental Neuroscience, 23,* 221–234.

Bischof, N. (1996). *Das Kraftfeld der Mythen.* München, Germany: Piper.

Bischof-Köhler, D. (1998). Zusammenhänge zwischen kognitiver, motivationaler und emotionaler Entwicklung in der frühen Kindheit und im Vorschulalter. In H. Keller (Ed.), *Entwicklungspsychologie* (pp. 319–376). Bern, Switzerland: Hans Huber.

Bowlby, J. (1969). *Attachment.* New York: Basic Books.

Brunner, R., Parzer, P., Schuld, V., & Resch, F. (2000). Dissociative symptomatology and traumatogenic factors in adolescent psychiatric patients. *Journal of Nervous and Mental Disease, 188*(2), 71–77.

Campos, J. J., & Stenberg, C. R. (1981). Perception, appraisal, and emotions: The onset of social referencing. In M. E. Lamb & L. R. Sherrod (Eds.), *Infant social cognition: Empirical and social considerations* (pp. 273–314). Hillsdale, NJ: Erlbaum.

Cassidy, J., & Shaver, P. R. (1999). *Handbook of attachment. Theory, research, and clinical applications.* New York: Guilford Press.

Cicchetti, D., & Cohen, D. J. (Eds.). (1995). *Developmental psychopathology.* New York: Wiley.

Cicchetti, D., & Walker, E. (2001). Stress and development: Biological and psychological consequences. *Developmental Psychopathology, 13,* 413–418.

Ciompi, L. (1997). *Die emotionalen Grundlagen des Denkens. Entwurf einer fraktalen Affektlogik.* Göttingen, Germany: Vandenhoeck & Ruprecht.

Cramer, B. (1986). Assessment of parent-infant relationship. In T. B. Brazelton & M. W. Yogman (Eds.), *Affective development in infancy* (pp. 27–38). Norwood, NJ: Ablex.

Damon, W., & Hart, D. (1982). The development of self-understanding from infancy through adolescence. *Child Development, 52,* 841–864.

Dornes, M. (1993). *Der kompetente Säugling.* Frankfurt, Germany: Fischer.

Dornes, M. (1998). *Der kompetente Säugling. Die präverbale Entwicklung des Menschen. Geist und Psyche.* Frankfurt, Germany: Fischer.

Evans, D. W., Brody, L., & Noam, G. G. (1995). Self-perceptions of adolescents with and without mood disorder: Content and structure. *Journal of Child Psychology and Psychiatry and Allied Disciplines, 36,* 1337–1351.

Evans, D. W., Brody, L., & Noam, G. G. (2001). Ego development, self-perception, and self-complexity in adolescence: A study of female psychiatric inpatients. *American Journal of Orthopsychiatry, 71*(1), 79–86.

Fiedler, P. (1995). *Persönlichkeitsstörungen.* Weinheim, Germany: Psychologie Verlags Union.

Fonagy, P., Gergely G., Jurist, E. L., & Target, M. (2002). *Affect regulation, mentalization, and the development of the self*. New York: Other Press.

Fraiberg, S. (1980). *Clinical studies in infant mental health: The first year of life*. New York: Basic Books.

Gray, J. A. (1982). *The neuropsychology of anxiety: An inquiry into the function of the septohippocampal system*. New York: Oxford University Press.

Greenberg, M. T. (1999). Attachment and psychopathology in childhood. In J. Cassidy & P. R. Shaver (Eds.), *Handbook of attachment* (pp. 469–496). New York: Guilford Press.

Harris, P. L. (1994). The child's understanding of emotion: Developmental change and the family environment. *Journal of Child Psychology and Psychiatry, 35*, 3–28.

Henderson, L. J. (1913). *The fitness of the environment*. New York: Macmillan.

Hinde, R. A. (1976). On describing relationships. *Journal of Child Psychology and Psychiatry, 17*, 1–19.

Kagan, J., Reznick, J. S., & Snidman, N. (1987). The physiology and psychology of behavioral inhibition in children. *Child Development, 58*, 1459–1473.

Kagan, J., & Snidman, N. (1999). Early childhood predictors of adult anxiety disorders. *Biological Psychiatry, 46*, 1536–1541.

Köhler, L. (1998). Einführung in die Entstehung des Gedächtnisses [Introduction to the origins of memory]. In M. Koukkou, M. Leuzinger-Bohleber, & W. Mertens (Eds.), *Erinnerung von Wirklichkeiten. Psychoanalyse und Neurowissenschaften im Dialog* (Vol. 1, pp. 131–222). Stuttgart, Germany: Verlag Internationale Psychoanalyse—Cotta.

Möhler, E., & Resch, F. (2000). Frühe Ausdrucksformen und Transmissionsmechanismen mütterlicher Traumatisierungen innerhalb der Mutter-Säuglings-Interaktion. *Praxis der Kinderpsychologie und Kinderpsychiatrie, 49*, 550–562.

Nigg, J. T. (2000). On inhibition/disinhibition in developmental psychopathology: Views from cognitive and personality psychology and a working inhibition taxonomy. *Psychological Bulletin, 126*, 220–246.

Papoušek, H., & Papoušek, M. (1987). Intuitive parenting: A dialectic counterpart to the infant's integrative competence. In J. Osofsky (Ed.), *Handbook of infant development* (2nd. ed., pp. 669–713). New York: Wiley.

Papoušek, M. (1994). *Vom ersten Schrei zum ersten Wort. Anfänge der Sprachentwicklung in der vorsprachlichen Kommunikation*. Bern, Switzerland: Hans Huber.

Papoušek, M. (2000). Persistent infant crying, parenting and infant mental health. In J. D. Osofsky & H. E. Fitzgerald (Eds.), *WAIMH handbook of infant mental health. Vol. 4: Infant mental health in groups at high risk* (pp. 415–453). New York: Wiley.

Parnas, J., & Carter, J. W. (2002). High-risk studies and neurodevelopmental hypothesis. In H. Häfner (Ed.), *Risk and protective factors in schizophrenia* (pp. 71–82). Darmstadt, Germany: Steinkopff.

Plomin, R., Coon, H., Carey, G., DeFries, J. C., & Fulker, D. W. (1991). Parent-offspring and sibling adoption analyses of parental ratings of temperament in infancy and childhood. *Journal of Personality 59*, 705–732.

Prohl, J., Resch, F., Parzer, P., & Brunner, R., (2001). Relationship between dissociative symptomatology and declarative and procedural memory in adolescent psychiatric patients. *Journal of Nervous and Mental Disease, 189*, 602–607.

Resch, F. (2001a). Der Körper als Instrument zur Bewältigung seelischer Krisen. Selbstverletzendes Verhalten bei Jugendlichen. *Deutsches Ärzteblatt, 98,* 2226–2271.

Resch, F. (2001b). Selbstentfremdung: Entwicklungsstörung oder Selbstfürsorge? *Beiträge zur Individualpsychologie, 26,* 99–116.

Resch, F., Brunner, R., & Parzer, P. (1998). Dissoziative Mechanismen und Persönlichkeitsentwicklung. In J. Klosterkötter (Ed.), *Frühdiagnostik und Frühbehandlung* (pp. 125–141). Berlin: Springer.

Resch, F., & Möhler, E. (2001). Wie entwickelt sich die kindliche Persönlichkeit? Beiträge zur Diskussion um Vererbung und Umwelt. In M. Wink (Ed.), *Vererbung und Milieu* (Heidelberger Jahrbücher, pp. 95–151). Heidelberg, Germany: Springer.

Resch, F., Parzer, P., Brunner, R., Haffner, J., Koch, E., Ölkers, R., et al. (1999). *Entwicklungspsychopathologie des Kindes- und Jugendalters. Ein Lehrbuch.* Weinheim, Germany: Psychologie Verlags Union.

Rosenbaum, J. F., Biederman, J., Bolduc, E. A., Hirshfeld, D. R., Faraone, S. V., & Kagan, J. (1992). Comorbidity of parental anxiety disorders as risk for childhood-onset anxiety in inhibited children. *American Journal of Psychiatry, 149,* 475–481.

Rothbart, M., & Ahadi, S. A. (1994). Temperament and the development of personality. *Journal of Abnormal Psychology, 103,* 55–66.

Rowe, D. C. (1997). *Genetik und Sozialisation. Die Grenzen der Erziehung.* Weinheim, Germany: Psychologie Verlags Union.

Sameroff, A. J. (1993). Models of development and developmental risk. In C. H. Zeanah (Ed.), *Handbook of infant mental health* (pp. 3–13). New York: Guilford Press.

Shahbazian, M. D., & Zoghbi, H. (2002). Rett syndrome and MeCP2: Linking epigenetics and neuronal function. *American Journal of Human Genetics, 71,* 1259–1272.

Stern, D. N. (1983). The early development of schemas of self, other and self with other. In J. D. Lichtenberg & S. Kaplan (Eds.), *Reflections on self psychology* (pp. 49–84). Hillsdale, NJ: Analytic Press.

Stern, D. N. (1985). *The interpersonal world of the infant.* New York: Basic Books.

Thomas, A., & Chess, S. (1977). *Temperament and development.* New York: Bruner/Mazel.

Van den Boom, D. C., & Hoeksma, J. B. (1994). The effect of infant irritability on mother-infant interactions: A growth-curve analysis. *Developmental Psychology, 30,* 581–590.

Zentner, M. R. (1998). *Die Wiederentdeckung des Temperamentes, eine Einführung in die Kindertemperamentsforschung.* Frankfurt, Germany: Verlag Fischer.

ZERO TO THREE. (2005). *Diagnostic classification of mental health and developmental disorders of infancy and early childhood: Revised edition (DC:0–3R).* Washington, DC: ZERO TO THREE Press.

CHAPTER 3

FACTS AND FIGURES: DATABASE OF THE
MUNICH INTERDISCIPLINARY RESEARCH
AND INTERVENTION PROGRAM
FOR FUSSY BABIES

Harald Wurmser
Mechthild Papoušek

INTRODUCTION

For many years, professionals have either ignored disorders of behavioral and emotional regulation in infancy (such as excessive crying, sleep and feeding disorders, chronic fussiness, excessive clinginess, and temper tantrums) or viewed them as harmless and transitory behaviors. As a result, parents have lacked access to professional counseling and treatment regarding these problems. Against this backdrop, the Munich Interdisciplinary Research and Intervention Program for Fussy Babies was inaugurated in 1991 in the Munich Center for Social Pediatrics. The Munich Program had two interrelated goals. The first was to improve the diagnostic and therapeutic care provided to families affected by infant and toddler behavioral disorders. The intention was to reduce the risk of longer term disorders in parent–infant relationships and to foster the social and emotional development of the child. The second aim was to analyze the conditions under which such disorders develop, their forms of manifestation, and their course and long-term effects. These efforts were designed to create an empirical database that would help to improve diagnostic procedures and therapeutic interventions.

This chapter describes the sociodemographic characteristics of more than 1,000 families who were treated in the program, and presents the main results regarding symptomatology, etiology, and typical course of the main disorders of behavioral and emotional regulation in early childhood. The results are based on parent interviews and systematic analyses of data on behavioral problems as they occur in the main interactional contexts, on the psychological state of the parents, and on the parent–child relationships.

METHODOLOGY

Data acquisition

Detailed descriptions of the standardized, interdisciplinary procedures for generating data in the program can be found in earlier publications (M. Papoušek & von Hofacker, 1995, 1998). In brief, data generation involved six components:

1. A pediatrician and a psychologist together conduct comprehensive semistructured diagnostic interviews (following Esser et al., 1990) on prenatal, perinatal, and postnatal distress resulting from somatic

and psychosocial risk factors. This team systematically gathers information about the parents' current psychological state, family relationships, and social support system and also collects general socio-demographic data.

2. Results of medical examinations complement findings from the developmental history of the child. These are essential to assess the level of neuromotor functioning and sensory processing and to diagnose pediatric and neurological disease.

3. Video-supported behavioral observation in our laboratory is at the core of the diagnostic procedure. The goal is to assess the infant's self-regulatory capacities and to evaluate the functionality of the parent–infant interaction in up to nine everyday contexts (settling to sleep, diapering, feeding, soothing, face-to-face dialogue, playing together, limit setting, boundary setting, and separation). The videotapes also permit a detailed analysis of the parents' repertoire of intuitive competencies, their behavioral expression, and attunement to the infant's communicative signals (M. Papoušek, 1996).

4. Parents keep a diary at home that complements behavioral observation in the laboratory setting. The reported amounts of crying and fussiness reflect the infant's capacity for self-regulation. A standardized prestructured 24-hour record is kept to determine the duration and circadian distribution of episodes of crying and fussiness, as well as of sleeping, waking, and feeding. This record is filled out by the parents over 5 consecutive days.

5. We use a battery of standardized questionnaires about the parents' perception of their child's temperament (Infant Characteristics Questionnaire [ICQ]; Bates, Freeland, & Lounsbury, 1979), postpartum depression (Edinburgh Postnatal Depression Scale [EPDS]; Cox, Holden, & Sagovsky, 1987), and the mother's attitudes and feelings toward her child (Maternal Childcare Attitudes and Feelings [EMKK]; Engfer, 1986; Engfer & Gavranidou, 1987). The EMKK yields information about the mother's psychological state (overstrain/exhaustion, depressiveness, frustration, anxious overprotection, rigidity, negative childhood memories, enjoyment of the child).

6. A pediatrician and psychologist independently use the Parent–Infant Relationship Global Assessment Scale (PIR-GAS; ZERO TO THREE, 1994, 2005) to assess the functional and adaptive quality of the mother–infant relationship. In the context of a multilevel diagnostic process, they rate each relationship on a 9-point scale that ranges from *well adapted to grossly impaired*. In case of scoring disagreements, the raters discuss their observations and interpretations until they achieve agreement.

To provide data for later scientific analyses, members of the staff systematically document each child's history, findings, and diagnoses, as well as the consultation and treatment provided and the overall progress of treatment.

Study Sample

Between the opening of the program in 1991 and 2004, about 3,000 families were referred for diagnostic assessment, counseling, and treatment. The sample being referred to in this book includes a total of 1,008 families who were referred to the program between 1994 and 1997. Follow-up data from occasional re-admissions encompass the time period from the families' first visit to the end of 2000. The results presented here are based on analyses of 701 families (69.5% of the total sample) for whom we had close to complete data sets. Three-hundred seven families were dropped from the study, primarily because of incomplete or missing questionnaires or because they were involved with the clinic too briefly to participate in all phases of data collection.

The 701 families whose data we analyzed did not differ markedly from the other 307 families in terms of their sociodemographic characteristics (sex distribution, nationality of the parents, marital status, birth order, age of the mother at childbirth, maternal occupation, primary caregiver, outside caregiver;

see Table 3.1). The present sample is thus largely representative of the 1,008 families in the total sample. It should be noted that no data were available on the educational level of the parents in the cases that were not considered. In addition, at their first visit, the children in the present sample were slightly, but significantly, younger than the children of the drop-out families. Because disorders of behavioral and emotional regulation in infancy and early childhood are age-related (see below), we assumed that behavioral problems in the second and third year were slightly underrepresented in the present sample in favor of disturbances in the first year.

To adequately address some of the research questions, we recruited participants in an age-matched nonclinical control group (sample of convenience); they were examined by the same staff, using the same procedures, as with the referred children. We also invited a subgroup of patients and a control sample for a follow-up exam at 30 months (see chapter 13).

RESULTS

This chapter describes the sociodemographic characteristics of the clinical sample in comparison to the population of Bavaria or the population of Germany as a whole. The chapter focuses on risk factors, symptomatology, and trajectories of early disorders of behavioral and emotional regulation—that is, common characteristics of crying, feeding and sleeping disorders, and other behavioral syndromes. Additional results regarding temperament, psychological state of the mother, and quality of the mother–infant relationship are included in chapter 4. Forms and techniques, duration, and success of treatment are described in chapter 12.

Sociodemographic Characteristics of the Sample

Age distribution. During the planning stage of the Munich Program, we expected that our consultation and treatment services would mainly attract families who were dealing with infant colic during the first months of life. Contrary to our expectation, however, the age range of the referred children at their first visit was between birth and 55 months (mean [M] ± standard deviation [SD]: 10.5 ± 7.1 months; see Table 3.1). Corresponding to the developmental crying peak reported around the 6th week of life (Alvarez & St. James-Roberts, 1996; St. James-Roberts & Halil, 1991), the age distribution among referred children reached an early peak between the 2nd and the 4th month, but further peaks were also evident in our sample at the 9th, 12th, 15th, and 18th months. Overall, 32.1% of the children who visited the program for the first time between 1994 and 1997 were between birth and 6 months, and 36.7% were between 7 and 12 months of age. Another 27.8% were examined for the first time during their second year, and 3.4% were first seen in their third year. Only a few children were seen for the first time at older ages.

Sex distribution. Slightly more than half of the children (55.2%) in our program were boys. However, this sex distribution is in line with the higher male birth rate (51.5%) in the Bavarian population as a whole in 1996 (Bayerisches Landesamt für Statistik und Datenverarbeitung [BLSD; Bavarian State Office for Statistics and Data Processing], 1997). In a similar vein, no clear indication of sex differences were found in representative community-based samples for the three most frequent disorders of

Table 3.1. Sociodemographic Data: Comparison of Families With Complete and Incomplete Data Sets.

	Cases with complete data (n = 701)	Cases with incomplete data (n = 307)	p
Age at first visit			≤ .001
Months M (±SD)*	10.5 ± 7.1	14.9 ± 10.8	
Sex			ns
Male	55.2%	59.9%	
Female	44.8%	40.1%	
Nationality of mother			ns
German	88.7%	90.8%	
Other	11.3%	9.2%	
Nationality of father			ns
German	85.5%	83.5%	
Other	14.5%	16.5%	
Marital status			ns
Married/living together	89.1%	88.6%	
Divorced/living apart	10.7%	11.4%	
Birth order			ns
1st child	67.9%	63.9%	
2nd child	26.0%	27.8%	
3rd child	4.9%	6.3%	
4th child	1.2%	1.7%	
5th child and above	0.0%	0.3%	
Age of mother at childbirth			ns
Under 20	0.6%	1.7%	
20–34	82.1%	83.9%	
35–39	15.2%	12.0%	
40 and above	2.0%	2.3%	
Employment of mother			ns
Full-time employment	1.4%	0.4%	
Part-time employment	16.3%	17.6%	
Not employed	82.2%	82.0%	
Primary caregiver			ns
Mother	85.0%	81.0%	
Other	15.0%	19.0%	
Outside caregiver			ns
Yes	8.0%	8.4%	
No	92.0%	91.6%	

Note. Families (n = 1008) were referred to the Munich Program between 1994 and 1997. ns = not significant (p > .05).

behavioral regulation in infancy—excessive crying, sleep disorders, and feeding disorders (Fegert et al., 1997; Lucassen et al., 2001; Richman, 1981; Wolke, 2000). Sex-specific differences in the prevalence of behavioral problems seem to develop only later, with boys developing higher rates of externalizing behavioral disorders and girls more frequently exhibiting psychosomatic disorders (Ihle & Esser, 2002).

Nationality of parents. Of mothers who brought their children to the program, 88.7% were German, as were 85.5% of the fathers; in 80.7% of families, both parents were German. The 11.3% of mothers who were not German came from Turkey (2.3%), the Balkans (2.3%), and other (6.8%) countries. The foreign-born mothers in our sample were representative of the proportion of foreign-born mothers in the Bavarian population in 1996 (11.4%; BLSD, 1997). However, the percentage of Turkish children in our sample (2.3%) was somewhat lower than that of Turkish chilren in Bavaria as a whole (4.5%).

Marital status. The majority of parents of the children in our sample were married (74.4%) at the time of the first contact. The rates for children growing up with unmarried parents who were living together (14.8%) or with single mothers (8.5%) were approximately twice the rate of unmarried parents in Bavaria in 1996 (12.8%; BLSD, 1997). Including the children of divorced parents (2.3% in our sample), a total of 10.8% of the children were being raised by single mothers, markedly less than the proportion of single mothers with minor children in Bavaria as a whole (18.4%; BLSD, 1997). However, we found a significant increase in the rate of single parenting as the age of the child increased (8.0% in the first year, 7.9% in the second year, 14.6% in the third year, 18.1% in the fourth year, and 25.0% in the fifth year or above), Mantel-Haenszel $X^2(1, N = 701) = 12.60, p \leq .001$.

Birth order. In 1997, 45.7% of children of married parents in Bavaria were first-born (BLSD, 1997). In our sample, 67.9% of the children were first-born. Conversely, the program registered percentages lower than those found in the Bavarian population for second-born (26.0% vs. 38.1%), third-born (4.9% vs. 12.3%), and fourth-born children (1.2% vs. 2.9%). These deviations are only partially explained by the particularly high proportion of first-borns with single mothers (79.7%) in our sample, because the rates of first-born children of married parents (67.6%) and of mothers separated from their husbands (62.5%) were also considerably higher than the figures for the Bavarian population as a whole. The possible explanation that regulation disorders are more prevalent in first-borns than in subsequent children has been rebutted by epidemiological studies of excessive crying (St. James-Roberts & Halil, 1991), sleep disorders (Lozoff & Zuckerman, 1988), feeding disorders (Lindberg, Bohlin, & Hagekull, 1991), and failure to thrive (Wilensky et al., 1996). Rather, parents of first-borns appear to be much more likely to seek professional help and counseling when their infants experience excessive crying and sleep disorders, probably because of the parents' lack of previous caregiving experience (Pollock, 1992; St. James-Roberts & Halil, 1991).

Maternal age. Mothers in our sample ranged in age from 19 to 44 years at the time they gave birth to the target child, with an average age of 30.4 ± 4.3 years. In our sample, 17.3% of the mothers were over 35 and 2.0% were over 40 years old. Nineteen-year-old mothers made up 0.6% of our sample. In Germany in 1996, 2.0% of all viable infants had mothers between 18 and 19 years of age, and 0.6% of all children were born to mothers under 18, according to data from the Statistisches Bundesamt [German Federal Statistics Office] (1999). Thus, children of adolescent mothers are underrepresented in our sample.

Maternal employment. As expected in Germany, mothers' employment was correlated with the age of their children. The rate of mothers employed full-time or part-time (n = 124 in our sample of 701 families) rose from 8.0% during the first half-year after the birth of a child to 20.2% during the second half-year, 26.0% in the third half-year, 23.6% in the fourth half-year, and 20.8% after the third year of life, Mantel-Haenszel X^2(1, N = 701) = 14.96, p ≤ .001. Almost all of the employed women (91.9%) were employed only part-time, most of them 1–2 days per week. The mother was the child's primary caregiver, regardless of the child's age, in 85.0% of the families. Only 8.0% of the mothers sought outside help with caregiving from nannies or out-of-home child care, most often in order to take a job. These figures are consistent with West German statistics for 1996 (Alt & Weidacher, 1996; Engstler, 1998). These show that, depending on educational level and employment, between 4.5% and 24% of parents with children under the age of 3 made use of such outside support.

Parental education. Most of the mothers (73.4%) and fathers (63.1%) of the children who were referred to the program had successfully completed some professional training after finishing elementary and secondary school. Relatively fewer mothers than fathers (18.8% and 31.3%, respectively) had completed high school and graduated from a technical college or university; 3.8% of mothers and 2.6% of fathers had not yet completed professional training after the final high-school examination (Abitur). A mere 0.3% of mothers and 0.5% of fathers had dropped out of school. For the year 1996, the BLSD (1997) published the following figures regarding the educational level of the population of Bavaria: Of all persons aged 20 to 44, 76.5% had completed elementary or secondary school; 16.0% of this age cohort had completed high school and graduated from a technical college or university. Only 4.1% had failed to complete elementary or secondary school. In our sample, fathers in particular had a markedly higher level of education than the population of Bavaria as a whole. Parents who had dropped out of school were underrepresented in our sample.

To summarize, the sociodemographic data show that sex distribution and percentage of foreign-born parents in our sample resembled those of the Bavarian population as a whole. However, first-borns were markedly overrepresented in our sample. Adolescent or single mothers and parents with a low level of education used our counseling services less often than other parents.

Clinical Syndromes of Behavioral and Emotional Regulation

As already mentioned, we originally expected that the Munich Program would be used predominantly by families of infants with colic within the first 3 months of life. Surprisingly, only a small minority (15.7%) of children were brought in during these first 3 months. Moreover, excessive crying was not the only disorder of concern to parents. At the first visit, the most frequent problems parents mentioned were sleep disorders; feeding disorders; dysphoric fussiness/disinterest in play (hereafter referred to as *dysphoric fussiness*); excessive crying; dysfunctional sleep–wake organization; excessive temper tantrums with conflicts over limit setting (hereafter referred to as *excessive defiance*); excessive clinginess with anxiety, social withdrawal, and/or intense separation anxiety (hereafter referred to as *excessive clinginess*); and aggressive/oppositional behavior (see Table 3.2). Less common were failure to thrive (3.3%) in the context of feeding problems, and head banging (2.0%) in the context of excessive defiance. Children with language delay, affective seizures, or sibling rivalry were extremely rare.

Table 3.2. Disorders of Behavioral and Emotional Regulation in Early Childhood).

Excessive crying	29.4%
Dysfunctional sleep-wake organization	25.8%
Chronic fussiness/motor restlessness/disinterest in play	30.1%
Feeding disorders	40.4%
Sleep disorders	62.8%
Excessive clinginess/social withdrawal/separation anxiety	12.3%
Excessive defiance	20.3%
Aggressive/oppositional behavior	6.8%

Note. Behavioral syndromes computed as percentage of the total sample ($n = 701$).

However, the numbers given in Table 3.2 as computed for the total sample represent a somewhat distorted picture. Most behavioral problems of early childhood are not distributed evenly across all ages but are clustered in particular developmental phases. For instance, excessive crying and dysfunctional sleep–wake organization are more or less confined to the first half-year of life, whereas sleep disorders were by definition diagnosed only above the age of 6 months. To take into account the age-dependency of individual syndromes, we also analyzed their distribution by individual age groups.

Phase Specificity of Clinical Syndromes

According to the scientific literature, development in infancy is not continuous but alternates between periods of consolidation and developmental spurts that are also termed *biobehavioral shifts*, *touchpoints*, *critical steps*, or *periods of qualitative transition* (see Figure 3.1). These periods are characterized by comprehensive reorganizational processes, which may be observed cross-culturally in physiological, affective, motor, cognitive, and social domains (Brazelton, 1999; Emde, 1985; Emde, Gaensbauer, & Harmon, 1976; Kagan, 1984; McCall, Eichorn, & Hogarty, 1977; H. Papoušek & Papoušek, 1984; Stern, 1985; Zeanah, Anders, Seifer, & Stern, 1989; see also chapters 1 and 4). The concept of touchpoints (Brazelton, 1999) postulates sensitive periods shortly before each impending developmental shift (around 3, 9, 12, and 18 months), in which critical regulatory tasks must be solved. Regulatory perturbations are more likely to occur in the particular behavioral domains that undergo major transitions at a given touchpoint. Parents are also more likely to seek help from their pediatrician during these sensitive periods (Brazelton, 1999).

In our sample, the predominance of certain syndromes at certain ages and the age-related course of these syndromes coincide remarkably well with the postulated touchpoints. For example, excessive crying predominates during the first 3 months (97.3% of that age group), during which postnatal adjustments and maturation of physiological processes are in the forefront. This behavior is seen less and less frequently over the rest of the first year.

Figure 3.1. Developmental Phases and Biobehavioral Shifts in Early Childhood.

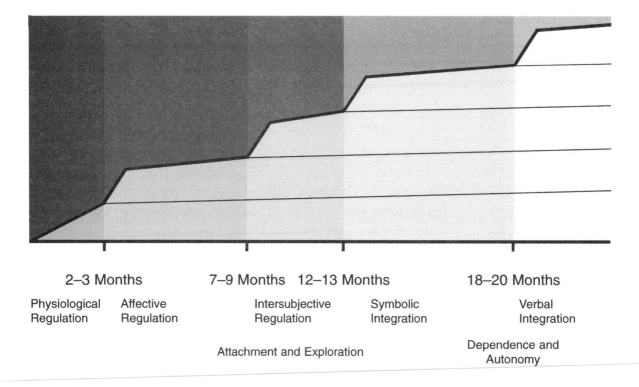

2–3 Months		7–9 Months	12–13 Months	18–20 Months
Physiological Regulation	Affective Regulation	Intersubjective Regulation	Symbolic Integration	Verbal Integration
		Attachment and Exploration		Dependence and Autonomy

As shown in Figure 3.2, dysphoric fussiness increases in frequency over the first 9 months and thus seems to replace excessive crying. We identified a peak of dysphoric fussiness in 45.0% of 7–9-month-olds in our sample, but this occurred only at rates between 30.2% and 35.8% in children older than 9 months. The rapid increase in the frequency of dysphoric fussiness up to its peak in the middle of the second half-year coincides with a developmental phase in which affective and attentional regulation processes and exploratory needs are predominant during the waking state. However, because self-produced locomotion is not yet possible, these developmentally appropriate needs may be frustrated and lead to extended periods of fussiness.

Dysfunctional sleep–wake organization is typically associated with excessive crying in the first 3 months (95.5% of the age group; see chapter 5). At about the sixth month, diurnal problems of sleep–wake organization give way to nighttime sleep disorders, which are the most frequent diagnoses in all age cohorts (between 81.9% and 90.8%; see Figure 3.3). Together with feeding disorders (the percentages vary around 40% in all age groups), these are the only syndromes for which no clear age correlation was found within the total sample. However, children with sleep disorders and/or feeding disorders undergo the same universal developmental processes that require multiple regulatory adjustments, so that in the context of these disorders the same age-related transitions may also be observed as discussed in the following paragraphs (see also chapters 6–8).

Excessive clinginess shows a bell-shaped association with age (see Figure 3.4). After peaking during the fourth quarter of the first year (21.4% of the age group), it remains a reason for referral during the

Figure 3.2. Age-Related Incidence of Excessive Crying and Chronic Fussiness.

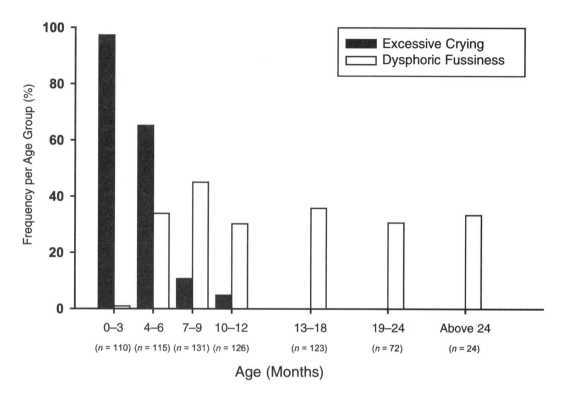

Figure 3.3. Age-Related Incidence of Sleep Disorders and Feeding Disorders.

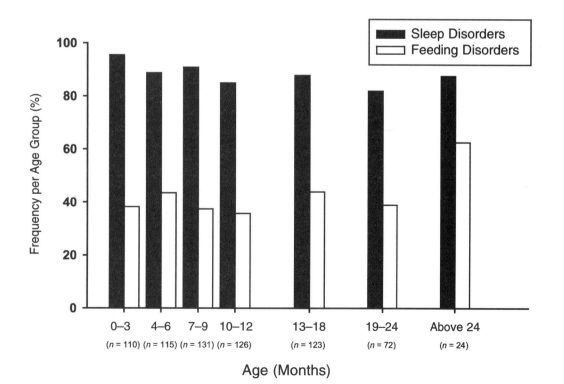

second year. Excessive clinginess appears as the child's attachment to his primary caregivers becomes established, and as fear of strangers and separation anxiety emerge. Maintaining a balance between physical closeness to the secure base and exploration of the environment continues to play a major role in the child's behavioral and emotional regulation in the second year. In the oldest group of children in our sample, however, the frequency of excessive clinginess dropped to 12.5%.

Excessive defiance and aggressive/oppositional behavior emerge as early as the second half of the first year, but only in a small percentage of children. Both syndromes gain in importance over the course of the second and third years, during a period in which self-awareness and goal-directed action develop, and the mother–child interaction is characterized by negotiation around autonomy issues and limit setting. In children above 24 months of age, excessive defiance and aggressive/oppositional behavior appear at a rate of 66.7% and 45.8%, respectively.

Overall, the results reported here illustrate the fact that behavioral syndromes emerge in close association with children's age or developmental phase. Each syndrome reflects the developmental tasks that await the child. However, the syndrome often persists beyond the usual developmental phase during which the task has been mastered (see chapter 4).

Co-Occurrence of Clinical Syndromes (Pervasiveness of Regulatory Problems)

Previously, it has been common for disorders of behavioral and emotional regulation in early childhood to be studied in isolation from each other. One of the first attempts to analyze the co-occurrence of

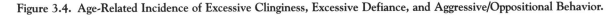

Figure 3.4. Age-Related Incidence of Excessive Clinginess, Excessive Defiance, and Aggressive/Oppositional Behavior.

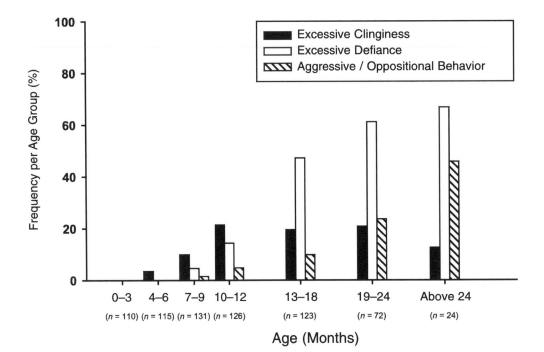

these syndromes was undertaken by Wolke, Meyer, Ohrt, and Riegel (1995). The authors studied the association between crying, sleeping, and feeding problems in a representative nonclinical sample of 5-month-old infants ($n = 430$) and found that only 14.6% of the infants exhibited more than one of these problems. Our clinical sample showed a much different picture: Our patients, the older ones in particular, suffered from up to seven different behavioral problems concurrently ($M \pm SD$: 2.3 ± 1.1).

Of infants younger than 3 months who were brought to the Munich Program, only 1.9% presented solely with excessive crying. Not a single baby who was brought to the program between 4 and 6 months of age had difficulty with excessive crying alone. Whereas Wolke et al. (1995) found little evidence of associations between crying, sleeping, and feeding problems in their nonclinical sample, these disorders were frequently combined in our sample. For example, 96.3% of the infants who presented with crying problems up to the age of 3 months also exhibited dysfunctional sleep–wake organization. We suggest that these problems together constitute the clinical diagnosis of excessive crying (see chapter 5). Nine out of 10 (90.7%) infants between the ages of 4 and 6 months who exhibited persistent crying also presented with dysfunctional sleep–wake organization or nighttime sleep disorders, depending on their age. During the first half-year of life, excessive crying co-occurred with feeding disorders in 41.2% of cases and with dysphoric fussiness in 13.2%.

Of the 440 children who presented with sleep disorders at their first visit, only 27.7% exhibited no other problems. Those syndromes co-occurring most frequently with sleep disorders included feeding disorders (36.6%), dysphoric fussiness (35.5%), excessive defiance (27.0%), and excessive clinginess (15.9%).

A similar pattern can be seen in the 283 children referred to the program because of feeding disorders. In only 8.1% of these children did this disorder present in isolation. In this group of children we observed concurrent problems with dysfunctional sleep–wake organization or sleep disorders (81.3%), excessive crying (31.4%), excessive defiance (23.3%), and excessive clinginess (13.8%).

None of the 142 children in our sample who presented with excessive defiance exhibited this symptom in isolation. Excessive defiance co-occurred with sleep disorders (83.8% of cases), feeding disorders (46.5%), dysphoric fussiness (45.8%), aggressive/oppositional behavior (26.1%), and excessive clinginess (21.8%).

Early Signs of Later Clinical Syndromes

In prospective studies of random samples, investigators have found associations between excessive crying during the first months of life and later behavioral problems such as feeding problems in the first (Shaver, 1974) and second years of life (St. James-Roberts, Conroy, & Wilsher, 1998), and sleep disorders in the second (St. James-Roberts et al., 1998; Wolke et al., 1995) and third years of life (Rautava, Lehtonen, Helenius, & Sillanpää, 1995). In the same vein, investigators have found associations between heightened anxiousness in 15-month-olds (St. James-Roberts et al., 1998) and daily temper tantrums at 3 years (Rautava et al., 1995). In one of our own prospective studies, we found clear indications that the clinical syndrome of excessive crying in early infancy is a precursor of clinically significant behavioral and emotional problems at 30 months (see chapter 13).

To investigate in a larger sample whether regulation disorders in the first half-year of life may be early signs of later behavioral problems, we analyzed retrospectively the individual case histories of the 476 children who came to the program for the first time when they were between 7 and 55 months of age. Only 9.9% of these children had not exhibited any behavioral problems during the first half-year of life. In 74.4% of the 414 children who were referred to us because of sleep disorders, dysfunctional sleep–wake organization had already been evident during the first 6 months. Excessive crying and feeding disorders also preceded later sleep disorders in 64.3% and 20.0% of infants, respectively.

Early excessive crying was not a predictor specifically of later sleep disorders. Excessive crying and dysfunctional sleep–wake organization had preceded later feeding disorders in 55.5% and 59.2%, respectively. In 42.4%, feeding disorders had already begun within the first 6 months of life. Moreover, excessive crying in combination with dysfunctional sleep–wake organization had also been evident within the first half-year of life in children with later excessive clinginess (69.5% of 82) and excessive defiance (64.8% of 142).

In a prospective study, we followed those infants who were referred for a second or third time to the Munich Program in order to find out how old they were when they returned and what kinds of problems they were presenting. Of the 225 infants who had been admitted for the first time during their first half-year of life between 1994 and 1997, 63 (28.0%) had been treated again as of the year 2000. Of the 52 children who had exhibited excessive crying during their first treatment at our program, 59.6% were seen for a second time, at an average age of 13.9 months (± 7.1 months) because of sleep disorders, 30.8% at 15.7 months (± 10.7 months) because of dysphoric fussiness, and 19.2% at 28.1 months (± 14.6 months) because of excessive defiance. Second visits because of feeding disorders (mean age [M ± SD]: 12.8 ± 4.3 months) were relatively rare (7.7%). Prospective data from third (in 6.8% of cases) and fourth treatments (in 2.0% of cases) were unsuitable for analysis because of the small sample sizes.

Duration of Individual Disorders Prior to the First Visit

The infants and young children in our sample had spent an enormous proportion of their short lifetimes with problems of behavioral and emotional regulation before their parents were informed and ready to avail themselves of our counseling and treatment services. Most parents had tried in vain to deal with the problems themselves. As discussed in the previous section, in the majority of cases infants' first behavioral problems had been early excessive crying and dysfunctional sleep–wake organization. From the onset of the first behavioral problems, an average of 9.2 months (± 6.6 months) had passed before the initial contact with the program.

The duration of problems before parents came to the program seems even more excessive in relation to the infant's age. On average, regulatory problems had affected more than 89.6% (± 21.2%) of the infant's lifetime; 67.0% of the parents reported that since the birth of their baby they had not experienced a single period of undisturbed, relaxed, and joyful togetherness. These figures illustrate the enormous burden that persistent regulatory problems place on parental resources and developing parent–child relationships.

[handwritten marginalia: Segment #; Sample of infants - toddlers = behavioral disorders; 30% prem / SGA / twins multiples / - ; Several birth complications]

Prenatal, Perinatal, and Postnatal Risk Factors

What conditions increase the risk of disorders of behavioral and emotional regulation? What makes these disorders pervasive and persistent? According to Scheithauer, Niebank, and Petermann (2000), an array of somatic, interactional, and interpersonal (psychosocial) factors may lead to maladaptive development in children. These factors are more often cumulative than isolated in their occurrence. Among these conditions, vulnerability factors may be distinguished from risk factors, depending on whether they pertain to characteristics of the individual child or of his environment.

We distinguish between primary (congenital, more or less unchangeable) and secondary (acquired, therefore more amenable to change) vulnerability factors, depending on the degree to which they may be affected by treatment. If it can be shown that modification of a factor changes the risk of developing a given disorder, this factor can be regarded as a causal risk factor. This definition clearly differs from the usual understanding of a causal factor as a necessary and sufficient condition for a specific diagnosis.

Depending on the time at which risk factors become manifest, we distinguish between prenatal factors (e.g., maternal age, prenatal stress, psychological disturbances, substance abuse), perinatal and immediate postnatal factors (e.g., birth complications, gestational age, birth weight), and later postnatal factors (e.g., health status during the first year of life; see Allen, Lewinsohn, & Seeley, 1998). Within these stages, we also distinguish between somatic and psychosocial factors.

The following sections summarize our results regarding risk factors identified during the medical examination of the child and semistructured interviews with the mother or both parents.

Prenatal organic risk factors. As Table 3.3 shows, 68.9% of the mothers in our sample exhibited at least one prenatal somatic risk factor. The percentage of mothers who were at least 40 years old when they gave birth and the percentage of mothers who smoked are comparable to the rates in the 2001 representative Bavarian Perinatal Survey (Bayerische Arbeitsgemeinschaft für Qualitätssicherung in der stationären Versorgung, Arbeitsgruppe Geburtshilfe [BAQ; Bavarian Task Force for Quality Assurance in Hospital Care, Obstetric Task Force], 2002). The rates of most of the somatic risk factors listed in Table 3.3, however, are between two and four times higher in our clinical sample. The extremely high rates of severe hyperemesis and premature labor that required medical treatment are particularly notable in our sample.

Prenatal psychosocial risk factors. How well pregnant mothers can adapt to life-changing events, as well as to acute and chronic stress, influences both their own psychological and physical health as well as the infant's emotional and behavioral development (Dunkel-Schetter & Lobel, 1998; cf. review by Wurmser, 2007; Wurmser et al., 2006). As early as the middle of the 20th century, Sontag (1941) identified a relationship between prenatal distress experienced by the mother and problematic feeding behavior in her infant. Sontag attributed these behavioral problems to irritability and hyperreactivity of the infant's autonomic nervous system.

The results of more recent studies have also pointed to the role of psychological stress during pregnancy in the etiological development of behavioral problems in infancy. Prospective studies have shown that significant prenatal risk factors for excessive infant crying include a problematic pregnancy, psychosomatic complaints (such as hyperemesis, pelvic pain, fatigue, headaches), maternal depression, partnership conflicts, frequent stress, social isolation, and other psychological problems during preg-nancy (Hoegdall, Vestermark, Birch, Plenov, & Toftager-Larsen, 1991; Rautava, Helenius, & Lehtonen, 1993; Rautava et al., 1995).

The psychological state of the pregnant mother is associated with additional infant characteristics. For example, in a prospective study, Field, Sandberg, Quetel, Garcia, and Rosario (1985) found associations between the level of a mother's prenatal anxiety and her newborn's hyperreactivity or limited capacity for self-regulation. Huttunen (1989) reported that the mother's prenatal psychological state (e.g., depression, nervousness, labile mood) is correlated with various dimensions of infant temperament, such as social withdrawal, irritability, negative emotionality, slow adaptability, distractibility, and high intensity. In addition, newborns and infants of mothers who have been suffering from prenatal

Table 3.3. Prevalence of Somatic Risk Factors: Comparison of the Present Clinical Sample With a Representative Sample.

	Clinical Sample (%)	Perinatal Survey (%)
Prenatal ≥ 1 risk factor	**68.9**	–
Previous miscarriages ≥ 2	9.0	3.7
Previous infertility treatment	7.4	2.5
Twins or triplets	6.3	1.7
Maternal age ≥ 40 years	2.0	2.9
Severe hyperemesis	17.3	0.4
Premature labor requiring tocolysis	20.3	5.6
Nicotine abuse	11.9	9.6
Cerclage	1.9	0.5
Gestosis	5.6	2.1
Perinatal ≥ 1 risk factor	**38.8**	–
Cesarean section	22.3	23.3
Forceps/vacuum	12.0	6.5
Amniotic infection syndrome	5.2	0.7
Premature birth (< 37th week)	10.6	4.8
Small for gestational age SGA (<10th percentile)	15.6	~10.1
Severe birth complications (child)	5.0	–
Severe birth complications (mother)	2.1	–
Postnatal ≥ 1 risk factor	**85.4**	–
Family atopy (first-degree relatives)	54.7	–
Manifest atopy (child)	18.2	–
Recurrent infections	28.6	–
Hospitalization	16.0	–
Neuromotor problems	33.9	–
Developmental disorders	3.1	–

Note. Clinical sample of the Munich Program (sample sizes according to available data [n = 689–700]). Representative sample from the Bavarian Perinatal Survey [n = 104,391]; BAQ, 2002.

depression are frequently irritable and exhibit immature sleep–wake organization, dysfunctional autonomic and endocrine regulation (e.g., elevated cortisol levels), neuromotor problems, and growth retardation (cf. Cohn, Matias, Tronick, Connell, & Lyons-Ruth, 1986; Field, 1998; Jones, Field, Davalos, & Pickens, 1997). Field and her colleagues (2002) attributed these phenomena to elevated stress hormone levels in the pregnant mother, with a potential negative effect on fetal development.

In a recent study of the effects of prenatal maternal stress on infant behavioral development during the first 6 months of life, we found that infants of mothers who experienced multiple negative life events in pregnancy exhibited more reactivity to mild stressors and diminished self-regulatory competencies in the neonatal period, more crying and fussing during the first 6 months of life, more distress to limitations and more fear at 3 months of life, and less soothability at 6 months of life (Wurmser, 2007; Wurmser et al., 2006).

Using standardized interventions with animals under experimental conditions, Schneider and her colleagues were able to further isolate the effects of prenatal stress from other factors. In a series of well-controlled studies of rhesus monkeys, these authors demonstrated that mothers who were subjected to repeated mild but unpredictable psychological stress during pregnancy (such as short-term transfer to an unfamiliar darkened and noisy room) gave birth to offspring with a particular pattern of disorders. These included neuromotor problems, such as delayed motor development and muscular hypotonia, and attentional problems (Schneider, 1992b; Schneider & Coe, 1993; Schneider, Coe, & Lubach, 1992; Schneider, Roughton, Koehler, & Lubach, 1999); impairment of behavioral organization (Roughton, Schneider, Bromley, & Coe, 1998) and cognitive functions (Schneider, 1992a); hyper-reactivity (Clarke & Schneider, 1993; Schneider, 1992c); and impaired social behavior (Clarke, Soto, Bergholz, & Schneider, 1996). Schneider et al. (1992) postulated that these problems in rhesus monkeys may be caused by hypercortisolism and its effects on cerebral development of the fetus (e.g., on neurons in the cerebellum, the vestibular nuclear complex, the hippocampus, and cortex). However, the specific physiological mechanisms have not yet been clarified.

Schneider's animal studies suggest a potential sensitive period of fetal development in which prenatal stress has a particularly deleterious effect on the maturation of the fetus. Schneider and colleagues (1999) compared the effects of maternal stress during the first and second half of pregnancy. The offspring of rhesus monkeys that had been stressed during early pregnancy exhibited lower birth weight, impaired neuromotor functioning (vestibular reactions, rotary nystagmus, motor coordination, regulation of muscle tone), and impaired cognitive functions (orientation, attention span) in comparison to a nonstressed control group and to a group of offspring that were delivered by mothers who had been stressed during the second half of pregnancy. These findings suggest that psychological stressors appear to affect embryonic and fetal development during the particular phase of pregnancy in which cortisol still passes easily across the placental barrier (Pepe & Albrecht, 1984, 1995).

In human studies, investigators have estimated that approximately 25% of all pregnant women experience prenatal stress, anxiety, or depression (cf. Norbeck & Tilden, 1983). In our clinical sample, 56.1% of mothers reported marked psychological or psychosocial stress during pregnancy (see Table 3.4). Stress, anxiety, and/or depression were almost twice as frequent in our sample (45.8%) than would be expected according to the estimates of Norbeck and Tilden (1983). The rate of prenatal partnership conflicts was nine times as high in our sample as in our own control group of expectant parents whose babies did not manifest regulation disorders (18.1% vs. 2.0% [n = 49]; M. Papoušek & von Hofacker, 1998; see also chapter 5).

According to Schuth (1989), even women who are eager to have a baby may experience ambivalent feelings and transient rejection of the child during pregnancy. Although approximately 30% of women reject their unborn child at the time their pregnancy is confirmed, this figure drops to about 5% at the time of birth (Netter, 1984). These data are consistent with the rate of unwanted pregnancies in our control group (6.1%; M. Papoušek & von Hofacker, 1998; see also chapter 5). Compared with these figures, the prevalence of primary unwanted pregnancy in our clinical sample is slightly elevated (see Table 3.4).

Somatic and psychosocial factors are known to be frequently confounded (cf. Esser, Laucht, & Schmidt, 1994). Taking this into account, we analyzed the interrelations between the most frequent prenatal somatic and psychosocial risk factors. Pregnant mothers with marked emotional distress (stress, anxiety,

Table 3.4. Prevalence of Psychosocial Risk Factors.

	Clinical Sample (%)
Prenatal ≥ 1 risk factor	**56.1**
Abnormal stress	23.2
Abnormal anxiety	25.7
Depression	6.3
Couple's conflicts	18.1
Unwanted pregnancy	10.2
Perinatal ≥ 1 risk factor	**23.2**
Subjective traumatic delivery	8.9
Early separation of mother and newborn	14.6
Postnatal ≥ 1 risk factor	**80.7**
Persistent severe couple's conflicts	49.4
Maternal psychological disturbances	47.4
Conflicts with families of origin	33.7
Distressing childhood experiences	37.3
Social isolation	30.1
Unresolved maternal trauma (loss, abuse)	16.1
Socioeconomic pressures	6.0
Migration-related cultural stressors	5.6
Maternal role conflicts	9.3
Chronic somatic disease in the mother	9.8
Other chronic stressors	6.7

Note. Clinical sample of the Munich Program (sample sizes according to available data [n = 689–701]).

or depression, or SAD [+]; n = 319) tended more frequently than nondistressed women (SAD [–]; n = 378) to experience severe hyperemesis (20.4% vs. 14.8%). However, this difference was not significant, $X^2(1, N = 697)$ = 3.73, p > .05. More than twice as many SAD (+) women reported premature labor requiring tocolysis than did SAD (–) women (29.8% vs. 12.4%), $X^2(1, N = 697)$ = 32.09, p ≤ .001; as well as two or more previous miscarriages (12.9% vs. 5.8%), $X^2(1, N = 697)$ = 10.41, p ≤ .001. Prior infertility treatment was not significantly greater in the SAD (+) women (8.8% vs. 6.3%), $X^2(1, N = 697)$ = 1.48, p > .05. Yet, the percentage of unwanted pregnancies in SAD (+) women was significantly above the rate for SAD (–) women (13.2% vs. 7.4%), $X^2(1, N = 697)$ = 6.35, p ≤ .05. Unwanted pregnancies were even more closely associated with prenatal couples' conflicts. Whereas 38.9% of the women (n = 126) in partnerships with severe conflicts rejected their pregnancy, this was true for only 3.7% of women (n = 571) who reported no problems with their partner, $X^2(1, N = 697)$ = 141.66, p ≤ .001.

To identify which risks tend to be associated with each other, we analyzed the factorial structure of all prenatal somatic and psychosocial pregnancy risk factors listed in Tables 3.3 and 3.4 using principal components analysis with varimax rotation. The analysis resulted in a solution with six factors: (a) Unwanted Pregnancy, Couples' Conflicts, Nicotine Abuse; (b) Multiple Pregnancy, Previous Infertility Treatment; (c) Abnormal Anxiety, Premature Labor Requiring Tocolysis, More Than Two Previous Miscarriages; (d) Gestosis, Cerclage, Prenatal Depression; (e) Maternal Age > 40, Abnormal Stress; and (f) Severe Hyperemesis. The load matrix points to positive correlations between individual pregnancy risks and their underlying components for each of the six factors. The combination of individual risks confirms the findings of Esser et al. (1994) that somatic and psychosocial risks are often interrelated.

Our findings demonstrate that mothers who were referred to the Munich Program experienced considerably more stress from both somatic and psychosocial pregnancy risks than did a representative sample of the Bavarian population or our own control group. Documented prenatal risks tend to accumulate and may become serious psychosomatic risks to the health of mother and baby.

Perinatal organic risk factors. According to recent data from the Bavarian Perinatal Survey (BAQ, 2002), 69.5% of mothers gave birth spontaneously; our clinical sample yielded a similarly high percentage (66.0%). The rates of Cesarean section were similar as well in both samples (see Table 3.3). However, the case histories of infants referred to the Munich Program showed significantly higher rates of forceps births or vacuum extraction as well as an increased incidence of amniotic infection syndrome and premature births. In addition, there was a higher incidence of children in our sample whose birth weight was below the 10th percentile (Thomson, Billewicz, & Hytten, 1968), that is, malnourished in utero, whereas the percentage of low birthweight babies in the Bavarian population as a whole was as expected. The birth weights of 9.1% of our children were under 2,500 g (61% for the premature births and 2.9% for infants born at term). We found severe intrauterine malnutrition (birth weight below the 3rd percentile) in 6.8% of premature infants and in 4.0% of term babies in our sample.

The mothers' overall prenatal distress (resulting from abnormal stress, anxiety, depression, and/or conflict) was significantly associated with premature births. Of the SAD (+) women, 16% gave birth before the 37th week of gestation, while this was true for only 6.1% of the SAD (–) women, $X^2(1, N = 697)$ =

17.67, $p \leq .001$. The percentage of small-for-date newborns below the 3rd percentile was slightly elevated for SAD (+) mothers (5.1% vs. 3.7%), although this difference failed to reach significance, $X^2(1, N = 691) = 0.73, p > .05$.

Perinatal psychosocial risk factors. Of the mothers in the clinical sample, 8.9% had experienced the birth of their child as traumatic (see Table 3.4). In a prospective study conducted by Rautava et al. (1993) on the effects of prenatal and perinatal risks, excessive infant crying was significantly associated with subjective birth trauma.

According to the Bavarian Perinatal Survey (BAQ, 2002), early transfer of the infant to another unit was documented for 10.4% of all newborns. In addition or in combination, 25.2% of all vaginal deliveries were followed by a transfer of the mother as a result of puerperal complications (anemia, fever, wound-healing problems, thrombosis). In our sample, early separation resulting from birth or puerperal complications of the mother and/or the infant occurred with comparable frequency (see Table 3.4).

In summary, the families in our clinical sample exhibited higher rates of forceps or vacuum extraction, amniotic infection syndrome, premature birth, and small for gestational age births than did families in the general Bavarian population. Surgical delivery by Cesarean section and early separation of mother and newborn, however, were not more frequent in our client base than in the Bavarian population as a whole.

Postnatal organic risk factors. By the time of their first visit to the program, 65.6% of the mothers had already weaned their infants or had bottle-fed them from birth. The duration of nursing varied considerably between 0 and 20 months ($M \pm SD$: 3.5 $\pm$ 3.5 months). Of the children who had already been weaned at the time of their first visit, 23.0% ($n = 457$) had been nursed not at all or less than 1 month, 38.6% only to the end of the first 3 months, 19.3% until 6 months, 12.5% until 9 months, and 6.6% for 10 months or longer.

The most frequent postnatal somatic vulnerability factors for infants in the present sample are listed in Table 3.3. Compared with the figures from our own control group, the infants' predisposition to allergic and/or asthmatic illnesses is markedly increased due to atopic problems in first-degree relatives (54.7% vs. 30.6%; see chapter 5). Manifest atopic problems, mostly in the form of mild symptoms of neuro-dermatitis and less often protein intolerance with gastrointestinal symptoms, were found in only 18.2% of clinical cases. Other somatic symptoms in the clinical sample included mild to moderate neuromotor problems in the form of transient asymmetries, hypertonia, and a delay in bodily self-righting. A particularly high proportion of manifest neuromotor problems was seen in infants with *excessive crying* (60.2% as compared with 22.4% in our control group; see chapter 5). A relatively high percentage of children also suffered from recurrent infections. Previous hospitalizations, developmental disorders, severe infectious diseases, gastroesophageal reflux, cardiac diseases, inguinal hernias, and genetic syndromes were found only rarely. We also analyzed whether these postnatal somatic risks were associated with the mothers' prenatal psychosocial stress during pregnancy. Infants of women who were particularly affected by prenatal stress, anxiety, or depression (SAD [+]) were at significantly higher risk of mild neuromotor problems than the infants of mothers without major prenatal distress (40.6% vs. 28.3%), $X^2(1, N = 697) = 11.58, p \leq .005$.

Postnatal psychosocial risk factors. Table 3.4 lists the most important psychosocial risks during the postnatal period. Engfer (1988) reported that even in families that were relatively unstressed, the parents experienced some deterioration of their partnership between the 4th and the 43rd month postpartum. In our sample, half of the mothers reported marked conflict in the partnership. In couples whose relationship had been strained even before the birth of their child (n = 126), conflict continued or worsened postnatally in 81.7% of these cases. By contrast, in families in which the partnership was not strained prenatally (n = 566), conflicts began in the postnatal phase in only 42.2% of the cases, $X^2(1, N = 692) = 64.39, p \le .001$. The postnatal increase in the rate of conflicted partnerships may be explained by both the typical challenges of postpartum adjustments (see chapter 4) and by the distress associated with their infant's regulation disorder.

Conflicts between parents have deleterious effects on children of all ages (Cummings & Davies, 1994; Grych & Fincham, 1990). Children who experience frequent conflicts between their mother and father are at higher risk of both externalizing disorders (aggression, oppositional and antisocial behavior) and internalizing disorders (anxiety, depression, social withdrawal, and somatic symptoms) than are children of couples whose relationship is less strained (Carlson, Tamm, & Hogan, 1999; Cummings & Davies, 1994; Davies & Cummings, 1994; Grych & Fincham, 1990).

Partnership conflicts are frequently associated with an elevated risk of psychological problems or mental disturbances in the partners, particularly with depression in women (Hammen, 1999). Partnership conflicts may also come to the fore before the emergence of a mental disorder, or be worsened by a manifest disorder (Herpertz-Dahlmann & Remschmidt, 2000). We observed psychological disturbances in mothers considerably more frequently in our clinical sample than in the control group (47.4% vs. 4.1%; see chapter 5). Psychological disturbances in the mother were significantly more frequent (61.0% vs. 33.8%) among couples who experienced marked conflicts after the birth of the child (n = 344) than among couples with unproblematic relationships (n = 352), $X^2(1, N = 696) = 51.79, p \le .001$. Among the mothers with psychological disturbances (n = 332), 56.3% suffered from postpartum depression, 46.4% from neurotic relational disturbances, 16.9% from personality disorders, and 8.2% from ongoing eating disorders (multiple mentions were possible). In addition to partnership conflicts and low socioeconomic status, affective disorders in the parents, (including the chronicity and severity of their psychopathology) have been shown to increase the probability of behavioral and emotional disorders in their children (Keller et al., 1986).

According to von Siebenthal and Largo (2000), other postnatal risk factors with prognostic significance for the development of the child include socioeconomic pressure, a child's experience of loss of a significant other, and migration-related cultural pressures. In addition to these factors, conflicts with the families of origin, social isolation, and mothers' distressing childhood experiences were much more frequent in our clinical sample than in the control group (see chapter 5). Interestingly, children of mothers who reported unresolved traumatic loss (n = 81) were far more likely than children of mothers without traumatic loss (n = 620) to exhibit excessive clinginess (19.8% vs. 11.3%), $X^2(1, N = 701) = 4.77, p \le .05$; as well as excessive defiance (30.9% vs. 18.9%), $X^2(1, N = 701) = 6.38, p \le .05$. Likewise, children of mothers who had experienced physical or emotional abuse (n = 44) were far more likely than children of mothers without such history (n = 657) to exhibit aggressive/oppositional behavior

(22.7% vs. 5.8%), $X^2(1, N = 701) = 18.56$, $p \leq .001$; as well as excessive defiance (40.9% vs. 18.9%), $X^2(1, N = 701) = 12.40$, $p \leq .001$. It is possible that the mother's specific experiences of her past are reenacted and reflected in the child's behavior problems during everyday mother–infant interactions (see chapter 8).

We performed principal components analysis with varimax rotation on all postnatal somatic and psychosocial risks listed in Tables 3.3 and 3.4 to identify which risks are interrelated and constitute factors of coherent risk. The analysis resulted in a solution with six factors: (a) Distressing Childhood Experiences of the Mother, Conflicts With the Families of Origin, Maternal Psychological Disturbances, and Unresolved Maternal Trauma; (b) Socioeconomic Pressure, Social Isolation, Migration-Related Culture-Specific Pressures, and Marked Partnership Conflict; (c) Infant Developmental Disorder, Neuromotor Problems, Hospitalization, and Chronic Stressors on the Mother; (d) Recurrent Infections and Manifest Atopy (Child); (e) Family Atopy (First-Degree Relatives) and Role Conflicts in the Mother; and (f) Chronic Physical Illness in the Mother. In each case, there is a positive correlation between the individual risks and the corresponding factors. In contrast to the prenatal risks, postnatal psychosocial and somatic risks mainly load on separate factors.

Overall, it has been shown that family atopies, neuromotor problems in the child, psychological disturbances in the mother, current conflicts with families of origin, distressing childhood experiences of the mother, and social isolation occur significantly more often in the clinical sample than in a control group without manifest regulation disorders. Postnatal risks tend to be cumulative, and to constitute separate factors of coherent psychosocial and somatic risk.

SUMMARY AND CONCLUDING REMARKS

The treatment and care provided by the Munich Interdisciplinary Research and Intervention Program are an important resource for distressed families with children experiencing behavioral and emotional regulation disorders. A review of more than 10 years of records shows that our sample is representative of the Bavarian population as a whole in terms of sex distribution and proportion of foreigners. The overrepresentation of first-borns in the client base may be attributed to their parents' lack of caregiving experience. As with all institution-based programs, the thresholds for seeking help may have been too high for a number of disadvantaged groups in need, as these families were clearly underrepresented. Our outpatient intervention services were enlisted less often than we had hoped by adolescent single mothers, working mothers, drug-addicted parents, parents with a low level of education and socio-economic status, and mothers with psychiatric disorders. That is, the program failed to serve precisely those groups in which one would expect to encounter a particularly high risk of behavioral and emo-tional problems and impaired parent–child relationships. Special home-based services need to be cre-ated for these multiple risk groups, or the admission threshold needs to be lowered for them at existing facilities. Moreover, programs should ensure that families with regulation disorders find specialized help substantially earlier than has been the case to date. On average, 9 months had passed before the highly distressed parents made their first visit to the program with their child. This is simply too long a delay because of the growing risks for the developing parent–child relationships and the child's social and emotional development.

In contrast to the Mannheim longitudinal risk study (Laucht et al., 1992), children with genetic syndromes, neurological and other developmental disorders, and multiple handicaps represented only a very small portion of our client base. Even when they exhibited regulation disorders, these children were treated in other programs in our center.

The kinds of behavioral syndromes presented by children at the Munich Program are related to specific ages or developmental tasks. If the parents were better prepared to understand what developmental tasks will be challenging a baby at a given time, escalating turbulence in the parent–child relationship could be prevented in many cases—or at least dealt with more effectively.

Disorders of behavioral and emotional regulation in infancy tend to be pervasive. They are characterized by the co-occurrence or sequential occurrence of different behavioral syndromes. Many problems that typically emerge during the second half-year of life or in later phases of early childhood development actually have precursors in the first half-year, mostly in the form of excessive crying and dysfunctional sleep–wake organization. Without timely intervention, these early disorders tend to persist and to pervade other behavioral domains. It is therefore important not to underestimate early excessive crying and to offer timely help with targeted counseling or even parent–infant psychotherapy.

The majority of families that made use of our specialized treatment services had already experienced severe distress during pregnancy and/or during and after the infant's birth; they were often exhausted by the excessive demands of the infant's long-standing behavioral problems. We have shown that prenatal, perinatal, and postnatal risks, both somatic and psychosocial, tend to accumulate and to be closely interconnected. Individual vulnerability and risk factors represent neither a necessary nor a sufficient condition for the development of a regulation disorder. However, all risk factors tend to drain the resources of the entire system in a more or less nonspecific manner. The high rates of prenatal psychosocial risks that increase the risk of regulation disorders and may jeopardize the mental health of infants and parents call for intensified preventive counseling and treatment services already during pregnancy.

The following chapter focuses on the specific mechanisms and processes by which vulnerability and risk factors are linked to the etiological development of disorders of behavioral and emotional regulation.

REFERENCES

Allen, N. B., Lewinsohn, P. M., & Seeley, J. R. (1998). Prenatal and perinatal influences on risk for psychopathology in childhood and adolescence. *Development and Psychopathology, 10,* 513–529.

Alt, C., & Weidacher, A. (1996). *Lebensphasen und Wohnungssituation junger Menschen in West und Ost, Diskurs 2* (pp. 15–20). München, Germany: DJI-Verlag.

Alvarez, M., & St. James-Roberts, I. (1996). Infant fussing and crying patterns in the first year in an urban community in Denmark. *Acta Paediatrica, 85,* 463–466.

Bates, J. E., Freeland, C. A., & Lounsbury, M. L. (1979). Measurement of infant difficultness. *Child Development, 50,* 794–803.

Bayerische Arbeitsgemeinschaft für Qualitätssicherung in der stationären Versorgung, Arbeitsgruppe Geburtshilfe. (2002). *Bayerische Perinatalerhebung, Jahresauswertung 2001,* München, Germany: Arbeitsgruppe Geburtshilfe. Available from www.baq-bayern.de/downloads/files/16_1_2001_online.pdf

Bayerisches Landesamt für Statistik und Datenverarbeitung. (1997). *Statistisches Jahrbuch für Bayern*. München, Germany: Landesamt.

Brazelton, T. B. (1999). How to help parents of young children: The touchpoints model. *Journal of Perinatology, 19*, 6–7.

Carlson, C. L., Tamm, L., & Hogan, A. E. (1999). The child with oppositional defiant disorder and conduct disorder in the family. In H. C. Quay & A. E. Hogan (Eds.), *Handbook of disruptive behavior disorders* (pp. 337–352). New York: Kluwer Academic/Plenum.

Clarke, A. S., & Schneider, M. L. (1993). Prenatal stress has long-term effects on behavioral responses to stress in juvenile rhesus monkeys. *Developmental Psychobiology, 26*, 293–304.

Clarke, A. S., Soto, A., Bergholz, T., & Schneider, M. L. (1996). Maternal gestational stress alters adaptive and social behavior in adolescent rhesus monkey offspring. *Infant Behavior and Development, 19*, 451–461.

Cohn, J., Matias, R., Tronick, E., Connell, D., & Lyons-Ruth, K. (1986). Face-to-face interactions of depressed mothers and their infants. In E. Tronick & T. Field (Eds.), *Maternal depression and infant disturbance. New directions for child development* (pp. 31–44). San Francisco: Jossey-Bass.

Cox, J. L., Holden, J. M., & Sagovsky, R. (1987). Detection of postnatal depression. Development of the 10-item Edinburgh Postnatal Depression Scale. *British Journal of Psychiatry, 150*, 782–786.

Cummings, E. M., & Davies, P. T. (1994). *Children and marital conflict: The impact of family dispute and resolution.* New York: Guilford Press.

Davies, P. T., & Cummings, E. M. (1994). Marital conflict and child adjustment: An emotional security hypothesis. *Psychological Bulletin, 116*, 387–411.

Dunkel-Schetter, C., & Lobel, M. (1998). Pregnancy and childbirth. In E. A. Blechman & K. D. Brownell (Eds.), *Behavioral medicine and women: A comprehensive handbook* (pp. 475–482). New York: Guilford Press.

Emde, R. N. (1985). The affective self: Continuities and transformations from infancy. In J. D. Call, E. Galenson, & R. L. Tyson (Eds.), *Frontiers of infant psychiatry* (Vol. 2, pp. 38–54). New York: Basic Books.

Emde, R. N., Gaensbauer, T. J., & Harmon R. J. (1976). Emotional expression in infancy: A biobehavioral study. *Psychological Issues Monograph, 10*(1, Serial No. 37). New York: International Universities Press.

Engfer, A. (1986). Antecedents of perceived behaviour problems in children 4 and 18 months of age—a longitudinal study. In D. Kohnstamm (Ed.), *Temperament and development in childhood* (pp. 165–180). Amsterdam: Swets & Zeitlinger.

Engfer, A. (1988). The interrelatedness of marriage and the mother-child relationship. In R. A. Hinde & J. Stevenson-Hinde (Eds.), *Relationships within families: Mutual influences* (pp. 104–118). Oxford, England: Clarendon.

Engfer, A., & Gavranidou, M. (1987). Antecedents and consequences of maternal sensitivity: A longitudinal study. In H. Rauh & H. C. Steinhausen (Eds.), *Psychobiology and early development. Advances in psychology* (Vol. 46, pp. 71–99). Amsterdam: North-Holland.

Engstler, H. (1998). *Die Familie im Spiegel der amtlichen Statistik* (3rd ed.). Bonn, Germany: Bundesministerium für Familie, Senioren, Frauen und Jugend.

Esser, G., Laucht, M., & Schmidt, M. H. (1994). Die Auswirkungen psychosozialer Risiken für die Kindesentwicklung. In D. Karch (Ed.), *Risikofaktoren der kindlichen Entwicklung* (pp. 143–157). Darmstadt, Germany: Steinkopff.

Esser, G., Laucht, M., Schmidt, M. H., Loffler, W., Reiser, A., Stohr, R. M., et al. (1990). Behaviour problems and developmental status of 3-month-old infants in relation to organic and psychosocial risks. *European Archives of Psychiatry and Neurological Sciences, 239,* 384–390.

Fegert, J. M., Schulz, J., Bergmann, R., Tacke, U., Bergmann, K. E., & Wahn, U. (1997). Schlafverhalten in den ersten drei Lebensjahren. *Praxis der Kinderpsychologie und Kinderpsychiatrie, 46,* 69–91.

Field, T. (1998). Maternal depression effects on infants and early interventions. *Preventive Medicine, 27,* 200–203.

Field, T., Diego, M., Hernandez-Reif, M., Schanberg, S., Kuhn, C., Yando, R., & Bendell, D. (2002). Prenatal depression effects on the foetus and neonate in different ethnic and socio-economic status groups. *Journal of Reproductive and Infant Psychology, 20,* 149–157.

Field, T., Sandberg, D., Quetel, T. A., Garcia, R., & Rosario, M. (1985). Effects of ultrasound feedback on pregnancy anxiety, fetal activity, and neonatal outcome. *Journal of Obstetrics and Gynecology, 66,* 525–528.

Grych, J. H., & Fincham, F. D. (1990). Marital conflict and children' adjustment: A cognitive-contextual framework. *Psychological Bulletin, 108,* 267–290.

Hammen, C. (1999). *Depression: Erscheinungsformen und Behandlung.* Bern, Switzerland: Hans Huber.

Herpertz-Dahlmann, B., & Remschmidt, H. (2000). Störungen der Kind-Umwelt-Interaktion und ihre Auswirkungen auf den Entwicklungsverlauf. In F. Petermann, K. Niebank, & H. Scheithauer (Eds.), *Risiken in der frühkindlichen Entwicklung: Entwicklungspsychopathologie der ersten Lebensjahre* (pp. 223–240). Göttingen, Germany: Hogrefe.

Hoegdall, C. K., Vestermark, V., Birch, M., Plenov, G., & Toftager-Larsen, K. (1991). The significance of pregnancy, delivery and postpartum factors for the development of infantile colic. *Journal of Perinatal Medicine, 19,* 251–257.

Huttunen, M. O. (1989). Maternal stress during pregnancy and the behavior of the offspring. In S. Doxiadis (Eds.), *Early influences shaping the individual* (pp.175–182). New York: Plenum Press.

Ihle, W., & Esser, G. (2002). Epidemiologie psychischer Störungen im Kindes und Jugendalter: Prävalenz, Verlauf, Komorbidität und Geschlechtsunterschiede. *Psychologische Rundschau, 53,* 159–169.

Jones, N. A., Field, T., Davalos, M., & Pickens, J. (1997). EEG stability in infants/children of depressed mothers. *Child Psychiatry and Human Development, 28,* 59–70.

Kagan, J. (1984). *The nature of the child.* New York: Basic Books.

Keller, M. B., Beardslee, W. R., Dorer, D. J., Lavori, P. W., Samuelson, H., & Klerman, G. R. (1986). Impact of severity and chronicity of parental affective illness on adaptive functioning and psychopathology in children. *Archives of General Psychiatry, 43,* 930–937.

Laucht, M., Esser, G., Schmidt, M. H., Ihle, W., Löffler, W., Stöhr, R. M., et al. (1992). Risikokinder. Zur Bedeutung biologischer und psychosozialer Risiken für die kindliche Entwicklung in den ersten beiden Lebensjahren. *Praxis der Kinderpsychologie und Kinderpsychiatrie, 41,* 274–285.

Lindberg, L., Bohlin, G., & Hagekull, B. (1991). Early feeding problems in a normal population. *International Journal of Eating Disorders, 10*, 395–405.

Lozoff, B., & Zuckerman, B. (1988). Sleep problems in children. *Pediatrics in Review, 10*, 17–24.

Lucassen, P. L. B. J., Assendelft, W. J. J., van Eijk, J. Th. M., Gubbels, J. W., Douwes, A. C., & van Geldrop, W. J. (2001). Systematic review of the occurrence of infantile colic in the community. *Archives of Disease in Childhood, 84*, 398–403.

McCall, R. B., Eichorn, D. H., & Hogarty, P. S. (1977). Transitions in early mental development. *Monographs of the Society for Research in Child Development, 42*(Serial No. 171).

Netter, P. (1984). Determinanten des Kinderwunsches und ihre Auswirkungen auf das Kind. In U. Tewes (Ed.), *Angewandte Medizinpsychologie* (pp. 382–390). Frankfurt, Germany: Fachbuchhandlung für Psychologie.

Norbeck, J. S., & Tilden, V. P. (1983). Life stress, social support, and emotional disequilibrium in complications of pregnancy: A prospective, multivariate study. *Journal of Health and Social Behavior, 24*, 30–46.

Papoušek, H., & Papoušek, M. (1984). Qualitative transitions in integrative processes during the first trimester of human postpartum life. In H. F. R. Prechtl (Ed.), *Continuity of neural functions from prenatal to postnatal life* (pp. 220–244). Oxford, England: Blackwell Scientific.

Papoušek, M. (1996). Die intuitive elterliche Kompetenz in der vorsprachlichen Kommunikation als Ansatz zur Diagnostik von präverbalen Kommunikations- und Beziehungsstörungen. *Kindheit und Entwicklung, 5*, 140–146.

Papoušek, M., & von Hofacker, N. (1995). Persistent crying and parenting: Search for a butterfly in a dynamic system. *Early Development and Parenting, 4*, 209–224.

Papoušek, M., & von Hofacker, N. (1998). Persistent crying in early infancy: A non-trivial condition of risk for the developing mother-infant relationship. *Child: Care, Health and Development, 24*, 395–424.

Pepe, G. J., & Albrecht, E. D. (1984). Transuteroplacental metabolism of cortisol and cortisone during mid and late gestation in the baboon. *Endocrinology, 115*, 1946–1951.

Pepe, G. J., & Albrecht, E. D. (1995). Actions of placental and fetal adrenal steroid hormones in primate pregnancy. *Endocrine Reviews, 16*, 608–648.

Pollock, J. I. (1992). Predictors and long-term associations of reported sleeping difficulties in infancy. *Journal of Reproductive and Infant Psychology, 10*, 151–168.

Rautava, P., Helenius, H., & Lehtonen, L. (1993). Psychosocial predisposing factors for infantile colic. *British Medical Journal, 307*, 600–604.

Rautava, P., Lehtonen, L., Helenius, H., & Sillanpää, M. (1995). Infantile colic: Child and family three years later. *Pediatrics, 96*, 43–47.

Richman, N. (1981). A community survey of characteristics of one- to two-year-olds with sleep disruptions. *Journal of the American Academy of Child Psychiatry, 20*, 281–291.

Roughton, E. C., Schneider, M. L., Bromley, L. J., & Coe, C. L. (1998). Maternal endocrine activation during pregnancy alters neurobehavioral state in primate infants. *American Journal of Occupational Therapy, 52*, 90–98.

Scheithauer, H., Niebank, K., & Petermann, F. (2000). Biopsychosoziale Risiken in der frühkindlichen Entwicklung: Das Risiko und Schutzfaktorenkonzept aus entwicklungspsychopathologischer Sicht. In F. Petermann, K. Niebank, & H. Scheithauer (Eds.), *Risiken in der frühkindlichen Entwicklung: Entwicklungspsychopathologie der ersten Lebensjahre* (pp. 65–97). Göttingen, Germany: Hogrefe.

Schneider, M. L. (1992a). Delayed object permanence development in prenatally stressed rhesus monkey infants (*Macaca mulatta*). *Occupational Therapy Journal of Research, 12*, 96–110.

Schneider, M. L. (1992b). The effect of mild stress during pregnancy on birthweight and neuromotor maturation in rhesus monkey infants (*Macaca mulatta*). *Infant Behavior and Development, 15*, 389–403.

Schneider, M. L. (1992c). Prenatal stress exposure alters postnatal behavioral expression under conditions of novelty challenge in rhesus monkey infants. *Developmental Psychobiology, 25*, 529–540.

Schneider, M. L., & Coe, C. L. (1993). Repeated social stress during pregnancy impairs neuromotor development of the primate infant. *Journal of Developmental and Behavioral Pediatrics, 14*, 81–87.

Schneider, M. L., Coe, C. L., & Lubach, G. R. (1992). Endocrine activation mimics the adverse effects of prenatal stress on the neuromotor development of the infant primate. *Developmental Psychobiology, 25*, 427–439.

Schneider, M. L., Roughton, E. C., Koehler, A. J., & Lubach, G. R. (1999). Growth and development following prenatal stress exposure in primates: An examination of ontogenetic vulnerability. *Child Development, 70*, 263–274.

Schuth, W. (1989). Kinderwunschmotive - Risiko für Mutter und Kind? In H. G. Hillemanns & H. Schillinger (Eds.), *Das Restrisiko gegenwärtiger Geburtshilfe* (pp. 318–326). Berlin: Springer-Verlag.

Shaver, B. A. (1974). Maternal personality and early adaptation as related to infantile colic. In P. M. Shereshefsky & L. J. Yarrow (Eds.), *Psychological aspects of a first pregnancy and early postnatal adaptation* (pp. 209–215). New York: Raven Press.

Sontag, I. W. (1941). The significance of fetal environmental differences. *American Journal of Obstetrics and Gynecology, 42*, 996–1003.

Statistisches Bundesamt. (1999). Wiesbaden: Schriftliche Information nach Anfrage (Berichtsjahr 1996).

Stern, D. N. (1985). *The interpersonal world of the infant.* New York: Basic Books.

St. James-Roberts, I., Conroy, S., & Wilsher, K. (1998). Stability and outcome of persistent infant crying. *Infant Behavior and Development, 21*, 411–435.

St. James-Roberts, I., & Halil, T. (1991). Infant crying patterns in the first year: Normative and clinical findings. *Journal of Child Psychology and Psychiatry and Allied Disciplines, 32*, 951–968.

Thomson, A. M., Billewicz, W. Z., & Hytten, F. E. (1968). The assessment of fetal growth. *Journal of Obstetrics and Gynaecology of the British Commonwealth, 75*, 903–916.

von Siebenthal, K., & Largo, R. H. (2000). Frühkindliche Risikofaktoren: Prognostische Bedeutung für die postnatale Entwicklung. In F. Petermann, K. Niebank, & H. Scheithauer (Eds.), *Risiken in der frühkindlichen Entwicklung: Entwicklungspsychopathologie der ersten Lebensjahre* (pp. 139– 155). Göttingen, Germany: Hogrefe.

Wilensky, D. S., Ginsberg, G., Altman, M., Tulchinsky, T. H., Ben Yishay, F., & Auerbach, J. (1996). A community based study of failure to thrive in Israel. *Archives of Disease in Childhood, 75*, 145–148.

Wolke, D. (2000). Fütterungsprobleme bei Säuglingen und Kleinkindern. *Verhaltenstherapie, 10*, 76–87.

Wolke, D., Meyer, R., Ohrt, B., & Riegel, K. (1995). Co-morbidity of crying and feeding problems with sleeping problems in infancy: Concurrent and predictive associations. *Early Development and Parenting, 4*, 191–207.

Wurmser, H. (2007). Einfluss der pränatalen Stressbelastung der Mutter auf die kindliche Verhaltensregulation im ersten Lebenshalbjahr. In K. H. Brisch & T. Hellbruegge (Eds.), *Die Anfänge der Eltern-Kind-Bindung* (pp. 129–156). Stuttgart, Germany: Klett-Cotta.

Wurmser, H., Rieger, M., Domogalla, C., Kahnt, A., Buchwald, J., Kowatsch, M., et al. (2006). Association between life stress during pregnancy and infant crying in the first six months postpartum: A prospective longitudinal study. *Early Human Development, 82,* 341–349.

Zeanah, C. H., Anders, T. F., Seifer, R., & Stern, D. N. (1989). Implications of research on infant development for psychodynamic theory and practice. *Journal of the American Academy of Child and Adolescent Psychiatry, 28,* 657–668.

ZERO TO THREE, Diagnostic Classification Task Force. (1994). *Diagnostic classification: 0–3. Diagnostic classification of mental health and developmental disorders of infancy and early childhood.* Arlington, VA: National Center for Clinical Infant Programs.

ZERO TO THREE. (2005). *Diagnostic classification of mental health and developmental disorders of infancy and early childhood: Revised edition (DC:0–3R).* Washington, DC: ZERO TO THREE Press.

CHAPTER 4

DISORDERS OF BEHAVIORAL AND EMOTIONAL REGULATION: CLINICAL EVIDENCE FOR A NEW DIAGNOSTIC CONCEPT

Mechthild Papoušek

INTRODUCTION: FIRST STEPS

When we first opened the Munich Program for Fussy Babies, the goals of our interdisciplinary clinical research group were rather modest. Our primary concern was to explore and hopefully explain one of the most frequent stressors in parent–infant relationships, that of the so-called infant colic. By offering affected families timely assistance, we also hoped to help relieve the burden of guilt on the mothers who are frequently blamed for their infant's problem. Secondary but equally important goals were to contribute to an understanding of early disturbances in preverbal communication between parents and infants, to identify precursors and conditions that may lead to later psychopathology, and to develop targeted approaches to prevention.

At the beginning, our small team was quickly overwhelmed by the unexpectedly broad age range and multiplicity of disorders of the children who came through our doors, all of whom had been referred to our program as fussy babies (see chapter 3, Table 3.2). What did colic at 3 months have to do with sleep disorders, feeding problems, and failure to thrive? And what was its relationship to early separation anxiety, temper tantrums, dysphoric mood, and motor agitation? The scientific foundations and research were sparse and spread across various disciplines and professional settings. Colic, feeding problems, and failure to thrive were primarily discussed within the rubrics of pediatrics and associated fields, such as infant psychosomatics and behavioral pediatrics (Brazelton, 1994; Wolke, Gray, & Meyer, 1994). Sleep disorders were the province of sleep medicine (Rabenschlag, 1998), stubbornness and oppositional behavior belonged to early childhood education, and anxiety and aggression were found in the realms of child psychiatry and psychoanalysis. It appeared that the unexpectedly diverse behavioral deviations in infancy had not yet been covered by developmental psychology or attachment research. Nor had infancy in and of itself been included in the area of empirical developmental psychopathology of childhood and adolescence (Resch, 1996). There had been several interesting interdisciplinary efforts, particularly in the areas of temperament research (Carey & McDevitt, 1995) and developmental pediatrics (Largo, 1993), in which early behavioral problems were explained in terms of a constitutionally determined variability of otherwise normal behavior. At the opposite pole, a new field of infant psychiatry—mainly influenced by psychodynamic parent–infant psychotherapy—had begun to establish itself and to assign psychiatric diagnoses to similar kinds of problems (ZERO TO THREE, 1994, 2005).

Interesting results were expected from the Mannheim prospective longitudinal risk study even though it included data points only at 3 and 24 months (Esser, Laucht, & Schmidt, 1995; see also chapter 14).

Against this background, the variety of disorders observed in the Munich Program challenged us to develop a clinically oriented interdisciplinary research approach based on infancy research.

The Discovery of Commonalities Among Crying, Sleeping, and Feeding Disorders

The attempt to integrate and synopsize the scattered research results, as well as our own clinical experience and findings, made it clear that crying, sleeping, and feeding problems in infancy include remarkable commonalities in spite of their differences in symptomatology:

1. They are among the most frequent problems seen in pediatric practice, and they affect between 20% and 25% of all physically healthy full-term infants in representative samples (see chapters 5–8).

2. In and of themselves, these disorders show a tendency toward chronological co-occurrence and sequential incidence (see chapter 3; von Hofacker & Papoušek, 1998; Wolke et al., 1994).

3. Such problems may lead parents to seek help, particularly when coinciding with the developmental challenges occurring at so-called touchpoints (Brazelton, 1994).

4. If seen as typical perturbations in infant development (see chapter 1), they are generally viewed as harmless and self-limiting ("children will grow out of it"), and therefore garner little attention.

5. Despite decades of research, the etiology of the problems generally cannot be traced unequivocally to an organic cause or to primary parental failure (St. James-Roberts, Conway, & Wilsher, 1995). In our own clinical sample, in contrast to epidemiological samples, the children and families are stressed by an accumulation of primarily nonspecific organic and psychosocial risk factors that may extend back to the prenatal period and may in specific cases include such factors as protein intolerance, traumatic birth, or emotional neglect as partial causes (see chapter 3).

6. In spite of the behavioral heterogeneity of the disorders, the profile of risk factors is remarkably similar, leading one to suspect that infants with crying, sleeping, and feeding disorders are found overwhelmingly in the same at-risk population. For example, similarly high rates of prenatal organic factors and abnormal degrees of prenatal stress, anxiety, depression, and unresolved conflicts, as well as ongoing stress caused by partnership conflicts between the parents, conflicts with the family of origin, social isolation, and limited resources in mothers with a psychological disorder, are striking in the three subgroups of the Munich sample.

The Clinical Research Paradigm of the Munich Program

The commonalities among the disorders generated many questions about the conditions under which they develop, their progress, and their prognosis in relation to the developmental processes and mechanisms that condition, trigger, sustain, exacerbate, and resolve them.

The clinical intervention program offered us a research paradigm that made use of the systematic and comprehensive interdisciplinary assessments, and of the documentation of findings, interventions, and progress for all infants referred to the Munich program. One of the goals of this approach was to create a comprehensive inventory of infantile disorders of behavioral and emotional regulation. In addition, we wanted to analyze the etiological conditions of individual disorders—as close as possible to their onset—and to do this within the systemic context of daily parent–infant interactions, family resources and stressors, and the dynamic, transactional development of infants, parents, and parent–infant relationships. Videotaped observation of the behavior of the child and parents during examination and treatment and in various contexts of daily interactions played a central role.

The research paradigm also permitted us to generate hypotheses in individual cases about the etiological conditions of the disorder and the interactional mechanisms that triggered and sustained them. These hypotheses were then tested in a targeted intervention and eventually adjusted according to the outcome achieved. All of this occurred in an ideal setting in which clinical and scientific goals were effectively merged.

In elaborating our approach we benefited from years of infancy research conducted by and with Hanuš Papoušek. Of particular value were understandings gained about the early development of basic behavior regulation, the infant's integrative capacities, intuitive parenting, and preverbal communication. The interdisciplinary nature of our approach (H. Papoušek & Papoušek, 1978), its developmental perspective (Emde, 1984), and its orientation based in dynamic systems theory (Smith & Thelen, 1993) were mainly stimulated by international infancy research.

DEVELOPMENTAL SYSTEMIC MODELS OF BEHAVIORAL AND EMOTIONAL REGULATION IN INFANCY

Self-Regulation in Living Organisms

The concept of regulation disorders builds on the psychobiological construct of self-regulation. Self-regulation in living systems includes self-controlled behavioral organization in the context of adaptation and in coping with the animate and inanimate environment while maintaining psycho-physiological balance (Bertalanffy, 1968). The model of the infant's fundamental adaptive response system developed by Hanuš Papoušek (H. Papoušek, 1967; H. Papoušek & Papoušek, 1979) in connection with research on early learning and integration processes gives central importance to the interplay between activating and inhibiting processes (see Figure 4.1). There are interesting parallels here to the neurophysiological behavior activation system (BAS) and the behavior inhibition system (BIS) described by Gray (1987). Other authors limit the term *self-regulation* to forms of behavior and processes that are self-soothing (Prudhomme-White, Gunnar, Larson, Donzella, & Barr, 2000; Rothbart, Derryberry, & Posner, 1994) and contrast it to sensory reactivity of the organism.

The Infant's Fundamental Adaptive Response System

Figure 4.1 gives a simplified overview of the system of basic adaptive behavior regulation (H. Papoušek & Papoušek, 1979) that is controlled by complex neuronal networks and includes somatic–autonomic, neuroendocrinological, sensory–motor, affective, motivational, and integrative subsystems (perception, emotional appraisal, cognitive processing, and control of actions). The model was derived from polygraphic tracings and observations of infant behavior in experimental learning situations (H. Papoušek, 1967).

Early integration of experience generally includes the regulation of arousal, activity, affect, and attention. The four A's are easily observable in the overall behavior of the infant. Their associated signals

Figure 4.1. The Infant's Fundamental Adaptive Response System.

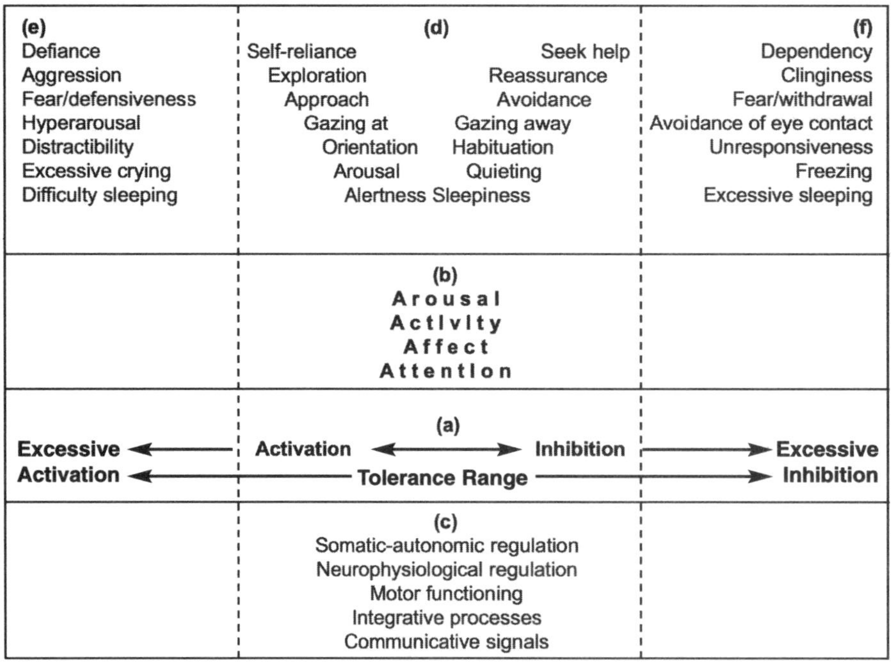

(e)	(d)	(f)
Defiance Aggression Fear/defensiveness Hyperarousal Distractibility Excessive crying Difficulty sleeping	Self-reliance Seek help Exploration Reassurance Approach Avoidance Gazing at Gazing away Orientation Habituation Arousal Quieting Alertness Sleepiness	Dependency Clinginess Fear/withdrawal Avoidance of eye contact Unresponsiveness Freezing Excessive sleeping
	(b) **Arousal** **Activity** **Affect** **Attention**	
(a)		
Excessive ←—————— **Activation** ←———	**Activation** ←——→ **Inhibition** **Tolerance Range** ———	——→ **Excessive** ——→ **Inhibition**
	(c) Somatic-autonomic regulation Neurophysiological regulation Motor functioning Integrative processes Communicative signals	

Note. Behavior regulation in coping with and adapting to an unknown event. (a) Interaction and balance between activating and inhibiting processes within tolerance limits (------); (b) psychological domains involved; (c) neuro- and psychophysiological systems included; (d) observable domains of behavior regulation; behavioral problems when tolerance limits are exceeded due to excessive activation (e), or excessive inhibition (f).

play a central role in nonverbal communication. Each encounter with a new and unknown event in which integration of the experience and control of adaptive physiological and motor reactions are required causes the four A's to become activated. At the same time, inhibiting processes keep the response in dynamic equilibrium within physiological tolerance limits.

One can easily observe this process in infants in everyday situations when they are confronted for the first time with an unknown or strange situation (see Figure 4.2a). When a newborn is placed in a bathtub for the first time, she initially responds with sympathetic arousal (wide-open eyes, rapid breathing), motor tension (closed fists), anxious affect (tenseness in the forehead and mouth areas), and orienting toward the face and voice of the caregiver (early forms of social referencing). Ideally, the baby then receives regulatory support from the mother's facial expression and vocal signals. This helps him to relax, feel more comfortable in each fresh encounter with the new situation, and integrate the many new sensations involved in bathing (see Figure 4.2b).

This interplay and balance between activation and inhibition may be observed over the course of infant development in many domains of behavioral and emotional regulation, as shown in Figure 4.1(d): alertness and sleepiness, arousal and quieting, gazing at and gazing away from, approach and avoidance, exploration and seeking reassurance from the secure base, relying on oneself and seeking help, striving for autonomy and re-approaching the secure base.

Figure 4.2a. Newborn Infant at Her First Bath.

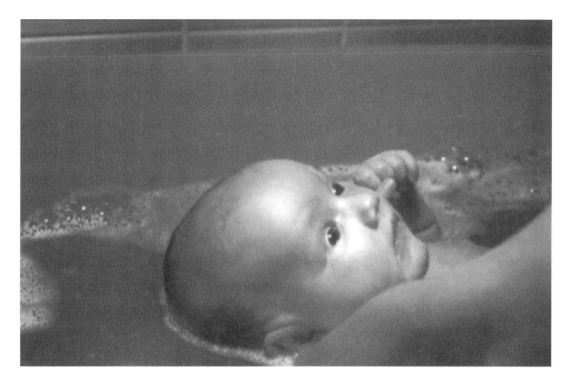

Figure 4.2b. Adjustment to the Novel Experience.

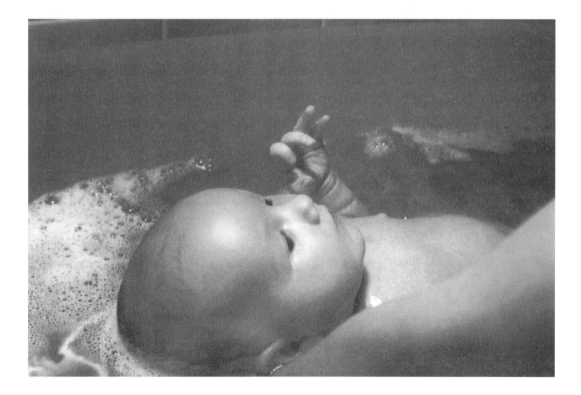

If there is an imbalance between activating and inhibiting processes (dysregulation), an excess of arousal or an excess of inhibition may exceed the tolerance limits, and maladaptations may result. This may lead, at one extreme, to hyperarousal, excessive crying, distractibility, anxious defensiveness, difficulty sleeping, defiance, or aggressive behavior; at the other extreme, the results may be excessive sleeping, freezing, general unresponsiveness, avoidance of eye contact, social withdrawal and avoidance strategies, excessive clinginess and inhibition of exploration, dependency, or giving up in the face of failure. It is not difficult to recognize the variety of disorders of behavioral and emotional regulation listed at the outset in such regulatory maladaptations (see also chapter 3, Table 3.2).

Phase-Typical Developmental Tasks in the First Years of Life

Basic regulation plays a role in all learning and adaptive processes in early development. Each developmental phase places new demands on the infant's capacity to regulate, which depends on the structural and functional maturity of the brain as well as the accumulated experiences that have already been integrated. Table 4.1 gives an overview of the most important phase-typical developmental tasks.

During the first 3 months, physiological adaptation processes are often so intense that they leave only small windows of opportunity for dialogue and interaction when the infant is in a quiet alert waking state. The most important regulation processes at this time involve the domains of nutritional intake and digestion, energy exchange, thermoregulation, and immunological adaptation. Behavioral organization concerns mainly the regulatory equilibrium in the behavioral states of the organism (nonalert waking activity, quiet or active alert waking, drowsiness, active sleep, and quiet sleep), and the regulation of transitions between waking and sleeping (Wolff, 1987). If transitional states such as fussiness and indeterminate sleep, inconsolable crying, and other problems with transitions between states predominate, this may be an expression of delayed maturation of sleep–wake organization (Emde, Swedberg, & Suzuki, 1975).

Successful solution of these initial regulatory tasks is indicated around the ages of 2 and 3 months by striking developmental progress (Dittrichová & Lapacková, 1964). This first biopsychosocial shift promotes regulation at a higher level of integration (Crockenberg & Leerkes, 2000; H. Papoušek & Papoušek, 1984). In addition to the necessary adjustments to nutritional intake, reorganization and consolidation of sleep, acceleration of learning, and new abilities for self-soothing, Emde (1984) has also stressed the emerging social capabilities (persistent eye contact, social smiling, melodious cooing) as the "awakening of sociability." This preverbal communication provides a framework for practicing reciprocal regulation of attention, positive affective arousal, and self-efficacy. In the same context, the infant practices ways to integrate experience in dialogue and play (H. Papoušek & Papoušek, 1987) and ways to explore the environment with eyes, hands, and mouth (Largo, 2003).

Another developmental shift occurs in the middle of the second half year (around 9 months), during which canonical babbling begins and object permanence, intentionality, fear of strangers, and crawling, among other things, occur at more or less the same time; all of these developments present parents with new challenges (Crockenberg & Leerkes, 2000; Emde, 1984; Emde, Gaensbauer, & Harman, 1976). The beginning of independent locomotion allows for the child's growing need for exploration—as well

Table 4.1. Adaptive Developmental Tasks of Early Childhood.

Age	Adaptive developmental tasks	Phase-typical problems
Birth to 3 months	Nutritional intake/digestion – Cycle of nutritional intake (hunger–satiation) – Coordinated sucking activity during nursing and bottle feeding Immunological adaptation Energy exchange/temperature regulation Regulation of behavioral states – Sleep–wake organization – Quiet alert waking state	Nursing/feeding problems Excessive crying associated with problems in sleep–wake organization, fussiness
3 to 7 months	Nutritional intake: supplementary feeding – Adaptation to a new mode, taste, consistency Consolidation of night sleep Regulation of attention, self-efficacy, affect, and integration of experience – In dialogue – In play	Feeding problems (e.g., sensory food aversion) Motor restlessness, unwillingness to play, dysphoric mood
7 to 9 months	Beginning of independent crawling Beginning of attachment to specific persons – Balance between attachment security and exploration – Interaction with the unfamiliar (strange surroundings, strange persons) Nutritional intake: weaning Sleeping through the night	Excessive clinginess Excessive fear of strangers, separation anxiety, fearfulness, social withdrawal, inhibited exploration Weaning problems Disruption of night sleep
15 to 18 months	Unlimited locomotion Vocabulary spurt Sleep: nightmares Nutritional intake: self-feeding Self-recognition, empathy, symbolic play Balance between dependency and autonomy Experience of social rules and limits ("no") Maturation of prefrontal inhibitory systems – Emotional regulation (tolerance for frustration, impulse control) – Goal-directed action	Motor restlessness Sleeping problems "Infantile anorexia" Excessive temper tantrums Conflict over limit setting Aggressive/oppositional behavior Impulsivity Disorganized activity

as its opposite, an increased need for closeness. Proximity seeking, fear of strangers, and separation anxiety are a sign of emergent attachment to specific caregivers. Among the most important long-term developmental tasks associated with this phase are the regulation of interpersonal distance, and the balance between exploration and the need for security, particularly in the face of unknown situations, strangers, and other novel experiences (see chapter 8).

A third biopsychosocial developmental shift begins around the middle of the second year of life and brings with it new regulatory challenges for both toddlers and parents. Independent walking offers a child an almost limitless range of exploration. Symbolic play and a spurt in vocabulary mark new levels of symbolization, language-mediated integration of experience, imagination, and representations of the self and attachment figures. Recognizing oneself in a mirror and the ability to empathize with the feelings and intentions of another person are among the other important milestones associated with this phase. At a motivational level, the interplay between the growing need for autonomy and the need for reassurance is first and foremost; in communication, it is the balance between dependency and autonomy, and the negotiation of social rules and limits. With the growing maturation and integration of the prefrontal neuronal inhibition systems, new developmental tasks come to the fore in the domains of emotional regulation (tolerance of frustration, impulse control) and goal-directed action (focused attention, persistence, flexibility).

Individual Variability in Infants' Self-Regulation: The Contribution of Temperament Research

There is considerable variability in children's ability to self-regulate and to accomplish the adaptive developmental tasks at hand. This variability has been the subject of research on temperament (Bates, Freeland, & Lounsbury, 1979; Carey & McDevitt, 1995; Kagan, 1997; Pauli-Pott, Ries-Hahn, Kupfer, & Beckmann, 1999; Rothbart et al., 1994; Zentner, 2000) ever since the groundbreaking research conducted by Thomas and Chess (1977, 1980). The various theories of temperament, if little else, agree in defining it as a largely stable inherited, biologically determined set of behavioral dispositions that underlies an individual's personal characteristics. In addition to these genetically anchored characteristics, the influence of prenatal factors on constitutional variability has recently gained increasing attention (Carey & McDevitt, 1995).

Traditionally, infant temperament has been measured by having parents fill out a questionnaire reporting on the behavior of their children in concrete everyday situations. The temperament dimensions resulting from factor analysis differ by author and questionnaire with regard to their number and specification. For example, Thomas and Chess (1977) first distinguished nine dimensions and, on further analysis, three prototypes. The *difficult temperament* (10% of the population) is characterized by irregular physiological functions, withdrawal from unknown stimuli, limited adaptability to change, and intense, mostly negative affective reactivity; the *slow-to-warm-up temperament* (15%) includes slightly negative reactivity to new stimuli and prolonged warm-up time; and the *easy temperament* (40%) is specified by regular rhythmicity, an easy approach to new stimuli, a high capacity for adaptation to change, and largely positive affect. According to Zentner (2000), the three prototypes have recently been referred to as *undercontrolled-impulsive*, *overcontrolled-inhibited*, and *ego-resilient*.

Rothbart et al. (1994) traced temperament dimensions primarily to differences in the balance between activating and inhibiting systems—to an imbalance between the excitability of the behavioral and physiological systems on the one hand and regulatory processes that serve to modulate arousal on the other (Prudhomme-White et al., 2000). In other words, temperament can also be related to a balance or a disturbance in the infant's fundamental adaptive response system (H. Papoušek & Papoušek, 1979). The development of extremes in one or several temperament dimensions may be associated with both elevated or decreased reactivity in the areas of the four A's (arousal, affect, attention, activity), or with decreased or excessive inhibitory counterregulation (see Figure 4.1).

Numerous studies of infant temperament have shown associations between extreme expressions of individual dimensions of temperament and problems in behavior regulation (Carey & McDevitt, 1995; Thomas, Chess, & Birch, 1968). Conversely, and with remarkable consistency, studies of infants who exhibit excessive crying, sleep disorders, or feeding disorders have shown significantly elevated scores in comparison with control groups on various subscales, particularly the *Fussy-Difficult* scale on the Infant Characteristics Questionnaire (ICQ; Bates et al., 1979) or the difficult temperament cluster according to Thomas and Chess (Atkinson, Vetere, & Grayson, 1995; Bithoney & Newberger, 1987; Carey, 1974; Chatoor, Ganiban, Hirsch, Borman-Spurrell, & Mrazek, 2000; Hagekull, Bohlin, & Rydell, 1997; Huffman et al., 1994; Lehtonen, Korhonen, & Korvenranta, 1994; Minde et al., 1993; M. Papoušek & von Hofacker, 1995, 1998; Richman, 1981; Scher, Tirosh, & Lavie, 1998; St. James-Roberts, Conroy, & Wilsher, 1998; Wolke, Skuse, & Mathisen, 1990).

Disorders of Behavioral and Emotional Regulation and Infant Temperament: Clinical Data

In our own clinical sample, we used the ICQ (Bates et al., 1979) to assess the *Fussy-Difficult, Adaptability,* and *Predictability* dimensions during the first year of life, and, during the second year of life, *Persistence* and *Sociability* in addition to *Fussy-Difficult* and *Adaptability*. We obtained completed temperament questionnaires for 308 of the 1- to 12-month-old infants and for 136 of the 1- to 2-year-olds. During the first half-year, 54% of infants who cried excessively were assessed by their mothers as *Unpredictable,* that is, their scores were more than two standard deviations from the standard mean of a representative control group (Bates et al., 1979). In 65% of infants, we found correspondingly extreme scores on the *Fussy-Difficult* scale, and in 11% on the *Unadaptability* scale. For infants in the second half-year, extreme scores on the *Unpredictability, Fussy-Difficult,* and *Unadaptability* scales still held at 26%, 28%, and 10%, respectively. For toddlers in the second year of life, the rates of extreme scores were 26% on the *Fussy-Difficult* scale, 6% on both the *Unadaptability* and the *Persistence* scales, and below 5% on the *Lack of Sociability* scale. Moreover, there was a significant association in all age groups between the proportion of fussy-difficult children and pervasiveness, that is, the number of dysregulated behavioral domains (feeding, sleep, diapering, dialogue, play, interpersonal boundaries, separation, limit setting). For example, the percentage of infants with extremely difficult temperaments rose from 9% of those with isolated symptoms to 88% of those with five or more dysregulated domains, Mantel-Haenszel $X^2(1, N = 308) = 55.81, p \le .001$. Toddlers in the second year of life also showed a significant trend in the proportion of those with extremely difficult temperament, Mantel-Haenszel $X^2(1, N = 136) = 22.97, p \le .001$, in relation to the number of problematic domains— albeit at a lower level (4% for one domain to 44% for five or more domains).

In summary, all age groups showed high rates of extreme scores, particularly with regard to the Fussy-Difficult dimension of temperament, which, together with the other dimensions, indicates clear impairment of self-regulation. It should be noted, however, that the high rates of extremes during the first 3 months do not permit us to draw conclusions about temperament because of the confounding effects of relative immaturity and constitutional factors. Only extreme expressions that persist beyond this age may be interpreted as a sign of a relatively stable behavioral disposition. In the absence of reliable objective measurements of temperament, parents' assessments of their infants' behavior in concrete everyday situations still provide the best approach, despite the dependence on the subjective perception of the parents.

In addition to possible genetic factors, all risk factors that could impair the infant's constitutional prerequisites for adaptive behavior regulation should be considered as potential causes of constitutional variability. In addition to transient immaturity before the first biopsychosocial shift and organic vulnerability factors (such as prematurity; small-for-gestational-age [SGA]; prenatal exposure to drugs, alcohol, or nicotine; and protein intolerance), these include constitutional impairments acquired in utero, particularly due to the high levels of physical and emotional stress, anxiety, and conflict in the pregnant mother (see chapter 3).

The goodness-of-fit model of temperament research. The presence of problematic temperamental characteristics in the majority of infants in the clinical sample does not, however, permit us to draw the conclusion that the causes of the disorder are primarily to be found in the child. Differences in temperament are variants of normal behavior and as such do not imply pathology (Thomas & Chess, 1977). Temperament research has convincingly shown that extreme expressions of temperament represent no more than a vulnerability factor in the context of developmental psychopathology and that the long-term outcome of the child largely depends on the goodness-of-fit between temperamental characteristics and the expectations, attitudes, competencies, and life circumstances of the social environment (Carey & McDevitt, 1995; Chess & Thomas, 1991; Zentner, 2000; see also chapter 1 as well as chapter 2).

This means that, as a determining factor, fit *or* misfit is at the heart of the matter and requires precise analysis of everyday situations in which it is negotiated. How can this quality be identified and diagnosed? Is it an either–or proposition? Is it written in stone forever? Is it like a key that must fit a lock precisely in order to function? Or is it itself a part and a result of dynamic transactional developmental processes?

These questions require a focus on the parents and everything that we know today about parental competencies in dealing with their infants or toddlers—in short, on the communication between parents and children in everyday interactions, on parent–infant communication at both the level of observable behavior and the subjective level of understanding, emotions, and representations.

PREVERBAL COMMUNICATION IN DAILY INTERACTION—THE ARENA IN WHICH DEVELOPMENTAL TASKS ARE MASTERED TOGETHER

The long phase of early childhood dependence implies that the infant cannot rely only on his own resources for mastering early adaptive and developmental tasks, but requires support from his parents or other primary caregivers. The challenges of infancy can only be mastered by the parents and their baby together. The arena of everyday interaction that includes soothing, feeding, putting to sleep, diapering, dialogue, and play is the context in which this coregulation takes place. The success of preverbal communication—the developing mutual understanding between parents and baby—is the precondition for the success of this process.

Intuitive Parenting

Parents come equipped with behavioral dispositions that are complementary to those of their infants, and that enable them to attune their behavior intuitively to the needs of their baby from moment to moment (H. Papoušek & Papoušek, 1987, 1995, 2002). When relying on their intuitive competencies, parents make themselves easy to understand for their baby by simplifying and highlighting the musical elements in their speech; in turn, they learn to read their baby's level of receptiveness or perceptual overload, self-regulatory capacities and difficulties as well as momentary needs and affective states, preferences, and interests from his behavior in the interaction. Guided by their infant's signals, parents seemingly know how to give their baby regulatory support that is attuned to his individual capacities and constraints. They do this by stimulating, soothing, and consoling him; by adjusting the type and intensity of stimulation in relation to his receptiveness and tolerance limits; and by conveying a sense of emotional reassurance, safety, and a secure base in stressful situations. They compensate for what the baby is not yet able to do, and offer him a framework within their interaction and dialogue in which he is able to test and practice his own maturing capacities for self-efficacy and self-regulation (M. Papoušek, 1994).

Adaptive functions of preverbal communication in "angels' circles." The developmental tasks of infancy, including occasional critical steps and perturbations of reorganizational phases, may be mastered together in the communicative interaction between the infant's and the parents' behavioral receptivity. A baby who cries from overfatigue is cradled in his mother's arm, where the sound of her voice and her gentle rocking soothes him and helps him relax; the baby quiets, snuggles into the mother's body, and eventually falls asleep. The mother, too, is able to relax along with her baby and recover from the alarming arousal elicited by her baby's crying. At the same time she receives one of the most beautiful responses imaginable from her baby—"I feel secure and sheltered with you"—feedback that strengthens her confidence in her intuitive competencies. Thus, mother and infant support each other, setting up a stable pattern of positive reciprocity in their communication and, at the same time, a mutually positive intersubjective experience—an "angel's circle." (This term has been adapted from the German counterpart as a contrast to the popularly-used term *Teufelskreis* or "devil's circle." *Angel's circle* is not intended to imply religious connotations but instead refers to the highly rewarding qualities and outcomes of positive parent–infant interactions. This concept and term are now being used in a variety of disciplines in Germany, and it is noteworthy that a recent special issue of the *Journal of Infant Mental Health* also included an article referring to a related concept, "angels in the nursery.")

Along these lines, the adaptive functions of preverbal communication include mutual mastering of phase-specific developmental tasks, building a secure attachment relationship, the early intersubjective integration of experience, and paving the way for speech development (H. Papoušek & Papoušek, 2002).

Coregulation and Vulnerability of Intuitive Parenting

One prerequisite for eliciting intuitive parental competencies and for their successful attunement is the readiness and capacity of the parents to give undivided attention to the preverbal communication of their infant. In addition, parents must allow themselves to be sufficiently emotionally available to be guided by the infant's signals, while at the same time relying on their own genuine competencies. The initial postnatal phase, during which parents and infant are getting to know each other, is particularly vulnerable to perturbation. This phase, shortly after birth, is a sort of orchestration phase during which the parents attune their intuitive program to respond to the individual needs of their baby. Occasional misunderstandings and discord may be unavoidable, and the parents' emotional bonding to their baby may in some cases take longer than expected.

The fact that coregulation is not always smooth and easy becomes clear when, for example, the baby cries inconsolably for no apparent reason during the first 3 months. If the parents have adequate resources, such phase-typical regulatory turmoil may be overcome step by step (Stifter, 2001). By contrast, parents and infants in the client base of the Munich Program hardly ever experienced an angel's circle, as described earlier. The parents—particularly the mother—of a baby who cries excessively, refuses food, or has developed a chronic sleep disorder may be at the end of their rope: They are highly vulnerable, they feel like failures, and their sense of themselves as mother and father may be very shaky. A baby whose self-regulatory capacities are impaired also affects the parents' trust in their intuitive competency (M. Papoušek, 2000). In situations that require soothing, communication can easily be derailed and turn into a dysfunctional vicious circle of escalating arousal (M. Papoušek & von Hofacker, 1995).

Unknowns in the Field of Clinical Infancy Research

What precisely is it that interferes with intuitive parenting? How are we to understand the high degree of psychological distress and overwhelmedness felt by these parents? Under what circumstances does the system of preverbal communication lose its protective and developmentally vital force? How does this system get derailed? How do dysfunctional interactional patterns and vicious circles develop? What role do the risk factors listed in chapter 3 play, either individually or cumulatively? By what interactional or psychodynamic mechanisms or processes do these risk factors have an impact on preverbal communication? What role do the parents' stressful or traumatic childhood experiences play? And by what means and under what conditions are parents' stressful or traumatic childhood experiences fatefully transmitted to the child? Although these questions play a central role in clinical work with parents and their infants with regulatory disorders, remarkably little research has been done on the interactional and psychodynamic control mechanisms of intuitive parenting.

Within our systemic developmental framework, four interrelated areas in which distressing factors can easily lead to impairment of intuitive parenting deserve particular attention: (a) the daily experience of interaction with the infant, (b) the adaptive developmental tasks on the part of the parents, (c) the motherhood constellation, and (d) the cumulative risk factors that affect the parents' psychological well-being.

The Daily Experience of Interactions With the Infant: Baby as Coregulator of the Parents' State of Well-Being and Intuitive Competencies

Probably the most important but often underrated influence on the intuitive competencies, state of well-being, and psychodynamic constellation of parents is their ongoing interaction with their baby, in which parental behavior is responded to with immediate positive or negative feedback. If the infant's behavioral response is positive, an angel's circle quickly develops in which the parents feel strengthened and self-efficacious in their intuitive competencies.

But what happens when the baby continues to cry inconsolably or rejects food? What happens when the baby resists being cuddled, stiffens in the parents' arms, and arches his back? What happens when the baby avoids eye contact, is consistently dissatisfied, demands to be nursed every hour at night, or strongly resists diapering? Parents quickly become exhausted, and depending on the extent of their psychological resources and distress, feelings of failure, helplessness, powerlessness, frustration, rage, fear of rejection, hopelessness, depression, and low self-esteem are likely to be triggered (M. Papoušek, 2000; M. Papoušek & Papoušek, 1990). They see their infant's behavior as proof positive that they are simply failures in the art of parenting.

The insecurity prompted by such negative feedback is, in and of itself, sufficient to cause parents to doubt their own intuitive competencies so that they end up mindlessly following one proffered recommendation after another—or slavishly following the rational "cookbook" instructions in this or that parenting manual.

The Parents' Adaptative Developmental Tasks During Their Transition to Parenthood

In the course of pregnancy, birth, and postpartum adjustment, the parents themselves regularly face a variety of adaptive developmental tasks (Gloger-Tippelt, 1988); these are summarized in Table 4.2.

Table 4.2. Parents' Adaptive Developmental Tasks.

Becoming emotionally connected to the child: Pre-, peri-, and postnatally	Gloger-Tippelt (1988)
Building self-confidence in their own intuitive parenting competencies	M. Papoušek (2001)
Postpartum physiological adjustments	
Transition to parenthood – From professional identity to identity in the parenting roles – From dyadic to triadic relationships	Petzold (1988); Fivaz-Depeursinge & Corboz-Warnery (2001)
Motherhood constellation – As psychodynamic reorganization – Revival of attachment and relationship experiences (implicit relational knowledge)	Stern (1995)
Finding a balance between the infant's needs and the parents' own needs Finding a balance between attachment and detachment Finding a balance between dependency and autonomy	Cierpka & Cierpka (2000)
Child-rearing competencies	Schneewind (2002)

The transition from the couple's relationship as a dyad to that of a triad, in which they must also identify with their new roles as parents, is often underestimated (Fivaz-Depeursinge & Corboz-Warnery, 2001; Schneewind, 2002).

These challenges offer parents a unique opportunity for their own development, both individually and as a couple. However, they may also lead to derailments in the form of unexpected crises and turmoil. Depending on lifestyle and social environment, developmental crises come about most frequently when the parents do not have or do not take the time to prepare themselves for their new roles, to adjust to the presence of their baby, and to allow themselves unoccupied hours for relaxation and well-being in the family. Traditional societies made provision for a protective social matrix in which the new mother was herself mothered and protected from stress during pregnancy and following childbirth. This social matrix has largely eroded in the industrialized world, leaving couples on their own.

The Motherhood Constellation as a Phase of Psychodynamic Reorganization

Stern (1995) in particular has investigated the psychodynamic reorganization that takes place during the transition to parenthood, in which the mother (and surely also the father, although this is less well understood) allows a psychodynamic constellation to develop in which new needs, sensitivities, fantasies, memories, fears, and behavioral motivations gain in importance. The mother's own experience of having been mothered is reactivated during this dynamic and vulnerable transition period. According to Stern, four themes take on importance in the mother's discourse with her own mother, with herself as mother, and with the baby, all of which may dominate her thoughts and feelings: (a) the life and thriving of her child ("Can I make my baby grow and thrive and keep my baby alive?"); (b) the theme of primary relatedness ("Can I relate naturally and intuitively to my baby? Can I allow myself to be in a state of primary preoccupation with my baby and assure an undisturbed psychic development?"); (c) the supporting matrix theme ("How can I create, permit, accept, and maintain a protective maternal support network for myself and my baby?"); and (d) the identity reorganization theme ("How will I find self-confidence and validation in my new role as a mother, parent, and wife? How do I reconcile this new role with my old identity as a daughter of my parents, as a partner, and as a working woman?").

Revival of the Mother's Experience of Her Own Attachment Relationships

In addition to her preoccupation with these themes, the mother's relationship with her own mother becomes reactivated and reorganized. The ongoing interaction with her baby with all of its sensations, feelings, perceptions, and thoughts functions as a "present remembering context" (Stern, 1995) in which memory traces of her preverbal experiences of relationship surface involuntarily out of procedural and episodic memory and unknowingly influence her communication with her baby. Eliciting signals may include a particular sensation (such as a smell), a perception, a peculiar behavior of the baby, or a particular feeling. Episodic images may emerge as well, often from later phases of childhood. But above all, the mother's implicit relational knowing is reactivated (Stern et al., 2002), as are communication patterns from her own preverbal past. These "schemas-of-being-with-mother" (Stern, 1995) along with their intrinsic affective dynamics represent the procedural know-how of preverbal communication as it was experienced and stored during everyday episodes of feeding, soothing, or settling to sleep. As a result, interaction with the baby evokes not only intuitive parenting, that is, the innate basic know-how of preverbal communication with a baby, but also the implicit relational knowing integrated during the mother's experience of being mothered as a child. If both types of knowing are in harmony, they will contribute to confidence in her intuitive competencies; on the other hand, if they are in conflict, intuitive parenting may be distorted, overlaid, or otherwise invalidated, although presumably not obliterated.

Risk Factors Within the Context of the Motherhood–Parenthood Constellation

Psychosocial risk factors may become more salient over the course of the psychodynamic reorganization that takes place during the transition to parenthood in that they intensify the themes of the motherhood constellation, bring out latent conflicts, and conjure up ghosts from the past.

As already described in detail in chapter 3, the clients of the Munich Program exhibit an accumulation of different but highly interconnected organic and psychosocial risk factors. Notable are the large proportions of ongoing distress in relationships with the partner (49%) and the family of origin (34%), the frequent lack of a supportive social matrix (30%), the frequency of distressing or traumatic childhood experiences (37%), and the high rate of psychological disturbances in the mother (47%) or in both parents. On the one hand, these largely relational risk factors are reciprocally related to the duration and pervasiveness of the infant's regulation disorder. On the other hand, they contribute significantly to a general decrease in both physical and psychological resources and in the parents' overall sense of well-being.

Psychological State of Mothers of Infants and Toddlers With Regulation Disorders: Clinical Data

To assess the mothers' psychological state, questionnaires were used that focused on the mothers' emotional attitudes towards their infant (Maternal Childcare Attitudes and Feelings [EMKK]; Engfer, 1984) and on postpartum depression (Edinburgh Postnatal Depression Scale [EPDS]; Murray & Carothers, 1990). Earlier research from our lab on the effects of excessive crying during the first half-year of life had already demonstrated significantly elevated strain on the marital relationship, on the mothers' self-confidence and sense of self-efficacy, and on the mothers' emotional attitudes towards their baby, depending on the amount of infant crying (M. Papoušek & von Hofacker, 1995, 1998). These results were replicated in the present clinical sample for the group of 1- to 6-month-old infants ($n = 196$) and complemented by Böhm's (2002) results for the group of 7- to 24-month-old babies ($n = 452$).

To compare the psychological state of the mothers of 1- to-6-month-old infants, we used a control group with infants of the same age without manifest regulation disorders ($n = 61$) and reference scores (means and cut-off values) from representative samples (Engfer, 1984; Murray & Carothers, 1990). In the second to fourth half-year, only normative reference scores from the standardized questionnaires were available for comparison. Highly significant differences ($p \leq .001$ in each case) were found during the first half-year on all subscales of the EMKK and on the EPDS in comparison with the control group. For example, mothers in the clinical group were significantly more distressed in terms of chronic exhaustion, depression, frustration, anxious overprotectiveness, and negative childhood memories than were those in the comparison group. Less striking but significant differences were also found for fear of rejection, rigidity, tendency to punish, and lack of delight in the child, but without distinctly deviating from the mean values in the normative control group.

In view of the high degree of individual variability in all areas of maternal well-being, the percentage of mothers with extreme scores was also computed. For the EPDS this involved a percentage of mothers with depression scores above the cut-off of 12 (Bergant, Nguyen, Heim, Ulmer, & Dapunt, 1998; Murray & Carothers, 1990), which indicates a clinically significant postpartum depression. For the EMKK, it involved the percentage that exceeded the 84th and 98th percentile (more than 1 or 2 standard deviations, respectively, above the mean scores for the control group). On the basis of the EPDS, we found an almost triple incidence of postpartum depression (31.1%) during the first half-year compared to the prevalence in the reference sample (11%; Bergant et al., 1998; Murray & Carothers, 1990). In the second, third, and fourth half-year, the incidence of depression was still approximately doubled (24.1%, 18.7%, and 23.6%, respectively). The rate of depressed mothers increased as more behavioral domains were affected by regulatory problems: It rose from 20.1% in cases of only one problematic domain to 52.4% in cases of five or more affected domains, Mantel-Haenszel $X^2(1, N = 701) = 19.67, p \leq .001$. On the EMKK as well, the scores and the proportions of high (above the 84th percentile) and extreme (above the 98th percentile) scores on the subscales of Chronic Exhaustion, Depressiveness, Frustration, and Anxious Overprotectiveness were significantly associated with the number of problematic domains ($p \leq .001$ in each case; see Figure 4.3). Moreover, depressiveness

Figure 4.3. Links Between Maternal Chronic Exhaustion and Number of Dysregulated Domains.

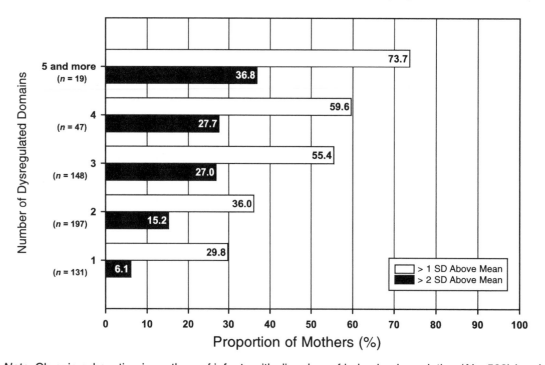

Note. Chronic exhaustion in mothers of infants with disorders of behavioral regulation ($N = 523$) in relation to the number of dysregulated behavioral domains. Percentage of mothers with extreme scores (> 1 and > 2 *SD* above the mean of the normative reference group; EMKK.
Source: Engfer, 1948.

decreased with the age of the child ($p \leq .005$), whereas overstrain ($p \leq .005$), rigidity ($p \leq .05$), and tendency to punish ($p \leq .001$) increased with the age of the child. Significant increases in depressiveness ($p \leq .005$) and frustration ($p \leq .001$) were noted, however, in relation to the relative duration of the disorder (i.e., the proportion of disordered months in relation to the child's lifetime).

It is evident from these data that depression and other impairments in the psychological condition of the mother are associated with the pervasiveness of regulation disorders as well as with infant age and the relative amount of time already spent together experiencing behavioral and emotional dysregulation.

Psychodynamic Regulation of Intuitive Parenting

Table 4.3 presents an overview of various risk factors for which we observed striking dysregulation or inhibition of intuitive parental competencies in the clients of the Munich Program, depending on the state of well-being and psychodynamic constellation of the parents.

Lasting impairment of intuitive communicative competencies may be caused by any psychological and biographical factors that diminish, inhibit, block, or distort the perception of, attention to, or emotional availability for the needs of the real baby (see Table 4.3). Chronic stress, severe exhaustion, and overstrain may elicit defense mechanisms, including reduced initiative, feelings of powerlessness, burnout, and emptiness, which for a time inhibit the parents' intuitive readiness to respond. Intense negative affects and/or entanglement in insoluble conflicts may so absorb the parents that they no longer perceive their baby's signals. When a mother suffers from even mild depression that inhibits her motivation to act and her vitality and that arouses feelings of emotional deadness, she may become mute while interacting with her baby; contingent responsiveness may cease, and in the end, regulatory attunement and support of the infant's needs may fail. This has been demonstrated in numerous studies of postpartum depression (for an overview, see M. Papoušek, 2002).

Particularly serious blocks in parental behavior may occur if the parents were themselves severely neglected or abused as children (Crittenden & DiLalla, 1988; Lyons-Ruth, 1987) or have had other traumatic experiences that could impinge on their ability to relate, such as life-threatening events surrounding the birth, the shock of giving birth to a handicapped child, or the loss of a significant other close to the time of pregnancy or birth. Psychodynamic defense mechanisms such as repression, denial, projective identification, or dissociation come into play here. All of these mechanisms may distort the parents' perception of the real baby and cancel out the parents' intuitive readiness to relate because of the reenactment of old conflicted relational patterns. Access to intuitive competencies may be completely blocked by defenses against threatening fear, grief, anger, or death wishes (Barth, 1998, 1999; Brazelton & Cramer, 1990; Dornes, 1997, 2000; Lieberman & Pawl, 1993; M. Papoušek & Wollwerth de Chuquisengo, 2003).

Under such circumstances, the revival of afflicted parental attachment and relational patterns, vividly described by Fraiberg, Adelson, and Shapiro (1975) as "ghosts in the nursery," may call forth these "visitors from the unremembered past" (see chapters 10–12). Instead of with the baby, the parents communicate with a "ghost" that is a representation of a repressed, unacceptable part of a parent's unconscious or a representation of a significant person from the past (Brazelton & Cramer, 1990).

Table 4.3. Interactional and Psychodynamic Factors Affecting the Regulation of Intuitive Parenting.

Lack of an initial orchestration phase in cases of early separation, due to –Prematurity, treatment in the intensive care unit –Inpatient psychiatric treatment of the mother because of postpartum disorder –Absent father –Late adoption **Unintelligibility of the baby's signals in cases of** –Severe developmental disorders, mental retardation, genetic syndromes, facial malformation –Negative feedback from a difficult infant	**Psychodynamic factors** that constrain, inhibit, block, distort, or abolish the parent's perception of, attention to, and emotional availability for the real baby, such as –Stress, overstrain, feelings of powerlessness in cases with minimal resources –Preoccupation with intense affect or unresolved conflicts –Retarded or agitated depression –Anxiety in relation to the baby's survival or thriving –Unresolved coping with the fate of a handicapped child –Unresolved mourning after loss of significant other –Unresolved trauma in the parent's childhood –Unresolved intergenerational conflict relating to autonomy and dependency –Psychotic disorders

The baby, with all his individual, sometimes difficult, behaviors and problems may himself become a co-actor in an imaginary drama that conjures up the past and, as if by fate, reenacts problematic patterns of relationship.

It is remarkable that so many parents are able to establish undisturbed communication with their baby with well-developed and intuitively attuned competencies in spite of severe traumatization and adverse experiences in their own attachment relationships. Such parents have learned to reflect upon and discuss their emotional experiences freely, or to admit their grief and anger, while at the same time trying to understand their parents' behavior from their perspective. What distinguishes them from parents who remain enmeshed in emotionally ambivalent relationship patterns or defend against access to their own unconscious affects and experience of relationship may possibly be differences in their attachment representations (difference between *secure-autonomous* as opposed to *enmeshed* or *dismissing*; Main, 2002). Fonagy, Steele, Moran, Steele, and Higgit (1993) emphasize the capacity for self-reflection and "mentalization," the parent's mind-mindedness, which can help to interrupt the intergenerational transmission of attachment experiences.

Vicious Circles of Preverbal Communication

Lasting impairment of the parents' intuitive capacity for attunement to the needs and signals of their infant increases the risk of creating a vicious circle of negative reciprocity in which the baby with his regulatory problems must do without the normal and intuitively attuned parental coregulation, and reciprocally, the parents lack the positive feedback signals from their baby that would reinforce their confidence in their own intuitive competencies.

One simple, but particularly frequent and distressing example of a vicious circle may occur when an infant avoids eye contact while the mother persists in forcing such contact (M. Papoušek, 1997). The more a constitutionally hyperreactive baby tries to protect himself from an excess of stimulation by averting his gaze, the more an insecure or depressive mother feels rejected, and the more intrusively she attempts to force the baby to look at her, again, the more the baby feels the need to withdraw. In the here and now, both sides contribute by their negative contingent responses to sustaining the problem so that it is pointless to look for the origin of the vicious circle. Repeated experience then leads to negative expectations on both sides, which accelerate derailment of communication the next time it is attempted.

Misunderstandings in preverbal communication are an everyday experience in all families and are usually soon resolved. However, because of both partners' negative contingent responsiveness, dysfunctional interactional patterns tend to become caught in a vicious circle of negative reciprocity, stabilizing there. Such vicious circles often persist and escalate, particularly in situations where resources are scarce and multiple risk factors are present. This is most likely to occur when the vicious circle represents an unconscious reenactment of a problematic relational pattern. Whereas angel's circles promote infant development and contribute to the development of a positive relationship, vicious circles represent a risk to development because pending developmental tasks remain unresolved, thereby making adaptation in other everyday domains difficult and blocking the way for successive developmental steps. Regulation problems persist, are exacerbated, or spill over into other domains (pervasiveness). As parents lose confidence in their own competencies, the preponderance of dysfunctional communication patterns contributes, over time and depending on pervasiveness, to unfavorable effects on the development of communication, language, play, and attachment, all the while distressing, disturbing, or even grossly impairing the parent–child relationship.

The Effect of Vicious Circles on Parent–Child Relationships: Clinical Data

In our clinical sample, we evaluated the quality of the mother–infant relationship based on the overall diagnostic assessments of experienced clinicians with the help of the Parent–Infant Relationship Global Assessment Scale (PIR-GAS; ZERO TO THREE, 1994). The 9-step scale (with scores from 90 to 10 in increments of 10) assesses the overall relationship with regard to its adaptive functions; to the duration, severity, and pervasiveness of dysfunctional interactional experiences; and to the quality and duration of positive relational experiences in the past. For computational reasons, scores of 90 to 70 were collapsed as *sufficiently adapted*, 60 to 40 as *distressed*, and 30 to 10 as *disordered*. A score of 40 (*disturbed*) was interpreted as a high risk for developing a relational disorder.

As Figure 4.4 shows, there was a significant association between the number of dysregulated interactional domains and the quality of the mother–infant relationship. The percentage of disordered relationships increased from barely 4% in cases of isolated regulatory problems to about 60% in the face of five or more dysregulated domains. There were also significant associations with infant age and the relative duration of the regulatory problem. The percentage of disordered relationships increased from 5% in the first half-year to 35% after the second year of life.

Because of the significance of the mother–infant relationship for the long-term prognosis of the psychological development of the child (see chapter 13), we also tried to analyze which factors contributed to its quality at the time of the first visit to our program. Using stepwise multiple regression analysis, we investigated which factors from our assessments contributed independently of each other to the

Figure 4.4. Links Between Quality of Mother–Infant Relationship and Number of Dysregulated Domains.

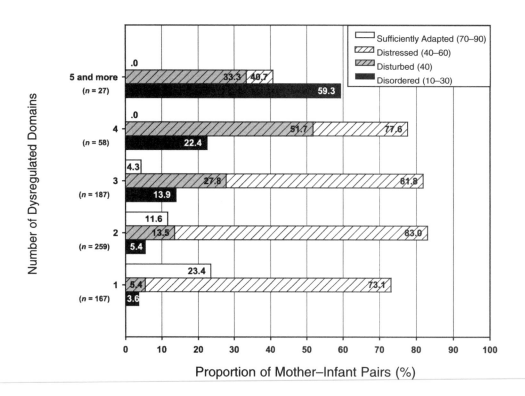

Note. Association between the quality of the mother–infant relationship (PIR-GAS; ZERO TO THREE, 1994) in disorders of behavioral and emotional regulation (*n* = 701) and the number of dysfunctional interactional domains.

variance in the quality of the relationship. The model in Figure 4.5 accounts for 52% of the variance to which infantile, maternal, and relationship variables contribute, $F(9, 752) = 91.2$, $p \leq .001$. On the infant's side, the variance is influenced by the number of dysregulated interactional domains (characterized by vicious circles), infant age and the proportion of disordered phases in relation to the infant's lifetime, and the postnatal cumulative somatic risks. On the side of the parents, partnership conflicts, the cumulative prenatal somatic and psychosocial risks as well as a distressed childhood, experiences of maltreatment, and psychological disturbance in the mother all contribute to the variance.

DISORDERS OF BEHAVIORAL AND EMOTIONAL REGULATION AS A DIAGNOSTIC CONCEPT

Figure 4.6 is an attempt to summarize and integrate the concepts, clinical experiences, and study results into a systemic model of the genesis and developmental dynamics of disorders of behavioral/emotional regulation and parent–infant relationships. On the infant's side, the fundamental adaptive response system or self-regulation may be affected by maturational processes, temperament, and multiple risk factors. On the parents' side, intuitive parenting may be directly affected by psychological state, which in turn may be influenced by multiple risk factors in the parents' health, biography, personality, and family relationships.

Figure 4.5. Links Between Quality of Mother–Infant Relationship and Risk Factors.

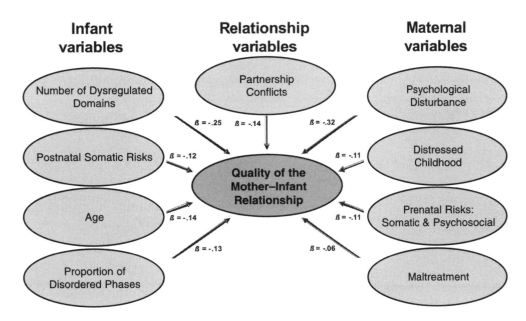

Note. Associations between the quality of the mother–infant relationship (PIR-GAS; ZERO TO THREE, 1994) and infant, maternal, and family variables. Stepwise multiple regression analysis ($R^2 = 0.52$; $F_{9;752} = 91.2$; $p \leq .001$).

In low-risk families, the innate positive reciprocity between infantile and parental dispositions in preverbal communication typically promotes angel's circles in everyday interactions. Angel's circles in preverbal communication serve a variety of adaptive functions such as conjoint mastering of developmental tasks, including behavioral and emotional regulation; they also facilitate procedural learning, early language acquisition, intersubjectivity, and secure attachment. Conversely, the system may become enmeshed in dysfunctional patterns of communication or vicious circles and end up in regulation and/or relationship disorders, as a result of scarce resources and adverse infantile and/or parental risk factors.

Direct focus on parent–infant communication in the context of soothing, putting to sleep, feeding, dialogue, and play, among other things, opens a clinical window (Stern, 1995) into the system of early dyadic and triadic relationships at both the level of observable patterns of communication and behavioral-emotional regulation and at the level of evoked representations. Thus, it provides a direct approach to the interactional mechanisms and processes involved in generating or maintaining the disorder in question, and, at the same time, to targeted consultation, and to parent–infant psychotherapy if needed.

Our systemic perspective founded in infancy research attempts to integrate pediatric, neurological, and constitutional aspects as well as concepts relevant to attachment, family systems, psychodynamics,

Figure 4.6. Disorders of Behavioral and Emotional Regulation and Parent-Infant Relationships: Communication–Centered Systemic Model.

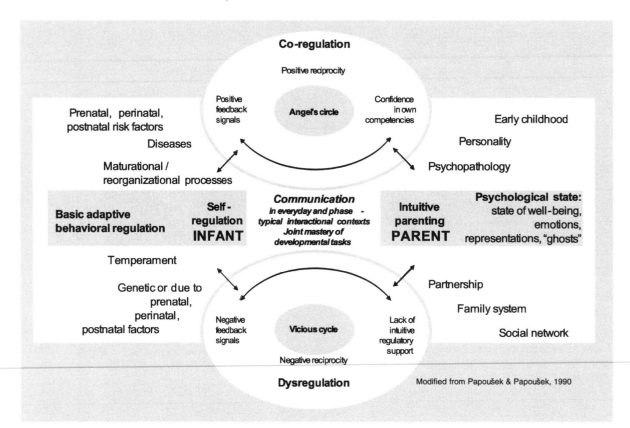

and psychosomatics into a common model of clinical developmental psychology of early childhood (M. Papoušek, 1999). The model takes account of the peculiarities of infancy (Emde, 1984; Sameroff & Emde, 1989), including (a) the high degree of intra- and interindividual variability; (b) the developmental dynamics conditioned by the tempo and intensity of maturational, adaptational, and learning processes; (c) discontinuities in developmental progress in connection with phase-typical developmental tasks; (d) the inseparable unity of the development of parent–infant relationships and infant mental health; (e) the role of the infant as co-creator of his own development and primary relationships; and (f) the central role of preverbal parent–infant communication and its adaptive functions. The model complements temperament research in that it examines the goodness-of-fit model at the level of everyday interactions and systematically incorporates the psychodynamics of individual parental variability (M. Papoušek, 1997; M. Papoušek & Wollwerth de Chuquisengo, 2003). It also complements existing concepts from attachment and psychodynamic theories in that it focuses more on the contribution of the child, the developmental dynamics and regulation of parental sensitivity, and preverbal communication processes during the first year of life (M. Papoušek, 1998; Schieche, 2001).

The Heterogeneity of Symptomatology and Severity of Regulation Disorders

The model forms the basis for the diagnostic and therapeutic approach of the Munich Interdisciplinary Research and Intervention Program. It has proved its validity over 15 years of clinical work with more than 3,000 infants and toddlers and their families. It takes into account the individual and phase-typical heterogeneity of behavioral manifestations of regulation disorders in infancy (see Table 4.4) as well as their developmental interrelatedness. Because of the commonalities that have been discussed in the beginning of this chapter in terms of etiology, developmental progress, and prognosis, one can easily treat this group of diverse syndromes as a whole under a common diagnostic category, namely *disorders*

Table 4.4. Proposal for a New Diagnostic Category: Disorders of Behavioral and Emotional Regulation.

Neutral term that stigmatizes neither the child nor the parents

One diagnosis for a complex of various behavioral syndromes that cannot yet be reliably separated from each other in terms of their etiological conditions, profiles of risk factors, progress, and prognosis.

Multiple behavioral syndromes related to phase-typical developmental tasks
- Excessive/persistent crying with problems of sleep–waking regulation
- Motor restlessness, dysphoric mood, attention problems, and inability to play
- Feeding disorder and failure to thrive
- Sleep disorder
- Excessive/persistent clinginess, anxiousness, and social withdrawal
- Excessive/persistent temper tantrums
- Aggressive/oppositional behavior

Etiological characteristics
- Extreme variants of normal constitutional variability of self-regulatory capacities
- Heightened demands on the parents' intuitive coregulatory competencies
- Impairment of infantile and/or parental competencies as a result of multiple risk factors
- Maladaptive dysregulated patterns of communication in interactional contexts that are relevant to the behavioral problems in question (e.g., dysfunctional feeding interactions in cases of feeding disorders)
- Escalation and persistence of otherwise transient perturbations with resulting failure in coregulating phase-typical developmental tasks

Diagnostic triad
- Infantile problems in behavioral and emotional regulation
- Dysfunctional communication patterns in relevant interactional contexts
- Excessive demands on the primary caregiver(s) and risk of adjustment disorder

Prognosis
- Transient in the context of adequate infantile and/or parental resources
- Persistent and escalating in the context of multiple risk factors and minimal infant and/or parent resources with growing risk of distressed/disordered parent–child relationships and/or increased risk of internalizing or externalizing behavior disorders in later childhood

of behavioral and emotional regulation (see Table 4.4). From a developmental perspective, the individual disorders are closely interrelated and are almost impossible to differentiate from each other in terms of their etiological conditions, profile of risk factors, developmental progress, involvement of parent–infant relationships and long-term outcome. However, given the state of the art, it is not yet known whether and to what extent subgroups of these disorders may have an identifiable neurobiological etiology. This may be true in particular for subgroups of infants with regulation disorders of sensory processing (ZERO TO THREE, 2005).

In terms of the severity of regulation disorders, we observed a wide range between transient perturbations occurring in the context of sufficient infantile and parental resources on the one extreme and persistent, pervasive, and distinctly maladaptive disorders in the context of cumulative risk factors and limited resources on the other extreme. The severity of the disorder may be particularly striking if one or more of the following developmental characteristics apply: (a) lasting failure to master earlier, still unresolved developmental tasks; (b) a preponderance of rigid vicious circles in everyday interactions with increasing strain on the parent–infant relationship; (c) endangerment or disorder in the development of attachment, autonomy, and the parent–child relationship; (d) distortion of parent–infant communication and relationships by the transmission of a parent's traumatic childhood experiences (Fraiberg et al., 1975).

Diagnostic Triad: A New Type of Patient

There are as yet no adequate diagnostic categories in the *International Classification of Diseases (Tenth Edition [ICD-10])* or *Diagnostic and Statistical Manual of Mental Disorders—Fourth Edition (DSM–IV)* classification systems for the construct of disorders of behavioral and emotional regulation. With regard to the infantile and parental adaptive developmental tasks, the closest approximation would be to Adjustment Disorders of Early Childhood (*ICD-10*: F43.2). In this form, it has already been accepted into the diagnostic guidelines of the German Society for Child and Adolescent Psychiatry, Psychosomatics, and Psychotherapy (von Hofacker et al., 2003).

In contrast to the medical disease model, primary caregivers and the context of developing parent–infant relationships are significantly taken into consideration in the diagnosis. At the center of the diagnosis is a triad of interrelated infantile, parental, and interactional distress symptoms (see Table 4.4), including (a) problems in behavioral and emotional regulation; (b) dysfunctional communication in relevant interactional contexts, leading to failures in the coregulation and joint mastery of developmental tasks; and (c) excessive demands on the primary caregiver(s), implying a risk of parental adjustment disorder. In contrast to the assorted (pseudo)diagnostic terms such as *difficult infant, sensory integration disorder, infantile neurosis, infant depression, minimal brain dysfunction, early-onset ADHD, disorders of sensory processing,* or *relationship disorder* used elsewhere to describe similar behavioral manifestations, the proposed term *disorders of behavioral and emotional regulation in infancy* is value neutral in that neither the infant nor the parents are stigmatized, and open in that the infant or toddler is not prematurely labeled with a psychiatric diagnosis. The disorder by itself does not yet reside in the infant, who may only, for example, contribute some constitutional vulnerability. Nor is it solely the result of parental failure (e.g., the result of a postpartum depression or other psychosocial stress on the parents). Rather, it is concretely anchored in the daily interactions between parents and infant, and thus in the developing parent–infant relationship. As a result, a new type of patient is at the heart of therapy: not a single person, but the dyadic or triadic relationships between the parents and their infant (Barth, 1998; Stern, 1995). This new patient requires us to rethink traditional medical presumptions.

Unresolved Problems of the Classification of Primary Infant Psychiatric Diagnoses

An interesting diagnostic approach is offered by the international task force in the ZERO TO THREE *Diagnostic Classification* (1994) and in its revised edition, *DC:0–3R* (ZERO TO THREE, 2005), which attempt to take into account the complexity of early childhood disorders by using a multiaxial system. The primary diagnosis is classified on Axis 1. In addition, the quality of relationship is classified on Axis 2; somatic, neurological, psychiatric, and developmental disorders on Axis 3; the type and extent of psychosocial stressors on Axis 4; and the emotional and social functioning of the child on Axis 5. This system thus connects with the existing *ICD-10* and *DSM-IV* diagnostic systems.

As mentioned in the *DC:0–3R* manual, reliable application of the system is still difficult for disorders in infancy. The main differences from our diagnostic approach are made particularly clear by the example of regulation disorders of sensory processing. According to the manual, this disorder is etiologically anchored in the child in the form of constitutionally based difficulties in responses to sensory stimulation. Similar to the goodness-of-fit model proposed by temperament research, the quality of the social environment and of everyday parent–infant interactions are simply considered as risk factors in relation to the long-term outcome but not as an integral part of the disorder.

Interestingly, there is considerable overlap between the types and diversity of behavioral manifestations as described in the manual and those included in the concept of regulation disorders of behavioral and emotional regulation. Part of the genetic developmental perspective is also similar in that attention is paid to the maturational and constitutional variability of infantile sensory processing (Benoit, 2000; Greenspan, 1992; Greenspan & Porges, 1984). But contrary to our concept, a primary disorder of sensory, sensory–motor, and organizational (regulatory) processing is seen as a pathognomic criterion that distinguishes it from affective disorders and other disorders on Axis 1 (DeGangi, DiPietro, Greenspan, & Porges, 1991; DeGangi, Porges, Sickel, & Greenspan, 1993; Greenspan & Wieder, 1993). As a result, isolated sleep disorders and isolated feeding disorders in the absence of disorders of primary sensory processing problems are excluded and given separate diagnoses. Moreover, early excessive crying, which we found to precede later regulatory manifestations in more than 70% of our clients, is still missing in the revised manual (Maldonado-Duran & Saudera-Garcia, 1996).

In a critical discussion of the sparse empirical data collected to date, Barton and Robins (2000) pointed to the continuing need for research to develop reliable measurement methods and objective differential diagnostic criteria, and to validate the diagnostic construct *regulatory disorders* and its four typological subgroups (hypersensitive-fearful/cautious, hypersensitive-negative/defiant, hyposensitive/under-responsive, sensory stimulation seeking/impulsive). We have consciously made our concept of disorders of behavioral and emotional regulation in infancy broad enough and more open-ended, so that further diagnostically reliable and valid distinctions may be elaborated based on growing empirical knowledge and improved diagnostic criteria and methods.

Our own experience has shown that reliable distinctions between the primary diagnoses on Axis 1 of the ZERO TO THREE *Diagnostic Classification* are methodically difficult to make given the state-of-the-art, and in terms of content they are only partially reproducible. This is especially true for the first and second years of life, which are particularly emphasized in our own concept of disorders of behavioral and emotional regulation in infancy. The disorder can be etiologically ascribed neither solely to the infant nor clearly attributed to partial aspects of the infant's preverbal mental development (such as to sensory processing, affects, attention, or attachment). As a result, we do not distinguish regulation disorders from primary disorders of affect. Differentiation from reactive attachment disorders can be difficult where the patient history lacks clear indications of maltreatment, severe neglect, or frequent interruptions in a relationship. In individual infants, etiologically defined diagnoses of posttraumatic stress disorder or adjustment disorder are less problematic because of their etiological connection with an identifiable event in the patient history. Similarly, disorders of relating and communicating may be easier to diagnose because of their specific psychopathology.

OUTLOOK AND PROPOSALS FOR FURTHER RESEARCH

The descriptive empirical database presented in this book may serve as an inventory of a broad but presumably incomplete spectrum of disorders of behavioral and emotional regulation in infancy. It raises a series of questions that need to be clarified in prospective longitudinal studies of homogeneous subsamples. The questions relate to:

- Neurophysiological correlates of individual constitutional variability in children,
- The role of prenatal stress factors in relation to the infant's regulatory capacities,
- The elaboration of valid measures of sensory processing difficulties in the infant,
- Interactional and psychodynamic regulation of intuitive parenting,
- The specific role of the father and triadic relationships,
- Connections between this model and constructs stemming from attachment theory and psychodynamics,
- The diagnostic differentiation and demarcation of clinically valid subgroups,
- Timely identification of early signs or predictors in the entire system of later psychopathology,
- The role of play and the lack of desire for play in the developmental psychopathology of ADHD, and
- The effectiveness of targeted preventive intervention with regard to psychiatric disorders of later childhood.

Clinical research in the field of developmental psychopathology of disorders of infant mental health is fascinating and still full of puzzles and unresolved questions. We hope that the open systemic concept of disorders of behavioral and emotional regulation and the clinical database presented in this book may provide foundations for further hypotheses to be tested and verified in future studies. The concept has stood the test of many years as a foundation for interdisciplinary diagnostics, counseling, and parent–infant psychotherapy of regulatory and relational disorders in infancy.

REFERENCES

Atkinson, E., Vetere, A., & Grayson, K. (1995). Sleep disruption in young children. The influence of temperament on the sleep patterns of pre-school children. *Child: Care, Health and Development, 21,* 233–246.

Barth, R. (1998). Psychotherapie und Beratung im Säuglings- und Kleinkindalter. In K. von Klitzing (Ed.), *Psychotherapie in der frühen Kindheit* (pp. 72–87). Göttingen, Germany: Vandenhoeck & Ruprecht.

Barth, R. (1999). Ein Beratungsangebot für Eltern mit Säuglingen und Kleinkindern - Konzeption und erste Erfahrungen der Beratungsstelle "Menschenskind." *Praxis der Kinderpsychologie und Kinderpsychiatrie, 48,* 178–191.

Barton, M. L., & Robins, D. (2000). Regulatory disorders. In C. H. Zeanah Jr. (Ed.), *Handbook of infant mental health* (2nd ed., pp. 311–325). New York: Guilford Press.

Bates, J. E., Freeland, C. A., & Lounsbury, M. L. (1979). Measurement of infant difficultness. *Child Development, 50,* 704–803.

Benoit, D. (2000). Regulation and its disorders. In C. Violato & E. Oddone-Paduzzi (Eds.), *The changing family and child development* (pp. 149–161). Aldershot, England: Ashgate.

Bergant, A. M., Nguyen, T., Heim, K., Ulmer, H., & Dapunt, O. (1998). Deutschsprachige Fassung und Validierung der "Edinburgh postnatal depression scale." *Deutsche Medizinische Wochenschrift, 123,* 35–40.

Bertalanffy, L. (1968). *Organismic psychology theory.* Barre, MA: Clark University Press/Barre Publishers.

Bithoney, W. G., & Newberger, E. H. (1987). Child and family attributes of failure-to-thrive. *Journal of Developmental and Behavioral Pediatrics, 8,* 320–326.

Böhm, S. H. (2002). *Die mütterliche Befindlichkeit und die Erziehungs- und emotionalen Einstellungen bei Müttern von Kindern mit frühkindlichen Regulationsstörungen.* Unpublished doctoral dissertation, Ludwig-Maximilians-University, Munich, Germany.

Brazelton, T. B. (1994). Touchpoints: Opportunities for preventing problems in the parent-child relationship. *Acta Paediatrica, Supplement, 394,* 35–39.

Brazelton, T. B., & Cramer, B. G. (1990). *The earliest relationship: Parents, infants, and the drama of early attachment.* Reading, MA: Addison-Wesley.

Carey, W. B. (1974). Night waking and temperament in infancy. *Journal of Pediatrics, 81,* 756–758.

Carey, W. B., & McDevitt, S. C. (1995). *Coping with children's temperament.* New York: Basic Books.

Chatoor, I., Ganiban, J., Hirsch, R., Borman-Spurrell, E., & Mrazek, D. A. (2000). Maternal characteristics and toddler temperament in infantile anorexia. *Journal of the American Academy of Child and Adolescent Psychiatry, 39,* 743–751.

Chess, S., & Thomas, A. (1991). Temperament and the concept of goodness of fit. In J. A. Strelau & A. Angleitner (Eds.), *Explorations in temperament: International perspectives on theory and measurement. Perspectives on individual differences* (pp. 15–28). New York: Plenum Press.

Cierpka, M., & Cierpka, A. (2000). Beratung von Familien mit zwei- bis dreijährigen Kindern. *Praxis der Kinderpsychologie und Kinderpsychiatrie, 49,* 563–579.

Crittenden, P. M., & DiLalla, D. L. (1988). Compulsive compliance: The development of an inhibitory coping strategy in infancy. *Journal of Abnormal Child Psychology, 16,* 585–599.

Crockenberg, S., & Leerkes, E. (2000). Infant social and emotional development in family context. In C. H. Zeanah Jr. (Ed.), *Handbook of infant mental health* (2nd ed., pp. 60–90). New York: Guilford Press.

DeGangi, G. A., DiPietro, J. A., Greenspan, S. I., & Porges, S. W. (1991). Psychophysiological characteristics of the regulatory disordered infant. *Infant Behavior and Development, 14*, 37–50.

DeGangi, G. A., Porges, S. W., Sickel, R. Z., & Greenspan, S. I. (1993). Four-year follow-up of a sample of regulatory disordered infants. *Infant Mental Health Journal, 14*, 330–343.

Dittrichová, J., & Lapacková, V. (1964). Development of the waking state in young infants. *Child Development, 35*, 365–370.

Dornes, M. (1997). *Die frühe Kindheit: Entwicklungspsychologie der ersten Lebensjahre.* Frankfurt, Germany: Fischer.

Dornes, M. (2000). *Die emotionale Welt des Kindes.* Frankfurt, Germany: Fischer.

Emde, R. N. (1984). The affective self: Continuities and transformations from infancy. In J. Call, E. Galenson, & R. L. Tyson (Eds.), *Frontiers of infant psychiatry* (Vol. 2, pp. 38–54). New York: Basic Books.

Emde, R. N., Gaensbauer, T. J., & Harmon, R. J. (1976). Emotional expression in infancy: A biobehavioral study. *Psychological Issues, Monograph No. 37.* New York: International Universities Press.

Emde, R. N., Swedberg, J., & Suzuki, B. (1975). Human wakefulness and biological rhythms after birth. *Archives of General Psychiatry, 32*, 780–783.

Engfer, A. (1984). *Entwicklung punitiver Mutter-Kind-Interaktionen im sozioökologischen Kontext.* Arbeitsbericht zum Antrag an die Deutsche Forschungsgemeinschaft auf Gewährung einer Sachbeihilfe. Institut für Psychologie, Persönlichkeitspsychologie und Psychodiagnsostik, University of Munich, Germany.

Esser, G., Laucht, M., & Schmidt, M. H. (1995). Der Einfluß von Risikofaktoren und der Mutter-Kind-Interaktion im Säuglingsalter auf die seelische Gesundheit des Vorschulkindes. *Kindheit und Entwicklung, 4*, 33–42.

Fivaz-Depeursinge, E., & Corboz-Warnery, A. (2001). *The primary triangle: A developmental systems view of mothers, fathers, and infants.* New York: Basic Books.

Fonagy, P., Steele, M., Moran, G., Steele, H., & Higgit, A. (1993). Measuring the ghost in the nursery: An empirical study of the relation between parents' mental representations of childhood experiences and their infants' security of attachment. *Journal of the American Psychoanalytic Association, 41*, 957–989.

Fraiberg, S., Adelson, E., & Shapiro, V. (1975). Ghosts in the nursery: A psychoanalytic approach to the problem of impaired infant-mother relationships. *Journal of the American Academy of Child Psychiatry, 14*, 387–422.

Gloger-Tippelt, G. (1988). *Schwangerschaft und erste Geburt: Psychologische Veränderungen der Eltern.* Stuttgart, Germany: Kohlhammer.

Gray, J. A. (1987). Perspectives on anxiety and impulsivity: A commentary. *Journal of Research in Personality, 21*, 493–509.

Greenspan, S. I. (1992). *Regulatory disorders. Infancy and early childhood: The practice of clinical assessment and intervention with emotional and developmental challenges.* Madison, CT: International Universities Press.

Greenspan, S. I., & Porges, S. W. (1984). Psychopathology in infancy and early childhood: Clinical perspectives on the organization of sensory and affective-thematic experience. *Child Development, 55*, 49–70.

Greenspan, S. I., & Wieder, S. (1993). Regulatory disorders. In C. H. Zeanah Jr. (Ed.), *Handbook of infant mental health* (1st ed., pp. 280–316). New York: Guilford Press.

Hagekull, B., Bohlin, G., & Rydell, A. M. (1997). Maternal sensitivity, infant temperament, and the development of early feeding problems. *Infant Mental Health Journal, 18,* 92–106.

Huffman, L. C., Bryan, Y. E., Pedersen, F. A., Lester, B. M., Newman, J. D., & del Carmen, R. (1994). Infant cry acoustics and maternal ratings of temperament. *Infant Behavior and Development, 17,* 45–53.

Kagan, J. (1997). Temperament and the reactions to unfamiliarity. *Child Development, 68,* 139–144.

Largo, R. H. (1993). Verhaltens- und Entwicklungsauffälligkeiten: Störungen oder Normvarianten? *Monatsschrift für Kinderheilkunde, 141,* 698–703.

Largo, R. H. (2003). Spielend Lernen. In M. Papoušek & A. von Gontard (Eds.), *Spiel und Kreativität in der frühen Kindheit* (pp. 56–75). Stuttgart, Germany: Pfeiffer bei Klett-Cotta.

Lehtonen, L., Korhonen, T., & Korvenranta, H. (1994). Temperament and sleeping patterns in colicky infants during the first year of life. *Journal of Developmental and Behavioral Pediatrics, 15,* 416–420.

Lieberman, A. F., & Pawl, J. H. (1993). Infant-parent psychotherapy. In C. H. Zeanah Jr. (Ed.), *Handbook of infant mental health* (1st ed., pp. 427–442). New York: Guilford Press.

Lyons-Ruth, K. (1987). Infants at social risk: Relations among infant maltreatment, maternal behavior and infant attachment behavior. *Developmental Psychology, 23,* 223–232.

Main, M. (2002). Organisierte Bindungskategorien von Säugling, Kind und Erwachsenen. In K. H. Brisch, K. E. Grossmann, K. Grossmann, & L. Köhler (Eds.), *Bindung und Seelische Entwicklungswege* (pp. 165–218). Stuttgart, Germany: Klett-Cotta.

Maldonado-Duran, M., & Saudera-Garcia, J. M. (1996). Excessive crying in infants with regulatory disorders. *Bulletin of the Menninger Clinic, 60,* 62–78.

Minde, K., Popiel, K., Leos, N., Falkner, S., Parker, K., & Handley-Derry, M. (1993). The evaluation and treatment of sleep disturbances in young children. *Journal of Child Psychology and Psychiatry, 34,* 521–533.

Murray, L., & Carothers, A. D. (1990). The validation of the Edinburgh Post-natal Depression Scale on a community sample. *British Journal of Psychiatry, 157,* 288–290.

Papoušek, H. (1967). Experimental studies of appetitional behavior in human newborns and infants. In H. W. Stevenson, E. H. Hess, & H. L. Rheingold (Eds.), *Early behavior: Comparative and developmental approaches* (pp. 249–277). New York: Wiley.

Papoušek, H., & Papoušek, M. (1978). Interdisciplinary parallels in studies of early human behavior: From physical to cognitive needs, from attachment to dyadic education. *International Journal of Behavioral Development, 1*(1), 37–49.

Papoušek, H., & Papoušek, M. (1979). The infant's fundamental adaptive response system in social interaction. In E. B. Thoman (Ed.), *Origins of the infant's social responsiveness* (pp. 175–208). Hillsdale, NJ: Erlbaum.

Papoušek, H., & Papoušek, M. (1984). Qualitative transitions in integrative processes during the first trimester of human postpartum life. In H. F. R. Prechtl (Ed.), *Continuity of neural functions from prenatal to postnatal life* (pp. 220–244). London: Spastics International Medical.

Papoušek, H., & Papoušek, M. (1987). Intuitive parenting: A dialectic counterpart to the infant's integrative competence. In J. D. Osofsky (Ed.), *Handbook of infant development* (2nd ed., pp. 669–720). New York: Wiley.

Papoušek, H., & Papoušek, M. (1995). Intuitive parenting. In M.-H. Bornstein (Ed.), *Handbook of parenting. Volume 2: Biology and ecology of parenting* (pp. 117–135). Mahwah, NJ: Erlbaum.

Papoušek, H., & Papoušek, M. (2002). Intuitive parenting. In M. H. Bornstein (Ed.), *Handbook of parenting. Volume 2: Biology and ecology of parenting* (2nd ed., pp. 183–203). Mahwah, NJ: Erlbaum.

Papoušek, M. (1994). *Vom ersten Schrei zum ersten Wort. Anfänge der Sprachentwicklung in der vorsprachlichen Kommunikation*. Bern, Switzerland: Hans Huber.

Papoušek, M. (1997). Entwicklungsdynamik und Prävention früher Störungen der Eltern-Kind-Beziehungen. *Analytische Kinder- und Jugendlichen-Psychotherapie, 28*(1), 5–30.

Papoušek, M. (1998). Das Münchner Modell einer interaktionszentrierten Säuglings-Eltern-Beratung und -Psychotherapie. In K. von Klitzing (Ed.), *Psychotherapie in der frühen Kindheit* (pp. 88–118). Göttingen, Germany: Vandenhoeck & Ruprecht.

Papoušek, M. (1999). Regulationsstörungen der frühen Kindheit: Entstehungsbedingungen im Kontext der Eltern-Kind-Beziehungen. In R. Oerter, C. von Hagen, G. Roeper, & G. Noam (Eds.), *Klinische Entwicklungspsychologie. Ein Lehrbuch* (pp. 148–169). Weinheim, Germany: Psychologie Verlags Union.

Papoušek, M. (2000). Persistent infant crying, parenting and infant mental health. In J. D. Osofsky & H. E. Fitzgerald (Eds.), *WAIMH handbook of infant mental health* (Vol. 4, pp. 415–453). New York: Wiley.

Papoušek, M. (2001). Intuitive elterliche Kompetenzen: Eine Ressource in der präventiven Eltern-Säuglings-Beratung und -Psychotherapie. *Frühe Kindheit, 4*, 4–10.

Papoušek, M. (2002). Auswirkungen der Wochenbettdepression auf die frühkindliche Entwicklung. In H. Braun-Scharm (Ed.), *Depression im Kindes- und Jugendalter* (pp. 201–229). Stuttgart, Germany: Wissenschaftliche Verlagsgesellschaft.

Papoušek, M., & Papoušek, H. (1990). Excessive infant crying and intuitive parental care: Buffering support and its failures in parent-infant interaction. *Early Child Development and Care, 65*(Special Issue), 117–126.

Papoušek, M., & von Hofacker, N. (1995). Persistent crying and parenting: Search for a butterfly in a dynamic system. *Early Development and Parenting, 4*(4), 209–224.

Papoušek, M., & von Hofacker, N. (1998). Persistent crying in early infancy: A non-trivial condition of risk for the developing mother-infant relationship. *Child: Care, Health and Development, 24*, 395–424.

Papoušek, M., & Wollwerth de Chuquisengo, R. (2003). Auswirkungen mütterlicher Traumatisierungen auf Kommunikation und Beziehung in der frühen Kindheit: Werkstattbericht aus 10 Jahren Münchner Sprechstunde für Schreibabys. In K. H. Brisch (Ed.), *Bindung und Trauma* (pp. 136–159). Stuttgart, Germany: Klett-Cotta.

Pauli-Pott, U., Ries-Hahn, A., Kupfer, J., & Beckmann, D. (1999). Konstruktion eines Fragebogens zur Erfassung des "frühkindlichen Temperaments" im Elternurteil. *Praxis der Kinderpsychologie und Kinderpsychiatrie, 48*, 231–246.

Petzold, M. (1988). *Paare werden Eltern: Eine familienentwicklungspsychologische Längsschnittstudie* (2nd. ed.). St. Augustin, Germany: Gardez.

Prudhomme-White, B., Gunnar, M. R., Larson, M. C., Donzella, B., & Barr, R. G. (2000). Behavioral and physiological responsivity, sleep, and patterns of daily cortisol production in infants with and without colic. *Child Development, 71*, 862–877.

Rabenschlag, U. (1998). *Kinder reisen durch die Nacht: Schlafen, Wachen, Träumen—Die gute Nacht für Kinder*. Freiburg, Germany: Herder.

Resch, F. (1996). *Entwicklungspsychopathologie des Kindes- und Jugendalters*. Weinheim, Germany: Psychologie Verlags Union.

Richman, N. (1981). A community survey of characteristics of one- to two-year-olds with sleep disruptions. *Journal of the American Academy of Child Psychiatry, 20*, 281–291.

Rothbart, M. K., Derryberry, D., & Posner, M. I. (1994). A psychobiological approach to the development of temperament. In J. E. Bates & T. D. Wachs (Eds.), *Temperament: Individual differences at the interface of biology and behavior* (pp. 83–116). Washington, DC: American Psychological Association.

Sameroff, A. J., & Emde, R. N. (Eds.). (1989). *Relationship disturbances in early childhood: A developmental approach*. New York: Basic Books.

Scher, A., Tirosh, E., & Lavie, P. (1998). The relation between sleep and temperament revisited: Evidence for 12-month-olds; a research note. *Journal of Child Psychology and Psychiatry, 39*, 785–788.

Schieche, M. (2001). Störungen der Bindungs-Explorations-Balance und Möglichkeiten der Intervention. In G. J. Suess, H. Scheuerer-Englisch, & W. K. P. Pfeiffer (Eds.), *Bindungstheorie und Familiendynamik. Anwendung der Bindungstheorie in Beratung und Therapie* (pp. 297–313). Gießen, Germany: Psychosozial-Verlag.

Schneewind, K. A. (2002). Familienentwicklung. In R. Oerter & L. Montada (Eds.), *Entwicklungspsychologie* (5th ed., pp. 105–127). Weinheim, Germany: Beltz Psychologie Verlags Union.

Smith, L. B., & Thelen, E. (Eds.). (1993). *A dynamic systems approach to development: Applications*. Cambridge, MA: MIT Press.

Stern, D. N. (1995). *The motherhood constellation: A unified view of parent-infant psychotherapy*. New York: Basic Books.

Stern, D. N., Sander, L. W., Nahum, J. P., Harrison, A. M., Lyons-Ruth, K., Morgan, A. C., et al. (2002). The Process of Change Study Group, Boston: Nicht-deutende Mechanismen in der psychoanalytischen Therapie: Das "Etwas-Mehr" als Deutung. *Psyche, 56* (Special Issue: Entwicklungsforschung, Bindungstheorie, Lebenszyklus), 974–1006.

Stifter, C. A. (2001). Life after unexplained crying: Child and parent outcomes. In R. G. Barr, I. St. James-Roberts, & M. R. Keefe (Eds.), *New evidence on unexplained early crying: Its origin, nature and management* (pp. 273–288). Skillman, NJ: Johnson & Johnson Pediatric Institute Round Table Series.

St. James-Roberts, I., Conroy, S., & Wilsher, K. (1995). Clinical, developmental and social aspects of infant crying and colic. *Early Development and Parenting, 4*, 177–189.

St. James-Roberts, I., Conroy, S., & Wilsher, K. (1998). Links between maternal care and persistent infant crying in the early months. *Child: Care, Health and Development, 24*, 353–376.

Thomas, A., & Chess, S. (1977). *Temperament and development*. New York: Brunner/Mazel.

Thomas, A., & Chess, S. (1980). *The dynamics of psychological development*. New York: Brunner/Mazel.

Thomas, A., Chess, S., & Birch, H. G. (1968). *Temperament and behavior disorders in childeren*. London: University of London Press.

von Hofacker, N., Barth, R., Bindt, C., Deneke, C., Jacubeit, T., & Papoušek, M. (2003). Regulationsstörungen im Säuglingsalter. In Deutsche Gesellschaft für Kinder- und Jugendpsychiatrie (Ed.), *Leitlinien zur Diagnostik und Therapie von psychischen Störungen im Säuglings-, Kindes- und Jugendalter* (2nd rev. ed., pp. 345–360). Köln,

Germany: Deutscher Ärzte Verlag.

von Hofacker, N., & Papoušek, M. (1998). Disorders of excessive crying, feeding, and sleeping: The Munich Interdisciplinary Research and Intervention Program. *Infant Mental Health Journal, 19*(2), 180–201.

Wolff, P. H. (1987). *The development of behavioral states and the expression of emotions in early infancy: New proposals for investigation*. Chicago: University of Chicago Press.

Wolke, D., Gray, P., & Meyer, R. (1994). Excessive infant crying: A controlled study of mothers helping mothers. *Pediatrics, 94*, 322–332.

Wolke, D., Skuse, D., & Mathisen, B. (1990). Behavioral style in failure-to-thrive infants: A preliminary communication. *Journal of Pediatric Psychology, 15*, 237–254.

Zentner, M. R. (2000). Das Temperament als Risikofaktor in der frühkindlichen Entwicklung. In F. Petermann, K. Niebank, & H. Scheithauer (Eds.), *Risiken in der frühkindlichen Entwicklung* (pp. 257–281). Göttingen, Germany: Hogrefe.

ZERO TO THREE. (1994). *Diagnostic classification: 0–3. Diagnostic classification of mental health and developmental disorders of infancy and early childhood*. Arlington, VA: National Center for Clinical Infant Programs.

ZERO TO THREE. (2005). *Diagnostic classification of mental health and developmental disorders of infancy and early childhood: Revised edition (DC:0–3R)*. Washington, DC: ZERO TO THREE Press.

CHAPTER 5

EXCESSIVE CRYING IN INFANCY

Margret Ziegler
Ruth Wollwerth de Chuquisengo
Mechthild Papoušek

CASE VIGNETTE

Reason for referral. Leon was brought to the Munich Program for Fussy Babies by his mother, Mrs. H., at the age of 3½ months because of severe bouts of crying. Ever since the 4th week of life, he had been crying or fussing for an average of 6 hours per day. All attempts at soothing Leon were met with resistance such as stiffening and pushing his mother away. Only rarely was his mother able to soothe him by rocking and carrying him around. Leon did not sleep much, and during his long waking phases he had to be carried constantly and demanded continual stimulation. The sleep log in Figure 5.1a, which the parents filled out before their first visit, shows a typical day: waking phases as long as 6

Figure 5.1a. Sleep Log Before Counseling.

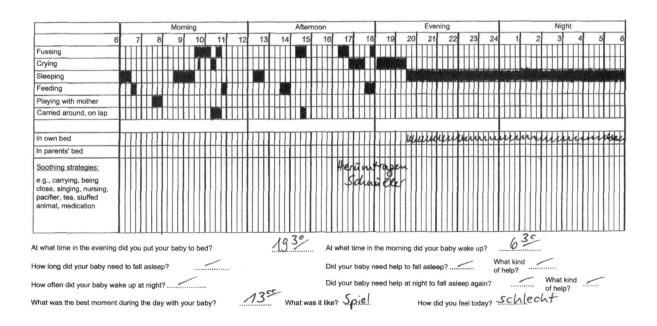

hours; short, infrequent sleep phases during the day; long phases of crying and fussiness, particularly toward evening; and hardly any time for mutual play. Leon slept for a total of only about 13 hours during this time.

Case history. Leon was the first child of an academic couple. After many years of longing for a child and trying unsuccessfully, the mother became pregnant at a time when they had become reconciled to a future without children. Both parents-to-be were delighted about the pregnancy, which proceeded without problems. A cesarean section was performed during the 38th week because of an abnormal fetal heartbeat during cardiotocography. A few days after delivery, the mother began to feel an inexplicable sadness, but her emotional state eventually improved. When the bouts of excessive crying began during the 4th week, she became depressed again. Her husband was unable to support her adequately because of pressure at work, and their families of origin lived far away.

Initial findings. Mrs. H. was at the end of her rope. She wept frequently, was deeply depressed, and occasionally felt tremendous anger toward her baby. She admitted that she frequently wished she could undo her pregnancy. Socially, she was completely isolated and saw no way out of her difficult situation.

During her first visit, the mother's exhaustion and depression were evident in the way she handled her crying baby. She was virtually unable to give Leon the support and security of body contact needed to soothe him. She held him at a distance, avoided eye contact, and stroked him absentmindedly with her fingertips. The feelings triggered in the mother by her son's incessant crying ranged from anger and aggression to inexplicable sadness and abandonment.

However, when Leon returned to a calm receptive state for a few minutes, his mother's affect changed immediately. Within the therapeutic setting, the mother was able for the first time to let herself become engaged in a dialogue. She was able to attune her voice and facial expression to Leon's signals and engaged in a relaxed dialogue with the infant, who was smiling and cooing. She enjoyed such moments of positive relatedness, which helped her to deal with the more stressful phases of crying. In addition, a planned extended visit to her mother who lived far away promised some support and relief.

As observed during the pediatric examination, Leon's behavioral regulation was still immature. Even the slightest acoustic and visual stimulation, such as the examiner's subtle attempts to establish visual contact with him, caused Leon to slip into a severe bout of crying, and it was almost impossible to bring him out of it.

Diagnosis. We diagnosed a disorder of behavioral and emotional regulation (F43.2, *ICD-10*), with excessive crying and problems with sleep–wake organization associated with postpartum depression in the mother.

Treatment and progress. Treatment included elements of mother–infant psychotherapy, developmental counseling, and guidance in mother–infant communication. Psychotherapy focused first on relieving the mother of her physical and psychological distress and supporting her plan to visit her mother. Before this trip, the therapist focused on detailed developmental counseling aiming at strategies to shield Leon from overstimulation, and to support a regular sleep–wake rhythm throughout the day.

Leon's crying and sleeping behavior changed considerably over the course of 1 week. His mother had managed despite her exhaustion and depression to follow some of the suggestions made during

Figure 5.1b. Sleep Log After Counseling.

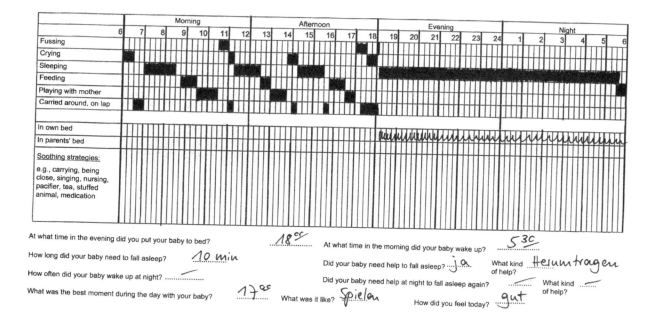

developmental counseling, thereby giving Leon the support necessary for his still immature regulatory capacities. Overall, Leon slept more. He began to show regular sleep phases during the day, and his waking phases became more stable, giving him more time to play with his mother (see Figure 5.1b).

Mother–infant psychotherapy focused on the memories and feelings of abandonment, sadness, and rage that were evoked by Leon's inconsolable crying. She herself had been an unwanted child. Her mother had not been prepared to give up her professional career; her father, whom she never really got to know, had left the mother during the pregnancy. After birth, Mrs. H. was raised by her grandmother. She had very positive memories of these first childhood years. Her grandparents were very loving, and she had plenty of playmates in the small village in northern Germany where they lived. She hardly got to know her mother. However, when she was 6 years old, her mother decided to take her back to Munich, against the wishes of her grandparents. For financial and professional reasons, her mother was unable to give up her career, and Mrs. H. was sent to a boarding school. She felt extremely unhappy and lonely there and developed a strong aversion to her mother. Only when Mrs. H. began to enter puberty and to rebel increasingly did her mother reduce her work hours. Slowly, over time, mother and daughter began to reconcile. Several years later, her mother moved back to the village where she had originally lived. In the meantime, Mrs. H. had gotten to know her future partner, and she decided to stay in Munich and work in a supervisory capacity at a respected corporation.

After her second appointment, Mrs. H. had to be counseled by telephone while she stayed with her mother. Mrs. H. had begun a homeopathic treatment for her depression; her mother cared for her around the clock and supported her in caring for Leon, which was a great relief for Mrs. H. Over the course of her stay she regained her strength and was able to take more pleasure in her little son. Soon, Leon developed more stable waking phases and a more regulated sleep–wake rhythm.

After 5 weeks with her mother, Mrs. H. made another attempt to live with her husband in Munich, a prospect that filled her with fears of renewed social isolation and overload. And, in fact, shortly after her return memories of the traumatic first months with her excessively crying baby were evoked again. She was afraid that Leon would suffer a relapse and imagined herself standing alone in the corner of the apartment, trying to console her crying infant. The feelings of loneliness returned, and Mrs. H. felt she was on the verge of another depression. Her husband's work situation had not improved during her absence, which led to increasing conflict. Because the relationship was important to both of them, they decided to live separately for a time. Mrs. H. moved back to live with her mother for 6 months; during this time her husband agreed to try to change his professional situation so that he would have more time for his family. In addition, they planned to move to a more family-friendly neighborhood.

While living with her mother, Mrs. H. continued to pursue treatment for her depression. Leon developed into an alert friendly little boy, who gave his mother and grandmother a great deal of pleasure. This time, things worked out well when she returned to Munich. The family moved to a new housing development with many other young families, and Mrs. H. quickly began to make friends. Her fear that Leon would relapse into his earlier crying problems resolved; she could see that he was more stable, and enjoyed his liveliness. Her husband had been able to arrange his work schedule so that he had more time and energy for his family. As a result the couple's relationship and overall family situation relaxed.

INTRODUCTION

From a psychobiological perspective, crying is an innate vocal signal of intense discomfort related to basic needs. It functions to alert the social environment both physiologically and psychologically and to motivate social partners to intervene immediately and provide physical closeness, safety, and intuitive regulatory support. But what happens when crying continues even though the infant's needs have been satisfied? Is the baby in pain? Is the mother incapable of soothing her infant?

In the pediatric literature, excessive crying is mentioned only under the rubric of 3-month colic and is described, if at all, as unexplained crying and fussing during the first 3 months of life. It is not attributed to a particular ailment in the classic sense. The bouts of crying are generally thought to be triggered by abdominal colic—overinflation of the still immature gastrointestinal tract—and treatment is prescribed accordingly. According to this line of reasoning, crying is harmless and resolves by the end of the third month without long-term consequences. Are such explanations helpful to an overstressed mother whose life revolves around nursing and carrying her excessively crying baby? Is such inconsolable crying really that harmless? After all, it has been shown that it may cause tremendous distress in the mother–infant relationship and in some cases can even lead to infant abuse and neglect. In this chapter we describe what is generally known about the mysteries of infant colic and provide recommendations based on many years of experience in the Munich Interdisciplinary Research and Intervention Program for Fussy Babies.

CLINICAL SYNDROME

The most important symptoms with regard to infant behavioral problems, parental distress, and parent–infant interaction are summarized in Table 5.1.

The core symptoms in infants include unexplained, inconsolable crying and long episodes of inexplicable fussiness. Paroxysmal bouts of severe crying with flexed knees, hypertonic extremities, overinflated

Table 5.1. Clinical Syndrome of Excessive Crying.

Infant behavioral problems
- –Unexplained inconsolable crying
- –Motor restlessness/fussiness
- –Irritability, sensory hyperreactivity
- –Motor hyperextension and tactile defensiveness
- –Urge to be in a vertical position, rejection of horizontal positions
- –Need to be carried around in upright position for vestibular and visual stimulation
- –Pseudo-stability as a result of distraction and new stimuli
- –Paradoxical "hunger" for stimulation (wide open eyes, seeking stimulation)
- –Or overanxiousness with anxious withdrawal
- –Inability to "turn off" stimulation when tired, to self-soothe, and to fall asleep
- –Cumulative sleep deficit with extremely short sleep phases during the day
- –Overfatigue and hyperreactivity with crying peak during evening hours
- –Absence of quiet alert waking states

Parental overload
- –Extreme fatigue, tension, exhaustion from continuous overload
- –Depressiveness, helplessness, feelings of failure
- –Vulnerability, powerless anger, feelings of being rejected
- –Inhibition of intuitive parenting
- –Neglect of own needs
- –Distress and conflict in couple's relationship

Interactional failure in the soothing context
- –Impeded handling in the face of motor restlessness and parental insecurity
- –Interruption of fussiness by carrying around and offering diversified stimulation
- –Ineffectiveness of normal soothing strategies during crying bouts
- –Dysfunctional interactions when soothing and settling to sleep with frequent changes in intense or bizarre soothing strategies
- –Interruption of stimulation triggers immediate crying, which is answered by intensified stimulation
- –When being held, "fighting against going to sleep" with motor restlessness, tactile rejection, and back-arching
- –Vicious circle of reciprocal escalating tension and arousal
- –By contrast, lack of angel's circles with intuitively attuned dialogues after successful soothing, or during quiet alert waking states

tummy, reddened face, and shrill hyperphonic/dysphonic crying (Lester, Boukydis, Garcia-Coll, & Hole, 1990) that do not respond to the usual soothing interventions naturally make one suspect abdominal pain. However, in nonclinical samples of infants with excessive crying, such colicky crying bouts make up only 11% of the average time spent crying and fussing during the day, compared to 28% normal crying and 61% fussing (St. James-Roberts, Conroy, & Wilsher, 1995).

The usual soothing strategies are ineffective. Carrying the baby around, frequently changing the baby's position so as to face the surroundings, typically brings relief neither to the infant nor to the parents. Parents use multiple, often dysfunctional, strategies to help their baby fall asleep: walking the baby, rocking, swaying, nursing for hours, extended excursions over cobblestones in a baby carriage, or even long rides at night on a highway without traffic lights. Many of these babies are remarkably receptive to visual stimuli; they absorb their surroundings with wide-open eyes; when they get tired, they cannot avert their gaze. The parents erroneously learn from their babies that they must constantly offer something new, discovering that intense visual and vestibular stimuli such as jumping on a gymnastics ball, changing position, or walking back and forth will interrupt fussiness and crying. Unfortunately, there is no lasting calming effect, and the baby begins to cry again as soon as the stimulation is withdrawn. Paradoxically, such babies seem to seek more and more stimuli even though they seem to be almost continually overstimulated. Parents soon discover that white noise such as the sound of a hairdryer, vacuum cleaner, electric toothbrush, or the sound of a car motor will also calm their crying baby temporarily. Left to themselves, the babies are almost always in a dissatisfied, fussy state that can at any moment turn into a full-blown bout of crying.

Motorically, these infants are notable for their restlessness, preference for vertical body positions, and defense against being laid down in a supine or prone position. It is often difficult to handle them and to hold them safely in close body contact because of moderate hypotonia in the trunk, hypertonic extremities, and a tendency for back-arching. They react intensely to external and internal stimuli (hyperreactivity) and are easily frightened and hypersensitive to sound (irritability). Some of these infants seem to be oversensitive and anxious and appear likely to burst into full-blown crying, for instance, if one only tries to elicit visual contact with them. The slightest environmental change can throw them out of a fragile equilibrium; to shield themselves from overstimulation, some of them may even switch into a state of excessive inhibition or brief freezing with sleep-like breathing and staring (H. Papoušek, 1969).

Generally, these behavioral problems exhibit a diurnal rhythm with more quiet waking and sleep in the morning and increasing fussiness, fatigue, overstrain, and crying toward the late afternoon and evening hours. In spite of overfatigue, these babies are barely able to fall asleep during the day, and if so only for short periods. They seem to fight against falling asleep in the parents' arms. Only late at night do they let themselves be put to sleep without immediate startles and awakenings. During the first months of life they still seem to experience a relatively undisturbed peaceful sleep between midnight and 6:00 in the morning. Often, a sleep deficit develops because they fall asleep so late and never compensate during the day.

Mothers of babies who cry excessively are generally on the job around the clock trying to satisfy their baby, while at the same time neglecting their own needs to a critical degree. Nevertheless, their baby's inconsolable crying and fussiness seem to certify to the mother that she is a failure and that she is incapable of meeting his basic needs. This causes her to feel insecure and "helpless in the baby's hands." Making matters more difficult is that many of these infants don't snuggle, but instead resist close body contact as if they were trying to struggle against their mother. In addition to helplessness and despair, the majority of mothers respond to the alarming effects of crying and their perception of powerlessness with anger, aggression, and even rejection of the child—which in turn may shock them and shatter their sense of self-worth (M. Papoušek & von Hofacker, 1995; St. James-Roberts, Conroy, & Wilsher, 1995). In the absence of severe psychosocial or biographical stressors, mothers are generally able to keep their aggressive impulses and fantasies under control so that they don't abuse their infant or neglect his basic needs. Similar dynamics affect fathers as well, to the extent that they partake in parenting. Unfortunately, all too often fathers abdicate responsibility and withdraw in the face of an excessively crying baby.

DEFINITIONS AND DIAGNOSTIC CRITERIA

According to international agreement, the scientific criteria for differentiating between normal and excessive crying at the age of 6 weeks draw on the "rule of threes": crying and fussing for more than 3 hours a day, for more than 3 days a week, and for more than 3 weeks in an infant who is well-fed and otherwise healthy (Wessel, Cobb, Jackson, Harris, & Detwiler, 1954). However, for clinical purposes, a criterion based alone on the duration of crying and fussing is clearly inadequate. The etiologically neutral term *excessive crying* has largely replaced earlier terms (*3-month colic, colicky crying, 5 o'clock crying*) as a label for the complex constellation of symptoms involving problems at the infant, parental, and interactional levels. In accordance with our current understanding, the syndrome is more appropriately classified as *syndrome of excessive crying* and an age-related subgroup of *disorders of behavioral and emotional regulation in early childhood*. The term *persistent excessive crying* is used when the problem persists beyond the age of 3 months (M. Papoušek & von Hofacker, 1995).

From a systemic perspective, neither the infant with regulatory problems, nor the overloaded mother who is no longer able to soothe him, can be viewed in isolation. The clinical syndrome of excessive infant crying is characterized by a triad of symptoms. The diagnostic triad includes (a) the infant's inconsolable crying with problems in sleep–wake organization, (b) the parents' overload and psychosocial distress, and (c) frequent interactional failure that maintains or exacerbates the behavioral problems (M. Papoušek, 2000).

Excessive crying that persists beyond the developmental spurt expected at the age of approximately 3 months takes on new qualities depending on the infant's progress in self-regulatory capacities. For example, crying may take on an instrumental quality in some situations. In addition, problematic crying shifts increasingly to nighttime, when the infant should be asleep. Persistent excessive crying should therefore be distinguished from excessive crying during the first months of life.

PREVALENCE AND EPIDEMIOLOGY IN REPRESENTATIVE SAMPLES

In a number of Western industrialized countries, the prevalence of excessive crying during the first 3 months in representative community-based samples has been reported to range between 16% and 29%

(Lehtonen, 1994; St. James-Roberts & Halil, 1991). The disparity mainly has to do with differences in definition, methods of assessment, and the particular age at which the data were collected. Wurmser, Laubereau, Hermann, Papoušek, and von Kries (2001) tried to ascertain, at least retrospectively, the prevalence of excessive crying in Germany based on an epidemiological telephone survey of representative households with children less than 3 years old. To date, this is the only investigation conducted in Germany, revealing that 21% of mothers reported excessive crying (fussing and crying for more than 3 hours per day) during the first months of their baby's life. Remarkably, 8.3%—that is, almost 40% of the excessively crying infants—were reported to have problematic crying that persisted beyond the third month of life.

Although it is generally assumed that male newborns and firstborns more frequently exhibit crying problems, such tendencies were not confirmed in large studies (Lehtonen, 1994; St. James-Roberts & Halil, 1991). However, mothers with firstborns tend to seek help more often because they are more likely to be unsettled by excessive crying than are more experienced mothers. Nevertheless, there is a clustering among siblings and twins (Lehtonen, 1994), which indicates that genetic factors and factors in the shared environment may be involved. According to most studies, maternal age, parental education, and socioeconomic status have no effect (Lehtonen, 1994).

CLINICAL SAMPLE REFERRED TO THE MUNICH PROGRAM

Clinical samples of families that are referred to a specialized program for excessively crying babies generally differ from epidemiological samples. On the basis of our data we may speculate that, within the universe of infants who fulfill the rule-of-threes, crying problems in clinical samples represent the most extreme manifestations influenced by cumulative somatic and psychosocial risk factors. We can only estimate the percentage of excessively crying infants whose parents seek help in relation to the overall prevalence of excessive crying and in comparison to the total infant population. We presume that if the overall prevalence is 20% on average (at the age of 6 weeks), about one fifth will present at a specialized clinical program, that is, approximately 4% of all infants.

Of the 701 infants examined in the Munich Program between 1994 and 1997 whose findings were analyzed in detail, 218 were referred between birth and 6 months of age because of excessive crying and dysfunctional sleep–wake organization (Sample B). Exactly 50% of the infants were more than 3 months old when they first came in. The mean age at first visit was 3.5 months (± 1.5); the mean duration of symptoms since their onset was 3.4 months (± 1.5). This means that in most cases, excessive crying had begun shortly after birth, leaving families with almost no unencumbered interaction time with their baby. The same was true for an earlier sample of 63 infants with excessive crying studied between 1992 and 1994 (Sample A; M. Papoušek & von Hofacker, 1995, 1998). At that time, we recruited a control group of 49 children from birth announcements in the local newspaper, matched for age, sex, and birth status, but without manifest crying problems; the control group children and their families were subjected to the same procedures as the referred families.

Data acquisition included (a) 24-hour diaries that parents filled out on five successive days, assessing duration and diurnal distribution of crying, fussing, sleeping, feeding, and play (see Figures 5.1a and b);

(b) a semi-structured medical and psychological diagnostic interview that inquired into developmental history as well as family risk factors and resources; (c) a comprehensive pediatric and neuropediatric examination; (d) questionnaires on the infant's everyday regulatory problems and temperament, maternal self-confidence, emotional state and attitude toward her infant, contentment in her partnership, and social network; and (e) spontaneous and videotaped behavioral observations of infant and parents during the medical examination and in interactional contexts relevant to the disorder (soothing when crying, settling to sleep, diapering, feeding, relaxed dialogue). The 24-hour diaries for 53 infants with excessive crying and 47 control babies of the same age without manifest crying problems were scientifically analyzed and compared (Schaumann, 2003). The following sections focus on the data related to somatic and psychosocial risks, sleep–wake organization, and infant temperament.

CONDITIONS OF SOMATIC AND PSYCHOSOCIAL RISKS IN A DEVELOPMENTAL CONTEXT

Pediatric Factors

Among the factors that contribute to excessive inconsolable crying, pediatric and neuropediatric disorders or illnesses are relatively rare events. Occasionally, they may be the sole cause of a crying problem, but often they are only part of a more complex set of risk conditions. In any case, it is important to identify pediatric disorders and to integrate their treatment into the therapeutic regimen as a whole (Gormally, 2001; Lehtonen, Gormally, & Barr, 2000).

Among the infants referred to our program, acute illnesses associated with increased crying (such as middle-ear infection, urinary tract infection, gastrointestinal infection, bone fractures, etc.) had previously been ruled out by the family pediatrician.

Gastrointestinal disorders that may lead to excessive crying in an otherwise healthy infant include lactose intolerance, cow's milk protein intolerance, and gastroesophageal reflux. Isolated fructose intolerance occurs only later when supplementary food is introduced.

Lactose intolerance. It is theorized that incomplete carbohydrate absorption (lactose) in the small intestine and fermentation in the large intestine lead to increased gas formation in the intestines. Studies measuring intestinal gas with radiological methods and measurement of the hydrogen content of the infant's exhaled air generally find no connection between excessive crying and increased intestinal gas (Barr, Clogg, Woolridge, & Tansey, 1987; Forsyth, 1997). However, intestinal gas may become transiently elevated as a result of air swallowed during excessive crying. Primary lactose intolerance is rarely found in infancy, but tends to be associated with massive diarrhea and failure to thrive.

Cow's milk protein intolerance. Cow's milk protein intolerance and allergy are considered a potential cause of excessive crying in a minority of infants. This condition, however, is typically associated with other somatic symptoms such as vomiting, abnormal stool (containing blood or mucous secretion), failure to thrive, eczema, or obstructive bronchitis. Given a positive history of allergy in first-order relatives, cow's milk protein intolerance may occur even in children who are nursed, because cow's milk protein (bovine beta-lactoglobulin) has been found in up to 75% of samples of breast milk from mothers who consume cow's milk products. The diagnosis is made on the basis of improvements in crying symptoms when the nursing mother drops cow's milk from her diet and/or begins to feed with hydrolysate formula, and when reexposure to cow's milk aggravates the symptoms. To date, available laboratory tests do not provide reliable results in young children. The results of many studies of the switch to a diet free of cow's milk either have not been reproducible or are contradictory (Barr et al., 1987; Lucassen et al., 1998). Notable is the extreme variation in the rates of improvement seen when cow's milk is eliminated, rates that fluctuate between 6% and 71%, depending on the sample selection (Forsyth, 1989; Iacono et al., 1991; Jacobsson, 1997). According to a critical review of the literature, several authors (Forsyth, 1997; Jacobsson, 1997; Treem, 2001) have come to the conclusion that the inconsistency of results is attributable to methodological flaws in terms of sample selection, diagnostic criteria, and control of spontaneous remissions around the age of 3 months. According to these authors, one may, at best, expect an improvement rate of 5% to 10% when cow's milk is eliminated from the diet. However, no conclusions may be drawn from this regarding a connection between cow's milk protein and excessive crying.

Gastroesophageal reflux. When taking a detailed case history or systematic examination, pediatricians may diagnose reflux esophagitis secondary to gastroesophageal reflux. The symptoms of gastro-esophageal reflux include frequent atonic, occasionally acid vomiting that occurs most frequently in the lying position and may occur at night many hours after feeding. Reflux-induced vomiting is typically associated with crying. Depending on the severity and duration of the symptoms, the vomitus may contain blood or hematin. Feeding problems are not uncommon, and severe forms may lead to failure to thrive. Respiratory problems may also be the primary symptom. In addition, affected infants often exhibit neurological symptoms with extreme hyperextension (Strassburg, Haug-Schnabel, & Mueller, 1990; Treem, 2001).

Conservative estimates of current research suggest that gastrointestinal problems are the sole cause of excessive crying in only 5% of infants (Lehtonen et al., 2000; Miller & Barr, 1991). However, they must be taken into consideration when additional premonitory symptoms are present such as extreme and high-pitched crying, extreme crying independent on time of day and night, persistence beyond the fourth month of life, recurrent choking and vomiting, stool irregularities, and failure to thrive (Gormally, 2001).

Functional abnormalities of the spinal column. Over the past several years we have seen hypomobile functional abnormalities of the cervical vertebral column, also called head-joint-induced functional asymmetry (KISS syndrome) as another potential cause of excessive crying. Constrained intrauterine positioning or birth complications may lead to painful restriction of mobility in the region of the cervical vertebral joints with asymmetrical positioning of the head and body. This disorder may be treated by manual therapy or physiotherapy, which may lead to immediate improvement in the crying symptoms (Biedermann, 2000). However, a large-scale double-blind nonclinical study has demonstrated that manual treatment of all infants with excessive crying without evidence of other clinical symptoms has no significant effect on crying behavior (Olafsdottir, Forshei, Fluge, & Markestad, 2001). In contrast, Biedermann (2000) postulated a success rate of 60%, given a correct initial diagnosis and targeted intervention.

Results From the Munich Program: Pediatric Findings

Among the client base of the Munich Program, pediatric disorders (postnatal somatic risk factors) of the gastrointestinal tract were found in only a few infants. Results concerning the most important postnatal risk factors found in our Sample B replicate the results of our earlier controlled comparative study (Sample A; M. Papoušek & von Hofacker, 1998; see Table 5.2).

Before their first visit, 33.3% of mothers had either not nursed at all or nursed for less than 1 month; another 5.2% had nursed for at least 1 month but had already weaned their infants before the first visit. There was no association between excessive crying and atopic disorders in family or infant. The referring pediatrician had usually already ruled out gastrointestinal disorders, or the infant's crying problem

The most prevalent perinatal + post natal rish factors

Table 5.2. Prenatal, Perinatal, and Postnatal Somatic Risk Factors.

Risk factor	Sample B	Sample A (M. Papoušek & von Hofacker, 1998)			
	Excessive crying (n = 218) %	Extreme crying (n = 37) %	Moderate crying (n = 26) %	Control group (n = 49) %	Mantel-Haenszel test[a] p
Prenatal					
Previous miscarriages	27.1	35.1	7.7	24.5	ns
Premature labor	19.3	27.0	7.7	6.1	≤ .01
Gestosis	6.4	5.4	7.7	6.1	ns
Nicotine abuse	14.7	18.9	23.1	6.1	≤ .05
Perinatal					
Premature birth (<37th week)	9.6	8.1	3.8	4.1	ns
Low birthweight (<2,500 g)	10.1	5.4	7.7	0.0	ns
Vacuum/forceps	12.8	18.9	7.7	12.2	ns
Cesarean section, planned or emergency	16.5	29.7	7.7	24.5	ns
Severe birth complications for infant	4.1	5.4	3.8	0.0	ns
Early separation/transfer to other unit	16.5	21.6	15.4	10.2	ns
Postnatal					
Nursing <1 month	33.3	24.3	26.9	8.5	ns
Family atopy	57.8	43.2	50.0	30.6	ns
Infant atopy (neurodermatitis, signs of cows milk intolerance)	12.8	8.1	23.1	12.2	ns
Neurological abnormalities	58.3	51.4	57.7	22.4	≤ .005
Hospital admissions	11.5	29.7	19.2	10.2	≤ .05

[a]One-tailed.

had not improved in spite of somatic treatment (e.g., switching to a cow's-milk-free diet, treatment of gastroesophageal reflux). Clinically relevant gastroesophageal reflux was newly diagnosed in only 0.9% of infants in the Munich sample.

However, as in Sample A (M. Papoušek & von Hofacker, 1998), prevailing mild neurological abnormalities were found in the form of asymmetries, irregular muscle tone, mild neuromotor delay, and occasional hypomobile functional problems of the vertebral column in a total of 58.3% of infants in the clinical sample. The majority of infants improved spontaneously as a result of improved handling by the parents, short-term physiotherapy, or manual therapy. Being carried continuously and lacking experience of being placed in supine or prone position on a firm surface seem to contribute to the slight neuromotor delay, which may be quickly made up for when the parents encourage such positioning during waking states. Manifest developmental disorders were seen in only 1.8% of infants.

Developmental Crying Curve and Individual Variability of Crying

A diagnosis of pediatric problems is certainly not sufficient to explain excessive crying. More light is shed on the matter when crying is studied from a developmental perspective. It has been shown in representative samples of healthy infants that the tendency to fuss and cry during the first 3 months is generally very high, and that the extent of daily crying and fussing reflects a high degree of individual variability (Barr, 1990; see Figure 5.2). The mean duration of crying and fussing typically peaks during the sixth week of life and decreases thereafter steadily to the twelfth week. In premature infants, daily amounts of crying follow the same developmental crying curve, with a peak during the sixth week corrected age. This finding in particular confirms that the natural course of early infant crying is closely linked to adaptation processes during the postnatal phase (Barr, Chen, Hopkins, & Westra, 1996).

Infants with excessive crying follow a predictable pattern: Increased crying and fussing usually begins during the first or second week of life, peaks during the sixth week, diminishes toward the end of the third month, and typically resolves with the onset of the first biopsychosocial developmental shift (see chapter 4). Thus, their fuss/cry behavior represents extreme manifestations of normal individual variability along the same developmental curve.

Regulatory Developmental Tasks During the First 3 Months

The first 3 months of life have been variously characterized in the literature as a phase of relative physiological immaturity (Prechtl, 1984) in which the newborn barely differs in his neuromotor development from the prenatal phase and is particularly dependent on his primary caregivers for regulatory support (M. Papoušek & Papoušek, 1990). It is a phase of intense physiological adjustments in relation to nutritional intake, metabolism, energy balance, thermoregulation, immunology, and chronobiology. The core developmental tasks during this phase include the regulation and cyclical alternation of stable behavioral states (sleep–wake organization including active sleep, quiet sleep, unfocused waking activity, quiet alert waking). The regulation of behavioral states is closely interrelated with the infant's fundamental adaptive response system, which controls the balance between activating and calming processes during perception and processing of environmental stimuli (see chapter 4). Development

Figure 5.2. Developmental Crying Curve in a Representative Sample.

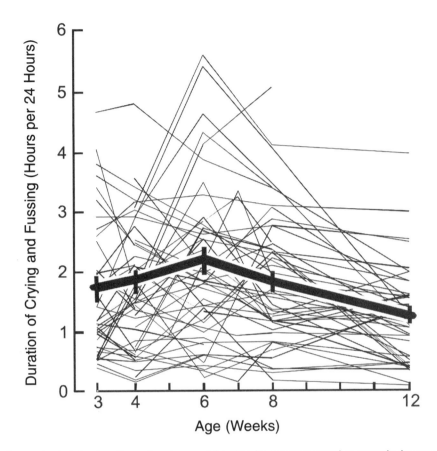

Note. Age-dependent daily duration of crying and fussing in a representative sample (means and individual variability). (Modified according to Barr, 1990.)

during the first 3 months is characterized by adaptational and reorganizational processes that may be turbulent at times, but are replaced by a maturational shift that brings about qualitative changes in all domains of development and self-regulation.

Infants with well-developed self-regulation are able early on to maintain a quiet alert waking state; they exhibit well-balanced excitability and reactivity in all sensory domains, with visual orientation and targeted attention. They are able to avert gaze from excessive stimulation when they become tired, soothe themselves by sucking their fingers, and have little trouble falling asleep. Infants who cry excessively, by contrast, exhibit problems with self-regulation. They can maintain a quiet alert waking state only for short periods of time, they are frequently overaroused, show no capacity for self-soothing, have trouble settling to sleep, or may even fight against falling asleep.

Recent research on nonclinical samples of excessively crying infants has shown reduction of total sleep time by more than 1 hour (Kirjavainen et al., 2001; St. James-Roberts, Conroy, & Hurry, 1997).

Polygraphic analyses of sleep state organization (Kirjavainen et al., 2001), on the other hand, have found no differences when comparing nonclinical excessively crying infants with a noncrying control group.

Sleep–Wake Organization

The data from our study on sleep–wake organization were extracted from the 24-hour diaries in which parents recorded the diurnal distribution and durations of crying, fussing, sleeping, and feeding for 5 days before the first visit (Schaumann, 2003). The clinical sample of 1- to 6-month-old infants with a clinical syndrome of excessive crying ($n = 53$) was subdivided into a group of 31 extreme criers who met Wessel's criteria (daily duration of crying and fussiness, 287 ± 120 minutes/24 hours) and a group of 22 moderate criers who did not meet the criteria (duration of crying and fussiness, 125 ± 44 minutes/24 hours). Their data were compared with data from an age-matched control group of 47 infants without crying problems (duration of crying and fussiness, 63 ± 40 minutes/24 hours).

In terms of diurnal distribution, both clinical groups showed an increase in the duration of crying and fussing over the entire day, with peaks in the afternoon or evening hours among the crying children (see Figure 5.3); extreme criers fussed and cried significantly more at all times of the 24-hour day in comparison with the other groups.

Figure 5.3. Diurnal Variation of Crying and Fussing.

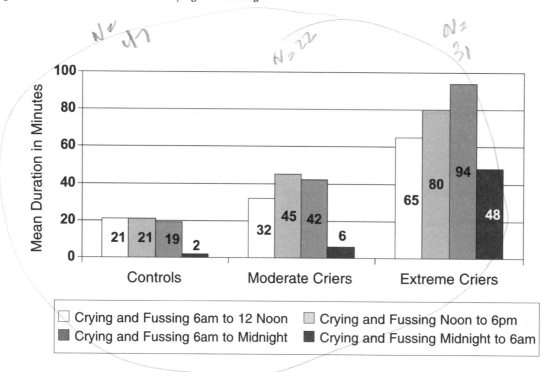

Note. Mean Duration of crying and fussing at various times of day.
Source: Schaumann, 2003.

The extreme group included 3 infants with the longest duration of crying and fussiness (450 minutes/24 hours). These infants exhibited a complete day–night reversal; that is, they were active and cried primarily at night and slept during the day until the early afternoon, albeit with frequent interruptions.

The amount of crying and fussing is interrelated with the extent of a relative sleep deficit (see Figure 5.4). Extreme criers sleep 90 minutes less than control infants (725 ± 98 minutes compared to 816 ± 71 minutes; $p ≤ .05$) and wake up twice as often at night (2.7 ± 2.5 times compared to 1.3 ± 1.0 times; $p ≤ .05$); they are awake at night for longer periods (61 ± 42 minutes compared to 29 ± 21 minutes; $p ≤ .05$), take longer to fall asleep (34 ± 23 minutes compared to 13 ± 11 minutes; $p ≤ .005$), and are carried around longer (138 ± 121 minutes compared to 34 ± 46 minutes; $p ≤ .001$). Other differences in the sleep data concern a shortening of the longest sleep phase and daytime sleep phases, more extensive soothing strategies (walking the baby, rocking, frequent nursing, extended car rides, etc.), and prolonged time for settling to sleep, which may last for hours well into the night.

A significant age-dependent increase in nighttime waking and changes in other sleep parameters are evident from 1 to 6 months of age across all groups (see Figure 5.5). Remarkably, except for short interruptions for feeding, even excessively crying infants generally sleep undisturbed between midnight and 6 a.m. during the first 3 months of life. However, this changes during the next 3 months. Whereas

Figure 5.4. Duration of Total Sleep.

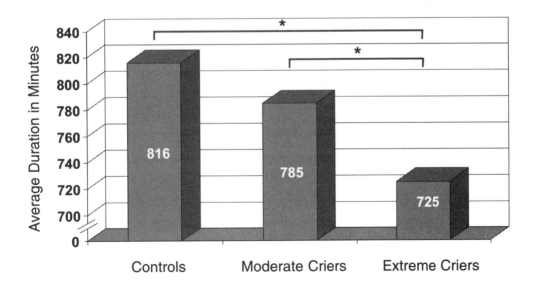

Note. Mean duration of total sleep per 24 hours in infants with normal, moderate, and extreme crying (Modified according to Schaumann, 2003). Kruskal-Wallis: $p ≤ .001$. *Mann-Whitney U test: $p ≤ .05$.

crying peaks during the first half of the night in 1- to 2-month-old excessively crying infants, the 3- to 4-month-old infants in the clinical sample exhibit signs of sleep consolidation with values close to those of the control group (with regard to the longest sleep phase, total sleep, duration of nighttime waking, and sleep between midnight and 6 a.m.). This consolidation is seen most clearly in the moderate criers, obviously because the majority of these infants were 3 to 4 months old and had already passed the peak period for crying and sleeping problems. Among the 1- to 2-month-old extreme criers, the most problematic sleep time is between 6 p.m. and midnight, whereas frequent awakenings and crying shift to the second half of the night in the 5- to 6-month-old subgroup (see Figure 5.5). Excessive crying that persists beyond the third and fourth month becomes associated with severe disruption of nighttime sleep. Conversely, 76.6% of infants and toddlers referred to the Munich Program because of a sleep disorder at an age older than 6 months had a history of early excessive crying during the first 3 months of life (see chapter 6).

Figure 5.5. Age-Dependent Changes in Nighttime Awakenings.

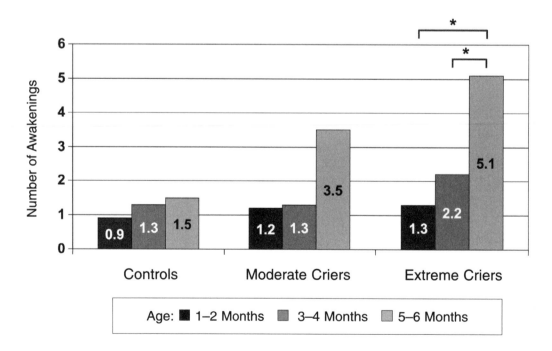

Note. Age-dependent changes in nighttime awakenings in infants with normal, moderate, and extreme crying (modified according to Schaumann, 2003). Kruskal-Wallis: $p \leq .005$. *Mann-Whitney U test: $p \leq .05$.

Factors Influencing Infant Self-Regulation

Excessive inconsolable crying and hyperreactivity on the one side, and inability to self-soothe and fall asleep without help on the other, may be viewed as behavioral manifestations of an imbalance between excitatory (arousing) and inhibitory (calming) processes (Lester, Boukydis, Garcia-Coll, Hole, & Peucker, 1992). The disturbed balance impedes the infant's regulation of stable waking and sleeping states and of smooth transitions between states (H. Papoušek & Papoušek, 1984; von Hofacker, Papoušek, Jacubeit, & Malinowski, 1999). It is still unclear, however, which neurophysiological factors and mechanisms underlie this regulatory imbalance. A number of interesting hypotheses are discussed in the following sections.

The so-called *sucrose hypothesis*. Barr and Young (1999) demonstrated experimentally that several drops of a sucrose solution have a two-phase soothing effect on the hunger cry of human newborns: a short-term effect associated with the taste stimulus and a long-term effect that extends beyond the stimulus. The long-term soothing effect of sucrose in animal experiments points to an intrinsic endorphin-dependent central soothing mechanism that is activated by the administration of sucrose. Infants with excessive crying or colic also interrupt their hunger crying in response to sucrose stimulation, but only as long as the taste stimulus is effective; the long-term effect is missing. The baby immediately begins to cry again, which indicates that the presumed central self-soothing mechanism may not be triggered in these infants. These findings are consistent with our own clinical observations that inconsolable excessive crying is only briefly interrupted by breast-feeding or other soothing interventions, including intense vestibular or acoustic stimuli; the crying resumes again as soon as the stimulus is withdrawn.

Transient immaturity or temperament? A number of standardized questionnaires regarding infant behavior in everyday situations are available for determining attributes of temperament. These are filled out by the parents; they provide information about consolability, fussiness/difficulty, predictability, adaptability, reactivity, and self-soothing. Infants from nonclinical samples who cry excessively score significantly higher with regard to almost all temperament dimensions than same-age infants without crying problems (Carey & McDevitt, 1995; St. James-Roberts, Conroy, & Wilsher, 1998b). The infants in our own clinical samples received even more unfavorable scores (M. Papoušek & von Hofacker, 1995, 1998). However, it is impossible to draw reliable conclusions regarding constitutional factors during the first 3 months because the behavioral effects of temperament and relative immaturity are confounded. What is crucial is the long-term stability of temperamental attributes beyond the 3-month maturational shift (see chapter 13).

Prenatally acquired constitutional factors. Constitutional variability, the biologically anchored innate behavioral dispositions of newborns, may be genetically determined or acquired during pregnancy. Table 5.2 lists the most prevalent somatic prenatal and perinatal risk factors. Here, too, the results from the Sample B confirm the findings of the earlier study (Sample A) from our lab (M. Papoušek & von Hofacker, 1998). Premature labor (with tocolysis) and nicotine abuse were the only prenatal somatic risk factors that were significantly more prevalent in comparison to the control group. Moreover, the percentage of excessively crying infants in whom one or more prenatal somatic risk factors were present

(73.1%) was particularly high. By contrast, there were no group differences with regard to perinatal risk factors.

Special attention must be paid to the rates of prenatal psychosocial risk factors and the high total rate of families in the present sample that were affected by one or more prenatal psychosocial risk factors (64.2%). The results for the most important prenatal psychosocial risk factors are summarized in Table 5.3. The subgroups of extreme and moderate criers in Sample A differed significantly from the control group in terms of a large number of psychosocial risk factors (M. Papoušek & von Hofacker, 1998). Particularly prominent factors included chronic stress and/or abnormal levels of maternal anxiety (50.9%). Maternal fears were related primarily to the infant (fear of miscarriage, prematurity, disease, or disabilities) and/or to changes in life circumstances associated with pregnancy and motherhood (economic pressures, autonomy, partnership, own health state, birth complications, or failure in the mother's role). Other relevant factors included unresolved partnership conflicts (30.0%), depression (6.4%), and unwanted pregnancy (10.1%).

Prenatal factors associated with stress, fears, depression, and unresolved conflicts represent a twofold risk for the infant's postnatal development: They may directly affect the infant's constitutional disposition for self-regulation and they may drain the resources of the mother. Associations between prenatal

Table 5.3. Prenatal and Postnatal Psychosocial Risk Factors.

Risk factor	Sample B	Sample A (M. Papoušek & von Hofacker, 1998)			
	Excessive crying (n = 218) %	Extreme crying (n = 37) %	Moderate crying (n = 26) %	Control group (n = 49) %	Mantel-Haenszel test[a] p
Prenatal					
Stress and anxiety	50.9	62.2	38.5	36.7	≤ .05
Manifest depression	6.4	8.1	3.8	0.0	≤ .05
Partnership conflicts	30.0	29.7	7.7	2.0	≤ .001
Conflicts with families of origin	16.1	18.9	3.8	6.1	≤ .05
Unwanted pregnancy	10.1	24.3	7.7	6.1	≤ .01
Postnatal					
Partnership conflicts	43.6	59.5	23.1	8.2	≤ .001
Conflicts with families of origin	36.2	35.1	34.6	12.2	≤ .01
Distressing childhood memories	39.9	27.0	30.8	16.3	ns
Social isolation	32.6	29.7	23.1	10.2	≤ .05
Socioeconomic problems	6.0	27.0	15.4	4.1	≤ .005
Single mother	7.8	13.5	3.8	0.0	≤ .005
Psychological disturbances in the mother	46.3	48.6	34.6	4.1	≤ .001

[a]One-tailed.

psychosocial risks and neonatal irritability have been frequently reported in the literature (Mulder et al., 2002; Murray & Cooper, 1997; Rautava, Helenius, & Lehtonen, 1993). This association has recently been confirmed by a series of experiments with rhesus monkeys, demonstrating that stress-induced activation of the hypothalamo-pituitary-adrenocortical axis and the release of stress hormones during pregnancy are causally involved in neonatal behavioral problems (irritability and mild neuro-motor immaturity; Schneider & Moore, 2000). In other words, symptoms found in rhesus monkeys were similar to those found in prenatally stressed mothers of excessively crying human infants. These studies point to prenatal stress as a potential causative factor in the etiology of infant irritability and excessive crying. Results of a comprehensive prospective study on the effects of prenatal stress on infant self-regulation confirm this assumption (Wurmser et al., 2006).

Parental failure? The still widespread assumption that excessive crying is primarily the result of inadequate parenting has been refuted by studies on representative samples. Analyses of mother–infant interaction and home observations show that maternal responsiveness does not differ between the groups of excessively crying infants and control infants (St. James-Roberts, Conroy, & Wilsher, 1998a). Even in one of our own clinical samples of infants with a syndrome of excessive crying ($n = 46$), we found that 60% of the mother–infant pairs showed well-attuned, intuitively guided communication during face-to-face interaction in comparison to 80% in the control group ($n = 47$; M. Papoušek, 1996). In contrast, dysfunctional interactional patterns were obvious in contexts of inconsolable crying in the majority of these mother–infant pairs. Because of the negative reciprocity between infant and mother in these situations, we cannot draw conclusions about a primary cause. However, the findings underscore the hypothesis that communication and interaction in the soothing context play a key role in understanding the syndrome of excessive crying (M. Papoušek & Papoušek, 1990).

A DEVELOPMENTAL, DYNAMIC SYSTEMS MODEL OF ORIGINS AND MAINTENANCE OF EXCESSIVE CRYING

Regulatory Functions of Intuitive Parenting

An important hallmark of infant self-regulation is that it is biologically preprogrammed to depend and rely on complementary regulatory support from primary caregivers (H. Papoušek & Papoušek 1987). Under favorable conditions, the initial self-regulatory constraints faced by the infant during the phase of relative physiological immaturity in the first 3 months will be accommodated by the parents. Thanks to their innate intuitive responsiveness, the parents are able to help their infant master the postnatal adaptational demands (see chapter 4).

Angel's circles and vicious circles of coregulation. Interestingly, the nature and extent of infant crying and its effects on the caregiver play a crucial role in the emergence of infant–caregiver coregulation. Infant crying is a powerful alarm signal due to its acoustic qualities and adaptive functions. It triggers alarm reactions in the social environment in the form of a measurable acute psychophysiological stress response (increased heartbeat, elevated blood pressure, sweating, psychological arousal). The psycho-physiological activation is accompanied by intuitively attuned soothing behavior (body contact in the parent's arm, gentle rhythmic stimulation, falling vocal melodies) and a strong motivation to identify and stop the cause of the crying. In response, the baby snuggles up, the crying resolves, and the baby quiets down—and with him, the mother as well. Positive feedback from the baby reinforces her confidence in her own intuitive competencies, while at the same time affording her a moment of intimate closeness and positive emotional relatedness with her baby, a moment of positive reciprocity— an angel's circle. This core experience may explain why attachment theory identifies infant crying as the most important attachment behavior.

Inconsolable crying, however, seems to turn this natural resource in early parent–infant relationships upside down. Good internal and external protective factors may enable the mother/parents to trust their intuitive competence and to either prevent derailment into inconsolable crying by quickly recognizing the infant's needs (e.g., need for being shielded from overstimulation, for rest, or for sleep) or to bridge the crying state by conveying a sense of security and calmness. Unfortunately, the persistent psychophysiological arousal resulting from the cries of an inconsolable infant makes it difficult even for competent and experienced parents to respond in a calm way.

What needs to be taken into account is that both parents, especially the mother (due to the motherhood constellation, postpartum psychophysiological adjustments, postpartum depression), are themselves in a vulnerable phase of intensive reorganization and adaptation. This is particularly true of parents experiencing the birth of their first child, who are also undergoing for the first time the transition to parenthood and the transition from dyad to triad (see also chapter 4).

The inconsolability of crying, with its escalating biological alarm functions, is a key to understanding the intense emotional effects on the parents and the high risk of dysfunctional interaction when all attempts at soothing have failed. The most frequent emotional effects of inconsolable crying on the parent and other caregivers are summarized in Figure 5.6. For example, the mother, and often the father as well, will exhibit all the signs of chronic exhaustion and overload (frayed nerves) as a consequence of persistent alarm and sleep deficit. The repeated daily experiences of infant inconsolability, stiffening when held, and occasional inaccessibility engender feelings of failure, diminished self-esteem, powerlessness, and depression. Almost all affected parents confess that feelings of helplessness in the face of increasing arousal and alarm occasionally turn into a state of aggressive feelings and powerless rage toward the infant, impulses that in turn evoke intense feelings of guilt and make the parents increasingly vulnerable. The intensity of aroused feelings may finally become fertile ground for the revival of latent conflicts with the partner or the families of origin, or over the mother's abandoned professional career. Moreover, memories and feelings of abandonment, fear, or rage experienced during their own childhood may easily be evoked in this context.

These effects are particularly problematic when insecurity, depression, exhaustion, or absorption by intense affect persistently inhibit or block intuitive parental competencies. The parents may do everything they can to soothe their infant, but are rendered silent in their attempts at dialogue and interaction with him. Hypersensitized by the crying, they barely perceive the subtle signals from the infant during more quiet states of alertness, thereby missing opportunities to enter into relaxed dialogue and play. As a consequence the dysregulated infants will miss the intuitive regulatory support from their parents, which they need in order to come to terms with a multitude of adaptational demands.

Dysfunctional communication patterns develop, first in the context of soothing, but eventually they may spill over into other everyday contexts as well. These are then maintained by negative reciprocity, or escalate into vicious circles of arousal and tension.

Psychosocial Stress Factors

Vicious circles of negative reciprocity tend to develop most frequently in the face of limited internal and external parental resources and persistent cumulative stress. We found during the postpartum period significantly increased rates of manifest partner conflicts, conflicts with the families of origin, distressing childhood memories, and social isolation in the clinical sample compared to the control group. Mothers of excessively crying infants are more apt to be socially isolated and are often left in the lurch by their partners, extended family, and social supports in general. Consistent with the previously discussed psychological effects of inconsolable crying, we found that almost all mothers (95.8%)

Figure 5.6. Effects of Inconsolable Crying on Parents and Other Caregivers.

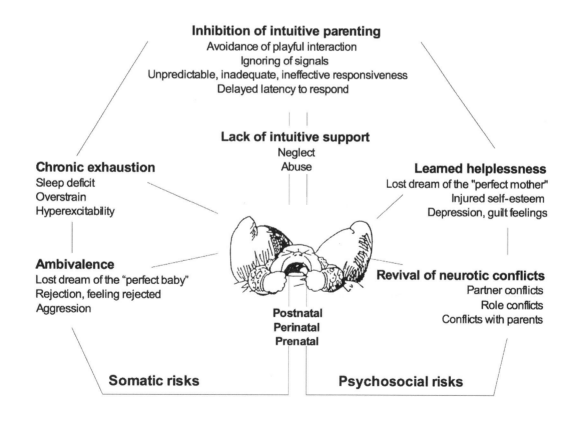

exhibited chronic exhaustion and overload. The 33.5% rate of postpartum depression was triple that found in representative samples of women at similar ages (11%; Murray & Carothers, 1990). In fact, more than 40% of mothers scored above the cutoff of 12 on the Edinburgh Postnatal Depression Scale, that is, the value that indicates depressive episodes requiring treatment. With few exceptions, these cases had been neither diagnosed nor treated before. Another 16.5% of mothers exhibited signs of neurotic relational disorders that in part became evident only after the birth of their child, and 6.4% exhibited personality disorders. In sum, 46.3% of all mothers in the clinical group exhibited psychological disturbances over and above their chronic exhaustion (see Table 5.3). These figures from the present large sample replicate the results of our earlier study (M. Papoušek & von Hofacker, 1998). Similarly, the rates for other postnatal psychosocial stress factors from the current sample also show a high proportion of multiple psychosocial stressors in comparison to the former control group without crying problems. In addition, the support and resources available to mothers in the clinical group in the face of sometimes extremely serious partnership conflicts (43.6%), conflicts with the families of origin (36.2%), and social isolation (32.6%) were very limited, although mothers with an excessively crying infant would have needed support more than anyone else.

Conditions leading to persistent crying. On the basis of our own clinical data, we hypothesize that excessive crying that persists beyond the third to fourth month is conditioned by an interaction between infant factors (e.g., difficult temperament) and parental factors (e.g., depression, lack of resources, cumulative psychosocial risks) at the level of dysfunctional interaction patterns in relevant daily contexts (see chapters 4 and 13). Under such circumstances, the risk for long-term distress in the parent–child relationship is particularly high.

DIAGNOSTIC ASSESSMENT

Close cooperation between psychologists and pediatricians at the Munich Program allows for both comprehensive medical and psychological assessment and well-coordinated counseling. At the first visit, detailed information is gathered on the presenting problems, possible risks and resources in the family, and the infant's history in relation to prenatal, birth, and postnatal development. The pediatric and neuropediatric examination is generally performed when the infant is in a relaxed waking state. It also serves to assess the infant's mental development and regulatory capacities. Videotaped observation allows us to evaluate parent–infant interaction in a variety of contexts, such as relaxed dialogue, soothing, diapering, feeding, and the still-face paradigm.

COUNSELING AND TREATMENT MODEL OF THE MUNICH PROGRAM

Studies of the Effectiveness of Widely Used Interventions

Internet sites and advice books for parents contain a bewildering array of behavioral tips and panaceas for excessive crying. CDs with recorded white noise from washing machines, vacuum cleaners, and hair dryers, intrauterine sounds, and maternal heart beat are on sale along with "baby classics." Various swings, water beds, and motorized cribs that simulate car noise and vibrations at 55 mph are extolled for their lasting soothing effects.

A short overview of scientifically evaluated treatment methods is meant to shed more light on a palette of interventions that has grown exponentially over the past decade. It must be said, however, that because of the high rate of spontaneous remissions at the age of about 3 months, the effectiveness of various treatments is extremely difficult to test reliably. Among the medical treatments, simethicone (Mylicon® Infant Drops, Genasyme® Drops, etc.), which is typically prescribed in German pediatric practices, has shown no significant effect in placebo-controlled double-blind studies (Lucassen et al., 1998). Apart from their unmistakable placebo effect, these drugs have the advantage of having no side effects. Hypoallergenic formula or dietary treatment of the nursing mother are to be recommended only when symptoms of cow's milk intolerance are present (see the section on pediatric conditional factors).

Many of the so-called "new baby therapies" (Harms, 2000) posit birth trauma as the primary cause for excessive crying. Treatment is targeted accordingly, with a broad spectrum of physically oriented relaxation methods and baby massage techniques, some of which are derived from the bioenergetics of Wilhelm Reich. Neither representative samples nor the particularly distressed clinical samples of the Munich Program exhibit significantly greater perinatal risk factors that might indicate an increased prevalence of birth trauma in infants with excessive crying (see chapter 3; Lehtonen, 1994). Serious birth complications or severe psychological birth trauma of the mother may occasionally promote excessive crying; however, it seems doubtful that this is a general cause of excessive crying that requires treatment. In addition, the fact that inconsolable crying usually begins during the second week of life and not right after birth would seem to speak against the birth trauma hypothesis. In any case, no outcome studies evaluating these forms of treatment have yet been conducted. However, specific manual treatment is indicated in cases of clear functional disorders of the vertebral column (see above).

Increased carrying of the infant has been shown to lead to a significant decrease of normal infant crying (Hunziker & Barr, 1986); however, this method has been shown to be ineffective in treating excessively crying infants, who already tend to be carried around for most of the day (Barr et al., 1991; St. James-Roberts, Conroy, & Wilsher et al., 1995). Although noise and movement simulators do have immediate soothing and sleep-inducing effects, these effects diminish with the cessation of stimulation (Sosland & Christophersen, 1991; Wolke, 1993).

In a few controlled studies, targeted advice given by pediatricians or trained laypersons has been shown to have a positive effect (see chapter 9). Significant symptomatic improvement has been demonstrated as a result of recommendations for parents to reduce stimulation or as a result of short-term separation of mother and baby to give them time to calm down (McKenzie, 1991). Sensitizing the parents to the infant's signals (Taubmann, 1984, 1988); clear structuring of feeding, sleep, and waking phases; and avoidance of overstimulation lead to a significant reduction in crying behavior in comparison with untreated control groups (Wolke, Gray, & Meyer, 1994). However, this positive effect is not seen when the parents receive advice only in written form without personal counseling and guidance (Parkin, Schwartz, & Manuel, 1993; St. James-Roberts, Hurry, Bowyer, & Barr, 1995).

The Munich Concept of Integrative Communication-Centered Parent–Infant Counseling and Psychotherapy

Psychological and physical relief for the parents. In building a positive therapeutic relationship with parents of excessively crying infants, it is important from the beginning to listen empathetically to and accept both parents with all their fears, feelings of guilt, desperation, frustration, and anger. Usually, these families have already made the rounds, seeking out professional and nonprofessional advice, and they generally feel completely undermined and guilty of not being able to care for their infants. In this context, information about the high prevalence of excessive crying often provides their first sense of relief by making them aware that they are not the only ones with such problems. In a similar vein, empathetic information on the alarming effects and emotional impact of inconsolable crying (see Figure 5.6) may afford considerable relief as well.

Providing physical relief often becomes a matter of primary concern because parents—and particularly the mother—may not have slept well for several weeks, and the daily stress under which they care for their infant leaves them exhausted and overwhelmed. It is important to find out with the parents what resources exist, both inside and outside the family, that might be used to afford them relief and support.

Developmental counseling. Proceeding on the assumption that excessive crying during the first 3 months is an expression of poorly regulated sleep–wake organization with overfatigue, hyperreactivity, and sleep deficit, detailed developmental counseling based on the individual sleep diaries are center stage, taking into account the development of crying, sleep–wake regulation, and soothing strategies. The concrete recommendations are summarized in Table 5.4. To support a regular sleep–wake rhythm, the parents are encouraged to reduce stimuli and to help the infant to fall asleep as soon as the first signs of fatigue appear, that is, as a rule of thumb, about 1 to 1^1/$_2$ hours after the last sleep episode. Exactly how the parents may best support their infant will be worked out with them or practiced together. The aim of this intervention is to avoid overstimulation, to help the infant to sleep more during the day, and to get the infant used to a regular 3- to 4-hour sleep–feed–wake–sleep cycle during the day. Feeding after waking up may be advantageous because it is often extremely difficult to feed an overstimulated and tired but hungry infant at the end of a long waking phase. In addition, rested and satiated infants take a greater interest in social interaction.

It is also important not to overstimulate the infant while he is in a fussy state of waking activity. The parents are encouraged instead to use the initially brief episodes of quiet alert waking in which the infant signals readiness for a relaxed dialogue and playful interchange.

The most difficult episodes of inconsolable crying in the afternoon and evenings may be bridged by walking the infant to sleep in a baby sling or baby carriage. In situations where the parent's arousal and anger build up in a vicious circle because of their unsuccessful soothing attempts, we recommend placing the crying infant in a secure spot (e.g., in his crib) for a short while so that the parent may take time out to calm down. This may eventually become an effective means to prevent an impulsive parent from shaking the baby or from other forms of infant abuse.

Effective ways of handling (holding and giving support with relaxed body contact, encouraging the baby to spend time in prone or supine positions, etc.) may be modeled and practiced with the parents.

In cases of extreme irritability, sensory hyperexcitability, and resistance, we recommend supportive sensory integration therapy. Physiotherapy is initiated as needed in case of neuromotor problems, as are pediatric treatments in case of a somatic disorder.

Guidance in parent–infant communication. The purpose of communication guidance is to enable parents and infant to understand each other in contexts of crying, attempts at soothing, and settling to sleep. Similar to what Barth (1998) described in her baby-reading lessons, we help the parent to find out what particular needs the infant is signaling with his fussing and crying. Once frequent needs like pain, hunger, wet diapers, or boredom have been ruled out, if the infant exhibits signs of fatigue or overstrain, and if the last sleep phase ended more than 1½ or 2 hours ago—as is usually the case—we then offer the parents concrete help with settling their infant to sleep in the here and now. To help an overstimulated, overly tired crying baby fall asleep, the room is darkened and the infant is shielded from

Table 5.4. Developmental Counseling for Parents of Excessively Crying Infants.

Reduce stimulation
- By avoiding overstimulation
- By creating shared moments of peaceful rest during the day

Avoid overfatigue
- By settling the infant to sleep at the first signs of fatigue, about 1–1½ hours after the last sleep episode

Initiate a well-regulated sleep–wake rhythm
- By striving for regular cycles of sleep and waking throughout the day (waking up from sleep, feeding [followed by a short nap in mother's arms], alert waking, settling to sleep)

Make use of quiet waking states
- For relaxed dialogue and play (experience of angel's circles), and responsive stimulation while being attentive to signs of fatigue and overload

Bridge the critical crying hours
- By walking the infant to sleep in a baby sling or baby carriage

Timeout for parents to relax
- By putting the infant down when feelings of arousal, exhaustion, and anger build up in a vicious circle
- By first relaxing yourself, then trying again to soothe the infant

There are no patented methods for soothing an infant and helping him fall asleep, but general rules are
- Be regular and consistent in your intervention; this is more important than what you do in particular.
- Proceed gently, without being hurried or abrupt.
- Avoid experimenting with ever-changing tips for intervention; try to stay with one strategy in order to get the infant used to regular sleep conditions.

all potentially disturbing stimuli and placed in a baby carriage or bassinet. To prevent the arousing effects of startles during transition to sleep, the infant is firmly wrapped in a cloth or his arms are gently held. The therapist gives the mother the necessary grounding, emotional support, and secure base and thus helps her stay with her preferred soothing strategy. The mother is encouraged not to pick the baby up before he is in a sound sleep and to overcome startles and prolonged crying by continuing her soothing behavior. Parents are usually able to get their infant to sleep in the therapeutic setting; at home alone, they often have a harder time. In such cases, we offer one or two home visits by a social worker. In general, it is easier for the parents to begin implementing such interventions in the home during the better-regulated morning hours.

Another goal of communication guidance is to create moments of emotional relatedness that are equally fulfilling for parent and infant as a positive counterpart to the many hours of inconsolable fussing and crying. Within the protective therapeutic environment, parents are sensitized and encouraged to engage in the short episodes during which the infant is alert and ready to interact. Even if these episodes of positive reciprocity are brief in the beginning, they represent an important first step for the parent–infant dyad to break the vicious circle of inconsolable crying with its long phases of negative reciprocity.

Parent–infant psychotherapy. If parents find it difficult to interpret their infant's crying correctly and to respond to it appropriately, it is important to find out what feelings the crying triggers in them and what motives they may attribute to the infant. Excessive crying, with its alarming and urgent qualities, may eventually evoke intense feelings and episodic memories from the parent's relational history. These may become superimposed on or distort the parent's perception of her or his real infant. For example, the crying may be interpreted as an aggressive act, as intentional screaming, or in an even more bizarre manner, as a psychotic expression of possession by a demon. And the parent will respond accordingly. In other parents (such as in the case vignette) the crying evokes deep feelings of abandonment or fear. Implicit memories of distressful relational patterns from the parent's own childhood may then be revived and reenacted with her own infant (Fraiberg, 1980; Fraiberg, Adelson, & Shapiro, 1975; Möhler & Resch, 2000). Parent–infant psychotherapy aims at enabling the parents to regain an undistorted perception of their infant and his needs. The therapy addresses the parent's attributions and inappropriate interpretation of infant signals, and helps the parent to become aware of their own unresolved experiences from the past that unintentionally made them perceive their infant in a distorted way.

Problems within the partner relationship frequently arise after the birth of the first child because of the many changes and challenges associated with the transition to parenthood (see chapter 4). The additional stress of excessive crying may cause the family system to get out of balance, which may lead to serious crises in the couple's relationship. The father is generally included in counseling and treatment if possible, and couples counseling may be offered as needed. When needed, individual, couples, or family psychotherapy, or support from social workers specializing in family issues are recommended and arranged.

Duration and success of interventions. The overall effects of treatment were globally evaluated at the final appointment. We coded *fully improved* when the infant's symptoms and the negative reciprocity in the parent–infant interaction had been successfully overcome. We coded *largely improved* when the negative reciprocities during interaction were overcome, the infant's problem behaviors had significantly diminished, and the family was on the right path toward solving the few remaining problems by themselves. Slight decreases in problem behavior were classified as *slightly improved*; no change as *lack of improvement*. The improvement rate in the present clinical population after conclusion of treatment was 48.4% fully improved and 44.2% largely improved, that is, an overall success rate of 92.6%. Slightly improved at the end of treatment was seen in 6.5% and lack of improvement in only 0.9%. A total of 4 sessions on average were needed for successful conclusion (first visit for diagnostic assessment included). In 56.7% of cases, only 1 to 3 sessions were needed; another 38.7% were successfully concluded within 4 to 10 sessions, similar to other short-term psychotherapies (see also chapter 12).

SUMMARY

Excessive infant crying is one of the most widespread disorders of infancy. Neither the infant alone nor the parents alone create the problem; an accumulation of risk factors on both sides contribute to impairments of infant self-regulation and/or of intuitive parental competencies. Preverbal parent–infant communication becomes dysfunctional, particularly in daily contexts of inconsolable crying and settling to sleep. The manifestations of inconsolable crying and its effect on the young family may take dramatic forms, with abuse and severe neglect being among the most extreme. Excessive crying generally resolves with the first maturational shift and rapid developmental dynamics by the end of the third month of life. It usually represents a transient, self-limiting condition that is quickly amenable to targeted counseling. However, crying problems may persist and lead to long-term distress in the parent–infant relationship and to disorders of behavioral and emotional regulation at the toddler stage in the presence of a difficult temperament and/or multiple psychosocial and biographical stressors and limited resources.

Treatment of excessive crying focuses on parent–infant communication and interaction in contexts of soothing and settling to sleep, while taking into account parental and infant somatic and psychosocial risk factors. Such treatment is a promising approach that may prevent later relational and behavioral disorders.

REFERENCES

Barr, R. G. (1990). The normal crying curve: What do we really know? *Developmental Medicine and Child Neurology, 32*, 356–362.

Barr, R. G., Chen, S., Hopkins, B., & Westra, T. (1996). Crying patterns in preterm infants. *Developmental Medicine and Child Neurology, 38*, 345–355.

Barr, R. G., Clogg, L. J., Woolridge, J. A., & Tansey, C. M. (1987). Carbohydrate change has no effect on infant crying behavior: A randomized controlled trial [Abstract]. *American Journal of Diseases of Children, 141*, 391.

Barr, R. G., Mc Mullan, S. J., Spiess, H., Leduc, D. G., Yaremko, J., Barfield, R., et al. (1991). Carrying as colic "therapy": A randomized controlled trial. *Pediatrics, 87*, 623–630.

Barr, R. G., & Young, S. N. (1999). A two phase model of the soothing taste response: Implications for a taste probe of temperament and emotion regulation. In M. Lewis & D. Ramsay (Eds.), *Soothing and stress* (pp. 109–137). Mahwah, NJ: Erlbaum.

Barth, R. (1998).Psychotherapie und Beratung im Säuglings- und Kleinkindalter. In K. von Klitzing (ed.), *Psychotherapie in der frühen Kindheit* (pp. 72–87). Göttingen, Germany: Vandenhoeck & Ruprecht.

Biedermann, H. (2000). KISS-Kinder. In T. Harms (Ed.), *Auf die Welt gekommen* (pp. 471–486). Berlin: Ulrich Leutner Verlag.

Carey, W. B., & McDevitt, S. C. (1995). *Coping with children's temperament.* New York: Basic Books.

Forsyth, B. W. C. (1989). Colic and the effect of changing formulas: A double-blind, multiple-crossover study. *Journal of Pediatrics, 115,* 521–526.

Forsyth, B. W. C. (1997). Infant formulas and colic: Where are we now? In H. S. Sauls & D. E. Redfern (Eds.), *Colic and excessive crying. Report of the 105th Ross Conference on Pediatric Research* (pp. 49–67). Columbus, OH: Ross Products Division, Abbot Laboratories.

Fraiberg, S. (1980). *Clinical studies in infant mental health: The first year of life.* New York: Basic Books.

Fraiberg, S., Adelson, E., & Shapiro, V. (1975). Ghosts in the nursery. *Journal of the American Academy of Child and Adolescent Psychiatry, 14,* 387–422.

Gormally, S. (2001). Clinical clues to organic etiologies in infants with colic. In R. G. Barr, I. St. James-Roberts, & M. R. Keefe (Eds.), *New evidence on unexplained early infant crying: Its origins, nature and management* (pp. 133–148). Skillman, NJ: Johnson & Johnson Pediatric Institute Round Table Series.

Harms, T. (2000). Emotionelle erste Hilfe – Grundlagen einer postnatalen Krisenarbeit mit Eltern und Säuglingen. In T. Harms (Ed.), *Auf die Welt gekommen* (pp. 189–229). Berlin: Ulrich Leutner Verlag.

Hunziker, U. A., & Barr, R. G. (1986). Increased carrying reduces infant crying: A randomized controlled trial. *Pediatrics, 77,* 641–648.

Iacono, G., Carroccio, A., Montalto, G., Cavataio, F., Bragion, E., Lorello, D., et al. (1991). Severe infantile colic and food intolerance: A long-term prospective study. *Journal of Pediatric Gastroenterology and Nutrition, 12,* 332–335.

Jacobsson, I. (1997). Cow's milk proteins as a cause of infantile colic. In H. S. Sauls & D. E. Redfern (Eds.), *Colic and excessive crying. Report of the 105th Ross Conference on Pediatric Research* (pp. 39–47). Columbus, OH: Ross Products Division, Abbot Laboratories.

Kirjavainen, J., Kirjavainen, T., Huhtala, V., Lehtonen, L., Korvenranta, H., & Kero, P. (2001). Infants with colic have a normal sleep structure at 2 and 7 month of age. *Journal of Pediatrics, 138,* 218–223.

Lehtonen, L. (1994). *Infantile colic.* Annales universitatis Turkunensis, Sarja – Ser. D., Medica-Odontologica, No. 151. Turku, Finland: Turku University.

Lehtonen, L., Gormally, S., & Barr, R. G. (2000). "Clinical pies" for etiology and outcome in infants presenting with early increased crying. In R. G. Barr, B. Hopkins, & J. A. Green (Eds.), *Crying as a sign, a symptom and a signal* (pp. 67–95). London: Mac Keith Press.

Lester, B. M., Boukydis, C. F. Z., Garcia-Coll, C. T., & Hole, W. T. (1990). Symposium on infantile colic: Introduction. *Infant Mental Health Journal, 11,* 320–333.

Lester, B. M., Boukydis, C. F. Z., Garcia-Coll, C. T., Hole, W, & Peucker, M. (1992). Infantile colic: Acoustic cry characteristics, maternal perception of cry, and temperament. *Infant Behavior and Development, 15,* 15–26.

Lucassen, P. L. B. J., Assendelft, W., Gubbels, J., van Eijk, J., van Geldrop, W., & Knuistingh-Neven, A. (1998). Effectiveness of treatments for infantile colic: Systematic review. *British Medical Journal, 316,* 1563–1569.

McKenzie, S. A. (1991). Troublesome crying in infants: Effect of advice to reduce stimulation. *Archives of Disease in Childhood, 66,* 1416–1420.

Miller, A. R., & Barr, R. G. (1991). Infantile colic. Is it a gut issue? *Pediatric Clinics of North America, 38,* 1407–1423.

Möhler, E., & Resch, F. (2000). Ausdrucksformen und Transmissionsmechanismen mütterlicher Traumatisierungen innerhalb der Mütter-Säuglings-Interaktion. *Praxis der Kinderpsychologie und Kinderpsychiatrie, 49,* 550–562.

Mulder, E. J. H., Robles de Medina, P. G., Huizink, A. C., Van den Bergh, B. R. H., Buitelaar, J. K., & Visser, G. H. A. (2002). Prenatal maternal stress: Effects on pregnancy and the (unborn) child. *Early Human Development, 70,* 3–14.

Murray, L., & Carothers, A. D. (1990). The validation of the Edinburgh Postnatal Depression Scale on a community sample. *British Journal of Psychiatry, 157,* 288–290.

Murray, L., & Cooper, P. J. (1997). The role of infant and maternal factors in postpartum depression, mother-infant interactions, and infant outcomes. In L. Murray & P. J. Cooper (Eds.), *Postpartum depression and child development* (pp. 111–135). New York: Guilford Press.

Olafsdottir, E., Forshei, S., Fluge, G., & Markestad, T. (2001). Randomised controlled trial of infantile colic treated with chiropractic spinal manipulation. *Archives of Disease in Childhood, 84,* 138–141.

Papoušek, H. (1969). Individual variability in learned responses during early post-natal development. In R. J. Robinson (Ed.), *Brain and early behavior. Development in the fetus and infant* (pp. 229–252). London: Academic Press.

Papoušek, H., & Papoušek, M. (1984). Qualitative transitions in integrative processes during the first trimester of human postpartum life. In H. F. R. Prechtl (Ed.), *Continuity of neural functions from prenatal to postnatal life* (pp. 220–244). Oxford, England: Blackwell Scientific.

Papoušek, H., & Papoušek, M. (1987). Intuitive parenting: A dialectic counterpart to the infant's integrative competence. In J. D. Osofsky (Ed.), *Handbook of infant development* (2nd ed., pp. 669–720). New York: Wiley.

Papoušek, M. (1996). Die intuitive elterliche Kompetenz in der vorsprachlichen Kommunikation als Ansatz zur Diagnostik von präverbalen Kommunikations- und Beziehungsstörungen. *Kindheit und Entwicklung, 5,* 140–146.

Papoušek, M. (2000). Persistent crying, parenting, and infant mental health. In J. D. Osofsky & H. E. Fitzgerald (Eds.), *WAIMH handbook of infant mental health* (Vol. 4, pp. 419–447). New York: Wiley.

Papoušek, M., & Papoušek, H. (1990). Excessive infant crying and intuitive parental care: Buffering support and its failures in parent-infant interaction. *Early Child Development and Care, 65,* 117–126.

Papoušek, M., & von Hofacker, N. (1995). Persistent crying and parenting: Search for a butterfly in a dynamic system. *Early Development and Parenting, 4,* 209–224.

Papoušek, M., & von Hofacker, N. (1998). Persistent crying in early infancy: A non-trivial condition of risk for the developing mother-infant relationship. *Child: Care, Health and Development, 24,* 395–424.

Parkin, P. C., Schwartz, C. J., & Manuel, B. A. (1993). Randomized controlled trial of three interventions in the management of persistent crying of infancy. *Pediatrics, 92,* 197–201.

Prechtl, H. F. R. (1984). Continuity and change in early neural development. In H. F. R. Prechtl (Ed.), *Continuity of neural functions from prenatal to postnatal life* (pp. 1–15). Oxford, England: Blackwell Scientific.

Rautava, P., Helenius, H., & Lehtonen, L. (1993). Psychosocial predisposing factors for infantile colic. *British Medical Journal, 307,* 600–604.

Schaumann, A. (2003). *Exzessives Schreien und Schlaf-Wach-Regulation im ersten Lebenshalbjahr.* Unpublished doctoral dissertation, Medical Faculty, Ludwig-Maximilians-University Munich.

Schneider, M. L., & Moore, C. F. (2000). Effect of prenatal stress on development: A nonhuman primate model. In C. Nelson (Ed.), *Minnesota Symposium on Child Psychology* (pp. 201–243). Mahwah, NJ: Erlbaum.

Sosland, J. M., & Christophersen, E. R. (1991). Does SleepTight work? A behavioural analysis of the effectiveness of SleepTight for the management of infant colic. *Journal of Applied Behavior Analysis, 24,* 161–166.

St. James-Roberts, I., Conroy, S., & Hurry, J. (1997). Links between infant crying and sleep-waking at six weeks of age. *Early Human Development, 48,* 143–152.

St. James-Roberts, I., Conroy, S., & Wilsher, K. (1995). Clinical, developmental and social aspects of infant crying and colic. *Early Development and Parenting, 4,* 177–189.

St. James-Roberts, I., Conroy, S., & Wilsher, K. (1998a). Links between maternal care and persistent infant crying in the early months. *Child: Care, Health and Development, 24,* 353–376.

St. James-Roberts, I., Conroy, S., & Wilsher, C. (1998b). Stability and outcome of persistent infant crying. *Infant Behavior and Development, 21,* 411–435.

St. James-Roberts, I., & Halil, T., (1991). Infant crying patterns in the first year: Normal community and clinical findings. *Journal of Child Psychology and Psychiatry, 32,* 951–968.

St. James-Roberts, I., Hurry, J., Bowyer, J., & Barr, R. G. (1995). Supplementary carrying compared with advice to increase responsive parenting as interventions to prevent persistent crying. *Pediatrics, 95,* 381–388.

Strassburg, H. M., Haug-Schnabel, G., & Mueller H. (1990). The crying infant—an interdisciplinary approach. *Early Child Development and Care, 65,* 153–166.

Taubmann, B. (1984). Clinical trial of the treatment of colic by modification of parent–infant interaction. *Pediatrics, 74,* 998–1003.

Taubmann, B. (1988). Parental counseling compared with elimination of cow's milk or soy milk protein for the treatment of infant colic syndrome: A randomized trial. *Pediatrics, 81,* 756–761.

Treem, W. R. (2001). Assessing crying complaints: The interaction with gastroesophageal reflux and cow's milk protein intolerance. In R. G. Barr, I. St. James-Roberts, & M. R. Keefe (Eds.), *New evidence on unexplained early infant crying: Its origins, nature and management* (pp. 165–176). Skillman, NJ: Johnson & Johnson Pediatric Institute Round Table Series.

von Hofacker, N., Papoušek, M., Jacubeit, T., & Malinowski, M. (1999). Rätsel der Säuglingskoliken: Ergebnisse, Erfahrungen und therapeutische Interventionen aus der "Münchener Sprechstunde für Schreibabies." *Monatsschrift für Kinderheilkunde, 147,* 244–253.

Wessel, M. A., Cobb, J. C., Jackson, E. B., Harris, G. S., & Detwiler, A. C. (1954). Paroxysmal fussing in infancy, sometimes called "colic." *Pediatrics, 14,* 421–434.

Wolke, D. (1993). The treatment of problem crying behavior. In I. St. James-Roberts, G. Harris, & D. Messer (Eds.), *Infant crying, feeding and sleeping: Development, problems and treatments* (pp. 47–79). New York: Harvester/Wheatsheaf.

Wolke, D., Gray, P., & Meyer, R. (1994). Excessive infant crying: A controlled study of mothers helping mothers. *Pediatrics, 94,* 322–332.

Wurmser, H., Laubereau, B., Hermann, M., Papoušek, M., & von Kries, R. (2001). Excessive infant crying: Often not confined to the first 3 months of age. *Early Human Development, 64,* 1–6.

Wurmser, H., Rieger, M., Domogalla, C., Kahnt, A., Buchwald, J., Kowatsch, M., et al. (2006). Association between life stress during pregnancy and infant crying in the first six months postpartum: A prospective longitudinal study. *Early Human Development, 82,* 341–349.

SLEEP DISORDERS: CURRENT RESULTS AND CLINICAL EXPERIENCE

Michael Schieche
Claudia Rupprecht
Mechthild Papoušek

CASE VIGNETTE

R*eason for referral.* Vera was 14 months old when her mother first brought her to the Munich Program for Fussy Babies. She was waking up crying as often as 10 times per night. Her mother responded by nursing her at least three times per night or carrying her around to soothe her and settle her back to sleep. By the second half of the night, the parents usually resorted to taking Vera into their own bed. In the evenings, her mother had to nurse her until she was in a sound sleep. The toddler's usual time for sleeping was between 10 p.m. and 8 a.m. Attempts to place Vera in her crib without nursing failed because of immediate intense crying. During the day, she generally slept again for about an hour and a half after her midday feeding. Even then, she required the mother's presence and nursing to fall asleep. Occasionally, her mother succeeded in sneaking out of the room without waking Vera up.

This sleep problem had persisted for a long time. By the time the little girl had begun to cry excessively during the first 3 months of life, her sleep–wake rhythm was already disordered, and she had not learned to fall asleep on her own. In addition, the mother reported that her daughter was extremely clingy during the day. Whenever she would leave the room Vera would immediately begin to cry. Even in her mother's presence, the child insisted on hanging onto her, and she would not tolerate having her father or older brother look after her. Although Vera was spoon-fed for her main meals, she requested to be nursed several times each day, primarily for soothing purposes rather than to satisfy hunger. Meanwhile, the parents' relationship was sorely strained by the nightly sleep disruptions. The father usually slept in another room but was unwilling to continue this arrangement long-term. Vera's mother felt ambivalent about change. She was completely exhausted, but she enjoyed Vera's need for closeness and their intimate body contact. The reason that she came in for counseling was that her two older sons, ages 4 and 6, had begun to exhibit escalating behavioral problems at home. They were rough-housing inside and became increasingly defiant and aggressive. All attempts to change the situation with her daughter failed as a result of Vera's intense crying. The mother was unable to cope with Vera's weeping, and therefore tended to give in to her daughter.

Initial observations. Vera sat on her mother's lap while the patient history was being taken, clung to her mother, and was hardly able to detach from her briefly even after a long warm-up phase. Whenever she began to whine, her mother would nurse her again.

Diagnosis. During the first visit, we diagnosed a regulation disorder with sleep-onset problems, night-waking problems, and excessive clinginess. At the time of the appointment, Vera had not yet learned to fall asleep and sleep through the night without her mother's extensive help (nursing, co-sleeping, carrying around). The excessive clinginess was linked to the very frequent nursing.

First steps. We first discussed with the mother whether, when, and to what extent she might decrease her nursing during the day and night, and what other soothing strategies she might use with Vera to help lessen her whining and crying. In the course of the discussion we dealt with the mother's ambivalence about Vera's current bedtime routines. The mother came from a large family and had always wanted four or five children of her own. But she now realized as a result of Vera's difficulties that this would probably be her last baby. In addition, the mother's family of origin lived far away. Because she missed the close contact with her own mother, she became deeply involved with her only daughter to maintain an intimate relationship with her. Although the father participated in child rearing, his work left him little time for the family. The mother regretted their lack of time for intimate togetherness as a couple. All of this had made it very difficult for her to detach step-by-step from her intense, almost symbiotic relationship with her daughter.

During developmental counseling it became clear to the parents that Vera was at an age when they could trust her with a certain autonomy and self-reliance. While discussing family resources, the mother hit upon the idea of asking the au pair who was living with the family to provide occasional respite care: Perhaps the girl could look after Vera in the evening and allow the parents to enjoy some long-awaited, undisturbed time together.

Further treatment. The father was then included in the treatment process. Observing a play situation involving Vera and her father helped the mother to recognize that her daughter was quite well regulated even when the mother was not present. This gave her more confidence in her husband's coregulatory competencies. As a result, the father began to assume the task of soothing Vera for several nights so that her mother would not have to nurse her and could catch up on her sleep in another room. Within only a few days this led to significant improvements in Vera's sleep problems. As a result, Vera was calmer and less whiny during the day as well. On the basis of this success, the mother decided to wean Vera over a 2-week period, which her daughter accepted without any trouble. The mother reported that Vera became increasingly autonomous and independent during the day and learned to be less clingy. Because Vera continued to wake up two to three times per night and quieted only when picked up and carried around by her parents, they were ready after detailed counseling for a behavior modification technique known as checking.

Since that time, Vera has been sleeping through the night, and the parents are satisfied with the overall situation. Vera has become more self-reliant, her mother has gained more energy for her two sons, and their behavior has improved rapidly as a result.

INTRODUCTION

This chapter deals with sleep-onset and night-waking disorders, by far the most frequent behavioral disorders of infancy. Like excessive crying during the first 3 months of life, sleep disorders during the first years of life have often been trivialized (Papoušek & von Hofacker, 1998). Their effects on family life, the developing parent–child relationships, and the couples' relationship are often overlooked or minimized. One-dimensional explanatory models, guidelines, and contradictory recommendations for resolving the problem predominate in parenting magazines—often without scientific basis. In the present chapter we therefore describe and try to define the phenomenon of infant sleep disorders on the basis of clinical data from the Munich Program. We then discuss the prevalence, course, and prognosis of infant sleep disorders as well as their genesis and developmental origins in their age-specific context. We conclude with a discussion of therapeutic interventions.

CLINICAL SYNDROME

Like all disorders of behavioral and emotional regulation, the clinical syndrome of sleep disorders is extraordinarily multifaceted depending on age and associated behavioral problems but is largely nonspecific with regard to risk factors, effects on the family, and long-term consequences (Papoušek, 2002). Individual manifestations arise most often in relation to age-dependent developmental tasks. Sleep disorders in early childhood mostly involve the infant's difficulty falling asleep on her own without parental assistance, giving in to her fatigue and biological need for sleep when tired, and/or going back to sleep without help after waking up at night (Ferber, 1987; Papoušek, 2002; Richman, 1981; Richman, Douglas, Hunt, Landsdown, & Levere, 1985). Depending on age, young children signal their problem by crying, fussing, calling their parents for help, or climbing into their parents' bed (co-sleeping). In general, brief awakenings at night are completely normal in infants. Scientific studies that use videosomnography and actometry have shown that infants wake up at night more frequently than parents suspect (Anders, 1978; Anders, Goodlin-Jones, & Sadeh, 2000; Minde et al., 1993; Sadeh, Lavie, Scher, Tirosh, & Epstein, 1991). Most infants wake up more than once per night, though for only 1 to 5 minutes (Anders et al., 2000). Gaylor, Goodlin-Jones, and Burnham (1998) used tape recordings to study the sleep behavior of infants between the ages of 3 and 12 months and also documented that infant waking was not noticed by sleeping parents. The authors stated that children awaken on average 2.3 times per night. According to Anders and Keener (1985), during the first 12 months of life most infants learn to soothe themselves after awakening, to develop their own strategies for going back to sleep, and to regulate the transition from waking to sleep on their own (Papoušek, 2002). However, infants with sleep problems seem to be unable to do this. They demand their parents' help by crying or calling, thereby disrupting the parents' sleep as well as their own.

Sleep behavior disorders of this kind represent the most frequent reason for parents to seek counseling at the Munich Program. More than 87% of the infants above the age of 6 months whom we see are brought in primarily because of sleep behavior disorders (see chapter 3).

SLEEP BEHAVIOR—CLINICAL DATA

To describe the clinical syndrome, we compared the first 100 sleep-disordered infants seen at the Munich Program (age range: 7 to 24 months; mean age: 12.2 ± 4.3 months) with 100 infants from a nonclinical control group. The latter convenience sample was not selected with regard to sleep problems, but included infants of the same age range (mean age: 12.1 ± 4.2 months; Oelschlegel, 2003; Vogt, 2003). The database in this comparison consists of the 24-hour sleep diaries that the parents kept for 5 days. An overview of the most important group differences is given in Figure 6.1.

According to Largo (1996), toward the end of the first year of life infants sleep approximately 12 hours during the night and 2 hours during the day. The total daily sleep time for a 13-month-old infant (an age close to the average age of our clinical sample) is approximately 14 hours. The range of individual sleep requirements varies considerably, for instance, between 12.5 and 17.5 hours per 24-hour period during the first half-year (Basler, Largo, & Molinari, 1980). At the end of the first year of life, short sleepers get along with only 11 hours of sleep per day, whereas long sleepers sleep as much as 16 hours. Analogous to the data from the Zurich longitudinal study (Largo, 1996), infants in our control group slept an average of 13.1 hours per 24-hour day. In contrast, infants who had been referred to the Munich Program because of a sleep disorder slept considerably less than the comparison group, that is, only 11.3 hours per 24-hour day (678 ± 76 minutes vs. 787 ± 71 minutes), $t(191) = -10.22$, $p \le .001$. At the same time, sleep-disordered infants exhibited significantly greater day-to-day fluctuations in total sleep than did control infants, $t(123.95) = 7.84$, $p \le .001$. On the basis of the 24-hour sleep diaries that are kept by the parents, we try to determine the individual infant's sleep requirement while taking into account whether the infant is well rested and in a good mood during the day.

Sleep-disordered infants in our clinical sample woke up crying or fussing more than four times per night on average, significantly more often than the control infants who woke up only once per night (4.1 ± 2.9 vs. 0.9 ± 1.0), $t(129.89) = 3.85$, $p \le .001$. In addition, infants in the clinical sample coslept in their parents' bed much longer each night than did infants in the control group, on average more than 3 hours (195 ± 230 minutes vs. 70 ± 164 minutes), $t(112.89) = 3.85$, $p \le .001$. One of the most taxing problems for parents was that their sleep-disordered toddlers were awake and crying at night for a total of almost 1½ hours (84 ± 56 minutes) and demanded help in getting back to sleep. This also represents a significant difference compared to the control infants, who lay awake for barely a quarter of an hour (15 ± 19 minutes), $t(109.86) = 11.18$, $p \le .001$. Most nocturnal waking for the clinical sample occurred during the second half of the night, between midnight and 6 a.m. (61 ± 45 minutes), whereas the control infants were awake after midnight for only 10 minutes on average (10 ± 13 minutes), $t(102.91) = 10.58$, $p \le .001$. Significant differences were also found for the amounts of fussing and crying in the morning (32 ± 34 minutes vs. 16 ± 14 minutes), $t(119.47) = 4.13$, $p \le .001$; in the afternoon (37 ± 47 minutes vs. 17 ± 18 minutes), $t(114.11) = 3.91$, $p \le .001$; and late evening hours (42 ± 32 minutes vs. 18 ± 16 minutes), $t(131.78) = 6.3$, $p \le .001$.

The clinical syndrome thus includes not only a shortening and increased intraindividual variability in total sleep time and frequent, lengthy night-waking periods with crying and calling for help, but also an impaired state of well-being during the day and evening. These characteristics present the parents with considerable demands, which they eventually feel unable to master. For this reason, we consider the

Figure 6.1. Symptoms of Sleep Disorders in a Clinical and a Community-Based Control Group.

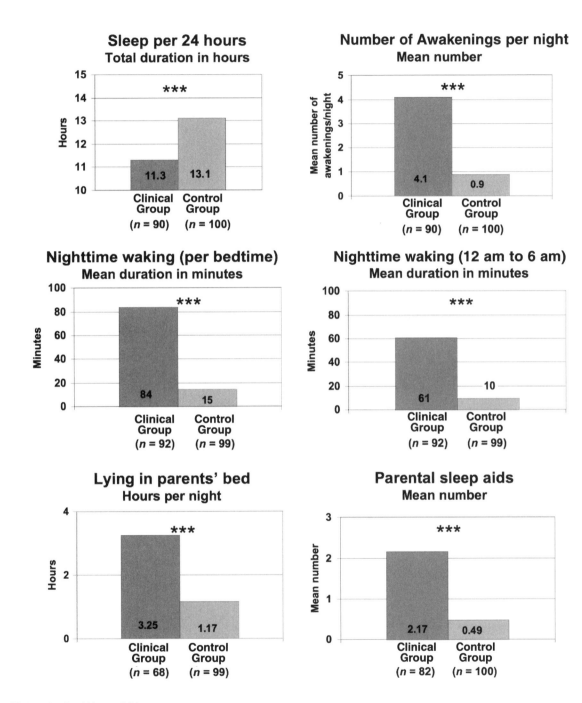

Note. t-tests; ***p ≤ .001.
Source: Vogt, 2003.

parents' affective reactions as an integral part of the clinical syndrome of infant sleep disorders. As Fegert and colleagues (1997) and Ferber (1987) emphasized, sleep disorders are associated with effortful, increasingly ritualized and often bizarre soothing and bedtime strategies and dysfunctional bedtime interactions (Papoušek, 2002). This expenditure of parental energy does not seem to have a marked effect on the time it takes the infant to fall asleep because the so-called sleep latency is still significantly longer in the clinical group than in the comparison group (26 ± 16 minutes vs. 16 ± 12 minutes), $t(89.33) = 4.22, p \le .001$.

What sleep aids or soothing strategies do parents use to support their infants? Most parents are extraordinarily caring and exhibit a wide repertoire of soothing strategies. The mother nurses any time the infant cries, parents offer tea or milk or pacifier; take the infant to their bed; soothe her with body contact, carrying, or singing; keep a nightlight on; play with their infant; or let her tug at the mother's ear lobes or hair (Papoušek, 2002). The soothing strategies are varied or combined in multiple ways to overcome their baby's apparent resistance to falling asleep or returning to sleep. In general, almost all infants between 7 and 24 months need some strategies to help them fall asleep. There are no differences between the children in the clinical group and the control group in this respect (97.8% vs. 96.0%), $X^2(1, N = 190) = 0.51$, ns. However, if we look at the number and type of sleep strategies, we find significant differences. Sleep-disordered infants depend on more parent-controlled sleep aids (2.2 ± 1.2 vs. 0.5 ± 0.7), $t(117.95) = 11.09, p \le .001$. These include nursing, bottle feeding, sitting by the bed, carrying around, holding hands, or other types of physical contact (stroking, etc.), medication (Sedinfant, Atosil, etc.) or other individualized support strategies (turning light on and off, singing and telling stories). These strategies typically do not come to a close with the end of a regular evening ritual. Rather, they continue as long as an infant successfully demands them, which means until she falls asleep.

Infants in the comparison group, in contrast, primarily make use of self-initiated sleep aids. They soothe themselves more often with a pacifier, their thumb, or some transitional object like a plush animal or a security blanket that they are able to control independently of their parents. Figure 6.2 gives an overview of the types and prevalence of sleep aids used in our clinical and community samples. A multivariate analysis of variance (MANOVA; a method that, according to Cohen and Cohen, 1983, may also be used on binary-coded variables such as the individual sleep aids), shows that the two groups differ significantly with regard to the kinds of sleep aids, Wilks's $F(6, 184) = 20.45, p \le .001$. Approximately 60% of infants in the community group fall asleep with a pacifier or thumb-sucking; about one third cuddle with a plush animal or security blanket. These self-controlled sleep aids are used far less frequently by infants with sleep disorders (28% pacifier, 2% plush animal or security blanket). Instead, they demand far more frequently the active support of their parents. Close to 70% fall asleep while being nursed or bottle-fed, as compared to less than 30% in the community group. More than half of the sleep-disordered infants are carried around or soothed by physical contact of one form or another, or they fall asleep in a parent's arms. This occurs in only 17% of the control families. A surprisingly high percentage of sleep-disordered infants, about 20%, had been given sleep medication, often with paradoxical effects. In contrast, drugs had been given to only 1 infant in the community group (1%).

Figure 6.2. Infant-Controlled and Parent-Controlled Sleep Aids.

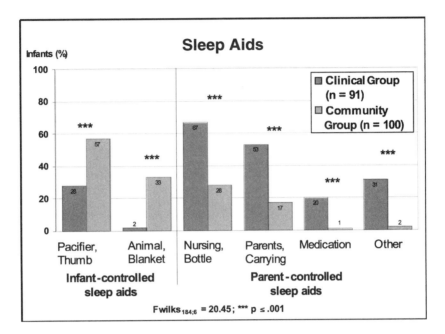

Note. Types of sleep aids used with sleep-disordered infants and community infants of the same age (multivariate analysis of variance with group as the independent variable and sleep aids as the dependent variable.)
Source: Vogt, 2003.

If the parents of sleep-disordered infants attempt to withdraw any of their supportive sleep aids, the infants regularly demand them back by crying. These bedtime interactions are the result of some reciprocal misunderstanding, of a dysfunctional pattern of communication which maintains or worsens the sleep disorder.

DEFINITION

To date, there is no uniform definition of *sleep disorders of early childhood*. The *ICD-10* criteria (Dilling, Mombour, & Schmidt, 1993) for nonorganic sleep disorders (F51: patient complaints about the duration and quality of sleep, exaggerated preoccupation with the sleep disorder during the day, increased anxiety and tension during transition to sleep, and impaired professional and social proficiency) at best apply to the parents. However, they are inappropriate, inadequate, and unhelpful when applied to early childhood sleep problems, because they describe intrinsic sleep disorders that are rare in childhood and adolescence (guidelines of the German Society for Child and Adolescent Psychiatry, Psychosomatics, and Psychotherapy, 2000).

The revised *DC: 0–3R* classification system (ZERO TO THREE, 2005) distinguishes disorders of initiating sleep (Sleep-Onset Protodyssomnia) and disorders of maintaining sleep (Night-Waking Protodyssomnia) in addition to the *DSM-IV-TR* (American Psychiatric Association, 2000) classifications of sleep terror, sleep-walking, breathing-related sleep disorders, and nightmare disorders. The present chapter deals with disorders of initiating and of maintaining sleep, but also includes younger infants between 7 and 12 months of age. Moreover, it addresses sleep problems that are associated with other primary diagnoses on Axis I of the ZERO TO THREE system such as disorders of affect, transient adjustment problems, posttraumatic stress disorder, and/or with a relationship diagnosis on Axis II. For the age range of 7 to 24 months, we prefer to speak of sleep disorders combined with regulatory problems in other domains because reliable diagnostic classification on Axis I is still difficult at this early age. As discussed in chapter 4, we also use a wider systemic definition of *sleep disorder* that also includes the parents' psychological state and criteria in the realm of parent–infant interactions.

In light of the high individual variability and rapid age-dependent changes in sleep and sleep behavior, a general definition of *sleep disorders of early childhood* is still difficult. Equally problematic are attempts to define criteria that demarcate pathological deviations and disorders in sleep behavior from transient perturbations brought about by developmental adjustments and demands (Basler et al., 1980). As is the case with disorders of behavioral and emotional regulation in general, the extraordinary heterogeneity of the clinical syndrome of sleep disorders in early childhood and their close association with age-specific developmental tasks render it difficult to define standard diagnostic criteria at present (Papoušek, 1999, 2002). Even though objective criteria have been defined in scientific publications, they are not applied in a uniform way. As a result, no universally accepted definition (such as the "rule of threes" for excessive crying; see chapter 5) has gained ground in the international literature. The diagnostic criteria vary greatly, depending on age, sample selection, and methods of data acquisition.

Anders and colleagues (Anders et al., 2000; Anders, Halpern, & Hua, 1992) have distinguished between sleep onset disorders and sleep maintenance disorders on the basis of videosomnographic studies of sleep development in term and preterm infants during the first years of life. They used two criteria in particular to assess a sleep maintenance disorder: the number and the duration of nighttime awakenings. For infants between the ages of 12 and 24 months, they defined a sleep maintenance disorder as involving two or more nighttime wakings and/or lying awake at night for more than 10 minutes. If the children are older (between 2 and 3 years), Anders and colleagues diagnose a sleep disorder when the child wakes up once or twice per night and/or nighttime waking lasts for more than 20 minutes. The diagnostic criteria they used for a sleep onset disorder are the time it takes for the child to fall asleep and the inability to fall asleep on her own, without extrinsic support. Accordingly, a sleep-onset disorder is diagnosed when 12- to 24-month-old infants need more than 30 minutes, or older children more than 20 minutes, to fall asleep, and the parents either stay with the child until she has fallen asleep or need to return to the child for comfort more than once.

Anders and colleagues (2000) generally differentiate between three levels of severity (perturbation, disturbance, and disorder), depending on the number of nights per week in which sleep problems occur as well as the duration of the sleep disorder. A perturbation is said to be present when the disorder occurs only 1 night per week and this problem continues for only 2 to 4 weeks. If 2 to 4 nights per week are affected for 2 to 4 weeks, they term this a disturbance. If the sleep problem lasts for at least 4 weeks and during more than 5 nights per week, a severe sleep disorder is diagnosed.

Wolke (1998) has distinguished between moderate sleep-maintenance problems (waking up once per night for at least 5 nights per week), a marked sleep-maintenance disorder (two or more awakenings in 5 or more nights per week), and a sleep-onset disorder (more than 60 minutes needed for the transition to sleep).

According to the *DC:0–3R* (ZERO TO THREE, 2005), the diagnosis of a sleep-onset disorder requires that there be significant difficulty falling asleep for at least 4 weeks, five to seven times per week. A night-waking problem is diagnosed when the child has significant difficulty in nighttime awakenings 5 to 7 nights per week at an age of 12 months or older.

Richman (1981; Richman et al., 1985) and Minde and colleagues (1993) used sleep diaries kept by the parents to diagnose a sleep problem. According to their criteria, a marked sleep maintenance disorder is diagnosed when the infant wakes up three or more times a night and/or lies awake for more than 20 minutes per waking episode, and/or is taken into the parents' bed. A marked sleep-onset disorder is diagnosed when an infant requires at least 30 minutes to fall asleep and/or needs the parents to stay with her. In addition, the problems must be present 5 or more nights per week and continue for more than 3 months (Minde et al., 1993; Richman, 1981; Richman et al., 1985).

Richman (1985) and Minde et al. (1993) created a sleep score for use in scientific studies and evaluation of treatment effects. It is composed of measures of sleep-onset time, wake-up time in the morning, duration of cosleeping, parental sleep aids, latency to fall asleep, and number and duration of nighttime waking episodes. However, the composition of the sleep score varies depending on the available database, even within the research groups, so that no uniform standard exists at present.

To create an objective measurement of the severity of a sleep disorder, and to evaluate changes over the course of treatment, our own team followed the previous work of Richman (1981) to produce a composite sleep score (Vogt, 2003) based on the 5-day sleep diaries from the previously mentioned clinical and community samples. To this end, all variables were used in which the clinical group of sleep-disordered infants differed clearly and significantly from the undiagnosed sample: number of disturbed nights per week, number and average duration of nighttime awakenings, and total sleep time. In contrast to the scores used by the former investigators, we also included a measure of sleep aids that contribute to or sustain the sleep problem, and the infant's state of well-being both during night and day: Number of parent-controlled sleep aids, duration of fussiness and crying between 6 a.m. and 6 p.m., and the duration of fussiness and crying between midnight and 6 a.m. On the basis of the distribution of these variables in our convenience sample of 100 children aged 7 to 24 months, we established 7 individual 6-point sleep scales. Specifically, the points (0 to 5) of these scales correspond with the 10th, 25th, 50th, 75th, and 100th percentile, respectively. Summing up the individual sleep scales yields a total sleep score.

A composite sleep score of 22 was set as the cutoff or criterion for diagnosing a marked sleep disorder as it corresponds approximately to the 80th percentile in the unselected community sample and is consistent with the prevalence rate of marked sleep disorders cited in the literature for unselected samples (see below). Composite scores greater than 22 were computed in 21.3% of the community sample and in 91.7% of the clinical sample, who thereby met the criterion for a marked sleep maintenance disorder (Vogt, 2003). Infants in the clinical sample had a mean composite sleep score of 29.1 ± 4.7, whereas infants in the community sample had a score of 15.8 ± 8.0, $t(152.49) = 13.74$, $p \leq .001$. These results demonstrate that the sleep score may provide a valid and useful quantitative measure for longitudinal studies and for the evaluation of therapeutic interventions in the future.

Unfortunately, the computation of the composite sleep score from sleep diaries is too time-consuming for clinical diagnosis in everyday practice. However, focusing on single individual sleep parameters is insufficient and inappropriate. For example, total sleep time as the sole diagnostic criterion in and of itself is neither useful nor indicative of a disorder; although it may be relatively stable in an individual child, it varies enormously among children. To determine whether an infant has slept enough, her state of well-being during the day must be considered (as in the composite sleep score). A lack of sleep is generally associated with abnormal sleepiness, fussiness, and motor restlessness during waking times. The sleep-disordered infants in our clinical sample cried and fussed significantly more (159 ± 89 minutes) than did those in the community group (56 ± 34 minutes), $t(122.05) = 8.07$, $p \leq .001$. Nevertheless, some sleep-disordered infants appear to be well regulated and inconspicuous during the day and are often viewed by outsiders as charming and highly sociable. In addition, current definitions of sleep disorders do not include a criterion of the parents' subjective and objective distress, an aspect that is indispensable for working with parents in a clinical setting. This is particularly important because sleep disorders in infants whose parents seek help have generally already been present for a long time. Thus, a chronic sleep deficit on the part of the parents diminishes their resources to an extent that must be taken into account in planning the intervention.

DIAGNOSTIC INSTRUMENTS AND DIFFERENTIAL DIAGNOSIS

Patient History Targeted to the Specific Disorder

It is absolutely essential to get a patient history from the parents that targets the specific problems in detail. This includes the infant's state of well-being during the entire day and night, the sleep habits of the family (e.g., who sleeps where?), nursing and nighttime feeding patterns, sleep settings and arrangements, housing conditions, sleep rituals, and the process and precise form of soothing interventions and other sleep aids, as well as patterns of bedtime interactions. The history should also determine when the sleep problem began, what triggered it, and its progress to date.

To assess a potential sleep deficit, it is important to observe and ask the parents about the infant's state of well-being during the day. Questions should also address disorders in other domains such as feeding or short-term separation in order to determine the pervasiveness of the regulatory problems. Questions regarding the infant's behavior in other contexts and observations of parent–infant interaction also provide relevant information about age-dependent conflict situations between the parents and child (excessive clinginess, conflicts over limit-setting or boundaries, etc.), which may also play a role in the sleep context. It is crucial to include both parents in the process. Each parent may have very different understandings and perceptions of the causes of the sleep disorder and what to do about it. If the parents' relationship has begun to suffer because of long-standing sleep problems, these differing perspectives may make it difficult for them to support each other and may even block progress.

Diagnostic Instruments

Videosomnography and actometry are frequently used diagnostic instruments for assessing sleep behavior in the home for scientific studies (Anders et al., 2000). Sleep logs or diaries that are kept by parents over several days (see chapter 5) are also favored. In comparison to the more objective videosomnography data, sleep logs provide an adequately reliable picture of problematic sleep, whereas parents whose infants sleep well tend to overestimate sleep time using this method (St. James-Roberts, Harris, & Messer, 1993). Missing in these reports are the short periods of waking in which the infants soothe themselves and return to sleep without disturbing the parents' sleep. Videosomnography is advantageous because it is noninvasive and may be used in the home to gain information about qualitative sleep characteristics such as stages of sleep, motor startles and agitation during sleep, type and amount of crying, parental intervention, and parent–infant interaction at bedtime. In contrast, sleep logs require much less expenditure in terms of equipment and time and are easier to analyze. For example, when nighttime awakenings are reported during which the infant appears to be alert and ready to play, sleep logs may be useful in determining whether the infant is lying in her crib too long in relation to her sleep requirements. On the basis of a Swiss clinical sample, Largo has drawn attention to this phenomenon as the most frequent cause of sleep problems (Largo, 1996). However, this phenomenon has rarely been seen in our clinical sample.

In recent years, sleep diaries have been complemented by home videos that the parents take during the worst part of the night. These videos may be particularly informative about bedtime interactions in the family. Commercially available video cameras or digital cameras are completely adequate for this purpose and may be mounted on a tripod in a corner of the bedroom so as to record interactions in real time or time-lapse. The latest generation of infrared cameras can even provide good pictures in the dark so that the normal routine is not disturbed.

Polygraphic EEG recordings and other invasive techniques in a sleep laboratory are only required when sleep apnea, risk of sudden infant death syndrome, seizures, or other organic brain disorders are suspected. One should be aware that the unfamiliar environment or false alarms given off by monitors and similar devices in the sleep laboratory may themselves disturb an infant's sleep, distort the picture, or even exacerbate the sleep disorder.

Night terrors (pavor nocturnus), which may also begin to occur toward the end of the first year of life, should be distinguished from the sleep problems and disorders described so far. According to Ferber (1987), infants with night terrors typically awake from deep sleep in a terrified state of mind during the first half of the night, cry or scream without actually becoming fully awake, are completely unresponsive, and may thrash about and reject physical contact and other soothing attempts. After about 10 to 15 minutes, they generally go back to sleep by themselves. Night terrors typically occur only once per night but may be associated with a sleep behavior disorder of the kind described above.

Pediatric Differential Diagnosis

In doubtful cases, acute and chronic diseases such as atopic dermatitis, epilepsy and other organic brain disorders, or obstructive sleep apnea syndrome must be ruled out by the pediatrician (von Hofacker, 1998; von Hofacker et al., 2000).

PREVALENCE, PERSISTENCE, AND AGE-DEPENDENT CO-OCCURRENCE WITH OTHER SYNDROMES

Prevalence

The prevalence of sleep disorders depends on the criteria used to diagnose them. Studies that utilize the above-mentioned criteria for a marked sleep disorder (three or more nighttime awakenings, for 5 or more nights a week, for at least 3 months) yield prevalence rates between 15% and 20% during the first 2 years of life (Minde et al., 1993; Richman, 1981). Using less stringent criteria (waking up only once per night), Wolke (1998) has found prevalence rates of 20% to 25% for moderate sleep-onset and sleep maintenance problems. Regular nighttime awakenings have been reported at the ages of 5 and 20 months in 22% (Wolke, 1994), at 12 months in 26% (Scott & Richards, 1990), and at 24 months in 29% of children studied (Laucht, Esser, & Schmidt, 1992). According to Anders et al. (1992), as many as 30% to 40% of 8-month-old infants are unable to go back to sleep on their own after waking up at night. A multicenter prospective longitudinal study conducted by Fegert and colleagues (1997) found that approximately 40% of infants between the ages of 6 and 36 months wake up their parents at least once per night on a regular basis; half of them do so several times per night. Sleep disorders are generally more frequent and last longer in infants who are nursed for a longer time and/or sleep in their parents' bedroom or bed (Fegert et al., 1997; Wolke, 1998; Wolke, Meyer, Ohrt, & Riegel, 1995).

Persistence

According to field studies conducted by Fegert and Wolke (Fegert et al., 1997; Wolke, 1994) only about 50% of parents feel disturbed by their infant's nighttime awakenings. However, subjective distress increases with the persistence of sleeping problems and may rise to extreme levels. More than half of the infants who exhibit a significant sleep disorder at 6 months continue to wake up repeatedly at night at 12 months, 75% of them at least once (Fegert et al., 1997). Sleep disorders diagnosed in 1-year-olds persist into the eighteenth month of life in 86% of infants and into the third year of life in between 50% and 70%. Sleep disorders still present in 3-year-olds tend to persist into school age (Jenkins, Owen, Bax, & Hart, 1980).

The persistence of sleep disorders was extraordinarily high in the Munich Program's clinical sample as well. As evident from the patient histories, the disorder had begun during the first 3 months of life with excessive crying and dysfunctional sleep–wake organization in more than three quarters (77.4%) of the infants who had been referred to the Munich Program because of sleep disorders (n = 393) between 7 and 24 months of age. The percentage of infants with early excessive crying and early sleep problems is even higher in cases of sleep disorders combined with regulatory problems in other behavioral domains (79.9% vs. 70.9%), $X^2(1, N = 393) = 3.62, p \le .057$. The high persistence of sleep disorders is also evident when we look at the duration of problems before the parents sought help. In isolated sleep disorders, sleep problems had persisted for almost 10 months (9.7 ± 4.4 months), and in combined disorders, almost 12 months (11.7 ± 4.8 months); the difference is highly significant, $t(391) = 3.38, p \le .001$. Calculated as a percentage of the infants' postnatal lifetimes, parents and their children with isolated sleep disorders had spent an average of 84% of their mutual postnatal life time sleeping poorly; for those with combined clinical disorders, the figures were as high as 90% of their mutual life time, $t(168.95) = 2.08, p \le .05$. This means that families with a 12-month-old infant with an isolated sleep disorder would have experienced more than 300 troubled nights, and those with an infant with a combined clinical disorder more than 328 sleepless nights before the parents sought or found help.

Age-Dependent Co-Occurrence With Other Clinical Syndromes

Isolated sleep disorders are rare (22.6%) among the 7- to 24-month-old infants who are referred to the Munich Program. Combined clinical syndromes, that is, sleep disorders associated with regulatory problems in other domains, are seen most frequently (77.4%). The situation looked somewhat different during the early years of our program (1991 to 1994), when more than half of the infants (53%) presented with relatively uncomplicated, isolated sleep disorders (von Hofacker & Papoušek, 1998). It is probably not by mere chance that the relative decrease of less complex sleep disorders in our client base coincided with the publication of a popular German parent book with the promising title *Every child can learn to sleep* (Kast-Zahn & Morgenroth, 1995, 2002), which is based on the Ferber method (Ferber, 1987). Ever since its appearance, many families have learned to manage isolated infant sleep problems simply by following the recommendations in the book.

In more complex cases in the Munich Program, sleep disorders in 7- to 24-month-old infants were associated with a syndrome of dysphoric restlessness/lack of interest in play (35.4%), excessive clinginess (17.0%), excessive temper tantrums (26.7%), aggressive-oppositional behavior (7.4%), and feeding disorders (35.4%). The co-occurrences exhibit significant age-related distributions, with the exception of feeding disorders, which consistently affect a good third of the sleep-disordered infants across the whole age range (see Table 6.1).

Dysphoric restlessness/lack of interest in play occurs in tandem with the sleep disorder in 44% of infants before the 10th month of life but then drops off steadily to a low of 25% by the end of the second year of life. As discussed in chapter 15, this syndrome can only partially be explained by direct effects of sleep deficit on the infant's state of well-being during the day.

About 20% of the infants who presented for the first time with sleep disorders at the age of 10 months or later also exhibited excessive clinginess. In younger sleep-disordered infants this syndrome was evident in only 9%. The increase in excessive clinginess therefore occurs at an age when the parents

Table 6.1. Age-Related Associations of Sleep Disorders With Other Clinical Syndromes.

Associated syndromes	Age at first visit					Trend test $(df = 1)^a$
	7–24 Total $(n = 393)$ %	7–9 months $(n = 190)$ %	10–12 months $(n = 107)$ %	13–18 months $(n = 108)$ %	19–24 months $(n = 59)$ %	
Dysphoric restlessness/ lack of interest in play	35.4	43.7	32.7	34.3	25.4	5.27*
Excessive clinginess	17.0	9.2	21.5	19.4	20.3	4.04***
Excessive temper tantrums	26.7	3.4	11.2	48.1	62.7	102.50***
Aggressive/oppositional behavior	7.4	1.7	5.6	7.4	22.0	19.54***
Feeding disorder	35.4	37.0	29.9	38.9	35.6	n.s.

^{a}Mantel-Haenszel trend test.
*$p \leq .05$. ***$p \leq .001$.

Note. Unpublished data from the Munich client database (multiple mentions possible).

and infant are facing new developmental tasks such as mastering separation anxiety and fear of strangers and regulating the balance between proximity and distance or between attachment and exploration (Schieche, 2001).

During the second year of life, the percentage of infants with associated excessive temper tantrums increased from 3% to 11% in the first year, to more than 48% during the third half-year and to over 63% during the fourth half-year. This impressive increase coincides with the child's increasing needs for autonomy (Erikson, 1976) and developmental tasks related to limit-setting. Association of sleep disorders with aggressive-oppositional behavior was rare until a significant increase after 18 months (22%).

DEVELOPMENTAL ORIGINS

What are the conditions that contribute to the development of sleep problems that then become full-blown sleep disorders, and under what conditions do these persist?

Early Development of Sleep–Wake Organization

Sleep disorders are closely linked to the development of sleep itself. Throughout the first year of life, the natural development of sleep is governed by rapid and remarkably complex maturational, adaptational, and reorganizational processes in the brain. Developmental progress involves the cyclical alternation between active rapid eye movement (REM) sleep and quiet non-REM sleep at 50- to 60-minute intervals; the steady decrease in REM sleep and indeterminate sleep in favor of quiet sleep; the shifting of the main sleep time to the night, of quiet sleep to the first half of the night, and of REM sleep to the second half; the transition from a polyphasic ultradian sleep–wake cycle to a biphasic circadian cycle; and external synchronization of the intrinsic circadian sleep–waking rhythm with the day–night cycle (Anders & Keener, 1985; Emde & Walker, 1976). Over the course of maturation and adaptation, the infant's regulation of transitions between waking and sleeping improves, the susceptibility to perturbation decreases, and the length of the longest uninterrupted sleep increases.

After the initial polyphasic sleep–wake organization with regular sleep–wake cycles is accomplished as a result of the 3-month developmental shift, the self regulatory capacity of infants to fall asleep and to sleep through the night improves considerably (Largo, 2000; Papoušek, 2002; see also chapter 5). Many of the above reorganizational processes evolve during the second half-year and are assumed to culminate during the seventh to ninth month of life. As a result, we again observe a clustering of night-time awakening and crying (Louis, Cannard, Bastuji, & Challamel, 1997). Infant sleep patterns are largely consolidated at 12 months, and at this time they are structurally very similar to those of adults.

Parental Sleep Aids and Communication During Bedtime Interactions

The most frequent causes of nonorganic sleep disorders in otherwise healthy infants and toddlers are related to the parents' readiness to maintain excessive regulatory support beyond the first 3 or 4 months when sleep aids were needed and helpful (especially in cases of excessive crying) or in contexts of illness, hospitalization, or an unfamiliar environment.

As already mentioned, sleep problems in our clinical sample originated most often (in 77.4%) during the first 3 months of life in the context of excessive crying with dysfunctional sleep–wake organization (Papoušek & von Hofacker, 1998). These infants in particular had required intense regulatory help for falling asleep. They had become accustomed to settling down only when rocked in their mother's arms, when in close physical contact with the mother, during nursing or bottle-feeding, when carried around, and/or when intense vestibular stimulation was provided.

Even when the initial regulation problems have been overcome as a result of the maturation spurt around 3 months, parents often continue to provide these sleep aids, which then become a familiar ritual. The infants get used to them, and as they develop may protest vehemently when these aids are withdrawn. In addition, they lack the experience of falling asleep without the expected help. Infants quickly learn to rely on familiar regulatory support during the transition to sleep, and they become both efficient and effective in demanding this familiar support by crying. Parent–infant bedtime interactions become increasingly dysfunctional over time. These patterns may be particularly tenacious in infants in whom breast- or bottle-feeding has become an established bedtime routine.

In the remaining quarter of infants in the clinical sample, sleep disorders began at a later age, particularly in the context of illness, inoculation, hospitalization, or moving to or vacationing in an unfamiliar environment. Here, too, the pattern is usually similar to that described above. The children initially signal a greater need for physical contact with their parents during the transition to sleep, receive the appropriate support from their responsive parents, but are unwilling to give up these comforting aids once the situation has calmed down and returned to the familiar routines. They cry, become clingy, or scream, making it difficult for the parents either to trust that their infant will again be able to fall asleep by herself, or to support the infant by conveying a clear sense of security.

If the parent–infant relationship was strained already during the first months of life by excessive crying, parents lose their sense of self-efficacy and confidence, which in turn may lead to depression, overload, and loss of self-esteem (Sarimski, 1993). The parents may become overwhelmed by a combination of exhaustion, anger, frustration, and feelings of failure and guilt. Guilt feelings, insecurity, and anxiousness may, in turn, contribute to some form of overprotectiveness or inconsistency during bedtime interactions (Sarimski, 1993).

Age-Related Developmental Tasks

Inadequate understanding of sleep requirements in infancy and of the infant's self-regulatory abilities to fall asleep and to sleep through the night often contribute to the development of sleep problems, as does a lack of clarity regarding the different age-related developmental tasks that may affect sleep behavior.

As described above, regulation of behavioral states and sleep–wake organization are of prime importance during the first half-year of life. Overstimulation and overload may increase the infant's difficulties with self-soothing and falling asleep when tired (Papoušek, 2002). During the second half-year, maintaining a balance between attachment and exploration and between proximity and distance become increasingly important, as does coping with separation anxiety and fear of strangers (Schieche, 2001; see also chapter 8). Bedtime interaction may also be affected by maternal sadness elicited in the context of weaning. During the second year of life, finding a balance between the infant's growing need for autonomy and renewed need for closeness and dependency take center stage (Erikson, 1976). Moreover, conflicts over limit-setting, rules, and boundaries have to be negotiated in many everyday contexts, including bedtime interactions. In the third year of life, children may begin to wake up from anxiety-provoking dreams, or to resist sleeping in their room because of frightening fantasies (Largo, 1996; see also chapter 1).

Infant Temperament

Numerous studies have demonstrated connections between sleep disorders and constitutional qualities that can make it difficult for the infant to master sleep-related developmental tasks (Anders et al., 2000; Carey & McDevitt, 1995; Minde et al., 1993; Richman, 1981). Dimensions of temperament such as fussiness/difficulty, unpredictability, hyperreactivity, inconsolability, unadaptability, and persistence may play a central role in this regard. Infants with sleep disorders are often easily distracted, and their sensory thresholds seem to be particularly low (Anders et al., 2000). They are also more demanding and less able to adapt to new situations. While awake, a generally elevated level of excitability and activity causes the infant to absorb an excess of stimuli and impressions that may not be adequately processed. This not only impedes falling asleep but may lead to restless sleep and frequent awakenings.

Risk Factors

Behavioral dispositions and problems with self-regulation that impede adaptation may be in part genetically determined, but they may also be acquired as a result of the influence of prenatal, perinatal, or even early postnatal risk factors. Both infants and parents in the present sample have been facing remarkable cumulative stress from such risk factors (see chapter 3). The amount of accumulated somatic and psychosocial risk is significantly related to the severity, duration, and pervasiveness of regulatory problems. The accumulation of somatic and psychosocial risk factors is significantly higher in sleep disorders that are part of a pervasive regulation disorder ($n = 278$) than in isolated sleep disorders ($n = 115$), $t(288.09) = 6.24$, $p \le .001$. In other words, for the clients of the Munich Program, the more risk factors accumulate, the more prolonged and severe the sleep disorder, and the greater the probability of pervasive regulatory problems.

Over and above the overall risk, some individual psychosocial factors appear to have a particularly unfavorable effect. These include conflicts in the parents' relationship (56% for combined, 37% for isolated sleep disorders), current conflicts with the families of origin (33% for combined, 17% for isolated sleep disorders), psychological disturbances in the mother (50% for combined, 23% for isolated sleep disorders), and distressing childhood memories (37% for combined, 18% for isolated sleep disorders; cf. von Hofacker & Papoušek, 1998). Somatic risk factors include perinatal and postnatal complications, medical reasons for monitoring, chronic atopic dermatitis, and obstructive apnea, among others (cf. Anders et al., 2000; Minde et al., 1993; Richman, 1981).

Another group of sleep disorders is associated with severe emotional neglect and attachment issues. In contrast to the majority of our clients, such cases primarily involve the infant's need for closeness and secure attachment as well as fears of rejection, abandonment, and separation. If the infants get too little attention and comfort during the day, they often try to make up at night for the closeness they have missed. Families with severe emotional neglect rarely seek outside help on their own; for many of these, a home-visiting intervention would have been more appropriate but unfortunately could not be provided by the Munich Program.

Similar needs and fears come to the fore when parents and infant must cope with other attachment-related challenges such as hospitalization, repeated separation, sudden loss of a significant other, adjustment to daycare, ambivalence about going back to work, or birth of a sibling.

Psychodynamic Themes Relevant to the Parents' Developmental Tasks

Psychosocial stressors may also revive parental psychodynamic themes with immediate effects on bedtime interactions and sleeping problems (Barth, 1999, 2003; see also chapter 10). Psychosocially distressed parents often have a hard time conveying the confidence and sense of security needed by the infant during the transition to sleep. The infant's nightly whining or crying all too easily evokes the parents' own need for being mothered, fear of abandonment, or vivid childhood memories of unresolved mourning, loss, or separation. When a parent is overly anxious and overprotective, or is involved with the infant in a symbiotic relationship without boundaries, wearisome nightly weaning problems and ambivalence around separation and attachment issues may arise. In addition, memories of frightening nighttime experiences may be evoked from those times when the parent as a child was desperately calling for help because of terrifying fantasies but received no comfort. In such situations, the parent may unconsciously project her own feelings onto the infant; this leads to distorted perceptions and misunderstandings of the real baby, and, in turn, to inappropriate or ambivalent reactions and dysfunctional communication patterns at bedtime (Barth, 1999; Papoušek, 2002; Papoušek & von Hofacker, 1998; see also chapter 10).

During the second year of life the parents, too, may increasingly deal with themes and unresolved conflicts around issues of dependency and autonomy (Barth, 1999). In some cases, the power struggles between parent and child about going to sleep seem to call forth unresolved dependency–autonomy conflicts with one or both of their own parents. The mother and/or father then may feel at the mercy of their own conflicted feelings of helplessness, rage, compassion, and self-blame.

In families in which partnership conflicts are not openly addressed, a sleep disorder in which the infant drives one of the parents out of the bedroom may be rigidly maintained. In such cases, the sleep disorder may take on the function of a placeholder that allows the parents to avoid coping with their smoldering conflict.

Thus, a variety of themes may be activated during nightly bedtime interaction depending on the developmental age of the child and the psychological constellation of one or both parents. The same themes may also dominate interactions in other everyday contexts and promote associated regulatory problems (excessive clinginess, conflict over limit-setting, excessive temper tantrums, etc.), which must be taken into account in the overall approach to sleep counseling and parent–infant psychotherapy.

THERAPEUTIC INTERVENTIONS

The starting point for counseling and treatment in our program is a systemic model that focuses on parent–infant communication during bedtime interactions. It is particularly important to have as precise an understanding as possible of the dysfunctional patterns of communication between parent and infant, and of the factors that produce and sustain these patterns. The detailed patient history, sleep logs, and home videos (if available) are the basis for this understanding. A treatment plan and concrete goals are worked out in collaboration with the parents (e.g., the parents hope that the infant will fall asleep and sleep through the night in her own bed or will sleep in her own bed in her parents' bedroom, or that the continual nursing will be replaced by a single feeding). The main modules of intervention include developmental counseling, guidance in communication in relation to bedtime interactions, and psychotherapy.

Developmental Counseling

In developmental counseling, the parents are given general information about sleep development, the typical phases of infant sleep, and the importance of a regular sleep rhythm. The sleep diaries are used to determine an infant's individual need for sleep and the most favorable sleep times (Largo, 1996; Wolke, 1999). It is crucial for the parents to recognize and respect the signs of fatigue, overfatigue, or sleep deficit and to adapt sleep time to the signaled needs of the infant. The older the child, the more easily the family will succeed in synchronizing the child's sleep rhythm with the daily routines of the other family members. Developmental counseling also focuses on assessing the infant's capacity for self-regulation and, if needed, on the impending developmental tasks related to attachment or autonomy issues.

Guidance in Communication at Bedtime

Guidance in communication also incorporates a modification of the behavioral self-help technique known as checking (Ferber, 1987; Kast-Zahn & Morgenroth, 1995, 2002), but with particular attention paid to communication between parents and infant and to their understanding of each others' needs and intentions in the context of settling the child to sleep in the evening and soothing during nighttime awakenings. In the beginning of the checking procedure, parents are encouraged to place the infant in her crib after a comforting, pleasantly shared evening ritual with close body contact, to say goodnight, and then to leave the room. If the infant begins to cry or scream, the parents reenter the room at short regular intervals, reassure her ("I'm right here, everything is okay. I'll look in on you again later"), but without offering any other sleep aids, and then leave the room again. If the infant continues to cry, this process is repeated at preset intervals until she falls asleep. This gives the infant the opportunity to learn to develop her own soothing and sleep strategies.

We have learned from our own experience that the success of this intervention crucially depends on whether and how this communication between parents and infant takes place, how the parents understand their infant's crying and needs, what messages they convey through their nonverbal behavior, and how they manage to convey a feeling of emotional security, predictability, and trust in their infant's capacity to fall asleep without their help. The quality of the evening ritual before placing the infant in the crib must also be addressed because it is important that one or both parents hold their infant in their arms or on their lap with undivided attention. It is important to close their day in mutual harmony and positive reciprocity, to jointly relax and experience proximity and emotional reassurance before parting for the night.

Psychotherapy

Undoubtedly, this process places high demands on the infant's capacity for regulation and learning and on the parents' emotional resources. This is why careful preparation of the intervention is key. It is important to include the father, to clarify together with him what the parents are ready to expect and demand from their infant and from themselves, and to encourage the father to actively participate in and support the intervention. The parents' feelings, fantasies, and associated memories that are elicited by the infant's nightly crying need to be addressed and clarified beforehand. The psychotherapy aims at understanding how the parents interpret their infant's crying and presumed inability to fall asleep on her own and what psychodynamically relevant themes make it difficult for them to convey unambiguous and unmistakable feelings of security and safety to their infant at bedtime (Barth, 1999; Papoušek, 2002). During these sessions, the parents may give voice to their own experiences with sleepless nights and nighttime feelings of abandonment. They may express fear that the intervention may traumatize their infant for the rest of her life; or they may attribute feelings of separation anxiety, loneliness, or despair to their infant's crying, thereby expressing their own needs for closeness and fear of separation or loss.

Prospects for Success of Sleep Interventions as a Component of Communication-Centered Parent–Infant Counseling and Psychotherapy

It is important during the preparatory stages of the intervention to weigh its demands on the infant and the parents against the chronic exhaustion and psychological strain long felt by the parents, including the negative effects on the parent–infant and partner relationships. The rapid success of the intervention reported in the literature (Sarimski, 1993; Wolke, 1999; see also chapter 9), as well as its positive repercussions on the infant's well-being during day and night, the parent–child-relationship, and family life in general speak in favor of the intervention.

The positive results have also been confirmed by our own clinical experience and study results (Barrera, 2003). The course of the sleep intervention per se as a central component of the overall communication-centered counseling and treatment (see chapter 12) was evaluated in a sample of 80 children between the ages of 6 and 28 months who were referred to the Munich Program because of an isolated sleep disorder or a sleep disorder combined with other syndromes. The infants' state of well-being during the day, sleep behavior, nighttime awakenings, and crying were documented and evaluated based on sleep logs filled out before the sleep intervention (5-night baseline) and over the course of the intervention (5 nights) and a global assessment of progress over a further 3 months. In comparison to the baseline nights, there was a highly significant improvement during the fourth and fifth night after the beginning of the intervention in terms of increases in the longest sleep phase, night sleep, and total sleep, as well as a decrease in the number and duration of awakenings. These improvements were also associated with a substantial decrease in parent-controlled sleep aids and a decrease in crying and fussing during the day. Contrary to our expectations, the objective stress caused by the intervention (as inferred by the extent of expected endless crying for many nights) generally proved minor and was limited to the first night in the majority of cases. Immediate improvement (in terms of falling asleep and sleeping through in their own crib without parental sleep aids) was observed in 79% of infants and remained stable for more than 3 months. Initial improvements were followed by a transient relapse in another 10% of infants, with subsequent improvement after another counseling session. The rate of failure, 8%, was low; another 13% experienced a relapse during the 3-month term after initial improvement.

Variants of the Intervention

If the parents decide against the intervention—perhaps because they feel less psychological strain or because previous attempts to apply the checking intervention on their own have failed—a stepwise variant may be considered, although in our experience it takes much longer to achieve the desired results (approximately 2 to 6 weeks). Using this procedure, the parents slowly reduce the level of attention and support given to their infant at night. For example, the mother reduces the continuous nightly nursing as a sleep aid to one or two feedings at night; she then switches from nursing to bottle-feeding, which the father may take charge of; the parents then switch from milk to water; they gradually reduce the amount of close physical contact; and they eventually leave the room before the infant is sound asleep.

We strongly advise against other strategies such as allowing the infant to cry herself to sleep as a way of extinguishing the behavior or prematurely rousing the infant from sleep before the expected spontaneous waking time. Medication should be considered only in extreme crisis situations, as it occasionally has paradoxical effects in young infants and may impede the development of age-appropriate sleep patterns if continued for too long.

Individual Adjustments to the Needs of Infant and Family

Within the context of communication-centered sleep counseling and psychotherapy, the selection and sequence of procedures is adjusted to the individual needs of infant and family. The following adjustments have proven to be the most successful:

- For isolated sleep disorders we recommend the approach described above, including developmental counseling, guidance in communication, and psychotherapeutic preparation of the sleep intervention after a positive bedtime ritual that strengthens the relationship. A more graduated approach may also be considered.

- If the sleep disorder is associated with a particularly difficult temperament, sensory integration therapy may provide additional support targeted to the infant's self-regulatory capacities.

- If the sleep disorder is associated with regulatory problems in relation to the attachment–exploration balance (e.g., excessive clinginess, extreme mother-centeredness, separation anxiety; see the case vignette at the beginning of the chapter), we recommend that treatment of the sleep disorder be postponed in favor of working first on proximity–distance regulation, attachment, and separation problems during the day. We use video-supported guidance in relation to communication and parent–infant psychotherapy as described in chapters 8 and 12. In addition to emphasizing positive reciprocity in the parent–infant relationship during play, video feedback may be used to practice regulating the balance between proximity and distance, setting boundaries, or dealing with short separations in every-day situations.

- If the sleep disorder is associated with marked attachment-related events such as the birth of a sibling, repeated separations, adjustment to day care, or disorders brought about by abrupt changes of primary caregivers or by emotional neglect, the attachment problems must be treated first with the help of communication guidance and parent–infant psychotherapy.

- If the sleep disorder is associated with general regulatory problems related to the autonomy–dependency balance (such as excessive temper tantrums and limit-setting difficulties), we recommend that the experience of positive reciprocity in the parent–child relationship during play be supported before limit-setting and handling of temper tantrums in typical everyday contexts are practiced with the help of video feedback.

- If "ghosts in the nursery" (Barth, 1999; Fraiberg, 1980) are evoked while the patient history is taken or in preparatory discussions of the sleep intervention, the focus should be on dispelling these ghosts from parent–infant communication with the help of psychodynamic parent–infant psychotherapy (see chapter 10). Such ghosts may be indicated, for instance, by distorted perceptions of the infant's crying, or projection onto the infant of intense feelings of abandonment or rage. If a parent suffers from unresolved psychodynamic conflict that extends well beyond the relationship with the infant, we encourage and mediate individual psychotherapy.

- If the sleep disorder occurs in the context of severe open or smoldering conflicts in the parents' relationship, both parents are invited for couples' counseling or referred to a couples' therapist.

REFERENCES

American Psychiatric Association. (2000). *Diagnostic and statistical manual of mental disorders* (4th ed., text revision). Washington, DC: Author.

Anders, T. F. (1978). Home recorded sleep in two and nine month old infants. *Journal of the American Academy of Child Psychiatry, 17,* 421–432.

Anders, T., Goodlin-Jones, B., & Sadeh, A. (2000). Sleep disorders. In C. H. Zeanah Jr. (Ed.), *Handbook of infant mental health* (2nd ed., pp. 326–338). New York: Guilford Press.

Anders, T. F., Halpern, L., & Hua, J. (1992). Sleeping through the night: A developmental perspective. *Pediatrics, 90,* 554–560.

Anders, T. F., & Keener, M. (1985). Developmental course of nighttime sleep-wake patterns in full-term and premature infants during the first year of life. I. *Sleep, 8,* 173–192.

Barrera, A. (2003). *Evaluation einer kommunikationszentrierten Behandlung von Schlafstörungen im Kleinkindalter.* Unpublished doctoral dissertation, Medical Faculty, Ludwig-Maximilians-University, Munich.

Barth, R. (1999). Schlafstörungen im Kontext der Autonomieentwicklung. *Monatsschrift für Kinderheilkunde, 147,* 488–492.

Barth, R. (2003). Schlafstörungen im Säuglings- und Kleinkindalter als Ausdruck einer ungelösten Trennungsproblematik. *Kinderpsychoanalyse, 11,* 41–57.

Basler, K., Largo, R. H., & Molinari, L. (1980). Die Entwicklung des Schlafverhaltens in den ersten Lebensjahren. *Helvetica Paediatrica Acta, 35,* 211–223.

Carey, W. B., & McDevitt, S. C. (1995). *Coping with children's temperament.* New York: Basic Books.

Cohen, J., & Cohen, P. (1983). *Applied multiple regression/correlation analysis for the behavioral sciences.* Hillsdale, NJ: Erlbaum.

Deutsche Gesellschaft für Kinder- und Jugendpsychiatrie und Psychotherapie, Bundesarbeitsgemeinschaft leitender Klinikärzte für Kinder- und Jugendpsychiatrie und Psychotherapie, Berufsverband der Ärzte für Kinder- und Jugendpsychiatrie und Psychotherapie (Eds.). (2000). *Leitlinien zu Diagnostik und Therapie von psychischen Störungen im Säuglings-, Kindes- und Jugendalter.* Köln, Germany: Deutscher Ärzte-Verlag.

Dilling, H., Mombour, W., & Schmidt, M. H. (1993). *Internationale Klassifikation psychischer Störungen. ICD-10 Kapitel V (F). Klinisch-diagnostische Leitlinien.* (2nd ed.). Bern, Switzerland: Verlag Hans Huber.

Emde, R. N., & Walker, S. (1976). Longitudinal study of infant sleep: Results of 14 subjects studied at monthly intervals. *Psychophysiology, 13,* 456–461.

Erikson, E. H. (1976). *Kindheit und Gesellschaft.* Stuttgart, Germany: Klett.

Fegert, J. M., Schulz, J., Bergmann, R., Tacke, U., Bergmann, K. E., & Wahn, U. (1997). Schlafverhalten in den ersten drei Lebensjahren. *Praxis der Kinderpsychologie und Kinderpsychiatrie, 46,* 69–91.

Ferber, R. (1987). Sleeplessness, night awakening, and night crying in the infant and toddler. *Pediatrics in Review, 9,* 69–82.

Fraiberg, S. (1980). *Clinical studies in infant mental health. The first year of life.* New York: Basic Books.

Gaylor, E. E., Goodlin-Jones, B. L., & Burnham, M. M. (1998, April). *Maternal perception of night awakenings and infant self-soothing behavior during first year of life*. Poster presented at the International Conference of Infant Studies, Atlanta, GA.

Jenkins, S., Owen, C., Bax, M., & Hart, H. (1980). Continuities of common problems in preschool children. *Journal of Child Psychology and Psychiatry, 25,* 75–89.

Kast-Zahn, A., & Morgenroth H. (1995). *Jedes Kind kann schlafen lernen*. Ratingen, Germany: Oberstebrink Verlag.

Kast-Zahn, A., & Morgenroth, H. (2002). *Every child can learn to sleep*. Ratingen, Germany: Oberstebrink.

Largo, R. (1996). *Babyjahre* (3rd ed.). München, Germany: Piper Verlag.

Largo, R. (2000). *Babyjahre* (4th ed.). München, Germany: Piper Verlag.

Laucht, M., Esser, G., & Schmidt, M. H. (1992). Verhaltensauffälligkeiten bei Säuglingen und Kleinkindern: Ein Beitrag zu einer Psychopathologie der frühen Kindheit. *Zeitschrift für Kinder- und Jugendpsychiatrie, 20,* 12–21.

Louis, J., Cannard, C., Bastuji, H., & Challamel, M.-J. (1997). Sleep ontogenesis revisited: A longitudinal 24-hour home polygraphic study on 15 normal infants during the first two years of life. *Sleep, 20,* 323–333

Minde, K., Popiel, K., Leos, N., Falkner, S., Parker, K., & Handley-Derry, M. (1993). The evaluation and treatment of sleep disturbances in young children. *Journal of Child Psychology and Psychiatry, 34,* 521–533.

Oelschlegel, P. (2003). Klinische Aspekte von Schlafstörungen im Säuglingsalter. Unpublished doctoral dissertation, Medical Faculty, Ludwig-Maximilians-University, Munich.

Papoušek, M. (1999). Regulationsstörungen der frühen Kindheit: Entstehungsbedingungen im Kontext der Eltern-Kind-Beziehungen. In R. Oerter, C. von Hagen, G. Röper, & G. Noam (Eds.), *Lehrbuch der klinischen Entwicklungspsychologie* (pp. 148–169). Weinheim, Germany: Beltz Verlag.

Papoušek, M. (2002). Störungen des Säuglingsalters. In G. Esser (Ed.), *Lehrbuch der klinischen Psychologie des Kindes- und Jugendalters* (pp. 80–101). Stuttgart, Germany: Thieme Verlag.

Papoušek, M., & von Hofacker, N. (1998). Persistent crying in early infancy: A non-trivial condition of risk for the developing mother-infant relationship. *Child: Care, Health and Development, 24,* 395–424.

Richman, N. (1981). A community survey of characteristics of one- to two-year-olds with sleep disruptions. *Journal of the American Academy of Child Psychiatry, 20,* 281–291.

Richman, N. (1985). A double-blind drug trial of treatment in young children with waking problems. *Journal of Child Psychology and Psychiatry, 26,* 591–598.

Richman, N., Douglas, J., Hunt, H., Landsdown, R., & Levere, R. (1985). Behavioural methods in the treatment of sleep disorders—a pilot study. *Journal of Child Psychology and Psychiatry, 26,* 581–590.

Sadeh, A., Lavie, P., Scher, A., Tirosh, E., & Epstein, R. (1991). Actigraphic home-monitoring of sleep-disturbed and control infants and young children: A new method for pediatric assessment of sleep-wake patterns. *Pediatrics, 87,* 494–499.

Sarimski, K. (1993). Aufrechterhaltung von Schlafstörungen im frühen Kindesalter: Entwicklungs-psychopathologisches Modell und Pilotstudie. *Praxis für Kinderpsychologie und Kinderpsychiatrie, 42,* 2–8.

Schieche, M. (2001). Störungen der Bindungs-Explorationsbalance und Möglichkeiten der Intervention. In G. J. Suess, H. Scheuerer-Englisch, & W. K. P. Pfeifer (Eds.), *Bindungstheorie und Familiendynamik. Anwendung der Bindungstheorie in Beratung und Therapie* (pp. 297–313). Giessen, Germany: Psychosozial-Verlag.

Scott, G., & Richards, M. (1990). Night waking in 1-year old children in England. *Child: Care, Health and Development, 16,* 283–302.

St. James-Roberts, I., Harris, G., & Messer, D. (1993). *Infant crying, feeding and sleeping. Development, problems and treatments.* New York: Harvester Wheatsheaf.

Vogt, A. (2003). *Schlafstörungen im Kleinkindalter.* Unpublished doctoral dissertation, Medical Faculty, Ludwig-Maximilians-University, Munich.

von Hofacker, N. (1998). Frühkindliche Störungen der Verhaltensregulation und der Eltern-Kind-Beziehungen. Zur differentiellen Diagnostik und Therapie psychosomatischer Probleme im Säuglingsalter. In K. von Klitzing (Ed.), *Psychotherapie in der frühen Kindheit* (pp. 50–71). Göttingen, Germany: Vandenhoeck & Ruprecht.

von Hofacker, N., & Papoušek, M. (1998). Disorders of excessive crying, feeding and sleeping: The Munich Interdisciplinary Research and Intervention Program. *Infant Mental Health Journal, 19,* 180–201.

von Hofacker, N., Riedesser, P., Berger, M., Jacubeit, T., Bindt, C., Papoušek, M., et al. (2000). Regulationsstörungen im Säuglingsalter. In Deutsche Gesellschaft für Kinder- und Jugendpsychiatrie und Psychotherapie, Bundesarbeitsgemeinschaft leitender Klinikärzte für Kinder- und Jugendpsychiatrie und Psychotherapie, Berufsverband der Ärzte für Kinder- und Jugendpsychiatrie und Psychotherapie (Eds.), *Leitlinien zu Diagnostik und Therapie von psychischen Störungen im Säuglings-, Kindes- und Jugendalter* (pp. 319–331). Köln, Germany: Deutscher Ärzte-Verlag.

Wolke, D. (1994). Häufigkeit und Persistenz von Ein- und Durchschlafproblemen im Vorschulalter: Ergebnisse einer prospektiven Untersuchung an einer repräsentativen Stichprobe in Bayern. *Praxis der Kinderpsychologie und Kinderpsychiatrie, 43,* 331–339.

Wolke, D. (1998). Probleme bei Neugeborenen und Kleinkindern. In J. Margraf (Ed.), *Lehrbuch der Verhaltenstherapie* (Vol. 2, pp. 463–480). Berlin: Springer Verlag.

Wolke, D. (1999). Interventionen bei Regulationsstörungen. In R. Oerter, C. von Hagen, G. Röper, & G. Noam (Eds.), *Lehrbuch der klinischen Entwicklungspsychologie* (pp.. 350–380). Weinheim, Germany: Beltz Verlag.

Wolke, D., Meyer, R., Ohrt, B., & Riegel, K. (1995). Co-morbidity of crying and feeding problems with sleeping problems in infancy: Concurrent and predictive associations. *Early Development and Parenting, 4,* 191–208.

ZERO TO THREE. (2005). *Diagnostic classification of mental health and developmental disorders of infancy and early childhood: Revised edition (DC:0-3R).* Washington, DC: ZERO TO THREE Press.

FEEDING DISORDERS AND FAILURE TO
THRIVE IN INFANTS AND TODDLERS

Nikolaus von Hofacker
Mechthild Papoušek
Harald Wurmser

CASE VIGNETTE

Case History

O take the nasty soup away!
I won't have any soup today:
I will not, will not eat my soup!
I will not eat it, no!

When little Mario was admitted with his mother to the parent–infant/toddler psychotherapy ward at Munich-Harlaching City Hospital at the age of 4 years, he had been acting out this classic scene from *Slovenly Peter* (Hoffmann, 1845) several times each day. Mario was born with cystic fibrosis. His development was punctuated by numerous infections—some of them quite serious—requiring a special diet and repeated hospitalizations. He failed to thrive and required supplementary tube feeding. His mother had fled from Kosovo, where she had been traumatized by the war and persecution, including the loss of several relatives. Mario's two older siblings had died in Kosovo with symptoms similar to his when they were toddlers. Mario's parents divorced while his mother was carrying him, and she was left to raise him alone. They arrived in Germany shortly after his birth. To date, their immigration status had not been resolved, and the question of repatriation to Kosovo recurred every 3 months.

Findings: Mario was an engaged little fellow who quickly opened up with his therapist, even though he seemed mildly depressed. Mario's mother was very concerned about his well-being. Her parenting style was somewhat permissive and she was inconsistent in setting limits. On the other hand, his constant limit testing quickly got on her nerves, causing her to become aggressive and tense. She showed clear signs of depressive exhaustion. She was in a permanent state of fear of being expelled from the country as a result of her unresolved immigration status. Should this happen, it would mean that Mario would no longer receive appropriate treatment, which, in his mother's eyes, would be tantamount to a death sentence. Her behavior in the feeding situation was also characterized by a certain permissiveness, at least as long as Mario was doing well physically. At those times, she tried to distract him with multiple toys to get him to eat. During phases in which Mario was not thriving and needed to increase his caloric intake, his mother felt tremendous pressure and would attempt to force-feed him, which led to conflicts between them. Mario reacted with panic and resistance whenever his mother tried to control the feeding situation.

Developmental origins: Because of Mario's underlying illness and his mother's own fears of losing him, which stemmed in part from her own traumatic biography, his mother had used a variety of strategies to motivate him to eat. When he was not suffering from an infection, Mario used his refusal to eat to manipulate his mother into offering an ever-increasing number of attractive distractions. When he was sick, however, feeding became associated with aversive experiences of being force-fed and of frequent tube feedings. He reacted with increasing resistance as soon as he recognized any attempts on the part of his mother to control the situation. Because of her own depressive exhaustion, she felt helpless and powerless and expected feeding to go badly. Mario's condition, his mother's distress, and dysfunctional interactional patterns all coincided in this feeding disorder. During Mario's periods of illness, there were clear signs of this being a posttraumatic feeding disorder.

Treatment: One goal of treatment was to correct the maladaptive interactional patterns in the feeding situation. The most important behaviors for the mother to modify involved avoiding distraction, a clear separation between play and feeding, and avoiding the use of pressure or force during feeding. The interaction-centered process was embedded in psychodynamic parent–child psychotherapy. Central themes involved processing emotionally charged events from the mother's history, particularly her grief over the death of Mario's siblings and her subsequent repeated traumatization. The question of her unresolved long-term immigration status was also a primary concern. From the perspective of attachment, it was clear that the mother would only be open to explore her own history effectively, including processing her traumatic past, if her basic needs for security and protection were guaranteed like those of her child. Ensuring the basic physical needs of her child was just as important to her, and this could best be accomplished by the interdisciplinary team of the parent–child psychotherapy ward. Once Mario's food intake had begun to increase as a result of therapy, and the feeding tube withdrawn, other themes began to emerge. At this point, the family dynamics of the parents' relationship, including the father's role in caring for the child, took on greater importance. However, the mother was only able to attend to these issues after her immediate fears and concerns about Mario had been successfully addressed. When after 4 weeks, Mario and his mother were discharged from the hospital, he was eating regularly, drinking high-calorie supplements, no longer needed to be tube fed, and even began to gain weight. After leaving the hospital, the mother decided to pursue psychotherapy on her own. A medical certificate verifying Mario's need for ongoing medical care in Germany qualified her for temporary legal resident status. As a result, she decided to visit the graves of her children in Kosovo in order to bid them farewell.

This case vignette illustrates the impact of early feeding disorders on the parent–child relationship:

Look at him, now the fourth day's come!
He scarce outweighs a sugar-plum;
He's like a little bit of thread;
And on the fifth day he was - dead. (Hoffmann, 1845).

The particular emotional impact derives from the complex intertwining of different factors: (a) at the somatic level, the infant must be adequately nourished so that he may thrive; (b) at the interactional level, the infant/toddler stubbornly refuses to eat, and conflicts between the parents and infant are increasingly exacerbated during feeding; (c) at the psychodynamic level, parental expectations, fantasies, and projections, particularly the fear that the infant might starve—in other words, the parents' own fears of separation and loss—all emerge. Each of these components plays a major role in early feeding disorders. It should be clear from the above why such disorders in early childhood so frequently lead to clinical manifestations, and why the emotional interplay between parents and infant is so heavily burdened, as are relationships between family members and the therapists charged with their care.

The present chapter is based on clinical experience and results from the Interdisciplinary Research and Intervention Program at the Munich Center for Social Pediatrics, as well as on clinical experience gained from the parent–infant/toddler psychotherapy ward at the Munich-Harlaching City Hospital.

CLINICAL SYNDROME

Symptoms and Signs in the Infant

The cardinal symptom is usually the persistent refusal to eat or a pronounced lack of desire to eat. Infants may initially react to the introduction of a variety of foods by looking disgusted, turning the head away, pushing the spoon aside, spitting out food or vomiting, or reacting with provocative choking or clenching of the jaws. Other infants look for or demand distraction in order to be fed. The infants are fed irregularly with short, but sometimes also overly long, intervals between feedings. The duration of the feeding and the amount of nutrition ingested fluctuate widely from feeding to feeding. Parents also report that it is difficult for them to recognize their infant's hunger signals, which is confirmed by clinical studies (Mathisen, Skuse, Wolke, & Reilly, 1989). The infant's eating behavior and abilities are often not age-appropriate (Wolke & Skuse, 1992).

Parents of infants with feeding disorders often report that they have additional regulatory problems such as chronic fussiness, excessive crying during early infancy, and sleep problems. As a result, such infants are often fed during sleep because that is when their state regulation becomes sufficiently stable and when they put up the least resistance.

Infants with a prior history of aversive orofacial experiences may react to all stimulation in the area of the face, mouth, and throat with anxious and even panicky resistance (posttraumatic feeding disorder; see "Traumatic Experiences in Infancy" below). In this particular manifestation, even the sight of a bottle or spoon may lead to vehement resistance. Such infants show a severe aversion to swallowing food that is in their mouth. This, too, leads to irregular feeding, the use of force in the feeding situation, and feeding during the transition to sleep or during sleep phases.

Feeding Interaction

The infant's problems become evident in everyday feeding interactions. In their attempts to get their infant or toddler to eat, the parents often intervene to control the situation, leaving little room for self-regulated feeding behavior on the part of the infant. While they react intensely to their infant's rejection of food (e.g., by force-feeding, constant demands, or offering distraction), their capacity to perceive their infant's more subtle positive signals (turning toward the spoon, etc.) becomes limited. Frequently, they fail to respond to signs of interest in food with reinforcing or rewarding signals. Negative affective signals and feedback from the parents begin to predominate in an ever-worsening vicious circle. The parents' prevailing mood becomes increasingly tense, depressive, and full of negative expectations at the beginning of each meal. Frequently, the parents no longer eat together with their infant and become completely fixated on his problematic eating behavior. As a result the parents no longer function as models of normal, relaxed, and unencumbered eating behavior.

Accordingly, the diagnostic experience and data from the Munich Program show the same triad of symptoms typical of other regulatory disorders: (a) infant problems of behavioral regulation (while feeding), (b) associated patterns of dysfunctional feeding interactions, and (c) parental adjustment disorders (chronic overstrain in one or both parents).

Feeding interactions generally mirror age-specific themes and developmental tasks of early childhood. As a result, feeding problems during the first 3 months are frequently associated with impaired regulation of behavioral states and modulation of arousal (Chatoor, Dickson, Schaefer, & Egan, 1985). Weaning during the second half-year of life and the transition to solid food represent new developmental tasks. On the level of parent–infant relationships, formation of attachment to the primary caregivers becomes a central developmental theme. During this phase, feeding disorders may manifest themselves as attachment problems in the form of separation difficulties between mother and infant (weaning), but also as limited reciprocity between the infant and his primary caregivers (Chatoor et al., 1985). Toward the end of the first year of life and beyond, the infant's increasing needs for autonomy and independence gain in importance as he attempts to participate actively in the feeding process. During this phase, feeding problems frequently manifest themselves as power struggles around control and autonomy in which parents either set unclear boundaries or place rigid limits on the infant's self-initiated participation in feeding. In return, the infant's rejection of food thereby reasserts his control over the parents (Papoušek, 2002).

DEFINITION

In clinical practice, a feeding disorder is generally said to exist when the parents seek help as a result of a subjectively perceived problem in feeding or nourishing their infant. However, because transient feeding problems occur frequently during infancy, a feeding disorder should only be diagnosed when it has persisted for more than 1 month.

The following criteria have been used as objective indications of a feeding disorder after the first 3 months of life (Ramsay, Gisel, & Boutry, 1993):

- Average duration of individual feedings ≥ 45 minutes and/or
- Interval between feedings < 2 hours.

A feeding disorder may also be associated with failure to thrive (FTT). The criteria for additional FTT (modified after O'Brien, Repp, Williams, & Christophersen, 1991; and Skuse, Wolke, & Reilly, 1992) are as follows:

- For infants with a birth weight at or above the 3rd percentile: weight loss to below the 3rd percentile and/or a change of more than two weight percentile graphs (e.g., from the 75th to below the 25th percentile) as a result of weight loss or stagnation over a period of at least 2 months (at less than 6 months of age) and at least 3 months (at more than 6 months of age);

- For infants with a birth weight below the 3rd percentile, any failure to gain weight that lasts for a month or longer should be viewed as FTT.

The distinction between mere organic and nonorganic thriving disorders has not been clinically substantiated and is therefore not clinically relevant. Children with so-called nonorganic failure to thrive (NOFT) show an increased incidence of mild organic problems such as oral-motor problems (Mathisen et al., 1989), and up to 40% of them have been found to be small/light for gestational age (SGA/LGA) at birth (Frank, 1985). Conversely, the so-called organic failure to thrive infants (OFT) show disturbed feeding interactions as often as do those with NOFT (Ramsay et al., 1993). Thus, to varying degrees, each subgroup of FTT has both somatic and interactional aspects, and the idea of diagnosing FTT as purely organic or nonorganic is obsolete.

EPIDEMIOLOGY, PREVALENCE, AND OUTCOMES

The data on prevalence rates are quite diverse because the diagnostic criteria and samples differ considerably. Transient feeding problems are frequent in infancy and are reported by every third parent of healthy infants during the first year of life (Forsyth & Canny, 1991; Martin & White, 1988). A study of a random sample using a feeding questionnaire found moderate feeding problems in 15% to 25% of infants during the first 2 years of life (Fergusson, Horwood, & Shannon, 1985). By contrast, severe persistent feeding problems of clinical significance were found in only 3% to 10% in random populations (Dahl & Sundelin, 1992; Lindberg, Bohlin, & Hagekull, 1991). In the population served by the Munich Program, depending on age, 35% to 50% of referred infants exhibited a feeding disorder during the first 2 years of life; during the third year, this figure rose to 60%.

FTT is less frequent than feeding disorders and is found in random populations in 3% to 4% (Drewett, Corbett, & Wright, 1999; Skuse, Wolke, Reilly, & Chan, 1995; Wilensky et al., 1996). In the client base of the Munich Program, FTT was present in 7%. According to a recent review (Wolke, 2000), sociodemographic factors such as social class, infant gender, parental age, number of siblings, and birth status, among others, have hardly any association with feeding disorders (Lindberg, 1994; Skuse et al., 1995; Wolke, 1999). Feeding problems are slightly more frequent in families from higher social status (Lindberg et al., 1991). On the other hand, a comprehensive epidemiological study showed that FTT occurs slightly more frequently among extremely disadvantaged (7.5%) and more well-to-do populations (8.2%), whereas they occur in only 3.8% of children from the middle classes between 18 and 30 months (Wright, Edwards, Halse, & Waterston, 1991).

The course of infant feeding disorders and FTT is partially dependent on whether the infant is able to thrive adequately over the long-term. FTT tends to be highly persistent, and over the long-term, an infant's physical, cognitive, and socioemotional development may be impaired in spite of intensive therapeutic intervention (Benoit, 2000; Drotar & Sturm, 1991; Wolke, 1994). Although inpatient admission to a pediatric clinic may significantly improve catch-up growth, the effect on psychosocial development is generally limited (Fryer, 1988). Both the birth weight of the infant and the height of the mother were shown to be significantly lower in infants and toddlers with FTT than in a control group, and these parameters combined with social status proved to be the best predictors of catch-up growth (Reif, Beler, Villa, & Spirer, 1995). In this study, which involved only medical interventions, cognitive development was impaired but improved depending on catch-up growth (Reif et al., 1995). In addition, children with FTT are at greater risk for child abuse, although this risk seems to be overestimated in the literature (Skuse et al., 1995).

Although feeding problems without FTT may also frequently persist up to the time of elementary school, they are apparently not associated with numerous other developmental problems (Dahl, Rydell, & Sundelin, 1994; Wolke, 2000). Infants with crying and feeding problems during the first 4 months of life are more frequently perceived by their parents as particularly vulnerable, particularly in cases where the parents have responded to the feeding problems by repeated changes in formula (Forsyth & Canny, 1991). Therefore, formula changes should be considered carefully and only implemented if there is a clear medical justification.

DEVELOPMENTAL ORIGINS

Infant Risk Factors

Somatic disease. Several organic factors may be directly involved in the development of feeding problems, including gastroesophageal reflux (Mathisen, Worrall, Masel, Wall, & Shepherd, 1999) and other disturbances involving the gastrointestinal tract, such as cystic fibrosis (Powers et al., 2002; Sanders, Turner, Wall, Waugh, & Tully, 1997). Other diseases may have an indirect effect, such as congenital heart disease (Clemente, Barnes, Shinebourne, & Stein, 2001) and renal and liver function disorders, among others. Overall, the incidence of organic factors is low, at least in epidemiological samples: Skuse et al. (1992) found etiologically relevant somatic factors in only 5.8% of infants and toddlers with FTT. In clinical samples, the incidence of organic factors as the sole cause for FTT was found to be 25% (Benoit, 2000). If the physical examination and laboratory tests (see "The Clinical and Differential Diagnostic Workup" below) show no obvious organic cause, the probability that such a cause will be found in subsequent, more extensive, examinations is low (Berwick, Levy, & Kleinermann, 1982; Skuse et al., 1992).

Regulatory disorders and constitutional factors. Infant regulatory problems, which are not necessarily confined to the feeding context, are more frequent than organic factors, and are found in the majority of feeding-disordered children already in early infancy. This is demonstrated by data from a sample of feeding-disordered infants and toddlers seen at the Munich Program (n = 283, age: 1 to 39 months). With a mean age at the first visit of more than 10 months (10.9 ± 7.5 months), over four-fifths of the infant's lifetime (8.9 ± 6.5 months) had been affected by regulatory problems in one or more domains.

Isolated feeding disorders were the exception in only 9% of the cases. Depending on age at first visit, the feeding disorder was associated with other age-specific developmental problems (see chapter 3). At all age levels, 71% to 93% simultaneously exhibited a disorder of circadian sleep–wake organization or night-waking disorder. Early excessive crying during the first 3 months co-occurred in 95%, and during the second 3 months, dysphoric fussiness was seen in 34%. During the second half-year, excessive clinginess was seen in 12% to 29% of infants. Excessive defiance was found in 46% of infants during the second year of life, and in up to 73% during the third year. After the end of the second year of life, oppositional-aggressive behavior increased from 11% to 40%.

The infant's behavior problems are closely associated with temperamental dimensions such as fussiness/difficulty, unpredictability, unadaptability, irritability, inconsolability, or stubbornness, as assessed in the Munich Program using the Infant Characteristics Questionnaire (ICQ; Bates, Freeland, & Lounsbury, 1979). During the first year of life, 56% of all feeding-disordered infants had extreme scores on the Fussy-Difficult scale; that is, more than two standard deviations above the mean of a normal sample. During the second year of life, 28% had similar extreme scores on the Fussy-Difficult scale and 14% on the Unadaptability scale. Such constitutional behavioral dispositions may make the regulation of nutritional intake considerably more difficult, particularly in response to new and changing environmental conditions, to new modes of feeding, to new consistencies of food, and to new tastes.

An array of infant behavioral characteristics are cited in the literature. For example, infants/toddlers with feeding disorders in the context of autonomy and dependency conflicts (infantile anorexia) have been described as particularly defiant, willful, and frequently forceful or provocative in the expression of their desires (Chatoor, Egan, Getson, Menvielle, & O'Donnell, 1988). Infants with FTT have been found to be more irritable, demanding, and less open socially (Wilensky et al., 1996; Wolke, Skuse, & Mathisen, 1990), as well as exhibiting more negative emotional signals. They have also been found to be SGA/LGA at birth and significantly more likely to show cognitive and motor developmental problems.

Neuromotor and oral-motor/sensory problems. The data from the Munich Program show that even primarily healthy feeding-disordered infants and toddlers exhibit a surprisingly high rate of mild transient neurological problems (43%). This is consistent with the findings of other authors who have reported increased incidences of mild neuromotor problems, particularly in infants with FTT (Goldson, 1989; Mathisen et al., 1989; Ramsay et al., 1993).

In the context of feeding disorders, oral-motor and sensory problems are now the focus of increased attention. According to Mathisen et al. (1989) these problems were found in 18% of feeding-disordered infants in a random sample, which was double the frequency of that in a comparison group. They most often take the form of hypotonia of the lips and masticatory muscles, which are often associated with hypersensitivity in the orofacial region and sensory aversion to touch by foods with certain textures, and with persistent tongue protrusion and other functional disorders of the tongue (e.g., inadequate lateralization of food by the tongue). They may also be evident as insufficient nonpersistent sucking, intolerance of age-appropriate food, and swallowing problems (Gisel, Birnbaum, & Schwartz, 2001; Mathisen et al., 1989; Ramsay et al., 1993).

Traumatic experiences in infancy. Traumatic learning experiences in infancy are an independent factor in the etiology of early feeding problems. As a result, any stimulation in the orofacial and pharyngeal region is potentially threatening because it is associated with unpleasant stimulation. This is often found in cases with congenital malformation of the oropharyngeal and gastrointestinal tract (e.g., esophageal atresia), in particular after surgical correction or after bouginage of a constricted esophagus. It is also prevalent in preterm or term infants who experienced long-term treatment in pediatric intensive care requiring intubation, suctioning, or artificial feeding via nasogastric tube. Infants who have a long history of vomiting as a result of severe gastroesophageal reflux may also develop anxiety-driven food refusal (Chatoor, Ganiban, Harrison, & Hirsch, 2001). Finally, force-feeding with firm holding, forcibly opening the infant's mouth, or feeding while the infant is crying may by itself turn feeding into a potentially threatening experience. The rejection of food develops in these children along the lines of classical conditioning; that is, the basically pleasant experience of feeding when hungry is associated with an adverse stimulus that triggers resistance to any stimulation in the orofacial area. These kinds of feeding problems are also called posttraumatic feeding disorders (Chatoor, Conley, & Dickson, 1988) because they are causally related to prior experiences with an obvious traumatic quality.

Developmental Origins: Parental and Family Risk Factors

The findings of the Munich Program point to an interplay between the infant's developmental risks described above and somatic and psychosocial risk factors affecting the parents. In some cases these factors extend back into pregnancy and may impair both the intuitive competencies of the parents during feeding as well as the infant's self-regulatory competencies (see Tables 7.1 and 7.2).

Somatic risk factors during pregnancy and the postpartum phase. Mothers of feeding-disordered infants and toddlers in the Munich sample experienced a range of somatic risk factors during their pregnancies, among which the comparatively high rate of premature labor (25%) with the pending risk of premature birth, and the rate of previous miscarriages (30%) are noteworthy. Such prior experiences in tandem with infant feeding difficulties may all too easily evoke parents' anxieties regarding separation and loss. In addition, 8% of mothers and/or infants experienced life-threatening events around delivery, 18% experienced postnatal separation due to immediate transferral of the neonate to a pediatric hospital, and 12% of mothers had experienced traumatic losses in their own prior histories.

Psychological and psychosocial risk factors during pregnancy and the postpartum phase. In his book *The Motherhood Constellation*, Daniel Stern (1995) illuminated the significance of maternal worries and fears about her infant during the postpartum period. Stern's term *motherhood constellation* describes the fundamental organizing principle of the maternal psyche with regard to her early relationship with her infant(s). He identified four themes that are central for mothers:

- The theme of life and growth
- The theme of primary relatedness
- The theme of the socially supportive matrix
- The theme of the reorganization of identity

Questions such as "Will I be able to feed my baby and keep him alive?", "Will I be able to build a relationship with him, even when he rejects my milk or nourishment?", and "Who will help me if I am unable to cope with my baby?" all interact intimately with maternal fears when the infant rejects nourishment.

Data from the Munich Program demonstrate, however, that similar maternal anxieties are often already part of a spectrum of prenatal psychosocial stressors (see Table 7.2). Almost two thirds of mothers (61%) of feeding-disordered infants/toddlers already suffered from excessive anxiety (28%), psychosocial stress (22%), or couples' conflicts (22%) during pregnancy. After birth, these distressing conditions are aggravated as they interact with the infant's feeding problems. Around the time of the first visit, 54% of parents reported marital conflicts, 43% conflicts with their family of origin, 43% reported

Table 7.1. Somatic Risk Factors for Feeding Disorders.

Somatic Risk Factors	Frequency (%)
Prenatal ≥ 1 risk factor	**77.9**
Hyperemesis	20.6
Previous miscarriages	29.8
Infertility treatment	9.9
Premature labor	25.2
Cerclage	2.1
Gestosis	3.2
Nicotine abuse	13.1
Perinatal ≥ 1 risk factor	**43.1**
Cesarean section	29.0
Vacuum/forceps	9.5
Severe birth complications (infant)	5.7
Severe birth complications (mother)	2.1
LGA/SGA (weight/height below third percentile)	7.4
Amniotic infection syndrome	6.4
Postnatal ≥ 1 risk factor	**86.8**
Familial atopic disease	55.2
Infant atopic disease	15.7
Recurrent infections	28.3
Hospitalization	21.6
Neurological problems	42.6
Developmental disorders	5.3

Note. LGA = large for gestational age; SGA = small for gestational age.
Unpublished data from the Munich Program; *n* = 283; age 1 to 39 months (multiple mentions possible).

distressing childhood experiences, and 33% inadequate social support and social isolation. A high incidence of psychological disturbances was evident among 61.5% of the mothers, including depressive syndromes (31%); neurotic, stress-related, and somatoform disorders (31%); and personality disorders (11%). About 17% of mothers reported some form of eating disorders during their own childhood or adolescence; 9% currently suffered from a manifest eating disorder.

Psychosocial family stress factors also may have a negative impact on the parent–infant relationship. For example, assessment by the clinicians in charge on the nine-step Parent-Infant Relationship Global Assessment Scale (PIR-GAS; ZERO TO THREE, 1994) showed that the relationship was moderately distressed in 36% of cases. It was considerably distressed and disturbed in 39% and disordered in 19%

Table 7.2. Psychosocial Risk Factors for Feeding Disorders.

Psychosocial Risk Factors		Frequency (%)
Prenatal	≥ 1 risk factor	**61.0**
Abnormal stress		22.3
Abnormal anxieties		28.0
Couples' conflicts		21.6
Depression		7.8
Unwanted pregnancy		13.1
Perinatal	≥ 1 risk factor	**25.8**
Subjective "traumatic" delivery		8.8
Early separation		18.0
Postpartum	≥ 1 risk factor	**85.3**
Couples' conflicts		54.4
Conflicts with families of origin		42.7
Distressing childhood experiences		42.7
"Broken home" biography		8.1
Socioeconomic risks		6.4
Social isolation		33.2
Role conflicts		12.0
Traumatic loss		12.0
Maternal psychological disturbances	≥ 1 disturbance	**61.5**
Postpartum depression/psychosis		30.7
Personality disorder		10.6
Neurotic relational disorder		31.1
Eating disorder, manifest		8.8
Eating disorder during childhood or adolescence		17.0

Note. Unpublished data from the Munich Program; n = 283; age 1 to 39 months (multiple mentions possible).

(von Hofacker & Papoušek, 1998). Only 5% of mother–infant relationships were assessed as sufficiently well-adapted. In the case of sleep-disordered infants, the quality of the mother–infant relationship was significantly more likely to be compromised when associated with a feeding disorder ($n = 228$) than when co-occurring with other regulatory problems or with no other problem ($n = 391$), $t(226.3) = -9.1, p \leq .001$.

Other clinical studies have also described an array of different parental, and especially maternal, psychological stress factors in connection with feeding disorders and FTT. For example, mothers of feeding-disordered infants and toddlers are more likely to have a history of separation and loss, and the mothers themselves are often relatively inexperienced in handling and caring for an infant (Dunitz & Scheer, 1991).

Mothers of infants with FTT in both clinical and nonclinical samples are significantly more likely to have a history of multiple risk factors and trauma, less social support, and more current stressors. They more frequently have negative perceptions of their infant and are more likely to have an insecure attachment representation, based on the Adult Attachment Interview. Several studies have found an increased incidence of mental illnesses such as depression, anxiety disorders, and personality disorders among these mothers, although these findings are not consistent (for a review, see Benoit, 2000). The notion that FTT is necessarily an indication of maternal neglect is lacking clear empirical evidence given the contradictory findings in the literature. In fact, Wolke (1996) described this notion as a myth.

Maternal eating disorders. The association of ongoing or prior maternal eating problems with infant feeding disorders has only recently been the subject of intensive research. One finding from a retrospective study by Conti, Abraham, and Taylor (1998) is notable: Thirty-two percent of mothers of small-for-date term infants reported clear signs of a clinically manifest eating disorder within the 3 months prior to pregnancy. In fact, infants of eating-disordered mothers have a higher incidence of low birth weight (Stein, Murray, Cooper, & Fairburn, 1996) and exhibit more nursing problems during the first year of life (Agras, Hammer, & McNicholas, 1999). Seventeen percent of infants of formerly anorectic mothers fail to thrive during the first year of life (Brinch, Isager, & Tolstrup, 1988). Problems and impairment in parental behavior and parental attitudes toward the infant are seen more frequently in eating-disordered mothers (Evans & LeGrange, 1995; Franzen & Gerlinghoff, 1997; Woodside, Shekter-Wolfson, Brandes, & Lackstrom, 1993), especially in the context of feeding interactions (Stein, Woolley, Cooper, & Fairburn, 1994; Stein, Woolley, & McPherson, 1999). These interactions are characterized by more frequent conflicts, less positive feedback from the mother, and more controlling–intrusive behavior that interferes with the infant's autonomy. The degree of conflict in the feeding situation has been shown to be the strongest predictor of the actual weight of the infant and explains 20% of the variance in infant weight (Stein et al., 1994, 1999). Eating-disordered mothers are more likely to experience their infant's eating behavior as problematic as he develops (Evans & LeGrange, 1995). Even mothers who do not have a clinical eating disorder exhibit dissatisfaction with their appearance, internalize an exaggeratedly slim ideal body image, or are obsessed with dieting (information gathered immediately after birth), along with a range of other parental markers that are important predictors of feeding and eating problems during the first 5 years of life (Stice, Agras & Hammer, 1999). Because the eating behavior of the parents represents an important model for the infant and toddler, these connections between maternal eating disorders, overt maternal eating behavior, and infant feeding problems must be taken seriously as potential developmental risks.

Data from the Munich Program support these findings: Among mothers with a history of eating disorders, distressed relationships were significantly more frequently shifted in the direction of disordered relationships (68% considerably distressed or disturbed, 32% disordered; see Figure 7.1) than in mothers without a history of eating disorders (78% distressed/disturbed, 16% disordered), $X^2(2, N = 281) = 10.07$, $p \leq .01$. Whereas 7% of the latter showed well-adapted mother–infant relationships, this was true of none of the mothers with a history of eating problems.

Distressing Factors in Parent–Infant Interactions and Relationships

Dysfunctional feeding interactions. In terms of the triad of symptoms described in the beginning of this chapter, infant and parental risk factors do not exert their influence in isolation but are evident in the interplay between the mother and infant during the actual feeding interactions. An array of dysfunctional infant and parent characteristics in the feeding situation have been described in the literature (Benoit, 2000; Boddy & Skuse, 1994; Bodeewes, 2003; Chatoor, Egan, et al., 1988; Chatoor, Getson, et al., 1997; Lindberg, Bohlin, Hagekull, & Palmérus, 1996; Papoušek, 2002; Sanders, Patel, Le Grice, & Shepherd, 1993; Sanders, Turner, Wall, Waugh, & Tully, 1997; Wolke et al., 1990). For example, the mothers of feeding-disordered infants more often use negative comments or intrusive

Figure 7.1. Effects of Maternal Eating Disorders on the Mother-Infant Relationship.

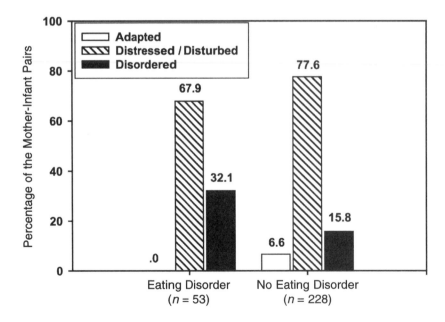

Note. Quality of mother-infant relationship (PIR-GAS) in infants with feeding disorders, dependent on the presence of an earlier or manifest eating disorder in the mother.

methods of control. Their behavior is less consistent, and they have a harder time picking up on their infant's signals. Not infrequently, such behavior patterns conceal deep-seated conflict constellations or ambivalences that are activated by the infant's food rejection. Accordingly, the literature draws attention to tension and dyadic conflicts in the feeding situation, and to bargaining during feeding interactions. Similar parenting characteristics are to be found in the feeding situations involving infants with FTT (Boddy & Skuse, 1994; Drotar, Eckerle, Satola, Pallotta, & Wyatt, 1990). However, none of the studies has demonstrated an unequivocal relationship between infant failure to thrive and specific problematic parental behaviors, neglect, parental psychopathology, and/or conflicted intrafamilial relational patterns. This lack of findings may be attributable to significant methodological problems and the lack of comparability among the studies. Insufficient longitudinal data that might shed light on the interplay among various factors may also be responsible (Benoit, 2000).

Clinically, we frequently see a vicious circle of escalating dysfunctional interactions: When an irritable or organically predisposed infant (e.g., one with a difficult temperament, low birth weight, primary organic disease) reacts to a spoonful of solid food with resistance or even panic (posttraumatic feeding disorder) instead of with curiosity and interest, many parents misunderstand this as a signal that their infant simply doesn't like the food that they have offered. As a consequence, some parents change food frequently out of concern that their infant may not thrive. Occasionally they even give up completely on age-appropriate food. If they fear the loss of their infant because of their own personal histories, some parents will relent while others will try to force-feed, which only exacerbates the problem. The parents increasingly lose self-confidence and their behavior toward their infant becomes increasingly inconsistent, especially when their intuitive capacities are already restricted. Although attempts to distract the infant may work initially, the infant quickly learns that refusal to eat actually makes mealtimes more interesting. In this way, distractions or offering a favorite food actually sustain and reinforce the infant's refusal to eat. The infant's refusal to eat, in combination with the parents' dysfunctional feeding behavior, creates a negatively reinforcing feedback loop. What the parents fail to grasp is that sticking with a particular new food in a careful and persistent manner without pressure would help the infant get used to its taste and consistency, which eventually would lead to acceptance.

It is noteworthy in this respect that the age between 4 and 8 months is a sensitive phase in which the infant develops a particular readiness and curiosity to explore and accept new food consistencies and tastes. They often become less accepting of these changes as they get older (Wolke, 1994). In addition, prolonged feeding of food that is not age-appropriate has adverse effects on oral-motor development, articulation, and speech development, and may damage teeth and gums (Lewis, 1982; O'Brien et al., 1991).

Feeding disorders, FTT, and attachment disorders. The numerous studies of the role of infant attachment in the development of feeding disorders and FTT in infancy may be summarized as follows:

1. Significantly increased rates of insecure disorganized attachment patterns are found in infants with nonorganic FTT from socially disadvantaged families as well as in socially heterogeneous groups (Brinich, Drotar, & Brinich, 1989; Crittenden, 1987; Valenzuela, 1990; Ward, Lee, & Lipper, 2000). If feeding-disordered infants above the age of 1 year and those without FTT are included, the rates of insecure attachment patterns are no longer elevated, although a moderate correlation between the severity of the feeding disorder and the attachment security has been reported (Chatoor, Ganiban, Colin, Plummer, & Harmon, 1998).

2. Mothers of FTT infants also more often exhibit insecure attachment representations (Adult Attachment Interview), particularly unresolved grief reactions (Benoit, Zeanah, & Barton, 1989; Coolbear & Benoit, 1999; Ward et al., 2000).

3. On the basis of the Working Model of the Child Interview (WMCI; Zeanah, Benoit, & Barton, 1993), parents of FFT infants are significantly more likely to exhibit inadequately balanced mental representations of their relationship to their infant (Coolbear & Benoit, 1999).

4. Brisch (2002) conceived of feeding problems as a potential manifestation of an attachment disorder. In his classification of attachment disorders he proposed a new category, *Attachment disorder with psychosomatic symptoms, Type VIIb*, which also includes infants and toddlers with feeding problems. However, this category lacks specificity, and detailed connections between attachment disorders and feeding disorders have yet to be studied.

CLASSIFICATION

Numerous attempts have been made to classify infant feeding disorders according to different criteria, but these efforts have often yielded limited clinical benefit (Burklow, Phelps, Schultz, McConnell, & Rudolph, 1998; Gisel & Alphonce, 1995; Wittenberg, 1990). Chatoor and colleagues (Chatoor, 2002; Chatoor, Dickson, et al., 1985) have vividly described the age-specific manifestations of early childhood feeding and eating disorders and have developed a classification scheme that complements these age-specific manifestations (*Feeding disorder of state regulation, Feeding disorder of caregiver-infant reciprocity,* and *Infantile anorexia*) with further categories, independent of age (*Sensory food aversion, Feeding disorder associated with concurrent medical condition,* and *Feeding disorder associated with insults to the gastrointestinal tract*). The last category in this classification system is identical with *Posttraumatic feeding disorder.* The combination of categories, some of which are specific to certain developmental stages, whereas others apply to all age groups, is somewhat problematic and makes the classifications somewhat inconsistent. Nevertheless, this system is of good clinical use. The classification system is integrated in the new revised version of the *Diagnostic Classification of Mental Health and Developmental Disorders of Infancy and Early Childhood* (DC:0–3R; ZERO TO THREE, 2005).

THE CLINICAL AND DIFFERENTIAL DIAGNOSTIC WORKUP

An integrated, interdisciplinary process is crucial from the very beginning to the diagnosis of feeding disorders in infancy. Once the somatic causes of feeding disorders and FTT have been ruled out, as is the common practice in pediatric services, and the staff has discussed with the parents the possibility of interactional and relational problems, the message that is often conveyed to the parents is the utter helplessness of the medical team in charge (*hierarchical, successive diagnostic workup*). The failure to make a clear diagnosis absolves the medical professionals of responsibility, which is then transferred to the next level of mental health specialists (psychologist, specialist in psychosomatic medicine, behavioral pediatrician, psychotherapist and psychiatrist, pediatric social worker, etc.). At this point, many parents come to feel that blame is being placed on them. Naturally, they reject this notion and seek out the services of another physician in the hope that he or she may perhaps uncover a somatic cause. This situation will not change until the somatic and psychosocial diagnostic workup is genuinely integrated from the beginning and runs in parallel at all levels (*parallel, simultaneous diagnostic workup*). Only then

Table 7.3. Specific Diagnostic Workup and Extended Diagnostic Measures for Feeding Disorders.

Specific diagnostic workup for feeding disorders

Nursing/feeding history, nutritional history, and growth history
  –Initial assessment of the impact of organic and interactional factors using a parent feeding questionnaire (von Hofacker, Eder, & Sobanski, 2002)

Feeding protocols
  –Infant behavior during feeding
  –Type, quantity, and frequency of nutrition offered

Growth measures (weight, height, head circumference)

(Video-supported) observation of infant/parent behavior and analysis of the feeding interaction (see Table 7.4)

(Video-supported) observation of infant/parent behavior and analysis of other interactive contexts (see Table 7.4)

Diagnostic workup of the parent–infant relationship
  –Semistructured interviews such as the WMCI

Feeding-specific parental stressors, attribution of meaning
  –Assessment of attribution of meaning by the parents and parental fantasies, fears, and expectations with regard to the feeding disorder
  –Assessment of the parents' psychological condition and psychosocial stressors, and, if needed, assessment and diagnostic workup of psychiatric disturbances: particularly in relation to maternal anxiety disorders, depressive syndromes, personality disorders, eating disorders
  –Prior experience of separation and loss

Extended diagnostic measures

Somatic laboratory and medical-technical procedures
  –Particularly in cases of FTT

Collecting information on the family's eating habits
  –Collecting information on the family's eating habits and its peculiarities
  –Collecting information on and diagnosis of earlier or manifest eating disorders in the mother (e.g., EDI [Garner et al., 1983]; EAT-26 [Garner et al., 1982])

Biographical history of each parent
  –In case of relevant unresolved problems in a parent's history

Marital relationship and family diagnostics
  –Assessment of family dynamics
  –Assessment of the significance and function of infant feeding problems in the context of the family relationships as well as changes brought about by them

---

Note. WMCI = Working Model of the Child Interview (Zeanah, Benoit, & Barton, 1993); FTT = failure to thrive; EDI = Eating Disorder Inventory; EAT-26 = Eating Attitudes Test.

will the parents believe that all etiologically significant factors—whether somatic, psychosocial, interactional, or relational—will be duly considered in the diagnosis.

The interdisciplinary diagnostic process involves collecting information and findings on all relevant aspects and domains (listed in Table 7.3) regarding the diagnostic triad: the infant, his parents and family, and parent–infant interactions. It is particularly important to observe the behavior of parents and infant during feeding interactions, over and above any co-occurring organic factors that require further diagnostic workup (see Table 7.4). Other interactional contexts, particularly a play situation, should also be observed in order to assess to what extent dysregulated interactions are confined to the feeding

Table 7.4. (Video-Supported) Behavioral Observation.

Feeding interaction at regular mealtime

Infant behavior:
  –Drinking/eating skills
  –Signals of hunger and satiation
  –Affective tone of child
  –Functional versus dysfunctional infant eating patterns (i.e., child's interest in nutritional intake/hunger versus refusal with demand for distraction, provocation, or anxious behavior

Parent feeding behavior:
  –Affective tone
  –Responsiveness to infant signals of hunger and satiation
  –Positive and negative feedback signals to the infant
  –Consistency of verbal and nonverbal communication patterns
  –Intrusive behavior in the feeding situation; degree of control of versus support for the infant's autonomy
  –Motivational support
  –Structuring of the feeding situation; limit setting
  –Modeling function

Parent–infant interaction and communication:
  –Functional or dysfunctional parent–infant interactions regarding infant-regulated appropriate nutritional intake, positive reciprocity, and a relaxed relationship in the feeding context
  –Extent of conflict and tension in the feeding interaction
  –Balance between feeding-related and non-feeding-related communication patterns

Interactions in other contexts

Mutual play

Further contexts depending on the presence of other regulatory problems
  –For example, setting limits

---

context or affect other contexts as well. A detailed assessment of parent–infant communication and qualitative aspects of the parent–infant relationship (e.g., using the WMCI) is of central importance in feeding disorders in particular. The goal is to determine the extent to which the feeding disorder is associated with immediate distress in the relationship or is already part of a manifest disorder in the parent–infant relationship.

A basic organic diagnostic workup, which includes laboratory tests (blood count, electrolytes, total protein, serum iron level, renal and liver function values, urine status) along with infant height, weight, and head circumference makes sense in all cases of FTT. However, before carrying out any extended diagnostic procedure, it is important to consider how irritating it may be for the infant and whether there is a clear medical justification for doing so. In any case, one should aim to keep the diagnostic workup as noninvasive as possible (Dunitz-Scheer et al., 2001).

TREATMENT

The integrative communication- and relationship-focused psychotherapeutic approach described in chapter 12 has become well established at the parent–infant/toddler psychotherapy ward at Munich-Harlaching City Hospital as well. It includes interventions that are targeted at changing dysfunctional behavioral and interactional patterns, as well as psychodynamically and family-oriented interventions. Although behavior modification alone may bring about quick changes, the drawback is that deeper psychodynamic and familial aspects that are often crucial in the development of feeding disorders are not adequately taken into account. Conversely, psychodynamic therapy alone neglects the tremendous effects that behavior modification can have on parental representations and psychodynamics and on the dynamics within the couple and the family as a whole.

Well-Established Communication- and Relationship-Focused Aspects of Intervention

Supportive and respectful therapeutic relationship. The insecurity and guilt often felt by parents of infants with feeding or eating problems is often great after their long and unsuccessful odyssey through a myriad of highly specialized care facilities. This makes it all the more important to provide an empathetic and respectful setting in which their intuitive parental competencies are recognized, valued, and appreciated, and in which their feelings of powerlessness and helplessness as well as their impulses to neglect or abuse their infant may be expressed without being blamed.

Adequate appreciation of physical aspects. Feeding problems always have a concrete physical aspect, namely, the parents' worries about whether their infant will thrive, regardless of whether these worries are founded or not. If these vital physical aspects (e.g., organic cofactors) are not adequately addressed in treatment (first theme of the motherhood constellation), the parents may come to believe that everything is being "psychologized," and that they are the only ones worried about their child's physical well-being. This is particularly true if the infant has a chronic illness. This state of affairs represents a roadblock in the parents' ability to trust, which is a major precondition for their allowing themselves to enter into a possibly stressful psychotherapeutic process.

Developmental counseling. Parents of infants with feeding problems are initially informed and advised about the normal development of eating behavior during the first year of life and the qualities and quantities of age-appropriate nutrition, as well as about the significance of hunger and satiation in the regulation of nutritional intake and how to recognize and distinguish hunger signals and satiation signals. We are often astonished at the distorted notions that parents have because of the abundance of so-called experts expounding in the media on issues of nutrition and thriving. It is crucial to take into account the particular developmental and psychological themes that are relevant to the infant at the moment, and how they are related to the feeding problem (e.g., autonomy needs vs. dependency). In developmental counseling, the introduction and age-appropriate adjustment of the feeding rules cited in Table 7.5 play a central role. The goal is to enable the infant to become aware of his own hunger and satiation signals and to use these signals for self-controlled regulation of nutritional intake.

Video-supported treatment of dysfunctional feeding interactions. Treatment of maladaptive and dysfunctional feeding patterns is central to interaction- and relationship-focused psychotherapy. Treatment is greatly supported by the use of video feedback from videorecorded feeding interactions. However, the use of this tool should be carefully implemented. In order to strengthen the parents' resources and intuitive competence, parents should first be shown and allowed to reexperience a successful feeding episode, regardless of how short it may be. This episode can then be used together with the parents to uncover what has helped to make this particular moment in the feeding situation enjoyable and free of conflict. In further steps, dysfunctional interactions can be viewed and a discussion may ensue as to why a particular interaction derailed and how it differed from the successful one. Moreover, progress in the therapy can be documented and used as feedback for the parents based on actual examples of interactions.

Interventions in posttraumatic feeding disorder and techniques of tube withdrawal in infants after long-term tube feeding. The procedure in cases of posttraumatic feeding disorders follows special rules, cited in Table 7.5, that take into account the traumatic etiology of the disorder. The effectiveness and practicability of alternate procedures such as flooding (the repeated overriding of the infant's resistance threshold by, for example, repeatedly touching his lips with a spoon) has not been adequately evaluated (Benoit & Coolbear, 1998; Benoit, Green, & Arts-Rodas, 1997).

It is possible to successfully wean infants from long-term tube feeding as part of a highly structured, multimodal therapeutic model (Chatoor, Ganiban, et al., 2001; Dunitz-Scheer et al., 2001). This is very important because long-term tube feeding may lead to oral-motor and sensory problems such as hypotonic lips and impaired mastication, immature sucking and swallowing coordination, and sensory hypersensitivity in the mouth area (Kamen, 1990; Schauster & Dwyer, 1996; Simpson, Schanler, & Lau, 2002).

Addressing other interactional contexts. Feeding disorders usually predominate over the day, leaving little time for dialogue and mutual play. The therapeutic support of mutual play creates a positive counterpart to stressful feeding interactions, and is therefore an effective approach to promoting attachment and healthy relationships (see chapter 12).

Concomitant regulation disorders in other interactional and regulatory contexts (such as sleep disorders) should be integrated into the treatment plan.

Addressing parental representations and the relational history with the child. Psychodynamically oriented psychotherapy is an indispensable supplement to interaction-centered therapy, particularly where feeding and FTT are at issue. This form of psychotherapy allows the parents to process their perceptions, interpretations, and affective experience of the feeding situation, and their fears around the infant's thriving and survival, and to include more deep-seated conflict constellations. This should especially be the case when parents are having trouble implementing the feeding rules, which can be seen as a hint of more deeply rooted parental defense (see chapter 11).

Video feedback in particular may be used constructively in this regard to help the parents reflect on the feelings, fantasies, beliefs, and expectations that are triggered by certain interactional episodes, particularly those involving conflict. This approach can be superior to traditional individual psychotherapy in

Table 7.5. Feeding Rules That Promote Age-Appropriate Nutritional Intake.

Feeding rules

–The parent determines when, how often, and what the infant is fed (age-appropriate, balanced diet); the infant determines how much he wants to eat

–Regular feedings with intervals between mealtimes

–Clear separation between mealtime and play time

–Support of the infant's active self-regulation by responding to his hunger and satiation signals

–No force-feeding; avoidance of distraction, pressure, or force

–Support and reinforcement of age-appropriate increasingly independent eating behavior

–Ignoring/setting limits for inappropriate eating behavior

Special rules for posttraumatic feeding disorders

–Avoidance of any aversive orofacial stimuli or unpleasant feeding-related experiences; no pressure or force-feeding

–Systematic desensitization by frequent offering of small quantities of food (every 1–2 hours in a quiet, relaxed, low-stimulus setting until a first sign of anxious reaction)

–Limiting feeding attempts to 10–15 minutes in order to minimize potentially aversive experience of frustrating feedings

–As a result, graduated reduction of the infant's resistance and graduated acceptance of food

–Concomitant oral sensorimotor training, desensitization of the orofacial region using soft toothbrushes, playing with spoons, touching mouth/lips with finger, etc.

–At the very beginning, playful relaxed exposure to food with differing tastes and consistencies outside the feeding situation (e.g., by leaving food around where the infant will find it by himself; Dunitz-Scheer et al., 2001)

---

identifying "ghosts in the nursery" (Fraiberg, Adelson, & Shapiro, 1975) and processing them therapeutically (such as transgenerational conflicts over dependency vs. autonomy that are reenacted in the feeding interaction; von Hofacker, 1998).

Addressing the family dynamics. Eating is a genuinely social process in human beings. Sharing a common meal is an expression of intimacy, closeness, and friendship. Because of the survival function of food, the theme of food and nutrition is associated with deeply rooted affects. It is not surprising that when observing a family at mealtime, one frequently becomes privy to significant behaviors, conflicts, and interactional patterns in an emotional intensity that is unusual in other settings. Everything gets put out on the table, so to speak. Working out the relational dynamics in the family, the relational constellations in which the infant feeding problems are imbedded, expands the therapeutic perspective from the dyad to the triad and beyond to complex family relationships and dynamics with their many resources and sensitive interfaces (Rosenfield, 1988).

Recruiting psychosocial resources. As in other regulatory disorders, a number of psychosocial stressors can be found in most of the families of feeding-disordered infants and toddlers. Therefore, in the therapeutic process emphasis should be placed on reducing parental and family distress as well as making use of overt or latent resources such as intuitive parental competencies (Papousek, 1998; also see chapter 12).

Choice of therapeutic setting. In the majority of feeding disorders (provided the infant is thriving adequately and does not have a traumatic history or severe organic impairment), the aspects described above may be treated in an outpatient setting with interaction-focused feeding counseling and therapy (von Hofacker et al., 2000). The focus here is on developmentally oriented counseling and support of the parents, the identification and treatment of dysfunctional interactional patterns during feeding, and the strengthening of family resources. Counseling and treatment are generally short term, usually 3 to 10 sessions.

A more comprehensive outpatient parent–infant psychotherapy (generally 10 to 25 sessions) is offered when the maternal/parental perception and interpretation of the infant" behavior is significantly impaired or distorted, intuitive parental competencies are severely restricted, and/or the mother–infant relationship is overtly disordered (e.g., as a result of low resources, severe psychological distress or mental illness, and particularly when the mother has an eating disorder). In such cases, individual psychotherapy, or couples therapy if needed, should also be considered.

Inpatient treatment for a feeding disorder is recommended

- When there is an immediate threat to the physical or mental well-being of the infant (e.g., in the case of severe FTT and/or severe psychopathology in the mother with threatening, distorted perceptions that are then projected onto the infant);
- In cases of a marked posttraumatic feeding disorder and/or weaning from tube-feeding;
- In cases of a marked pervasive disorder of behavioral and emotional regulation;
- When the infant has significant difficulties because of somatic/constitutional conditions (e.g., chronic organic disease, prematurity, difficult temperament);
- When there is danger of neglect and/or abuse;

- When the psychosocial environment is severely stressed or in cases of social isolation;
- When the mother's intuitive competencies are severely restricted, and in cases of relational disorders caused by depression or other mental illness;
- When outpatient treatment fails.

Inpatient admission makes it possible, among other things, to carefully monitor the caloric intake and the somatic status of the infant. Frequently, the mother or both parents experience delegating this function to the treating pediatrician as a real relief.

Inpatient units for parent–infant psychotherapy require a specially trained interdisciplinary team that includes a nursing staff to support the parents, primarily the mother, in their own competencies. A trusted and supportive parent figure with whom the mother can build a "good-grandmother transference" (Stern, 1995) can be an important first point of reference for her.

Duration and Outcome of Treatment

Evaluation of treatment outcome in the present sample of the Munich Program. In the present sample, treatment of the 283 feeding-disordered infants required on average 6.6 sessions/treatment days (including diagnostic workup; $SD = 8.3$) up to the concluding assessment. The number of sessions was significantly related to the degree of impairment of the mother–infant relationship, $F(2, 277) = 11.8$, $p \leq .001$. For relationships scored as *sufficiently adapted* (PIR-GAS 90-70), the duration averaged 2.4 sessions ($SD = 1.2$); for *stressed/disturbed* relationships (PIR-GAS 60-40), 5.8 sessions ($SD = 6.5$); for *disordered* relationships (PIR-GAS 30-10), 11.2 sessions ($SD = 13.2$) (see also chapter 12). Thirty infants (11%) in the sample received inpatient treatment at least once. In two thirds of these cases, treatment lasted between 4 and 15 days; the duration for the other infants varied from 16 up to 55 days in exceptional cases.

The success of treatment was assessed globally at the conclusion of treatment, in relation to the feeding symptoms, other concomitant regulatory problems, and relief of distress for the mother–infant relationship (see chapter 12). Overall, 37.7% of cases were assessed as *completely improved*, 48.4% as *largely improved* (e.g., the feeding situation was relaxed and the child ate on his own accord, but the amount eaten and weight gain were still not optimal), 10.7% as a *slightly improved*, and 3.6% as *unimproved* (because of premature discontinuation of treatment). The degree to which the feeding problem could be positively affected by the therapy was also significantly related to the quality of the mother–infant relationship, $X^2(6, N = 283), = 42.5, p \leq .001$. In well-adapted relationships, 80% of the feeding disorders were completely improved and 20% largely improved. For distressed/endangered relationships, these figures were 42% and 48%, respectively. Only 9% and 57%, respectively, of feeding disorders with disordered relationships showed such improvement.

Further studies. Randomized studies have compared various forms of intervention for infants and toddlers who fail to thrive (home-based, family-centered, parent-centered, general counseling, multimodal treatment approaches), but have not shown any single method to be superior. In general, only very limited positive effects on the long-term nutritional status and developmental and socioemotional outcomes for the child have been found (for a review, see Benoit, 2000; Wolke, 2000). Overall, approaches that seek to differentially reinforce positive eating behavior while ignoring unwanted behavioral patterns have best been validated empirically (Kerwin, 1999; see chapter 9 for a detailed discussion of evidence-based treatments of feeding disorders without FTT).

SUMMARY AND OUTLOOK

The described results and clinical experience show that infant feeding disorders and FTT are generally part of a complex constellation of symptoms consisting of infant problems and parental overstrain, as well as dysfunctional interactions in the feeding situation (diagnostic triad). Because of their tendency to persist and to affect the parent–infant relationships in the long run, these symptoms should be recognized, taken seriously, and treated as early as possible. They should be treated comprehensively, that is, with a multimodal interdisciplinary approach in order not to impair the further development of the infant, particularly in cases in which the infant fails to thrive and/or the mother has an eating disorder. The treatment of infant feeding disorders is thus particularly important because it may help to prevent long-term and more severe disorders of the child's physical, mental, and socioemotional developmental and of the parent–child relationship.

REFERENCES

Agras, S., Hammer, L., & McNicholas, F. (1999). A prospective study of the influence of eating-disordered mothers on their children. *International Journal of Eating Disorders, 25*, 253–262.

Bates, J. E., Freeland, C. A. B., & Lounsbury, M. L. (1979). Measurement of infant difficultness. *Child Development, 50*, 794–803.

Benoit, D. (2000). Feeding disorders, failure to thrive, and obesity. In C. H. Zeanah (Ed.), *Handbook of infant mental health* (pp. 339–352). New York: Guilford Press.

Benoit, D., & Coolbear, J. (1998). Post-traumatic feeding disorders in infancy: Behaviours predicting treatment outcome. *Infant Mental Health Journal, 19*, 409–421.

Benoit, D., Green, D., & Arts-Rodas, D. (1997). Posttraumatic feeding disorders. *Journal of the American Academy of Child and Adolescent Psychiatry, 36*, 577–578.

Benoit, D., Zeanah, C., & Barton, M. L. (1989). Die Bedeutung der Bindungssicherheit vom Kind zur Mutter für die psychische und physische Entwicklung von gedeihschwachen Kindern. *Praxis der Kinderpsychologie und Kinderpsychiatrie, 38*, 70–77.

Benoit, D., Zeanah, C., & Barton, M. L. (1989). Maternal attachment disturbances in failure to thrive. *Infant Mental Health Journal, 10*, 185–202.

Berwick, D. M., Levy, J. C., & Kleinermann, R. (1982). Failure to thrive: Diagnostic yield of hospitalisation. *Archives of Disease in Childhood, 57*, 347–351.

Boddy, J., & Skuse, D. H. (1994). Annotation: The process of parenting in failure to thrive. *Journal of Child Psychology and Psychiatry, and Allied Disciplines, 35*, 401–424.

Bodeewes, T. (2003). *Fütterinteraktion zwischen Mutter und Kind bei füttergestörten und nicht-füttergestörten Kindern.* Unpublished doctoral dissertation, Medical Faculty, Ludwig-Maximilians-University, Munich, Germany.

Brinch, M., Isager, T., & Tolstrup, K. (1988). Anorexia nervosa and motherhood: Reproductional pattern and mothering behaviour of 50 women. *Acta Psychiatrica Scandinavica, 77*, 98–104.

Brinich, E. B., Drotar, D. D., & Brinich, P. M. (1989). Die Bedeutung der Bindungssicherheit vom Kind zur Mutter für die psychische und physische Entwicklung von gedeihschwachen Kindern. *Praxis der Kinderpsychologie und Kinderpsychiatrie, 38*, 70–77.

Brisch, K. H. (2002). Klassifikation und klinische Merkmale von Bindungsstörungen. *Monatsschrift für Kinderheilkunde, 150*, 140–148.

Burklow, K. A., Phelps, A. N., Schultz, J. R., McConnell, K., & Rudolph, C. (1998). Classifying complex pediatric feeding disorders. *Journal of Pediatric Gastroenterology and Nutrition, 27*, 143–147.

Chatoor, E. (2002, July). *Diagnostic criteria of feeding disorders of infancy and early childhood*. Paper presented at the Congress of the World Association for Infant Mental Health, Amsterdam.

Chatoor, I., Conley, C., & Dickson, L. (1988). Food refusal after an incident of choking: A posttraumatic eating disorder. *Journal of the American Academy of Child and Adolescent Psychiatry, 27*, 105–110.

Chatoor, I., Dickson, L., Schaefer, S., & Egan, J. (1985). A developmental classification of feeding disorders associated with failure to thrive: Diagnosis and treatment. In D. Drotar (Ed.), *New directions in failure to thrive: Implications for research and practice* (pp. 235–258). New York: Plenum Press.

Chatoor, I., Egan, J., Getson, P., Menvielle, E., & O'Donnell, R. (1988). Mother-infant interactions in infantile anorexia nervosa. *Journal of the American Academy of Child and Adolescent Psychiatry, 27*, 535–540.

Chatoor, I., Ganiban, J., Colin, V., Plummer, N., & Harmon, R. J. (1998). Attachment and feeding problems: A reexamination of nonorganic failure to thrive and attachment insecurity. *Journal of the American Academy of Child and Adolescent Psychiatry, 37*, 1217–1224.

Chatoor, I., Ganiban, J., Harrison, J., & Hirsch, R. (2001). Observation of feeding in the diagnosis of posttraumatic feeding disorder of infancy. *Journal of the American Academy of Child and Adolescent Psychiatry, 40*, 595–602.

Chatoor, I., Getson, P., Menvielle, E., Brasseaux, C., O'Donnel, R., Rivera, Y., et al. (1997). A feeding scale for research and clinical practice to assess mother-infant interactions in the first three years of life. *Infant Mental Health Journal, 18*, 76–91.

Clemente, C., Barnes, J., Shinebourne, E., & Stein, A. (2001). Are infant behavioral feeding difficulties associated with congenital heart disease? *Child: Care, Health and Development, 27*, 47–59.

Conti, J., Abraham, S., & Taylor, A. (1998). Eating behavior and pregnancy outcome. *Journal of Psychosomatic Research, 44*, 465–477.

Coolbear, J., & Benoit, D. (1999). Failure to thrive: Risk for clinical disturbance of attachment? *Infant Mental Health Journal, 20*, 87–104.

Crittenden, P. (1987). Non-organic failure to thrive: Deprivation or distortion? *Infant Mental Health Journal, 8*, 51–64.

Dahl, M., Rydell, A. M., & Sundelin, C. (1994). Children with early refusal to eat: Follow-up during primary school. *Acta Paediatrica, 83*, 54–58.

Dahl, M., & Sundelin, C. (1992). Feeding problems in an affluent society. Follow-up at four years of age in children with early refusal to eat. *Acta Paediatrica Scandinavica, 81*, 575–579.

Drewett, R. F., Corbett, S. S., & Wright, C. M. (1999). Cognitive and educational attainments at school age of children who failed to thrive in infancy: A population-based study. *Journal of Child Psychology and Psychiatry and Allied Disciplines, 40,* 551–561.

Drotar, D., Eckerle, D., Satola, J., Pallotta, J., & Wyatt, B. (1990). Maternal interactional behavior with nonorganic failure-to-thrive infants: A case comparison study. *Child Abuse and Neglect, 14,* 41–51.

Drotar, D., & Sturm, L. (1991). Psychosocial influences in the etiology, diagnosis, and prognosis of nonorganic failure to thrive. In H. E. Fitzgerald, B. M. Lester, & M. W. Yogman (Eds.), *Theory and research in behavioral pediatrics* (pp. 19–59). New York: Plenum Press.

Dunitz, M., & Scheer, P. J. (1991). Diagnostik und Therapie der frühen Mutter-Kind-Störung, die sogenannte Gedeihstörung des Säuglings. *Monatsschrift für Kinderheilkunde, 139,* 465–470.

Dunitz-Scheer, M., Wilken, M., Lamm, B., Scheitenberger, S., Stadler, B., Schein, A., et al. (2001). Sondenentwöhnung in der frühen Kindheit. *Monatsschrift für Kinderheilkunde, 149,* 1348–1359.

Evans, J., & LeGrange, D. (1995). Body size and parenting in eating disorders: A comparative study of the attitudes of mothers towards their children. *International Journal of Eating Disorders, 18,* 39–48.

Fergusson, D. M., Horwood, L. J., & Shannon, F. T. (1985). Relationship between family life events, maternal depression and child rearing problems. *Pediatrics, 73,* 773–788.

Forsyth, B. W. C., & Canny, P. F. (1991). Perceptions of vulnerability 3 1/2 years after problems of feeding and crying behavior in early infancy. *Pediatrics, 88,* 757–763.

Fraiberg, S., Adelson, E., & Shapiro, V. (1975). Ghosts in the nursery: A psychoanalytic approach to the problems of impaired infant-mother relationships. *Journal of the American Academy of Child and Adolescent Psychiatry, 14,* 387–422.

Frank, D. A. (1985). Biologic risks in "nonorganic" failure to thrive: Diagnostic and therapeutic implications. In D. Drotar (Ed.), *New directions in failure to thrive.* Implications for research and practice (pp. 17–26). London: Plenum.

Franzen, U., & Gerlinghoff, M. (1997). Parenting by patients with eating disorders: Experiences with a mother-child group. *Eating Disorders, 5,* 5–14.

Fryer, G. E. (1988). The efficacy of hospitalization of nonorganic failure-to-thrive children: A meta-analysis. *Child Abuse and Neglect, 12,* 375–381.

Garner, D., Olmsted, M. P., Bohr, Y., & Garfinkel, P. E. (1982). The eating attitudes test: Psychometric features and clinical correlates. *Psychological Medicine, 12,* 871–878.

Garner, D., Olmsted, M. P., & Polivy, J. (1983). The development and validation of a multidimensional eating disorders inventory for anorexia nervosa and bulimia nervosa. *International Journal of Eating Disorders, 2,* 15–34.

Gisel, E. G., & Alphonce, E. (1995). Classification of eating impairments based on eating efficiency in children with cerebral palsy. *Dysphagia, 10,* 268–274.

Gisel, E. G., Birnbaum, R., & Schwartz, S. (2001). Feeding impairments in children: Diagnosis and effective intervention. *International Journal of Orofacial Myology, 24,* 27–33.

Goldson, E. (1989). Neurological aspects of failure to thrive. *Developmental Medicine and Child Neurology, 31,* 816–826.

Hoffmann, H. (1845). Der Struwwelpeter. Mit 15 schön kolorierten Tafeln für Kinder von 3 - 6 Jahren. In H. Hoffmann, *Lustige Geschichten und drollige Bilder*. Frankfurt, Germany: Literarische Anstalt.

Kamen, R. S. (1990). Impaired development of oral-motor functions required for normal oral feeding as a consequence of tube feeding during infancy. *Advances in Peritoneal Dialysis. Conference on Peritoneal Dialysis, 6*, 276–278.

Kerwin, M. L. E. (1999). Empirically supported treatments in pediatric psychology: Severe feeding problems. *Journal of Pediatric Psychology, 24*, 193–214.

Lewis, J. A. (1982). Treatment of feeding difficulties. In P. Accardo (Ed.), *Failure to thrive in infancy and early childhood* (pp. 265–296). Baltimore: University Park Press.

Lindberg, L. (1994). *Early feeding problems: A developmental perspective. Acta Universitatis Upsaliensis, 44*. Uppsala, Sweden: Acta Universitatis Upsaliensis.

Lindberg, L., Bohlin, G., & Hagekull, B. (1991). Early feeding problems in a normal population. *International Journal of Eating Disorders, 10*, 395–405.

Lindberg, L., Bohlin, G., Hagekull, B., & Palmérus, K. (1996). Interactions between mothers and infants showing food refusal. *Infant Mental Health Journal, 17*, 334–347.

Martin, J., & White, A. (1988). *Infant feeding 1985*. London: Her Majesty's Stationary Office.

Mathisen, B., Skuse, D., Wolke, D., & Reilly, S. (1989). Oral-motor dysfunction and failure to thrive among inner-city infants. *Developmental Medicine and Child Neurology, 31*, 293–302.

Mathisen, B., Worrall, L., Masel, J., Wall, C., & Shepherd, R. W. (1999). Feeding problems in infants with gastro-oesophageal reflux disease: A controlled study. *Journal of Paediatrics and Child Health, 35*, 163–169.

O'Brien, S., Repp, A. C., Williams, G. E., & Christophersen, E. R. (1991). Pediatric feeding disorders. *Behavior Modification, 15*, 394–418.

Papoušek, M. (1998). Das Münchner Modell einer interaktionszentrierten Säuglings-Eltern-Beratung und –Psychotherapie. In K. von Klitzing (Ed.), *Psychotherapie in der frühen Kindheit* (pp. 88–118). Göttingen, Germany: Vandenhoeck & Ruprecht.

Papoušek, M. (2002). Störungen des Säuglingsalters. In G. Esser (Ed.), *Lehrbuch der klinischen Psychologie und Psychotherapie des Säuglingsalters* (pp. 80–101). Stuttgart, Germany: Thieme.

Powers, S. W., Patton, S. R., Byars, K. C., Mitchell, M. J., Jelalian, E., Mulvihill, M. M., et al. (2002). Caloric intake and eating behavior in infants and toddlers with cystic fibrosis. *Pediatrics, 109*, 75–80.

Ramsay, M., Gisel, E. G., & Boutry, M. (1993). Non-organic failure to thrive: Growth failure secondary to feeding-skills disorder. *Developmental Medicine and Child Neurology, 35*, 285–297.

Reif, S., Beler, B., Villa, Y., & Spirer, Z. (1995). Long-term follow-up and outcome of infants with non-organic failure to thrive. *Israel Journal of Medical Sciences, 31*, 483–489.

Rosenfield, S. (1988). Family influence on eating behavior and attitudes in eating disorders: A review of the literature. *Nursing Practice, 3*, 46–55.

Sanders, M. R., Patel, R. K., Le Grice, B., & Shepherd, R. W. (1993). Children with persistent feeding difficulties: An observational analysis of the feeding interactions of problem and non-problem eaters. *Health Psychology, 12*, 64–73.

Sanders, M. R., Turner, K. M. T., Wall, C. R., Waugh, L. M., & Tully, L. A. (1997). Mealtime behavior and parent-child interaction: A comparison of children with cystic fibrosis, children with feeding problems, and nonclinical controls. *Journal of Pediatric Psychology, 22,* 881–900.

Schauster, H., & Dwyer, J. (1996). Transition from tube feedings to feedings by mouth in children: Preventing eating dysfunction. *Journal of the American Dietetic Association, 96,* 277–281.

Simpson, C., Schanler, R. J., & Lau, C. (2002). Early introduction of oral feeding in preterm infants. *Pediatrics, 110,* 517–522.

Skuse, D., Wolke, D., & Reilly, S. (1992). Failure to thrive. Clinical and developmental aspects. In H. Remschmidt & M. Schmidt (Eds.), *Child and youth psychiatry: European perspectives. Volume 2: Developmental psychopathology* (pp. 46–71). Stuttgart, Germany: Huber.

Skuse, D., Wolke, D., Reilly, S., & Chan, I. (1995). Failure to thrive in human infants: The significance of maternal well-being and behavior. In C. Price, R. P. Martin, & D. Skuse (Eds.), *Motherhood in human and non-human primates: Biosocial determinants* (pp. 162–170). Basel, Switzerland: Karger.

Stein, A., Murray, L., Cooper, P., & Fairburn, C. G. (1996). Infant growth in the context of maternal eating disorders and maternal depression: A comparative study. *Psychological Medicine, 26,* 569–574.

Stein, A., Woolley, H., Cooper, S. D., & Fairburn, C. G. (1994). An observational study of mothers with eating disorders and their infants. *Journal of Child Psychology and Psychiatry and Allied Disciplines, 35,* 733–748.

Stein, A., Woolley, H., & McPherson, K. (1999). Conflict between mothers with eating disorders and their infants during mealtimes. *British Journal of Psychiatry, 175,* 455–461.

Stern, D. N. (1995). *The motherhood constellation.* New York: Basic Books.

Stice, E., Agras, S. W., & Hammer, L. D. (1999). Risk factors for the emergence of childhood eating disturbances: A five-year prospective study. *International Journal of Eating Disorders, 25,* 375–387.

Valenzuela, M. (1990). Attachment in chronically underweight young children. *Child Development, 61,* 1984–1996.

von Hofacker, N. (1998). Fallbeispiel einer Fütterstörung im Säuglingsalter. In M. Schulte-Markwort, B. Diepold, & F. Resch (Eds.), *Psychische Störungen im Kindes- und Jugendalter. Ein psychodynamisches Fallbuch* (pp. 1–8). Stuttgart, Germany: Thieme Verlag.

von Hofacker, N., Eder, S., & Sobanski, P. (2002). *Elternfragebogen zur Fütter- und Essanamnese im Säuglings- und Kleinkindalter.* Unpublished manuscript.

von Hofacker, N., & Papoušek, M. (1998). Disorders of excessive crying, feeding, and sleeping: The Munich Interdisciplinary Research and Intervention Program. *Infant Mental Health Journal, 19,* 180–201.

von Hofacker, N., Riedesser, P., Berger, M., Jacubeit, T., Bindt, C., Papoušek, M., et al. (2000). Leitlinie Regulationsstörungen im Säuglingsalter. In Deutsche Gesellschaft fuer Kinder- und Jugendpsychiatrie et al. (Eds.), *Leitlinien zur Diagnostik und Therapie von psychischen Störungen im Säuglings-, Kindes- und Jugendalter* (pp. 319–331). Köln, Germany: Deutscher Ärzteverlag.

Ward, M. J., Lee, S. S., & Lipper, E. G. (2000). Failure-to-thrive is associated with disorganized infant-mother attachment and unresolved maternal attachment. *Infant Mental Health Journal, 21,* 428–442.

Wilensky, D. S., Ginsberg, G., Altman, M., Tulchinsky, T. H., Yishay, F. B., & Auerbach, J. (1996). A community-based study of failure to thrive in Israel. *Archives of Disease in Childhood, 75*, 145–148.

Wittenberg, J. V. (1990). Feeding disorders in infancy: Classification and treatment considerations. *Canadian Journal of Psychiatry, 35*, 529–533.

Wolke, D. (1994). Feeding and sleeping across lifespan. In M. Rutter & D. Hay (Eds.), *Development through life: A handbook for clinicians* (pp. 517–557). Oxford, England: Blackwell.

Wolke, D. (1996). Failure to thrive: The myth of maternal deprivation syndrome. *The Signal, 4*, 1–6.

Wolke, D. (1999). Interventionen bei Regulationsstörungen. In R. Oerter, C. von Hagen, & G. Röper (Eds.), *Klinische Entwicklungspsychologie* (pp. 351–380). Weinheim, Germany: Beltz.

Wolke, D. (2000). Fütterungsprobleme bei Säuglingen und Kleinkindern. *Verhaltenstherapie, 10*, 76–87.

Wolke, D., & Skuse, D. (1992). The management of infant feeding problems. In P. J. Cooper & A. Stein (Eds.), *Feeding problems and eating disorders in children and adolescents* (pp. 27–59). Chur, Switzerland: Harwood Academic.

Wolke, D., Skuse, D., & Mathisen, B. (1990). Behavioral style in failure-to-thrive infants—a preliminary communication. *Journal of Pediatric Psychology, 15*, 237–254.

Woodside, D. B., Shekter-Wolfson, L. F., Brandes, J. S., & Lackstrom, J. B. (1993). *Eating disorders and marriage: The couple in focus.* New York: Brunner/Mazel.

Wright, C. M., Edwards, A. G., Halse, P. C., & Waterston, A. J. (1991). Weight and failure to thrive in infancy. *Lancet, 377*, 365–366.

Zeanah, C. H., Benoit, D., & Barton, M. L. (1993). *Working Model of the Child Interview.* Unpublished manuscript. Providence, RI: Brown University.

ZERO TO THREE. (1994). *Diagnostic classification: 0–3. Diagnostic classification of mental health and developmental disorders of infancy and early childhood.* Washington, DC: ZERO TO THREE.

ZERO TO THREE. (2005). *Diagnostic classification of mental health and developmental disorders of infancy and early childhood: Revised edition (DC:0–3R).* Washington, DC: ZERO TO THREE.

CHAPTER 8

CLINGING, ROMPING, THROWING TANTRUMS: DISORDERS OF BEHAVIORAL AND EMOTIONAL REGULATION IN OLDER INFANTS AND TODDLERS

Mechthild Papoušek
Nikolaus von Hofacker

CASE VIGNETTE

Reason for referral. Adam was brought in for the first time at the age of 22 months by his single mother. The immediate reason was an embarrassing event in her self-help group for single mothers that she found somewhat painful: When she reprimanded Adam for having pushed another child, he demanded to be nursed in full view of everyone in the group. The mother had every intention of weaning him, but she was at the end of her rope and simply felt unable to do so.

Adam's extreme crying had been evident even in the neonatal unit. Because of his crying and fussiness, she had carried him close to her body for months and nursed him whenever he seemed unhappy. He would only fall asleep snuggled up to her body. Even now, he continued to require close physical contact at her breast to sleep, although he woke up each night as many as eight times, only to fall asleep again at her breast. At any occasion during the day (when bored or frustrated, for example) he would beseech his mother with his eyes to be nursed; this typically occurred more than 20 times per day, and Adam whined bitterly whenever she would not give in to him. He cried regularly during diapering and while being dressed. At mealtimes, he played listlessly with his food, spit out what he had chewed, and demanded mashed food. He was unable to play alone and demanded his mother's constant attention and entertainment. His behavior was particularly provocative when she was on the telephone, at which times he might flood the bathroom, empty drawers onto the floor, or tear down the curtains. Some days Adam's mother would just let him have his way in order to prevent an escalation; other times she would lose her patience and scream. Whenever she attempted to set some limits, he would immediately cry bitterly and calm down only at her breast.

The mother, who was almost 40, looked completely exhausted and depressed. She reported premenstrual depression with an inability to sleep as well as episodes of bulimia. At home things were getting beyond her control, as she felt less and less capable of managing her son's behavior; she reported becoming extremely irritable and inconsistent, and sometimes screaming at him.

Observations and findings. During the first visit, Adam immediately began to explore the room, focusing on toys, the office computer, and the video unit. Whenever he became bored or limits were set, he immediately sought out his mother's lap. She readily allowed him to nurse and spoke to him softly and with warmth or stroked his head in order to appease him.

Adam cried desperately, resisting the medical examination, while his mother attempted in vain to comfort him. His crying stopped immediately when the pediatrician showed him a set of stacking blocks, which he began to play with, showing a great deal of fine-motor skill and persistence. He had no trouble when his mother left the room for a short time, but he cried again as soon as she returned. When interacting and playing with the examiner, he seemed calm and content.

Adam was physically healthy, and his motor, mental, and receptive language skills were age-appropriate, although his expressive language was somewhat delayed (minimal, difficult to understand vocabulary). Although he seemed insecure and inhibited initially, he was friendly and cooperative after a considerable warm-up time, particularly with males.

When he and his mother played together, he tended to follow her suggestions passively but gave up quickly whenever something didn't work out for him. In spite of her depressive exhaustion, Adam's mother showed adequate intuitive competencies during play, although she immediately helped him whenever he experienced difficulties in order to spare him frustration. In a semistructured boundary- and limit-setting situation during solitary play next to the mother (the mother is asked to encourage the child to play alone, to withdraw her attention and focus on a magazine, and to make sure that the child complies with certain off-limit areas such as the microphone, curtains, and humidifier), the mother was barely able to let Adam out of her sight. He immediately began to explore the off-limit areas insistently, throwing his mother challenging glances. Winning these little power struggles seemed to please him greatly. His mother, rather halfheartedly and indecisively, pleaded with him to stop. She then tried a sharper tone of voice but in the end gave up helplessly while Adam discovered the next off-limits area.

Prior history. Although the mother had wanted a child for many years, her pregnancy was burdened by depression and ambivalence because of massive conflicts with Adam's father. After the birth, the mother succeeded in putting at least some geographical distance between herself and the father; however, she continued to feel at the mercy of his authoritarian, intrusive, and demeaning behavior. The father never had contact with his son.

The mother herself had been deposited with her grandmother by her single working mother and had been lovingly cared for by her for the first 3 years of life until her grandmother's death. In spite of her mother's remarriage, she was shunted off for another year, this time to the step-grandmother, at whose hands she experienced only strict rules, beatings, and rejection. Her own mother did not treat her much better when she took her back at preschool age and even today provides no support. Regarding her own mother, she said "I never experienced anything good from my mother."

Diagnosis. Adam's pronounced generalized disorder of behavioral and emotional regulation had existed since birth. During the second year of life, this came to include excessive clinginess, lack of interest in play, excessive defiance, and aggressive/oppositional behavior along with a chronic sleep disorder and eating problems. These problems had developed within a symbiotically enmeshed mother–child relationship and seemed to be confined to the mother–child context. The child gave evidence of functional impairment of age-appropriate play, expressive language, and self-regulation. He had still not mastered the developmental tasks of regulating sleep, age-appropriate nutritional intake, or his needs for attachment and autonomy.

Treatment. Given the complexity of the disorder, the treatment goals were developed with the mother step-by-step, particularly her desire to wean Adam and have him sleep through the night. The goals of intervention included weaning during the day, strengthening age-appropriate self-efficacy, autonomy, and compliance; perseverance and expressive language competency during play; the introduction and clarification of rules and limits; behavioral and emotional boundaries in concrete everyday contexts; strengthening of self-regulatory strategies; and weaning during the transition to sleep and nighttime sleep. Central to the problem was a deep-seated disorder of the balance between attachment/dependency and autonomy in the mother–child relationship. The mother's behavior seemed to be determined by a strong need for closeness and a simultaneous fear of autonomy, which she associated only with threatening and denigrating experiences in her life. For his part, Adam sought to satisfy his age-appropriate needs for autonomy regressively by exacerbated attachment behavior or provocative power struggles.

In spite of her depression and the enmeshed relationship with her son, the mother had a remarkable capacity for self-reflection and good intuitive competencies, presumably the result of her positive attachment relationship with her grandmother during her first 3 years of life. These internal resources greatly facilitated treatment.

The first step was to foster positive relational experiences with the help of video-supported communication-centered guidance and developmental counseling. In this context, the mother quickly learned to recognize Adam's need for autonomy and mastery and to support his initiatives, affective self-regulation, self-esteem, perseverance, and verbal communication. Video feedback of the boundary- and limit-setting situation opened her eyes to the extent to which her ambivalent stance toward permissiveness versus control and her empathy and guilt came to the fore in her communication with Adam. During the next session, a therapeutic frame was selected in which the mother, right after a positive play experience with Adam, was asked to divert her attention from him for a while so that she could focus on talking with the therapist and addressing her own feelings and representations. The mother and therapist had come to an understanding beforehand that they could trust Adam to be able to continue playing by himself next to the mother.

However, Adam stopped playing immediately and began to cry pleadingly, reaching up toward his mother and demanding to be nursed. This situation elicited his mother's compassion and an immense demand on herself to be a loving mother ("He's suffering and needs me right now. He won't be able to get over his sense of abandonment without my help. He's looking for love, and I'm refusing it to him. He needs to know that his mother is there for him every second…"). This compassion, only understandable as projective identification with Adam, made it extremely difficult for her to gradually disengage her attention from her son. The therapist's persistent attempts to direct the mother's attention to her own needs enabled her to recall episodes from her childhood when she pleadingly stretched her arms toward her busy mother, who pushed her away, or when she was beaten because her mother was annoyed. She also remembered waking up from nightmares, crying in panic for help, but instead being hit for disturbing others in the family.

To the extent that the mother succeeded in addressing her own childhood suffering, Adam—still crying—turned away from his mother, observed himself crying in the mirror, stopped crying, and finally took his favorite toy from the therapist and began to play. As became evident during the next few sessions, Adam's whining and clinginess had several facets. On the one hand, it evoked her own feelings of abandonment and protest against the loss of her grandmother. On the other hand, situations in which Adam cried because she was unwilling to give in to him also repeated fear-laden childhood experiences of complete helplessness in which she had been screamed at, blamed, denigrated, and humiliated.

The session just described was a turning point for mother and child that made it easier for her to set clear limits, set affective boundaries between Adam's and her own needs in particular situations, and, step by step, wean her son. Adam learned to accept limits, comply with her requests, and play with greater endurance and pleasure. He became more independent and content, began to speak more, and to flourish whenever he succeeded in age-appropriate behavior.

During this communication-centered mother–child psychotherapy, which lasted a total of 10 sessions, the mother herself was encouraged to begin individual psychotherapy in order to continue to deal with her own painful relational history.

DISORDERS OF BEHAVIORAL AND EMOTIONAL REGULATION BEYOND EARLY INFANCY

During the second half of the first year of life, disorders of behavioral and emotional regulation begin to affect new age-related domains. Figures 8.1 and 8.2 show the most frequent behavioral syndromes and their frequency distribution in the sample of 701 children described in chapter 3 who were referred to the Munich Program for the first time during their second half-year (Figure 8.1) or during their second, third, or fourth year of life (Figure 8.2). Figures 8.3 and 8.4 depict age-dependent changes in the prevalence of individual behavioral manifestations from the second half-year to the fourth year of life: (a) for children at their first visit (Figure 8.3), and (b) for the subgroup of these children who were referred a second time because of a later relapse or new behavioral problems after initially successful treatment (Figure 8.4).

The percentage of children with sleep disorders during the second half-year (88.3%) and during the second to fourth year of life (85.8%) remained the most prominent of all syndromes, with an almost unchanged rate. The rate of feeding disorders showed some increase from 36.7% to 44.5% (see also chapter 3); the percentage of lack of interest in play reached its peak during the second half-year (37.7%) and then receded slightly to 33.5% (for more on this syndrome, see chapter 15). New behavioral syndromes also became evident: excessive clinginess/fearfulness and/or extreme separation anxiety, which peaked during the fourth half-year (Figure 8.3), then receded into the background, but increased during the fourth year of life in children who were referred for a second time (Figure 8.4). The rates of excessive defiance began to increase dramatically during the third half-year, being evident in up to as many as two thirds of the age group in the third year; defiance was thus the most frequent reason for referral next to sleep disorders after the end of the second year. Aggressive/oppositional behavior

Figure 8.1. Disorders of Behavioral and Emotional Regulation During the Second Half-Year.

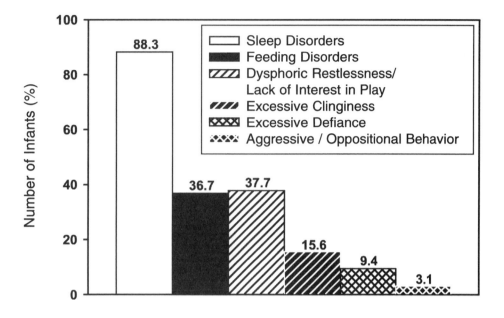

Figure 8.2. Disorders of Behavioral and Emotional Regulation in the Second to Fourth Years of Life.

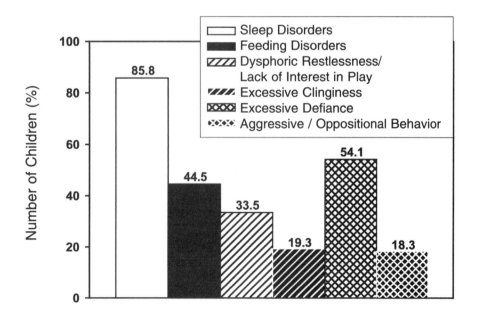

Figure 8.3. Age-Related Distribution of Syndromes of Behavioral and Emotional Regulation at the First Referral.

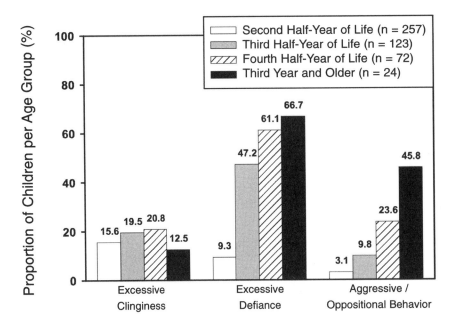

Figure 8.4. Age-Related Distribution of Syndromes of Behavioral and Emotional Regulation at the Second Referral.

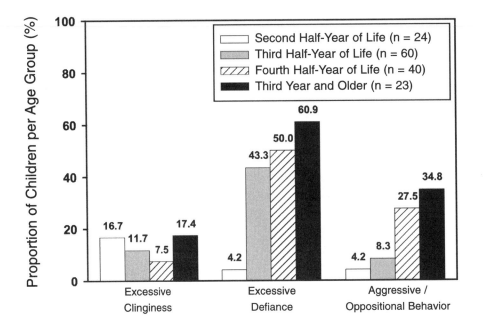

accompanied defiance in a significantly smaller percentage of children beginning after the third half-year. The frequency profile of syndromes at a second referral (due to relapse or new problems) was remarkably similar, although sleep or feeding disorders that had been treated successfully during the initial therapeutic intervention had largely disappeared.

There is an extensive literature on emotional and behavioral disorders among preschoolers. However, although the behavioral problems of late infancy and toddlerhood have been analyzed and discussed in terms of their potential role in developmental psychopathology, they have only rarely been investigated as clinically relevant disorders (Belsky, Hsieh, & Crnic, 1998; Belsky, Woodworth, & Crnic, 1996; Calkins, 2002; Crockenberg & Leerkes, 2000; Laucht, 2002; Laucht, Esser, & Schmidt, 1993; Minde & Tidmarsh, 1997; Zeanah, Boris, & Scheeringa, 1997). A growing number of investigations and prospective longitudinal studies of emotional and social development in the areas of developmental psychology (Biringen, Emde, Campos, & Appelbaum, 1995; Bischof-Köhler, 1998; Rauh, 2002), temperament research (Derryberry & Rothbart, 2001; Olson, Bates, Sandy, & Lanthier, 2000; Pettit & Bates, 1989; Pettit, Bates, & Dodge, 1997), attachment research (Cassidy, 1994; Sroufe, 1983), family research (Schneewind, 2002), and emotion research (Friedlmeier & Holodynski, 1999) have all contributed important information.

This chapter presents a descriptive overview of the present results and experiences from our own clinical program. Excessive clinginess, defiance, and aggressiveness occurred in the majority of referred children in association with sleep disorders and frequently with feeding disorders and dysphoric fussiness as well. In three fourths of cases the syndromes had been preceded by a long history of distressing dysfunctional interactions that began with excessive crying during the first 3 months of life. Given these associations and their temporal relation to age-dependent regulatory developmental tasks, it appears justifiable to include these problems of emotional regulation in the overarching diagnosis disorders of behavioral and emotional regulation of early childhood, especially because the same remises apply to them as discussed in chapter 4:

1. The infants' behavioral difficulties represent extreme variants of phase-typical developmental phenomena (fear of strangers, separation anxiety, temper tantrums); although normal distributions of these behaviors are available by now, a categorical diagnostic demarcation of pathological deviations from normal manifestations is neither possible nor justified (Fegert, 1996; Largo, 1993).

2. The child's behavior problems are anchored in day-to-day parent–child interactions and cannot be separated from the communicative and relational patterns in which they originate, tend to worsen, and persist.

3. As with crying and sleep and feeding disorders, the clinical relevance and need for treatment ensue from the diagnostic triad of behavioral problems, dysfunctional interactional patterns, and psychophysical overburdening of the primary caregiver(s). The growing distress and endangerment of the parent–child relationships tend to increase with age and duration of the problem (see chapter 4).

4. Severity of the disorder depends on (a) the absolute and relative duration of the current and earlier regulatory problems (persistence); (b) the number of affected domains with dysfunctional, negatively contingent patterns of communication (pervasiveness); (c) the degree to which earlier and current developmental tasks are mastered and to which the child's self-regulatory functioning is impaired as a result (with regard to self-soothing, falling asleep and sleeping through the night, self-feeding, etc.); (d) the accumulation of risk factors in the parent–child system; and (e) the burden placed on the developing parent–child relationships, including the quality of attachment (Anders, 1989; Campbell, 1995; von Hofacker, Papoušek, Resch, & Lehmkuhl, in press).

CLINICAL SYNDROME

Excessive Clinginess

The child is remarkable for her insistence on constant physical contact, demands which are in some cases tinged with fear or panic but are most often expressed by instrumental crying and vehement clinging to the primary caregiver. Children who have not yet been weaned demand breast-feeding in this context. The behavior gives the impression of overly activated attachment behavior, completely out of proportion to the context and stress that may have triggered it. The observations that closeness and physical contact alone do not always lead to soothing and that clinginess and fussing continue on the mother's lap indicate that attachment behavior is activated in the service of other needs such as the need to overcome boredom and lack of interest in play and the desire for undivided parental attention and entertainment.

This may be easily observed in the counseling context with the parents. The child clings, whines, or cries incessantly on the parent's lap until she has achieved her goal of undivided attention. The thread of counseling conversation is interrupted as the parent ambivalently switches her attention back and forth between the child and the counselor, incapable of assessing the child's actual need or of clarifying the situation for herself and for the child. The counselor is often effectively excluded in the process.

According to the parents, the child clings to the mother's legs while she tries to cook or momentarily diverts her attention to other household activities. Or the child insists on being held whenever her mother gives way to one of her own neglected needs, such as taking time out to drink a cup of tea, leaf through the newspaper, telephone a friend, take a shower, or go to the bathroom. Even when sitting on a parent's lap, the child effectively prevents any conversation between the parents.

The parents are often conspicuous for their insecure or ambivalent behavior in dealing with their child's excessive demands for contact. They exhibit a high level of dysfunctional responsiveness, mixed messages, halfhearted attempts to meet their child's demands, automatic stroking with increasing tension and suppressed anger while alternating between caring attention and rejection. Communication fails because the parents have difficulties reading their child's actual needs from her inappropriate and exaggerated attachment behavior. They are also unable to trust that she will be able to play by herself for a while in their presence or fail to support her in such age-appropriate behavior. Notably, they are often only physically present but not emotionally available, due to their permanent engagement with the child. They also find it hard to acknowledge any of their own modest needs or to divert their attention for a while in order to create space for themselves. Dysfunctional patterns of communication develop easily in day-to-day contexts in which short-term withdrawal of attention would be appropriate or needed: The child learns to escalate her demands until her parents give in, and as a result fails to develop her own capacity for self-regulation in exploration and play. Because of her constant nagging for attention, the parents soon reach their limits of tolerance and in the end give up on their own needs as well as their needs as a couple.

Excessive Fearfulness and Social Inhibition

In unfamiliar surroundings, when meeting strangers or encountering unknown toys, the child exhibits an extremely long warm-up time and sustained inhibition in exploring, playing, and making social contact. Tense and motionless, she anxiously observes the surroundings or stranger (therapist) and seeks the physical shelter of her primary caregiver where she eventually calms down but without taking up social contact. Even when the therapist attempts a careful approach, the child is likely to withdraw fearfully, avert her gaze, hide her face, and suddenly cry or even scream. There may also be an associated generalized anxiousness that is triggered by loud noises, unknown or uncontrollable objects, certain animals, bearded men, or peers who are motorically more advanced. In a mother–child playgroup the child may not leave her mother's lap, even after a warm-up time.

Excessive Separation Anxiety

During the second half-year, the infant becomes increasingly reliant on keeping the primary caregiver within sight. Some children cry even in their familiar home whenever the caregiver is out of sight or leaves the room. If such children are always picked up immediately and carried everywhere, this normal phase-typical behavior pattern may be maintained up to the second and third year of life, particularly in the case of extremely anxious children or overprotective parents. If the mother needs to leave the child in the care of another trusted primary caregiver (father, grandmother, nanny) for a certain period of time, the child will respond with excessive age-inappropriate separation reactions such as excessive clinginess and panicky crying or sobbing, which become more reinforced than diminished by extended farewell rituals with overly sensitive maternal attention and affection. If the mother feels extremely insecure, anxious, and guilty, her attempts to console the child are usually unsuccessful because she conveys anything but security to the child. A mother's own ambivalence and futile attempts at detachment eventually lead to a complete avoidance of separation situations of any kind. The mother's resulting dependence, in turn, will elicit feelings of resignation, frustration, and potential conflict.

Excessive Defiance

The child exhibits frequent, intense, and long temper tantrums that are incommensurate with the situation. In general, tantrums may be triggered by any situation that leads to frustration and anger. They include situations in which the child is restrained from her intended actions and goals, in which she does not succeed in achieving her goal or getting what she wants, or in which she is confronted with unexpected limits and rules. Her intense affective arousal is discharged through outraged crying, throwing herself on the floor, hitting everything within close range, and even autoaggressive behavior or aggressive behavior directed at objects and caregivers such as head-banging, hitting, kicking, throwing toys, and the like.

In typical everyday interactional contexts (e.g., refusal of a desired object, restricting the child's mobility for her own protection, introducing rules and limits in social contexts such as in a crowded supermarket, forbidding behaviors) the parents typically exhibit insecurity, ambivalence regarding rules and limits, inconsistency, permissiveness, and helpless compliance with their child's will. They will do anything to keep the peace. They are not able to cope with their child's growing assertiveness, her need to explore, and her increasing penchant for saying "No." They capitulate out of fear of an impending temper tantrum, thereby giving up on their well-intentioned attempts at socializing their child. In the process, the child learns that anger and assertiveness pay off: Eventually she gets what she wants.

Once an uncontrollable temper tantrum has begun, some parents immediately give in or try—generally unsuccessfully—to explain, argue, negotiate, bribe, or promise their way out of further escalation. In other cases, defiance quickly elicits and escalates the parent's anger and provokes an authoritarian style of child rearing with inappropriate strictness, severe threats, emotional abusiveness, and punishment.

Aggressive/Oppositional Behavior

In oppositional behavior, the opposite of compliance and cooperation, the child intentionally refuses to follow rules or to accept limits. If requested to do things she deems unpleasant, or if forbidden to do something attractive she wants to do, she will simply ignore or refuse to obey. The child will challenge the caregiver with a provocative stare, willfully overturn objects on a shelf, tear at curtains, smear the bathtub with lipstick, and do precisely what she has been told not to do, obviously with the goal of getting attention, testing limits, or, with less responsive parents, triggering authentic anger. Such behavior most frequently develops when the child has been subjected to an unpredictable and inconsistent child-rearing style that oscillates between permissiveness (laissez-faire style) and overbearing control and is maintained by what Patterson (1982) described as a dysfunctional communication pattern of coercive cycles. A vicious circle of negative reciprocity is set in motion when the child's negative assertive behavior forces the parents to give in (to prevent escalation and a temper tantrum) until finally their dammed up anger explodes and they force their child to submit and obey by using threats and punishments.

Aggressive behavior in which the child willfully throws objects around, occasionally destroying them, is often described by parents as associated with provocative behavior and temper tantrums. Other behaviors such as biting, scratching, shoving, hitting, or snatching toys away are often observed when toddlers begin to play with peers, or in sibling relationships. These pseudo-aggressive behaviors become particularly problematic when they result in the child being ostracized by peers, and thus prevent normal socialization. Aggressive behavior may also occur in close physical contact with the parents. At an earlier age, such contact may have often been an expression of the child's joy in exploration. Occasionally, it may also occur in association with excessive clinginess.

Sleep Disorders and Feeding Disorders

As already mentioned in the previous chapters, similar developmental themes come to the fore during late infancy and toddlerhood in the context of persistent or first-time sleep disorders and feeding disorders, which at this age may also influence communication patterns during the day. Attachment themes (need for physical closeness, separation, and detachment) may come up during the second half-year when putting an infant to sleep and attempting to soothe him at night, particularly if associated with weaning. During the second year of life, conflicts over boundaries and limit setting may predominate in the context of unresolved dependency–autonomy conflicts (see also chapter 10); during the third year of life and later, nighttime waking and nightmares may become a major theme. Similarly, feeding interactions may be marked by deep-seated attachment themes (a mother's fear of losing the child, due to failure to thrive or after having experienced a life-threatening event) and increasingly by power struggles (over self-feeding) and unresolved conflicts involving issues of dependency and autonomy (see also chapter 11).

PREVALENCE AND PROGNOSIS

Epidemiological studies conducted in the United States (Achenbach, 1992), England (Richman, Stevenson, & Graham, 1975), the Netherlands (Koot & Verhulst, 1991), and Germany (Fegert, 1996) have determined the prevalence rates of behavioral problems in 2 1/2- and 3-year-old toddlers based on standardized behavior checklists filled in by the mothers. The prevalence rates reflect the percentage of children with extreme values above the 98th percentile on at least one of the behavioral or emotional subscales that were ascertained by factor analysis (Fegert, 1996; Laucht, 2002). The prevalence rates obtained using the Child Behavior Checklist/2-3 (CBCL/2-3; Achenbach, 1992), are remarkably similar for the American (12.0%), Dutch (12.6%), and German (11.6%) populations. With regard to individual subscales, rates between 2.3% (aggressive behavior) and 3.0% (somatic problems) have been found. Because of widespread stereotypes in the social valuation of male and female behavior in children, Fegert (1996) also ascertained sex-specific factor models with five factors for boys (Aggressive-Acting Out, Irritable-Fussy, Frustration-Intolerance, Fearful-Shy, and Sleep Problems) and five factors for girls (Aggressive, Irritable-Oppositional, Fearful-Shy, Depressive Somatic, and Sleep Problems).

Behavioral problems in toddlers were assessed in the Mannheim longitudinal risk study using a detailed standardized parent interview (Laucht, 2002; see chapter 14). As expected, the overall rate of behavioral problems in this at-risk sample (somatic and psychosocial stressors) of 2-year-olds was appreciably increased (19.1%) and showed significant sex differences (23.8% in boys, 15.4% in girls). Numerous studies have documented that the well-known sex differences in later childhood (to the boys' disadvantage) appear as early as the toddler stage. Boys are more often aggressive and hyperactive and less cooperative and compliant (Sanson, Oberklaid, Pedlow, & Prior, 1991). Our own data also documented sex differences in the frequency of aggressive/oppositional behavior during the second year of life (19.8% for boys vs. 9% for girls), $X^2(1, N = 213) = 4.48, p \le .05$, but not in any of the other regulatory problems.

Behavior problems in 2- to 3-year-olds exhibit remarkably high rates of persistence into preschool or school age: Approximately 60% of children who were assessed as having behavior problems at the age of 2 to 3 years obtained the same problem scores in later childhood (Campbell, 1995; Laucht, 2002; Richman et al., 1975; see chapter 14).

DEVELOPMENTAL ORIGINS

Emotional Development

All of the clinical problems described at the beginning of this chapter as well as those assessed with behavioral checklists represent extreme expressions of negative affects/emotions and of problems in affective/emotional regulation. To understand how they develop, it is necessary to look at the early development of affects and emotions. The difficulties, however, begin as soon as we try to define *affect* or *emotion*, because their definitions differ widely depending on the theory of emotion referenced (see Dornes, 2000; Friedlmeier & Holodynski, 1999). If we look at the most common definitions in the abundant literature, both terms seem to be used interchangeably, particularly in relation to infancy and toddlerhood, and so they are used synonymously in this chapter.

Affects/emotions represent innate psychobiological reactions of the organism that have been studied empirically in terms of their expressive components, their subjective experiential components (feelings), their peripheral-physiological components, and lately also their central neurobiological components. At all levels, nonspecific aspects of affective arousal (intensity, affect dynamics) may be distinguished from emotion-specific qualitative aspects (e.g., anger vs. joy). From a dynamic systems perspective, emotions are a central part of an overarching system of integrative processes (H. Papoušek & Papoušek, 1979, 1999) that include both information processing (sensory perception, affective appraisal, learning, cognitive processes) and the regulation of behavioral responses or action. From a functional perspective, emotions provide the organism with some basic affective appraisal when confronted with an unknown event, and, by activating corresponding physiological systems and behavioral dispositions, prepare the organism to recruit appropriate coping behaviors (e.g., approach or withdrawal; Holodynski, 1999a). From the perspective of social communication, the expressive components of emotions function as an appeal in social contexts; that is, affects become signals that are perceived, interpreted, and responded to by the social partner according to her inherited, individually acquired, and culturally nuanced communicative competencies.

The psychophysiological affective reactivity is subject to considerable individual variability (*constitution* or *temperament*), especially in relation to its arousal components such as excitability and self-regulated modulation of arousal (Rothbart, Derryberry, & Posner, 1994), but also in relation to specific affective qualities such as anxious-inhibited temperament (Kagan, 1997), negative emotionality (Thomas, Chess, & Birch, 1968), and aggressiveness (Shaw, Gilliom, & Giovanelli, 2000).

Affects/emotions develop and become differentiated with regard to the child's conscious awareness, their functions as signals, and their evaluative and action-regulating functions (Friedlmeier, 1999; Holodynski, 1999b). Notably, the development and differentiation of emotion regulation depend on communication with the primary caregiver in a twofold sense, regarding both the dynamic regulation of emotional arousal and the action-regulating function of the emotions. The development of emotion regulation occurs in discernible steps, beginning in the first months of life with predominantly parent-led interactional regulation. This is followed by phases in which the infant becomes an increasingly active and intentional participant in interactional coregulations, and continues to the final transition from interactional to innerpsychic regulation during the late toddler and preschool ages (Friedlmeier, 1999; Holodynski, 1999b; Sroufe, 1996; Thompson, 1994).

The infant and her parents are well equipped with complementary psychobiological dispositions for successful interactional regulation (H. Papoušek & Papoušek, 1987). The newborn has only basic self-regulatory capacities to control arousal; however, she is equipped with a repertoire of discrete facial expressions of the so-called basic emotions (interest, distress, happiness, sadness, surprise, disgust, anger, fear), with an alarming vocal signal, crying, and with complex body language that expresses her psycho-physiological state of well-being. The infant's expressive affective behavior differentially elicits intuitive parental competencies, that is, complementary psychobiologically anchored behavioral dispositions and strategies for regulating the infant's level of affective arousal.

With the first developmental spurt (see chapter 4), the infant begins to incorporate visual, facial, and vocal expressions during playful face-to-face dialogues with her parents with a growing sense of self-efficacy. The infant's capacity to express and perceive emotions becomes increasingly refined through the interplay with the parents' intuitive affective communication (simplified and contrast-rich facial and vocal expressions, modulation of affective arousal, contingent responsive mirroring of the infant's affective behavior and attribution of meaning). The infant recognizes commonalities between her own and her parents' facial expressions and contingent relations between the expressive behavior and her subjective experience of affective state. Repetitive patterns of emotional regulation during preverbal early communication are stored in the infant's procedural memory as implicit relational knowing (Stern, 1985). These patterns later become an important matrix for the infant's internal working model of attachment. At the same time, crying and other involuntary behavioral expressions of emotional states develop into communicative signals that express distinctive emotions (anger, frustration, sadness, fear, abandonment, etc.), and the infant becomes capable of instrumental and intentional communication of these different emotions directed at the caregiver.

Age-Related Developmental Tasks: 7 to 9 Months

After a phase of comprehensive reorganization processes, infant development undergoes a further shift around the middle of the second half-year and allows a new level of integrative processes and self-regulation. This shift has been described as "discovery of intersubjectivity" (Stern, 1985; Trevarthen, 1980), the beginning of focused (Emde, 1984) or person-specific attachment (Bowlby, 1969), or the beginning of the awareness of self-efficacy (Crockenberg & Leerkes, 2000). New motor and vocal capabilities as well as new cognitive competencies, emotional regulation, and communicative capacities all contribute to this shift.

Self-controlled locomotion and self-righting expand the scope of exploration and play. The infant's increasing need for exploration is no longer limited by what her little arms can reach, but she now tries to conquer distant objects and the entire room (H. Papoušek, 2003; see also chapter 4, Table 4.1). If the capacity for locomotion lags behind the infant's impulse to explore, boredom and frustration may result, as well as a need to be carried around and passively entertained.

New cognitive competencies (object- and person permanence; for a review, see Rauh, 2002) enable the infant to access from memory previously integrated experiences with herself and her primary caregivers. The infant integrates models or representational schemes, which she can now use intentionally to guide her actions and regulate her emotions, even in the absence of her caregivers.

Emotional regulation in contexts of preverbal communication gains a new intersubjective dimension during this phase (Stern, 1985). The child becomes aware of her own feelings, interests, desires, and intentions as well as of the feelings and intentions of others. She directs her attention preferentially to where the primary caregivers focus their attention (*joint attention*; Tomasello, 1995), to the emotions with which they react to new events (*social referencing*; Campos & Stenbert, 1981), and to how they handle objects and events in the environment (*observational learning*; Gopnik, Kuhl, & Meltzoff, 2001). Particularly in unfamiliar or otherwise unsettling situations, the infant orients herself by referencing back toward the parent's emotional appraisal in order to learn how to evaluate the situation, and is then guided by this in her own emotional reactivity and behavior regulation (such as approach or withdrawal; Campos & Stenbert, 1981). Thus, contingent and clear emotional signals in the parent's face, gestures, and voice become important means of regulatory support.

Affective attunement (Stern, 1985) has similar functions. This aspect of intuitive parental competencies manifests itself in immediate emotional empathy with the infant's momentary experience. The parents perceive and match the affective dynamics of their infant's actions and imitate these in another modality, usually vocally or with other affective expressions. They thus mirror the dynamic qualities of the child's emotional engagement, her efforts, kinetic energy, surprise, disappointments, or relief. This form of contingent emotional attunement paves the way for the infant to become aware of her own subjective experience, to recognize the commonalities between her experience and her parents' emotional expressions, and to share her feelings with her parents. The relative intensity of the parents' affective attunement also contributes to the modulation of arousal, and can encourage and reinforce or dampen the infant's activity and exploration.

The intersubjective dimension of communication depends on the emotional availability of the parents (Emde, 1984) and thus on an emotionally unrestricted access to their intuitive parenting competencies. It is important in this respect that the parents let themselves engage in the infant's subjective perspective and, relying on their own competencies, allow themselves to be guided by their infant's signals (see chapter 4). During this phase, the child becomes increasingly receptive to the affective state, feelings, and emotional stances of her primary caregivers. Unfortunately, this applies as well to a parent's potential depression, anxiousness, specific fears, or anger, as well as to emotional reactions that are consciously displayed and seem artificial, overexaggerated, or false, because they are not affectively attuned to the child's emotional experience.

Another new component of intersubjective emotional regulation is *intentional communication*, or the ability to direct goal-oriented wishes, intentions, and needs to the primary caregiver. Intentional communication functions as a directed appeal that is meant to elicit a specific desired action from the primary caregiver. If the child feels generally successful in these attempts, she will develop a sense of effectance and self-confidence at a new level of intersubjective relatedness and will begin to trust that she will be able to achieve her own goals.

Intentional communication of negative feelings such as fear, frustration, and anger takes on particular significance for the emergence of attachment. Recurrent communication patterns are crucial particularly in situations where a distressed infant turns to her attachment figure seeking proximity, security, and regulatory support. In these contexts, the infant builds up self-regulatory strategies for interpsychic and intrapsychic regulation of negative affects. The learned attachment strategies have been observed, analyzed, and classified in attachment research, using the standardized Strange Situation. If the child reliably experiences that her crying is heard and receives regulatory support, her closeness to the primary caregiver will function as a secure base to which she may trustingly communicate negative feelings (*secure attachment*) and receive regulatory support. If the child is rejected when she cries, the primary caregiver's protective proximity will only be secure if the child learns to minimize or completely hide her negative feelings in order to avoid renewed rejection (*insecure-avoidant attachment*). If the primary caregiver responds inconsistently or unpredictably to the infant's crying, or is emotionally unreachable, the child learns to secure protective closeness by exaggerated attachment behavior with escalating clinginess, demandingness, and crying, even though she now runs the risk of triggering hidden or open rejection (*insecure-ambivalent attachment*).

Developmental Aspects of Anxiety and Fears

Anxiety or fear unfold as a new emotional system in close connection with the beginning of independent locomotion and person-specific attachment, and may serve adaptive protective functions. Anxiety and fear are triggered during this phase by separation from the secure base of the primary caregiver or when dealing with unknown situations or strangers. Anxiety and fear come into play whenever the unknown is perceived as threatening. These affects elicit immediate motor inhibition with simultaneous cortical arousal and increased vigilance and attention for analyzing the threatening situation, as well as peripheral physiological activation and tension and a disposition toward withdrawal and flight.

A variety of explanatory models can be found in the literature about the fear of strangers emerging around the age of 7 to 9 months (see Rauh, 2002). It may be viewed to some extent as the converse of person-specific attachment and intimacy with the primary caregiver. It is theorized that the anxiety caused by the stranger results from the newly acquired capacities for intersubjective emotional regulation, which at this stage is only possible within the finely attuned person-specific communication with the familiar attachment figure.

Uncertainty and separation anxiety, as well as a need for security and regulatory support in the safe haven of the attachment relationship, are elicited by increasing distance or separation from the primary caregiver. The regulation of proximity to and distance from the primary caregiver in relation to the antagonistic needs for security and exploration of the environment is one of the central developmental tasks that need to be mastered jointly by parents and infant during this phase.

Age-typical triggers of extreme separation anxiety include repeated experiences of separation or hospitalizations, a strange environment when moving to a new home or going on vacation, overload in infant play groups, abrupt changes of the caregiver, being placed in day care, reentry of the mother into the workforce, or loss of a significant attachment figure. It is crucial in such situations that the infant's fears can be successfully regulated through parent–infant interpsychic communication.

During the second year of life, generalized anxiousness about the unknown accompanied by social inhibition and withdrawal has mainly been attributed to temperamental factors such as unadaptability, low thresholds to stimuli, or social withdrawal. Kagan (1994, 1997) conducted extensive prospective longitudinal studies of the anxious-inhibited temperament with regard to its neurobiological and psychophysiological correlates, genetic factors, behavioral aspects, and developmental course in the context of parent–child relationships. It is especially interesting at the behavioral level that these infants had exhibited generalized negative hyperreactivity to a series of unknown stimuli (strong motor arousal and crying) at the age of 4 months, but began to exhibit the complete picture of social inhibition only during the second year of life (Kagan, 1997). The anxious-inhibited temperament exhibits remarkable stability and continuity from toddlerhood to preschool age. Thus, children who react negatively and anxiously to new situations and even to known but discrepant stimuli at the age of 14 and 21 months have a high probability of being socially inhibited at the age of 4 1/2 years (Fox, Henderson, Rubin, Calkins, & Schmidt, 2001).

Age-Related Developmental Tasks: Second Year of Life

Increased mobility, and independent walking and climbing in particular, opens up an almost endless potential for exploration at the beginning of the second year of life, and infants take on this new challenge with a sense of enthusiasm, self-efficacy, and willfulness, even though they inevitably come up against limits. The parents frequently need to step in for the child's safety and when the child's activities conflict with the rules of the social environment (Emde, 1984). These changes are associated with a comprehensive affective reorganization and new developmental tasks for the parents (Biringen et al., 1995).

Progress in motor skills, vocalization, emotionality, communication, and integration of experiences that depend on maturation provide the conditions for a third comprehensive transformational phase during the middle of the second year of life in which the growing needs for autonomy become the central theme. This developmental shift brings about new levels of regulation and integrative processes related to the development of self, social communication, verbal integration, and action organization (Bischof-Köhler, 1998; Crockenberg & Leerkes, 2000; Emde, 1984; Rauh, 2002; Stern, 1985).

The child discovers herself as initiator and agent of her own actions with her own desires, intentions, and goals, and begins to plan and organize goal-directed actions purposefully with an eye toward results. The anticipated results now become more important than the action itself, which is a clear departure from just a few months earlier. The child's intensive emotional involvement is also fed by her needs for autonomy and self-efficacy, her mastery motivation, her desire to do and have things herself, and her self-assertion and self-conscious willfulness (Bischof-Köhler, 1998). The child now passes through a phase during which she may become fixed on a goal but still lacks flexibility and is unwilling to allow herself to be distracted from the pursuit of that goal. As a consequence, she appears particularly stubborn and strong-willed at this stage. If the child is prevented from accomplishing her goals by objective or subjective restraints, or by some protective or educational intervention, she may easily fall into a motivational void (Heckhausen, 1987) and become completely disorganized. If she isn't immediately presented with an alternative action, her anger and rage coupled with aggressive tendencies may increase rapidly and end up in a full-blown temper tantrum.

Temper tantrums are often part of the phase-typical developmental perturbations at this age. Thus, in a random sample of first-born boys aged 15 and 21 months, Belsky and colleagues (1996) observed marked problems with tantrums in 62% at one or both ages. Tantrums tend to decrease in intensity and frequency over the course of the third year of life as action competence and linguistic capacities increase—unless they are maintained by dysfunctional communication patterns.

Conflicts between the child's intentions and goals and those of the parents are unavoidable in day-to-day interactions between parents and their child, mostly in connection with scaffolding and teaching the child to adapt to the rules and conventions of social life, and in relation to limits, cultural norms, and values.

Interpsychic emotion regulation enters a new phase with the ability for delayed imitation of complex actions during the second year of life and with the child's growing tendencies to identify with the primary caregiver. The child begins to acquire and internalize the emotions and behaviors of her parents by observational learning, the significance of which is often underestimated.

A similar transition from interpsychic regulation to intrapsychic self-regulation occurs with the child's growing readiness to cooperate and comply with the everyday "dos" and "don'ts," with her readiness to adopt the parents' goals and to follow their requests or demands to stop doing something enjoyable or to do something that is not (Crockenberg & Leerkes, 2000; Kochanska, Coy, & Murray, 2001). Communication is needed to find a balance between one's own goals and those of the other person, to negotiate compromise, or to clarify which goal takes priority in one context or another. Empirical studies have justifiably distinguished between adaptive *committed compliance* and maladaptive *compulsive compliance* (Crittenden & DiLalla, 1988; Kochanska et al., 2001). Committed compliance can develop without problems when it builds on secure attachment relationships in which the child has an easy time identifying with and accepting the goals of the primary caregiver.

Numerous studies have shown, however, that secure attachment alone is not sufficient for mastering the developmental challenges of the second year of life without problems. The child-rearing competencies of the parents are just as critical, that is, their capacity to deal with both the need of the child to assert herself and her need for appropriate limits (Crittenden & DiLalla, 1988). Longitudinal studies have shown that problems of emotional and behavioral regulation in toddlers and preschool children generally depend on both the attachment pattern formed during the first year of life and the subsequent interaction patterns (Crockenberg & Leerkes, 2000).

Open and sympathetic parental communication about negative emotions such as anger, disappointment, rage, defiance, and aggressiveness is one of the new challenges brought on by "the terrible twos" (Gopnik et al., 2001). This is an age of increased vulnerability, low tolerance of frustration, and once again, increased needs for emotional security and physical closeness. Toddlers occasionally express these needs in aggressive forms of proximity-seeking, clinginess, and demands for attention, understanding, and acceptance. Marked temperamental differences in the child's capacity for self-regulation of intense affective arousal (impulsivity, negative emotionality) may lead to greater difficulty during this time.

The child's needs for autonomy interact with her awakening consciousness of self. Around the middle of the second year of life, the child will recognize herself as a figurative "I" in the mirror (Bischof-Köhler, 1989). Her new mental capacities of symbolization and representation of past and present experiences open for the child an inner world of mental activities and imagination. This enables her to integrate experiences and test out solutions to conflicts in her fantasies and/or in symbolic play (Bischof-Köhler, 1998). The development of self-recognition also coincides with the emergence of empathy. The child begins to understand the feelings and intentions of the social partner, to interpret them from the other person's mental perspective, and to respond accordingly with prosocial behavior (Bischof-Köhler, 1989). The capacity to evaluate oneself and one's own behavior from the perspective of the social partner begins to develop toward the end of the second year of life. This includes role expectations and social standards (as a boy or girl, as competent or incompetent, as acceptable or unacceptable, as good or bad), and the ability to adapt to the rules and standards of social life. This also enables the child to predict the behavior and expectations of her primary caregiver. Interestingly, new self-referencing emotions such as self-esteem, mastery-related satisfaction, pride, and embarrassment also develop during the second year of life; shame and guilt feelings begin to be seen in the third and fourth year.

Developmental Aspects of Anger and Aggression

From a psychobiological perspective, anger and rage are part of an adaptive system of self-assertion. These emotions are typically elicited at this age by uncontrollable limitations on spontaneous or goal-oriented action or expectations, including restrictions on the child's freedom to move, abrupt interruption of a pleasurable activity, withdrawal of an attractive object, postponement of an expected reward, failure of an intended playful action, or restriction of exploratory activities. Anger activates psychophysiological and behavioral dispositions to ward off and overcome the obstacles in question.

Aggressive forms of behavior such as biting, scratching, kicking, hitting, pulling hair, pushing, or snatching toys away, as well as later physical attack and fighting, are part of the normal repertoire of young boys and girls. Such behaviors typically increase rapidly between 12 and 17 months and can be found in 80% of children at 17 months (Tremblay, 1999). They peak at the age of 2 and then decrease significantly until about the age of 5 (Shaw et al., 2000; Shaw, Owens, Giovanelli, & Winslow, 2001). In most cases, these early forms of aggressive behavior are generally not problematic in their narrow sense, that is, as aggression targeted at a person or object with the intention of destroying, injuring, or intimidating. Rather, they are mostly in the service of curiosity, exploration, demands for attention and contact, or needs for autonomy and self-assertion, and are not necessarily associated with anger. For instance, snatching a toy away from another child is primarily directed at the toy and not at the child. Within the child's own play room, arguments over "mine" and "yours" may trigger aggressive behavior. Physically aggressive behavior is significantly more common among boys, among toddlers with siblings, and in groups of young children where there are numerous opportunities for conflict around toys. Girls, on the other hand, are known to dominate in verbal rather than physical aggressiveness.

The question posed by the increase in aggression-like behavior during the second year of life is less under which conditions aggressive behavioral problems originate, but rather what causes such problems to be maintained beyond the second and third years of life. Persistence of true aggressive behavior is usually associated with severe problems in the family, such as a failure of parental child-rearing competencies, aggressive modeling within the family, or conflict-laden parent–child relationships with emotional abuse and rejection of the child. Aggressive behavior disappears in the majority of children as they gain in language and social competency. Shaw and colleagues (2000, 2001), however, reported on a group of boys from the lower socioeconomic class who had exhibited extreme scores on the CBCL scale Externalizing Behavior at the age of 2 years, and who continued to obtain extremely high rates of persistent aggressive behavioral problems at early school age.

According to comprehensive literature reviews (Campbell, 1995; Crockenberg & Leerkes, 2000; Shaw et al., 2000), the following factors have been shown to contribute to the persistence of aggressive behavior into the preschool years: sex (boys); temperament (negative emotionality, impulsivity, low tolerance for frustration); disorganized attachment; antisocial behavior of the father before the child's birth; depression and other mental disorders in the mother; couples' conflicts; ongoing physical aggression and violence in the family; experience of violence in the mother's childhood; poverty; and social disadvantage.

THE PARENTS' DEVELOPMENTAL TASKS AND CHILD-REARING COMPETENCIES

As their infant develops, parents can count on facing numerous new challenges. Toward the end of the first year of life—often in connection with weaning—the mother enters a new phase of detachment that may elicit sadness, fears, and occasional feelings of abandonment. "Letting go" is more difficult if early infancy was characterized by excessive crying and extremely ambivalent feelings toward the baby and toward her maternal role, or if the mother still feels deprived of the expected harmony and intimacy in the early mother–infant relationship she had always dreamed of.

Parallel to this development, the mother's long-deferred needs for autonomy also begin to stir around the beginning of the second year. A transition to part-time day care and part-time work may satisfy her need for some independence and self-efficacy. Yet she must also find the appropriate time for the baby and for herself, she must be able to delegate responsibilities, and she must learn to deal successfully with situations involving separation from her infant.

Understandably, this may become problematic when the mother and infant have experienced traumatic separation episodes before, such as after a premature birth, early postpartum separation or hospitalization, life-threatening events, and diseases. Other risk factors include a parent's attachment-related traumatic experience of separation, loss, or abandonment; a parent's anxiety disorder; unresolved dependency–autonomy conflicts with the families of origin; and/or a symbiotic parent–infant relationship. Such distressing conditions may cause the parents, in particular the mother, to lose the balance between their own need for closeness and their mostly neglected desire for autonomy.

During the second year of life, the child's own need for autonomy places increasing demands on the parents' child-rearing competencies, which frequently takes them by surprise and causes them to feel overwhelmed. They have to figure out how to navigate their way through this particular set of problems and negotiate their child-rearing goals and styles in the heterogeneous context of family, societal, and cultural expectations and demands. The widely recognized goals of child rearing during this phase of life consist of (a) the necessity of setting certain limits on the child's kinetic energy and exploratory needs in order to keep her safe, (b) presenting rules for living with other people, (c) feeding the child an age-appropriate and healthy diet, (d) practicing habits of bodily care, (e) providing for a regular daytime schedule and adequate sleep time, (f) fostering the child's independence, and (g) supporting the child in developing into an independent, competent, and social human being (Schneewind, 2002).

Frequently, the parents find themselves caught between their desire to continue satisfying every wish of their child and the growing pressures of having to socialize their child— that is, the need to place certain reins on the child's spontaneous development, to set limits, and to expect the child to cope with challenges, demands, and occasional frustrations. In this process, qualitatively different child-rearing styles sometimes develop very early that are in conflict with the parents' own deliberate intent or principles, often without their awareness. In family research, following Maccoby and Martin (1983), four prototypical child-rearing styles have been distinguished: an autonomous-authoritative style (accepting, clearly structured), an authoritarian style (rejecting, controlling, exercising power), a neglecting style (rejecting, giving little or no guidance), and a permissive style (accepting, no demands, little guidance; Schneewind, 2002). Numerous original studies and an array of review studies of the current literature have come to the conclusion that an autonomous authoritative child-rearing style characterized by warmth, firm but fair limits and controls, and understandable explanations has the best chance of achieving the above child-rearing goals—even with constitutionally difficult children (Campbell, 1995; Crockenberg & Leerkes, 2000; Laucht, 2002). By contrast, child-rearing styles in which the parents' behavior is negatively controlling, unpredictable, inconsistent, or uninvolved are associated with an increased incidence of noncompliance, excessive defiance, oppositional behavior, and poor internalization of parental standards. If an authoritarian child-rearing style is combined with a lack of emotional availability and warmth, the child will experience parental attention only in reaction to her aversive behavior, whereas her prosocial behavior is ignored or responded to with derogatory signals. Such interaction patterns provide conditions in which noncompliance and aggressive behavior are maintained (Dumas & Wahler, 1985).

Infant and Parental Risk Factors: Clinical Data

The behavioral problems observed in late infancy and toddlerhood may be viewed as extreme variants of normal early childhood problems of behavioral and emotional regulation that appear in an aggravated form as the child deals with phase-typical developmental tasks or critical life events (birth of a sibling, hospitalization, moving, or beginning day care). Multiple prenatal, perinatal, and postnatal organic and psychosocial stressors contribute to exacerbation and persistence of what are generally transient problems. The stressors either compromise the child's self-regulation or the parents' psychological condition and their communicative and child-rearing competencies, and thus create and maintain dysfunctional parent–infant interactions (see the systemic model in chapter 4). This is confirmed by the clinical data from the Munich Program.

It is particularly interesting for those involved in prevention and treatment efforts to know whether the risk factors for excessive clinginess/fearfulness, excessive defiance, and aggressiveness differ from each other. This question has been difficult to answer because of the frequent co-occurrence of these syndromes and their even more frequent co-occurrence with dysphoric restlessness, sleep disorders, and feeding disorders. The following procedure was used to cope with this problem. First, the relevant age group for each particular syndrome was singled out from the entire sample of 701 families. Then, the partial sample with the particular syndrome was compared with the remaining subjects of the same age group with regard to temperament (Infant Characteristics Questionnaire [ICQ]), the mother's emotional state (Maternal Childcare Attitudes and Feelings [EMKK] and Edinburgh Postnatal Depression Scale [EPDS]), and the quality of the mother-child relationship (Parent–Infant Relationship Global Assessment Scale [PIR-GAS]), as well as the most common risk factors (for information on the scales, see chapter 3). This analysis yielded a number of interesting differences among the syndromes.

As expected, the partial sample clinginess–fearfulness–separation anxiety (age $\geq$ 4 months; n = 86) was characterized by temperamental difficulties with significantly less favorable scores on the Inadaptability scale than in the control sample (n = 503) and a sixfold increase in extreme manifestations on this scale (defined as > 2 SDs above the standard mean) as compared to the control sample (18% vs. 3%; $p \leq$ .01). In terms of the mothers' emotional state, the EMKK revealed significantly elevated scores on the subscales Fearful Overprotectiveness ($p \leq$ .001) in addition to differences on the scales Depressiveness ($p \leq$ .01) and Distressing Childhood ($p \leq$ .05). The EPDS Depression scale more frequently showed signs of a clinically relevant depression (defined as scores above the cut-off; 12: 39% vs. 28%). The quality of the mother–child relationship was more frequently classified as disordered according to the PIR-GAS (24% vs. 10%; $p \leq$ .001). Among the psychosocial stressors, significantly elevated rates were found for severe couples' conflicts (47% vs. 27%; $p \leq$ .001), unresolved traumatic loss in the mother's prior history (19% vs. 11%; $p \leq$ .05), and conflicts in the mother–child relationship (19% vs. 7%, $p \leq$ .001).

By contrast, the partial group of children with excessive defiance (age $\geq$ 7 months; n = 141) differed from the other children in the age group (n = 333) in terms of temperament mainly on the Fussy-Difficult scale ($p \leq$ .001): the percentage of extreme scores was four times as high as in the control group (38% vs. 12%; $p \leq$ .001). In addition, their mean scores on the Stubborn and Unsociable scales differed significantly from those of the rest of the age group ($p \leq$ .01 and $p \leq$ .05, respectively). Chronic overstrain ($p \leq$ .001), tendency to punish ($p \leq$ .001), and frustration ($p \leq$ .01) were significantly more pronounced in the mothers of defiant children, in addition to slightly elevated scores of depressiveness ($p \leq$ .05), lack of pleasure in the child ($p \leq$ .05), and rigidity ($p \leq$ .05). Here, too, the percentage of disordered mother–child relationships on the PIR-GAS was elevated to the same extent as in the fearful group (24% vs. 9%; $p \leq$ .001). Among the specific psychosocial stressors in the defiant group, the percentage of severely disturbed couples' relationships was more than double that of the control group (51% vs. 24%; $p \leq$ .001). Just as clearly elevated were the percentages of ongoing severe intergenerational conflicts with the families of origin (32% vs. 17%; $p \leq$ .001), of violence experienced by the mother in her own childhood (13% vs. 5%; $p \leq$ .005), and conflicts in the mother–child relationship (20% vs. 5%; $p \leq$ .001).

Remarkably, there were no specific differences in temperament in the partial group of children with aggressive/oppositional behavior (age $\geq$ 12 months; n = 40) when compared to the control group

(n = 213). However, elevated rates of emotional distress in these mothers were all the more evident, with marked differences in the mean scores and in the rates of extreme scores on the subscales Chronic Overstrain ($p \leq .001$), Depressiveness ($p \leq .001$), Anxious Overprotectiveness ($p \leq .001$), Frustration ($p \leq .05$), Distressing Childhood ($p \leq .005$), and Tendency to Punish ($p \leq .05$). Among the specific psychosocial stressors, by far the highest rates (as compared to the other syndromes) were found for severe couples' conflicts (64% vs. 31% in the control group; $p \leq .001$), severe intergenerational conflicts (42% vs. 17%; $p \leq .001$), violence experienced by the mother in her own childhood (22% vs. 7%; $p \leq .001$), and conflicts in the mother–child relationship (29% vs. 8%; $p \leq .001$). The rate for disordered relationships on the PIR-GAS was 38% as opposed to 13% ($p \leq .001$).

The data clearly show that the three syndromes are more than merely extreme manifestations of normal phase-typical behavior problems. Rather, the problems should be seen in the context of multiple psychosocial risk factors with significant impairment of the psychological resources of the mother and the families, infants' temperament problems, and a high percentage of early manifest disorders of the mother–child relationship. The highest accumulation of psychosocial stressors was found in families of children with aggressive/oppositional behavior.

The pronounced impairment of the mother–child relationship is not surprising given the long duration of regulation problems that were present since birth in the majority of cases and the dysfunctional interactional patterns evident in many interactional domains. In addition, the level of self-regulatory functioning was distinctly impaired in the domains of earlier developmental tasks that had still not been mastered, namely falling asleep and sleeping through the night, self-feeding, and self-initiated play. In many cases, the regulatory balance between attachment and exploration had not yet been achieved as well.

The behavioral syndromes are tied almost exclusively to the relational context with its dysfunctional patterns of communication in which the interactional regulation fails in one way or another, and which maintains or even worsens the disorder. Over and above the dysfunctional interactional patterns in social encounters with strangers, separation contexts, or boundary-setting and limit-setting situations, the following patterns of disturbed emotional relatedness may also be distinguished (M. Papoušek & von Hofacker, 2002): lack of relatedness (underinvolved), symbiotic relatedness (overinvolved), anxiously overprotective relatedness (anxious–tense), enmeshed-conflicted relatedness (angry–hostile), and covert or overt rejection (abusive).

The observed relational patterns are very often a part of a conflict-laden multigenerational family system with unresolved intergenerational conflicts over dependency and autonomy on the part of one or both parents, which are then reenacted in the parents' child-rearing styles and in interactions with the child (Cierpka & Cierpka, 2000). However, the child also makes an important contribution with her individual temperamental difficulties, which impede the coregulation of developmental tasks in daily interactions from earliest infancy.

DISORDER-SPECIFIC DIAGNOSTIC PROCEDURES

As in crying, sleeping, and feeding disorders, the medical and psychological procedures focus on the diagnostic triad: presenting behavioral problems of the child, the psychological state of the mother and father in their roles as parents and partners, and the parent–child communication and relationships during joint play and in contexts that are relevant to the behavioral and relational problems (von Hofacker et al., 2003).

Behavioral observations of the child during the counseling sessions with her parents play a central role. They focus on the child's exploratory and play behavior; her social contact with parents, pediatrician, and therapist; and on the parents' emotional relatedness to the child and to each other. In addition, video-supported behavioral observations are indispensable, both in interactional contexts that are relevant to the behavioral problems and in standardized semistructured challenging situations such as the medical examination. These are critical for evaluating the child's self-regulatory competencies, affective and attentional regulation, frustration tolerance, and context-appropriate behavior (see Table 8.1 for details).

DISORDER-SPECIFIC COUNSELING AND TREATMENT

Counseling and treatment follow the model of communication-centered parent–infant counseling and psychotherapy as detailed in chapter 12. Developmental counseling that is geared to the phase-specific developmental and child-rearing tasks and to the observable strengths and weaknesses of the child has generally proven to be an effective part of the intervention. In cases of isolated excessive defiance, early forms of aggressiveness, fearfulness, or clinginess that have been triggered by current life events, simple (video-supported) interaction guidance with a focus on communication may be sufficient to solve the behavioral problems and unburden the parents and their relationship with the child. However, whenever the parent–child relationship is extremely distressed, endangered, or even manifestly disordered, communication-centered relational psychotherapy becomes the core of the therapeutic process. This approach integrates the behavioral level of parent–infant interactions and the representational level of the parents' psychological distress, relational representations, and psychodynamic processes (see chapter 12).

The therapy emphasizes the play context for strengthening the quality of the parent–child relationship, and aims at reinforcing adaptive communication patterns and dissolving maladaptive patterns. Interactional contexts that are most relevant to the behavioral problems (e.g., limit setting) are chosen for dissolving vicious circles and improving behavioral and emotional coregulation. Video-supported psychotherapy in both contexts can contribute a great deal toward addressing and clarifying the parents' feelings of insecurity, ambivalence, fear, frustration, or anger evoked by the child's behavior, and to identify the parents' and the infant's immediate needs. The therapy becomes particularly effective when the resolution of a maladaptive vicious circle or interactional conflict is not only elaborated verbally but played out and practiced in the here and now of the therapeutic situation. Such a procedure allows the therapist to directly address the specific individual problems of the child or the psychodynamic barriers in the parents. The session is concluded with consideration of how the positive interactional experience may be carried over into the family's everyday life at home. Various aspects of this video-supported communication-centered relational therapy are listed in Table 8.2 for each of the regulatory syndromes.

Table 8.1. Diagnostic Assessment of Parent–Child Communication and Relationships During Late Infancy and Toddlerhood (With or Without Video Analysis and Video Feedback).

Observation and video recording in semistructured interactional contexts:

–Choice of age-typical observational episodes relevant to the presenting behavioral problems: free play – catching soap bubbles – teaching/seeking help with difficult tasks – playing alone next to the "working" parent – limit setting – cooperation/cleaning up – separation/reunion (see also Zeanah et al., 2000)

Joint access with the parent(s) to the observable interaction:

–(1) Selection and focus on positive sequences; (2) selection and focus on dysfunctional sequences

Interactional context	Behaviors of particular interest
Play:	–Infant curiosity, interest in exploration, initiative, persistence, visual contact, seeking help; –Parental support, affective attunement, joint focused attention, verbal and nonverbal communication related to the play focus, directive, intrusive behavior
Unfamiliar surroundings: (Treatment room at first visit)	–Proximity-distance regulation, warm-up time, readiness to explore, reassuring looks –Unambiguousness of parental messages, emotional reassurance
Solitary free play: (Parent sits near the child and reads or fills out a questionnaire; child plays on the floor	–Play competencies, regulation of attention, seeking proximity, demanding mother's attention, clinginess, provocative behavior; –Unambiguous parental messages, contingencies of gaze and attentional focus, (toward or away from child), clarity of boundaries and limits, positive and negative contingencies, functional and dysfunctional communication patterns
Parental requests: ("dos," cleaning up)	–Compliance when cleaning up –Clarity of parent's request, positive and negative contingencies, functional and dysfunctional communication patterns
Limit setting: ("don'ts," previously negotiated with therapist)	–Compliance, ignoring the parent's "no," limit testing –Clarity/unambiguousness of setting boundaries and limits, positive and negative contingencies functional and dysfunctional communication patterns
Separation (only as long as tolerable) **and return:**	–Seeking proximity upon return/avoidance/ambivalence; soothability, returning to play, indications of the child's attachment strategies –Quality of soothing, quality of body contact, distraction

Joint access to representational level:

–Empathetic entering into the parents' subjective experience of the episodes, of certain infant behaviors, of the parents' own role and behaviors;

–Perception of and attribution of meaning to infant signals (positive and negative);

–Addressing feelings, associations, memories, and fantasies evoked by concrete child behaviors or associated with concrete parental behaviors

Standardized assessment of the parent–child relationship:

–Parent–Infant Relationship Global Assessment Scale (ZERO TO THREE, 2000), a 9-step scale for evaluating parent–child relationships, based on global clinical assessment of the chronicity, severity, and pervasiveness of regulatory problems, dysfunctional interactional patterns, the degree of emotional distress, and the impairment of the infant's level of functioning

One rule has proven to be particularly important in this work: Each demand placed on the child and the parents must be balanced by a positive relational experience guided by the child's needs and interests and characterized by positive reciprocity, relatedness, and the parents' undivided attention. It is recommended that the day be structured into brief situations alternating between short play episodes led by the child with undivided parental attention and emotional availability, episodes in which the child plays alone in the parent's sight while the parent is focusing on something else, and episodes in which the child is included in household activities.

Table 8.2. Disorder-Specific Aspects of Video-Supported Counseling and Communication-Centered Relational Therapy.

Behavioral syndrome (relevant interactional context)	Therapeutic focus
Excessive clinginess (solitary free play)	–Providing clear, unambiguous messages (understandable for the child) that the child should play by herself for a short time while the parent pays full attention to some important matter. The parent should not respond to the child's demands for attention in this context. –Conveying security and calmness while consistently encouraging self-initiated exploration and play –Clarifying the child's momentary need for proximity or attention –Clarifying and dealing with the parents' feelings, memories, and images evoked by the context –Addressing and working through parental fears that may be evoked related to former distressing or traumatic experiences of separation and loss, fears around thriving and survival, and the parents' possible unfulfilled needs for closeness and emotional security –Learning to trust the child's ability to play by herself –Helping the parent to support the child's motivation to play at home, first in close proximity for a short time, then progressively longer and more distant
Separation anxiety (separation and return of the primary caregiver)	–Conveying security before and after separation –Practicing how to separate and return in brief episodes with clear advance notice and warm attention given upon reunion –Addressing and dealing with the parents' feelings and memories elicited by the separation situation and soothing upon return –Supporting the parents in conveying security, safety, and closeness to their child in order to provide corrective attachment experiences –Addressing and working through parental fears related to former distressing or traumatic experiences of separation and loss, fears around thriving and survival, and the parents' unfulfilled needs for closeness and emotional security
Fearfulness, social inhibition (observation during first visit and medical examination)	–Helping the parent to perceive and understand the child's signals and regulatory difficulties –Allowing sufficient warm-up time, encouraging initiatives for exploration and social contact –Supporting contact and social relationships with one or two peers

continued

Table 8.2. Disorder-Specific Aspects of Video-Supported Counseling and Communication-Centered Relational Therapy (*continued*).

Behavioral syndrome (relevant interactional context)	Therapeutic focus
Excessive defiance (limit setting, requests, solitary free play)	–Negotiating "dos" and "don'ts," rules and limits between both parents and with the therapist –Friendly, clear, and consistent introduction and implementation of requests, social rules, and limits –Building bridges that permit the child to retreat without losing face in case of temper tantrums or failure to obey rules; at the same time, supporting and promoting the child's self-regulatory capacities (e.g., making available a pacifier or transitional object); rituals of reconciliation after a power struggle or temper tantrum –Parental timeout if needed in order to defuse anger and avoid escalation –Avoiding derogatory negative feedback to the child; instead, supporting feelings of self-esteem, self-efficacy, and mastery –Addressing and dealing with parents' feelings and memories related to their own parents' child-rearing styles and the affects elicited by the temper tantrum
Aggressive/oppositional behavior (any instance of spontaneous aggressive behavior, such as during limit setting. solitary play, return upon separation)	–Modeling, encouraging, and supporting prosocial behavior –Friendly, clear limit setting in cases of aggressive behavior and guidance in prosocial behavior –Understanding the child's negative affects and accepting the child, while at the same time rejecting her aggressive behavior –Avoiding harsh verbal or physical discipline, being aware of observational learning –Supporting and enhancing feelings of self-esteem –Addressing and working through parental experiences of aggression and violence during childhood or currently in the families of origin or in the couples' relationship, as well as feelings and memories elicited by the child's aggressive behavior or associated with specific parental behaviors

SUMMARY AND OUTLOOK

This chapter presents a phenomenological description of the most common syndromes of behavioral and emotional dysregulation that were observed co-occurring with sleep disorders, feeding disorders, and dysphoric restlessness/disinterest in play among the clients of the Munich Program between ages 9 and 30 months. The syndromes typically coincide with age-related developmental tasks that are discussed in relation to parent–child communication and its role in the interpsychic regulation and growing self-regulation of behavior and emotion. They may be distinguished from extreme variants of normal phase-typical behavioral problems by the overall amount of resulting distress in the family system as evidenced by (a) the duration, severity, and pervasiveness of the behavioral problems; (b) the parents' psychological distress; (c) distress and endangerment of the parent–child relationships; (d) the accumulation of biological and psychosocial stressors; and (e) impairment of the child's emotional and social functioning.

Because of the frequent co-occurrence of individual syndromes, the question remains to what extent they may represent early manifestations of discrete disorders. This is particularly interesting with regard to the later internalizing and externalizing disorders among preschool- and school-age children. Nevertheless, distinguishable etiological constellations are evident in both the literature and our own data in terms of differences in temperamental qualities, profiles of the mothers' psychological state and personality, relational patterns in the family, and the profile of psychosocial stressors. Many questions remain to be investigated, including the specific role of the father and the father–child relationship in terms of his contribution to mastering the developmental tasks during this phase of life and to the development of disorders of behavioral and emotional regulation.

The documented tendency of regulation disorders to persist over the long term remains a cause for major concern. For example, unfavorable outcomes have been documented by prospective longitudinal studies for subgroups with extreme manifestations of social inhibition/anxiety (Kagan, 1997), and for oppositional and aggressive behavior from the beginning of the third year of life into preschool- and school-age (Shaw et al., 2000; see chapter 14). Such results make it all the more important to use the knowledge gained from parent–infant counseling and psychotherapy to unburden affected families, especially during the vulnerable periods in which emotion regulation, attachment, and autonomy are developing. Communication-centered relational therapy can be used effectively to strengthen the resources available to both parents and infants, and to foster positive relational experiences, particularly in the context of demanding developmental tasks and difficult child-rearing situations.

REFERENCES

Achenbach, T. M. (1992). *Manual for the Child Behavior Checklist/2-3 and 1992 profile*. Burlington: University of Vermont.

Anders, T. F. (1989). Clinical syndromes, relationship disturbances and their assessment. In A. J. Sameroff & R. N. Emde (Eds.), *Relationship disturbances in early childhood* (pp. 125–144). New York: Basic Books.

Belsky, J., Hsieh, K., & Crnic, K. (1998). Mothering, fathering, and infant negativity as antecedents of boys' externalizing problems and inhibition at 3 years: Differential susceptibility to rearing experience. *Development and Psychopathology, 10*, 301–319.

Belsky, J., Woodworth, S., & Crnic, K. (1996). Trouble in the second year: Three questions about family interactions. *Child Development, 67,* 556–578.

Biringen, Z., Emde, R. N., Campos, J. J., & Appelbaum, M. I. (1995). Affective reorganization in the infant, the mother, and the dyad: The role of upright locomotion and its timing. *Child Development, 66,* 499–514.

Bischof-Köhler, D. (1989). *Spiegelbild und Empathie.* Bern, Switzerland: Hans Huber.

Bischof-Köhler, D. (1998). Zusammenhänge zwischen kognitiver, motivationaler und emotionaler Entwicklung in der frühen Kindheit und im Vorschulalter. In H. Keller (Ed.), *Lehrbuch Entwicklungspsychologie* (pp. 319–376). Bern, Switzerland: Hans Huber.

Bowlby, J. (1969). *Attachment and loss* (Vol. 1). New York: Basic Books.

Calkins, S. D. (2002). Does aversive behavior during toddlerhood matter? The effects of difficult temperament on maternal perceptions and behavior. *Infant Mental Health Journal, 23,* 381–402.

Campbell, S. B. (1995). Behavior problems in preschool children: A review of recent research. *Journal of Child Psychology and Psychiatry, and Allied Disciplines, 36,* 113–149.

Campos, J. J., & Stenbert, C. R. (1981). Perception, appraisal, and emotions: The onset of social referencing. In M. E. Lamb & L. R. Sherrod (Eds.), *Infant social cognition: Empirical and social considerations* (pp. 273–314). Hillsdale, NJ: Erlbaum.

Cassidy, J. (1994). Emotion regulation: Influences of attachment relationships. *Monographs of the Society for Research in Child Development, 59*(2–3, Serial No. 240), 228–249.

Cierpka, M., & Cierpka, A. (2000). Beratung von Familien mit zwei- bis dreijährigen Kindern. *Praxis der Kinderpsychologie und Kinderpsychiatrie, 49,* 563–579.

Crittenden, P. M., & DiLalla, D. L. (1988). Compulsive compliance: The development of an inhibitory coping strategy in infancy. *Journal of Abnormal Child Psychology, 16,* 585–599.

Crockenberg, S., & Leerkes, E. (2000). Infant social and emotional development in family context. In C. H. Zeanah Jr. (Ed.), *Handbook of infant mental health* (2nd ed., pp. 60–90). New York: Guilford Press.

Derryberry, D., & Rothbart, M. K. (2001). Early temperament and emotional development. In A. F. Kalverboer & A. Gramsbergen (Eds.), *Handbook of brain and behaviour in human development* (pp. 967–987). Dordrecht, the Netherlands: Kluwer Academic.

Dornes, M. (2000). *Die emotionale Welt des Kindes.* Frankfurt, Germany: Fischer Taschenbuch-Verlag.

Dumas, J., & Wahler, R. G. (1985). Indiscriminate mothering as a contextual factor in aggressive-oppositional child behavior: "Damned if you do and damned if you don't." *Journal of Abnormal Child Psychology, 13,* 1–18.

Emde, R. N. (1984). The affective self: Continuities and transformations from infancy. In J. Call, E. Galenson, & R. L. Tyson (Eds.), *Frontiers of infant psychiatry* (Vol. 2, pp. 38–54). New York: Basic Books.

Fegert, J. M. (1996). Verhaltensdimensionen und Verhaltensprobleme bei zweieinhalbjährigen Kindern. *Praxis der Kinderpsychologie und Kinderpsychiatrie, 45,* 83–94.

Fox, N. A., Henderson, H. A., Rubin, K. H., Calkins, S. D., & Schmidt, L. A. (2001). Continuitiy and discontinuity of behavioral inhibition and exuberance: Psychophysiological and behavioral influences across the first four years of life. *Child Development, 72,* 1–21.

Friedlmeier, W. (1999). Emotionsregulation in der Kindheit. In W. Friedlmeier & M. Holodynski (Eds.), *Emotionale Entwicklung: Funktion, Regulation und soziokultureller Kontext von Emotionen* (pp. 198–218). Heidelberg, Germany: Spektrum Akademischer Verlag.

Friedlmeier, W., & Holodynski, M. (Eds.). (1999). *Emotionale Entwicklung: Funktion, Regulation und soziokultureller Kontext von Emotionen.* Heidelberg, Germany: Spektrum Akademischer Verlag.

Gopnik, A., Kuhl, P. K., & Meltzoff, A. N. (2001). *The scientist in the crib: Minds, brains, and how children learn.* New York: William Morrow.

Heckhausen, H. (1987). Emotional components of action: Their ontogeny as reflected in achievement behavior. In D. Görlitz & J. F. Wohlwill (Eds.), *Curiosity, imagination, and play* (pp. 326–348). Hillsdale, NJ: Erlbaum.

Holodynski, M. (1999a). Emotionale Entwicklung und Perspektiven ihrer Erforschung. In W. Friedlmeier & M. Holodynski (Eds.), *Emotionale Entwicklung: Funktion, Regulation und soziokultureller Kontext von Emotionen* (pp. 1–26). Heidelberg, Germany: Spektrum Akademischer Verlag.

Holodynski, M. (1999b). Handlungsregulation und Emotionsdifferenzierung. In W. Friedlmeier & M. Holodynski (Eds.), *Emotionale Entwicklung: Funktion, Regulation und soziokulturelle Entwicklung* (pp. 30–51). Heidelberg, Germany: Spektrum Akademischer Verlag.

Kagan, J. (1994). *Galen's prophecy: Temperament in human nature.* New York: Basic Books.

Kagan, J. (1997). Temperament and the reactions to unfamiliarity. *Child Development, 68,* 139–144.

Kochanska, G., Coy, K. C., & Murray, K. T. (2001). The development of self-regulation in the first four years of life. *Child Development, 72,* 1091–1111.

Koot, H. M., & Verhulst, F. C. (1991). Problem behavior in Dutch children aged 2-3. *Acta Psychiatrica Scandinavica, 83*(Suppl. 367), 1–37.

Largo, R. H. (1993). Verhaltens- und Entwicklungsauffälligkeiten: Störungen oder Normvarianten? *Monatsschrift für Kinderheilkunde, 141,* 698–703.

Laucht, M. (2002). Störungen des Kleinkind- und Vorschulalters. In G. Esser (Ed.), *Lehrbuch der klinischen Psychologie und Psychotherapie des Kindes- und Jugendalters* (pp. 102–118). Stuttgart, Germany: Thieme.

Laucht, M., Esser, G., & Schmidt, M. H. (1993). Psychische Auffälligkeiten im Kleinkind- und Vorschulalter. *Kindheit und Entwicklung, 2,* 143–149.

Maccoby, E. E., & Martin, J. A. (1983). Socialization in the context of the family: Parent-child interaction. In P. H. Mussen (Ed.), *Handbook of child psychology* (Vol. 4, pp. 1–101). New York: Wiley.

Minde, K., & Tidmarsh, L. (1997). The changing practices of an infant psychiatry program: The McGill experience. *Infant Mental Health Journal, 18,* 135–144.

Olson, S. L., Bates, J. E., Sandy, J. M., & Lanthier, R. (2000). Early developmental precursors of externalizing behavior in middle childhood and adolescence. *Journal of Abnormal Child Psychology, 28,* 119–133.

Papoušek, H. (2003). Spiel in der Wiege der Menschheit. In M. Papoušek & A. von Gontard (Eds.), *Spiel und Kreativität in der frühen Kindheit* (pp. 17–55). Stuttgart, Germany: Pfeiffer bei Klett-Cotta.

Papoušek, H., & Papoušek, M. (1979). The infant's fundamental adaptive response system in social interaction. In E. B. Thoman (Ed.), *Origins of the infant's social responsiveness* (pp. 175–208). Hillsdale, NJ: Erlbaum.

Papoušek, H., & Papoušek, M. (1987). Intuitive parenting: A dialectic counterpart to the infant's integrative competence. In J. D. Osofsky (Ed.), *Handbook of infant development* (2nd ed., pp. 669–720). New York: Wiley.

Papoušek, H., & Papoušek, M. (1999). Symbolbildung, Emotionsregulation und soziale Interaktion. In W. Friedlmeier & M. Holodynski (Eds.), *Emotionale Entwicklung. Funktion, Regulation und soziokultureller Kontext von Emotionen* (pp. 135–155). Heidelberg, Germany: Spektrum Akademischer Verlag.

Papoušek, M., & von Hofacker, N. (2002). Leitlinie R. Sozialpädiatrie: Störungen der frühen Eltern-Kind-Beziehungen. In R. Reinhardt (Ed.), *Leitlinien der Deutschen Gesellschaft für Kinder- und Jugendmedizin* (Section R6, pp. 1–10). München, Germany: Urban & Fischer.

Patterson, G. R. (1982). *Coercive family processes*. Eugene, OR: Castalia.

Pettit, G. S., & Bates, J. E. (1989). Family interaction patterns and children's behavior problems from infancy to age 4 years. *Developmental Psychology, 24*, 413–420.

Pettit, G. S., Bates, J. E., & Dodge, K. A. (1997). Supportive parenting, ecological context, and children's adjustment. *Child Development, 68*, 908–923.

Rauh, H. (2002). Vorgeburtliche Entwicklung und frühe Kindheit. In R. Oerter & L. Montada (Eds.), *Entwicklungspsychologie* (5th ed., pp. 131–208). Weinheim, Germany: Beltz, Psychologie Verlags Union.

Richman, M., Stevenson, J., & Graham, P. J. (1975). Prevalence of behavior problems in 3-year-old children: An epidemiological study in a London borough. *Journal of Child Psychology and Psychiatry, and Allied Disciplines, 16*, 277–287.

Rothbart, M. K., Derryberry, D., & Posner, M. I. (1994). A psychobiological approach to the development of temperament. In J. E. Bates & T. D. Wachs (Eds.), *Temperament: Individual differences at the interface of biology and behavior* (pp. 83–116). Washington, DC: American Psychological Association.

Sanson, A., Oberklaid, F., Pedlow, R., & Prior, M. (1991). Risk indicators: Assessment of infancy predictors of pre-school behavioural maladjustment. *Journal of Child Psychology and Psychiatry, 32*, 609–626.

Schneewind, K. A. (2002). Familienentwicklung. In R. Oerter & L. Montada (Eds.), *Entwicklungspsychologie* (5th ed, pp. 105–127). Weinheim, Germany: Beltz, Psychologie Verlags Union.

Shaw, D. S., Gilliom, M., & Giovanelli, J. (2000). Aggressive behavior disorders. In C. H. Zeanah, Jr. (Ed.), *Handbook of infant mental health* (2nd ed., pp. 397–411). New York: Guilford Press.

Shaw, D. S., Owens, E. B., Giovanelli, J., & Winslow, E. B. (2001). Infant and toddler pathways leading to early externalizing disorders. *Journal of the American Academy of Child and Adolescent Psychiatry, 40*, 36–43.

Sroufe, L. A. (1983). Infant-caregiver attachment and patterns of adaptation in preschool: The roots of maladaptation and competence. In M. Perlmutter (Ed.), *Minnesota Symposium in Child Psychology* (Vol. 16, pp. 41–81). Hillsdale, NJ: Erlbaum.

Sroufe, L. A. (1996). *Emotional development: The organization of emotional life in the first early years*. New York: Cambridge University Press.

Stern, D. N. (1985). *The interpersonal world of the infant*. New York: Basic Books.

Thomas, A., Chess, S., & Birch, H. G. (1968). *Temperament and behavior disorders in children*. London: University of London Press.

Thompson, R. A. (1994). Emotion regulation: A theme in search of definition. In N. A. Fox (Ed.), The development of emotion regulation: Biological and behavioral considerations. *Monographs of the Society for Research in Child Development, 59* (2–3, Serial No. 240), 25–52.

Tomasello, M. (1995). Joint attention as social cognition. In C. Moore & P. J. Dunham (Eds.), *Joint attention: Its origins and role in development* (pp. 102–130). Hillsdale, NJ: Erlbaum.

Tremblay, R. E. (1999). The search for the age of "onset" of physical aggression: Rousseau and Bandura revisited. *Criminal Behavior and Mental Health, 9,* 8–23.

Trevarthen, C. (1980). The foundations of intersubjectivity: Development of interpersonal and cooperative understanding in infants. In D. R. Olson (Ed.), *The social foundation of language and thought: Essays in honor of Jerome Bruner* (pp. 316–342). New York: Norton.

von Hofacker, N., Papoušek, M., Resch, F., & Lehmkuhl, U. (in press). Psychische Störungen im Kleinkindalter (2./3. Lebensjahr). In Deutsche Gesellschaft für Kinder- und Jugendpsychiatrie und –Psychotherapie (Ed.), *Leitlinien zu Diagnostik und Therapie von psychischen Störungen im Säuglings-, Kindes- und Jugendalter* (3rd ed.). Köln, Germany: Deutscher Ärzte-Verlag.

Zeanah, C., H., Jr., Boris, N. W., & Scheeringa, M. S. (1997). Psychopathology in infancy. *Journal of Child Psychology and Psychiatry, and Allied Disciplines, 38,* 81–99.

Zeanah, C. H., Jr., Larrieu, J. A., Heller, S. S., & Valliere, J. (2000). Infant–parent relationship assessment. In C. H. Zeanah, Jr. (Ed.), *Handbook of infant mental health* (2nd ed., pp. 222–235). New York: Guilford Press.

ZERO TO THREE. (2005). *Diagnostic classification of mental health and developmental disorders of infancy and early childhood: Revised edition (DC:0–3R).* Washington, DC: ZERO TO THREE Press.

EVALUATION OF BEHAVIOR THERAPY APPROACHES TO CRYING, FEEDING, AND SLEEP DISORDERS

Klaus Sarimski

INTRODUCTION

Infants are faced with a vast array of adaptive challenges during the first 2 years of life, including regulation of nutritional intake, behavioral states, sleep–wake organization, and affect and attention, as well as the achievement of balance between attachment and exploration and between dependency and autonomy. Infants can master these normal developmental tasks only with their parents' help, and only when the parents and infant become attuned to each other in their early interactions.

The quality of these interactions is determined by the infant's constitutional disposition for adaptation and self-regulation, by complementary support from his parents, and by the integration and subjective evaluation of experiences recalled from previous interactions. The parents' appraisal of their relationship with their baby is influenced by their hopes, fears, significant childhood experiences, current psychosocial stressors, and many other factors. The development of disorders of behavioral and emotional regulation and their consequences in early infancy may be understood as a failure of coregulation in mastering these developmental tasks (Sarimski & Papoušek, 2000). These failures become manifest in symptoms of extreme irritability (excessive crying), feeding disorders, or sleep disorders that may occur in isolation or in combination and may distress parents and child to such a degree that they seek professional help.

EVIDENCE-BASED TREATMENT

As in other areas of pediatrics and pediatric psychology, decisions regarding psychotherapy should consider and explicitly take into account all available knowledge. Efforts at an evidence-based therapeutic approach require familiarity with the results of scientific studies that were planned and conducted with sufficient methodological care to enable conclusions about the effectiveness of a particular therapeutic intervention in question. However, the practitioner in the field is hardly in a position to review all of the studies published each year. Practitioners depend on systematic reviews and meta-analyses that summarize and evaluate the original studies pointing out those areas in which the current knowledge base is still inadequate and where further study is needed to address immediate clinical questions.

Such systematic reviews should consider all studies that are available at the time of publication in various databases (such as MEDLINE or PsycLIT). These studies are evaluated according to criteria elaborated by groups of experts and approved as methodological standards for evaluating psychotherapeutic intervention (Task Force on Promotion and Dissemination of Psychological Procedures, 1995):

- Substantial growth in knowledge resulting from a clear framing of hypotheses and appropriate study design;

- Transparent information on the recruitment of samples, exclusion criteria, and study conditions (similar to those in practice);

- Use of valid instruments for assessment;

- Attempts to minimize systematic distortions of results by means of objective diagnostic criteria and the control of potential intervening variables (control groups);

- Adequate group sizes in a control-group design in order to establish clinically relevant effects ("power" of the study), or choice of a single-case study design in which the effect of the intervention compared to baseline is unambiguously controlled with regard to other potential factors;

- Duration and completeness of follow-up adequate for drawing conclusions with regard to the stability of effects.

These criteria justify conclusions about which psychotherapeutic procedures are *well-established, probably effective*, or *promising* (see Table 9.1). The same criteria have been used to evaluate therapeutic interventions for crying, sleeping, and feeding disorders. They are summarized in this chapter on the basis of four current reviews and meta-analyses that were published in recognized international journals or books (Kerwin, 1999; Lucassen et al., 1998; Mindell, 1999; Wolke, 1993). In addition to a description of the intervention, these articles define the behavioral disorder in question, describe how the therapeutic success was evaluated, and which other conditional factors may have accounted for the success.

A methodologically convincing demonstration of therapeutic effectiveness presupposes that the therapeutic goals and procedure have been precisely set, that individual components of therapeutic effects

Table 9.1. Criteria for Evaluating the Effectiveness of Therapeutic Procedures.

Procedure	Criteria
Well-established procedure	At least two randomized control-group studies or at least nine single-case studies with a multiple-treatment-reversal design that demonstrate the procedure's superiority to placebo or alternative form of treatment or its equivalence with already established forms of treatment (detailed description of patients and procedure; at least two independent investigators)
Probably effective procedure	At least two studies that demonstrate the superiority of the intervention in comparison with a control group (waiting list), or at least one study that meets the criteria for well-established procedures
Promising procedure	At least one control-group study and at least one less well-controlled study by an independent investigator, or at least two controlled studies with small samples, or conducted by the same investigator

Source: Task Force on Promotion and Dissemination of Psychological Procedures, 1995.

are isolated, that as many intervening variables as possible are neutralized, and that behavioral changes are measured objectively. These requirements are best met by models of behavior therapy. It is considerably more difficult to reduce the complexity of the treatment process in psychodynamic, family systems, or hypnotherapeutic approaches in a way that would allow objective assessments of relevant changes and analysis of the effective components of treatment. This does not mean that the models mentioned cannot be effective. Based on the state-of-the-art, the practitioner will be called upon to develop a treatment model that combines a particular well-established therapeutic procedure with auxiliary methods of support for the family in order to deal with the complexities of a particular case.

EXCESSIVE CRYING

Excessive crying is defined as episodes of crying, irritability, or fussing that total more than 3 hours per day, occur more than 3 days per week, and have lasted for more than 3 weeks. The parents' inability to calm the baby causes them to doubt their own intuitive capacity to create a positive relationship, and quickly leads to a vicious circle of dysfunctional or ineffective efforts at calming by the parents and missed opportunities for self-regulation by the baby (Papoušek & von Hofacker, 1998).

Systematic reviews by Wolke (1993) and Lucassen et al. (1998) reported on a total of 27 studies of the treatment of excessive crying; however, not all of these meet the criteria for adequate control and sufficient time intervals for follow-up. Most of the studies relate to the effects of nutritional changes and medication. The switch to a diet free of cow's milk or substituting a hypoallergenic alternative was shown to be effective in a subgroup of infants in two controlled studies; no clear-cut effect was shown, however, in controlled studies in which soy milk was substituted. In his review, Wolke (1993) indicated that no more than 10% to 15% of babies who cry excessively react positively to such nutritional changes. This estimate is based on one of the two studies, both of which were judged to be methodologically flawless. Of 17 treated infants who cried excessively, only 2 showed a positive effect when switched to hypoallergenic milk. However, given the size of the sample, the generalization of this result is problematic. According to Lucassen and colleagues (Lucassen et al., 1998), excessive crying should not be treated with medication because of the potential for adverse side effects in this age group.

Four of the studies evaluated in the two systematic reviews used a behavior therapy approach (Table 9.2). Evaluation of the therapeutic interventions is generally based on a daily diary in which the parents enter the child's sleeping, waking, and crying times in 15-minute increments over a 24-hour period. The reliability of diary-based data was checked in a study by Drummond et al. (1999), who hid a small recording device in a teddy bear that was constantly with the child. Crying times recorded by this method are generally about one third less than the times entered by parents in their daily diaries. The difference does not necessarily represent an overestimate by the parents but may simply reflect their tendency to record as one episode several brief crying bouts that follow each other in rapid succession with pauses in between. The 15-minute increments also introduce an element of inexactitude.

Behavioral intervention consists of reducing excessive stimulation, promoting the parents' ability to react to the infant's signals, and supporting the baby's capacity for self-regulation. McKenzie (1991) advised parents of babies who cried excessively to reduce their (usually ineffective) efforts to calm the

Table 9.2. Studies of Behavior Therapy for Infants With Excessive Crying.

Study	Number of infants	Dropouts (%)	Mean age (weeks)	Baseline rate of crying/fussing (hours per 24 hours)
McKenzie (1991)	42	7	10	—
Parkin et al. (1993)	38	16	7	5.7
Taubman (1988)	20	5	6 (<12)	3.2
Wolke et al. (1994)	92	0	13 (<26)	5.8

Note. The dash indicates no data were available.

infant by rocking, carrying, diapering, and so on, and tested the effect of this measure by asking the parents to estimate amount of crying on a 7-step rating scale. However, because of the subjectivity of the estimates, the reliability of results of this study is questionable.

Taubman (1988) advised the parents of 20 infants to try to attune their interactions to the infant's signals and needs. The parents recorded the infant's crying continuously, and advice was offered on the basis of these running records; however, there is little detail about what advice was given. The frequency and duration of crying were compared over a period of 9 days with a control group that had been switched from cow's milk formula to hypoallergenic milk. The control group was then switched back to cow's milk formula, and the control-group parents in their turn were given advice about how to attune their interactions to their infant's signals and needs. Figure 9.1 shows a significant reduction in the duration of daily crying that is dependent on getting advice. The effect was replicated in the original control group during a second therapy phase. But there are methodological questions here too. Because there was no untreated control group, there is no way to determine whether the rate of crying in the time period cited would have diminished anyway—as a result of maturation, for example. It would also have been desirable to know whether and how the parents translated the recommendations for better attunement into practice, to determine whether the changes in crying rates were actually attributable to them.

Wolke, Gray, and Meyer (1994) studied the effect of a complex behavioral approach on the rate of crying. They compared three groups: a first group of 21 infants (average age 3.4 months) whose parents received behavioral counseling in a booklet and over the telephone (an average of 2.9 calls), a second group of 27 infants whose parents received only empathetic support over the telephone (empathy group), and an untreated control group of 44 infants. Follow-up was done 3 months after the advice period.

Counseling included information about the normal development of crying and sleep regulation. The parents were encouraged to establish a regular daily structure for their babies' feeding, sleeping, and playing times and for outdoor activities. They were also advised to reduce overstimulation by finding appropriate forms of stimulation (social play) and soothing. They were advised against continuous

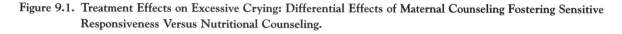

Figure 9.1. Treatment Effects on Excessive Crying: Differential Effects of Maternal Counseling Fostering Sensitive Responsiveness Versus Nutritional Counseling.

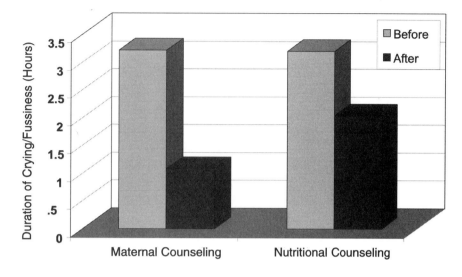

Source: Taubman, 1988.

rocking and carrying, frequent feeding, or driving around in a car to calm the infant. The parents were asked to distinguish as well as possible among various causes for crying and not to react immediately to the first signs of fussing or crying. Depending on the cause, they were asked to wait for 1 to 2 minutes to give the infant the opportunity to practice self-regulation. There was a significantly greater reduction in crying times (51% compared to baseline) in the counseling group than in both the empathy group (about 39%) and control group (about 32%; see Figure 9.2). The positive effect of behavioral counseling was evident too in questionnaires on the babies' temperament that the parents filled out before and after treatment and in the parents' self-ratings of whether the advice they received helped to reduce the problems and improve the relationship with their infant.

FEEDING DISORDERS

Clinically relevant feeding disorders must be distinguished from completely normal perturbations that occur in many families in the context of feeding situations. Transitional periods in particular, such as when an infant is getting used to spoon feeding or solid food, are often difficult to negotiate.

Feeding disorders only require treatment in cases in which there is a persistent lack of appetite, regular choking or vomiting, extreme pickiness, complete food refusal and/or failure-to-thrive. In such cases, feeding can become extremely time-consuming, with frequent feeding attempts at short intervals and/or feeding that may only be possible if accompanied by playful distractions or by pressure and force. The normal regulation of the feeding interaction by which the parents intuitively adjust their feeding behavior to the infant's signals of hunger and satiation has turned into a vicious circle. Dysfunctional

Figure 9.2. **Treatment Effects on Excessive Crying: Differential Effects of Interactional Counseling Versus Empathetic Support.**

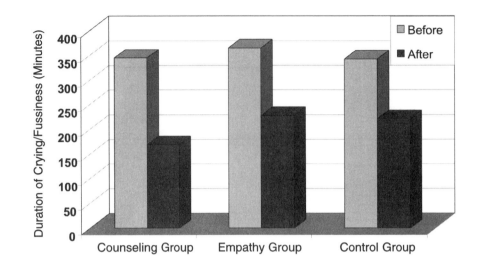

Source: Wolke, Gray, & Meyer, 1994.

feeding interactions become associated with deep-seated self-doubt in the mother about her mothering competency, and, in many cases, the mother–infant relationship becomes severely distressed (Coolbear & Benoit, 1999; Lindberg, Bohlin, Hagekull, & Palmerus, 1996; Papoušek, 2002; von Hofacker & Papoušek, 1998).

The risk of developing a feeding or eating disorder is significantly increased in infants with physical illnesses, malformations, mental or physical handicaps, or severe oral-motor dysfunction resulting from extreme immaturity at birth or highly stressed early development (for instance during treatment in a neonatal intensive care unit). Extreme cases, often with failure-to-thrive, require invasive procedures such as tube feeding, or inpatient admission. However, feeding and eating disorders that require intensive treatment also occur in children without severe physical problems (see chapter 7).

The following description of the effectiveness of behavior therapy is limited to the subgroup of children with feeding disorders that are not primarily organic. This does not rule out the possibility that slight delays in oral-motor maturity or a particularly high level of irritability play a role in the interplay between these and social and interactional factors in the genesis of these feeding disorders. Such cases may require additional medical treatment such as in the case of gastroesophageal reflux or oropharyngeal sensorimotor dysfunction.

The systematic review by Kerwin (1999; see Table 9.3) includes 29 studies that tested the effectiveness of behavioral treatment. Studies were excluded that involved medication, surgery, tube feeding, or oral-motor treatment. The majority of studies on the effectiveness of behavior therapy relate to severe feeding and eating disorders in children with mental retardation or complex medical problems. These

Table 9.3. Studies of Behavior Therapy for Feeding Disorders.

Study	Number/Age	Problems/Design	Intervention	Follow-up
Thompson et al. (1977)	n = 1 / 30 months	Selective food refusal/ multiple baseline rate	Differential attentiveness	6 months
Werle et al. (1993)	n = 3 / 21–53 months	Selective food refusal/ multiple baseline rate	Differential attentiveness	—
Turner et al. (1994)	n = 20 / 18–60 months	Various eating problems/ control group	Differential attentiveness	3–4 months
Benoit et al. (1997)	n = 24 / 2–34 months	Posttraumatic feeding disorder/pre–post comparison	Systematic desensitization	—

Note. The dash indicates no data were available.

will not be discussed here either. Only four studies concern infants and toddlers with feeding disorders that did not exhibit such complicating conditions. One of these was a single-case study.

Three of the studies were based on the operant conditioning model. In this model, behavioral change is brought about by the adult's differential attention to the desired versus the problematic behavior. The studies relate to children whose general or selective food refusal is attributable primarily to unfavorable learning processes in parent–infant feeding interactions. The fourth study follows the classic conditioning model. Here, the infant learns to accept food in small steps according to the principle of systematic desensitization with the help of relaxation techniques. This study relates to children for whom the feeding situation has become traumatic (resulting, for example, from the use of intubation or other aversive medical manipulations).

Success is measured by an increase in caloric intake or the quantity of (previously rejected) food ingested over the course of treatment, or by weight gain over a longer period of time. In the case of severe disorders, videotaped observation of the feeding situation in the clinical setting or at home is generally used for diagnostic assessment and control of progress. Daily logs are used to monitor quality of food, amount of food intake and the frequency of problematic behavior (vomiting, persistent crying, etc.). Some authors also apply standardized questionnaires such as the Infant Feeding Behavior Check-list (Benoit & Green, 1995), which records positive and negative behaviors in the feeding interaction.

In operant conditioning interventions, social attention and enthusiastic praise whenever the baby accepts food are generally combined with short-term withdrawal of attention (by ignoring avoidant behavior or crying, turning away or interruption of feeding) when the baby responds with problematic behavior. Once the child is mobile, he is prevented from leaving the table during mealtime and is denied between-meal snacks. These interventions were conducted and evaluated in toddlers (age > 18 months). Experience with this procedure has not been reported for younger infants. In all cases, the parents were trained in using these techniques in feeding interactions with their child (direct and written instruction, practicing the procedure in simulated situations, feedback by the therapist during or after meal times, regular video-based supervision). The number of therapy sessions varied between 4 and 14. Follow-up in two of three studies showed that the changes were stable over 3 to 6 months. One study compared the effectiveness of the behavioral procedure with nutritional counseling (Turner, Sanders, & Wall, 1994). The other two studies examined the effectiveness in comparison to baseline obtained over the course of 3 to 10 observational sessions before the commencement of treatment (Thompson, Palmer, & Linscheid, 1977; Werle, Murphy, & Budd, 1993). On the basis of these studies, differential attention to adaptive eating behavior is considered a promising procedure for children with feeding and eating disorders without complex medical problems.

The treatment of feeding disorders that are characterized by anxious food aversion is grounded in the experience gained in the behavioral treatment of anxiety disorders using systematic desensitization and stimulus exposure. In individual therapy sessions, the child is offered food and calmly encouraged to open his mouth without forcing him to eat. The adult attempts to calm the child by stroking him, singing, or talking in a friendly manner whenever he accepts a bit of food on his lips or in his mouth. If the child begins to choke or back-arch, an attempt is made to calm him and the feeding process is resumed, but with a reduced amount. This procedure is repeated three to four times per day. The therapeutic process is very time-consuming (10 to 130 sessions). To achieve some progress requires a great deal of patience, which may be unavailable to the highly stressed parents. For this reason, the procedure is often more successful in an inpatient setting. It is not promising in children in whom a severe neurological disorder impairs swallowing.

Benoit, Green, and Arts-Rodas (1997) reported on the treatment of 24 children (average age: 19.1 months) with posttraumatic feeding disorder, 15 of whom required tube feeding (nasogastric tube or percutaneous endoscopic gastric tube). Treatment lasted 10 sessions on average (range = 2–21 sessions). Success was evaluated according to the following clinical criteria: increase in the oral ingestion of food and liquids, improvement in cooperation during mealtimes, steady weight gain, commencement of oral feeding (in cases of complete food refusal), acceptance of a greater variety of tastes and consistencies (in cases of partial food refusal), or reduction in the dependence on tube feeding (in tube-fed children). The procedure described above led to clinical improvement in 17 of 24 cases (71%). The improvement was evident as well in a standardized behavioral assessment of feeding situations using the Infant Feeding Behavior Checklist (scores of 37.67 vs. 26.19 before and after treatment, respectively).

SLEEP DISORDERS

Difficulties falling asleep and sleeping through the night are part of the daily caregiving routine with infants and toddlers. Most children learn to fall asleep by themselves or to fall asleep again after waking up in the middle of the night. However, some children develop the habit of falling asleep with a long delay and/or only with the help of their parents. Others wake up several times during the night and immediately begin to cry. Their parents have trouble calming them unless they take the baby into their bed. Such children have either not yet learned how to self-regulate the transition to sleep, or they have unlearned it. The tolerance of individual parents for problems of sleep onset and night waking in their children differs greatly. Once the problems have become consolidated, the nightly stress may become so exacerbated that families seek professional help.

In some cases, information about individual variability and development of sleep during the first years of life and the changes in physiological sleep organization, sleep rhythms, and sleep duration is sufficient to promote normal sleep behavior (Basler, Largo, & Molinari, 1980; Largo & Hunziker, 1984; see also chapter 6). In other cases, behavioral treatment may be required to change the child's sleep habits. Mindell (1999) provides a systematic review of a total of 41 studies. Investigations that included children with physical or mental handicaps or school-age children were excluded. Table 9.4 lists the studies that had a control group or multiple base-rate design and (at least in part) evaluated children below the age of 2. Single-case studies and studies in which no baseline sleep behavior was reported were excluded.

The majority of studies using behavior therapy for sleep onset and night waking disorders are based on the operant conditioning model. The child's protest against falling asleep by himself, or his request for closeness and parental support after waking up, are viewed as learned behavior patterns that have been involuntarily reinforced by the parents. The goal of treatment is to attenuate this behavior pattern so that the child eventually learns to fall asleep by himself.

In general, measures of success include the time it takes to fall asleep in the evening, the average frequency of nighttime waking, or the relative frequency of "problematic nights" as reported in sleep logs filled out by the parents. The reliability of the parents' log entries was checked in several studies by using tape recorders or actometry devices that were left on throughout the night (France, Blampied, & Wilkinson, 1991; Sadeh, 1994).

Table 9.4. Studies of Behavior Therapy for Infants With Sleep Onset and Night Waking Disorders.

Study	Number/Age	Problems/Design	Intervention	Follow-up
Rickert & Johnson (1988)	n = 33 / 6–54 months	Sleeping through/control group	Extinction scheduled awakenings	1.5 months
Seymour et al. (1989)	n = 45 / 9–60 months	Falling asleep and sleeping through/control group (waiting list)	Extinction	3 months
France et al. (1991)	n = 45 / 7–27 months	Sleeping through/control group	Extinction	3–24 months
Pritchart & Appleton (1988)	n = 31 / 9–42 months	Falling asleep and sleeping through/control group	Gradual extinction	3 months
Lawton et al. (1991)	n = 6 / 6–14 months	Falling asleep and sleeping through/multiple baseline	Gradual extinction	4 months
Mindell & Durand (1993)	n = 6 / 18–52 months	Falling asleep and sleeping through/multiple baseline	Gradual extinction	1 month
Sadeh (1994)	n = 50 / 9–24 months	Sleeping through/control group	Gradual extinction	0.75 months
Adams & Rickert (1989)	n = 36 / 18–48 months	Falling asleep/control group	Gradual extinction	1.5 months

To elicit the desired changes in behavior, the parents must reduce the amount of attention they give their infant while he is falling asleep or waking up at night. This may be done all at once or step-by-step (total or gradual extinction). The principle of extinction implies that the parents learn to ignore consistently their child's attention-getting behavior. This may mean in practical terms that if the child has gotten up after the usual bedtime ritual, the parents should quietly and consistently take him back to bed. If he starts to cry at night they should not pick him up and console him, with the assumption, of course, that there is nothing physically or emotionally wrong with him. Several studies have confirmed the effectiveness of this procedure in comparison with an untreated control group (Table 9.4).

Rickert and Johnson (1988) reported in a study of 33 children (age range: 6–54 months) that the frequency of nighttime waking dropped to twice per week within several weeks due to extinction as compared to eight times in the control group (Figure 9.3). France and colleagues (1991) treated 45 children (age range: 7–27 months), assigning them to three subgroups. The procedure in the first subgroup consisted of instructing the parents in how to extinguish attention-getting behavior. In the second subgroup, this procedure was combined with sleep medication (trimeprazin); in the third subgroup with a placebo. The parent logs were checked against a recording device. The therapeutic principle of extinction was successful in all children, and the success proved stable. The most rapid changes were seen in children in whom behavioral therapy was combined with sleep medication.

It is understandably difficult for the parents to follow through with this procedure consistently. They are unsure whether the sleep problems might not be caused by fears and feelings of abandonment. They want to protect their child and make him feel emotionally secure but recognize that what they have done up to now has not brought about the desired changes. They feel helpless and fear that they may lose their child's trust if they leave him alone at night and do not respond reliably to his crying or other signals. This means that only a fraction of parents are able to commit to this procedure or to pursue it consistently. Unfortunately, no dropout figures have been reported in the literature.

Several variations on this procedure have been developed to test whether stable success may be achieved by other means. In the gradual extinction method, the parents enter the nursery at preset intervals to check on their child. This allows him to feel that he is not being abandoned; however, the parents insist that he is to sleep in his own bed and to fall asleep by himself. Pritchart and Appleton (1988), for example, instructed the parents to wait at least 20 minutes after the bedtime ritual before reentering the nursery. If the child wakes up at night, the parents are instructed to make sure that nothing is physically wrong, then leave the nursery again, and not return at less than 10-minute intervals. This procedure was shown to be successful in the group of 31 children between the ages of 9 and 42 months.

Lawton, France, and Blampied (1991) adapted the interval at which parents look in on their child according to individual needs. First, they determined how much time on average the parents devoted to their child during the transition to sleep or when he woke up at night. They then asked the parents to reduce this time by one-seventh every 4 days. Unless absolutely necessary, the parents didn't set foot in the nursery again after the twenty-eighth day. In 4 of 7 children treated using this procedure, the frequency and duration of nighttime crying decreased significantly and remained stable at least until a follow-up examination 3 months later. Mindell and Durand (1993) used a similar form of gradual

Figure 9.3. Progress in Treatment of Night Waking Disorders Using Extinction Versus Scheduled Awakening.

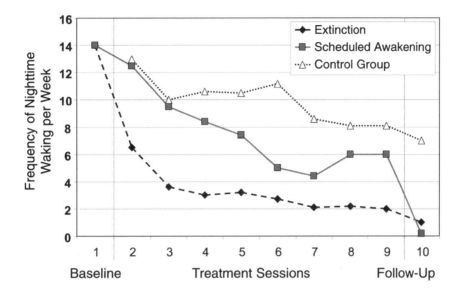

Source: Modified according to Rickert & Johnson, 1988.

extinction, instructing the parents to increase the time they waited to reenter the nursery by 5 minutes from night to night to a maximum of 20 minutes. This procedure led to a reduction in transition-to-sleep problems in 6 children between the ages of 18 and 52 months. After a short period, 5 of these children also began to sleep through the night.

The success of treatment depends in part on whether the parents can be assured in counseling that the procedure will not endanger their relationship with their baby. On that account, Chadez and Nurtius (1987) combined behavior therapy with detailed parent counseling in order to understand how they viewed their child's sleeping problem and to help them to overcome their fears. France (1992) complemented the behavioral intervention with systematic observation of parent–infant interactions during the day and showed that the infant's daytime mood improved significantly as a result of the intervention, and that the quality of the parent–infant relationship did not suffer.

Another procedure, so-called scheduled awakenings, has proved just as successful as systematic extinction in a controlled study and in several single-case studies, even though it takes longer. The procedure is based on the assumption that the time of waking up from sleep can be influenced by classical conditioning. The first step is to establish a baseline when the child typically wakes up at night. The parents are then instructed to awaken the child at least 15 minutes before these "habitual" wake-up times, give him something to drink and/or change diapers as usual. The frequency with which this is done depends on the frequency of his spontaneous awakenings. The point in time at which he is awakened is then postponed stepwise by 30 minutes, to let the child sleep increasingly longer from the moment he falls asleep. In a group of 11 children between the ages of 6 and 54 months, Rickert and Johnson (1988) achieved a similar reduction in nighttime waking over an average period of 8.8 weeks as in a control group treated by the method of extinction.

There is a suggestion that consolidation of infant sleep disorders can be prevented if the child becomes accustomed from early on to being put in his crib while he is still awake instead of falling asleep while being carried around or nursed. Two studies on large samples ($n = 164$ and $n = 169$) speak to the effectiveness of preventive counseling (Adair, Zuckerman, Bauchner, Philipp, & Levenson, 1992; Kerr, Jowett, & Smith, 1996). Infants whose parents received such advice when they were 3 to 4 months old slept through the night significantly more often at the age of 9 months than control infants whose parents had not been counseled.

STATE-OF-THE-ART SUMMARY

The literature reviews have shown that persistent feeding and sleep disorders and their developmental precursor, excessive crying in early infancy, can be effectively treated. The reported studies, which meet the methodological standards for demonstrating the effectiveness of therapeutic procedures, are based on models of behavior therapy. The procedures for treating the three behavioral syndromes have in common that the interaction between the parent and child is structured clearly and consistently in order to foster the child's capacity for self-regulation and help him learn which behaviors are reinforced by the parents, and which are ignored.

Such conscious structuring of interaction in the therapeutic setting constitutes a considerable intrusion in the relational system of parent and child and may contradict the parents' intuitive forms of responsiveness. The effectiveness of this procedure should not lead to the conclusion that the capacity for affective self-regulation, independent falling asleep or sleeping through the night and cooperation during feeding can only be learned in this manner. Nevertheless, such structuring has been shown to be helpful in cases in which the normal coregulation between infant self-regulation and the parents' intuitive regulatory support in mastering these developmental tasks have failed and distressing dysfunctional interaction patterns have become consolidated.

The effectiveness studies neither justify the conclusion that behavioral structuring of interaction is the only way to treat disorders of behavioral regulation, nor that it is suitable for all families. There is enough evidence to assume that many ways exist for changing dysfunctional interactional patterns and failed attunement between infant signals and parental responses. Different "windows" may be opened for helping parent and infant to become attuned to each other in soothing, feeding, or bedtime interactions in a consistent positive way (Papoušek, 1998; see also chapter 12).

Psychotherapeutic interventions that focus on the parents' relational representations and attitude toward their infant, and which help them to resolve distorted perceptions of infant behavior or blockage in their relationship that result from stressors in their own past, can be just as effective (see chapters 10, 11, and 12). Comparative studies have shown that both behavioral and psychodynamic approaches can successfully resolve early relational disorders between the parent and child (Cramer et al., 1990). Unfortunately, there are to date few studies of the therapeutic effectiveness of approaches other than behavioral therapy that deal explicitly with the symptoms of excessive crying, feeding or sleeping disorders, and that use objective measures and designs that meet the methodological standards for evaluating the effectiveness of psychological therapies.

In clinical practice, a combined treatment approach is often necessary. Here, behavioral intervention, psychotherapy, developmental counseling, and support that helps the parents to overcome the particular challenges they face are integrated with the goal of strengthening their confidence in their own competency and helping them to resolve blockages in their relationship with their child that result from their own past experience. This reflects the increasing openness of behavioral therapy to elements of cognitive, interactional, and systems approaches that has become commonplace in many areas of pediatric psychotherapy over the past several years.

REFERENCES

Adair, R., Zuckerman, B., Bauchner, H., Philipp, B., & Levenson, B. (1992). Reducing night waking in infancy: A primary care intervention. *Pediatrics, 89*, 585–588.

Adams, L., & Rickert, V. (1989). Reducing bedtime tantrums: Comparison between positive routines and graduated extinction. *Pediatrics, 84*, 756–759.

Basler, K., Largo, R., & Molinari, L. (1980).Die Entwicklung des Schlafverhaltens in den ersten fünf Lebensjahren. *Helvetica Paediatrica Acta, 35*, 211–223.

Benoit, D., & Green, D. (1995, October). *The Infant Feeding Behaviors—Rater checklist: Preliminary data*. Poster presented at the 42nd annual meeting of the American Academy of Child and Adolescent Psychiatry. New Orleans, LA.

Benoit, D., Green, D., & Arts-Rodas, D. (1997). Posttraumatic feeding disorders. *Journal of the American Academy of Child and Adolescent Psychiatry, 36*, 577–578.

Chadez, L., & Nurtius, P. (1987). Stopping bedtime crying: Treating the child and the parents. *Journal of Clinical Child Psychology, 16*, 212–217.

Coolbear, J., & Benoit, D. (1999). Failure to thrive: Risk for clinical disturbance of attachment? *Infant Mental Health Journal, 20*, 87–104.

Cramer, B., Robert-Tissot, C., Stern, D., Serpa-Rusconi, S., deMuralt, M., Besson, G., et al. (1990). Outcome evaluation in brief mother-infant psychotherapy: A preliminary report. *Infant Mental Health Journal, 11*, 278–300.

Drummond, J., Letourneau, N., Neufeld, S., Harvey, H., Elliott, R., & Reilly, S. (1999). Infant crying and parent-infant interaction: Theory and measurement. *Infant Mental Health Journal, 20*, 452–465.

France, K. (1992). Behavior characteristics and security in sleep-disturbed infants treated with extinction. *Journal of Pediatric Psychology, 17*, 467–475.

France, K., Blampied, N., & Wilkinson, P. (1991). Treatment of infant sleep disturbance by trimeprazine in combination with extinction. *Journal of Developmental Behavior and Pediatrics, 12*, 308–314.

Kerr, S., Jowett, S., & Smith, L. (1996). Preventing sleep problems in infants: A randomized controlled trial. *Journal of Advanced Nursing, 24*, 938–942.

Kerwin, E. (1999). Empirically supported treatments in pediatric psychology: Severe feeding problems. *Journal of Pediatric Psychology, 24*, 193–214.

Largo, R., & Hunziker, U. (1984). A developmental approach to the management of sleep disturbances in the first three years of life. *European Journal of Pediatrics, 142*, 170–173.

Lawton, C., France, K., & Blampied, N. (1991). Treatment of infant sleep disturbance by graduated extinction. *Child and Family Behavior Therapy, 13*, 39–56.

Lindberg, L., Bohlin, G., Hagekull, B., & Palmerus, K. (1996). Interactions between mothers and infants showing food refusal. *Infant Mental Health Journal, 17*, 334–347.

Lucassen, P., Assendelft, J., Gubbels, J., van Eijk, J., van Geldrop, W., & Knuistingh, N. (1998). Effectiveness of treatments for infantile colic: Systematic review. *British Medical Journal, 316*, 1563–1569.

McKenzie, S. (1991). Troublesome crying in infants: Effect of advice to reduce stimulation. *Archives of Diseases in Children, 66*, 1416–1420.

Mindell, J. (1999). Empirically supported treatments in pediatric psychology: Bedtime refusal and night wakings in young children. *Journal of Pediatric Psychology, 24*, 465–481.

Mindell, J., & Durand, V. (1993). Treatment of childhood sleep disorders: Generalization across disorders and effects on family members. *Journal of Pediatric Psychology, 18*, 731–750.

Papoušek, M. (1998). Das Münchner Modell einer interaktionszentrierten Eltern-Säuglings-Beratung und –Psychotherapie. In K. von Klitzing (Ed.), *Psychotherapie in der frühen Kindheit* (pp. 88–118). Göttingen, Germany: Vandenhoeck & Ruprecht.

Papoušek,, M. (2002). Störungen des Säuglingsalters. In G. Esser (Ed.), *Lehrbuch der klinischen Psychologie des Kindes- und Jugendalters* (pp. 80–101). Stuttgart, Germany: Thieme.

Papoušek,, M., & von Hofacker, N. (1998). Persistent crying in early infancy: A nontrivial condition of risk for the developing mother-infant relationship. *Child: Care, Health and Development, 24*, 395–424.

Parkin, P., Schwartz, C., & Manuel, B. (1993). Randomized controlled trial of three interventions in the management of persistent crying of infancy. *Pediatrics, 92*, 197–201.

Pritchart, A., & Appleton, P. (1988). Management of sleep problems in pre-school children. *Early Child Development and Care, 34*, 227–240.

Rickert, V., & Johnson, C. (1988). Reducing nocturnal awakening and crying episodes in infants and young children: A comparison between scheduled awakenings and systematic ignoring. *Pediatrics, 81*, 203–212.

Sadeh, A. (1994). Assessment and intervention for infant night waking: Parental reports and activity-based home monitoring. *Journal of Consulting and Clinical Psychology, 62*, 63–68.

Sarimski, K., & Papoušek, M. (2000). Eltern-Kind-Beziehung und die Entwicklung von Regulationsstörungen. In F. Petermann, K. Niebank, & H. Scheithauer (Ed.), *Risiken in der frühkindlichen Entwicklung* (pp. 199–222). Göttingen, Germany: Hogrefe.

Seymour, F., Brock, P., During, M., & Poole, G. (1989). Reducing sleep disruptions in young children: Evaluation of therapist-guided and written information approaches: A brief report. *Journal of Child Psychology and Psychiatry, and Allied Disciplines, 30,* 913–918.

Task Force on Promotion and Dissemination of Psychological Procedures. (1995). Training in and dissemination of empirically-validated psychological treatments: Report and recommendations. *Clinical Psychologist, 48,* 3–23.

Taubman, B. (1988). Parental counseling compared with elimination of cow's milk or soy milk protein for the treatment of infant colic syndrome: A randomized trial. *Pediatrics, 81,* 756–761.

Thompson, R., Palmer, S., & Linscheid, T. (1977). Single-subject design and interaction analysis in the behavioral treatment of a child with a feeding problem. *Child Psychiatry and Human Development, 8,* 43–53.

Turner, K., Sanders, M., & Wall, C. (1994). Behavioural parent training versus dietary education in the treatment of children with persistent feeding difficulties. *Behaviour Change, 11,* 242–258.

von Hofacker, N., & Papoušek, M. (1998). Disorders of excessive crying, feeding, and sleeping: The Munich Interdisciplinary Research and Intervention Program. *Infant Mental Health Journal, 19,* 180–201.

Werle, M., Murphy, T., & Budd, K. (1993). Treating chronic food refusal in young children: Home-based parent training. *Journal of Applied Behavior Analysis, 26,* 421–433.

Wolke, D. (1993). The treatment of problem crying behavior. In I. St.James-Roberts, G. Harris, & D. Messer (Eds.), *Infant crying, feeding, and sleeping* (pp. 47–79). New York: Harvester Wheatsheaf.

Wolke, D., Gray, P., & Meyer, R. (1994). Excessive infant crying: A controlled study of mothers helping mothers. *Pediatrics 94,* 322–332.

CHAPTER 10

"GHOSTS IN THE BEDROOM"— PSYCHODYNAMIC ASPECTS IN THE TREATMENT OF SLEEP DISORDERS

Renate Barth

INTRODUCTION

Difficulties getting to sleep and frequent nighttime waking are among the most common behavioral problems in early childhood (Barth, 1999a, 2000b; Deutsche Gesellschaft für Kinder- und Jugendpsychiatrie und Psychotherapie et al., 2003; Fegert et al., 1997; Wolke, Meyer, Orth, & Riegel, 1994). The main difficulty is that the child is unable to regulate her sleep behavior. Children with sleep-onset disorders cannot fall asleep on their own and need extensive help from their parents. Children with night-waking disorders cannot go back to sleep without their parents' help when they wake up during light sleep stages. In both cases, the child is unable to fall asleep by herself, and the parents find it difficult to support their child in mastering this developmental step.

Many mothers and fathers seem to believe that sleeping is something that the child either can or cannot do, or that—if they wait long enough—she will be eventually able to do on her own. However, this is only partially true. Although infant development is driven by maturation processes, it is largely shaped within the context of the interaction and relationship with the parents (Papoušek, 1999; Stern, 1986, 1995; Winnicott, 1984/1965). Many babies have good self-regulatory capacities that enable them to learn quickly how to fall asleep by themselves. However, if the parents fail to support these capacities—that is, if they allow their baby to get used to falling asleep in their arms, next to them in their bed, or only when being rocked in the baby carriage—then the child learns that sleep is something that comes from outside herself rather than something she regulates herself. Sleeping problems are the result.

Such sleep disorders are eminently treatable. In many cases, developmental guidance or even self-help manuals lead to rapid success (Barth, 2000a, 2000b; Mindell, 1999; Wolke et al. 1994; see also chapter 5). The aim of these approaches is to support parents in fostering the ability of their child to fall asleep by herself (see chapter 9).

Nevertheless, parents are not always helped by interaction-focused counseling or advice alone. In these families, infant sleep disorders are typically associated with parental feelings of aloneness, abandonment, helplessness, powerlessness, disappointment, aggression, desire for love, rivalry, and the like. An observer is often left with the feeling that something emotionally significant is being negotiated between the parents and their child, the meaning of which is not immediately obvious. How are these interactions to be understood? To answer this question, this chapter looks at such sleep disorders from a psychodynamic perspective and as an expression of unconscious separation problems. Case vignettes are used to substantiate our hypotheses.

THE PROBLEM

Mrs. A. describes her 9-month-old son's sleep disorder as follows:

> Lucas only falls asleep at my breast. When I carefully place him in his crib, he wakes up immediately and starts screaming. I then nurse him for a while or carry him around, and it just goes on like that. At night he wakes up every 1 or 2 hours. Sometimes he doesn't want to go back to sleep at all. At these times, I take him to bed with me and my husband sleeps in the child's bedroom. But even then I don't get any peace and rest. Things aren't any different during the day. Lucas has no sleep rhythm at all and takes short naps for half an hour at the most. I try to be responsive to him one hundred percent, but he still won't fall asleep. I'm at the end of my rope. Recently, I got so angry that I began to scream at him. I even slapped him once. Now I've got a guilty conscience. If only I knew what is wrong with him. I'm doing everything I can for him.

This mother describes a typical scenario of sleep disorders in infancy and toddlerhood. It includes the following characteristic elements:

- The parents

  –Have inappropriate or no assumptions about why their child sleeps so poorly;

  –Extend themselves beyond their limits to meet their child's presumed needs;

  –Are at the end of their rope and feel exhausted, helpless, and desperate;

  –Have frequent aggressive feelings toward their child that may, in extreme cases, lead to loss of impulse control; and

  –Feel guilty, after which they are particularly permissive in order to make things right again.

- The child

  –Does not get her needs met adequately (how is she supposed to understand why she is constantly put at her mother's breast when she is actually tired rather than hungry?);

  –Is chronically overtired and therefore fussy; and

  –Gets no appropriate support in mastering an important developmental step (i.e., learning to fall asleep by herself).

Both parents and child spend a great deal of time with negative emotions in these unfortunate interactions. The psychological strain is considerable.

SEPARATION AND INDIVIDUATION

Much of the psychoanalytic and developmental psychological literature deals with the question of how the child moves from initial dependence on her parents in the direction of independence. The fetus is closely bonded with the mother, and the mother with the fetus. Birth interrupts this state and initiates—at least physically—their separation from each other. Some authors have viewed this as the first experience of fear and trauma in humans (Freud, 1975/1923; Rank, 1998/1924).

Under favorable circumstances, birth is the beginning of a development toward autonomy that eventually allows the child to live a life of her own independent of her parents. However, this does not happen automatically; rather, it involves coming to terms with conflicting intrapsychic tendencies. On the one hand, there is the desire for individuation and progression that is associated with obstacles and frustrations (Grunberger, 1988). On the other hand, it is tempting to take the easy path of avoiding life's challenges and remaining in a merged "symbiotic" state or to regress into that state as soon as difficulties arise. A number of authors have described the desire to return to a state of narcissistic bliss and omnipotence within the womb as a universal human fantasy (Chasseguet-Smirgel, 1988; Ferenczi, 1982/1924; Grunberger, 1988). It may be possible to approach this idealized state at the level of fantasy during pregnancy or in the emotionally merged state of early parenthood. By identifying with her fetus or baby, the mother is able to reexperience the primordial feeling of oneness with her own mother. The child, too, experiences a constant internal struggle between progression and regression. New developmental steps are typically associated with regression during which the child seems to be younger in some areas than she really is (Brazelton, 1995). It is at such times that transient sleep disorders often occur.

To retain for a time the pleasant feeling of symbiosis after birth, parents, and particularly mothers, often try to spare their infant all frustration and to allow her to slip from one behavioral state into the next—without encouraging the child's own coping strategies (Grunberger, 1988). This is obvious, for example, when a crying baby, while being breast-fed or bottle-fed, begins to relax snuggled up to her parent's body and slowly falls asleep—without any effort on her part. Such mother–infant pairs often appear to be psychologically connected by an invisible umbilical cord. A postnatal phase of symbiotic mergence—if transient— is often viewed as fostering development. However, it is important that the parents' initially intense adaptation to their infant's needs eventually tapers off (Winnicott, 1984/1965). Parents understand this intuitively. They generally curtail the help they offer as they increasingly trust that their child will work things out herself. Such age-appropriate withholding of immediate support and the temporary frustration that it causes are generally believed to promote development.

Nevertheless, the development of autonomy is not invulnerable to disorder, as this German nursery rhyme illustrates:

Little Hans
All at once
Out into the world he runs.
Walking stick,
Hat so slick,
Made him feel real big.
But his mother is so sad,
No little boy at home she had.
Hans so fit,
Thought of it,
And return he did.[1]

---

[1] Translation by Waltraud Knudsen.

Little Hans tries to detach from his mother and goes out into the wide world dressed with hat and stick. What adventures will he have? Little Hans, unfortunately, will never find out because his mother can't bear to see him go. She has a very hard time in his absence. Little Hans turns his back on autonomy and goes back home to mother.

Does Little Hans feel good about this? Probably not. Wouldn't it be reasonable to assume that he returns full of anger without allowing himself to openly express his emotional state, given his mother's vulnerability? If he shows his anger, she might cry even more, and that would make him feel guilty. Instead, he probably swallows his anger and pretends to be getting along. Why does he do that? Perhaps he fantasizes that his mother might die without him. In that case, he would have killed her, thus proving that he is a bad person. After all, he has long been unconsciously harboring aggressive feelings toward his mother, who restricts whatever he tries to do. In other words, he saves himself from his own guilty conscience by being particularly nice. Little Hans's unconscious conflict may be expressed as follows: Either my mother dies and I live, or the other way around. He decides to save her life, at the same time giving up his own.

But perhaps he also gives up his desire for autonomy because he realizes that as a result of his merged state things will not be easy for him all by himself. And so—using the excuse that "my mother needs me"—he can go back home without having to face his own separation anxieties and shortcomings. In this case, his return may be interpreted as an attempt to rescue himself.

SLEEP AS ONE OF THE FIRST POSTNATAL SEPARATION THEMES

Falling asleep and waking up imply separation and reunion. Whenever parents put their child to bed without making themselves available during the transition to sleep, they are initiating a form of separation: "You are going to sleep now, and we are going to do something else" (Daws, 1989; Sadeh & Anders, 1993). As soon as the child wakes up, parents and child resume the contact that was interrupted by sleep.

On the other hand, an infant who falls asleep by herself shows her parents that they are no longer needed in this realm, thereby initiating a separation of her own. This may be perceived as a joyful event; it may, however, trigger feelings of tender melancholy or sadness because it may seem that the young baby is gone forever. Some parents actually perceive this developmental step as an act of abandonment by the infant. Furman (1982) considered this psychological abandonment by the child to be one of the most difficult and threatening aspects of motherhood. She expressed this poignantly in the title of her article: "Mothers have to be there to be left."

I have previously advanced the hypothesis that the self-regulation of sleep is vulnerable to disorder precisely because it implies separation (Barth, 1999b, 2002, 2003). The infant must learn how to cope with feelings triggered by the transient absence of her parents, and to use the capacity for self-soothing to fall asleep by herself. This may at first include thumb-sucking, tossing and turning to find a comfortable position, or focusing on a light source. After a few months, we begin to observe the transitional phenomena (such as babbling) described by Winnicott (1994/1951) and the use of transitional objects.

In his well-known account of the wooden reel game played by a 1½-year-old boy, Freud (1975/1920) drew attention to the coping processes by which infants deal with experiences of separation.

However, fostering infant self-regulation also implies separation for the parents because they must loosen or even give up the merged form of relationship. This becomes particularly problematic when the parents' excessive closeness to the child has a defensive quality.

SYMBIOSIS AS DEFENSE

The term defense refers to psychological activities with the goal of avoiding unpleasant feelings like shame, guilt, and particularly anxieties. Defense mechanisms protect the ego by keeping painful or unsettling feelings and perceptions from becoming conscious. In addition, they enable an indirect short-term discharge of tension or satisfaction, which, however, provides merely a neurotic pseudo-solution and leads to complications in the long run.

It is important to distinguish between intrapsychic and interpersonal defense mechanisms (Mentzos, 1988). Intrapsychic defense mechanisms like repression, displacement, projection, splitting, and so on are purely psychological processes (e.g., someone is projectively perceived as being clingy). In the case of interpersonal defense mechanisms, however, real objects are chosen in order to behave in a particular way (actual clinging, for example), or these real objects are forced to behave that way within a particular interaction.

If the excessive closeness that the parents foster with their sleep-disordered infant or toddler has a largely defensive character, it is mainly a defense of the interpersonal type, that is, a symbiotic defense (Barth, 2002; Eckstaedt, 1989; Greenacre, 1971/1959; Halberstadt-Freud, 1993; Khan, 1977). It operates in combination with other defense mechanisms, especially projective identification (Ogden, 1988), and involves two steps: The parents (a) project a part of their own self, in this case their own excessive need for closeness, onto their child and (b) force the child interactionally to think, feel, and behave according to the projection. Since the child is unable to withstand the compelling nature of this unconscious process, she actually becomes clingy and seeks constant closeness. By giving in to their child's apparent wishes, the parents themselves are no longer alone. As a result, they no longer need to face their own separation anxieties.

GHOSTS IN THE NURSERY

Selma Fraiberg's (1980) "ghosts in the nursery" is a vivid description of how unconscious conflicts in the parents are reenacted in current interactions with their infant. She defined ghosts as "visitors from the unremembered past of the parents," and as "uninvited guests at the christening," and described how the infant is made to embody a particular ghost through the parents' interaction with her. Fraiberg (1980) distinguished between two types of ghosts.

1. *The baby has become a representative of an aspect of the parental self that is repudiated or negated.*

   Such projection of self-representations causes the parent to describe her infant as if she were or felt precisely the same as the parent ("My child is just like me"). Both positive and negative aspects of a parent's self may be projected onto the child.

2. *The baby has become a representative of figures within the parental past.*

> In such cases, an object representation is projected onto the infant, and the parent perceives her infant as feeling or thinking just like a significant person from her past ("My child is just like my mother/father/brother/sister," etc.).

These ghosts are illustrated by the two case vignettes below. These are not meant to be thorough clinical depictions; rather, they point out the connection between observable interactions and the projections in which they are grounded.

The Baby Has Become a Representative of an Aspect of the Parental Self That Is Repudiated or Negated

Case vignette 1. Mrs. B. reported having repeatedly used the book *Jedes Kind kann schlafen lernen* ([*Every child can learn to sleep*]; Kast-Zahn & Morgenroth, 2002/1995) to help her deal with her 1½-year-old daughter's sleep problem. However, she never pursued the given advice consistently because the child got sick each time. Her daughter would fall asleep only at her breast or in the baby carriage and wake up frequently during the night. She suffered from frequent colds and from croup. "Sleep and illnesses, those are my problems. Nothing else matters." The child's croup was treated with cortisone. Mrs. B. and her husband had also taken their daughter to the hospital several times. Mrs. B. said, "Actually, my fear of the situation is worse than the situation itself." As soon as her child seemed to be the least bit ill, she would run over and scoop her up into her arms. Her fear of life-threatening illness had begun at around the time of her daughter's birth. In the beginning, she constantly looked in to see if her daughter was still breathing. Now her fears revolved around disease.

When asked about her own history, Mrs. B. said, among other things, "My parents were divorced, and I lived with my mother. My mother always had to work long hours. She was independent and managed her own newsstand. Our apartment was in the same building, but several stories up. I was alone the entire day, even as an infant. My mother only occasionally came upstairs to see how I was doing."

In the countertransference I felt sorry for Mrs. B and for the little child she described, and I tried to imagine how she must have felt experiencing hunger or pain or other kinds of distress and not having anyone respond to her crying. It seemed reasonable to assume that she was overwhelmed by strong feelings of abandonment and hatred as well as by a sense of existential threat because of her total helplessness and dependence. I verbalized my impressions and offered as an explanation that Mrs. B. had experienced this situation of aloneness as life-threatening at such an early age and that she was now projecting these old feelings of abandonment and fear of death onto her child. In the mother's perception of her child, I continued, her daughter felt just as alone, abandoned, and threatened when going to sleep by herself as she herself had as a small child. Mrs. B. was taken aback, but confirmed this interpretation when she replied, "Perhaps I was always afraid of dying when no one was around." As a result of our conversation she began to gain access to her own childhood and to memories and feelings of a past long gone that was now being resurrected as a ghost.

A consistent scenario that was reenacted several times during our counseling session now became understandable. The child had repeatedly put toy pieces into her mouth and made sounds as if she were choking. Each time, her mother reacted with alarm and immediately went over to take the toy pieces out of her daughter's mouth. I interpreted this as follows: "Your child is enacting in the here and now precisely the theme that we are talking about. She is showing us how it feels to be unable to breathe and close to dying in order to get saved." Mrs. B. noted with surprise that such interactions had happened frequently at home. She canceled the second appointment because her child was now sleeping well.

This example illustrates that the ghost in the bedroom came from the mother's own painful unresolved feelings, which she had projected onto her child. This projection was prompted by her daughter's croup with its (apparently) life-threatening symptoms. Mrs. B. was unaware that she was interpreting the separation associated with her child's falling asleep by herself in relation to her own history—that is, as a situation of total abandonment and life-threatening experiences, even though her daughter's situation with two sufficiently available parents was completely different from her own. In addition, it may have been difficult for her to separate from her daughter and let her fall asleep by herself because she might then have felt too similar to her own mother, with similarly "bad" characteristics. Change began to occur as soon as Mrs. B. gained emotional access to her own separation trauma. Her new awareness enabled her to correct her distorted projective perceptions so that she no longer saw the short-term separation in sleep as life-threatening. This enabled her to help her daughter learn to fall asleep on her own within a few days. According to her, the process had been quite easy.

Ghosts of this sort are quite common. Essentially, the parents perceive their sleep-disordered child as just as helpless and lonely as they once had been themselves. The existential fear of fragmentation, helplessness, and object loss comes to the fore and is combined with powerless rage. These feelings are defended against by a strong desire for symbolic fusion with the maternal object and are projected onto the child. The child is now the one who cries for permanent parental closeness at bedtime, and the parent no longer has to perceive and deal with her own activated separation anxieties.

The Baby Has Become a Representative of Figures Within the Parental Past

Case vignette 2. Mr. C. reported that he had done "everything, but really absolutely everything" to teach his 1-year-old son to fall asleep on his own. "Nothing, absolutely nothing" worked. Each night he had to get into his son's bed for hours. "If I so much as move a muscle to leave, he immediately cries."

I asked Mr. C. how he experienced the interactions with his son around bedtime. He said, "It seems so unfair. I give him everything, and he just gets cranky. It really makes me angry. I play with him, read him bedtime stories, listen to one music cassette after another, and then I even crawl into bed with him. But he's still not satisfied."

When I asked him whether these feelings reminded him of anything, Mr. C. started to talk about his father, whom he had tried so hard to please. But it had never been enough. His father yelled at him for the slightest "infraction," and nothing was good enough. "Just like my son," Mr. C. said, surprised. "It doesn't matter what I do, he just keeps crying. What am I supposed to do? A few nights ago I had it up to here and yelled back at him. I even hit him, just like my father used to do. That really frightened me. I never wanted to do something like that. But nothing seems to work. Bedtime is just a nightmare."

The ghost in the bedroom was Mr. C.'s father. Mr. C. projected his father's negative qualities onto his son and repeated the same painful relationship. He was struggling for his son's recognition in the present just as he had with his father in the past. He was trying to reenact old scenarios with new actors and to bring them to a better end. Without a "good" outcome he experienced the relationship as endangered and was unable to separate from his son for the night and allow him to sleep. His son, however, was unable to give him the recognition he desired because this theme was irrelevant to him given his developmental needs. He fussed and cried for completely different reasons, namely, that he was chronically overtired and wasn't getting the support he needed to master an important developmental step (learning to fall asleep independently). He presumably had no idea what his father wanted from him. Mr. C., for his part, also identified with his son and wanted to be the committed and loving father he had never had. If he set even the slightest limits, he presumably felt himself to be the "bad" father, whom he had railed against his entire life.

Once Mr. C. recognized his contribution to the sleep problem, he arrived at a much more realistic interpretation of his son's signals and was soon able to teach him how to fall asleep by himself.

PARENT–INFANT PSYCHOTHERAPY

The specific method for treating ghosts in the nursery is parent–infant psychotherapy (Fraiberg, 1980). Generally, the infant and parents are treated together because the problem is viewed as inherent to the relationship. Stern (1995) made the point effectively when he said that the "patient" is the parent–child relationship and not the child, mother, or father alone.

In parent–infant psychotherapy the primary issue always revolves around whom the baby represents and which old relational patterns are being reenacted. The goal is to identify ghosts from the parents' past, and to free the child from the parents' projections. As stated by Brazelton and Cramer (1989), once psychological energy can be redirected and suppressed feelings such as grief or envy can be released, attachment to a realistically perceived baby becomes possible and the baby stops being symptomatic. Clinical experience has shown that this sort of limited therapeutic goal can often be achieved within a few sessions (Barth, 1998, 1999b, 2003; Ludwig-Körner et al., 2001; Stern, 1995; see also chapters 5 and 12). If success is not rapid, this form of treatment alone will probably not be sufficient. A comprehensive treatment of parental conflicts is not a goal of parent–infant psychotherapy. If parents wish to further explore their own issues, individual psychotherapy or couples therapy may be recommended.

SUMMARY

Sleep disorders are among the most frequent complaints of parents with infants or toddlers. Many parents solve the problem on their own or make use of self-help approaches or behavioral advice. This chapter dealt with families in which such interventions do not bring about improvement.

The hypothesis was advanced that the regulation of infant sleep is vulnerable to disorder because it embodies the theme of separation for both the child and the parents. The child has to learn to regulate herself and to use self-soothing strategies to fall asleep. Parents need to support this process by introducing age-appropriate frustrations, rather than making themselves available as sleep aids at bedtime.

The symbiotic relationship that can be observed between parents and their severely sleep disordered children is understood as an unconscious parental attempt to defend against their own conflicts (Barth, 2002, 2003). The aggressive feelings, which are inevitably associated with these overly close relationships, are typically manifested in occasional impulsive acts, as was the case with Mr. C. These parents use their children as a sort of interpersonal defense and thus avoid being confronted with their own painful feelings. They need the child to need them (Lebovici, 1990). One female patient whom I recently began to treat in analysis once said to me, "When I first came to see you, I thought that I would be the happiest person in the world if my daughter finally fell asleep by herself. Now I wish the old days were back because when she began to sleep independently of me, that's when my problems really started to show." By that time, my patient had developed a neurotic anxiety disorder. In severe cases, symbiotic defense may not be resolvable within the framework of parent–infant psychotherapy. Elsewhere I have described a group of mothers for whom improvement in their child's sleep disorder— and with it a loosening of their symbiotic relationship—was so threatening that they terminated therapy (Barth, 2002).

The conflicts that parents defend against may take many forms (Barth, 1998, 1999b, 2002, 2003; Brazelton & Cramer, 1989). Fraiberg (1980) vividly elaborated two types of ghosts in the nursery: first, the baby as a representative of an aspect of the parental self that is repudiated or negated, and second, the baby as a representative of figures within the parental past. In this chapter, such ghosts have been illustrated with case vignettes.

REFERENCES

Barth, R. (1998). Psychotherapie und Beratung im Säuglings- und Kleinkindalter. In K. v. Klitzing, (Ed.), *Psychotherapie in der frühen Kindheit* (pp. 17–27). Göttingen, Germany: Vandenhoek & Ruprecht.

Barth, R. (1999a). Ein Beratungsangebot für Eltern mit Säuglingen und Kleinkindern – Konzeption und erste Erfahrungen der Beratungsstelle MenschensKind. *Praxis der Kinderpsychologie und Kinderpsychiatrie, 48*, 178–191.

Barth, R. (1999b). Schlafstörungen im Kontext der Autonomieentwicklung. *Monatsschrift Kinderheilkunde, 147*, 488–492.

Barth, R. (2000a). "Baby-Lese-Stunden" für Eltern mit exzessiv schreienden Säuglingen – das Konzept der "angeleiteten Eltern-Säuglings-Übungssitzungen". *Praxis der Kinderpsychologie und Kinderpsychiatrie, 49*, 537–549.

Barth, R. (2000b). Präventive Konzepte für Eltern mit Säuglingen und Kleinkindern am Beispiel der Beratungsstelle MenschensKind. *Frühförderung interdisziplinär, 19*, 1–9.

Barth, R. (2002). Mutter-Kind-Symbiose bei Schlafstörungen: Eine psychoanalytische Betrachtung zum Ausschluss des Dritten. In K. Steinhardt, W. Datler, & J. Gstach (Eds.), *Die Bedeutung des Vaters in der frühen Kindheit*. Gießen, Germany: Psychosozial Verlag.

Barth, R. (2003). Schlafstörungen im Säuglings- und Kleinkindalter als Ausdruck einer ungelösten Trennungsproblematik. *Kinderanalyse, 1*, 41–57.

Brazelton, T. B. (1995). *Ein Kind wächst auf: Das Handbuch für die ersten sechs Lebensjahre*. Stuttgart, Germany: Klett-Cotta.

Brazelton, T. B., & Cramer, B. G. (1989). *The earliest relationship—Parents, infants, and the drama of early attachment.* Redding, MA: Addison-Wesley.

Chasseguet-Smirgel, J. (1988). *Zwei Bäume im Garten.* München, Germany: Verlag Internationale Psychoanalyse.

Daws, D. (1989). *Through the night.* London: Free Association Books.

Deutsche Gesellschaft für Kinder- und Jugendpsychiatrie und Psychotherapie (Eds.). (2000). *Leitlinien zur Diagnostik und Therapie von psychischen Störungen im Säuglings-, Kindes- und Jugendalter.* Köln, Germany: Deutscher Ärzte Verlag.

Eckstaedt, A. (1989). *Nationalsozialismus in der "zweiten Generation".* Frankfurt, Germany: Suhrkamp Verlag.

Fegert, J., Schulz, J., Bergmann, R., Tacke, U., Bergmann, K., & Wahn, U. (1997). Schlafverhalten in den ersten drei Lebensjahren. *Praxis der Kinderpsychologie und Kinderpsychiatrie, 46,* 69–91.

Ferenczi, S. (1982). Versuch einer Genitaltheorie. In S. Ferenczi (Ed.), *Schriften zur Psychoanalyse* (Vol. 2, pp. 317–400). Frankfurt, Germany: Fischer. (Original work published 1924)

Fraiberg, S. (1980). *Clinical studies in infant mental health: The first year of life.* New York: Basic Books.

Freud, S. (Ed.). (1975). Jenseits des Lustprinzips. *Studienausgabe* (Vol. 3, pp. 213–272). Frankfurt am Main, Germany: Fischer. (Original work published 1920)

Freud, S. (1975/1923). Das Ich und das Es. In S. Freud, *Studienausgabe* (Vol. 3, pp. 273–330). Frankfurt am Main, Germany: Fischer. (Original work published 1923)

Furman, E. (1982). Mothers have to be there to be left. *The Psychoanalytic Study of the Child, 37,* 15–28.

Greenacre, P. (1971). On focal symbiosis. In L. Jessner & E. Pavenstedt (Eds.), *Emotional growth* (Vol. 1, pp. 145–161). Madison, CT: International Universities Press. (Original work published 1959)

Grunberger, B. (1988). *Narziß und Anubis* (Vol. 2). München, Germany: Verlag Internationale Psychoanalyse.

Halberstadt-Freud, H. C. (1993). Postpartale Depression und die Illusion der Symbiose. *Psyche, 47,* 1041–1062.

Kast-Zahn, A., & Morgenroth, H. (2002). *Jedes Kind kann schlafen lernen* [Every child can learn to sleep]. Ratingen, Germany: Oberstebrink & Partner. (Original work published 1995)

Khan, M. M. R. (1977). Symbiotische Omnipotenz. In M. M. K. Khan (Eds.), *Selbsterfahrung in der Therapie, Theorie und Praxis* (pp. 100–113). Zürich, Switzerland: Kindler.

Lebovici, S. (1990). *Der Säugling, die Mutter und der Psychoanalytiker: Die frühen Formen der Kommunikation.* Stuttgart, Germany: Klett-Cotta.

Ludwig-Körner, C., Derksen, B., Koch, G., Wedler, D., Fröhlich, M., & Schneider, L. (2001). *Primäre Prävention und Interaktion im Bereich der frühen Eltern-Kind-Beziehung.* Unpublished working materials, Fachbereichs Sozialwesen der Fachhochschule Potsdam, Germany.

Mindell, J. A. (1999). Empirically supported treatments in pediatric psychology: Bedtime refusal and night waking in young children. *Journal of Pediatric Psychology, 24,* 465–481.

Mentzos, S. (1988). *Interpersonale und institutionalisierte Abwehr.* Frankfurt, Germany: Suhrkamp.

Ogden, T. H. (1988). Die projektive Identifikation. *Forum der Psychoanalyse, 4,* 1–21.

Papoušek,, M. (1999). Regulationsstörungen der frühen Kindheit: Entstehungsbedingungen im Kontext der Eltern-Kind-Beziehung. In R. Oerter, C. von Hagen, C. Röper, & G. Noam (Eds.), *Klinische Entwicklungspsychologie* (pp. 148–169). Weinheim, Germany: Psychologie Verlags Union.

Rank, O. (1998). *Das Trauma der Geburt und seine Bedeutung für die Psychoanalyse*. Gießen, Germany: Psychosozial-Verlag. (Original work published 1924)

Sadeh, A., & Anders, T. F. (1993). Sleep disorders. In C. H. Zeanah Jr. (Ed.), *Handbook of infant mental health* (pp. 305–316). New York: Guilford Press.

Stern, D. N. (1986). *The interpersonal world of the infant*. New York: Basic Books.

Stern, D. N. (1995). *The motherhood constellation*. New York: Basic Books.

Winnicott, D. W. (1984). Von der Abhängigkeit zur Unabhängigkeit in der Entwicklung des Individuums. In D. W. Winnicott (Ed.), *Reifungsprozesse und fördernde Umwelt* (pp. 106–119). Frankfurt, Germany: Fischer Taschenbuch. (Original work published 1965)

Winnicott, D. W. (1994). Übergangsobjekte und Übergangsphänomene. In D. W. Winnicott (Ed.), *Von der Kinderheilkunde zur Psychoanalyse* (pp. 300–319). Frankfurt, Germany: Fischer Taschenbuch. (Original work published 1951)

Wolke, D., Meyer, R., Orth, B., & Riegel, K. (1994). Häufigkeit und Persistenz von Ein- und Durchschlafstörungen im Vorschulalter: Ergebnisse einer prospektiven Untersuchung an einer repräsentativen Stichprobe in Bayern. *Praxis der Kinderpsychologie und Kinderpsychiatrie, 9*, 331–339.

CHAPTER 11

"GHOSTS AT THE DINING TABLE": PSYCHODYNAMIC ASPECTS OF THE TREATMENT OF FEEDING DISORDERS

Tamara Jacubeit

INTRODUCTION

From day one, the acts of feeding and being fed are ones of intimate relatedness, loving care, joy and satisfaction, rapid development, and happy experiences. However, they also have the potential—sometimes from the very beginning—of becoming an arena of struggle characterized by force, fear, rage, refusal, and despair. A satiated and satisfied baby compensates his mother for her struggles to calm him through a hard night; a baby who refuses food may cause his mother to despair and even lose self-control.

Feeding is the context in which the child's basic need for nutrition, his desire for exploration, self-assertion, and striving for autonomy come together with a central theme of the motherhood constellation, namely that of life and growth (Stern, 1995). First-time mothers are intensely preoccupied with whether they will be able to nourish their baby adequately and to ensure healthy development, and they may experience a certain level of anxiety with regard to their child's survival. The baby may also elicit feelings in his mother that have their origins in her own childhood. There are always two who are hungry in a feeding disorder: the baby, whose mother is unable to nourish him adequately, and the mother, who is herself in need of a loving, nurturing mother (Berger, 1990). Anna Freud (1946/2006) pointed out that nutritional intake represents a developmental path in which the infant gradually develops an intrapsychic differentiation between mother and food. This entails a growing sense of identity in the child with regard to his own body and his own capacities in the feeding context. At the same time, eating may also become an arena for a long-term "struggle for love" between mother and child (Diephold, 1983).

Feeding and being fed are a joint ritual that occurs several times each day. Neither parent nor child can avoid it, and they must relate to each other during feeding; otherwise the baby would starve. Thus feeding becomes a stage for joint repetitive enactments. These scenarios are directed by conscious child-rearing attitudes and the parents' relational experiences from their own childhoods that are unconsciously transferred onto the child, along with the child's personality, his development, and his increasing expectations and ever-expanding experience. If one of the parents' scripts is overly rigid and inflexible, marked by early trauma and/or unresolved intrapsychic conflicts, and if the other partner is unable to assist or compensate with a script of his own, the baby will have little opportunity to participate constructively in the staging of his own drama. On the contrary, he will lend to the enactment his own dynamic that goes beyond refusing food and by behavior that is otherwise problematic and age-inappropriate. This sets the stage for a vicious circle.

This is how experiences from the parents' history may create a negative scenario at mealtimes and direct a daily drama, which the parents and the child jointly enact. Selma Fraiberg (1980, p. 164) called this constellation "ghosts in the nursery," who turn up as "uninvited guests at the christening . . . from the unremembered past." These ghosts prevent the parents from perceiving their baby's own specific characteristics and wishes, or they unconsciously force the baby to embody a ghost. The parents' past is reenacted in current interactions. Because feeding interactions are recurrent and unavoidable, they easily provide the stage for such scenarios. The driving forces behind these observable interactions between the parent and the child are the parents' imagined, conscious, or unconscious fantasies (Brazelton & Cramer, 1989; Lebovici, 1990). These fantasies may take on various guises. The baby may appear to the parents as a ghost from their past and represent a person who played an important role in their history. Their relationship to their baby repeats relational patterns from the past, or the baby r epresents an aspect of a parent's unconscious. When the therapist attempts to decipher the script by exact behavioral observation and exploration of the parents' fantasies during the diagnostic process, it is common to find that the various facets of the imagined interaction are superimposed on each other.

In some cases, the baby's development and food intake is so impaired as a result of organic disease or sensory-motor problems that he has little tolerance or leeway for participating in a joint scenario. In such cases, the parents need a high degree of flexibility and adaptability in their behavior and can hardly follow their own scripts. Otherwise, interactional disorders may become intertwined with the child's basic organic feeding problems.

Parents, too, may be so compromised by stressful events such as the prospect of a life-threatening disease of their baby (even in cases with no current symptoms) or by conflicts in the couple's relationship that they are unable to experience the emotionally charged feeding situation without being flooded by powerful affects that they find difficult to integrate.

Of course, the feeding situation is not only a potential battleground, but rather a daily recurring context for intuitive parental care, and for practicing fine-motor control and manual skills, regulation of attention, exploration, and autonomy as well as intense communication and regulatory processes between the parents and child. Long-lasting feeding and eating disorders in early childhood not only harm the parent–child relationship, but they also endanger the physical and psychological development of the child. Therefore, psychotherapy must focus not only on sufficient nutritional intake and bodily growth but also on healthy psychological development of the child along with age-appropriate eating behavior and satisfactory parent–child interactions.

From a psychodynamic perspective, the unconscious dynamics of the feeding scenario—the "inner script"—is just as interesting as the observable interaction. Psychotherapeutic interventions, whether they proceed from observable interactions or from the parents' fantasies and unconscious processes, will only be successful if they permit the child with his own specific developmental dynamic to become a creative coproducer of the scenario.

Sleep disorders in infancy and toddlerhood frequently involve problems with separation in which the parents and child practice and master the process of detachment in daily recurring bedtime scenarios (Barth, 2003). In the case of eating, the central developmental theme has to do with whether both sides are able to negotiate issues of autonomy in dyadic and later in triadic interactions and to learn to integrate these flexibly. Diagnostically, it is important to distinguish between the child's behavior against the backdrop of his developmental state and what this behavior triggers in his parents. Disorders of nutritional intake in the youngest infants, for example, may be explained in terms of difficulties modulating arousal and adapting to new foods or circumstances. If, on the other hand, the baby refuses to eat toward the end of the second half-year of life, this usually involves integration of the baby's need for autonomy. Refusal can be an expression of his frustration at not being able to self-feed either because he lacks the age-appropriate motor coordination or because the parents restrict his activities. Parents—particularly mothers—who cannot adequately interpret their child's behavior may experience such refusal as a rejection of their lovingly prepared food, and sometimes even of their own person. The theme of autonomy may be reactivated in the parents in this situation, depending on how well they have resolved their own earlier conflicts over autonomy and have learned to tolerate the need for autonomy in others. This may trigger reactions that are completely independent of the child's developmental state and the pending developmental tasks that remain for him to master.

These aspects are illustrated by the following vignettes and descriptions of feeding interactions from psychotherapeutic work done with three families. The feeding interactions were videotaped during the diagnostic and/or therapeutic process in the treatment room, in the absence of the therapist. The parents (in one case an older sibling was involved as well) were informed of the videotaping, and they gave their consent. It is impossible to relate all of the observable details caught on a videotape. In addition, it is unavoidable that some interpretative terms will slip into the description of behavior. (The description of videotaped action is italicized in the text.)

EATING AND FEEDING AS A JOINT DEVELOPMENTAL TASK

We present a successful feeding interaction to show the great potential that such a scene has for many aspects of the baby's development, for the mother's self-esteem, and for the joint mastery of conflict negotiation. This example will help illustrate how flexibly an intuitively responsive mother must deal with her infant's behavioral patterns if feeding is to succeed.

> *Nina (barely 10 months old) sits expectantly in a highchair in front of a full plate. She shows her mother by smacking her lips and moving her arms that she is hungry and wants to start eating right away. She tries to grab the full spoon several times. Her mother doesn't let her, but offers her a second empty spoon instead that Nina doesn't use for eating, but throws under the table. In spite of her frustration, Nina allows herself to be fed several spoonfuls of pabulum. Then she begins to explore the table by tapping it with both hands. Her mother first answers with some vocal imitation, ignoring her tapping and holding the full spoon within her daughter's visual field. She eats another spoonful and then begins to tap on the table and the plate as well. Her mother cleans her hands and patiently continues to feed her. Nina becomes fussier, eats very slowly with low appetite, twists in her chair, and refuses to open her mouth.*

The observer witnesses an escalating interpersonal conflict. The mother's wish to get her daughter to eat as much as possible leads to patient but stoic behavior that hardly leaves room for the infant to act on her own. The infant, for her part, would like to try eating independently with the spoon. Initially, this conflict leads to provoking behavior and increasing refusal by the daughter. A power struggle ensues with refusal and the potential for intrusive feeding if the mother doesn't stop feeding and trust that her child will eat enough later on or let her daughter play with the spoon. However, the mother and her daughter find a novel solution to this tense situation that becomes successful for both.

> Nina signals her mother by turning her head away and clenching her mouth that she has no intention of eating anymore. Her mother places the full spoon at the edge of the plate. She offers Nina a cup of water, which Nina drinks. While her mother is busy putting the cup away, Nina tries to grasp the full spoon and to bring it to her mouth. This time, her mother doesn't take the spoon out of her hand but helps her by guiding her hand so that her daughter can put the spoon into her mouth herself.

If she had tried to take the spoon away, Nina would have protested vociferously. On the other hand, if her mother hadn't helped her, Nina would almost certainly not have been able to get the spoon into her mouth. At this time, Nina's motor skills were not yet up to the task of translating this complex behavioral pattern into action. The result would have been frustration and anger. Within a few fractions of a second, the mother intuitively chose a third and this time successful path.

> The mother praises her daughter's almost independent action much more expressively than before and promptly changes her feeding behavior. This time, she refills the spoon but does not try to feed Nina herself. Rather, she places the spoon on the edge of the plate and waits until Nina grabs the spoon and then helps her guide it into her mouth. Almost immediately Nina begins to eat more quickly and with observable pleasure. The mother begins to talk more, look more relaxed, and praise her daughter frequently. "Wait until daddy finds out!" she says to her daughter proudly.

Nina's pleasure in her own action was now just as much a motive for eating as hunger itself. Her mother was clearly delighted by her daughter's developmental step and adapted her behavior to her child immediately. The mother and child together found a novel solution to this potentially escalating interpersonal conflict resulting in pleasurable eating and a successful developmental step for the child, and pride and satisfaction for the mother.

Feeding situations are particularly susceptible to escalating conflict because they cannot be avoided during the first year of life, as illustrated by the previous example. With settling to sleep, by contrast, the child will eventually fall asleep by himself without regulatory support, simply because of exhaustion. Bodily care can be provided without the baby's cooperation, and the parents and child can avoid playing together. Because of this difference, the feeding situation may turn into an arena for power struggles, misunderstandings, and conflicts, but also provide a space in which the infant develops and both parties feel satisfied by arriving together at a common solution.

The feeding scene just described, which took less than 10 minutes, included great potential for conflict but also created a space for the infant's psychological development, for the mother's feelings of self-esteem, and for positive interpersonal processes. If a mother cannot respond flexibly to the rapidly developing and changing behavior of her child but reacts to his attempts at autonomy with rigid or unpredictable patterns, recurrent conflict at mealtimes is almost assured.

Frequently, parental behavioral patterns and the feeding scenarios that are enacted together with the infant are a manifestation of the parents' (usually the mother's or primary caregiver's) unresolved conflicted relationships. Such constellations are described in Case Vignettes 2 and 3 in this chapter. By contrast, Case Vignette 1 shows a situation in which the mother does not restage an old conflict from her past but deals with a difficult feeding situation in the present and is so flooded by ambivalent feelings toward her baby that she feels compelled to draw on defense mechanisms to control her own affect. This has the effect of blocking her own intuitive maternal competencies.

"I WILL NOT EAT YOUR ANGER AND FEAR"

Case Vignette 1

The child just described had been referred for the first time by outpatient gastroenterology to parent–infant psychotherapy at the age of 3 months. Although Nina suffered from a genetic disease (cystic fibrosis) and her health was compromised as a result of various complications in the past, the girl's present observable rejection of food could not be attributed to organic causes alone, particularly because it was observable only during the day.

At the first appointment, the mother and Nina were brought in by the mother's grandparents. Nina's father had refused to come in. Nina was sleeping peacefully in her baby chair. Her mother reported increasing problems with feeding. Whenever Nina was given her bottle during the day she began to cry. She drank better at night when she was half asleep, but overall she wasn't drinking enough. When asked about her daughter's birth and the time immediately thereafter, her mother related a terrible story. She reported in a factual and emotionally detached manner that her daughter had been delivered by emergency Cesarean section because Nina had a bowel obstruction (ileus) that required several operations and care in the intensive care unit because of a sequence of life-threatening events. She was eventually diagnosed with cystic fibrosis, a serious genetic disease. While the mother was talking, Nina woke up. The mother responded intuitively in a way that allowed Nina to take her time waking up and to become included in the conversation. She happily played with her mother's fingers, laughed, looked around curiously, and engaged with the therapist. In spite of the cystic fibrosis and more than 2 months in an intensive care unit, Nina's development was appropriate for her age. She did not seem the least disturbed by what her mother was talking about. This means that Nina's mother had been able to integrate her own embarrassment and affect in such a way that her intuitive behavior was not impaired. As a therapist, however, I was shocked and felt great sadness at hearing this story and felt increasing anger at the father, who was obviously leaving his wife in the lurch—perhaps as an expression of his own attempt to deal with his daughter's disease.

Nina became a bit more fussy after about a half hour. Because the mother had assumed that Nina would be getting hungry since she hadn't eaten for a few hours, counseling was interrupted, and feeding was videotaped without the therapist being present in the room.

First, Nina's mother changes her diaper. In the process, she expertly takes care of her daughter's artificial anus. The two of them talk and laugh the whole time. Baby talk, greeting reactions, and happy gurgling are evident. Finished with diapering, her mother picks Nina up in order to get the prewarmed bottle. Nina becomes increasingly fussy. The mother sits down and tests the temperature of the milk. In the meantime, Nina begins to cry. The mother places the nipple in Nina's mouth. The mother says, "What are you fussing about," several times, always in a calming tone. However, Nina does not calm down, and spits out the nipple. The mother removes the bottle for a moment, but does nothing to change the situation and looks increasingly tense. She again puts the nipple into Nina's mouth, this time visibly against Nina's will. Nina cries even more and almost chokes. The mother takes the nipple out of Nina's mouth again and begins to walk around trying to divert Nina's attention to objects in the room, all the while holding Nina in the feeding position in her arms. The mother's speech becomes more rigid. She tries to give her daughter the bottle again while walking around, but Nina intensifies her crying. After a few minutes, she brings her daughter to the upright position, but she can't hold her crying infant securely enough, who squirms and arches her back. Nevertheless, Nina calms down somewhat. The mother puts her in the feeding position again and gives her a teaspoon of medication with a little water. Nina tolerates this well and stops crying. But as soon as the mother places the nipple into her mouth again, Nina begins to cry with increasing intensity. Her mother walks around some more, talking in monotone and with increasing volume in response to her baby's crying. Nina back-arches so much in the process that there seems to be no chance of calming her unless the mother stops trying to feed her. However, her mother tries again and again to feed her, holding her ever more precariously. This escalating situation only ends with the intervention of the therapist. Nina calms down in her baby carriage and immediately falls asleep, exhausted.

In the beginning of feeding it was still unclear why Nina began to cry, whether she wanted to eat or not, or whether she was hungry and her mother simply didn't feed her fast enough. The mother was unable to tolerate her infant's refusal and to stop the feeding. Rather, she became increasingly rigid, loud, and tense, and seemed to have lost her intuitive ease and forgotten the calming strategies observed during the initial interaction. As she reported later, this situation swamped her with powerful feelings toward Nina. Anger at her refusal to eat and an underlying rage about her child's severe disease became mixed with fear that her child might starve or die as a result of the disease. The mother had to defend against powerful aversive impulses and death wishes aimed at her child. However, she was unable to extricate herself from this increasingly derailed situation because this would only have increased her fears. Her stereotypical question, "What are you fussing about," was a projection of her own impulses.

The mother's intrapsychic dilemma led to a selective blockage of her intuitive maternal competencies, so that she was unable to help her baby regulate herself specifically in the feeding situation. Nevertheless, she was more than able to provide regulatory support in other situations. During feeding, the mother's affects became condensed in an unbearable way. Her fear and anger were aggravated by the knowledge that the child's life expectancy depended on how well she thrived during her first years of life.

During the 2 months at the hospital, the mother had been completely competent, reliable, and loving. However, during the 3 weeks after discharge, she had become increasingly overloaded and exhausted. There was little support at home. Her parents blamed her for her daughter's refusal to eat because she always ate better when her grandmother took over. Nina's father paid little attention to either of them and in particular did nothing to help his wife with feeding.

As soon as Nina had fallen asleep we resumed the dialogue we had begun, the goal of which was to give the mother some psychological relief. On the basis of a positive "good-grandmother transference" (Stern, 1995), the mother was reminded of her own very good maternal skills. We encouraged her to trust her child's signals, even during the feeding situation, and only to feed her when she was clearly signaling hunger, at least until the situation improved. One of the mother's conscious or preconscious grandiose fantasies was addressed during the session. Like other mothers of severely ill children, Nina's mother hoped that Nina would be cured by good mothering, especially by good feeding, even though she understood very well the genetic cause and incurability of the disease.

What was significant for the mother was the opportunity to find in the therapist someone with whom she could talk calmly for the first time about the life story of her little daughter, someone who would listen with empathy and without being overwhelmed. Giving parents space to talk about their child in a therapeutic relationship can by itself become a helpful intervention. It enables them to step out of their close involvement with their child and their entanglement with their own early experiences (the "ghosts"). By reporting their child's biographical history to another person, they are able to look at their child from a more distant position. It is particularly important in cases of severely ill children like Nina to pay close attention to the narrative history. This helps the parents to appreciate what is healthy in their child, to prevent themselves from being flooded by their fears, and to learn how to defend against them more efficiently (Jacubeit, 2001).

The tense feeding situation settled down very quickly. Three days after our first outpatient session, the mother announced proudly that feeding was no longer a problem. It should be said, however, that as Nina's needs for autonomy increased, critical situations in the feeding context reappeared repeatedly. Nevertheless, these were resolved in the course of prolonged family psychotherapy.

The mother's inner emotional state had become apparent only in a certain interactional context with the baby where it severely impeded the baby's capacity for self-regulation. With severely ill babies this typically occurs in the feeding situation, where both sides experience emotionally intense relatedness and the mother's affects become condensed. In such cases, therapeutic intervention in the form of crisis intervention has the primary goal of reinstating the mother's intuitive competence in the feeding context in order to protect the child from the mother's "indigestible" affects.

"LITTLE BOYS DON'T SURVIVE"

Case Vignette 2

The pediatrician referred Florian to our program because of a feeding disorder with neither an apparent organic cause nor evidence of failure to thrive, but with inadequate nutritional intake and increasing stress on the mother. A few days later Florian's mother came to the clinic in an agitated state with her 9-month-old son and reported, among other things, that Florian had neither eaten nor drunk any fluids that day. Florian was awake and, in spite of not having eaten for at least 8 hours, readily engaged with the therapist. He was somewhat small for his age, but lively and with advanced psychomotor development. The little boy crawled all over the office and pulled himself up onto his feet wherever he could.

After a short exploratory dialogue, we decided with the mother to videotape first their morning feeding or nursing ritual and to continue the dialogue thereafter.

> In the video room the mother takes Florian in her arms after opening her blouse. He is calm, has a pacifier in his mouth, and his eyes are wide open. His mother walks around the room rocking him gently and humming a song. "There is still too much light in here," she says and leans over Florian so that the ceiling lights don't shine in his eyes. Florian remains calm but somewhat tense. His tiny arms are stretched toward her and his fists are closed. The mother gently removes the pacifier from his mouth and turns him to her breast. He takes the nipple into his mouth, but without sucking on it. He gets a bit cranky and turns his head to the side. His mother gives him the pacifier again and walks around the room rocking her son. Florian remains calm but lies somewhat tensely in her arms. When the mother attempts for the second time to turn him toward her breast, Florian puts the pacifier, which had been jammed between his sweater and his chin, back into his mouth. The mother continues to walk around the room with Florian. Suddenly, she stops, goes over to her handbag, and takes out a bottle of milk. At first Florian does not react, and the mother continues to rock him with the bottle in her hand. The mother sits down, takes the pacifier out of his mouth, and replaces it with the bottle. He begins to suck, but immediately starts to fuss. Startled, his mother says, "Uh-oh, I forgot the cap." She immediately gives Florian the pacifier and takes the cap off the bottle. When she gives Florian the bottle again, he drinks tensely and looks expectantly into her face. Neither of them can relax. The mother fails to react to his eye contact or drinking; her facial expression remains impassive. After sucking several times, Florian sits up and suddenly begins to cry. His mother gives him the pacifier and rocks him again. He calms down. This alternation between bottle feeding and rocking with the pacifier continues for another 45 minutes.

At first it was unclear to the observer (and probably to the mother and baby as well) whether the issue was eating or sleeping. The mother thought that Florian only ate when he was asleep. In many respects she acted as if she were taking care of a very young baby. She prepared the food as if for a newborn; the bottle had a newborn nipple (its milk flow simply was not fast enough, which explained Florian's negative reaction after the first sucks). The mother soothed him before taking him to her breast as one does with a newborn who cannot suck because he is too aroused. In play situations, the mother stimulated her son with toys the way one does with a little baby but did not allow him to play by himself. This inappropriate interactional behavior, which was not attuned to his capacities and needs, can be understood against the backdrop of severe trauma in the mother's childhood, as is discussed below. However, the fact that she behaved this way was also provoked by Florian's behavior. He passively endured his mother's behavior and soothed himself with his pacifier. It would have been more age-appropriate if he had demonstrated increasing fussiness to his mother as a sign that he wanted to eat immediately. Hungry children at this age generally have little tolerance for frustration. But Florian did not react to his mother's frustrating attempts at nursing with fussiness and massive rejection; he seemed to take a wait-and-see attitude and let himself be rocked. Presumably, he had a basic understanding of what would happen had he begun to cry loudly: His mother would probably have become so irritated and confused that he would not have gotten anything to eat. Typical ritualized patterns of interaction such as this are represented by the infant in what Stern (1986, 1995) called the "schema-of-being-with." Florian adapted his behavior to that of his mother to such an extent that his own desires and capacities of affect expression, which were observed in his interactions with other people, hardly came into play. According to Winnicott (1965), we can observe here the origins of a "false self." The mother mistakenly interprets the boy's passivity and inhibited expressiveness as lack of interest in her and responds according to her own misconception. However, the boy's actual affective state is very different. Over the long term, this discrepancy may lead to the development of pathological self-representations (Fonagy & Target, 2002).

In observing the interpersonal regulatory processes at work here, it became clear that by giving up his own vitality, Florian no longer communicated to his mother what he wanted and was able to do. This contributed to her distorted perception of him as an infant or little baby.

Another aspect of the feeding interaction, the mother's unconscious refusal to feed her child, became even clearer a few hours later at lunchtime. In the morning she tried to give him her breast, although (as it turned out) she was no longer producing milk. She then offered him a bottle with a cap and a nipple that was too small. At noon she began feeding by putting a bib on him. She then tried to get him to take a vitamin tablet with water while they were sitting on the floor. Only then did she begin to prepare pabulum. Florian sat expectantly at her feet without any signs of impatience, although he must have felt hungry, having only had 80 ml of milk that morning. His mother then placed him in a high chair, showed him the pabulum and then a vial containing drops of medicine that she wanted to give him first. Florian let it all happen and played with his feet. He ate the pabulum better than his mother had expected. Her comment: "You're trying to annoy me; I don't get it." She was attributing purposeful intent to his eating better than usual, inferring that he was trying to anger her because the situation was being videotaped. In other words, she was attributing capacities to him that he could not possibly have had at this point in his development. Here, too, his mother seemed to deny him food aggressively while projecting her own aggressive impulses onto him.

The key to this behavior was revealed during the evening feeding when the father was present. He supported his wife and child as well as he could, given the pressures of his professional life. He did chores around the house and cooked—something that the mother was no longer able to do because she was so exclusively focused on preparing food for Florian and feeding him. The videotape described below was also taken in our facility; the parents tried to reproduce the situation as it usually developed at home.

Florian sits on his father's lap looking out into the room. He is being held and fed by his father in such a way that there is no face-to-face interaction, and no possible dyadic situation can develop. After a few spoonfuls, Florian refuses to eat; he squirms on his father's lap and turns away from him. The father has difficulties holding him firmly enough. After a short conversation between the parents, the mother gets up, begins to sing an old folk tune, and accompanies her singing with creative finger games and dance movements. As soon as his mother begins to sing Florian beams, opens his mouth, and continues to eat.

Over the next several days we were able to piece together details from the mother's biographical history. Her parents had considered her a "replacement" for a brother who had died during the first weeks of life. As a small child she experienced the death of two younger brothers who also died during their first year. She had to watch how her mother, who was emotionally unavailable to her, had lovingly but unsuccessfully cared for and fed her little brothers. She must have felt rage at her mother along with powerful feelings of envy and possibly even a desire to kill—which in a way may have become reality in her mind. Thanks to her caring father she nonetheless developed into a psychologically healthy person, as far as we could assess.

The song she sang, a kindergarten dance, was probably not an accidental choice. "Come little brother, come dance with me, I am reaching with my hands to you . . . ." This was where her own early experiences with her brothers and her noticeable desire for a relationship with her own son condensed despite of her unconscious refusal to feed him properly.

Why were a lively little boy and an engaged father, who cared for both his son and his wife, unable to change the mother's script and enact a relaxed scenario together? Florian had severely curtailed his needs and vitality in the eating and play situation because he experienced that refusal and protest seriously irritated his mother and triggered behavior that was incomprehensible and unpredictable behavior for him. The father obviously had a good sense that a dyadic feeding situation, which probably would have succeeded between himself and Florian, would have excluded his wife and further destabilized her. She would presumably have been flooded by a revival of her early feelings of being excluded as a third wheel from the mother–brother dyad, now in the father–son dyad. At the same time, she found it difficult to develop positive maternal self-esteem because when she was a little girl she saw that her mother was unable to save her little boys despite heroic efforts. Intuitively, the father had included his wife in the scenario in such a way that her singing enabled Florian to eat.

Diagnostically, the mother can be said to have suffered an emotional crisis with disintegration and severe regression. In order to function as well as she could and control her death fantasies, she had to deny the actual developmental state of her son and treat him as if he were a newborn or a much older boy.

In the framework of crisis intervention, we helped the mother learn to feed her son in an age-appropriate manner. The goal was to enable Florian to reactivate his communicative capabilities in interactions with his mother or learn how to guide his mother's feeding through signals of hunger and satiation. The feeding situation quickly turned into a satisfying and pleasurable experience for both of them. During the 5 days of inpatient therapy, the mother's early history had been reconstructed and the "ghost of the dead brothers" brought to life as part of the diagnostic assessments. It was, however, important to counterbalance the risk that the mother would be flooded intrapsychically by the affects associated with her history. We focused on stabilizing the mature defensive structures that had helped her to live a psychologically healthy life before the birth of her son. In spite of our psychodynamic understanding of the cause of the feeding disorder, we used an interaction-centered approach (von Hofacker & Papoušek, 1998): The goal of therapy was not to deal with her traumatic experiences, but rather to exorcise the "ghost" from the current feeding situation, to enable the mother and infant to experience positive age-appropriate interactions, and to stabilize the mother.

Shortly after Florian's first birthday, the mother came in for a follow-up session and reported, relieved and with a certain self-irony, that everything was now all right because, after all, he had survived his first year.

"I Hate My Little Sister"

Case Vignette 3

Eighteen-month-old Carmen was brought in by her parents because she was never hungry, ate hardly anything, and eating was a constant battle. The parents suspected an organic disease, although Carmen had been examined several times by the family pediatrician and in the hospital, with no pathological findings. The parents arrived for the initial appointment with Carmen and her 4-year-old sister Carola. While the parents talked, the girls explored the room, and Carmen indiscriminately dragged toys out of the closet without examining or playing with them. She didn't say a word, ran around the room, and disturbed her sister whenever she began to play. Carmen turned to her mother several times with a toy in hand. Without responding to her or asking what she wanted, the mother gave her something to drink. In short order, the children had made a shambles of the room, and the parents, rather than intervening, asked Carola to play with her younger sister. All family members seemed angry at each other: Carola at her younger sister whom she was supposed to supervise; the mother at both children, who regularly trashed their living room and now the therapy room; the father at the mother, because she forced him to come home for all mealtimes. Carmen's uncontrolled behavior may be interpreted as a sign of anger because no one was attending to her and helping her to deal with the counseling situation.

Mealtimes at home lasted more than an hour because otherwise Carmen wouldn't eat and drink enough. The mother reported that she wanted the father to be present in order to prevent herself from hitting the children, particularly Carmen, when she caused trouble at mealtimes.

The biographical history of the children hinted at details that were best discussed without the girls present, and so the session was ended and the family was asked to come in for a second session. Given the difficult initial meeting, it seemed more promising to focus on the presenting symptom, that is, Carmen's eating disorder, than to address more problematic relational issues too early in the process. We therefore discussed with the parents the possibility of videotaping a mealtime during the second session, which is described below.

The mother prepares the table, distributes the food that she has brought on the children's plates, and asks the father to put bibs on both daughters. The parents don't eat (like at home where they also do not eat with the children). Both children come to the table upon their mother's request. Carmen crawls up onto a normal chair, but her mother lifts her into a highchair. Even before the older sister and parents have sat down, Carmen is given a plateful of noodles with tomato sauce and a spoon. She starts to eat all by her self. Both parents overlook Carmen's independent eating, even though she is sitting between both parents and next to her sister. The parents talk to their older daughter, sometimes even simultaneously. Carmen stops eating several times and interrupts the intense conversation between her sister and her parents by a vocal request, whereupon the mother gives her a glass of water. Each time this happens, her mother turns her entire upper body toward her daughter but promptly turns away from her as soon as Carmen starts eating again. Both parents ignore their daughter's independent eating, nor do they respond to her with any facial expression or speech until Carmen has finished most of her meal and has begun to squirm and climb out of her chair. Her mother offers to feed her and places Carmen on her lap, even though she has clearly signaled that she doesn't want any more. The mother tries to put the spoon in her mouth, which Carmen rejects. Her mother sets her down on the floor, and then stands up with a full spoon in hand and runs after her trying to feed her. When Carmen refuses, her mother sets her down on her now empty seat and tries to feed her there. The father offers to continue feeding Carmen and gets up. The mother takes a seat next to Carola, who angrily pushes her aside. The mother moves to the next seat. Carmen is now fed in all imaginable places (under the table, on a hobby horse, in the play area) by both parents, who alternate with each other and discuss the situation. By contrast, Carola, left alone at the table, quietly continues to eat until she asks her parents for permission to finish her meal and get up. A few minutes later the mother tells her unexpectedly, "Carola, please sit down back at the table. Your sister hasn't finished yet!" Carola refuses and continues to play. In the meantime, Carmen is sitting on her mother's lap and is fed and praised by her father for each spoonful that she eats. This bizarre dance ends with Carola playing alone in the play area, Carmen snuggling on her mother's lap, and the parents discussing the meal.

Various aspects of intrafamilial interaction are clearly delineated in this feeding scene. First, Carmen's desired behavior, that is, the fact that she was eating a substantial portion by herself, was completely ignored. Meanwhile, the parents were communicating simultaneously with the older daughter. At a later point in time, the older daughter was completely excluded while the parents together fed her younger sister. At no time was there a dyadic situation, which would have been appropriate in this setting, or any flexibility in their communications. One of the children is excluded at each given time, which must have elicited envy in them and caused them to disturb each other in more or less subtle ways. Carola is expected to take over the parents' role (looking after the little sister while she plays, or remaining seated at the table so that Carmen would eat although she was already full). All in all, the children controlled the situation and choreographed the parents' dance, which centered around them.

The conflicts between the parents that were evident here were clarified during the third session at which the children were not present. The couple had been married for many years and had sought in vain to have a child. Pregnancy occurred only after the mother underwent intensive fertility treatment, which was both physically and psychologically extremely stressful for her. The pregnancy and Carola's birth and development were not unusual. Both parents agreed that they only wanted one child and were satisfied with their little threesome. However, 2 years later the mother became pregnant again. This meant to her on the one hand that it was personally satisfying to be able to get pregnant without medical help, but on the other hand it meant a disturbance in their family planning. After much discussion, the parents decided against an abortion, although their relationship with their second child remained highly ambivalent.

This became clear in the interaction described above. At first they ignored Carmen's independent eating, and she was not integrated into the family circle. As soon as she decided to stop eating, the parents forced themselves on her in an attempt to get her to eat some more. During this phase of the interaction, her older sister was excluded. In addition to their ambivalence, the parents were also acting as if they had only one child, as they had originally planned. The mother's relationship with her own younger sister was significant in this regard. Because her sister had always had a hard time eating, she got more attention from their mother. According to the mother, she continued to be the favorite daughter.

Therapy was difficult because the mother repeatedly enacted rivalries in the therapeutic relationship as well so that it was almost impossible to establish a positive and therapeutically helpful transference. The parents were not ready to see the connection between the mother's early relationship with her own sister and their current difficulties with Carmen. When the therapist tried to help the parents achieve healthy control over mealtimes while allowing the children to determine how much to eat, the mother exhibited anxieties that were incommensurate with the situation. She fantasized that Carmen might die within a few hours if she didn't eat or drink. These severe fears, which were clearly dysfunctional in relation to an 18-month-old child, threatened to impede the child's own independence. They may most likely be understood as a defense against other more powerful impulses, possibly including the wish that her own younger sister would die, transferred onto her own daughter.

The ghost of the hated sister was so alive in the mother that, although she claimed that her older daughter should never experience something similar (therefore only one child), she provoked a powerful sibling rivalry both at mealtimes and in many other day-to-day situations, such as when the children played.

In the end, this family was not able to come to an understanding of the psychodynamic connections between the "drama" at mealtimes and the mother's early experiences. It was, however, possible to enable them to be more relaxed at the dining table by setting up mealtime rules together with the family. This primarily pedagogical counseling approach (Kast-Zahn & Morgenroth, 2000) is of course not sufficiently effective by itself in cases of "stubborn ghosts" and irrational and projected fears, as was the case here.

Nevertheless, the mother was able to become involved in short-term parent–toddler psychotherapy that focused on Carmen's play and speech development and was presumably less threatening to her. This therapy emphasized not only developmental aspects but also improvement of the mother–child relationship. It was important to help the mother differentiate between her younger daughter and her younger sister in her mental representations. This was not achieved by addressing the mother's fantasies in this case, but rather by facilitating concrete positive experiences of playing together with Carmen.

Summary

Ghosts tend to "do mischief" (Fraiberg, 1980) at the dining table in more than a few families. The result is the emergence of dramas that are distressing for the child and the parents and that endanger the parent–child relationship and the child's development. The primary goal in treating feeding disorders should be to create a more relaxed atmosphere in the feeding interactions as quickly as possible in order to prevent escalating vicious circles from leading to impulsive acts by the parents or persistent food refusal by the child. In addition to diagnosing the psychodynamic processes, observing the mealtime scenarios, and analyzing the transference and countertransference in the therapeutic setting, a detailed analysis of the child's eating behavior in relation to his developmental state should be a sine qua non in psychodynamic and psychoanalytic parent–infant psychotherapies as well (Wolke & Skuse, 1992).

Von Klitzing (2003) has stressed the importance of including the father as the third member of the triad in therapy during early childhood. In two of the case histories described, the function of the father as part of the mealtime scenario was evident, as was his supportive role in stabilizing problematic situations and preventing destructive derailments. These aspects should not be underestimated and must be taken into account when doing such therapeutic work.

Pedrina (2001) invited parent–infant psychotherapists with a psychoanalytic approach to collaborate with other professionals in an interdisciplinary manner. Close cooperation with a pediatrician is almost always necessary in treating families with infants and toddlers experiencing feeding disorders; otherwise, an exclusively psychodynamic approach has the potential to endanger the baby somatically, particularly in cases of failure to thrive.

References

Barth, R. (2003). Schlafstörungen im Säuglings- und Kleinkindalter als Ausdruck einer ungelösten Trennungsproblematik. *Kinderanalyse, 11*, 41–57.

Berger, M. (1990). Zur Psychodynamik frühkindlicher Essstörungen. In J. Wiesse (Ed.), *Psychosomatische Medizin in Kindheit und Adoleszenz* (pp. 43–62). Göttingen. Germany: Vandenhoeck & Ruprecht.

Brazelton, T. B., & Cramer, B. (1989). *The earliest relationship: Parents, infants, and the drama of early attachment.* Reading, MA: Addison-Wesley.

Diephold, B. (1983). Essstörungen bei Kindern und Jugendlichen. *Praxis der Kinderpsychologie und Kinderpsychiatrie, 32*, 298–304.

Fonagy, P., & Target, M. (2002). Neubewertung der Entwicklung der Affektregulation vor dem Hintergrund von Winnicotts Konzept des "falschen Selbst." *Psyche, 56*, 839–862.

Fraiberg, S. (1980). *Clinical studies in infant mental health. The first year of life.* New York: Basic Books.

Freud, A. (2006). Das psychoanalytische Studium der frühkindlichen Essstörungen. In U. Jongbloed-Schurig (Ed.), *Ich esse meine Suppe nicht. Psychoanalyse gestörten Essverhaltens* (pp. 22–36). Frankfurt, Germany: Brandes Apsel Verlag. (Original work published 1946)

Jacubeit, T. (2001). Wenn ich schon überlebe, muss ich auch lebendig werden dürfen. Aus der psychotherapeutischen Arbeit mit chronisch kranken Säuglingen und Kleinkindern. In F. Pedrina (Ed.), *Beziehung und Entwicklung in der frühen Kindheit* (pp. 81–102). Tübingen, Germany: Edition Discord.

Kast-Zahn, A., & Morgenroth, H. (2000). *Jedes Kind kann richtig essen*. Ratingen, Germany: Oberstebrink & Partner.

Lebovici, S. (1990). *Der Säugling, die Mutter und der Psychoanalytiker: die frühen Formen der Kommunikation.* Stuttgart, Germany: Klett-Cotta.

Pedrina, F. (2001). Psychoanalytische Interventionen mit Eltern und Babys in interdisziplinären Kontexten. Eine Einführung. In F. Pedrina (Ed.), *Beziehung und Entwicklung in der frühen Kindheit* (pp. 11–29). Tübingen, Germany: Edition Discord.

Stern, D. N. (1986). *The interpersonal world of the infant.* New York: Basic Books.

Stern, D. N. (1995). *The motherhood constellation.* New York: Basic Books.

von Hofacker, N., & Papoušek, M. (1998). Disorders of excessive crying, feeding, and sleeping: The Munich Interdisciplinary Research and Intervention Program. *Infant Mental Health Journal, 19,* 180–201.

von Klitzing, K. (2003). Wann braucht ein Säugling einen Psychoanalytiker? Von der Erforschung zur Therapie früher Beziehungen. *Kinderanalyse, 11,* 3–19.

Winnicott, D. W. (1965). Ego distortion in terms of true and false self. In D. W. Winnicott (Ed.), *The maturational processes and the facilitating environment* (pp. 140–152). New York: International Universities Press.

Wolke, D., & Skuse, D. (1992). The management of infant feeding problems. In P. Cooper & A. Stein (Eds.), *Feeding problems and eating disorders in children and adolescents* (pp. 27–59). New York: Harwood Academic.

CHAPTER 12

INTEGRATIVE COMMUNICATION-
CENTERED PARENT–INFANT
COUNSELING AND PSYCHOTHERAPY:
THE MUNICH MODEL

Ruth Wollwerth de Chuquisengo
Mechthild Papoušek

ORIGINS AND BASIC CHARACTERISTICS OF THE TREATMENT MODEL

The treatment model of the Munich Interdisciplinary Research and Intervention Program for Fussy Babies is based on many years of research by Hanuš Papoušek on the infant's behavioral regulation, preverbal learning, and integration of experience (H. Papoušek, 1967; H. Papoušek & Papoušek, 1979a, 1979b) and by Hanuš and Mechthild Papoušek on preverbal communication (M. Papoušek, 1994) and intuitive parenting (H. Papoušek & Papoušek, 1987). The therapeutic program was inspired by two clinicians (in pediatrics and in psychiatry/psychotherapy) engaged in finding an empirical approach to early deviations and disorders in parent–infant communication; understanding their causes, characteristics, and outcomes; and developing effective intervention methods.

Anchored in interdisciplinary infancy research and theories of complex biological systems (Bertalanffy, 1968; Smith & Thelen, 1993), the approach seeks to deal with the characteristics specific to infancy. This means taking into account (a) the developmental dynamics of early maturation, adaptation, and learning processes, as well as their extraordinary individual variability; (b) the close interrelations between the infant's behavior and somatic functions (sensory-motor, autonomic, organic); (c) the primary caregiving relationship as the matrix for infant development during the first years of life, with its transactional dynamics and complexity of reciprocal influences between infant and parents; and (d) the various adaptive functions of early communication with regard to the joint regulation of adaptive developmental tasks and the construction and integration of a common experiential world, attachment, and language.

Building on the results of temperament research (Carey & McDevitt, 1995) and research on infant crying (for an overview, see M. Papoušek, 1985), the model focused primarily on excessive crying during the first 3 months of life (M. Papoušek & Papoušek, 1990). However, the surprising diversity of behavioral syndromes observed in the Munich Program, the unexpected extension of the age range to include the first 2 years and occasionally even the third year of life, and the large percentage of psychological problems in the parents soon required that the initial concept be further elaborated upon and expanded. The model had to be differentiated step by step to meet the rapidly growing demands and to incorporate the findings of the associated research projects.

As a result, a systemic model of parent–infant counseling and psychotherapy was developed in the early 1990s by the interdisciplinary staff of the Munich Program. It is conceived of as an interdisciplinary, interaction-centered treatment approach with a primary focus on parent–infant communication and the interplay between the infant's integrative and self-regulatory capacities and the parents' intuitive competencies (M. Papoušek, 1998).

The interdisciplinary nature of the approach is realized on the one hand in daily practice by close cooperation of the pediatrician and psychologist/psychotherapist in charge and other professionals. On the other hand, these professionals try to keep up with and integrate current interdisciplinary research in pediatrics, the neurosciences, developmental neurology, developmental psycho(bio)logy, attachment research, psychiatry, and psychotherapy. The fact that the staff members come from very different psychotherapeutic training backgrounds (psychodynamic, family systems, body-oriented, interlocutory, integrative, and behavior therapies) means that therapeutic elements and techniques from various schools could be integrated into the model from the very beginning. Important confirmation came from the writings of psychodynamic parent–infant psychotherapists (in particular, Brazelton & Cramer, 1989; Fraiberg, 1980; Lieberman & Pawl, 1993; Muir, 1992; Stern, 1995) and the closely related work on interaction guidance (McDonough, 1993). All of these confirmed many of our own findings and enriched and deepened our psychotherapeutic work at the level of parent–infant communication. With the foundation of the German-speaking Association of Infant Mental Health in 1996, exchanges among a growing number of German-speaking parent–infant therapists (Barth, 1998, 1999, 2000, 2003; Pedrina, 2001; von Klitzing, 1998) helped to further elaborate and clarify the approach.

Formally, the model may be classified among the solution-focused and resource-oriented short-term therapies, but with an intermittent treatment schema (Stern, 1995) that is tailored to the individual needs of the child, the parents, and their relationship. It tries to recruit the most important resource of early childhood, the psychobiologically anchored intuitive competencies of the parents in their attunement to the integrative competencies of their infant, which together form the basis for the experience of positive reciprocity in interaction.

The primary role of the counselor or therapist consists of creating a secure base for the parents and infant in the role of a good grandmother ("good grandmother transference;" Stern, 1995) and in strengthening the parents' own genuine competencies. The empathic and supportive therapeutic relationship may function as a corrective positive emotional relationship, or it may occasionally serve as the context in which relational patterns are reenacted and resolved by working through transference and countertransference in the relationship.

The presence of the infant with her current needs and interests makes it possible to anchor counseling and psychotherapy in the actual communication and relational experience in the here and now (Barth, 1998), to include the baby as an active cocreator of her early relationships, and to ensure that her genuine needs for security and self-efficacy are perceived and responded to appropriately (infant-led parent-infant psychotherapy; Cohen, Muir, & Lojkasek, 2003).

A case vignette has been selected to illustrate the overall approach. The example is exceptional with regard to its long intermittent treatment schedule (see Table 12.1, see p. 267). However, that is why this particular case is well suited to illustrate the integration of the various components of parent–infant counseling and psychotherapy.

CASE VIGNETTE

The case comprises four self-contained treatment episodes in which the parents sought help intermittently when their son was 6, 13, 20, and 30 months of age.

First Treatment Episode

Reason for referral. Paul was brought in and treated for the first time at the age of 6 ½ months. Paul's parents considered him a difficult infant from the day he was born. He was only content when carried around and entertained, but did not tolerate close body contact or cuddling. Although Paul had become accustomed to falling asleep by himself during the first 3 months of life, sleep problems developed during a vacation, when the parents' relatives convinced them to carry Paul around and nurse him to sleep. At the time of his first visit, Paul was waking up nightly every hour or two and could only be settled to sleep after being nursed or carried. He was cranky and fussy during the day and constantly had to be attended to. The parents had previously begun to use the behavioral techniques recommended by Ferber (Ferber, 1987; Kast-Zahn & Morgenroth, 1995) with good success until the mother's parents so criticized them that they felt forced to give up on this approach.

Case history. Paul was his parents' first child. Both parents were academics, and the birth was planned and wanted. During her pregnancy, the mother suffered from ongoing fear that she might lose the child because of two previous miscarriages. During the 24th week of pregnancy she was prescribed bed rest because of a suspected amnion rupture, which only heightened her anxiety. The child was delivered at term by Cesarean section because of protracted labor. Ever since the birth the mother had suffered severe mood swings, which had become even more extreme recently because of an accumulating sleep deficit.

Findings. Both parents seemed extremely exhausted and insecure during the first visit. They reported that Paul's nightly crying was eliciting increasingly aggressive impulses toward him. In contrast to the parents' description, Paul showed good self-regulatory capacities and readiness for social interaction. He played persistently on the floor or on his father's lap. In spite of their exhaustion and sleep deprivation, both parents responded sensitively to Paul's needs.

Paul seemed behaviorally well-regulated during the videotaped mother–infant interaction as well. He explored with his eyes, mouth, and hands a ring-shaped object with great interest and concentration. In spite of this, Paul's mother offered him new toys in rapid succession, seeking to divert his attention, but thereby getting in the way of his own exploratory activity. When the therapist introduced a context of solitary play (while the mother was to read in the same room) both mother and Paul did surprisingly well, presumably because Paul found the new surroundings to be sufficiently stimulating.

Diagnosis. We diagnosed a disorder of behavioral and emotional regulation with fussiness and lack of interest in play during the day and learned sleep-onset and night-waking problems that had been perpetuated by the parents' extensive use of sleep aids. The mother suffered from mild postpartum depression with marked insecurity, dependence on the judgment of relatives, and ambivalent feelings toward the child. Distressing dysfunctional communication patterns were evident at bedtime and during play. According to the therapist's observations, there were no signs of Paul having a difficult temperament.

Therapeutic intervention. A communication-centered therapeutic sleep intervention was prepared in a supportive psychotherapeutic session devoted to clarifying and strengthening the parents' child-rearing attitudes and feelings in relation to the sleep problems, limiting their dependence on their relatives' interference, and clarifying their communication patterns around bedtime. The parents perceived Paul's crying as a protest against any attempts to wean him from the strategies they had used before to help him go to sleep. After extensive developmental counseling, the parents agreed that given his state of development they should trust him to be able to fall asleep in his bed by himself after nursing and a sleep ritual with close body contact and undivided maternal attention. They were ready to support him during the transitional phase of getting used to the new rule, reassure him at regular intervals with clear signals, and convey a sense of security, but all that without taking him out of his crib or providing other sleep aids.

The parents' efforts to put this sleep intervention into practice at home and convey a clear, warm, and consistent reassurance to their son were successful in short order (see chapter 6). During the first night, Paul fell asleep quietly after only minor protest, waking up again only twice and going back to sleep within 5 minutes each time. Paul was well-balanced during the day and was soon able to get involved in play with age-appropriate endurance.

Video-supported guidance in communication during mother–infant play and solitary play enabled the parents to appreciate how well Paul was able to play by himself. They realized their own intrusiveness and learned to take their infant's lead. Couples counseling that focused on the transition to parenthood and its challenges and developmental tasks was included to strengthen the parents' self-confidence in their child-rearing competencies. The parents felt relieved and satisfied after three sessions and were clearly more confident in the way they handled their son, who continued to fall asleep and sleep through the night reliably.

Second Treatment Episode

Reason for referral and recent history. Paul was brought in again by his mother at the age of 13 months, this time because of chronic fussiness, disinterest in playing alone, and occasional aggressive behavior toward his mother and other children in his play group. The mother found it very hard to deal with the fact that Paul's liveliness was perceived as rude and disruptive by everyone with whom he came in contact. Again, Paul demanded constant entertainment from his mother, but rejected physical contact whenever his mother tried to hug or hold him closely. The times she could enjoy being with him were rare. In spite of homeopathic treatment, she continued to suffer from premenstrual and postmenstrual depressive episodes to which Paul reacted with increased crankiness and demands for attention, which in turn triggered angry feelings in her.

Paul's current behavior problems once again evoked memories of the mother's own childhood. She had experienced her own parents as very strict and rejecting. They had no time for her needs. As a result, she was all the more determined to make sure that Paul got the care that had been denied to her and to be available for him. However, she increasingly realized that in the process she was confronted with her own psychological and physical limits. Whenever she tried to set some boundaries, she felt guilty about neglecting or traumatizing him. Occasionally she felt powerless, at his mercy, and angry at the same time. She became aware that she tended to compare Paul unfavorably with other same-age children in the play group, and that she had a hard time defending him. Here, too, she saw parallels to her own childhood. The situation was exacerbated at this time by the fact that her parents were once again interfering, which repeatedly led to conflicts with her husband. A Family System Test (FAST) was administered independently to both parents to analyze with them the relationships within the family. The parents were asked to place wooden figures on a checkerboard by which they could symbolize their relative closeness, distance, and social hierarchy among the family members. In creating a "typical situation" (current family relationship constellation) the parents placed Paul high above all other family members in the hierarchy, whereas the boundaries in relation to proximity and distance with the mother's family of origin were blurred. In setting up an "ideal situation" (the desired family relationship constellation) they placed Paul on the same level with themselves and clearly distanced themselves from the mother's family of origin.

Diagnosis. Once again, Paul's problems of behavioral regulation with chronic fussiness and disinterest in play occurred in the context of maternal depression and an ambivalent mother–child relationship with blurred boundaries. At the family level there was a lack of boundaries in relation to the mother's family of origin, with unresolved conflicts over dependency and autonomy, and resultant marital conflicts.

Therapy. The therapy began with a module of video-supported guidance in a joint mother–infant play session where both mother and Paul did remarkably well. The mother responded sensitively to Paul's initiatives, interests, and needs. Paul showed positive mastery motivation and repeatedly sought visual contact with his mother to share his joy. With the help of video feedback the therapist reinforced the mother in the quality of their joint play and worked with her to set appropriate boundaries for herself in order to help him play alone. In a similar vein, developmental counseling focused on how to structure the day and alternate between periods of joint play with undivided maternal attention and periods of solitary play with clear boundaries.

With the help of the FAST test, the therapist worked with the parents in a couples' counseling session to find ways to reverse the family hierarchy, unburden the couple's relationship and establish appropriate boundaries toward the mother's family of origin. The mother was encouraged to begin individual psychotherapy to deal with the distressing experiences and unresolved conflicts of her childhood and ongoing conflicts with her family of origin.

The mother was remarkably capable of putting the therapist's recommendations into practice over the course of treatment. She reported that she had been successful in maintaining her ground in the presence of her parents in a limit-setting situation with Paul, to remain consistent and create more space for protecting herself against her parents' interference. Furthermore, she reported that her relationships with Paul and her husband had become considerably more relaxed and that she was much more able to enjoy playing with her son. Paul became more even-tempered during the 4 weeks of treatment (five sessions) and learned to play alone happily for longer periods of time.

Third Treatment Episode

Reason for referral and recent history. Paul was brought in again at the age of 20 months because of increasingly aggressive behavior such as biting and hitting other children, particularly when his mother was also present. These problems were not evident, however, when the mother was alone with Paul. While his mother was describing Paul's aggressive behavior, he bit her several times as if to demonstrate. When the therapist asked his mother about his positive traits and behavior, he immediately ended his provocative behavior, stood in front of his mother, and confirmed each positive statement she made with a categorical "yes."

During the session, it turned out that not only had Paul been attending a nursery school in the morning for 3 months (because of the mother's work schedule) but also that several afternoons a week his mother had been taking him to different play groups and to visit friends of hers who had children the same age. Behavioral observation in the nursery school and reports by the teachers confirmed the mother's report that Paul's provocative behavior occurred only when she was present and that he was generally a quiet and even withdrawn child who rarely drew attention for negative behavior.

The therapist concluded that Paul's aggressive and provocative behavior was related to problems in the mother–child relationship. Paul seemed to be signaling that he was being overextended by having to cope with so many different groups of children and adults and that he needed more of his mother's undivided attention and closeness.

Therapy. The first step in developmental counseling was to reduce Paul's social schedule because it was clear that the many groups and visits were having a negative effect on him and that there were few opportunities for undisturbed time together with his mother. Further steps aimed at ensuring a positive quality of their interactions during the free time they could now spend together.

With regard to Paul's aggressive behavior toward other children, the therapist invited one of the mother's friends to come in with her son for a joint videotaped peer session. In the subsequent video-supported relational psychotherapy, the therapist again addressed themes that were rooted in the mother's childhood, in particular her tendencies to compare Paul unfavorably with other children and to subordinate herself to the judgment of others.

Both the reduction in Paul's schedule of social activities and the video-supported communication-centered relational therapy quickly led to a relaxation in the relationship between Paul and his mother, and Paul's aggressive behavior vanished. Treatment was concluded after five sessions.

Fourth Treatment Episode

Reason for referral and recent history. Paul was brought in again by both parents at the age of $2\frac{1}{2}$ years. A baby brother, Robin, had been born 3 months earlier. Paul was extremely envious of his little brother and tried to get his parents' attention by provocative and aggressive behavior toward him. Paul was rapidly becoming the problem child of the family. As a result of the birth of her second son, the mother became aware of how difficult and stressed her relationship with Paul had been from the very beginning. Right after Robin was born she experienced a deep emotional bonding to the baby, and she received a lot of positive feedback from him. In contrast, her memories of Paul's birth were negatively charged. After the Cesarean, she had seen Paul only fleetingly and felt hardly any emotion. A few hours later when he was placed on her belly, she had been unable to soothe him as he cried and came to see herself as failure. She felt disappointed and hurt. In her relationship with Robin she experienced for the first time how intense and fulfilling a mother–baby relationship can be, and this without the enormous effort she had to invest in order to satisfy Paul. She realized that she had never really been able to enter into a close positive relatedness with Paul and had always felt a certain distance from him.

Because of his escalating behavioral problems Paul's parents had brought him to spend the weekend with his godmother, with whom he had a good relationship. When his mother dropped him off, she was shocked to realize that she felt herself freed as if from a cage. She spent a very lovely and relaxed weekend with her husband and Robin. But as soon as the parents picked Paul up again, the interactions between mother and son escalated. Paul screamed and behaved provocatively, and his mother screamed back at him. This episode made it clear to her that something had to be done.

Therapy. Over several sessions, the psychotherapist worked with the mother on the mother–child relationship (psychodynamic relational psychotherapy), which had become increasingly tense and enmeshed. More and more traumatic memories from her childhood began to emerge, in particular of her parents' extremely strict and hypercritical child-rearing attitudes that suppressed all her liveliness in the home. Denying her own vitality, disappointment, and rage, she had her whole life tried to adapt to her mother's expectations. This was a strategy that simply could not accommodate Paul, with his liveliness and rebelliousness. In fact, he seemed to represent all of the unacceptable parts of her own personality that she had warded off, to which she had no emotional access, and which she rejected in her unconscious identification with her mother.

Extremely painful early memories were revived over the course of therapy. Paul's behavior kept eliciting feelings of helplessness and powerless rage in his mother similar to those her own mother had elicited in her when she was a child. These feelings evoked memories of a mother who was never available to her, whom she could not approach, who rejected her, and who never had time for her when she needed mothering. She visualized herself as a little girl seeking proximity to her mother, who was busy serving a customer in the family shop without taking the least notice of her. This image suddenly became linked to the present as she allowed herself to identify with Paul's current role in the family and to experience the intense loneliness of her little son. She suddenly realized that, as a result of her depression and her critical and distancing comparisons with other children, she was precisely as emotionally unavailable to Paul as her mother had been in relation to her. As she portrayed these haunting images she was overcome by feelings of intense sorrow, to which she gave full rein. The dam was broken, and the "ghost of the past" that she had warded off for so long was banished from her relationship with Paul. She became increasingly able to attend to and accept Paul with all facets of his personality and behavior and to empathize with him.

From that time on, she became increasingly able to take pleasure in Paul's liveliness. She made a conscious effort to allow Paul to do things that she had not been permitted to as a child (such as splashing water, pouring juice in a glass, etc.), and she took pleasure in Paul's surprising carefulness. She began to experience her relationship with him more positively and intensely and felt how she was growing in the process herself. After nursery school, a beaming Paul would run toward her as soon as she appeared, greeting her with a loud "Mama." He also began to seek physical closeness and tender affection with her.

Short-term music therapy was used to strengthen the mutual positive relatedness and enjoyment by using the medium of sound. As a result, the house resounded with the singing and playful noise as they enjoyed each other's liveliness. At their concluding session, both parents noted how much more relaxed the atmosphere in the family had become.

After the fourth and final treatment episode, which required a total of seven sessions, the mother–child relationship continued to develop positively. At a follow-up session 2 1/2 years later, the mother reported no further problems, except for the minor scrapes typical for a 5-year-old.

MODULES OF COMMUNICATION-CENTERED PARENT–INFANT COUNSELING AND PSYCHOTHERAPY

The integrative treatment model attempts to deal with a broad spectrum of behavioral syndromes with all the differences associated with age, severity, pervasiveness, and impairment of the parent–infant relationships—a spectrum between transient developmental problems on the one side and chronic pervasive disorders in the context of severe attachment and relational disorders and/or mental illness in the primary caregiver on the other. The therapeutic spectrum ranges from basic developmental counseling all the way to psychodynamic psychotherapy.

The point of departure for counseling and therapy is the interdisciplinary diagnostic analysis of the behavioral manifestations and the immediate and distant conditions of their origin. The assessment includes infant regulatory capacities (developmental level, strengths and difficulties, temperament, level and quality of solitary play), amount and quality of parental distress (physical and emotional well-being, resources and stress factors, the couple's relationship, family and social network), and parent–infant communication and relationships (patterns of communication in disorder-related interactional contexts and joint play, availability and attunement of intuitive parental competencies, infant readiness to interact and attachment behavior, and quality of dialogue and play).

The goal of treatment is discussed and coordinated with the parents beforehand. The goal is always threefold, corresponding to the diagnostic triad (see chapter 4), namely, resolving the behavioral problem as quickly as possible, unburdening the parents, and supporting positive interactions and relational experiences. Three main interrelated modules are important in achieving these: developmental counseling, supportive psychotherapy, and video-supported guidance in communication. These are complemented as needed by psychodynamic communication-centered relational therapy. The type, extent, and emphasis given to each module are individually tailored to the symptoms, the psychosocial situation, and the needs of the family.

Developmental Counseling

Grounded in the scientific advances of infancy research, developmental counseling conveys general information about relevant aspects of infant development (sleep needs, separation anxiety, temper tantrums, self-regulation, learning, individual variability, intentionality, play, etc.), and applies these specifically to the problems and developmental tasks at hand (settling to sleep, introduction of rules, self-feeding, etc.). The therapist and the parents together determine the infant's observable strengths and weaknesses, her individual developmental level and phase-specific needs, and address the challenges ahead while taking into account the parents' expectations, child-rearing attitudes, and competencies. Developmental counseling may be effectively used to give the parents emotional access to and a better understanding of their infant's interpersonal perspective and experience, and of her needs, signals, and interests (for detailed description of the disorder-specific themes of counseling, see chapters 5–8 and 15).

Supportive Psychotherapy

The parents' physical and psychological well-being is at the center of supportive resource-oriented psychotherapy. It is important to include the father in the sessions. The focus is on creating a positive, accepting, and appreciative therapeutic relationship that allows time and space for empathizing with the parents' accumulated disappointments, fears, grief, vulnerabilities, anger, and long-neglected needs. This offers the parents a secure base and, if needed, paves the way for corrective attachment experiences. Other focal points are the developmental tasks faced by the parents in their transition to parenthood (motherhood and fatherhood constellation, postpartum adjustments, transition from dyadic to triadic relationships and from the couple's relationship to a coparenting relationship; see chapters 4 and 7). A number of fundamental psychodynamic themes of early parenthood may be brought up in this context and picked up again during the further course of the therapeutic process. The themes may include the parents' fears about their baby's thriving and survival, needs for being mothered themselves, exaggerated expectations and pressures to be perfect parents and associated fears of failure, and problems relating to dependency and autonomy. Over and above the current and chronic stressors, supportive psychotherapy aims at identifying and strengthening the parents' intuitive competencies and resources in the child, the parents' personalities, the family, and the social environment.

Interaction Guidance in Parent–Infant Communication

Therapy at the level of parent–infant communication is mainly directed at observable parent–infant interactions or those described by the parents. Of particular interest are the patterns of communication in contexts in which the behavioral problems in question are the most evident (for instance, feeding interactions, settling to sleep, playing together, or limit-setting). The therapist draws the parents' attention to observable communication patterns during the session and regularly uses videotaped observations. The goal is to replace dysfunctional communication patterns that are marked by negative contingency between the infant's and the parents' behavior (e.g., the mother offers food, the infant rejects, the mother distracts the infant, the infant automatically opens her mouth, the mother offers the next spoon, etc.) with functional patterns (infant signals hunger, mother offers a spoonful of food, infant opens her mouth and eats, mother continues feeding until infant refuses because of satiation). The parents can also learn how to recognize signals in their infant's behavior, to better understand the needs and interests that the infant expresses, and to find more intuitive ways of responding. The "baby-reading lessons" developed by Barth (2000) provide a good example of this approach.

Communication is also regularly videotaped and observed in the context of relaxed dialogue or play in order to encourage and strengthen experiences of positive reciprocity and relatedness. This is particularly important in families with a difficult infant in order to balance the overwhelming experiences of negative reciprocity. The protective frame of the therapeutic relationship should foster positive relational experiences in which the baby is sensitively supported in her self-regulatory capacities, needs for security, self-efficacy, exploration, and autonomy. Similarly, the parents get positive feedback from their baby's response and experience self-efficacy and growing confidence in their intuitive communicative capacities (see below for more details on video-supported therapy).

Psychodynamic Communication-Centered Relational Therapy

Communication-centered relational therapy that incorporates the parents' unconscious psychodynamics is indicated whenever the three elements of developmental counseling, supportive psychotherapy, and video-supported guidance in parent–infant communication have reached their limits: (a) in cases of explicit problems in the parents' emotional relatedness or acceptance of the infant; (b) when intuitive parenting is distinctly impaired and the parents' perception of the baby and emotional availability are markedly inhibited, blocked, or distorted; (c) when the parents only speak disparagingly of their child, label her as the family's trouble maker or black sheep, or attribute evil intentions to the child; or (d) when the parent–child relationship is endangered (neglecting-depriving, fearful-tense, symbiotic, entangled-conflictual, covertly or openly rejecting; M. Papoušek & von Hofacker, 2003).

Within the protective frame of the therapeutic relationship, the goal of psychodynamic communication-centered relational therapy is to resolve psychodynamic blockages and distortions in early communication during actual interactions with the baby, to release inhibited intuitive competencies, and to enable the parents to engage with their baby in the here and now.

In the majority of cases, the use of video-supported behavioral observation, video feedback, and microanalytic focus on short videotaped communication segments (see below) may expedite and intensify the therapeutic process. The focus on concrete behavior in communication opens immediate access to the parents' sensitivities, feelings, representations, associations, and memories.

Psychodynamic communication-centered relational therapy during play. One variant of relational therapy has proved particularly effective when a parent refuses to be videotaped because of strong feelings of anxiousness and vulnerability, such as in parents with deep-seated relational disorders, severe depression, or borderline disorders. This variant is similar to Greenspan's (1992) "floortime" and to infant-led infant–parent psychotherapy known as "watch, wait, and wonder" (Cohen et al., 2003; Muir, 1992). Here, communication-centered relational therapy takes place on a play mat without videotaping. By her immediate presence on the floor, the therapist provides a secure base for parent and infant, thereby creating a space for fresh communicative experiences and a starting point for psychodynamic therapy.

Integration of the Above Modules

Barth (1998) has conceptualized developmental counseling, interaction guidance in the form of baby-reading lessons, and psychodynamic parent–infant psychotherapy as interrelated but separate approaches to treatment, each with their own indications. In the Munich Program, the boundaries among the therapeutic modules are fluid over the course of therapy or even within a particular session. The emphasis placed on one or the other is tailored to the individual family and used flexibly, depending on the current needs of the child (regulating behavioral state, hunger, prevalent behavioral problems) and the parents (degree of distress, pending developmental tasks) and on positive or symptomatic interactional patterns that are observed.

Integration of Other Modules in Collaboration With Specialists in Other Fields

Other modules can be integrated into the individual treatment plan as needed by members of the staff, such as was done in collaboration with specialists from other units of the Center for Social Pediatrics in Munich, or in a practice near the family's place of residence.

Occupational therapy (sensory integration) has proven effective in supporting sensory processing and self-regulation in cases of pronounced temperamental difficulty. This can be assessed independently of parent–infant interactions, for instance during the medical exam (irritability, inconsolability, tactile defensiveness, and other signs of sensory hyperreactivity or hyporeactivity, motor restlessness, unadaptability, extreme distractibility, or impulsivity).

Mild neuromotor problems and delayed motor self-righting (e.g., in association with constant carrying) may be effectively treated by counseling in proper handling. If this fails to yield results after a few weeks, physiotherapy is recommended in consultation with the family pediatrician. In cases of a childhood illness, medical treatment is prescribed or initiated in agreement with the family pediatrician.

Collaboration with social service units may be needed in cases of multiple psychosocial problems (social isolation, housing problems, financial debts, regulation of paternal visits after separation, maternal mental illness, etc.) and when home visits are required to help the parents to put into practice what was elaborated in the counseling sessions.

Couples counseling sessions are offered in cases of acute escalating or chronic couples' conflicts. The goal here is to work out effective solutions and/or motivate the couple to seek couples' or family counseling beyond the parent–infant therapy.

Whenever the therapeutic process uncovers more deep-seated psychodynamic problems in one or both parents (depression requiring psychiatric treatment, borderline disorders, anxiety or obsessive-compulsive disorders, among others) that go well beyond impairment of the parent–child relationship, parents are encouraged to seek additional help in the form of individual psychotherapy.

Figure 12.1 illustrates the integrative multimodal therapeutic model with the main therapeutic modules that may be viewed as different ports of entry into the system as described by Stern (1995). Parent–infant communication in everyday interactional contexts represents the core of the model, relating directly to the infant's self-regulation and developmental dynamics; to the parents' intuitive competence, emotional state, and representations; and to the patterns of family relations. The degree of impairment and distress in the parent–infant relationship and the parents' psychological conditions determine which level of communication receives priority in the intervention, either the level of observable behavior or that of parental feelings and representations.

COMMUNICATION AS INTERFACE BETWEEN THE BEHAVIORAL AND REPRESENTATIONAL LEVELS OF PARENT–INFANT INTERACTION

The currently rich literature on psychodynamic parent–infant psychotherapy provides an impressive source of case vignettes and valuable experiences that contribute significantly to the current understanding of psychodynamic processes involved in early dysfunctional communication and relational disorders (Barth, 1998, 1999, 2002, 2003; Beebe, 2003; Brazelton & Cramer, 1989; Fraiberg, 1980;

Figure 12.1. Integrative Communication-Centered Parent–Infant Counseling and Psychotherapy: The Munich Model.

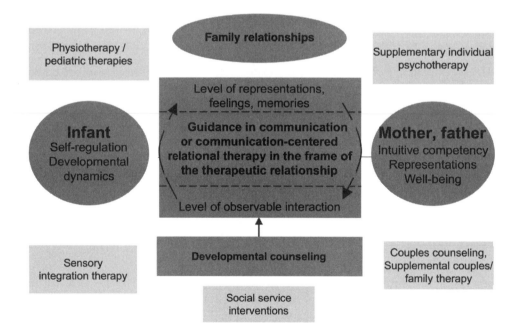

Lieberman & Pawl, 1993; Lojkasek, Cohen, & Muir, 1994; Lyons-Ruth, 1998; Pedrina, 1998, 2001; Stern, 1995; von Klitzing, 1998).

In her inimitable way, Selma Fraiberg has described the effects of psychodynamic processes on parent–infant communication:

> In every nursery there are ghosts. They are the visitors from the unremembered past of the parents, the uninvited guests at the christening. Under favorable conditions, these unfriendly and unbidden spirits are banished from the nursery and return to their subterranean dwelling place. . . . This does not say that ghosts cannot invent mischief from their burial places. . . . the intruders from the parental past may break through the magic circle in an unguarded moment, and a parent and his child may find themselves reenacting a moment or a scene from another time with another set of characters. (Fraiberg, Adelson, & Schapiro, 1980, pp. 164–165)

The ghost becomes the parent's communicative partner in place of the infant, as a representative of some repressed part of the parents' unconscious or as a representative of a significant person from the parent's past (Brazelton & Cramer, 1989). The parent ends up communicating with the ghost instead of with her baby. Yet, the baby with her individual and occasionally difficult temperament and behavior problems can become a co-actor in an imaginary drama that conjures up the parent's past and fatefully reenacts earlier problematic relational patterns (M. Papoušek & Wollwerth de Chuquisengo, 2003; see also chapters 10 and 11). The intrusion of ghosts into the arena of everyday interactions should be suspected whenever parents have excessive difficulty in perceiving their infant's signals, capacities, and needs, in interpreting them from the infant's perspective, or in responding to them appropriately. In such cases, parents may perceive the signals in a distorted way, remain entrapped in projective attributions of meaning, or describe the child in pejorative terms (Brazelton & Cramer, 1989; Fraiberg, 1980; Fraiberg et al., 1980; Möhler & Resch, 2000). The goal of analytic parent–infant psychotherapy is to uncover and make conscious these projections from the past, and to pave the way for unencumbered parent–child interactions in the present. Although the presence of the child is recommended in analytic parent–infant psychotherapies (Fraiberg et al., 1980), treatment focuses primarily on the parent's representations, childhood memories, and unconscious fantasies and conflicts.

By contrast, interaction-centered psychotherapies seek to improve the quality of parent–infant interaction directly (see, for example, Field, 1984; McDonough, 1993; Muir, 1992). The parents are sensitized to their infant's signals at the level of observable interaction. If this occurs in the context of a trusting and supportive therapeutic relationship, projectively distorted perceptions may be resolved, and positive changes at the representational level may be promoted by this approach as well. The parents learn to interpret their infant's signals correctly, and to respond to them appropriately. In turn, they may experience their baby's positive feedback. The infant's cuddling, visual attention, eye contact, and smiling, in turn, help to release their intuitive competencies from inner psychic inhibition and blockages (M. Papoušek, 1998).

In one of the first careful evaluation studies (Robert-Tissot et al., 1996), different approaches and methods of parent–infant therapies were randomly applied and compared (interaction guidance and psychodynamic mother–infant psychotherapy). Although the types of therapy differed considerably in their theoretical underpinnings and therapeutic techniques, the results were remarkably similar given the same duration of treatment. Using either approach, the rates of behavioral symptoms (such as sleeping or feeding problems) decreased over the course of therapy. Mother–child interaction improved significantly, and the mothers came to view their children as well as their own child-rearing competencies considerably more positively. Differential effects were barely noticeable: Mothers in the "interaction guidance" group showed somewhat better attunement in play with their children, whereas mothers in the psychotherapy group exhibited better self-esteem.

More distinct differential effects were found in a comparative randomized intervention study with weekly sessions over 5 months (Cohen, Lojkasek, Muir, Muir, & Parker, 2002), in which psychoanalytic mother–infant therapy was compared with infant-led infant–mother psychotherapy (watch, wait, and wonder) based in attachment and psychodynamic theory (Cohen et al., 2003; Muir, 1992). Improvements in infant symptoms, maternal distress, and quality of mother–infant interaction were seen immediately upon conclusion of treatment in both treatment groups. The positive effects remained stable or continued to improve until the follow-up examination 6 months after the conclusion of treatment.

It is noteworthy that by the end of treatment, a decrease in maternal depression, advances in infant cognitive and emotional development, and an increase in the rate of securely attached infants were found only in the watch, wait, and wonder group. Similar changes were also seen in mother–infant pairs in the psychoanalytic group, but only 6 months later at the follow-up examination. Nevertheless, one differential effect persisted: The mothers in the watch, wait, and wonder group were more self-confident in interactions with their children, and the level of subjective maternal distress between the end of treatment and the follow-up examination was significantly lower. The authors attribute these differential effects to the active inclusion of the infant as initiator in the infant-led watch, wait, and wonder therapy (Cohen et al., 2002).

In summary, these studies signify that interaction-focused and psychoanalytic parent–infant psychotherapies achieve surprisingly similar effects at both the level of observable interactional behavior and the level of parental representations. The results confirm Stern's (1995) theory that access to the system (which he depicts as a kind of house with many doors) is possible through different ports of entry because the individual rooms of the house are connected with each other. In other words, the parents' representations and the observable parent–child interactions are not unconnected; they interact in continuous reciprocal exchange and influence each other.

INTEGRATIVE COMMUNICATION-CENTERED PARENT–INFANT COUNSELING AND PSYCHOTHERAPY: THE MUNICH MODEL

Preverbal communication provides both a starting point and a focus of counseling and psychotherapy because it includes the level of observable signaling behavior as well as the level of subjective experience, representations, conscious and unconscious affects, and fantasies and needs. The ease with which the therapeutic process flows between the levels of observable behavior and of inner representations and the levels of present interactions and of relational patterns from the past makes earlier controversies and categorical demarcations between behavior therapy and psychodynamic models seem outdated. Attention now turns to the dynamic interrelations between both levels in the domains of preverbal communication.

Parent–infant interactions are the daily arena in which psychobiologically anchored infant and parent competencies become attuned and are practiced and negotiated in recurrent and ever-changing scenarios. This interplay must endure in the face of multiple organic and psychosocial risk factors that can impede infant self-regulation and the parents' ability to provide regulatory support. This is also the arena in which the psychodynamic processes described in the literature exert their influence by affecting mutual understanding and behavioral attunement, and in which they become accessible to observation and experience: as "ghosts haunting the nursery" (Fraiberg et al., 1980), as reenactment of relational patterns (Brazelton & Cramer, 1989), as transgenerational transmission of attachment patterns (Gloger-Tippelt, 1999), or as psychodynamic defense mechanisms such as repression, denial, dissociation, and projective identification (Möhler & Resch, 2000), which distort or even abolish the parents' innate procedural knowledge of how to communicate with their baby.

A microanalytic approach to viewing video segments of parent–infant communication together with the parent is particularly suitable for gaining immediate access to the parent's current emotional states, feelings, perceptions, fantasies, and memories that are elicited in the here and now of the interaction (Beebe, 2003; Downing, 2003; M. Papoušek, 1998; Stern, 1995). Precise observation of preverbal communication as the interface between the behavioral and the representational levels, between present and past, and between the parents' current relationship with their baby and their own prior relational history opens a door to the level of presymbolic procedural integration of the parent's early attachment relationship. The implicit relational knowledge (Stern, 1995; Stern et al., 2002) stored in procedural memory may be unconsciously evoked in the present communication with their baby but may also be revived, relived, and experienced in a new way with their baby (Beebe, 2003; Lyons-Ruth, 1998; M. Papoušek & Wollwerth de Chuquisengo, 2003).

In contrast to traditional psychodynamic psychotherapies, a communication-centered approach seeks to include the infant/toddler as an active partner in the therapeutic process. At the presymbolic level, the goal is to create a space within a secure therapeutic relationship to experience new ways of relating. As is the case with the infant-led watch, wait, and wonder approach (Muir, 1992), a protected play space is created in which the attention of the mother/father and therapist (merely in a supportive role in the background, occasionally giving the baby voice) is focused on the current needs, interests, or regulatory problems of the child. The therapy makes use of and strengthens the infant's own initiative in exploration and play, her engagement and communication with the parent, and her intrinsic motivations with regard to eliciting contingent parental responses, closeness and security, self-efficacy, self-regulation, and autonomy. It builds on the rewarding power of the infant's smile, her bright eye contact and appealing comfort sounds that may help to weaken or invalidate the psychodynamic mechanisms that have inhibited, distorted, or blocked the parents' intuitive ability to respond. Communication-centered psychotherapy aims at releasing the parents' psychobiologically anchored implicit relational knowledge (H. Papoušek & Papoušek, 1987; Stern, 1995; Stern et al., 2002) and at strengthening it in its contingent attunement to the infant's signals. The potential of intuitive parental competencies is used in turn to provide the baby with optimally attuned regulatory support.

Video-Supported Guidance in Parent–Infant Communication and Psychodynamic Relational Therapy: Interventional Steps

Video-supported microanalysis of behavior in interactional sequences that are prototypical of a particular parent–infant dyad is used routinely in the Munich Program for diagnostic assessment, for video-supported guidance in communication and psychodynamic communication-centered relational therapy. Specific interactional sequences are selected and then viewed and analyzed together with the parents. Video feedback with its technical potential for repetition and pausing, still framing, slow motion, and time-lapse replay of selected sequences makes it possible for the parents to relive and become aware of particular interactional patterns and their meanings. However, this procedure must be used with caution because each video image intrudes into the most private and intimate sphere of the parent in question (M. Papoušek, 2000). Therefore, a secure and protective therapeutic relationship is an indispensable precondition for any video-supported intervention.

1. Videotaping

When videotaping parent–infant interactions, it is important to ensure that the infant is in an alert waking state in order to have the best possible conditions for positive and mutually rewarding interactions. The still-face paradigm developed by Tronick and his colleagues (1978) can be used with infants during the first half-year. It includes a spontaneous parent–infant dialogue, followed by a 2-minute episode of unresponsiveness and withdrawal of attention by the parent, and then a resumption of dialogue. With older children, a joint session of free play interaction is recorded followed by an episode of solitary play during which the parent is asked to convey to the child her own momentary interest and need (reading or filling out a questionnaire next to the child), followed by resumption of joint play. Other problem-specific interaction contexts are videotaped, depending on the behavioral problem, such as feeding, limit setting, separation situations, cooperation while cleaning up, and so forth. Home videos made by the parents are welcome for treatment of dysfunctional bedside interactions or behavior problems that only show up in the home.

2. Preparing the parent(s) for video feedback

Seeing oneself on video may elicit feelings of strangeness, embarrassment, or self-blaming, or may even hurt, particularly when it happens for the first time. It is therefore worthwhile to address the parents' experience and feelings either directly after an observed situation has been videotaped or just before viewing it with the parent(s), and to help them deal with any vulnerabilities. It is also important to clarify whether the videotaped interaction has been similar to what they typically experience at home.

We recommend viewing the videotape with the parents during a subsequent session, after the therapist has been able to analyze it thoroughly. Moreover, it is often easier for the parents to become involved in the emotional processes elicited by the video feedback if the child is not present at the session.

3. Microanalytic identification of positive and negative interaction sequences

Clinical assessment scales for parent–infant communication such as those developed in the Munich Program (M. Papoušek, 1996) or other instruments may be used to identify sequences of positive and negative reciprocity, and to analyze them for use in communication-centered counseling and psychotherapy with the parents.

Example of a sequence of positive reciprocity ("angel's circle"): A 3-month-old infant signals by averting her gaze that she needs to rest. The mother stops stimulating her for a short time and waits until her infant renews eye contact. When this happens, the mother responds with a smile and a greeting reaction, whereupon the infant smiles back.

Example of a sequence of negative reciprocity ("vicious circle"): A 3-month-old infant signals by averting her gaze that she needs to rest. The mother intensifies her efforts to get her baby's attention. The baby responds with active avoidance of visual contact and becomes increasingly restless, cranky, and resistant, whereupon the mother reacts even more intrusively (M. Papoušek, 2000).

Exactly why these two mothers respond so differently to the same behavior in their infant may have to do with the availability and attunement of the mothers' intuitive competencies, with preceding interactional experiences with their infant, and with the feelings, attributions, fantasies, and implicit relational patterns elicited in the mother by the infant's behavior.

Microanalysis helps to decode the flowing and subtle details of parent–infant communication, the mutual "dance" (Brazelton & Cramer, 1989). It is often difficult to determine whether and to what extent the infant's temperament (e.g., irritability, low arousal threshold, among others) or parental factors (e.g., depressive inhibition of intuitive competencies, distorted perception, among others) are the primary cause of the derailment of parent–infant communication. Most often, both sides contribute by their behavior to maintaining maladaptive interaction patterns.

4. Viewing a sequence of positive reciprocity

The actual therapy begins with positive and mutually rewarding interaction sequences. This offers ample opportunities for the therapist to strengthen the parents' vulnerable self-esteem, to restore their trust in the infant's capacities and self-confidence in their intuitive competencies, and to help them enjoy being together with their infant. At the same time, the emphasis on positive sequences and the appreciation and respect conveyed by the therapist may bolster their trust in the therapeutic relationship.

The parents and therapist look at the positive segments repeatedly, which allows the parents to relive these seemingly rare moments of attunement and to experience them emotionally. The therapist carefully probes for the parents' feelings and associations. Even subtle feelings of relaxation, joy, surprise, or pride may be reinforced by the therapist's affective attunement. Further on in the session, the parents are encouraged to identify with their infant and to experience how their own behavior is perceived from the infant's perspective.

5. Integration of positive interactions into daily life at home

Toward the end of the session an attempt is made to relate the positive experience to the real infant and to daily life. Therapist and parents together consider whether and under which conditions the parents have experienced similar positive situations at home and what strategies may help them to enjoy more positive reciprocity at home.

Several schools of therapy that use video feedback when working with socially disadvantaged and highly stressed families focus exclusively on positive interaction sequences. These include video home training (Leist, 1998) and interaction guidance (McDonough, 1993). Our own experience has shown that this is very effective at the beginning of treatment and with parents who seem particularly vulnerable and have received much negative feedback from their family and acquaintances. In the Munich Program, however, the initial focus on positive sequences is typically followed by a joint analysis of difficult interaction sequences that are directly related to the behavioral problems.

In contrast to many parent training programs that follow principles of behavior therapy and in which the parents are given concrete behavioral instructions, the Munich Program only does this in exceptional cases. Field (1984) gave examples of global behavioral instructions in a controlled evaluation study of interactional coaching of mothers suffering from postpartum depression. In this study, intrusive overstimulating mothers were given the simple instruction, "Do nothing other than imitate everything that your baby does," with the consequence that the mothers paused more often, observed their infants more, and responded more contingently to their baby's signals. This, in turn, led to more initiative on the part of the baby. In underinvolved mothers who afforded too little stimulation, the recommendation, "Do everything you can to get your baby to look at you" increased the mothers' stimulation, with the consequence that the babies began to show more interest and make more eye contact. The effect on the mothers in turn was that their often blocked intuitive competencies were freed up little by little by their infant's behavior.

6. Viewing a sequence of negative reciprocity together

When viewing a short segment of a dysfunctional interaction pattern, it is advantageous to first address the parents' representational level of associated feelings and to find out which specific behaviors on the part of the infant (such as gaze aversion, keeping the mouth firmly closed while being fed, clinginess, pulling mother's hair) trigger which affects, memories, or fantasies in the parent. Conversely, the parent may later be encouraged to identify with the baby and to reflect closely from the baby's perspective what the parent's response brings about in the baby at the behavioral and emotional level.

The parents and the therapist then look for negatively contingent relations at the behavioral and representational level and for the psychodynamic mechanisms that may trigger, sustain, or resolve the dysfunctional communication pattern or vicious circle. It is amazing how often parents are able to recognize the mechanisms of negative reciprocity and to identify double messages, ambivalence, or signs of overstimulation or understimulation in their own responses. Attempts are then made to find ways to break the vicious circle of negative reciprocities and to test out and practice alternative behaviors within the therapeutic context.

The ghosts in the nursery, that is, the psychodynamic mechanisms of distorted perception, repressed affects, unconscious reenactment, or projective identification that may be uncovered in this context, must be addressed and treated with the main goal of expelling the ghost reliably from the present communication and relationship with the real baby (see chapters 10 and 11). Once this goal is achieved, parents may find appropriate help for dealing with unresolved psychodynamic problems in individual psychotherapy.

7. Translating positive change into daily life at home

The last step consists of elaborating with the parents how they can translate these new and mutually positive interactions into daily life.

GLOBAL EVALUATION OF THERAPEUTIC SUCCESS IN THE MUNICH SAMPLE

Prevalence and Distribution of the Individual Therapeutic Modules

The results of an evaluation of 701 children treated in the Munich Program between 1994 and 1997 are summarized in Figure 12.2, which gives an overall view of how often each therapeutic module discussed in this chapter was used in the sample as a whole. In the majority of sessions various modules were combined, and the transition from one to the other was sometimes quite fluid.

Figure 12.2. Prevalence and Distribution of Therapeutic Modules (Multiple Mentions Are Possible). Sample From the Munich Interdisciplinary Research and Intervention Program for Fussy Babies (*n* = 701).

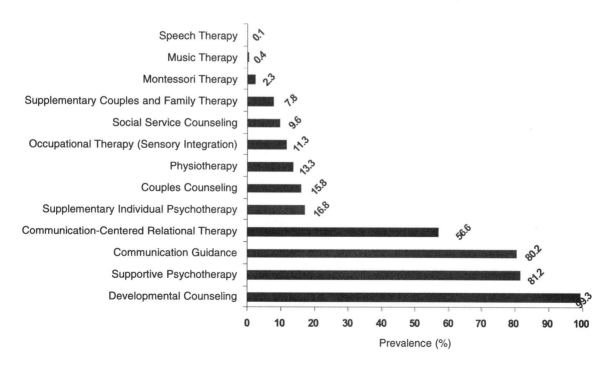

The three basic modules of developmental counseling (99%), supportive psychotherapy (81%), and guidance in communication (80%) were implemented in most of the cases. In addition, psychodynamic communication-centered relational therapy was needed in more than half of the cases (57%). In 17% of cases, the mother began parallel individual psychotherapy outside the Center. Individual sessions in the form of couples or family counseling were offered to 16% of the families, while 8% were referred for couples or family counseling outside the Center. Other parent-related modules of the program included social service counseling and family assistance (10%). Additional modules with a direct focus on supporting the child included occupational therapy (11%) or physiotherapy (13%) as well as speech therapy, music therapy, and Montessori therapy in isolated cases for specific reasons.

It was obvious that the amount of distress in the parent–child relationship played an important role in the choice of and emphasis placed on particular therapeutic modules. Figure 12.3 illustrates the relation between the type and focus of therapeutic interventions and the quality of the mother–child relationship as assessed with the Parent–Infant Relationship Global Assessment Scale (PIR-GAS; ZERO TO THREE, 1994). Independent of the quality of the mother–child relationship, developmental counseling, supportive psychotherapy, and communication-centered therapies remained the primary focus. The more distressed the relationship between mother and child, the more important were additional parent-focused therapeutic elements such as couples' counseling and individual psychotherapy. In cases of the most highly distressed relationships (such as in the case of mental illness in the mother), child-focused modules such as occupational therapy and physiotherapy were also recommended significantly more often. Indications for targeted support of the child are particularly strong when the child has a

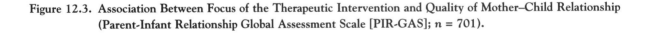

Figure 12.3. Association Between Focus of the Therapeutic Intervention and Quality of Mother–Child Relationship (Parent-Infant Relationship Global Assessment Scale [PIR-GAS]; *n* = 701).

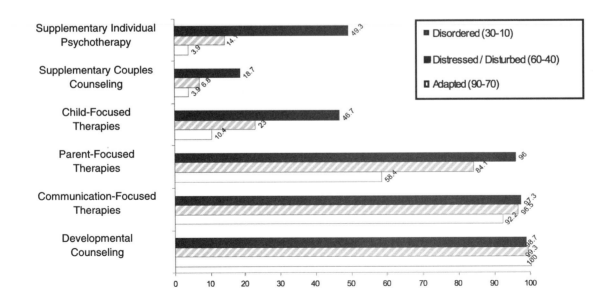

Source: ZERO TO THREE, 1994.

"difficult" temperament or neuromotor problems that pose extra challenges to the parents' child-rearing abilities, as these may contribute in and of themselves to deterioration in the parent–infant relationship.

Success of Treatment

Associated studies conducted as part of the Munich Program were designed to study the developmental genesis and manifestations of disorders of behavioral and emotional regulation but not to evaluate the effects of specific therapeutic interventions. Only a general assessment of the success of treatment was made at the concluding session of the first (and usually the only) treatment phase. The criteria for success included elimination of the behavioral problem, resolution of dysfunctional interaction patterns, and unburdening of the parents; that is, positive changes in all three areas of the diagnostic triad. Complete improvement was realized when the child's symptoms subsided (such as remission of the crying problem, regular sleep–wake cycles during the day, falling asleep by herself, sleeping through the night), when the negative reciprocity in the parent–child interaction was successfully eliminated (relaxed feeding situation with infant control of feeding by signaling hunger and satiation), and when the parents felt relieved and strengthened in their competencies. Treatment outcome was classified as largely improved when the negative interaction spirals were eliminated, the child's symptoms significantly decreased, and the family was well on its way to resolving on their own whatever problems remained (such as waking once per night after a reduction from 10 times per night). Slight decreases in symptoms were classified as slightly improved; no changes as not improved.

Together, the complete and largely improved categories yielded a success rate of 89.9%. Slight improvement was seen in 7.7%, partly because the parents were not ready or unable to change something for the better, partly because of more severe mental illness in the mother or overwhelming couples' problems that permitted only some relative improvement in parent–child communication and in the child's symptoms. In 2.4% of cases, the parents terminated before the start of treatment, in which case there was presumably no change.

The success of treatment depended significantly on the degree of distress/disorder in the mother–child relationship (PIR-GAS). Improvement rates of 75.7% (completely improved) and 21.6% (largely improved) were achieved in cases where the mother–child relationship was well adapted (90 to 70 on the scale). In distressed/disturbed relationships (60 to 40) the improvement rates were 46.0% (completely improved) and 45.7% (largely improved). When the mother–child relationship was disordered (30 to 10) complete improvement was seen in only 8.0% of cases, whereas the percentages for slight (24.0%) and no improvement (6.7%) were relatively high in this group. In most cases, termination of treatment was the cause for the lack of success (Figure 12.4).

Duration of Treatment

As shown in Figure 12.5, the duration of treatment needed from the initial presentation to the achievement of therapeutic success was relatively short given the many complex and difficult cases. On average, treatment was successfully concluded after 3.9 sessions including the initial diagnostics. In 38% of

Figure 12.4. Relation Between Treatment Success and Quality of Relationship.

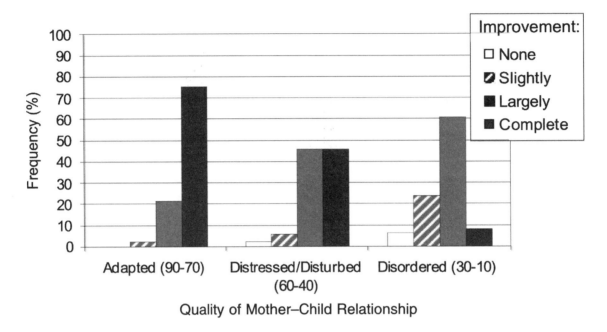

Note. $X^2(6, N = 701) = 89.55, p \leq .001$.
Source: PIR-GAS, ZERO TO THREE, 1994.

Figure 12.5. Number of Sessions During First Treatment Episode.

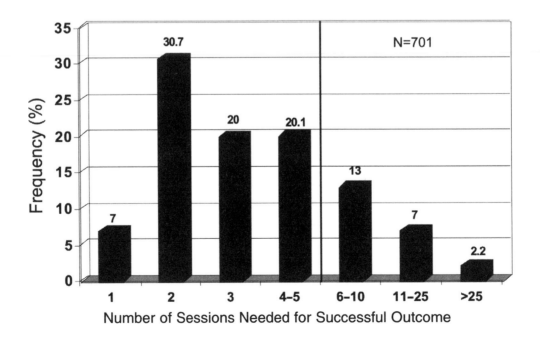

all families, 1 to 2 sessions were adequate; another 20% required 3 sessions, and another 20% 4 to 5 sessions. In a further 13% of cases, improvement occurred within 6 to 10 sessions; that is, within the official time frame of short-term focal therapies (Figure 12.5).

If we examine the number of sessions required in relation to the quality of the mother–child relationship (PIR-GAS), there are significant differences here as well, as indicated by an analysis of variance, $F(1, 694) = 27.98, p \le .001$. In well-adapted mother–child relationships, the desired outcome was seen in 90% of cases during the first 3 sessions; in distressed relationships this occurred in approximately 65%, and in disordered mother–child relationships in fewer than 50% of cases. By contrast, treatments that lasted more than 10 sessions were seen almost exclusively in cases of disordered mother–child relationships. In these cases, treatment was often conducted in the form of a supportive companionship over a long period of time with intermittent brief therapies.

Intermittent Treatment Scheme With Readmittance to the Program

As shown in Table 12.1, only about a quarter of treated children reentered the program because of regulatory problems in the context of later developmental perturbations. Third and fourth presentations were the exception throughout the time span under consideration.

It is worth noting that second, third, and fourth treatment episodes were concluded considerably more quickly on average than were the initial treatments. One session sufficed for 41% of all children presenting a second time; only two sessions were required to stabilize the children in an additional 21% of cases.

Other schools of parent–infant psychotherapy (Stern, 1995) also use an episodic treatment plan oriented to the needs of the families. This is specifically tailored to the phase-typical developmental tasks of early childhood and meets the needs of families seeking help in resolving developmental perturbations (Largo, 1992) during phases of enhanced vulnerability, or touchpoints (Brazelton, 1994; see chapters 3 and 4). The relatively short intervention is also an attempt not to label parents and child as patients that permanently require treatment but to support and trust them in mastering regulatory developmental tasks that have become temporarily derailed.

Table 12.1. **Percentage of Readmitted Children and Number of Treatment Sessions in Cases of Readmittance.**

Readmittance to the program	% of sample	Mean number of sessions	Mean age (months)
Second treatment	26.7	2.1	24.6
Third treatment	6.7	2.5	31.6
Fourth treatment	1.9	2.9	41.4

SUMMARY

The integrative model of communication-centered parent–infant counseling and psychotherapy represents an interdisciplinary, developmentally oriented systems concept. The core of the system is constituted by parent–infant communication in interactional contexts that are relevant to the presenting behavioral problems and the parent–infant relationships. Counseling and psychotherapy directly address patterns of communication at the interface between observable interaction and the parents' conscious and unconscious affects, representations, and memories. The therapeutic procedure, that is, the choice of and emphasis given to individual counseling and treatment modules is tailored to the specific needs of the individual family. Since its initial tentative trials in 1991, the model has proven itself effective in a broad array of regulatory and relational disorders of early childhood.

The goal of therapy is to rapidly transform dysfunctional communication patterns that are stressful for both parents and children into mutually rewarding interactions. If the vicious circle of escalating negative reciprocity can be broken and reversed, the parents' self-confidence in their intuitive competence will be strengthened by positive feedback from their infant. They will feel more secure in interactions with their infant and become able, led by the baby's signals, to support her self-regulatory capacities more efficiently than before and to coregulate and master the pending developmental tasks.

The new dynamics in the family constellation that result from the birth of a child and the developmental dynamics of the child during the first years of life make it possible to achieve rapid and lasting changes within a relatively short period of time. The fact that relatively few sessions are needed, as well as the overwhelmingly gratifying treatment outcomes, suggest that the model is well suited to meet the needs of young families, the rapid developmental trajectories of the infant during the first years of life, and the needs of the still fragile parent–infant relationship in cases of disorders of behavioral and emotional regulation.

REFERENCES

Barth, R. (1998). Psychotherapie und Beratung im Säuglings- und Kleinkindalter. In K. von Klitzing (Ed.), *Psychotherapie in der frühen Kindheit* (pp. 72–87). Göttingen, Germany: Vandenhoeck & Ruprecht.

Barth, R. (1999). Ein Beratungsangebot für Eltern mit Säuglingen und Kleinkindern - Konzeption und erste Erfahrungen der Beratungsstelle "Menschenskind." *Praxis der Kinderpsychologie und Kinderpsychiatrie, 48,* 178–191.

Barth, R. (2000). "Baby-Lese-Stunden" für Eltern mit exzessiv schreienden Säuglingen. *Praxis der Kinderpsychologie und Kinderpsychiatrie, 49,* 537–549.

Barth, R. (2002). Mutter-Kind-Symbiose bei Schlafstörungen: Eine psychoanalytische Betrachtung zum Ausschluss des Dritten. In K. Steinhardt, W. Datler, & J. Gstach (Eds.), *Die Bedeutung des Vaters in der frühen Kindheit* (pp. 142–158). Gießen, Germany: Psychosozial Verlag.

Barth, R. (2003). Schlafstörungen im Säuglings- und Kleinkindalter als Ausdruck einer ungelösten Trennungsproblematik. *Kinderanalyse, 11,* 41–57.

Beebe, B. (2003). Brief mother-infant treatment: Psychoanalytically informed video feedback. *Infant Mental Health Journal, 24,* 24–52.

Bertalanffy, L. (1968). *Organismic psychology theory*. Barre, MA: Clark University Press with Barre Publishers.

Brazelton, T. B. (1994). Touchpoints: Opportunity for preventing problems in the parent-child relationship. *Acta Paediatrica, 394*(Suppl.), 35–39.

Brazelton, T. B., & Cramer, B. (1989). *The earliest relationship: Parents, infants, and the drama of early attachment*. Redding, MA: Addison-Wesley.

Carey, W. B., & McDevitt, S. C. (1995). *Coping with children's temperament*. New York: Basic Books.

Cohen, N. J., Lojkasek, M., Muir, E., Muir, R., & Parker, C. J. (2002). Six-month follow-up of two mother-infant psychotherapies: Convergence of therapeutic outcomes. *Infant Mental Health Journal, 23*, 361–380.

Cohen, N. J., Muir, E., & Lojkasek, M. (2003). "Watch, wait and wonder"—ein kindzentriertes Psychotherapieprogramm zur Behandlung gestörter Mutter-Kind-Beziehungen. *Kinderanalyse, 11*, 58–79.

Downing, G. (2003). Video-Mikroanalyse-Therapie: Einige Grundlagen und Prinzipien. In H. Scheuerer-Englisch, G. J. Suess, & W.-K. P. Pfeiffer (Eds.), *Wege zur Sicherheit: Bindungswissen in Diagnostik und Intervention* (pp. 51–68). Gießen, Germany: Psychosozial Verlag.

Ferber, R. (1987). Sleeplessness, night awakening, and night crying in the infant and toddler. *Pediatrics in Review, 9*, 69–82.

Field, T. (1984). Interactions between infants and their postpartum depressed mothers. *Infant Behaviour and Development, 7*, 517–522.

Fraiberg, S. (1980). *Clinical studies in infant mental health: The first year of life*. New York: Basic Books.

Fraiberg, S., Adelson, E., & Shapiro, V. (1980). Ghosts in the nursery: A psychoanalytic approach to the problem of impaired infant-mother relationships. In S. Fraiberg (Ed.), *Clinical studies in infant mental health: The first year of life* (pp. 164–196). New York: Basic Books. (Originally published in 1975)

Gloger-Tippelt, G. (1999). Transmission von Bindung über die Generationen. *Praxis der Kinderpsychologie und Kinderpsychiatrie, 48*, 73–85.

Greenspan, S. I. (1992). *Regulatory disorders. Infancy and early childhood: The practice of clinical assessment and intervention with emotional and developmental challenges*. Madison, CT: International Universities Press.

Kast-Zahn, A., & Morgenroth, H. (1995). *Jedes Kind kann schlafen lernen*. Ratingen, Germany: Oberstebrink & Partner.

Largo, R. (1992). Die normalen Krisen der kindlichen Entwicklung. *Kindheit und Entwicklung, 1*, 72–76.

Leist, M. (1998). Video-home-training: ein ressourcenorientiertes Angebot für verhaltensauffällige Kinder und ihre Familien. *Verhaltenstherapie und psychosoziale Praxis, 30*, 69–88.

Lieberman, A. F., & Pawl, J. H. (1993). Infant-parent psychotherapy. In C. H. Zeanah Jr. (Ed.), *Handbook of infant mental health* (1st ed., pp. 427–442). New York: Guilford Press.

Lojkasek, M., Cohen, N., & Muir, E. (1994). Where is the infant in mother-infant intervention? *Psychotherapy, 31*, 208–220.

Lyons-Ruth, K. (1998). Implicit relational knowing: Its role in development and psychoanalytic treatment. *Infant Mental Health Journal, 19*, 282–289.

McDonough, S. C. (1993). Interaction guidance: Understanding and treating early infant-caregiver relationship disturbances. In C. H. Zeanah Jr. (Ed.), *Handbook of infant mental health* (1st ed., pp. 414–426). New York: Guilford Press.

Möhler, E., & Resch, F. (2000). Ausdrucksformen und Transmissionsmechanismen mütterlicher Traumatisierungen innerhalb der Mütter-Säuglings-Interaktion. *Praxis der Kinderpsychologie und Kinderpsychiatrie, 49,* 550–562.

Muir, E. (1992). Watching, waiting and wondering: Applying psychoanalytic principles to mother-infant intervention. *Infant Mental Health Journal 13,* 319–328.

Papoušek, H. (1967). Experimental studies of appetitional behavior in human newborns and infants. In H. W. Stevenson, E. H. Hess, & H. L. Rheingold (Eds.), *Early behavior: Comparative and developmental approaches* (pp. 249–277). New York: Wiley.

Papoušek, H., & Papoušek, M. (1979a). The infant's fundamental adaptive response system in social interaction. In E. B. Thoman (Ed.), *Origins of the infant's social responsiveness* (pp. 175–208). Hillsdale, NJ: Erlbaum.

Papoušek, H., & Papoušek, M. (1979b). Lernen im ersten Lebensjahr. In L. Montada (Ed.), *Brennpunkte der Entwicklungspsychologie* (pp. 194–212). Stuttgart, Germany: Kohlhammer.

Papoušek, H., & Papoušek, M. (1987). Intuitive parenting: A dialectic counterpart to the infant's integrative competence. In J. D. Osofsky (Ed.), *Handbook of infant development* (2nd ed., pp. 669–720). New York: Wiley.

Papoušek, M. (1985). Umgang mit dem schreienden Säugling und sozialpädiatrische Beratung. *Sozialpädiatrie in Praxis und Klinik, 7,* 294–300, 352–357.

Papoušek, M. (1994). *Vom ersten Schrei zum ersten Wort. Anfaenge der Sprachentwicklung in der vorsprachlichen Kommunikation.* Bern, Switzerland: Hans Huber.

Papoušek, M. (1996). Die intuitive elterliche Kompetenz in der vorsprachlichen Kommunikation als Ansatz zur Diagnostik von präverbalen Kommunikations- und Beziehungsstörungen. *Kindheit und Entwicklung 5,* 140–146.

Papoušek, M. (1998). Das Münchner Modell einer interaktionszentrierten Säuglings-Eltern-Beratung und -Psychotherapie. In K. von Klitzing (Ed.), *Psychotherapie in der fruehen Kindheit* (pp. 88–118). Göttingen, Germany: Vandenhoeck & Ruprecht.

Papoušek, M. (2000). Einsatz von Video in der Eltern-Säuglings-Beratung und –Psychotherapie. *Praxis der Kinderpsychologie und Kinderpsychiatrie, 49,* 611–627.

Papoušek, M., & Papoušek, H. (1990). Excessive infant crying and intuitive parental care: Buffering support and its failures in parent-infant interaction [Special issue]. *Early Child Development and Care, 65,* 117–126.

Papoušek, M., & von Hofacker, N. (2003). Störungen der frühen Eltern-Kind-Beziehungen. In D. Reinhardt (Ed.), *Leitlinien der Deutschen Gesellschaft für Kinderheilkunde und Jugendmedizin, Section Sozialpädiatrie (R9)* (pp. 1–10). München, Germany: Urban & Fischer.

Papoušek, M., & Wollwerth de Chuquisengo, R. (2003). Auswirkungen mütterlicher Traumatisierungen auf Kommunikation und Beziehung in der frühen Kindheit. Werkstattbericht aus 10 Jahren Münchner Sprechstunde für Schreibabys. In K. H. Brisch (Ed.), *Bindung und Trauma* (pp. 136–159). Stuttgart, Germany: Klett-Cotta.

Pedrina, F. (1998). Eltern-Kind-Therapien bei postpartalen Depressionen. In K. von Klitzing (Ed.), *Psychotherapie in der frühen Kindheit* (pp. 132–153). Göttingen, Germany: Vandenhoeck & Ruprecht.

Pedrina, F. (Ed.). (2001). *Beziehung und Entwicklung in der frühen Kindheit: Psychoanalytische Interventionen in interdisziplinären Kontexten*. Tübingen, Germany: Edition Discord.

Robert-Tissot, C., Cramer, B., Stern, D., Serpa, S. R., Bachmann, J.-P., Palacio-Esposa, D., et al. (1996). Outcome evaluation in brief mother-infant psychotherapies: Report on 75 cases. *Infant Mental Health Journal, 17*, 97–114.

Smith, L. B., & Thelen, E. (Eds.). (1993). *A dynamic systems approach to development: Applications*. Cambridge, MA: MIT Press.

Stern, D. N. (1995). *The motherhood constellation*. New York: Basic Books.

Stern, D. N., Sander, L. W., Nahum, J. P., Harrison, A. M., Lyons-Ruth, K., Morgan, A. C., et al. (2002). The Process of Change Study Group, Boston: Nicht-deutende Mechanismen in der psychoanalytischen Therapie: Das "Etwas-Mehr" als Deutung [Special issue: Entwicklungsforschung, Bindungstheorie, Lebenszyklus]. *Psyche, 56,* 974–1006.

Tronick, E. Z., Als, H, Adamson, L., Wise, E., & Brazelton, T. B. (1978). The infant's response to entrapment between contradictory messages in face-to-face interaction. *Journal of Child Psychiatry, 17*, 1–13.

von Klitzing, K. (1998). *Psychotherapie in der frühen Kindheit*. Göttingen, Germany: Vandenhoeck & Ruprecht.

ZERO TO THREE. (1994). *Diagnostic classification: 0–3. Diagnostic classification of mental health and developmental disorders of infancy and early childhood*. Arlington, VA: National Center for Clinical Infant Programs.

CHAPTER 13

LONG-TERM RISKS OF PERSISTENT EXCESSIVE CRYING IN INFANTS

Harald Wurmser
Mechthild Papoušek
Nikolaus von Hofacker

INTRODUCTION

Pediatric manuals frequently refer to excessive crying in infants as 3-month colic, describing it as a harmless and transient behavioral problem of early childhood. Exhausted, frustrated, or worried parents may find this positive assessment of the course of excessive crying encouraging. A literature search for evidence of its benign course, however, shows that the research is sparse and the results are not clear-cut. As a result, the description of the outcome of excessive infant crying in pediatric manuals appears to be incomplete or even inadequate and premature.

The comprehensive literature review done by Lehtonen, Gormally, and Barr (2000) and our own systematic search on MEDLINE and PsycINFO yielded 14 prospective studies, published between 1967 and mid-2002, on the sequelae of excessive infant crying. Two of these studies (Keefe, Kotzer, Froese-Fretz, & Curtin, 1996; Shaver, 1974) included insufficient follow-ups (maximum of 4 to 5 months after diagnosis of the crying problem) and are therefore not considered in the following overview. The most important features and results of the remaining 12 studies are summarized in Table 13.1.

In 7 of these studies, data about an ongoing crying problem between the ages of 0 and 6 months were collected prospectively either by using behavior logs or by questioning the parents (Castro-Rodriguez et al., 2001; Elliott, Fischer, & Ames, 1988; Elliot, Pedersen, & Mogan, 1997; Lehtonen, Korhonen, & Korvenranta, 1994; Räihä, Lehtonen, Korhonen, & Korvenranta, 1996, 1997; Räihä, Lehtonen, & Korvenranta, 1995; Stifter & Bono, 1998; Stifter & Braungart, 1992; Stifter & Spinrad, 2002; St. James-Roberts, Conroy, & Wilsher, 1995, 1998a, 1998b; Wolke, Rizzo, & Woods, 2002). Cases were defined according to the daily duration of crying (mostly using the criteria of Wessel, Cobb, Jackson, Harris, & Detwiler, 1954). In another 5 studies, information on infant behavior was collected retrospectively by means of interviews or questionnaires after the crying problem had been resolved (Forsyth & Canny, 1991; Forsyth, Leventhal, & McCarthy, 1985; Oberklaid, Sanson, Pedlow, & Prior, 1993; Rautava, Helenius, & Lehtonen, 1993; Rautava, Lehtonen, Helenius, & Sillanpaa, 1995; Sloman, Bellinger, & Krentzel, 1990; Wolke, Meyer, Ohr, & Riegel, 1995). As a result, the possibility of memory bias cannot be ruled out. The age range of the children included in these studies was between 3 and 8 months at the time the groups were formed. Again, cases were defined according to the duration of crying or the degree of parental distress caused by infant crying. After cases and controls were defined, prospective data on the behavior and development of the child, the mother's well-being, the quality of parent–child interactions, and characteristics of family life were collected in all 12 studies but with varying numbers of data points (one to six follow-ups) and over widely variable periods of time (10 months to 13 years).

The results of three studies (Elliott et al., 1988, 1997; Stifter & Bono, 1998; Stifter & Braungart, 1992; Stifter & Spinrad, 2002) are open to only limited interpretation because of very small sample sizes, particularly in the case groups ($10 \leq n \leq 14$). The authors of these studies found that excessive infant crying has only transient effects, if any, on the later behavior of the child, his development and attachment security, the psychological well-being of the mother, the quality of parent–child interactions, and family life in general. However, in contrast to the earlier study (Stifter & Braungart, 1992), Stifter and Spinrad (2002) reported increased negative reactivity and decreased capacity for self-regulation, as behavioral manifestations of infant temperament, at the ages of 5 and 10 months in infants who had cried excessively in the first months of postnatal life. Because of these contradictory results and the inadequate power associated with the small sample sizes of the studies summarized above, one cannot conclude with certainty that the course of infant crying is benign.

All of the remaining studies had markedly larger sample sizes and covered adequate follow-up intervals. All of them point to a positive prognosis for infant crying in terms of later physical health and motor, cognitive, and social development. For example, former infant criers and controls without a crying problem had comparable frequencies of allergies up to adolescence (Castro-Rodriguez et al., 2001) and similar weight gains over the course of the first year of life—except for transient differences during the first 16 weeks of life (Lehtonen et al., 1994). With regard to motor, cognitive, and social development during the first 3 years, either no differences were found between children who had previously cried excessively and children in control groups (Lehtonen et al., 1994; Rautava et al., 1995; St. James-Roberts et al., 1995, 1998a, 1998b) or differences were limited only to the first half-year of life (Sloman et al., 1990).

By contrast, most of the studies that have examined infant temperament have shown that in comparison to children in control groups, children who previously had cried excessively continued to be viewed as more difficult by their parents over the course of the first year of life (Sloman et al., 1990), the second year of life (St. James-Roberts et al., 1995, 1998a, 1998b), and even up to the age of 8 to 10 years (Wolke et al., 2002). However, this is not reflected in infant behavior under laboratory conditions. Thus, for example, St. James-Roberts and colleagues (1995, 1998a, 1998b) did not find any group differences in terms of reactivity between 5-month-old children who had previously cried excessively and age-matched controls when tested with a sequence of visual, auditory, and tactile stimuli increasing stepwise in intensity.

The findings for behavioral development are not uniform. Fifteen-month-old children who had previously cried excessively seem to have rates of irritability, temper tantrums, and frustration that are similar to those of control group children (St. James-Roberts et al., 1995, 1998a, 1998b). Likewise, although children with behavioral problems (excessive crying, feeding problems) during the first 4

Table 13.1. Methods and Findings of Prospective Studies on the Developmental Outcomes of Excessive Infant Crying.

	Elliott et al. (1988, 1997)	Stifter & Braungart (1992); Stifter & Bono (1998)	Stifter & Spinrad (2002)	Lehtonen et al. (1994); Räihä et al. (1995, 1996, 1997)
Sample size Criers group Control group	10 72	10 10	14 102	59 58
Age at group assignment	6–8 weeks	3, 4, and 5 weeks	6 weeks	Birth–11 weeks
Study design	Prospective	Prospective	Prospective	Prospective
Assessment method	Questionnaire	Telephone interview	Behavior log	Behavior log
Criteria for group assignment	Criteria of Wessel et al. (1954)	Criteria of Wessel et al. (1954)	(a) Mean duration of crying > 86 minutes/day or (b) Mean duration of crying and fussing combined > 221 minutes/day	Modified criteria of Wessel et al. (1954)
Age at follow-up	2–4 years	5, 10, and 18 months	5 and 10 months	3, 4, 8, 12, and 36 months
Methods of follow-up	–Questionnaires –Behavioral observation	–Behavioral observation –Developmental test –Questionnaires	–Behavioral observation –Questionnaires	–Interview –Pediatric examinations –Developmental test –Questionnaires
Effects on the child	None	None	At 5 and 10 months: –Negative reactivity (+) –Self-regulatory competencies (–) (in boys, but not in girls)	At 3, 12, and 36 months: –Maternal global assessment of "Difficult" temperament (+)
Effects on the mother	None	At 5 months: –Self-efficacy (–)	None	Not tested

Table 13.1. Methods and Findings of Prospective Studies on the Developmental Outcomes of Excessive Infant Crying *(continued)*.

	St. James-Roberts et al. (1995, 1998a, 1998b)	Wolke et al. (2002)	Castro-Rodriguez et al. (2001)	Rautava et al. (1993, 1995)
Sample size Criers group Control group	67 93	64 64	90 893	338 866
Age at group assignment	4–6 weeks	2–6 months	1–2 months	3 months
Study design	Prospective	Prospective	Prospective	Retrospective
Assessment method	Questionnaire, behavior log, audio recording	Behavior log	Pediatric examinations, parent reports	Questionnaire
Criteria for group assignment	Modified criteria of Wessel et al. (1954)	Modified criteria of Wessel et al. (1954)	Unknown	Item value > 3 on a 5-point rating scale (1 to 5)
Age at follow-up	5 and 15 months	8–10 years	2, 3, 6, 8, 11, and 13 years	3 years
Methods of follow-up	–Behavior log –Questionnaires –Developmental test –Behavioral observation	–Questionnaires –Teacher assessment of school performance	–Case history –Allergy testing	–Questionnaires –Developmental test
Effects on the child	At 5 months: –Duration of crying/fussing (+) –"Difficult" temperament (+) At 15 months: –"Difficult" temperament (+) –Adaptability (–) –Stubbornness (+) –Eating problems (+) –Night time awakenings (+) –Anxiety (+)	–Hyperactivity (+) –Conduct problems (+) –School performance (–) –Negative emotionality (+) –Difficult/demanding (+) –Adaptability (–) –Eating problems (+)	None	–Daily temper tantrums (+) –Sleeping problems (+)
Effects on the mother	At 15 months: –Depression (+) –Time spent on soothing strategies (+) –Stress in routine care (+) –Tendency to respond to infant crying (–)	None	Not tested	–Stress caused by housework (+)

Table 13.1. Methods and Findings of Prospective Studies on the Developmental Outcomes of Excessive Infant Crying (*continued*).

	Forsyth et al. (1985, 1991)	Wolke et al. (1995)	Sloman et al. (1990)	Oberklaid et al. (1993)
Sample size Criers group Control group	$85 \leq n \leq 126$ 242	138 292	37 179	358 1,583 (= total cohort)
Age at group assignment	4 months	5 months	6 months	4–8 months
Study design	Retrospective	Retrospective	Retrospective	Retrospective
Assessment method	Telephone interview	Interview	Interview	Questionnaire
Criteria for group assignment	Degree of subjective stress on the mother (moderate to strong)	–Duration of crying > 2 hours per day –Above-average extent of crying –Inconsolability –Parental stress caused by the infant's crying problem	Modified criteria of Wessel et al. (1954)	Overall score ≥ 75th percentile
Age at follow-up	3.5 years	20 and 56 months	12, 18, and 24 months	4 to 5 years
Methods of follow-up	Questionnaires	Interview	–Questionnaires –Behavioral observation –Developmental tests	Questionnaire
Effects on the child	–Perceived vulnerability (+) –Behavioral problems (+) –Allergies (+)	At 20 months: –Nighttime awakenings (+) At 56 months: –One parent sleeps in bed with child (+)	At 6 months: –Withdrawal (+) –Tension (+) –Irritability (+) –Cognitive development (–) –Motor development (–)	–Behavioral problems (+)
Effects on the mother	Not tested	Not tested	At 6 months: –Stress (+) –Responsiveness (–) –Adequate stimulation of the child (–)	Not tested

months of life are significantly more likely to be viewed by their mothers as vulnerable at the age of 3½ years compared to children without early behavior problems, the groups do not differ in terms of attention span, behavioral regulation, or sociability at this age (Forsyth & Canny, 1991; Forsyth et al., 1985). However, indications have been found that excessive infant crying is associated with eating problems and elevated anxiety at 15 months (St. James-Roberts et al., 1995, 1998a, 1998b) as well as daily temper tantrums at the age of 3 years (Rautava et al., 1993, 1995). Furthermore, several studies have consistently shown marked associations between excessive infant crying and sleeping problems in the second year of life (St. James-Roberts et al., 1995, 1998a, 1998b; Wolke et al., 1995) as well as in the third year of life (Rautava et al., 1993, 1995). Our own clinical data show that regulatory disorders in toddlerhood (sleeping and feeding disorders, excessive clinginess, tantrums, aggressive/oppositional behavior) frequently have begun with early excessive infant crying (see chapter 3).

Wolke and colleagues (2002) conducted one of the few studies with follow-up into school age. The authors compared 64 children who at the age of 2 to 6 months ($M \pm SD = 3.8 \pm 1.3$ months) had met modified criteria according to Wessel et al. (1954) and had participated in an intervention study because of their crying problems, with an age- and sex-matched classroom control group without a history of infant crying problems ($n = 64$). Comparisons were made regarding the frequency of external-izing behavioral problems at the age of 8 to 10 years. At the initial presentation, 7.8% of the infants in the clinical group exhibited an isolated crying problem, whereas 92.2% of the children had additional, concurrent behavioral problems (sleeping and/or feeding problems). Excessive crying persisted in 87.5% of the children in the clinical group beyond the usual first 3 months of life. Follow-up examination at the age of 8 to 10 years (9.7 ± 0.6 years) revealed that the children who had previously cried exces-sively scored significantly higher for hyperactivity and conduct problems on a validated questionnaire (filled out by the child, parents, and teachers). They also performed less well in school than did chil-dren in the control group, according to their teachers. With regard to hyperactivity, the group of children who had previously cried excessively exhibited scores in the borderline/clinical range (scores > 80th percentile) significantly more frequently than did the control children. In 18.9% of the children who had previously cried excessively and 1.6% of the control children, hyperactivity values on the questionnaires filled out by children, parents, and teachers were above the cutoff. Children who had previously cried excessively also exhibited higher rates of conduct problems in the borderline/clinical range, according to parent reports (45.3% vs. 17.2%) and child reports (32.8% vs. 7.8%). To date, Wolke et al. (2002) have reported the most unfavorable developmental prognosis for excessive infant crying in a clinical sample.

Several studies have also looked at whether and to what extent excessive infant crying affects the mother's well-being and family life. It should surprise no one that mothers of infants who cry exces-sively find taking routine care of their babies and meeting their babies' demands more distressing during the first 5 to 6 months postpartum than do mothers in control groups (Sloman et al., 1990; St. James-Roberts et al., 1995, 1998a, 1998b). However, mothers of infants who cry excessively also experience depression even in the clinical range significantly more frequently during the first 5 months postpartum than do mothers of children in control groups (St. James-Roberts et al., 1995, 1998a, 1998b). What remains unclear, however, is whether the depression was elicited by the child's crying problem or whether it had existed prior to birth. At any rate, Wolke and colleagues (2002) did not find any difference 8 to 10 years later between the rates of depression among mothers whose children cried excessively as infants and those of the mothers of children in control groups.

Compared with control families, families with babies who cry excessively show significantly more problems in terms of the quality of family life during the first 3 months postpartum (Räihä et al., 1995) and also at 12 months postpartum (Räihä et al., 1996). Even 3 years postpartum, parents of babies who cried excessively still report dissatisfaction with family life (Rautava et al., 1993, 1995). The studies conducted by Rautava and colleagues (1993, 1995) indicate, however, that the couples' relationship may have been stressed even during pregnancy.

Further studies on the effects of excessive infant crying are definitely needed, given the sparse and somewhat contradictory data. The observed connections between excessive infant crying and later disorders in behavioral regulation in the clients of our program motivated us to collect follow-up data at 30 months (Papoušek, Wurmser, & von Hofacker, 2001), the results of which are presented in the next section.

FOLLOW-UP STUDY

The clinical group that took part in the follow-up study consisted of 60 infants (57% boys) who had been brought to our program with a crying problem between the ages of 1 and 6 months (average age: 4.1 ± 1.5 months). We compared these infants with a control group of similar age and sex distribution (n = 45; 3.7 ± 1.3 months; 49% boys) that was recruited from birth announcements in a local newspaper. According to reports by the mothers, 24% of the control infants had been affected by a transient crying problem at about 6 weeks. However, this problem had already been resolved by the time of recruitment.

The clinical group was further divided into two subgroups according to mean daily durations of crying and fussing on 5 successive days, as documented on behavior logs provided by the parents at the initial appointment (1 to 6 months postpartum). One group consisted of infants with extreme crying (n = 30; termed *extreme criers*) who cried or fussed for more than 3 hours on average per day over 5 days (a more stringent variant of the criteria of Wessel et al., 1954); the other group consisted of infants with moderate crying (n = 30; *moderate criers*) who also presented with a crying problem, but who cried or fussed on average less than 3 hours per day. The children in both the clinical groups and the control group were followed up at the age of 30 months.

Methods and results of the initial examination have been presented in detail in earlier publications (Papoušek & von Hofacker, 1995, 1998; see also chapter 5) and, therefore, are only briefly summarized here.

Main Findings of the Initial Examination 1 to 6 Months Postpartum

It should be noted in connection with the typical course of excessive infant crying that 95% of the infants in all groups were older than 6 weeks at the time of recruitment and that 60% were older than

3 months. Although the majority of these infants had therefore already reached the mean crying peak at 6 weeks or the developmental spurt at the age of 3 months, the analysis of the behavior logs still showed an average daily duration of crying and fussing of 4.6 ± 1.3 hours for the extreme criers, 2.2 ± 0.5 hours for the moderate criers, and 1.1 ± 0.7 hours for the control group infants. The average duration of crying and fussing correlated negatively with total duration of sleep, which was also obtained from the behavior logs. By contrast, it correlated positively with various measures of an immature circadian and ultradian sleep–wake organization. In addition, the daily duration of crying and fussing correlated positively with the Fussy/Difficult, Unpredictable, and Unadaptable temperament scales on the Infant Characteristics Questionnaire (ICQ; Bates, Freeland, & Lounsbury, 1979).

Clear group differences were seen in the semistructured neuropediatric and psychological interview done at the initial examination, which focused on the pediatric and developmental history of the infants and served to sum up the prenatal, perinatal, and postnatal stresses caused by medical and psychosocial risk factors (psychological state of the mother, her childhood experiences, and the quality of couple and family relationships, as well as satisfaction with the social support received). Differences were also found on the standardized questionnaires. The main results are summarized as follows:

- The developmental neurological examination of the extreme and moderate criers showed signs of neuromotor immaturity significantly more frequently when compared with the control group.

- Compared with the control mothers, mothers of extreme criers were more stressed by organic, and particularly by psychosocial, risk factors, both prenatally and postnatally.

- On questionnaires (Maternal Childcare Attitudes and Feelings [EMKK; Engfer & Gavranidou, 1987]; Belastung der Partnerschaft [BELPAR, cited in Sarimski, 1993]; Maternal Self-Confidence Scale [MSCS; Lips, Bloom, & Barnett, 1990]; Edinburgh Postnatal Depression Scale [EPDS; Cox, Holden, & Sagovsky, 1987]), mothers in the clinical groups exhibited higher values on the following scales: Depressiveness, Exhaustion, Frustration, Anxious Overprotection, and Stress in the Parents' Relationship. By the same token, these mothers exhibited lower levels of confidence in their maternal competencies. In addition, the mothers in the clinical groups suffered significantly more frequently from postpartum depression requiring treatment (EPDS scores > 12; Cox et al., 1987).

On the basis of all of the information collected at the initial examination, including videotaped mother–child interactions in typical daily contexts, an additional expert assessment (Parent-Infant Relationship Global Assessment Scale [PIR-GAS]; ZERO TO THREE, 1994) evaluated the functional and adaptive quality of the mother–child relationship on a 9-point scale (from *well adapted* to *severely disordered*). The group comparison showed that the mother–child relationship was far more frequently distressed (85.5% vs. 10.2%) or disordered (6.5% vs. 0.0%) in the clinical dyads than in the control dyads.

The families in our clinical sample were thus characterized by a higher percentage of persistent and pervasive regulatory problems, multiple prenatal and postnatal stressors, and considerable psychological strain on the part of the mother, as well as considerable distress in the mother–child relationship. By contrast, in representative community-based samples, the crying problem is frequently limited to the first 3–4 months of life, and the stress on the affected families is generally low (Lehtonen et al., 2000).

Therapeutic intervention. After collecting the data, a pediatrician and a psychologist conducted an interaction-centered intervention with the families in the clinical groups that was tailored to the individual stressors and needs of the families. Among other things, this intervention was aimed at consolidating sleep–wake organization and unassisted falling asleep (see chapter 5). Depending on the individual situation, the intervention was supplemented by additional therapeutic modules and techniques. The intervention was continued until the infant's condition improved completely or until the parents had been provided with enough strategies and resources to deal on their own with whatever minor behavioral problems remained ("largely improved"). At the end of treatment, the therapists assessed therapeutic success on the basis of the duration of crying and fussing, the quality of each infant's sleep–wake organization, the psychological state of the mother, and the quality of the mother–child interaction. After the intervention, 72.9% of the 60 families in the clinical groups were assessed as completely improved, 22.0% as largely improved, 3.4% as slightly improved, and 1.7% as unimproved, mainly because of lack of compliance.

Methods of Follow-Up

Sample. A total of 83 families with infants having a crying problem and 57 control families without a crying problem were invited to participate in a follow-up examination 30 months postpartum and asked to fill out the sleep logs and questionnaires (see below) they had been sent earlier. The 60 families in the clinical groups and the 45 families in the control group that filled out and returned this material represent 72.3% and 78.9%, respectively, of the original groups. There were no differences in the dependent variables gathered at the initial examination between the participating and nonparticipating families.

Sleep log. Analogous to the initial examination, the follow-up behavior logs filled out by the parents for 24 hours over 5 successive days served to determine the duration of sleep and the child's circadian sleep rhythm. Information about the average duration of daytime and nighttime sleep as well as nightly bedtimes, sleep times, and waking times was extracted from the logs in order to determine indices of problematic sleep behavior based on 5-point scales according to Richman (1981) and Minde et al. (1993): (a) the number of nights with at least one waking episode over the entire 5-day observation period, (b) average number of waking episodes per night, (c) average duration of the waking episodes per night, (d) number of nights with bedtime routine problems (conflicts over going to bed), (e) average duration of bedtime routines (the time that it takes to put the child to bed), (f) number of nights with sleep-onset problems, (g) average time it takes to fall asleep at night, and (h) number of nights during which the child sleeps in the parents' bed. A principal components analysis with varimax rotation was conducted based on a covariance matrix of the data for all 105 children. This analysis yielded a solution with four factors that explain up to 80% of the variance in the original scores: (a) Sleep-Onset Problems, (b) Sleep Maintenance Problems, (c) Bedtime Routine Problems, and (d) Sleeping in Parents' Bed. Factor scores were calculated for each of these 4 factors for all participants.

Standardized questionnaires. The parents filled out a version of the ICQ (Bates et al., 1979) adapted for children older than 24 months, in which the following temperament dimensions were quantified: fussiness/difficulty, stubbornness, unadaptability, irregular rhythm, and dependence. To determine behavioral and emotional problems, the parents were asked to fill out the Child Behavior Checklist/2-3 (CBCL/2-3; Achenbach, Edelbrock, & Howell, 1987). This clinical questionnaire screens six problem areas: aggressive behavior, destructive behavior, sleep problems, somatic problems, anxiety/depression, and social withdrawal. Combining two of these primary scales yields secondary scales for externalizing (aggressive behavior + destructive behavior) and internalizing problems (anxiety/depression + social withdrawal). To assess the severity of behavioral and emotional problems, T values were used that were calculated from a large German epidemiological normative group consisting of 751 toddlers 30 months of age (Fegert, 1996).

RESULTS OF THE FOLLOW-UP AT 30 MONTHS POSTPARTUM

Child Temperament (ICQ)

Former extreme criers, moderate criers, and controls differed significantly at follow-up on fussiness/difficulty, $F(2, 102) = 5.5, p \leq .01$ (see Figure 13.1), and stubbornness, $F(2, 102)2 = 4.0, p \leq .05$. No group differences were found with regard to unadaptability, irregular rhythm, or dependence. The correlation coefficients between the values of the initial examination and the follow-up indicate a low-to-moderate stability in unadaptability ($r = .29$) and in fussiness/difficulty ($r = .46$; see Table 13.2).

Behavioral and Emotional Problems (CBCL/2-3)

At the age of 30 months, former extreme criers, moderate criers, and controls differed on five of the six scales of the CBCL/2-3: Aggressive Behavior, $F(2, 102) = 3.8, p \leq .05$; Anxiety/Depression, $F(2, 102) = 5.1, p \leq .01$; Sleep Problems, $F(2, 102) = 3.6, p \leq .05$; Somatic Problems, $F(2, 102) = 4.4, p \leq .05$; and

Figure 13.1. Temperament in Former Extreme and Moderate Criers and Controls at 30 Months.

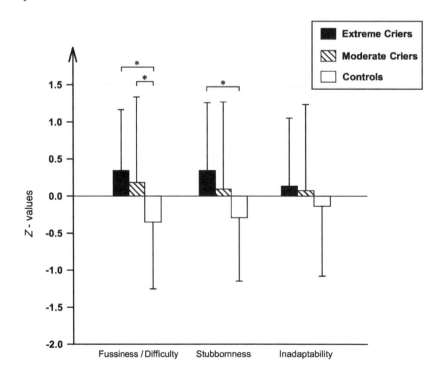

Note. ICQ; one-way *ANOVA* (M ± *SD*). *p ≤ .05 (two-tailed); post hoc Duncan's multiple range tests.

Table 13.2. Correlations Between Initial Examination (1–6 Months) and Follow-Up (30 Months).

1–6 months	Child temperament (ICQ)			Sleep log					Emotional and behavioral problems (CBCL/2-3)		
	Fussiness/difficulty	Inadaptability	Stubbornness	Sleeping (min/24h)	Sleep-onset problems	Sleep maintenance problems	Bedtime routine problems	Sleep in parents' bed	Sleep problems	Externalizing problems	Internalizing problems
Behavior log											
Crying (min/24h)	—	—	—	-.26**	—	—	.25**	—	—	—	—
Fussing (min/24h)	.22*	—	.32***	-.24*	—	—	.18*	—	.24**	.32***	.35***
Crying and fussing (min/24h)	.20*	—	.29***	-.29***	—	—	—	—	—	.23*	.27**
Sleeping (min/24h)	-.18*	—	-.21*	.22*	—	-.21*	—	—	-.23*	—	-.18*
Infant temperament (ICQ)											
Fussiness/difficulty	.46***	—	.21*	-.28***	—	.21*	—	—	.25**	.37***	.34***
Unpredictability	.30***	.19*	.24*	-.18*	—	.20*	—	—	.25**	.31***	.25**
Inadaptability	.31***	.29***	.19*	-.21*	—	—	—	—	.25**	.29***	.27***

Note. ICQ = Infant Characteristics Questionnaire (Bates, Freeland, & Lounsbury, 1979); CBCL/2-3 = Child Behavior Checklist/2-3 (Achenbach, Edelbrock, & Howell, 1987); min/24h = minutes per 24 hours.

*$p \leq .05$.   **$p \leq .01$.   ***$p \leq .005$.

Social Withdrawal, $F(2, 102) = 4.4$, $p \leq .05$. There also were group differences on the secondary scales for externalizing, $F(2, 102) = 3.9$, $p \leq .05$, and internalizing problems, $F(2, 102) = 6.0$, $p \leq .005$ (see Figure 13.2). Compared with the children in the control group, former extreme criers had significantly higher T values for aggressive behavior, sleep problems, and social withdrawal, as well as for externalizing problems, whereas former moderate criers had higher T values on the Somatic Problems subscale. Both former extreme criers and moderate criers exhibited higher T values on the Anxiety/Depression subscale and the internalizing problems secondary scale than did the controls. No significant group differences were seen in destructive behavior.

The CBCL/2-3 (Achenbach et al., 1987) is frequently used in psychiatric diagnosis as a screening instrument to identify behavioral and emotional problems in toddlers. According to Fegert (1996), a T value ≥ 70 exceeds the 98th percentile of the normative sample on each of the six subscales and both of the secondary scales, and indicates behavioral and emotional problems in the clinical range requiring treatment. Table 13.3 shows the percentage of children in the clinical and control groups exhibiting behavioral and emotional problems in the clinical range based on this cutoff. The percentages of children requiring treatment for behavioral and emotional problems were significantly higher in the former clinical groups than in the control group with regard to the aggressive behavior (18.3% vs. 4.4%; $p \leq .05$), anxiety/depression (18.3% vs. 2.2%; $p \leq .01$), and social withdrawal (11.7% vs. 0.0%; $p \leq .01$) subscales and with regard to the internalizing problems secondary scale (15.0% vs. 2.2%; $p \leq .05$). By

Figure 13.2. Behavioral and Emotional Problems in Former Extreme Criers and Controls at Age 30 Months.

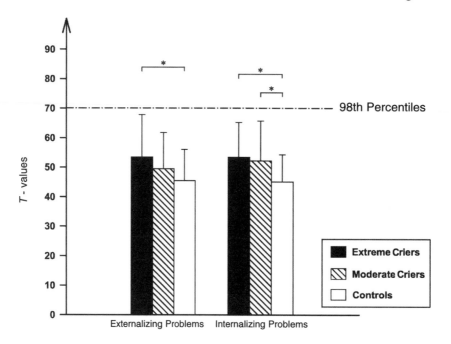

Note. CBCL/2-3; one-way *ANOVA* (*M ± SD*). *$p \leq .05$ (two-tailed); post hoc Duncan's multiple range tests. A *T*-value ≥ 70 exceeds the 98th percentile of the normative sample (Fegert, 1996) and indicates behavioral and emotional problems in the clinical range.

Table 13.3. Percentages of Behavioral and Emotional Problems in the Clinical Range in the Former Clinical and Controls Groups.

	Clinical groups (n = 60)	Controls (n = 45)	Chi-square	p[a]
Aggressive behavior	18.3	4.4	≤ 4.6	≤.05
Anxiety/depression	18.3	2.2	≤ 6.6	≤.01
Destructive behavior	6.7	6.7	0.0	ns
Sleep problems	10.0	4.4	1.1	ns
Somatic problems	11.7	4.4	1.7	ns
Social withdrawal	11.7	0.0	≤ 5.6	≤.01
Internalizing problems	15.0	2.2	≤ 4.9	≤.05
Externalizing problems	15.0	6.7	1.8	ns

[a]One-tailed tests.

contrast, the frequencies of problems in the clinical range were comparable in all groups with regard to destructive behavior, sleep problems, somatic problems, and externalizing problems. It should be noted that 10.0% of the children in the former clinical groups but none of the children in the control group exhibited both internalizing and externalizing problems in the clinical range.

Of the total of 105 children tested, 26 (24.8%) exhibited emotional or behavioral problems in the clinical range on at least one of the six CBCL/2-3 syndrome scales at the age of 30 months. This group is referred to below as CBCL+. The other 79 children (CBCL–) did not exceed the 98th percentile on any of the subscales. Twice as many children from the former clinical groups belonged to the CBCL+ group as did the control children (31.7% vs. 15.6%), $X^2(1, N = 105) = 3.6$, $p \leq .05$ (one-tailed test). Moreover, 11.7% of the former clinical groups (compared to none of the control children) exceeded the 98th percentile on three or even more of the syndrome scales, $X^2(3, N = 105) = 6.4$, $p \leq .05$ (one-tailed test). In the epidemiological survey conducted by Fegert (1996) to standardize the CBCL/2-3 on a German sample (n = 751), 11.6% of the children exhibited emotional or behavioral problems on at least one of the scales at the age of 30 months. Summarizing the results of epidemiological studies, Laucht (2002) estimated the prevalence of psychological disorders in toddlerhood to be between 5% and 15%. While the control group is located at the upper end of this range, the prevalence in the former clinical groups is increased by a factor of two.

Sleep Behavior (Sleep Log)

A total of 92 sleep logs had been completely and correctly filled out and were available for analysis (Leupold, 2001). The differences in total sleep time per 24 hours that were observed at the initial examination between former extreme criers, moderate criers, and controls were no longer evident at the follow-up examination. However, former extreme criers exhibited significantly shorter daytime sleep than did moderate criers and controls, $F(2, 86) = 3.6$, $p \le .05$. The correlation coefficient of total sleep time between the two data points was low but significant ($r = .22$, $p \le .05$; see Table 13.2). Although former extreme criers reached significantly higher values on the Sleep Problems syndrome scale of the CBCL/2-3 than did moderate criers or controls, no significant differences between the three groups were found on any of the eight indices for problematic sleep behavior according to Richman (1981) and Minde et al. (1993), nor on any of the four sleep factors derived from them. However, significant associations were found in the database for the overall sample between the CBCL/2-3 Sleep Problems primary scale and either the total sleep time derived from the logs or the Sleep Maintenance Problems factor ($r = -.48$ and $r = .51$, respectively; $p \le .005$; see Table 13.4).

There was no significant association between the success of treatment among the former excessive and moderate criers and either the primary or secondary scales of the CBCL/2-3. Also, success of treatment was not associated with the values derived from the sleep logs. However, the power of these analyses is low because of the low number of partially, slightly, and unimproved cases (see section on Therapeutic Intervention).

As the matrix in Table 13.4 shows, most of the outcome variables at the follow-up examination 30 months postpartum were significantly intercorrelated. Particularly high correlation coefficients were found between fussiness/difficulty, inadaptability, and stubbornness, on the one hand, and externalizing and internalizing problems, on the other. The correlation coefficients between the values derived from the sleep logs and child temperament or the scales of the CBCL/2-3 were mainly low but significant.

Predictors for the Outcome Variables

In our search for early signs of behavioral and emotional problems at the age of 30 months, we first correlated the infant, maternal, and relationship variables from the initial examination with the outcome variables from the follow-up (see Tables 13.2 and 13.5). The duration of fussing and the sum of crying and fussing durations were each positively associated, whereas total sleep time in infancy was negatively associated with fussiness/difficulty and stubbornness as well as with externalizing and internalizing problems at the age of 30 months (see Table 13.2). Overall, infant behavior variables correlated weakly with the indicators for sleep problems at the age of 30 months derived from the log entries. Infant temperament dimensions correlated negatively with subsequent total sleep time and positively with sleep problems (CBCL/2-3) as well as with externalizing and internalizing problems.

The psychological state of the mother and the relationship variables at the time of the initial examination were each significantly correlated with later fussiness/difficulty and stubbornness (see Table 13.5). Both the degree of maternal self-confidence as well as the quality of the mother–child relationship were negatively correlated with these temperament dimensions. In addition, the mothers' feelings of frustration and rejection by her child during the first half-year of life were significantly associated with the measures derived from the sleep logs at the follow-up examination. With the exception of the feeling of rejection, all measures of the psychological state of the mother, the level of stress in the parents' relationship, and the quality of the mother–child relationship were significantly correlated with externalizing and internalizing problems at 30 months.

Table 13.4. Intercorrelation Matrix of Variables at the Follow-Up 30 Months Postpartum.

30 months	Child temperament (ICQ)			Sleep log					Emotional and behavioral problems (CBCL/2-3)		
	Fussiness/ difficulty	Inadaptability	Stubbornness	Sleeping (min/24h)	Sleep-onset problems	Sleep maintenance problems	Bedtime routine problems	Sleep in parents' bed	Sleep problems	Externalizing problems	Internalizing problems
Child temperament (ICQ)											
Fussiness/difficulty	1										
Inadaptability	.48***	1									
Stubbornness	.49***	—	1								
Sleep log											
Duration of sleeping (min/24h)	-.23*	—	-.23*	1							
Sleep-onset problems	—	—	.23*	—	1						
Sleep maintenance problems	.24*	—	.20*	-.42***	—	1					
Bedtime routine problems	—	—	—	—	—	—	1				
Sleep in parents' bed	.18*	—	—	—	—	—	—	1			
Behavioral and emotional problems (CBCL/2-3)											
Sleep problems	.35***	—	.34***	-.48***	—	.51***	—	—	1		
Externalizing problems	.73***	.27***	.58***	-.34***	.23*	.26**	—	—	.44***	1	
Internalizing problems	.59***	.55***	.32***	-.25**	—	—	—	—	.41***	.62***	1

Note. ICQ = Infant Characteristics Questionnaire (Bates, Freeland, & Lounsbury, 1979); CBCL/2-3 = Child Behavior Checklist/2-3 (Achenbach, Edelbrock, & Howell, 1987); min/24h = minutes per 24 hours.

*p ≤ .05. **p ≤ .01. ***p ≤ .005.

Table 13.5. Correlations Between Maternal and Relationship Variables at Initial Examination and Outcome Variables at Follow-Up.

| | Child temperament (ICQ) | | | Sleep log | | | | | Emotional and behavioral problems (CBCL/2-3) | | |
1–6 months	Fussiness/ difficulty	Inadaptability	Stubbornness	Sleeping (min/24h)	Sleep-onset problems	Bedtime routine problems	Sleep maintenance problems	Sleep in parents' bed	Sleep problems	Externalizing problems	Internalizing problems
Psychological state of the mother											
Depressiveness (EMKK)	.37***	—	.25**	—	—	—	—	—	—	.34***	.24**
Frustration (EMKK)	.45***	.19*	.34***	-.20*	.19*	—	.21*	—	.25**	.47***	.34***
Exhaustion (EMKK)	.34***	—	.26***	—	—	—	—	—	—	.34***	.25**
Rejection (EMKK)	.20*	—	—	—	.21*	.21*	.22*	.21*	—	—	—
Maternal self-confidence (MSCS)	-.42***	—	-.33***	—	—	—	-.20*	-.24*	-.27***	-.35***	-.29***
Relationship variables											
Marital dissatisfaction (BELPAR)	.35***	.19*	—	—	—	—	—	—	—	.39***	.35***
Mother–child relationship (PIR-GAS)	-.33***	—	-.19*	—	—	—	—	—	—	-.23*	-.32***

Note. ICQ = Infant Characteristics Questionnaire (Bates, Freeland, & Lounsbury, 1979); CBCL/2-3 = Child Behavior Checklist/2-3 (Achenbach, Edelbrock, & Howell, 1987); EMKK = Maternal Childcare Attitudes and Feelings (Engfer & Gavranidou, 1987); MSCS = Maternal Self-Confidence Scale (Lips, Bloom, & Barnett, unpublished manuscript); BELPAR = Belastungen in der Partnerschaft (cited in Sarimski, 1993); PIR-GAS = Parent–Infant Relationship Global Assessment Scale (ZERO TO THREE, 1994); min/24h = minutes per 24 hours.

*p ≤ .05. **p ≤ .01. ***p ≤ .005.

To determine the role of potential etiological factors for psychological disorders at the age of 30 months, the 26 CBCL+ children with and the 79 CBCL– children without behavioral and emotional problems in the clinical range were compared with regard to early infant, maternal, and relationship variables.

CBCL+ and CBCL– children did not differ in infancy in terms of duration of crying and fussing. However, the CBCL+ children scored significantly higher on the temperament scales Fussiness/Difficulty, $t(103) = 3.6$, $p \leq .001$ (one-tailed test); Unpredictability, $t(45) = 1.9$, $p \leq .05$ (one-tailed test); and Unadaptability scales, $t(34) = 2.8$, $p \leq .005$ (one-tailed test) scales at initial examination than did CBCL– children (see Figure 13.3).

In addition, CBCL+ mothers were significantly more depressed, $t(103) = 2.3$, $p \leq .05$ (one-tailed test), and frustrated, $t(103) = 3.7$, $p \leq .001$ (one-tailed test), during the first half-year of their child's life according to their EMKK scores (Engfer & Gavranidou, 1987) and had significantly lower scores for self-confidence (MSCS; Lips et al., 1990), $t(44.8) = -2.8$, $p \leq .005$ (one-tailed test) than did CBCL– mothers. In particular, CBCL+ mothers scored significantly higher, $t(103) = 2.6$, $p \leq .005$ (one-tailed test) on the depression scale (EPDS; Cox et al., 1987). There were no significant differences between the CBCL+ mothers and the CBCL– mothers in the scores on the other maternal scales (pleasure with infant, exhaustion, anxious overprotection, punitive tendencies, rejection by the child, and rigidity; all EMKK [Engfer & Gavranidou, 1987]). Significantly higher values had been found for CBCL+ mothers than for CBCL– mothers, $t(32) = 2.1$, $p \leq .05$ (one-tailed test), with regard to cumulative psychosocial stress (the sum of weighted prenatal and postnatal risks).

Finally, both the parents' relationships (BELPAR; Sarimski, 1993), $t(31.6) = 3.1$, $p \leq .005$ (one-tailed test), and the mother–infant relationships (PIR-GAS; ZERO TO THREE, 1994), $t(103) = -2.5$, $p \leq .01$ (one-tailed test), at the initial examination were significantly more distressed in the CBCL+ families than in the CBCL–families.

Multiple stepwise regression analyses were performed using all available information regarding prenatal, perinatal, and postnatal stressors caused by medical and psychosocial risk factors as well as infant, maternal, and relationship variables at the initial examination. These variables were entered as predictors in order to determine which factors best predict behavioral and emotional problems at the age of 30 months. The results of these analyses are depicted in Figures 13.4 and 13.5. The regression model best suited to predict externalizing problems explains 35% (adjusted R^2) of the variance and contains only one maternal factor but five infant predictors (see Figure 13.4): maternal frustration, infant characteristics of sleep–wake organization (total duration of crying, total duration of fussing, total sleep time), fussiness/difficulty, and the cumulative postnatal medical risk factors on the side of the infant. Conversely, with regard to internalizing problems, maternal variables (depression, frustration, anxious overprotection, prenatal anxieties) proved to be the most important independent predictors along with the quality of the mother–child relationship, stresses in the parents' relationship and fussiness/difficulty in the infant (see Figure 13.5). This model explains 36% (adjusted R^2) of the variance in the dependent variable. The Sleep Problems primary scale on the CBCL/2-3 is significantly predicted by maternal depressiveness, rejection by the child, pleasure with infant, postpartum depression, and quality of the social support system. Inadaptability and total duration of fussing at the time of the initial examination

Figure 13.3. Infant Temperament in Children With and Without Behavioral and Emotional Problems in the Clinical Range.

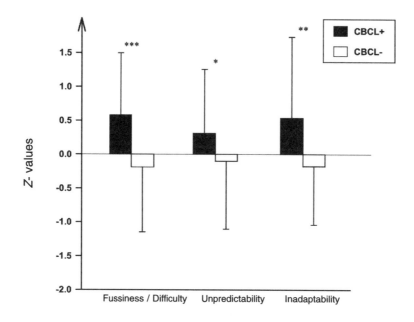

Note. (CBCL+) includes children with behavioral/emotional problems in the clinical range in at least one of the six CBCL/2-3 syndrome scales; (CBCL-) includes children who did not exceed the 98th percentile on any of the scales. ($M \pm SD$).

Figure 13.4. Prediction of Externalizing Problems at 30 Months From Early Infant, Maternal, and Relationship Variables

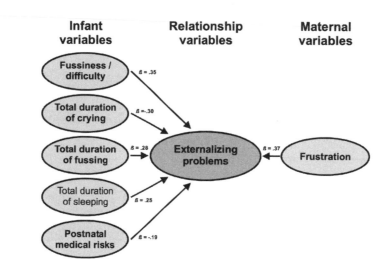

Note. CBCL/2-3. Multiple stepwise regression analysis. (Adjusted R^2 =.35; $F(6, 98)$ = 10.5, $p \leq$ .001.)

Figure 13.5. Prediction of Internalizing Problems at 30 Months From Early Infant, Maternal, and Relationship Variables.

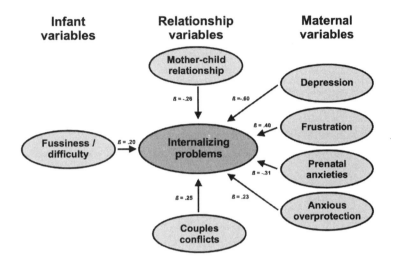

Note. CBCL/2-3. Multiple stepwise regression analysis. (Adjusted R^2 = .36; $F(7, 97)$ = 9.5, $p \leq$ .001.)

are the only infant characteristics in this regression model, which explains 27% (adjusted R^2) of the variance in the dependent variable.

Finally, we conducted a logistic regression analysis to predict belonging to either the CBCL+ or CBCL– groups. The only significant predictors were infant fussiness/difficulty and conflicts in the parents' relationship, $X^2(2, N = 105)$ = 18.1, $p \leq$ .001 (two-tailed test).

DISCUSSION

The results of this follow-up examination show that infants who had attended the Munich Program within the first 6 months of life for a crying problem and been treated together with their parents were still viewed as more difficult and stubborn at the age of 30 months than were control children who had not had a crying problem in infancy. In addition, former criers exhibited higher scores for aggressive behavior, anxiety/depression, sleep problems, somatic problems, and social withdrawal as well as for externalizing and internalizing problems on a validated and standardized screening instrument used to detect behavioral and emotional disorders in toddlerhood. They were also far more likely to be rated in the clinical range for aggressive behavior, anxiety/depression, social withdrawal, and internalizing problems. With the exception of a shorter duration of daytime sleep among the former extreme criers, the groups did not differ with regard to indicators for sleep problems at follow-up as derived from the behavior logs. Both internalizing and externalizing problems were predictable from the initial diagnostic data.

To date, a total of 13 longitudinal studies of the development of excessive infant crying have been published, including our own follow-up study. In only 1 of these studies (Wolke et al., 2002) a clinical sample of children was followed up whose families had sought out a self-help group because of excessive crying. Wolke et al. (2002) reported that children who had once cried excessively exhibited more frequent hyperactivity and conduct problems in the clinical range at the age of 8 to 10 years than did an age- and sex-matched control group. The other studies primarily recruited community-based samples. Except for later sleep problems, these studies found only sporadic associations between excessive infant crying and later behavioral problems (Rautava et al., 1993, 1995; St. James-Roberts et al., 1995, 1998a, 1998b; Wolke et al., 1995).

Differences Between Clinical and Nonclinical Samples

In summary, it is notable that an unfavorable prognosis of excessive crying is most evident in studies conducted on clinical samples. Obviously, the degree of infant crying or fussing alone is inadequate for identifying infants at elevated risk for later emotional or behavioral problems. Presumably, other characteristics in which clinical populations and community-based samples differ need to be considered for the prognosis. In our sample, we observed that the crying problem persisted markedly beyond the first 3 months of life in 60% of the infants seen by us and that it was frequently accompanied by other regulatory disorders. The study conducted by Wolke et al. (2002) also pointed out the role of the persistence and pervasiveness of excessive infant crying for the development of hyperactivity and conduct problems. Neither persistence nor pervasiveness of the crying problem as moderating factors were included in any of the studies on community-based samples. Furthermore, our data show that families with a crying problem are also characterized by multiple prenatal and postnatal risks, psychological problems in the mother, inadequate or exhausted resources, and markedly distressed mother–child relationships (Papoušek & von Hofacker, 1995, 1998; see also chapter 5). The community-based samples in the nonclinical studies, on the other hand, came from populations that were less stressed (Lehtonen et al., 2000).

Effects of Early Interventions

Nonclinical prospective studies have repeatedly shown connections between excessive infant crying and sleep problems in toddlerhood (Rautava et al., 1993, 1995; St. James-Roberts et al., 1995, 1998a, 1998b; Wolke et al., 1995). Children who had previously cried excessively exhibited higher scores for sleep problems on the CBCL/2-3 in our follow-up study as well. However, the former criers did not differ from the controls either in the frequency of sleep problems in the clinical range or in indicators for problematic sleep behavior as based on parents' behavior log entries. This may point to a potential long-term preventive effect of the therapeutic intervention aimed at consolidating sleep–wake organization and falling asleep independently. For ethical reasons, however, it was not possible to study the developmental outcomes of excessive infant crying in relation to an untreated control group, which means that our follow-up study cannot distinguish between developmental and therapeutic effects. The study conducted by Wolke and colleagues (2002), on the other hand, reported on the behavioral development of an untreated control group. In this study, families with infants who cried excessively were grouped into three treatment conditions (behavioral counseling, empathic support, no treatment; Wolke, Gray, & Meyer, 1994). Although behavioral counseling, which like empathic support was done by trained nonspecialists over the telephone, proved superior, with a reduction in the duration of crying and fussing at a follow-up 3 months after the invention, the children in all three groups continued to cry or fuss markedly more than the normal criers. When Wolke and colleagues (2002) followed up at 8 to 10 years, they found no treatment effects on the degree of externalizing problems. Exhausted and frustrated parents may well find the sharing of experiences in a self-help group to be comforting and reinforcing. However, the work of nonspecialists, even over the telephone, appears not to be comparable to that performed by skilled counselors and personnel in a specialized program. The lack of treatment effects on the degree of externalizing problems in the study conducted by Wolke and colleagues (2002) may therefore be attributed less to the excessive criers' resistance to therapy than to the low long-term effectiveness of counseling by nonspecialists.

Explanatory Models

A number of possible explanations suggest themselves for the connections between excessive crying and later behavioral and emotional problems. Both early infant crying and later behavioral and emotional problems may, for example, be manifestations of a difficult temperament (Thomas, Chess, & Birch, 1968). In this model, infant behavioral problems develop into later problematic behavior because of relatively stable predisposing factors. Carey (1984) and Lester, Boukydis, Garcia-Coll, and Hole (1990) also argued that excessive infant crying is an early manifestation of constitutional characteristics. One generally accepted definitional criterion of temperament is the stability of individual characteristics over time (Goldsmith et al., 1987). In the present study and other studies in which data were collected by questionnaire (Sloman et al., 1990; St. James-Roberts et al., 1995, 1998a, 1998b; Wolke et al., 2002) the significant differences between excessive criers and controls in difficult temperament have been reported to persist into childhood. This seems to be consistent with the thesis advanced by Carey (1984) and Lester and colleagues (1990). In addition, the results of our regression analyses show that infant fussiness/difficulty and the stresses in the parents' relationship are significant predictors of their classification into groups with and without later behavioral and emotional problems in the clinical range. By the same token, infant fussiness/difficulty proved to be a significant and independent predictor for both externalizing and internalizing problems at the age of 30 months. Interestingly, different groups of variables contributed to the predictability of these two problems. Whereas, with the exception of maternal frustration, externalizing problems were explained primarily by infant characteristics, internalizing problems were primarily predicted by early maternal variables and the quality of the mother–child relationship, as well as by the parents' relationship. In terms of the temperament approach, these results may be interpreted as indications that aggressive/destructive behavior is primarily a manifestation of stable constitutional factors, whereas internalizing tendencies also involve relationship and environmental factors. Other authors have also reported on significant associations between dimensions of temperament and externalizing as well as internalizing behavioral problems (Caspi, Henry, McGee, Moffitt, & Silva, 1995; Colder, Mott, & Berman, 2002; Keenan, Shaw, Delliquadri, Giovannelli, & Walsh, 1998; Tschann, Kaiser, Chesney, Alkon, & Boyce, 1996).

Our results, however, also indicate that both externalizing and internalizing problems cannot be explained exclusively by the infant's temperament, but by the interplay of infant, maternal, and relationship variables. This is consistent with our dynamic systems model of the development of infant behavioral disorders (see chapter 4). Above and beyond this, we found only low to moderate—though significant—stability for inadaptability and fussiness/difficulty over the time span of our follow-up study ($r = .29$ and $r = .46$, respectively).

One possible reason for the low stability of these dimensions of temperament might be that temperamental characteristics during the first months of life are hardly distinguishable from adaptive problems related to maturation. Early on, Emde, Gaensbauer, and Harmon (1976) pointed to the cooccurrence of inexplicable fussiness during the first 3 months of life and maturational processes. Postnatal neurophysiological adjustments and reorganizational processes during the early months promote qualitatively new cognitive and social capacities. After the transformative phase of the first months of life, the crying problem usually resolves itself in the process of a biopsychosocial developmental shift (Emde et al., 1976) at the age of 2 to 3 months (Barr, Konner, Bakeman, & Adamson, 1991; St. James-Roberts, Bowyer, Varghese, & Sawdon, 1994; St. James-Roberts & Halil, 1991).

According to the double-hit hypothesis advanced by Lehtonen and colleagues (2000) the further course of excessive infant crying varies with the specific conditions in the infant's environment. In this model, unfavorable developmental trajectories are not the consequence of stable constitutional characteristics, but rather are the result of the interplay between infant characteristics and those of the surroundings. Similar to the goodness-of-fit model advanced by temperament researchers, the development of later behavioral problems is primarily dependent on how the parents deal with the difficult early postpartal adaptation phase, and how they react to their child's transient crying problems that are related to maturation. In this view, the association between excessive infant crying and later behavioral problems is conditioned by the characteristics of the parent–child interaction. Persistently dysfunctional and maladaptive reaction patterns of the parents to their child's behavior, and therefore unfavorable developmental outcomes, may be expected when already stressed parents are additionally confronted with a crying problem; in contrast, the prognosis for children with unstressed parents who have adequate resources is not necessarily negative.

The double-hit hypothesis does not, however, take into consideration that psychosocial stressors not only make it difficult for parents to interact appropriately, but may also lead to increased reactivity and decreased self-regulatory competencies in the infant as a result of prenatal endocrine influences on fetal brain development (Wurmser, 2007; Wurmser et al., 2006). In other words, prenatal stress may possibly underlie both difficult infant temperament and the inhibition or poor attunement of intuitive parental competencies. Our developmental dynamic systems model (Papoušek & von Hofacker, 1995; see also chapter 4) greatly expands on the double-hit model by including complex transactions between infant prenatal, perinatal, and postnatal factors and the family environment.

IMPLICATIONS FOR CLINICAL PRACTICE

On the basis of the existing body of research, the differences between clinical and nonclinical samples have important implications for clinical practice. For infants whose parents seek counseling and treatment for excessive crying, the probability of developing later behavioral and emotional problems seems to be increased if (a) the crying problem persists beyond the usual first 3 months of life, (b) the crying problem occurs in the context of other disorders of behavioral regulation such as feeding problems and/or dysphoric-motor restlessness, (c) the affected families are stressed by multiple prenatal and postnatal risk factors, and (d) signs of impaired or disordered parent–child relationships with regard to their functional and adaptive quality are present. The results of clinical studies have shown that the role of so-called 3-month colic should not be underestimated as a transient infant behavioral problem. Nuanced counseling and treatment that is tailored to individual stresses and needs is particularly important in cases in which the risk factors cited here are clustered together.

REFERENCES

Achenbach, T. M., Edelbrock, C., & Howell, C. T. (1987). Empirically based assessment of the behavioral/emotional problems of 2- and 3-year-old children. *Journal of Abnormal Child Psychology, 15*, 629–650.

Barr, R. G., Konner, M., Bakeman, R., & Adamson, L. (1991). Crying in !Kung San infants: A test of the cultural specificity hypothesis. *Developmental Medicine and Child Neurology, 33*, 601–610.

Bates, J. E., Freeland, C. A. B., & Lounsbury, M. L. (1979). Measurement of infant difficultness. *Child Development, 50*, 794–803.

Carey, W. B. (1984). "Colic"—primary excessive crying as an infant-environment interaction. *Pediatric Clinics of North America, 31*, 993–1005.

Caspi, A., Henry, B., McGee, R. O., Moffitt, T. E., & Silva, P. A. (1995). Temperamental origins of child and adolescent behavior problems: From age three to age fifteen. *Child Development, 66*, 55–68.

Castro-Rodriguez, J. A., Stern, D. A., Halonen, M., Wright, A. L., Holberg, C. J., Taussig, L. M., & Martinez, F. D. (2001). Relation between infantile colic and asthma/atopy: A prospective study in an unselected population. *Pediatrics, 108*, 878–882.

Colder, C. R., Mott, J. A., & Berman, A. S. (2002). The interactive effects of infant activity level and fear on growth trajectories of early childhood behavior problems. *Development and Psychopathlogy, 14*, 1–23.

Cox, J. L., Holden, J. M., & Sagovsky, R. (1987). Detection of postnatal depression. Development of the 10-item Edinburgh Postnatal Depression Scale. *British Journal of Psychiatry, 150*, 782–786.

Elliott, M. R., Fisher, K., & Ames, E. W. (1988). The effects of rocking on the state and respiration of normal and excessive cryers. *Canadian Journal of Psychology, 42*, 163–172.

Elliott, M. R., Pedersen, E. L., & Mogan, J. (1997). Early infant crying: Child and family follow-up at three years. *Canadian Journal of Nursing Research, 29*, 47–67.

Emde, R. N., Gaensbauer, T. J., & Harmon, R. J. (1976). Emotional expression in infancy: A behavioral study. *Psychological Issues: A Monograph Series, 10*. New York: International Universities Press.

Engfer, A., & Gavranidou, M. (1987). Antecedents and consequences of maternal sensitivity. A longitudinal study. In H. Rauh & H. C. Steinhausen (Eds.), *Psychobiology and early development* (pp. 71–99). Amsterdam: Elsevier Science.

Fegert, J. M. (1996). Verhaltensdimensionen und Verhaltensprobleme bei zweieinhalbjährigen Kindern. *Praxis der Kinderpsychologie und Kinderpsychiatrie, 45,* 83–94.

Forsyth, B. W. C., & Canny, P. F. (1991). Perceptions of vulnerability 3¹/₂ years after problems of feeding and crying behavior in early infancy. *Pediatrics, 88,* 757–763.

Forsyth, B. W. C., Leventhal, J. M., & McCarthy, P. L. (1985). Mothers' perceptions of problems of feeding and crying behaviors. A prospective study. *American Journal of Diseases of Children, 139,* 269–272.

Goldsmith, H. H., Buss, A. H., Plomin, R., Rothbart, M. K., Thomas, A., Chess, S., Hinde, R. A., & McCall, R. B. (1987). Roundtable: What is temperament? Four approaches. *Child Development, 58,* 505–529.

Keefe, M. R., Kotzer, A. M., Froese-Fretz, A., & Curtin, M. (1996). A longitudinal comparison of irritable and nonirritable infants. *Nursing Research, 45,* 4–9.

Keenan, K., Shaw, D., Delliquadri, E., Giovannelli, J., & Walsh, B. (1998). Evidence for the continuity of early problem behaviors: Application of a developmental model. *Journal of Abnormal Child Psychology, 26,* 441–452.

Laucht, M. (2002). Störungen des Kleinkind- und Vorschulalters. In G. Esser (Ed.), *Lehrbuch der Klinischen Psychologie und Psychotherapie des Kindes- und Jugendalters* (pp. 102–118). Stuttgart, Germany: Thieme Verlag.

Lehtonen, L., Gormally, S., & Barr, R. G. (2000). "Clinical pies" for etiology and outcome in infants presenting with early increased crying. In R. G. Barr, B. Hopkins, & J. Green (Eds.), *Crying as a sign, a symptom and a signal: Clinical, emotional and developmental aspects of infant and toddler crying* (pp. 67–95). London: Mac Keith Press.

Lehtonen, L., Korhonen, T., & Korvenranta, H. (1994). Temperament and sleeping patterns in colicky infants during the first year of life. *Journal of Developmental and Behavioral Pediatrics, 15,* 416–420.

Lester, B. M., Boukydis, C. Z., Garcia-Coll, C. T., & Hole, W. T. (1990). Colic for developmentalists. *Infant Mental Health Journal, 11,* 321–333.

Leupold, S. (2001). *Implikationen von exzessivem Schreien im Säuglingsalter für spätere Verhaltensmerkmale bei Kindern im Alter von 30 Monaten. Eine Follow-Up-Erhebung.* Diplomarbeit, Psychological Faculty, Ludwig-Maximilians-Universität Munich.

Lips, N. H., Bloom, K., & Barnett, H. (1990). *Psychometric evaluation of a new scale to measure maternal self-confidence.* Unpublished manuscript.

Minde, K., Popiel, K., Leos, N., Falkner, S., Parker, K., & Handley-Derry, M. (1993). The evaluation and treatment of sleep disturbances in young children. *Journal of Child Psychology and Psychiatry, 34,* 521–533.

Oberklaid, F., Sanson, A., Pedlow, R., & Prior, M. (1993). Predicting preschool behaviour problems from temperament and other variables in infancy. *Pediatrics, 91,* 113–120.

Papoušek, M., & von Hofacker, N. (1995). Persistent crying and parenting: Search for a butterfly in a dynamic system. *Early Development and Parenting, 4,* 209–224.

Papoušek, M., & von Hofacker, N. (1998). Persistent crying in early infancy: A non-trivial condition of risk for the developing mother-infant relationship. *Child: Care, Health and Development, 24,* 395–424.

Papoušek, M., Wurmser, H., & von Hofacker, N. (2001). Clinical perspectives on unexplained early crying: Challenges and risks for infant mental health and parent-infant relationships. In R. G. Barr, I. St. James-Roberts, & M. R. Keefe (Eds.), *New evidence on unexplained early infant crying: Its origins, nature and management* (pp. 289–316). Skillman, NJ: Johnson & Johnson Pediatric Institute Round Table Series.

Räihä, H., Lehtonen, L., Korhonen, T., & Korvenranta, H. (1996). Family life 1 year after infantile colic. *Archives of Pediatric and Adolescent Medicine, 150,* 1032–1036.

Räihä, H., Lehtonen, L., Korhonen, T., & Korvenranta, H. (1997). Family functioning 3 years after infantile colic. *Journal of Developmental and Behavioral Pediatrics, 18,* 290–294.

Räihä, H., Lehtonen, L., & Korvenranta, H. (1995). Family context of infantile colic. *Infant Mental Health Journal, 16,* 206–217.

Rautava, P., Helenius, H., & Lehtonen, L. (1993). Psychosocial predisposing factors for infantile colic. *British Medical Journal, 307,* 600–604.

Rautava, P., Lehtonen, L., Helenius, H., & Sillanpaa, M. (1995). Infantile colic: Child and family three years later. *Pediatrics, 96,* 43–47.

Richman, N. (1981). A community survey of characteristics of one- to two-year-olds with sleep disruptions. *Journal of the American Academy of Child Psychiatry, 20,* 281–291.

Sarimski, K. (1993). Aufrechterhaltung von Schlafstörungen im frühen Kindesalter: Entwicklungs-psychopathologisches Modell und Pilot-Studie. *Praxis der Kinderpsychologie und Kinderpsychiatrie, 42,* 2–8.

Shaver, B. A. (1974). Maternal personality and early adaptation as related to infantile colic. In P. M. Shereshefsky & L. J. Yarrow (Eds.), *Psychological aspects of a first pregnancy and early postnatal adaptation* (pp. 209–215). New York: Raven Press.

Sloman, J., Bellinger, D. C., & Krentzel, C. P. (1990). Infantile colic and transient developmental lag in the first year of life. *Child Psychiatry and Human Development, 21,* 25–36.

Stifter, C. A., & Bono, M. A. (1998). The effect of infant colic on maternal self-perceptions and mother-infant attachment. *Child: Care, Health and Development, 24,* 339–351.

Stifter, C. A., & Braungart, J. M. (1992). Infant colic: A transient condition with no apparent effects. *Journal of Applied Developmental Psychology, 13,* 447–462.

Stifter, C. A., & Spinrad, T. L. (2002). The effect of excessive crying on the development of emotion regulation. *Infancy, 3,* 133–152.

St. James-Roberts, I., Bowyer, J., Varghese, S., & Sawdon, J. (1994). Infant crying patterns in Manali and London. *Child: Care, Health and Development, 20,* 323–237.

St. James-Roberts, I., Conroy, S., & Wilsher, K. (1995). Clinical, developmental and social aspects of infant crying and colic. *Early Development and Parenting, 4,* 177–189.

St. James-Roberts, I., Conroy, S., & Wilsher, K. (1998a). Links between maternal care and persistent infant crying in the early months. *Child: Care, Health and Development, 24,* 353–376.

St. James-Roberts, I., Conroy, S., & Wilsher, K. (1998b). Stability and outcome of persistent infant crying. *Infant Behavior and Development, 21,* 411–435.

St. James-Roberts, I., & Halil, T. (1991). Infant crying patterns in the first year: Normal community and clinical findings. *Journal of Child Psychology and Psychiatry, 32,* 951–968.

Thomas, A., Chess, S., & Birch, H. G. (1968). *Temperament and behavior disorders in children.* New York: New York University Press.

Tschann, J. M., Kaiser, P., Chesney, M. A., Alkon, A., & Boyce, W. T. (1996). Resilience and vulnerability among preschool children: Family functioning, temperament, and behavior problems. *Journal of the American Academy of Child and Adolescent Psychiatry, 35,* 184–192.

Wessel, M. A., Cobb, J. C., Jackson, E. B., Harris, G. S., & Detwiler, A. C. (1954). Paroxysmal fussing in infancy, sometimes called "colic." *Pediatrics, 14,* 421–434.

Wolke, D., Gray, P., & Meyer, R. (1994). Excessive infant crying: A controlled study of mothers helping mothers. *Pediatrics, 94,* 322–332.

Wolke, D., Meyer, R., Ohr, B., & Riegel, K. (1995). Co-morbidity of crying and feeding problems with sleeping problems in infancy: Concurrent and predictive associations. *Early Development and Parenting, 4,* 191–207.

Wolke, D., Rizzo, P., & Woods, S. (2002). Persistent infant crying and hyperactivity problems in middle childhood. *Pediatrics, 109,* 1054–1060.

Wurmser, H. (2007). Einfluss der pränatalen Stressbelastung der Mutter auf die kindliche Verhaltensregulation im ersten Lebenshalbjahr. In K. H. Brisch & T. Hellbruegge (Eds.), *Die Anfänge der Eltern-Kind-Bindung* (pp. 129–156). Stuttgart, Germany: Klett-Cotta.

Wurmser, H., Rieger, M., Domogalla, C., Kahnt, A., Buchwald, J., Kowatsch, M., et al. (2006). Association between life stress during pregnancy and infant crying in the first six months postpartum: A prospective longitudinal study. *Early Human Development, 82,* 341–349.

ZERO TO THREE. (1994). *Diagnostic classification: 0–3. Diagnostic classification of mental health and developmental disorders of infancy and early childhood.* Arlington, VA: National Center for Clinical Infant Programs.

PROBLEMS OF BEHAVIORAL AND EMOTIONAL REGULATION: PRECURSORS TO PSYCHIATRIC DISORDERS IN LATER CHILDHOOD?

Manfred Laucht
Martin H. Schmidt
Günter Esser

INTRODUCTION

In their efforts to create a taxonomy of psychiatric problems in children, psychopathologists usually come up with two basic groups of disorders. *Categorical* classification systems of psychiatric disorders, such as the World Health Organization's (1990) *International Statistical Classification of Diseases and Related Health Problems—Tenth Revision (ICD–10)* or the American Psychiatric Association's (1994) *Diagnostic and Statistical Manual of Mental Disorders—Fourth Edition (DSM–IV)*, distinguish between behavior disorders and emotional disorders. Included among the behavior disorders are attention deficit hyperactivity disorders, conduct disorders, and oppositional-defiant disorders; emotional disorders include separation anxiety, phobias, social anxiety, and depressive disorders.

Similar distinctions are made when *dimensional* approaches to classification are used, such as that of Achenbach (1991). Achenbach derived two basic dimensions of disorders from comprehensive empirical studies and statistical analyses. The externalizing dimension includes aggressive and antisocial behavior problems, while the internalizing dimension comprises problems such as social withdrawal, somatic complaints, and anxious-depressive behavior.

Comparative cultural studies have shown that both groups of disorders are detectable and stable across cultures (Döpfner et al., 1996; Verhulst & Achenbach, 1995), although they may be perceived completely differently within any particular culture. Thus, behavior disorders are constantly in the limelight, whereas emotional disorders are seldom seen as a problem by the public. This difference in selective attention is mirrored in the current research as well. Although our understanding of the conditions leading to the development of behavior disorders is relatively sophisticated (Stoff, Breiling, & Maser, 1997), we lack fundamental knowledge about the social and psychological contexts of emotional disorders (Shaw, Keenan, Vondra, Delliquadri, & Giovannelli, 1997).

These considerations notwithstanding, researchers and psychopathologists must ask whether such purely descriptive categories are corroborated by differential etiologies and specific pathogeneses. One interdisciplinary approach that has introduced a developmental dimension into psychopathology and seeks to create a bridge between developmental psychology and clinical psychology has begun to deal with precisely such questions. In a seminal article, Sroufe and Rutter (1984) summarized the tasks facing developmental psychopathology as follows: "The developmental psychopathologist is concerned with the origins and time course of a given disorder, its varying manifestations and development, its precursors and sequelae, and its relation to non-disordered patterns of behavior" (p. 18). According to the authors, central questions for developmental psychopathology include the following, among others: At what age does a disorder begin? How do the frequency and manifestations of a disorder change over its developmental course? How stable is a disorder in the transition from childhood to adolescence? And what are the developmental precursors of later disorders? (see also Costello & Angold, 1995).

Longitudinal assessments that illustrate the chronological characteristics of a disorder promise answers to such questions. The data from prospective longitudinal studies of birth cohorts are particularly well-suited because they reflect child development from birth over a longer period of time. Sroufe and Rutter (1984) stressed this when they wrote, "Generally, these studies will require costly and taxing longitudinal research. But in the end, such research can yield valuable information for guiding early intervention and primary prevention" (p. 27).

The issue of developmental precursors of later disorders is addressed in this chapter, presenting the results of a prospective longitudinal study that examines the significance of infant regulatory problems as possible precursors of behavior disorders in later childhood. Questions studied in this investigation include the following: (a) What is the developmental outcome of infant regulatory problems into school age? (b) How can groups at risk for developing later behavior disorders be identified? (c) What influence do dysfunctional interactional patterns in early mother–child interactions have as potential moderators of the developmental outcome? (d) What role do infant risk factors (pre- and perinatal complications, family adversity) play as copredictors of later behavior disorders?

THE MANNHEIM STUDY OF AT-RISK CHILDREN

More than 20 years ago, a research group at the Mannheim Central Institute of Mental Health began to study so-called "at-risk children" (Esser et al., 1990; Laucht, Esser, & Schmidt, 1989). The focus of their interest was children whose development seemed to be particularly jeopardized by early stress factors such as prematurity or mental illness in the mother or father. The cornerstone of this prospective longitudinal study following the long-term development of at-risk children was begun with the support of the Deutsche Forschungsgemeinschaft (German Research Foundation), and came to be called the Mannheim Study of At-Risk Children (Laucht, Esser, & Schmidt, 2000b). The primary goals of this research were to provide answers to questions such as: Which children are particularly at risk? Which developmental functions become disordered, and to what degree? How and when do developmental impairments become manifest? How persistent are early disorders, and what consequences do they have? Are organic or psychosocial risk factors more important for the outcome, and how do they interact? How do early risk factors interact with individual and family characteristics? And, which children are protected from the adverse consequences of early risk?

Sample

To study these questions, the Mannheim Study of At-Risk Children followed a cohort of 362 children (184 girls and 178 boys born between 1986 and 1988) and their parents over the course of the children's development into adulthood. Data were collected at regular intervals (at 3 months and at 2, 4½, 8, 11, and 15 years), beginning in 1986 with a current follow-up assessment in young adulthood (19 to 20 years). The study sample was selected such that children with organic risk factors (mild to severe pre- and perinatal complications) and children with psychosocial risk factors (unfavorable family situations to a lesser or greater extent) were overrepresented. Both types of factors were combined in the design of the study, resulting in a broad range of risk constellations that encompassed both a group without any risk factors and—at the other extreme—a group that was highly stressed by both organic and psychosocial risks. More detailed information about sample selection may be found in several publications (Laucht, Esser, & Schmidt, 1997; Laucht et al., 2000b). A total of 324 children without mental or motor disabilities for whom complete longitudinal data were available were included in the current analysis.

Study variables

Risk factors. The stress to a child posed by factors that jeopardize development was determined at the time of birth. Organic risk factors were defined as pre- and perinatal problems related to medical complications during pregnancy, delivery, and the neonatal period (such as gestosis, asphyxia, or seizures). To quantify the level of stress, a cumulative risk index was created that reflected the number of complications ranging from 0 to 9. *Psychosocial* risk factors were determined from an array of family adversity factors present at birth based on information given by the parents at the initial assessment. The list comprised problems relating to the parents (such as mental illness), the partnership (such as disharmony), and the family's living conditions (such as chronic difficulties). Analogous to the procedure for quantifying the organic risk factors, a cumulative risk index was formed in which the number of psychosocial stress factors affecting a family were added up (for a precise definition of the risk criteria, see Laucht et al., 1997).

Problems of behavioral and emotional regulation. Because the notion of disorders of behavioral and emotional regulation was largely unknown at the time the Mannheim Study of At-Risk Children began, and because there was no standardized diagnostic procedure or empirically based classification of psychiatric disorders in infancy, we developed our own procedure that was based on both traditional infant pediatrics and on the infant temperament model. A parent interview, which was constructed along the lines of the Mannheim Parent Interview (MPI; Esser et al., 1990) for early infancy, was conducted at the age of 3 months to diagnose sleep, feeding, and digestive problems. In addition, a larger number of behavior problems were observed by experts in various situations, and the parents were interviewed about them as well (see Laucht, Esser, & Schmidt, 1992).

The basis for the selection of behavioral dimensions was the temperament model advanced by Thomas, Chess, and Birch (1968). Table 14.1 shows a list of the selected temperament dimensions and the behavior problems derived from them. Generally, a negative deviation on one dimension corresponded to a problem behavior; in several cases in which both extremes of a dimension have negative implications (e.g., in the level of motor activity), we derived two problem behaviors (hypoactivity and hyperactivity). Behavioral evaluations were collected in two ways, first from information gathered in a highly structured parent interview, and second based on behavioral observations in four standardized situations on two different days in a familiar environment (at home) and in an unfamiliar environment (the clinic). This procedure had the advantage that our evaluation of an infant was dependent on neither the parents' information alone nor on one-time observations. The evaluations were completed by trained raters on a 5-point scale. Agreement between two raters was satisfactory to high (mean kappa = .68, range = .51–.84). If the evaluation of a child in the majority of situations showed a problematic deviation from the mean of a scale, a behavioral characteristic was judged as disturbed.

Table 14.1. Behavior Problems in Infancy.

	Behavioral dimension	Behavior problem
1	Motor activity	Hypoactive, hyperactive
2	Daily rhythm	Irregular
3	Affective quality	Dysphoric
4	Sensitivity	Hypersensitive
5	Intensity of response	Apathetic, irritable
6	Attention	Uninterested, distractible
7	Approach to new situations	Anxious
8	Adaptability to change	Delayed
9	Adaptability to stress	Low tolerance of stress
10	Social contact	Withdrawn

Four problem patterns were established using principal components analysis (Laucht, Esser, & Schmidt, 1993). Three of these (accounting for most of the common variance) were included in the group definitions below: an Irritability factor (dysphoric, hypersensitive), a Hyporeactivity factor (apathetic, uninterested), and a factor of Somatic Regulatory Problems (sleep, feeding, and digestive problems). Infants who exhibited above-average values (> 1 SD) on one of these factors were classified as regulatory-disordered (n = 120, corresponding to 37.0%). Infants with above average values on the Irritability factor and the Somatic Regulatory Problems factor were assigned to a group with multiple regulatory problems (n = 55, corresponding to 17.0%). This definition deviates considerably from the definitions of regulatory disorders that have since found their way into the literature and that underlie this book; that is, those that are not based on empirically determined cutoff values but on diagnostic criteria formulated by experts. To express this difference semantically, we discuss *regulatory problems* in this chapter in contradistinction to *regulatory disorders*.

Child psychiatric disorders. Age-adjusted versions of the MPI (Esser, Blanz, Geisel, & Laucht, 1989) were used to determine externalizing and internalizing problems in children after the age of 2 years. The MPI is a proven highly structured interview instrument from which conclusions may be drawn based on parent information about a child's emotional and behavioral problems. Two groups of measures of psychiatric problems were created from the information gained:

1. *Categorical measures:* (a) expert clinical assessment of the severity of a psychological impairment on a 7-point scale and (b) diagnostic assessment of all children classified as disturbed according to *ICD-10* (WHO, 1990) research criteria;

2. *Continuous measures:* diagnosis-specific symptom scores representing the sum of all problems that are characteristic of externalizing disorders (hyperkinetic and conduct disorders) and internalizing disorders (emotional and developmentally specific disorders).

Early mother–child interaction. Mothers and infants were observed in a videotaped semistandardized setting to assess the quality of the early mother–child interaction. The observation session, which lasted 10 minutes, was done at the age of 3 months in a playing and nursing situation in our video lab. Two different coding procedures, both developed by us, were used by trained raters to code the videotapes:

1. The Mannheim Rating Scales of Mother-Child Interaction in Infancy (Esser, Scheven, Petrova, Laucht, & Schmidt, 1989) is a qualitative rating system assessing the mother's and infant's behavior in an interaction situation. The rating system, which is based on models put forward by Field (1980) and Keller, Gauda, and Miranda (1980) consists of eight 5-point scales to assess maternal behavior (emotion, tenderness, vocalization, lack of verbal restriction, congruence, variability, responsiveness/ sensitivity, stimulation) and five scales for assessing infant behavior (emotion, vocalization, direction of gaze, reactivity, readiness to interact). Ratings on each scale were made every minute, resulting in a total of 130 ratings per dyad. Scores were formed by adding up the ratings for each scale over the entire interaction time.

2. The qualitative assessment was complemented by a microanalytic procedure assessing, to the second, the occurrence and duration of precisely defined behaviors of the mother and child (Mannheim Category System for the Microanalysis of Early Mother-Child Interaction; Jörg et al., 1994). The following behaviors were coded: vocalization (negative, positive, off), facial expression (positive, neutral, negative), and direction of gaze (face-to-face, toy, other) of both mother and child, as well as the posture (close, distant) and activity of the mother (playing, diapering, neither). In addition to this microanalytic assessment, longer lasting and more complex behavioral and interactional patterns were coded using interval coding. We subsequently used the maternal responsiveness scale, assessing contingent and appropriate responses by the mother to the behavior of the child. Here, we distinguished between responses within three communication channels: vocal (e.g., the mother consoles verbally or vocally), mimic (e.g., the mother imitates the child), and motor (e.g., the mother reacts by kissing her infant's tummy). The presence of this behavior pattern was coded at 15-second intervals. The codings were added up for the total interaction time across the three communications channels, resulting in an overall score.

RESULTS

Prognosis of Children With Problems of Behavioral and Emotional Regulation

A first glance at the long-term social-emotional development of infants with regulatory problems that extend into school age yielded a relatively positive outcome. Figure 14.1 shows the rates of psychiatric problems at the ages of 2 to 11 years in the group of children with infant behavioral and emotional regulation problems (n = 120) and of the control group of children who were undisturbed in infancy (n = 204). Although the children who had been disturbed in infancy exhibited higher rates of psychiatric problems at all assessments, the rates were only slightly elevated (significantly higher only at the preschool age) in comparison to the control group.

The low risk for persistence of infant problems became clear when we looked at the developmental course (see Figure 14.2). Of the 120 infants with regulatory problems, 33 (approximately one-quarter) were assessed as psychiatrically disordered at the age of 11; the other three-quarters had no psychiatric problems at this age. However, because the risk of becoming psychiatrically disordered at the age of 11 among previously undisturbed infants was only marginally lower (20%), the increase in relative risk (from one-fifth to one-fourth) was well below the level of statistical significance.

A more detailed analysis, however, revealed that this apparently favorable result represented only one side of the prognosis for problems of behavioral and emotional regulation and that there were subgroups

Figure 14.1. Psychiatric Problems in Children With Behavioral and Emotional Regulation Problems (at 3 Months) From Infancy to School-Age.

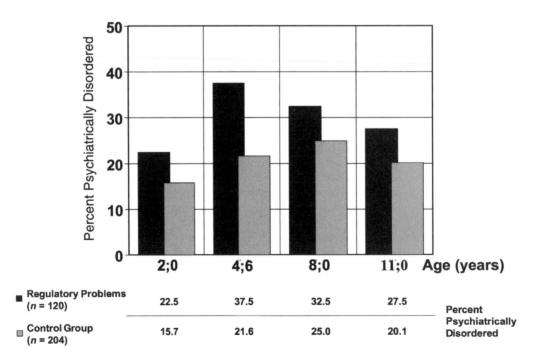

	2;0	4;6	8;0	11;0	
■ Regulatory Problems (*n* = 120)	22.5	37.5	32.5	27.5	Percent Psychiatrically Disordered
▢ Control Group (*n* = 204)	15.7	21.6	25.0	20.1	

with significantly increased risk for later developmental disorders. One at-risk group that we studied more closely in the following analyses consisted of infants with multiple regulatory problems who were both more frequently dysphoric and irritable and who suffered more frequently from sleep, feeding, and digestive problems. Infants with these symptoms (n = 55, corresponding to 17.0% of our sample) showed significantly more externalizing (hyperkinetic, oppositional, and aggressive) behavior problems over their entire development from the age of 2 to 11 than did children in the control group (see Figure 14.3). The number of internalizing (anxious and depressive) problems was also elevated over the observational period (see Figure 14.4).

Problems of Behavioral and Emotional Regulation and Mother–Child Interaction

Early problems of behavioral regulation not only manifested themselves in behavior problems, but they also had a deleterious effect on interactions between mother and child. In the playing and nursing scenes that we videotaped (using the Mannheim Rating Scales), significant differences in the behavior of both partners in comparison to the control group were observed. The mothers of infants with multiple regulatory problems were overall less sensitive and responsive (p < .01), they laughed (p < .01) and vocalized less with their child (p < .001), and they were more restricted in their behavior (p < .01), and stimulated their child less (p < .001). For their part, the infants smiled at their mothers less (p < .05) and were less responsive (p < .05).

Figure 14.2. Course of Psychiatric Problems From Infancy to School-Age.

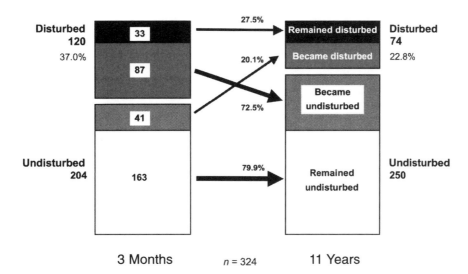

Figure 14.3. Externalizing Problems in Children With Multiple Regulatory Problems (at 3 Months) From Infancy to School-Age.

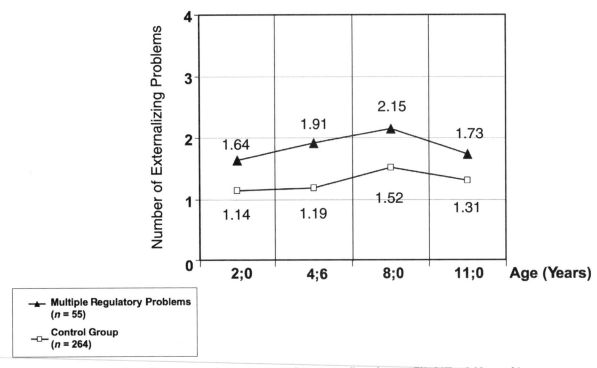

Note. Two-way repeated measures ANOVA: main effect of group, $F(1, 317) = 6.93$, $p < .01$.

Figure 14.4. Internalizing Problems in Children With Multiple Regulatory Problems (at 3 Months) From Infancy to School-Age.

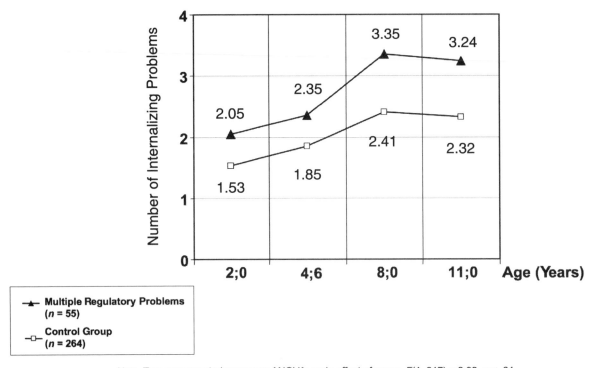

Note. Two-way repeated measures ANOVA: main effect of group, $F(1, 317) = 6.93$, $p < .01$.

We further analyzed whether such impairments in the mother–child interaction had any significance for the long-term prognosis of regulatory problems, in particular, whether their presence contributed to a particularly unfavorable outcome and their absence to a more favorable development. Figure 14.5 shows the number of psychiatric problems from 2 to 11 years in children with and without multiple regulatory problems for two subgroups, those with a more harmonious mother–child interaction (sum of all maternal rating scales ≥ median) versus those with a less harmonious interaction (sum < median). As can be seen, belonging to the group of infants with multiple regulatory problems and to the group with less harmonious early interactions was associated with increased problems over the course of the development. The negative effects seemed to be cumulative: The children who belonged to both groups exhibited the most unfavorable development with the most psychiatric problems.

The effects of infant regulatory problems and the (negative) quality of early mother–child interactions were not additive for all interactional characteristics. Two examples demonstrate that both factors may interact in their long-term consequences and may exacerbate each other. Infants with multiple regulatory problems whose mothers were relatively unresponsive to their babies had a particularly negative outcome with an increase in externalizing problems over the course of development (see Figure 14.6). This effect of maternal responsiveness (< median vs. ≥ median) was seen only in the infants with multiple regulation problems, but not in the undisturbed control group (as indicated by a statistically significant interaction).

This result in the form described here was limited to girls, with boys exhibiting precisely the opposite pattern (see Figure 14.7). Among boys, a high level of maternal responsiveness to infants with multiple

Figure 14.5. Psychiatric Problems in Children With Multiple Regulatory Problems (at 3 Months) From Infancy to School Age: Effect of the Quality of Early Mother–Child Interaction.

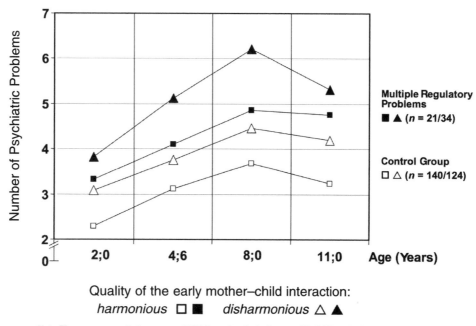

Note. Three-way repeated measures ANOVA: main effect of group, $F(1, 315) = 12.62$, $p < .001$; main effect of mother-child interaction, $F(1, 315) = 5.87$, $p < .05$; interaction effect, $F(1, 315) = 0.01$, *ns*.

Figure 14.6. Externalizing Problems of Girls With Multiple Regulatory Problems (at 3 Months) From Infancy to School Age: Effect of Maternal Responsiveness in Early Interaction.

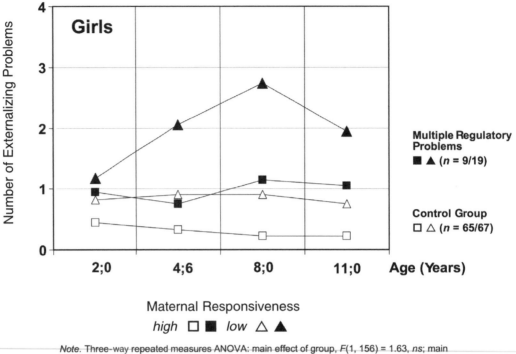

Note. Three-way repeated measures ANOVA: main effect of group, $F(1, 156) = 1.63$, *ns*; main effect of responsiveness, $F(1, 156) = 12.05$, $p < .001$; interaction effect, $F(1, 156) = 15.86$, $p < .001$.

Figure 14.7. Externalizing Problems of Boys With Multiple Regulatory Problems (at 3 Months) From Infancy to School Age: Effect of Maternal Responsiveness in Early Interaction.

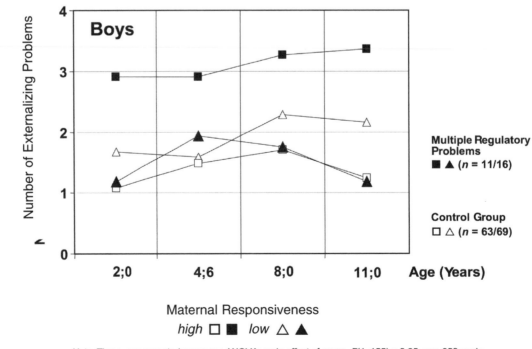

Note. Three-way repeated measures ANOVA: main effect of group, $F(1, 155) = 3.85$, $p = .052$; main effect of responsiveness, $F(1, 155) = 2.41$, *ns*; interaction effect, $F(1, 155) = 10.12$, $p < .005$.

regulatory disorders was associated with a higher number of externalizing problems starting at the age of 2 years. This finding may indicate that girls with regulatory problems were more sensitive to a lack of maternal responsiveness, whereas the development of boys with regulatory problems tended to be impaired more by a higher degree of responsiveness.

Problems of Behavioral and Emotional Regulation and Early Developmental Risks

Various studies have shown that there is an increased rate of problems in early behavioral regulation in infants whose mothers experienced pregnancy and delivery complications, or in infants born into psychosocially disadvantaged families (see, for example, Papoušek, 2002; von Hofacker, Jacubeit, Malinowski, & Papoušek, 1996). Our results were consistent with these findings (see Figure 14.8), indicating that the relative risk (odds ratio) for a number of pre- and perinatal complications as well as family adversity factors in the group of infants with multiple regulatory problems was significantly increased. Thus, infants with a very low birth weight (<1,500 g) were represented in this group three times more frequently than normal-weight babies. In addition, the percentage of infants in this group who grew up in overcrowded living conditions (as an indicator of poverty) was elevated by almost the same factor.

Psychosocial risk factors play a particularly important role in the prognosis of problems of behavioral and emotional regulation. Figure 14.9 presents the number of psychiatric problems between the ages of 2 and 11 in two groups of children: children with versus without multiple problems and children with a low versus high level of psychosocial risk. As can be seen, belonging to the group with regulatory

Figure 14.8. Relative Risk (Odds Ratio [OR]) of Multiple Infant Regulatory Problems Depending on Perinatal and Psychosocial Risk Factors.

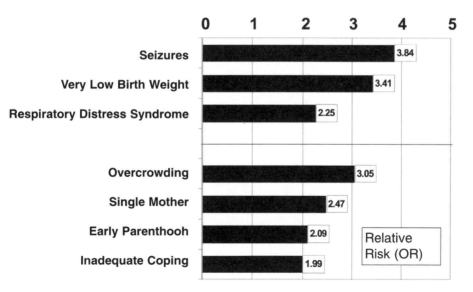

problems and to the group under psychosocial stress was associated with an increased number of psychiatric problems. The children who as infants suffered from regulatory problems while experiencing psychosocial risks had the highest number of later problems.

More detailed analyses revealed specific interactions between regulatory problems and family adversity. We found an increased risk for developing attention deficit/hyperactivity disorder (ADHD) symptoms in a subgroup of infants with multiple regulatory problems whose parents (particularly whose mothers) had experienced particularly stressed childhoods, such as growing up in broken homes. Figure 14.10 shows that children in this group exhibited a higher number of ADHD problems (such as hyperactivity or impulsivity) starting at the age of 2.

A more precise description of the jeopardized development of children with multiple regulatory problems, which would also document the predictive value of this condition, requires assessment of the relative significance of this predictor. Our analyses (see Figure 14.11) indicated that although the independent contribution of multiple regulatory problems in infancy was statistically significant in terms of predicting behavior disorders in later childhood, their effect was rather marginal as compared to other predictors. By far the most important predictor was found to be early psychosocial risk factors in the family (in particular a low level of education in the parents, followed by mental illness in one of the parents). By comparison, multiple infant regulatory problems contributed only a modest amount to the prediction.

Figure 14.9. Psychiatric Problems in Children With Multiple Regulatory Problems: Effect of Psychosocial Risk Factors.

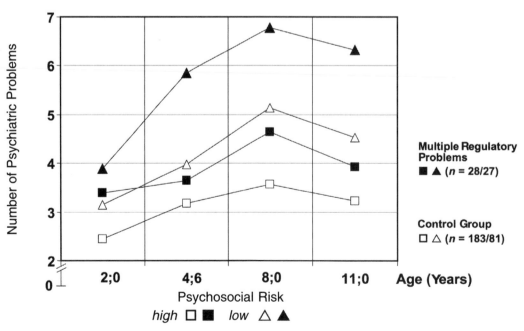

Note. Three-way repeated measures ANOVA: main effect of group, $F(1, 315) = 11.96$, $p < .001$; main effect of psychosocial risk, $F(1, 315) = 18.85$, $p < .001$; interaction effect, $F(1, 315) = 1.27$, ns.

Figure 14.10. ADHD Problems in Children With Multiple Regulatory Problems: Effect of Maternal Broken Home History.

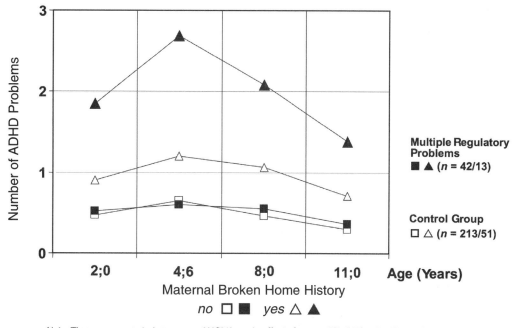

Note. Three-way repeated measures ANOVA: main effect of group, $F(1, 315) = 15.59$, $p < .001$; main effect of broken home, $F(1, 315) = 53.81$, $p < .001$; interaction effect, $F(1, 315) = 13.48$, $p < .001$.

Figure 14.11. Specific Contribution of Regulatory Problems in Infancy (Percentage of Explained Variance) to the Prediction of Psychiatric Problems at the Age of 11 After Controlling for Psychosocial Risk Factors (Hierarchical Multiple Regression).

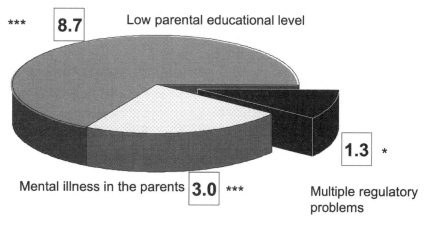

$***p < .001$. $*p < .05$.

Summary and Conclusions

Problems of behavioral and emotional regulation are a widespread phenomenon in infancy. In the form defined here, we made this diagnosis in more than one third of all 3-month-olds in our at-risk sample, in which obstetric and psychosocial risks were overrepresented. Half of these cases involved isolated problems (such as increased irritability or hyporeactivity, feeding problems, or sleep problems); the other half included problems in several areas of behavioral regulation.

When we looked at the outcome of infants with regulatory problems from infancy to school-age, we found an overall favorable prognosis for isolated regulatory problems. The rate of psychiatric disorders in this group was only slightly above that of the control group (and only significantly different during the transition to kindergarten at 4.5 years). By contrast, infants with multiple regulatory problems were at increased risk for later psychiatric disorders. Analyses revealed that they had significantly more externalizing (hyperkinetic, aggressive, and oppositional) symptoms over the entire course of their development as well as more internalizing (anxious and depressive) problems than did the control group.

Problems of behavioral and emotional regulation were in many cases associated with impairment in early mother–child interaction. Dysfunctional interactional patterns were manifested in, among other things, significantly shortened phases of positive interaction (e.g., reciprocal smiling), but also in less sensitivity and responsiveness by the mother, in comparison with the group of undisturbed infants. The presence of dysfunctional interactions increased the risk of later problems and therefore contributed to an unfavorable outcome. In addition to this nonspecific association, which was found to the same extent in the undisturbed control group, we also identified interactional patterns in the infants who previously had regulatory problems that are specifically associated with an increase in externalizing disorders. Depending on gender, completely opposite associations were observed. Whereas low responsiveness on the part of the mother increased the number of externalizing problems over the course of development in girls with multiple regulatory problems, in boys, this tended to be the case when the mother was highly responsive. This means that the outcome of problems of behavioral and emotional regulation in girls is more negatively affected by deprivation in the early mother–child interaction, and in boys by relative overstimulation. One possible explanation for this result may be derived from the fact that with regard to their cognitive and socioemotional abilities, girls have a developmental advantage over boys (Keenan & Shaw, 1997). This may explain why girls react more sensitively to a lack of maternal responsiveness, whereas boys may become overloaded by a high level of maternal responsiveness. This finding implies a gender-specific effect of dysfunctional interactional patterns on the prognosis for problems of behavioral and emotional regulation.

As in other studies, problems of early behavioral regulation accumulated when additional developmental risk factors were present (von Hofacker et al., 1996). This was particularly true for multiple regulatory problems that occurred increasingly in infants who were born with pre- and perinatal risks or who grew up in psychosocially disadvantaged families. Thus, a very low birth weight (<1,500 g) and living in poverty increased the risk of multiple regulatory problems. The presence of other developmental risk factors (particularly psychosocial ones) increased the probability of a negative outcome, with the children who had both regulatory problems and high levels of psychosocial stress having the worst prognosis.

The predictive significance of infant regulatory problems for later behavior problems should, however, not be overestimated. Their relative contribution in concert with other early predictors turned out to be comparatively low. Psychosocial risk factors in the family (such as a low level of education or mental illness in the parents) proved to be a far more significant predictor of later externalizing and internalizing disorders in children. The effects of these factors are mediated and moderated by the quality of the early mother–child interaction and result in particularly unfavorable prognostic constellations (Laucht et al., 2000b; Laucht, Esser, & Schmidt, 2002). The stability of regulatory problems increases considerably as early as toddlerhood (2 years), and their contribution to the long-term prognosis of later psychiatric disorders continues to grow (Laucht, Esser, & Schmidt, 2000a).

The research on risk factors in infancy has revealed that the disadvantageous consequences of early developmental risks are not inevitable, but are dependent on other developmental conditions that may play a considerable role in the transmission and mediation of harmful effects. From this perspective, the outcome for problems of behavioral and emotional regulation becomes more unfavorable the more generalized the disorder is, the more the early interaction is impaired, the more organically stressed the child is, and the more adverse the family living conditions are (see Papoušek, 1999). One important target group for preventive and early intervention is that of psychosocially disadvantaged families with multiple stress factors in which developmental problems and risks accumulate. There is a particular need for targeted support that is tailored to the problems and needs of this group and that will be accepted by these families, many of whom are seen as "hard to reach." This may, for example, involve regular home-based care. Because unfavorable development is heralded early on in dysfunctional parent–child interactions and because intervention in this context is both promising as well as relatively low threshold and noninvasive, infancy is a particularly good point at which to intervene. One example of a comprehensive early intervention program for infants and toddlers is the Early Head Start Program in United States, which specifically targets socially disadvantaged families (Early Head Start National Resource Center, 2001).

REFERENCES

Achenbach, T. M. (1991). *Manual for the Child Behavior Checklist/4-18 and 1991 Profile*. Burlington: University of Vermont.

American Psychiatric Association. (1994). *Diagnostic and statistical manual of mental disorders* (4th ed.). Washington, DC: Author.

Costello, E. J., & Angold, A. (1995). Developmental epidemiology. In D. Cicchetti & D. J. Cohen (Eds.), *Developmental psychopathology* (Vol. 1, pp. 23–56). New York: Wiley.

Döpfner, M., Schmeck, K., Poustka, F., Berner, W., Lehmkuhl, G., & Verhulst, F. (1996). Verhaltensauffälligkeiten von Kindern und Jugendlichen in Deutschland, den Niederlanden und den USA. *Nervenarzt, 67*, 960–967.

Early Head Start National Resource Center. (2001). *Early Head Start Program strategies: Socializations for infants and toddlers in the Early Head Start home-based program option*. Washington, DC: ZERO TO THREE.

Esser, G., Blanz, B., Geisel, B., & Laucht, M. (1989). *Mannheimer Elterninterview - Strukturiertes Interview zur Erfassung von kinderpsychiatrischen Auffälligkeiten*. Weinheim, Germany: Beltz.

Esser, G., Laucht, M., Schmidt, M., Löffler, W., Reiser, A., Stöhr, R.-M., et al. (1990). Behaviour problems and developmental status of 3-month-old infants in relation to organic and psychosocial risks. *European Archives of Psychiatry and Neurological Sciences, 239*, 384–390.

Esser, G., Scheven, A., Petrova, A., Laucht, M., & Schmidt, M. H. (1989). Mannheimer Beurteilungsskalen zur Erfassung der Mutter-Kind-Interaktion im Säuglingsalter (MBS-MKI-S). *Zeitschrift für Kinder- und Jugendpsychiatrie, 17*, 185–193.

Field, T. M. (1980). Interactions of preterm and term infants with their lower- and middle-class teenage and adult mothers. In T. M. Field, S. Goldberg, D. Stern, & A. M. Sostek (Eds.), *High-risk infants and children: Adult and peer interactions* (pp. 113–132). New York: Academic Press.

Jörg, M., Rose, F., Dinter, R., Villalba-Yantorno, P., Esser, G. Schmidt, M. H., & Laucht, M. (1994). Kategoriensystem zur Mikroanalyse der frühen Mutter-Kind-Interaktion. *Zeitschrift für Kinder- und Jugendpsychiatrie, 22*, 97–106.

Keenan, K., & Shaw, D. (1997). Developmental and social influences on young girls' early problem behavior. *Development and Psychopathology, 121*, 95–113.

Keller, H., Gauda, G., & Miranda, D. (1980). *Beobachtung, Beschreibung und Interpretation von Eltern-Kind-Interaktionen im ersten Lebensjahr.* Bericht Nr. 80-9, Institut für Psychologie, Technische Hochschule Darmstadt.

Laucht, M., Esser, G., & Schmidt, M. H. (1989). Verhaltensauffälligkeiten und Entwicklungsstörungen im Säuglingsalter: Einfluss von organischen und psychosozialen Risikofaktoren. In H. M. Weinmann (Ed.), *Aktuelle Neuropädiatrie 1988* (pp. 416–420). Berlin: Springer.

Laucht, M., Esser, G., & Schmidt, M. H. (1992). Verhaltensauffälligkeiten bei Säuglingen und Kleinkindern: Ein Beitrag zu einer Psychopathologie der frühen Kindheit. *Zeitschrift für Kinder- und Jugendpsychiatrie, 20*, 22–33.

Laucht, M., Esser, G., & Schmidt, M. H. (1993). Adverse temperamental characteristics and early behavior problems in 3-months-old infants born with different psychosocial and biological risks. *Acta Paedopsychiatrica, 56*, 19–24.

Laucht, M., Esser, G., & Schmidt, M. H. (1997). Developmental outcome of infants born with biological and psychosocial risks. *Journal of Child Psychology and Psychiatry, 38*, 843–854.

Laucht, M., Esser, G., & Schmidt, M. H. (2000a). Externalisierende und internalisierende Störungen in der Kindheit: Untersuchungen zur Entwicklungspsychopathologie. *Zeitschrift für Klinische Psychologie und Psychotherapie, 29*, 284–292.

Laucht, M., Esser, G., & Schmidt, M. H. (2000b). Längsschnittforschung zur Entwicklungsepidemiologie psychischer Störungen: Zielsetzung, Konzeption und zentrale Ergebnisse der Mannheimer Risikokinderstudie. *Zeitschrift für Klinische Psychologie und Psychotherapie, 29*, 246–262.

Laucht, M., Esser, G., & Schmidt, M. H. (2002). Heterogene Entwicklung von Kindern postpartal depressiver Mütter. *Zeitschrift für Klinische Psychologie und Psychotherapie, 31*, 127–134.

Papoušek, M. (1999). Regulationsstörungen der frühen Kindheit. In R. Oerter, C. v. Hagen, G. Röper & G. Noam (Eds.), *Klinische Entwicklungspsychologie* (pp. 148–169). Weinheim, Germany: PVU.

Papoušek, M. (2002). Störungen des Säuglingsalters. In G. Esser (Ed.), *Lehrbuch der Klinischen Psychologie und Psychotherapie des Kindes- und Jugendalters* (pp. 80–101). Stuttgart, Germany: Thieme.

Shaw, D., Keenan, K., Vondra, J. I., Delliquadri, E., & Giovannelli, J. (1997). Antecedents of preschool children's internalizing problems: A longitudinal study of low-income families. *Journal of the American Academy of Child and Adolescent Psychiatry, 36,* 1760–1767.

Sroufe, L. A., & Rutter, M. (1984). The domain of developmental psychopathology. *Child Development, 55,* 17–29.

Stoff, D. M., Breiling, J., & Maser, J. D. (Eds.). (1997). *Handbook of antisocial behavior.* New York: Wiley.

Thomas, A., Chess, S., & Birch, H. G. (1968). *Temperament and behavior disorders in children.* New York: University Press.

Verhulst, F. C., & Achenbach, T. M. (1995). Empirically based assessment and taxonomy of psychopathology: Cross-cultural applications. *European Child and Adolescent Psychiatry, 4,* 61–76.

von Hofacker, N., Jacubeit, T., Malinowski, M., & Papoušek, M. (1996). Diagnostik von Beeinträchtigungen der Mutter-Kind-Beziehung bei frühkindlichen Störungen der Verhaltensregulation. *Kindheit und Entwicklung, 5,* 160–167.

World Health Organization. (1990). *International statistical classification of diseases and related health problems—Tenth revision (ICD–10).* Geneva, Switzerland: Author.

CHAPTER 15

DYSPHORIC FUSSINESS AND DISINTEREST IN PLAY IN INFANCY: PRECURSORS OR EARLY MANIFESTATIONS OF ADHD?

Mechthild Papoušek

CASE VIGNETTE

R*eason for referral.* Dominic was brought in by both parents for the first time at the age of 12 months because of frequent vomiting, refusal to eat, difficulty sleeping, and motor restlessness. Ever since an intestinal infection 2 months earlier, he had been vomiting several times per day whenever he became excited, regardless of the reason. Vomiting could be triggered by his delight at seeing his father come home from work, by a coughing fit, or simply by crying. He refused food during the day and took milk only when everything around him was completely tranquil. Repeated pediatric examination found no evidence of reflux or any other organic cause for his complex symptoms. His weight and height were normal for his age.

In spite of his mother's presence and numerous, varied strategies to help him fall asleep, Dominic still needed about 2 hours to settle down at night, and even then he repeatedly woke up crying from a restless sleep. During the day, he was unpredictable, tired, and unable to engage in anything by himself for even a moment. He fussed whenever he felt physically constrained. He would cry when being placed in a high chair or car seat, or during diapering, which could only be done standing. Although his parents were completely exhausted and under enormous stress 24 hours a day, they still took pleasure in his usually sunny nature.

Prior history. Dominic was the first child of a professionally highly involved academic couple. The pregnancy was wanted and relatively uncomplicated, although the birth had to be initiated prematurely by Cesarean section at 36 weeks because the mother's health was at risk due to pre-eclampsia with HELLP syndrome. The immediate period after birth was not only clouded by the mother's transiently dangerous condition but also by the newborn's weak sucking and growing refusal to nurse. The mother felt under considerable pressure because of her fear that Dominic might not thrive, and so she began to feed him pumped breast milk drop by drop. To everyone's astonishment, she finally succeeded with great patience to get Dominic used to breast-feeding and nursed him for 6 months. However, his pronounced motor restlessness, hyperexcitability, and distractibility at mealtimes still remained a cause for alarm and could only be alleviated by intense rocking while sitting on a large gymnastics ball. Despite this strategy, he would end up choking and vomiting. The transition to solid food at 6 months required constant distractions and games. Only when he began to crawl did Dominic show signs of a real appetite. Nevertheless, ever since the critical perinatal period, feeding remained his most vulnerable domain in terms of regulatory demands.

This little boy, always curious and alert, required a great deal of attention during the day. His mother succeeded in entertaining him, tried to avoid excessive excitement, and tried to keep a regular rhythm during the day. After occasional pleasurable excursions or visits with relatives, he was extremely erratic and irritable in the evening and had a hard time falling asleep. When he finally was asleep, he remained restless and woke up frequently.

Family history. The family history is interesting in that the father himself had been hyperactive as a child and a sort of fidgety class clown in school. Into adolescence he was a creative and intelligent boy but restless and erratic. Dominic's mother came from a large family; she was the older sister in a brood of younger brothers, among them a particularly hot-tempered one, so she had had sufficient experience in dealing with boys.

Behavioral observations and findings. In the unfamiliar surroundings of the consultation room, Dominic proved to be a curious and primarily happy little boy who was socially quite engaging. At the age of 12 months he was physically healthy and thriving; his motor, mental, and language skills were age-appropriate. Dominic was extremely active while we discussed his history with his parents. He crawled around the room, eagerly and breathlessly exploring everything, or pulled himself up precariously, balancing his little body on the furniture. No sound from the street or hallway escaped his attention. He never spent more than a minute or so on a given toy and eventually became increasingly erratic and irritable. His mother got down on the floor with him and quickly calmed him, and as a result he was able to play for a reasonably long time with building blocks, which he manipulated with good fine-motor skills.

Dominic was alert and interested in what the physician was doing during his medical examination. In the end, however, despite his mother's skills at distracting him, she had a hard time restraining him for diapering and dressing. Nevertheless, she remained remarkably calm, carrying out the task with a sort of friendly determination.

During feeding at his regular mealtime, he showed no appetite whatsoever and tried with all his might to wriggle out of his high chair. Both parents offered puppets and picture books to get him to sit still, while his mother followed his erratic head movements with a spoon. Occasionally, she was actually able to trick him into opening his mouth.

Both the mother–child and the father–child relationships were characterized by a warm, open, and caring connectedness in which closeness and distance were flexibly regulated. Dominic repeatedly engaged with his mother or father. Both parents, particularly his mother, showed an intuitive understanding of how difficult it was for Dominic to take in and process the flood of stimuli from outside. He had always been an extremely sensitive infant who, according to his mother, would act out any kind of hyper-arousal through his stomach. She felt empathy because as a child and adolescent she also had stomach problems whenever things got tense. Both parents, however, were quite worried about the recent escalation in symptoms.

Diagnosis. We diagnosed a disorder of behavioral and emotional regulation with ongoing feeding problems and vomiting, sleep-onset and night-waking problems, and motor restlessness. In addition to a potential genetic component for attention deficit/hyperactivity disorder (ADHD) in the family, we found clear signs of constitutional difficulties with sensory processing (high levels of visual and auditory excitability and hyperreactivity, heightened susceptibility to stimuli, distractibility, high activity level), which was largely compensated for by intuitively competent and supportive parents. Interestingly, the family doctor had documented in the patient record a prospective diagnosis of ADHD at the age of 1 year!

Treatment. During the following three sessions we focused on treating the feeding and sleep disorders. With the father's help, the mother was able to implement the rules and recommendations that we worked out together with amazing success.

Thanks to the mother's empathy and intuitive competencies, she had already developed optimum strategies for helping Dominic with motivation, endurance, and regulation of attention and arousal during play. We gave her reassurance in reducing the number of toys in his playroom, in supporting Dominic's sense of self-efficacy and mastery motivation, and in structuring playtime and rest periods. We also encouraged her to support joint focused attention, avoid overstimulation, and reduce distractions.

Supplementary sensory integration therapy was a component of treatment that greatly helped Dominic to deal with his sensory processing problems. Within a few weeks, the entire home situation calmed down, and we agreed to continue sensory integration therapy, combined with follow-up sessions with us at longer intervals.

Further course. The further development was characterized by alternation between periods of stabilization and periods of disorganization lasting for several weeks, at the end of which the parents regularly noted a significant spurt in their son's development. Destabilization was triggered by infections, difficult adaptive demands, and age-related developmental tasks associated with the second and third years of life.

Dominic felt exhilarated by the new experiences that became available to him once he began independent walking. He often got so excited that he acted as if he were in a trance, running around fearlessly whenever he went outside and crying as soon as he had to go back home. In contrast, when his mother went shopping he had no trouble sitting still in his stroller, which his mother had gotten him used to early on. He was usually quiet in the apartment as well and had learned to engage in play by himself for short periods. However, whenever he felt flooded by intense feelings, whether joy, overstimulation or overfatigue, or rage and defiance because limits had been set, he threw a tantrum, during which he flung himself to the floor. His mother tried to cope differentially with his outbursts: In cases of real defiance, she gave him time to calm down while she placed some distracting toys within his reach. If this happened in the context of overfatigue, she would soothe him; if it occurred after a short episode of separation, she would try to convey to him a sense of closeness and security.

Toward the end of his second year, he had a severe relapse brought about by a family trip to the grandparents that was complicated by an infection. At this time he began again to refuse food and to vomit, and his sleeping disorder and former inability to engage in play returned. His parents were particularly alarmed by Dominic's increasingly aversive and aggressive behavior and by his impulsivity. When he became excited, even in positive situations, he would hit and bite other children, his parents, and even his favorite stuffed animal. He regularly awoke as a result of nightmares (a new phenomenon) and lashed out even though he had learned to fall asleep in a relaxed state after his bedtime ritual. His mood would swing from enthusiasm to enraged rejection. Outside, he again would run away without any caution at all. During this period, his mother introduced a timeout place in his narrow traveling bed, where he learned to calm down promptly. When he became overly excited at home, Dominic found a way to create a timeout by himself, withdrawing with his stuffed animal to a special corner of the room nicely furnished by his mother. During this difficult period he would come to his sensory integration therapy sessions bubbling with anticipatory delight, but he would then quickly calm down by seeking out and retreating to a narrow tub filled with little plastic balls. Afterwards, he could concentrate better and become more engaged with the other children in the room.

Just short of his third birthday, after a longer period of stability, Dominic underwent another transient period of turbulence, this time associated with his entry into two new play groups. He had, in the meantime, learned to protect himself from overstimulation by withdrawing to his little timeout island. Outside the home, he got used to taking his mother's hand when necessary, actively participating in shopping with her, and coping with longer trips without becoming emotionally derailed. He was mostly in good spirits and showed persistence and enduring attention while playing by himself; he spoke more and began to sing. However, he again started to have severe tantrums in which he became completely disorganized. He was increasingly aggressive, even toward his best friend. He frequently had no idea what he wanted or what to do with himself. At night he would lie in bed for hours completely awake, obviously trying to process the day's events. Even during the day, he was occupied with past events, sometimes events in the distant past. Increasingly he began to reflect on his impulsive behavior, aggressive outbursts, and the rules of social behavior, which his mother patiently practiced with him.

Overall, Dominic's development was remarkably positive in spite of repeated relapses, because he was growing up in a particularly supportive environment with secure attachment relationships with his parents. Their own resources and intuitive competencies enabled his parents to support Dominic in building self-regulatory competencies with only occasional counseling sessions and without the need for more extensive psychotherapy. With his parents' help and with sensory integration therapy, Dominic learned to test out and consolidate his own regulatory strategies for dealing with affective arousal, impulse control, attention regulation, and goal-oriented actions. Only his further development will indicate just how helpful these learned strategies have been for mastering future developmental tasks.

DISORDERS OF BEHAVIORAL AND EMOTIONAL REGULATION AND ADHD— UNRESOLVED QUESTIONS

Parents' Fears

One of the most frequent fears that parents express about their regulation-disordered infant or toddler is that their child may develop ADHD or may already suffer from ADHD. Many parents read the currently widespread literature on ADHD and worry that their child's natural liveliness, fidgeting, or restlessness might be the first symptoms of hyperactivity. They interpret their infant's persistent fussiness and bursts of full-blown crying for no apparent reason as signs of impulsivity. Or, they worry themselves with visions of a hyperactive schoolchild when their 5-month-old baby is only irritable or distracted during nursing. They feel confirmed in their fears when, in his second year of life, their child scampers about at full speed or wanders around aimlessly, constantly demands entertainment, throws toys or a tantrum, or quickly gives up playing when frustrated. As time goes by, they may discover among their relatives a little tyrant who has already begun to be treated medically for ADHD and whose behavior looks increasingly similar to that of their own baby.

Inconclusive Data

To date, research has not yet given conclusive answers to these understandable fears. Because the empirical data are still fragmentary, it is not possible to give parents reliable advice. The professional literature and retrospective case histories of children with ADHD indicate that in the majority of cases the problem began in infancy in the form of inconsolable crying, sleep disorders, feeding problems, irritability, tactile aversion, moodiness, and a high activity level; in toddlerhood, symptoms often included aimless and restless motor activity, severe tantrums, and inadequate impulse control (Döpfner, 2000; Skrodzki, 2002; Steinhausen, 2000). From a clinical perspective, we assume that only a subgroup within the large pool of children with disorders of behavioral and emotional regulation is at increased risk of developing ADHD in the preschool or school years. However, because of scarce data there is no way yet to estimate how many children, with which early signs and under which conditions, will later develop ADHD. Therefore, it would be disastrous to draw the general conclusion that disorders of behavioral and emotional regulation per se are precursors or early symptoms of ADHD, as has, unfortunately, been done on occasion (Dunitz-Scheer, Schein, Fuest, Oswald, & Scheer, 1998; ZERO TO THREE, 1994). Classifying the behavior of such children as early onset attention deficit/hyperactivity disorder (EOADHD) or labeling them as incurable troublemakers ("Fidgety Phils") is equally problematic. It is far more important to define the particular risk constellations under which ADHD might develop from initial regulatory disorders.

The only prospective study of infants who formerly cried excessively (cited in chapter 13) pointed to two potential predictors of ADHD at school age: the persistence of the crying problem beyond the developmental shift at 3 months and the pervasiveness, that is, its association with sleep problems and other regulatory problems (Wolke, Rizzo, & Woods, 2002). However, if we were to simply use these criteria, more than two-thirds of the infants who were referred to the Munich Program would be at high risk for developing ADHD at school age. In the sample studied by Wolke and colleagues, 19% of the children (about one fifth of the children who had cried excessively) had scores on the hyperactivity scale in the preclinical or clinical range at the age of 8 to 10, according to agreement on parent, teacher, and self-assessments. Compared to the control group, risk in the study sample showed a 16-fold increase. These results add weight to our questions regarding which children, with which behavioral problems and under which conditions—among the multiple organic and psychosocial risk factors and/or relationship problems—are at particular risk and therefore require extra attention.

Disinterest in Play Among Children With Disorders of Behavioral and Emotional Regulation

With these questions in mind, the Munich Program has for quite some time been looking closely at a particular behavioral manifestation that is observed in a subgroup of regulation-disordered infants and toddlers, and which, in its symptomatology, is suggestive of ADHD: a conspicuous lack of interest in play coupled with dysphoric fussiness and motor restlessness (M. Papoušek, 2003). Early crying, sleep, and feeding disorders are primarily related to basic psychophysiological regulatory processes. Clinginess, anxiousness, temper tantrums, and aggressive behavior represent problems of emotional regulation. By contrast, the observed lack of interest in play seems to be related to motivational problems of attention regulation, information processing, and control of goal-oriented action.

This syndrome of disinterest in play combined with dysphoric fussiness and motor restlessness was observed in 209 children (35.4%) of the overall sample of 590 regulation-disordered infants and toddlers between the ages of 4 and 36 months. These symptoms seemed to replace excessive crying between 3 and 6 months, peaked at the age of 7 to 9 months in 45% of cases, but was still observed in about one third of children who were referred for the first time at a later age. It was the sole reason for the referral in only 1.4% of these cases and was most typically associated with sleep disorders followed by regulatory problems in a number of other behavioral domains (see Table 15.1).

Research on this syndrome and its potential associations with later ADHD is only beginning and has hardly been mentioned in the clinical literature to date. However, it must be taken seriously because it concerns an important domain of adaptive developmental processes in early childhood.

This chapter summarizes our clinical observations and preliminary findings over many years and analyzes them in relation to basic developmental aspects of attention (Ruff & Rothbart, 1996) and play (H. Papoušek & Papoušek, 1999; H. Papoušek, Papoušek, & Bornstein, 2000; M. Papoušek & von Gontard, 2003) and integrates them into our overall model of disorders of behavioral and emotional regulation. We describe early problems of attention regulation within the everyday arena of parent–infant interactions and play (H. Papoušek & Papoušek, 1984; H. Papoušek, Papoušek, & Kestermann, 2000); identify phase-specific perturbations in attentional development; analyze conditions, mechanisms, and processes that favor and maintain attentional problems in infancy and toddlerhood; and indicate approaches to early preventive intervention.

EARLY DEVELOPMENT OF ATTENTION REGULATION

Like affects or emotions, attention is not easy to define because of its close interrelationship with integrative processes. Attention comprises functionally and structurally distinguishable systems: *vigilance*, the general degree of alertness, which determines the overall provision of energy for information processing, and *selective attention*, which focuses information processing like a spotlight on a particular task to the exclusion of irrelevant, distracting interference (Spitzer, 2002). Under favorable conditions, perception and integrative processes are directed selectively at a particular source of information, a single action, task, or goal until enough information has been gathered, the action has been accomplished, the problem has been solved, or a particular goal has been reached. From a neurobiological perspective, selective modification of the strength of synaptic transmission in the involved neuronal networks provides for the capacity to process the information. Functionally, selective attention includes the identification of the targeted focus, a state of alert focused attention, and central executive control functions. Two structurally different systems are involved here: (a) the posterior orienting/investigative system with a spatial orienting network in the parietal cortex and an object recognition network in the temporal cortex, and (b) the anterior superordinate prefrontal networks of higher level control.

Ruff and Rothbart (1996) have provided a comprehensive overview of a large number of experimental studies on the early development of attention that relate, in particular, to visual attention in infancy. This overview is essential to an understanding of early attentional problems. The development of the attentional systems in infancy and toddlerhood is subject to particularly striking processes of maturation and differentiation that continue well into later childhood.

Attention Regulation in Newborns

In newborns, attention, as a state of general vigilance, is primarily organized in a subcortical homeostatic system in close association with the regulation of arousal and behavioral state (Gardner, Karmel, & Flory, 2003). Although an alert waking state is rare in newborns, visual attention is nevertheless selective and organized even at this age (Wolff, 1987). Stimulus selection is determined by innate preferences (human face and voice) and by physical characteristics (intensity, brightness, contrast). Even in newborns, a visible stimulus elicits not only visual orientation and fine ocular scanning movements, but at the same time triggers a complex orienting response (OR) involving a state of alertness with general physiological arousal as well as cortical and autonomic preparedness of the organism to perceive, process, and respond to the information (see also chapter 4, Figure 4.1: The infant's fundamental adaptive response system; H. Papoušek & Papoušek, 1979). This state is associated with facial expressions of interest and with active inhibitory processes that suppress irrelevant motor reactions, decelerate heart rate, and decrease vagal tone. Another interesting phenomenon in very young infants is the so-called *obligatory looking*, a state of intense visual attention that may last for several minutes from which the infant cannot free himself and which may even abruptly end in crying. In addition, healthy newborns are able to regulate their state of arousal by selective attention in that they direct their visual attention to stimuli with less intensity when their internal arousal level is already high (e.g., before mealtime), whereas they prefer more intensive stimuli when their arousal level is low (e.g., after a mealtime) (Gardner & Karmel, 1983). In early social interactions, infants regulate their arousal level by gazing at their partner or averting their gaze.

Functions and Development of the Posterior Attentional System

Parallel to the maturation and differentiation of the peripheral sensory systems, the posterior orienting/investigative system begins to function with the first developmental spurt at 2 to 3 months. Attention is selectively triggered in the form of an OR by everything that is new and unknown in the infant's surroundings (response to novelty) or that deviates in a surprising way from what is already familiar (response to discrepancy). The focus of visual attention continues to depend on salient or particularly attractive characteristics of the stimulus: Early on, these include colorful and contrasting stimuli, patterns, movements, and regularities; with increasing motor development, the tangible objects become more appealing; and in the second half-year, objects that are spatially remote command the infant's attention.

Maturation of the posterior attention system enables rapid orientation with novel objects, as well as recognition of objects and becoming familiar with the environment. The orienting response decreases as soon as the new object has been taken in and integrated. Repeated exposure inhibits the OR by means of an involuntary active process called habituation, which protects the organism from being flooded by irrelevant stimuli. The attention span devoted to novel visual or auditory events is generally short (in the range of seconds). It decreases with age and becomes faster as the infant processes information more efficiently. One of the few early predictors of the development of cognitive and linguistic competencies appears to be the efficiency of this early habituation process (Bornstein & Sigman, 1986).

It is possible that in overly alert infants this may promote a sort of hunger for sensory stimulation, or distractibility. As soon as the novelty value of an object decreases and is outweighed by the novelty value of a competing stimulus, the spotlight of attention is diverted to the new stimulus. If the OR subsides without being reactivated by something new, a state of low-intensity arousal occurs that may be perceived as unpleasant or a state of boredom, which may be dissipated by renewed sensory activation of a state of alert focused attention.

Experiments have demonstrated that activation of an orienting response in infants experiencing a state of discomfort can have a calming effect; for example, providing a distracting stimulus can keep their negative affective arousal under control by means of some inhibitory mechanism, However, the effect lasts only as long as the stimulus is presented and retains adequate novelty value. As soon as the stimulus is withdrawn or the infant becomes habituated to it, the negative affective arousal returns to the original level. In other words, there is no persistent calming effect (Harmon et al., 1995, cited in Ruff & Rothbart, 1996). Activation of the posterior attentional system may thus function as an active regulatory mechanism for dealing with negative arousal and affective states.

Parents, of course, take advantage of this by distracting their cranky or crying baby with varied toys and stimulation; infants, in turn, soon develop a pronounced sensory hunger and discover how to request diversified stimulation and entertainment from their parents to satisfy that need.

Whereas attention is mainly controlled by external events during the first 9 months, the magnitude of the orienting response to external stimuli decreases after that time and gives way to the initiation and maintenance of attention by internal cognition-related factors such as intention, goal-directedness, or mastery motivation. Fortunately, the maturing brain provides more effective regulatory mechanisms. With the development of the ability to grasp, attention is sustained by manual, oral, and visually coordinated exploration of the object world. Novel features of objects (texture, weight, taste, and form) and their details become interesting. Over time, cognitive incentives (the discovery of regularities, concept formation, memory functions, expectation, and anticipation) and emotional appraisal gain in importance.

Between 3 and 9 months, sustained focused attention is regulated most efficiently by *intrinsic motivational processes* connected with self-agency and self-efficacy (H. Papoušek, 1969). This was also demonstrated in experiments conducted by Watson (1972). A 3-month-old infant soon becomes habituated when merely looking at a wind-up mobile suspended from the ceiling. If the mobile is randomly set in motion by the current of air, the infant's attention appears to be sustained by actively tracking the patterns of motion and an interest in predictable regularities (personal observation). However, if the infant is given the opportunity to control the movement of the mobile himself by using his own arms and legs, the *discovery of contingency* triggers a state of particularly intense and persistent attention with targeted exploration and positive emotions. The motivating experience of self-efficacy seems to nullify the effects of habituation, and inhibitory mechanisms may protect the infant from distraction. At the same time, self-efficacy represents an important basic experience for the further development of intentionality and planned, goal-oriented activity during play.

Although an infant's attention may occasionally be caught by self-efficacious exploration of a mobile for up to half an hour, the attention generally lasts for only 2–3 minutes per object during the process of active exploration. Nevertheless, the now familiar object may be temporarily replaced by another object and then again become the focus of attention when different aspects of it are explored.

Functions and Development of the Anterior Attentional System

Longer-lasting activation of attention and persistence only becomes possible with further progress in cognitive functions and with the maturation of the anterior attentional system. This process is closely interrelated with the early development of the so-called executive functions, of self-initiated intentional action, working memory, and goal-oriented behavior, as well as planning and execution of sequential actions. Important components of the anterior attentional system include inhibitory control mechanisms of motor functions, interfering affective impulses, and internal and external distractors.

Intrinsic motivational and reward systems continue to be of central importance in focusing and maintaining attention. These systems include needs for autonomy and self-efficacy with regard to the realization of one's own goals, pleasure in success and mastery motivation, expectation of positive or negative reinforcement, desire for social acceptance, and cognitive needs. When attention to some goal-directed action is activated, the anterior system acts on the networks of the posterior orientation/exploration system by inhibiting habituation to stimuli and events that are significant to a goal and by blocking orienting responses to irrelevant stimuli and events that distract from the goal.

The maturation of the prefrontal attentional networks begins between the ages of approximately 9 and 12 months and is associated with achievements of the second biopsychosocial shift (see chapters 4 and 8). It begins with the development of intentionality, joint and triangular attention, and awareness of the attentional focus and intention of others. Only during the middle of the second year of life does this system consolidate as infants begin to develop an inner world of representation and imagination, the capacity to symbolize, and language. The child then will no longer plan his actions and goals on the basis of physically available information alone, but will begin to use symbolic and linguistic representations in planning. Between 18 and 30 months, the child develops the capacity to suppress irresistible impulses such as the urge to unwrap a present immediately or the temptation to touch an attractive but forbidden object. The development of the highly complex executive functions continues and becomes increasingly nuanced as the child grows into school age and adolescence.

Attention Regulation in Parent–Infant Communication

From his very first encounter with his mother after birth, the infant's achievement of eye contact and the regulation of visual attention play a central role in parent–infant interactions. The parents' repertoire of intuitive competencies is rich in tactile, vocal, facial, and visual behavioral dispositions that allow them to stimulate and modulate their infant's attention and to respond to it contingently (H. Papoušek & Papoušek, 1987; M. Papoušek, 1994). It also permits them to attune the form, timing, and intensity of their stimulation and responses to their infant's momentary receptivity. Of primary importance is the mutual attention in early parent–infant dialogues, a context in which the infant begins to practice how to focus, maintain, and regulate attention by gazing at or away from his social partner. His parents also play an irreplaceable role in mediating experience with the immediate and distant environment by directing their infant's attention to various aspects of that environment, offering him objects for exploration, and structuring his play space. Parents support their infant's attention and meet his needs for self-efficacy by giving him time and space to follow his own initiatives and by letting themselves be guided by his interest.

During the second half-year, a new phase of mutual regulation of attention takes on central importance. Parent and child can now negotiate how to achieve a joint focus of attention on a single object or event. This occurs in the context of joint play and in other day-to-day interactional contexts. The child develops the capacity for triangular attention; that is, the capacity to direct his attention to a desired object, to the caregiver as an agent of help, and to his own intention to obtain the object. He learns to read and follow the orientation of his parent's attention from pointing, gaze direction, and body language. At about the same time, the availability of an attachment figure as a secure base and the regulation of closeness and distance gain in importance for the infant's readiness to direct his attention to novel experiences in the distant environment, particularly when increased motor skills allow him to explore on his own.

During the second year of life, the child focuses his attention increasingly on the goals of his intentional actions. In social contexts, these actions are particularly aimed at anything new and exciting, including previously unreachable objects that are fragile or unsafe, and those things that his parents or siblings love and treasure. The joint regulation of attention has reached a new level where parent and child must learn to negotiate conflicts of interest, and parents are on the move to guide their child with strategies of diverting his attention to something unproblematic, or of setting limits. Attentional regulation may become particularly difficult in this developmental phase because the amount of energy the child invests in attaining a particular goal is still high and relatively inflexible. The relative immaturity of the anterior attentional system means that the child's attention is not always amenable to being diverted.

The Significance of Play in the Development of Attention Regulation

In addition to parent–infant interactions, play is the most important context of infant experience in which attentional regulation unfolds. To date, this aspect of play has received remarkably little attention in clinical models of developmental psychopathology. As with communication, infants have a fundamental psychobiological need for play (H. Papoušek & Papoušek, 1977; H. Papoušek, Papoušek, & Bornstein, 2000; M. Papoušek & von Gontard, 2003). Play is the arena in which the child learns by his own initiative and integrates his experiences with the environment. The infant has a genuine need to familiarize himself with persons, objects, and events in his surroundings. He seeks to understand them, to gain some control over them and to detect rules and connections among them. The infant's interest in play, and his motives to focus and maintain attention, derive from intrinsic motivations, curiosity, exploratory needs, his joy in discovering something familiar, and in discovering rules and connections. The child's fulfillment of expectations; his need for agency, self-efficacy, and doing things himself; and his mastery motivation all play important roles as well. Self-initiated solitary play or interactional play with others provides the foundation (Crockenberg & Leerkes, 2000) upon which the child from early on tries out and practices his attentional functions, basic fine- and gross-motor skills, intentional or goal-oriented action, problem-solving strategies, symbolic and linguistic competencies, and maturing executive functions. Alternating between playing together and playing alone provides an arena in which the gradual transition from interactional attention regulation to intrapsychic self-regulation of attention may be observed.

CLINICAL SYNDROME OF DYSPHORIC FUSSINESS/DISINTEREST IN PLAY

A syndrome of discontent, fussiness, and inability or disinterest in playing alone for short periods was observed at all ages in more than a third of the children who were referred to the Munich Program. This occurred in addition to a prevalence of other disorders of behavioral and emotional regulation such as crying, sleeping or feeding problems, and problems with regulating boundaries or setting limits. In the everyday experience of these children and their parents there is—in spite of a full agenda of activities, an abundance of toys, and plenty of action—neither time nor space for leisurely self-initiated exploration and play.

Parent Complaints

The parents report that their infant is unable to play by himself, demands their attention constantly, is permanently discontent and cranky, cannot be put down or left alone for a minute, and insists on being carried around and entertained at all times. The child is fidgety and bored at home, runs around aimlessly, fusses, or clings to his mother's legs all day. He quickly loses interest in new toys and pulls toys down off their shelves and tosses them around. He cannot pay attention even when they play together, and gives up quickly and runs off. Only television and forbidden objects or locations capture his attention, such as the remote control, the computer, or cosmetics in the bathroom.

The parents themselves often feel that the "walls are closing in on us" at home. Even though they are involved with their child around the clock, they come to feel that they aren't doing enough and put incredible energy into a diversified entertainment program. This is exhausting business; the parents lose their intuitive playfulness, run out of ideas, and often can't think of any way to play with their child. Often these parents had never experienced play in their own childhoods.

Infant Behavioral Problems

According to our observations, the infant's disinterest in play is often associated with problems in basic regulation of arousal, attention, motor organization, impulse control, and motivation.

Problems in basic regulation of arousal and vigilance. Play, in the sense of active exploration, is not yet expected during the first months of life. Some infants with excessive crying, however, do have problems with attentional regulation and the processing of stimuli due to an impaired homeostatic balance of activating and quieting processes and resulting problems in their sleep–wake organization (see chapter 4): On the one hand they exhibit an elevated arousal level with general irritability or hyperreactivity in individual sensory modalities, such as hypersensitivity to noise, touch, or arm restraint and close body contact. On the other hand, consolability, self-soothing, and self control of sensory input by gaze aversion are distinctly impaired. In addition, dysphoric fussiness, irritability, fatigue, and overstimulation are often the expected consequences of a cumulative sleep deficit.

These infants are only occasionally in a stable and alert state shortly after waking up. They typically fight against being placed in a horizontal position and prefer a vertical position on the shoulder of the parent, which may activate their vigilance system. They learn to regulate their waking state by orienting to visual stimuli. And thus, after about the third month, many of these infants become particularly alert, engaged, and bright "lookers" with wide open eyes and an unquenchable thirst for new stimuli. Even if they are already in an overstimulated, dysphoric, or fussy state, the orienting response to a new stimulus is enough to help them shift to a positive state of alert focused attention. However, as soon as the orienting response diminishes as a consequence of habituation, they quickly relapse into their previous fussy state. The infant's positive response to being stimulated while in a fussy state encourages the parents to keep offering fresh stimuli. This may lead to a dysfunctional interaction pattern that easily becomes a risk in the long-term.

When crying problems persist beyond the first developmental spurt around the age of 3 months, the infant's preference for being in a vertical position remains and is linked with a strong preference for varied visual stimuli. Such children demand, by fussing or crying, to be walked and carried around, sit or stand upright on the parent's lap—any position that will give them a clear line of vision. In order to satisfy their presumed needs, some parents place them prematurely in a sitting position or a walker. Such infants fail to discover the appeal of self-initiated play in a relaxed position on a solid floor, of coordinated manual-oral-visual exploration, of investigating their own bodies, or of practicing newly emerging motor patterns that are relevant for the development of independent locomotion. Instead, they learn to satisfy their need for self-efficacy by instrumental crying and fussing, and their parents, if only to get a moment's peace, respond contingently by picking them up and carrying them around.

Problems of attention regulation. Hypersensitivity and hyperreactivity to sensory input are primarily a manifestation of low sensory thresholds or a generally elevated arousability in response to sensory stimulation. Children with these characteristics seem to perceive the environment with highly sensitive antennae so that no background noise from next door or the street escapes them. In play, they are easily distracted by competing stimuli. In addition, "sensory hunger" may constantly divert their attention to everything novel in the environment. If such children are exposed to an abundance of toys, their arousal level escalates and their ability for selective attention declines even further.

During the second and third years of life, distractibility and the ability to persevere in play depend increasingly on the functioning of the maturing anterior attentional system and the development of executive functions. Children who suffer from disinterest in play often focus their attention only briefly and superficially, alternating quickly among toys and failing to complete anything they set out to do. Their attention continues to be steered externally by the novelty value of environmental events, that is, by the posterior attentional system, instead of being regulated by intrinsic motivational and cognitive factors. Premature abandonment of their play activities and sudden breakdowns of attention are frequently observed in association with their experiences of failure.

Problems of motor organization. A generally high level of spontaneous motor activity, motor liveliness, and need to move about are not necessarily signs of motor disorganization. Nor is it problematic when an infant lapses into temporary phases of motor restlessness and discontent before fully mastering the ability to crawl reliably or to walk independently. It may become difficult to curtail the normal enthusiasm with which the toddler typically responds to the broader horizons once he has become mobile. Fortunately for the child, the elation he feels upon mastering a new motor competency makes it easier for the parents to cope in a positive way with the challenges and perturbations posed by the child's occasional needs for motor discharge.

A toddler's craving for stimulation and uncontrollable motor discharge becomes problematic when it is associated with a lack of caution and leads to risk-taking behavior and accident-proneness. Motor restlessness in states of boredom may also become problematic if associated with aimless running or jumping about, roughhousing, rages, and chaotic throwing or destroying of toys.

During the first months of life, a subgroup of infants with excessive inconsolable crying may exhibit motor hyperreactivity with frequent back-arching, trembling, and uncoordinated movements, and motor restlessness in a parent's arms when "fighting against falling asleep." All of these are signs of a generally elevated level of arousal.

Some toddlers exhibit problems in gross-motor coordination in the form of clumsiness, frequently bumping into things and stumbling. Clumsiness as well as some infants' aversive responses to physical closeness or restraint may be caused by problems with sensory processing of tactile, proprioceptive, or vestibular information.

Impulse control. Excessive, inconsolable crying indicates an early inability to self-soothe and to inhibit arousal. Three-fourths of children with disinterest in play in the second year also show the typical symptoms of the terrible twos, with their uncontrollable temper tantrums, outbursts of anger, and aggressive impulses (see chapter 8). The capacity for self-control of affective impulsivity, however, can be expected to develop only in the years that follow.

Impairment of intrinsic motivations to play. Infants and toddlers with disinterest in play and dysphoric fussiness typically exhibit states of boredom, lack of interest, and aimlessness as soon as they are left for a while to play on their own. In infancy, they get bored lying in their crib or infant seat and will fuss or cry unless they are picked up and carried around. Older infants and toddlers may show little initiative to play with an object by themselves for more than a few seconds. After very little time, they will have scattered their toys on the floor and carelessly stumble over them. Similarly, they show little interest in playing with their parents. Rather than settling themselves on the floor to join in the play, they either watch passively as their parents stack blocks, or immediately knock them down. The slightest frustration is followed by giving up, angrily throwing their toys in the corner, and running off. Curiosity, short-lived appeal of novelty, and seeking varied high-intensity stimulation seem to provide the overriding motivations for attention regulation and integration of experience in the second and third years of life for these children. Their needs for self-efficacy, exploration, success, and mastery have no opportunity to be satisfied or to be fostered and strengthened by a scaffolding social environment.

CONDITIONS THAT PROMOTE THE DEVELOPMENT OF DISINTEREST IN PLAY

In the following section we discuss the conditions under which early problems of basic regulation of arousal and attention, of motor organization, of affective control, and of motivation arise and eventually lead to the clinical syndrome of disinterest in play. With regard to the role of this syndrome in the genesis of ADHD, we then ask whether and to what extent a lack of experience with self-initiated play during the first years of life may contribute to the manifestation of ADHD symptoms seen later in the preschool or school years.

Clinical Data

The overall clinical sample of 590 regulation-disordered infants and toddlers between the ages of 4 and 36 months includes only 1.4% children in whom this syndrome was observed in isolation. In the great majority, the syndrome was associated with multiple problems of behavioral and emotional regulation. Nevertheless, a comparison of the subsample of children with disinterest in play ($n = 209$; 35.4%) to those without the syndrome ($n = 381$; 64.6%) yields some interesting figures. For example, disinterest in play is the only regulation disorder among all those studied that exhibits a small but significant sex difference in the expected direction (60.5% boys compared to 39.5% girls; $p \leq .05$). By contrast, the percentage of boys and girls in the remaining group (53.0% and 47.0%) does not deviate significantly from the expected values. More than 90% of infants and toddlers with disinterest in play after the first half-year had cried excessively during the first months of life.

It is important to bear in mind again that the syndrome of disinterest in play and dysphoric mood occurred in isolation only sporadically in 1.4% of children in both age groups, but was generally associated with sleep disorders and other regulatory problems (see Table 15.1). During the first year of life, associated regulatory problems were similarly distributed between children with disinterest in play and those in the control group. At the toddler age, however, association with excessive defiance and aggressive-oppositional behavior was significantly increased in the play-disordered group. It should also be noted for both age ranges that the subgroup of children with disinterest in play exhibited a significantly higher number of dysregulated domains, and should therefore be viewed as generally more distressed.

Table 15.1. Associated Regulatory Problems in Infants and Toddlers With and Without Disinterest in Play.

Infants and toddlers with disorders of behavioral and emotional regulation Total sample (N = 590)	4–12 months (n = 372)		13–36 months (n = 218)	
	With disinterest in play (n = 136)	Without disinterest in play (n = 236)	With disinterest in play (n = 73)	Without disinterest in play (n = 145)
Excessive crying (%)	25.7	25.5	4.1	0.7
Sleep disorder (%)	89.0	88.1	78.4	89.7
Feeding disorder (%)	38.2	39.1	43.2	44.8
Excessive clinginess (%)	14.7	10.2	17.6	20.0
Excessive defiance (%)	8.8	5.1	71.6	44.8[a]
Aggressive/oppositional behavior (%)	5.9	0.0	28.4	13.1[b]
Mean number of dysfunctional domains[c]	3.0	1.7[a]	3.6	2.1[a]

[a] Chi square ($p \leq .001$); [b] Chi square ($p \leq .01$); [c] t test ($p \leq .001$).

Further comparative results are summarized in Table 15.2, separately for infants between the ages of 4 and 12 months and for the older children from 13 to 36 months.

On the basis of the particularly pronounced regulatory problems in relation to arousal, attention, activity, affect, and difficulties in information processing, significant constitutional and probably also organic risk factors were to be anticipated. This assumption has been confirmed for qualities of temperament, which were assessed by the mothers with the help of the Infant Characteristics Questionnaire (ICQ; Bates, Freeland, & Lounsbury, 1979). Both age groups of children with disinterest in play exhibited significantly higher rates with extreme manifestations (>2 SDs above the standard mean): in infancy on the Fussy-Difficult, Unpredictable, and Unadaptable subscales and in toddlerhood on the Fussy-Difficult-Demanding and Unsociable scales. Yet, the presumptions of increased rates of prenatal, perinatal, or postnatal organic risk factors in the infant, or of prenatal psychosocial stressors, have not been confirmed (for assessment of risk factors, see chapter 3). No differences in frequencies were found between the two groups except for a higher rate of prenatal depression in the play-disordered group. Mild neurological problems were diagnosed slightly more frequently during the first year of life (41.1% vs. 30.5%). The lack of clear organic risk factors may be explained by the fact that children with organic developmental disorders and genetic syndromes were underrepresented in the population seen by the Munich Program (see chapter 3).

On one of our own problem behavior checklists, the children with disinterest in play exhibited the following problems significantly more often than the children in the control group (in about two thirds vs. one third, respectively): irritability, rapidly escalating negative arousal, inability to self-soothe, low tolerance of frustration, moodiness, distractibility, and (in 85% vs. 49%) demanding attention and entertainment. Unfortunately, there are to date no objective measures of infants' behavioral dispositions available for reliable use in a clinical setting.

By far the most pronounced differences between the children who had difficulties playing and children in the control group were in the areas of psychosocial risk factors, the psychological condition of the mother, and family relationships (see Table 15.2). Highly significant differences were found in the frequencies of prenatal depression, which is generally a rare condition. In addition, the overall rate of mothers with postnatal mental health problems was high, approaching 73% during the second and third years of their infants' lives, and included depressive episodes, personality disorders, and neurotic relational disorders. Compared to the control group, the rates of personality disorders and neurotic disorders were notably high in mothers of infants in this clinical subgroup who were referred after their first year of life. By contrast, the mothers' self-ratings of emotional well-being and attitude toward their infants were significantly more problematic on all subscales of the EMKK (Engfer, 1984) only during the first year of life. In addition, the rates of extreme scores (>2 SDs above the mean of the reference sample) were significantly elevated on the subscales Depressiveness, Overstrain, Frustration, and Tendency to Punish in the group of infants with disinterest in play. The same held true for the depression scores on the Edinburgh Postnatal Depression Scale (Murray & Carothers, 1990) in the first year, which were found considerably more often (42.1% vs. 25.8%) in the clinically significant range above the cutoff value of 12. This did not, however, apply to the mothers of 2- and 3-year-old children, where the high rates of psychosocial stressors did not affect the mother's self-ratings to the same extent (see Table 15.2). In both age groups, the subgroup with disinterest in play had to cope with a significantly higher burden of pronounced couples conflicts and unresolved intergenerational conflicts with the families of origin. In addition, the rate of serious conflicts in the mother–child relationship was approximately four times as high as in the control group. Similar results—with regard to the quality of the mother–child relationship—were obtained using the Parent–Infant Relationship Global Assessment Scale (PIR-GAS; ZERO TO THREE, 1994). Disordered relationships were seen in both age groups twice as often as in the control group; that is, in 1 of 8 mother–infant dyads in the first year of life and in 1 of 4 mother–child dyads in this group during the second and third years of life.

In summary, the subgroup of children with dysphoric fussiness/disinterest in play is characterized by especially pervasive regulatory problems, by particularly extreme expressions of infant temperament, particularly high rates of relationship conflicts and psychological problems in the mother, and—especially in toddlerhood—a rather high rate of disordered mother–child relationships. Precisely where the original cause of the problem lies differs from case to case and often cannot be teased out because of the long intertwined developmental history. The distressed relationships or the mothers' psychological problems may make it impossible for the child and the parents to engage in exploration and play. Conversely, a child with extreme temperamental difficulties who persistently demands attention and entertainment while exhibiting sleep disorders, eating problems, and conflicts over limit setting may cause a mother to decompensate psychologically, throw the family into disarray, and burden the mother–child relationship. From a systems perspective, we must assume a dynamic transactional interplay between infantile, maternal, and family factors that begins with early inconsolable crying and contributes to a later emergence and persistence of multiple disorders of behavioral and emotional regulation, including the syndrome of dysphoric fussiness/disinterest in play in particularly severe cases. This assumption is supported by the results of our follow-up study of infants with early excessive crying at the age of 30 months as detailed in chapter 13. To date, prospective longitudinal studies are still lacking that would analyze more precisely and objectively the infant's self-regulatory capacities and the mechanisms and processes in day-to-day interactions, and specify the causes and effects of the clinical syndrome of dysphoric fussiness/disinterest in play.

Dysfunctional Patterns of Communication During Mother–Child Play

Interesting information may be obtained from close clinical observation and video-based analysis of parent–infant play interactions. Most parents—mothers far more than fathers—in the subgroup of children who incessantly request attention and entertainment give in to their child's demands; they neglect their housework and other duties, disregard their own personal needs, and carry the infant around. This pattern most often begins during the first months of life when the baby cries excessively. Parents want to do well as mothers and fathers, and want to satisfy their baby's needs. They are afraid of doing something wrong or of missing anything that would advance their child's development; they want to do a better job than their own parents and therefore put tremendous pressure on themselves. They often just want to stop the crankiness and crying that seem to confirm their own failure and evoke feelings of hurt, helplessness, anger, or rage. It is important to realize that simply carrying an infant or toddler around without relating to each other, or the time spent merely sitting next to the child in play seems to satisfy neither the parent nor the child, who, in his passive role, continues to fluctuate between crankiness and insatiability.

Impaired expression of intuitive parental competencies. When taking a closer look at play interactions, it becomes clear that it is not simply the amount of play time that is at issue, but the quality of communication within the play context that is important. Within this context, the mother's psychological state has a far greater impact than in other situations. The repertoire of intuitive parental behaviors of the parents may be diminished, inhibited or blocked, or may come across as stereotypical, unnaturally effusive, or forced. Intuitive playful elements are missing, such as the capacity for contingent responsiveness, playful variations, games with buildup and release of positive affective arousal, creative ideas, and all of the small encouragements needed to overcome difficulties (H. Papoušek, 2003). In many cases, a striking speechlessness or complete lack of communication are apparent. The parents seem tense, listless, or bored, become emotionally unavailable, and fail to respond to the child's initiatives. They remain caught up in their own thoughts and worries or become absorbed by intense affects and unresolved conflicts (M. Papoušek, 2003). Fathers are often more relaxed at play, but sometimes they become so involved in whatever game is being played that they, too, fail to perceive the child's initiatives, capacities, and interests. Impairment of intuitive parenting also implies that the parent's communicative behavior becomes inaccessible to the infant. When speaking, the parents' language resembles that of adult-directed speech: It is complex, often too soft, and unrelated to the play context. It often lacks both the prototypical melodies of motherese and the typical dialogue patterns of turn-taking and repetition with variation. Stimulation is rapid and with frequent alternations, but without the repetitions and pauses that would allow the child to take in, process, and participate effectively in this dialogue.

Table 15.2. Comparison of Infants and Toddlers With and Without Disinterest in Play.

Infants and toddlers with disorders of behavioral and emotional regulation Total sample (N = 590)	4–12 months (n = 372)		13–36 months (n = 218)	
	With disinterest in play (n = 136)	Without disinterest in play (n = 236)	With disinterest in play (n = 73)	Without disinterest in play (n = 145)
ICQ				
(% > 2 SDs above standard mean)				
4–12 months:				
Fussy/difficult (%)	57.3	23.7***		
Unpredictable (%)	37.7	25.9*		
Unadaptable (%)	19.2	4.5*		
13–24 months:				
Fussy/difficult/demanding (%)			41.7	15.7**
Unsociable (%)			10.0	2.1*
Prenatal psychosocial stressors				
Prenatal depression (%)	11.1	5.5*	8.2	2.8*
Postnatal psychosocial stressors				
Couples' conflicts, unresolved (%)	27.2	22.1*	45.7	36.6*
Intergenerational conflicts, unresolved (%)	32.8	17.4**	27.5	16.7*
Distressing childhood, severe (%)	33.3	26.5	38.6	24.6*
Mother–child relational conflict, severe (%)	14.7	3.8***	21.6	5.5***
Mother–child relationship PIR-GAS:				
% disordered (10–30)	12.5	6.4	25.7	13.2
% distressed/disturbed (40–60)	83.8	78.7	74.3	75.0
% adapted (70–90)	3.7	14.9*	0.0	11.8*
Psychological problems in mother				
% total	60.3	37.3*	73.0	38.6***
% Depression	37.5	22.0*	33.8	13.8***
% Neurotic disorder	25.0	16.5	39.2	26.2*
% Personality disorder	5.9	2.5	18.9	6.2***
% Eating disorder	5.3	4.6	3.0	3.7
Psychological condition of mother (EMKK)				
(% > 2 SDs above standard mean)				
Depressivity	34.5	21.6*	32.7	24.1
Overstrain	31.0	10.3*	23.6	20.9
Frustration	21.6	9.0**	16.4	9.0
Tendency to punish	6.5	2.2*	13.7	14.4
Postnatal Depression Scale (EPDS)				
(% > clinical cutoff of 12)	42.1	25.8**	28.8	23.3

Note. ICQ = Infant Characteristics Questionnaire (Bates, Freeland, & Lounsbury, 1979); EMKK = Maternal Childcare Attitudes and Feelings (Engfer & Gavranidou, 1987); EPDS = Edinburgh Postnatal Depression Scale (Cox, Holden, & Sagovsky, 1987).

Chi-square: $*p \leq .05$; $**p \leq .01$; $***p \leq .001$.

Impaired attunement of the intuitive parenting repertoire to the child's initiatives and signals. With regard to the adaptive functions of play as self-directed learning, the parents' ability to attune their play behavior to the initiatives, capacities, and signals of their child is crucial (M. Papoušek, 2003). Most often, infants' disinterest in play is associated with a lack of emotional relatedness in parent–infant play interactions and a lack of responsive contingent attunement to the infant's signals. The many facets of impaired attunement are described in the following paragraphs.

To begin with, parent–infant play can only function well if the parent adjusts to the infant's momentary *receptivity* and *tolerance limits*. If signs of tiredness, overstimulation, need for rest, or aversion are overlooked or misinterpreted as signs of rejection, the parents' encouragements to play may quickly become overstimulating and overwhelming. Problems of attunement to the infant's receptivity and tolerance limits are often associated with a lack of intuition for creating an appropriate framework in relation to structuring the day (lack of regular rest periods and sleep, a full schedule of social events) and the play environment (play room stuffed with toys, television turned on, inappropriate room furnishings for a child, and so forth).

Parents who have a strong need for control or feel pressured to create a "superbaby" have difficulties allowing their child to take the initiative. Well-meaning stimulation may turn into *directive controlling* behavior if the parents ignore their child's interests, thwart his goal-oriented actions, or seek to determine how the child is to play with an object. Directive controlling behavior inevitably leads to power struggles during play in the second year of life, particularly with hyperreactive impulsive infants. When this happens, play may be abruptly terminated by a temper tantrum.

In addition, parental directivity may threaten a core aspect of communication during the second half-year: the *joint focus of attention* on objects or actions in the play context. A joint attentional focus enables both parents and child to communicate and share their intentions and feelings, cooperate in play, refer to and name what they are doing, and gradually construct a common ground of shared experience (M. Papoušek, 1994). All of this is lacking when the parents, for whatever reason, follow their own agenda without engaging with the focus of their child's attention and intentions. As a consequence, the child quickly loses the motivation to play, becomes passive or bored, runs off, or protests and provokes conflict. In parents who are extremely stressed psychologically, thwarting a child's initiative may become invasive and intrusive; they physically intrude into the child's intimate body space or play space, impede his spontaneity, or try to direct his movements despite his resistance.

Many highly stressed and insecure parents are guided in their approach by the developmental stage of same-age infants in the neighborhood, by normative standards, by parenting manuals, or by toy advertisements much more than by their own infant's spontaneous interests and feedback. Paying attention to their infant's signals instead would enable them to infer which developmental themes are motivating him to try out and practice freshly acquired or emerging skills (as in the zone of proximal development; Vygotsky, 1978). Often, the demanding challenges that parents pose to a not-quite-ready child go nowhere but simply overload and discourage him. Unrealistic expectations, impatience, or even disappointment about what the child is not yet able to do are transmitted back to the child, inhibiting his motivation to play and confidence in his own capacities.

Only undivided attention will permit the parents to perceive where, at what time, and to what extent the child needs assistance when playing, in a way that does not imperil his experience of self-efficacy and success but rather supports his self-confidence. If instances of intuitive encouragement and assistance are lacking, the child will easily become discouraged and give up, particularly if he already has a low frustration tolerance and is quickly derailed when faced with failed attempts. Assistance in small doses is therefore an important regulatory help that parents can provide to promote longer bouts of attention. Attention and motivation drop at precisely the moment in which the child feels not up to the next step towards an intended goal; every decrease in motivation renders the child more receptive to competing distractors from the environment. By contrast, focused attention is given a boost when a small hurdle is successfully surmounted with unobtrusive assistance.

The various facets of *deficient contingent attunement* described above are directly related to the core issues of disinterest in play. They inhibit the child's intrinsic motivations to play and fail to intuitively support experiences of self-efficacy, goal-oriented action, and self-directed exploration, as well as success and mastery. If parents are too exhausted, too depressed, too absorbed in their own unresolved conflicts, or too overwhelmed to engage in play with their baby, they will also overlook his subtle signs of contentment and joy at success. They will neither perceive nor share emotionally and value what motivates their child, his eagerness and kinetic energy, his seriousness, tension and efforts, his unavoidable disappointments and failures, his joy and pride in accomplishment, and his relaxing pauses for recovery. This turns the hours spent in play together into a joyless and dispiriting exercise for the child and the parent, and in the process deprives the parents of an important source of positive child-rearing experiences.

Such degradation of play may also be evident in some parents' attempts to enliven their child's willingness to play by external rewards and promises ("If you will play now, I'll buy you an ice cream cone later") or by threats and punishments ("If you don't play now, you won't be allowed to watch TV today").

Instead, the baby is stimulated, his sensory hunger satisfied temporarily. Toddlers are kept occupied, passively entertained, or held off with a succession of new toys. Play activities serve to immediately satisfy the child's curiosity and hunger for stimulation and to eliminate boredom, following one simple rule: "keep the child quiet." Television and computer games serve the same purpose.

In order to overcome his own state of fidgetiness, dysphoria, and boredom, the child learns to seek out high-intensity sensory input and diversified, mostly passive entertainment. As a result, he remains stuck at a superficial level of sensory processing and play. There is little opportunity to further develop the basic experiences of contingency and self-efficacy into intentional, goal-oriented action, deepened exploration, mastery motivation, self-guided learning, and creative symbolic play. If maturation of the brain is truly experience-dependent, these children miss the chance to try out and practice the newly emerging executive functions of the anterior attentional system at a time when the neurobiological prefrontal networks are about to mature. The immediate consequences include problems of attention regulation, a lack of persistence, motor restlessness and self-soothing with constant sucking on a pacifier or bottle, as well as stagnation in the development of symbolic representation, play, and language competencies.

Dysphoric Fussiness/Disinterest in Play—Precursors or Early Symptoms of ADHD?

At least with regard to a core group, the extensive literature on ADHD points to a more or less one-sided etiology in which genetic, neurobiological, or constitutional factors play a decisive role, while psychosocial environmental conditions are ascribed a mere modulating influence on the severity and course of the disorder (Döpfner, 2000; Moll & Rothenberger, 2001; Steinhausen, 2000). The neurobiological basis is assumed to imply a functional deficit in the neuronal networks of the prefrontal cortex, in particular the dopaminergic regulatory systems that include the anterior attentional system with its motivational subsistence and inhibitory executive functions. Other authors place a greater emphasis on developmental aspects in the psychosocial environment and its structural and functional effects on brain development in children with a presumed genetic or constitutional vulnerability for ADHD (Carey, 2002; Hüther & Bonney, 2002; M. Papoušek, 2003). These authors search for early risk factors in parent–child relationships as starting points for therapeutic approaches to effective prevention. The case study at the beginning of this chapter gives an interesting example of potential gene–environment interaction. It describes a young child who presumably has been born with a genetic neurobiological vulnerability to ADHD, and in whom relational and environmental factors have played a positive compensatory role (see below).

It is not clear at present what significance the syndrome of dysphoric fussiness/disinterest in play—as part of an early disorder of behavioral and emotional regulation—has for the psychopathological development of ADHD in a core group, or in the broad spectrum of later attentional, hyperactive, and impulsive behavioral disorders. Targeted clinical studies are needed to determine the long-term consequences of a lack of age-appropriate play on attention regulation, mastery motivation, and learning capacity in school-age children. The observed problems draw attention to a potentially sensitive early phase of neurobiological maturation in which the primary attention regulation by the posterior cortical networks increasingly comes under the motivational and inhibitory control of the prefrontal networks, where it is complemented by new goal-oriented and task-oriented motivations and cognitive competencies. Infants and toddlers who have been referred to the Munich Program because of early problems with hyperexcitability, impaired stimulus processing, sensory hunger, and disinterest in play may be particularly vulnerable during this transitional phase between the 9th and the 18th month of life. At this point, their expanded locomotor space allows them to find an abundance of novel stimulation and thereby satisfy their sensory hunger. If this form of information processing is not complemented by focused exploratory complemented by beginning symbolic play, the development of phase-specific functions such as intentionality, triangular focused attention, delayed imitation, goal-oriented action, and problem solving may be compromised. The third developmental shift around the middle of the second year can lead to stabilization of these capacities in the third year of life, with an advancement of frontal executive functions. If a supportive environment for play continues to be absent, however, it is to be expected that important developmental progress involving emotional regulation and impulse control, motor organization, goal-oriented sequential planning, adequate attention span, and the acquisition of symbolic and linguistically integrated mental representations will be impeded (Bischof-Köhler, 1998).

Moreover, the structural and functional maturation of the complex prefrontal networks will become even more vulnerable if the child does not experience the necessary emotional security in early attachment relationships, and is repeatedly exposed to uncontrollable emotional distress in problematic relationships (Hüther & Bonney, 2002; Rothenberger & Hüther, 1997). However, studies on the effects of attachment quality on task orientation and endurance over the course of the second year of life have yielded inconsistent results; unfavorable effects are found particularly in children with insecure-ambivalent attachment (Crockenberg & Leerkes, 2000). More distinct associations have been found between early parental scaffolding and support of infant self-efficacy, and infants' endurance and competence in play in their second and third year (Frodi, Bridges, & Grolnick, 1985).

To conclude, in a majority of children with disinterest in play described in this chapter the long-term risks may be increased in two specific respects: (a) as a result of a chronic lack of age-appropriate play experience, and (b) as a result of disorders in the mother–child and other family relationships. In one of the few nuanced longitudinal studies that included analysis of mother–child play, Campbell, Ewing, Breaux, and Szumowski (1986) showed that only 30% of the sample of 46 children who were brought by their parents because of pronounced attentional problems in mother–child play, impulsivity, and motor restlessness met the *Diagnostic and Statistical Manual of Mental Disorders—Third Edition* criteria for ADHD at 6 and 9 years. In contrast, the behavior of the remaining children had normalized by school-age. The case vignette presented at the beginning of this chapter describes a child with a presumed neurobiological vulnerability for ADHD. In this case, however, the mother's continuing support of attention regulation and self-regulatory strategies in play and the sympathetic accepting parent–child relationships facilitated an overall positive development.

The syndrome of dysphoric fussiness/disinterest in play contributes considerably to ongoing tension in the parent–child relationship and may impede the development of attentional, emotional, and mental functions. This risk may be reduced, however, with a relatively small investment in targeted therapeutic intervention. The clinical syndrome of dysphoric fussiness/disinterest in play in the context of other problems of behavioral and emotional regulation deserves our full attention for its own sake, even if the connection postulated here between a lack of positive experience in play in infancy and later ADHD symptoms is not confirmed in future studies.

DISORDER-SPECIFIC DIAGNOSTIC ASSESSMENT

Specific diagnostic measures focus on behavioral observations of spontaneous play both alone and together with mother and father, if possible in dyadic and triadic contexts. Videotaped interactions provide unique advantages for microanalytic diagnostics of contingent interrelations between infant and parent behavior. The medical examination offers opportunities to observe and analyze behavioral manifestations of the child's constitutional characteristics with regard to self-regulation, reactivity, stimulus processing in various sensory modalities, and motor coordination. This procedure is complemented by further diagnostics in collaboration with occupational therapists trained in sensory integration therapy. Unfortunately, there are as yet no standardized and validated clinical diagnostic procedures for these aspects.

DISORDER-SPECIFIC COUNSELING AND THERAPY

Overall, counseling and treatment follow the model of communication-centered parent–infant counseling and psychotherapy presented in chapter 12. At the end of the first session, a stepwise treatment plan that takes into account all current regulatory problems of the child is developed with the parents, and these problems are then treated in succession depending on their urgency. If the parents feel up to it, we often recommend treating a sleep disorder first in order to eliminate the potential effects of a sleep deficit on the infant's sense of well-being and regulatory capacities during waking times. This approach also improves the physical resources available to the parents and child. If the mother–child relationship is particularly tense and conflicted, it makes sense to begin with communication-centered relational therapy at the level of parent–child play. Once the child's lack of interest in play is overcome, it becomes possible for both parent and child to experience positive relatedness, which then makes it easier to resolve existing boundary and limit-setting conflicts. Because disinterest in play is associated with excessive defiance in 71.6% of infants and with aggressive/oppositional behavior in 28.4%, parallel treatment of these problems of emotional regulation and impulse control are particularly important from a preventive perspective.

Video-supported behavioral observation of infants both playing alone and in interaction with a parent provides an excellent starting point for disorder-specific developmental counseling and communication-centered relational therapy with a focus on joint play. The elements of this kind of play therapy are summarized in Table 15.3. Such resource-oriented play therapy, with or without the use of video feedback (see chapter 12), has proven to be very effective in the treatment of dysphoric fussiness/disinterest in play.

In our program, the overall therapeutic investment was significantly higher in the play-disordered group, with a more frequent focus on communication-centered relational therapy (71.4% vs. 43.2%) and more frequent supplemental treatments such as sensory integration therapy (17.1% vs. 5.0%), interventions by social workers (13.3% vs. 5.0%), and longer term individual psychotherapy (25.2% vs. 12.6%). During the child's second and third years of life, couples counseling as an integrated part of the Munich Program (28.4% vs. 14.5%), or external couples therapy (18.9% vs. 6.9%) were needed significantly more often.

The success of treatment (for criteria, see chapter 12) was particularly encouraging during infancy, with 40.7% completely improved and 53.3% largely improved. Only 4.4% showed only slight improvement, but these infants came from severely stressed multiproblem families; 1.5% showed no improvement because the family dropped out. The rate of complete improvement in the older children was significantly lower (28.8%), and the rate of slight improvement was higher (15.1%).

OUTLOOK

This chapter summarizes the experiences, targeted observations, and initial data from our clinical work with families in which infants and toddlers were experiencing disorders of behavioral and emotional regulation. It draws attention to a phenomenon that has to date been relatively overlooked, namely, that an increasing number of infants and toddlers appear to grow up with a striking lack of experience with play. If we assume that infant play as self-regulated learning and integration of experience is one of the fundamental adaptive psychobiological needs and elementary life patterns of the growing child, this phenomenon should be profoundly alarming to child health professionals, particularly in view of the growing number of attentional, learning, and language disorders that are diagnosed at preschool or school age. Unlike attachment, this aspect of early deprivation has not been adequately addressed

Table 15.3. Disorder-Specific Developmental Counseling and Video-Supported Communication-Centered Relational Therapy.

Therapeutic frame and treatment goals:

–Supportive therapeutic relationship

–Stress-free space and time for play, for experiencing positive reciprocity and relatedness

–Discovering and strengthening infant and parent competencies

–Strengthening the child's intrinsic motivation for self-initiated play through affective attunement: self-efficacy, joy in exploration, mastery motivation

–Relieving the pressure on the parents to constantly entertain their child and accelerate his development

–Strengthening the parents' trust in their intuitive playfulness and resolving inhibitions and blockages to intuitive parenting

Video-supported approach to play therapy:

–Discovering, reliving, and enjoying sequences of positive reciprocity in parent–infant play, and sequences of concentrated self-directed play by the child alone; gaining self-confidence and trust in the child's competencies

–Recognizing, understanding, and valuing the child's preferences, interests, developmental themes, motivations, and strengths in play

–Recognizing and understanding the child's signals of receptivity, tolerance, limits, and overload in play

–Identifying reciprocal contingencies in functional "angel's circles" and dysfunctional vicious circles in parent–infant play

–Addressing and working through the parent's subjective feelings, memories, and thoughts evoked by the context of play

–Practicing undivided attention and emotional availability in short episodes of parent–infant play; addressing and working on disturbing affects

Supplementary developmental counseling:

–Informing about the role of play in the child's development

–Orienting the parent to the child's developmental level and his individual strengths and weaknesses

–Budgeting time and structuring the day, including episodes of joint play with undivided attention and emotional availability and episodes of playing alone

–Adopting a "watch, wait, and, wonder" attitude that supports the child's initiatives, offering help only if needed or requested, and engaging in play-related communication

–Protecting the child from overstimulation, creating peaceful timeouts during the day, sleeping enough, allowing time to recover, and permitting boredom

–Taking time for themselves and the couple's relationship to meet their own basic needs

either in the current discourse around early education or in models of developmental psychopathology in child psychiatry.

The phenomenon of disinterest in play, observed in the context of other regulatory problems, seems to be promoted by the way of life and the Zeitgeist of our fast-paced, media-oriented, overstimulating society, which is characterized by a continuous glut of information full of rapid, exciting, and sensational stimuli, hectic and overly booked schedules, and a lack of time for relaxation and leisure. Our lives are built around market-driven consumption and, in relation to children, by pressures to advance their academic achievements. Parents are overwhelmed by an abundance of parenting magazines and books, and an overabundance of noncreative but arousing toys or so-called educational toys for even the smallest infants. American authors speak of a "high-speed society" and a "rapid-fire culture" (DeGrandpre, 2002) that favors new forms of fast but superficial communication and information processing via television, computers, cell phones, and the like. These influences have already begun to extend into pregnancy, the postpartum transition, and infancy, making it difficult for parents to adjust to their baby's slower tempo, receptive capacities, and peculiar needs.

A good one third of the infants and toddlers with disorders of behavioral and emotional regulation may well be predisposed to develop the syndrome of disinterest in play because of some constitutional disposition, adverse family environment, dysfunctional parent–infant interactions, and persistent pervasive regulatory problems. The syndrome of disinterest in play by itself with its accompanying features—distractibility, sensory hunger, dysphoric fussiness, and motor restlessness—and the resulting deprivation of self-initiated play suggest that children with these problems may well form a special risk group with regard to ADHD.

The developmental trajectories presented here need to be verified in prospective clinical studies focusing on the early development of attention and play in the context of parent–infant relationships in both clinical and nonclinical populations. The effectiveness of targeted therapeutic interventions should be evaluated as well. In addition, the phenomenon of disinterest in play should lead to interdisciplinary studies involving neurobiologists, molecular biologists, clinical developmentalists, and child psychiatrists in order to improve current knowledge about the developmental psychopathology of ADHD, the most frequent psychiatric disorder of childhood. The sooner it becomes possible to identify the mechanisms and processes involved in the origins and maintenance of problems of attention regulation, goal-directed action, and impulse control, the easier it will be to develop targeted preventive treatment strategies.

It is not our intention to pathologize the behavioral syndrome of disinterest in play, or to provide evidence for a diagnosis of early-onset attention deficit hyperactivity disorder (EOADHD). Rather, we wish to draw the attention of specialists and parents to the significance of play as a unique resource for infant development and early parent–child relationships and to counteract disturbing influences early on. Given the pressures brought about by the current societal Zeitgeist, the psychobiological predispositions in infants and parents in favor of the development of play have become precious and threatened commodities. Increasingly missing in modern societies are emotional security, true leisure, and an environment that encourages parents to engage in play, communication, and positive relatedness with their infant. In addition, children need to be insulated at an early age from overstimulation, the pressure to become a superbaby, television, and other dangers of fast-paced and technologically oriented societies. To create a protective space in which play remains an elementary facet of life and learning, and an indispensable right of the child, may well be one of the most important tasks of caregiving and child rearing today. In this regard, a therapeutic approach at the level of parent–child play is one of the most mutually rewarding interventions, and—we hope—one of the most effective forms leading to long-term preventive outcomes.

REFERENCES

Bates, J. E., Freeland, C. A., & Lounsbury, M. L. (1979). Measurement of infant difficultness. *Child Development*, 50, 794–803.

Bischof-Köhler, D. (1998). Zusammenhänge zwischen kognitiver, motivationaler und emotionaler Entwicklung in der frühen Kindheit und im Vorschulalter. In H. Keller (Ed.), *Lehrbuch Entwicklungspsychologie* (pp. 319–376). Bern, Switzerland: Hans Huber.

Bornstein, M. H., & Sigman, M. D. (1986). Continuity in mental development from infancy. *Child Development*, 57, 251–274.

Campbell, S. B., Ewing, L. J., Breaux, A. M., & Szumowski, E. K. (1986). Parent-referred problem three-year-olds: Follow-up at school-entry. *Journal of Child Psychology and Psychiatry*, 27, 473–488.

Carey, W. B. (2002). Is ADHD a valid disorder? In P. S. Jensen & I. Cooper (Eds.), *Attention deficit hyperactivity disorder: State of the science, best practices*. Kingston, NI: Livre Research Institute.

Cox, J. L., Holden, J. M., & Sagovsky, R. (1987). Detection of postnatal depression. Development of the 10-item Edinburgh Postnatal Depression Scale. *British Journal of Psychiatry*, 150, 782–786.

Crockenberg, S., & Leerkes, E. (2000). Infant social and emotional development in family context. In C. H. Zeanah Jr. (Ed.), *Handbook of infant mental health* (2nd ed., pp. 60–90). New York: Guilford Press.

DeGrandpre, R. (2002). *Die Ritalin-Gesellschaft: ADS - eine Generation wird krank geschrieben*. Weinheim, Germany: Beltz Verlag.

Döpfner, M. (2000). Hyperkinetische Störungen. In G. Esser (Ed.), *Lehrbuch der klinischen Psychologie und Psychotherapie des Kindes- und Jugendalters* (pp. 172–196). Stuttgart, Germany: Thieme.

Dunitz-Scheer, M., Schein, A., Fuest, B., Oswald, Y., & Scheer, P. (1998). *EOADHD: Early onset attention deficit disorder*. Unpublished manuscript.

Engfer, A. (1984). Entwicklung punitiver Mutter-Kind-Interaktionen im sozioökologischen Kontext. *Arbeitsbericht zum Antrag an die Deutsche Forschungsgemeinschaft auf Gewährung einer Sachbeihilfe*. Institut für Psychologie, Persönlichkeitspsychologie und Psychodiagnostik, Universität München.

Engfer, A., & Gavranidou, M. (1987). Antecedents and consequences of maternal sensitivity: A longitudinal study. In H. Rauh & H. C. Steinhausen (Eds.), *Psychobiology and early development. Advances in psychology* (Vol. 46, pp. 71–99). Amsterdam: North-Holland.

Frodi, A., Bridges, L., & Grolnick, W. (1985). Correlates of mastery related behavior: A short term longitudinal study of infants in their second year. *Child Development*, 56, 1291–1298.

Gardner, J., & Karmel, B. Z. (1983). Attention and arousal in preterm and full-term neonates. In T. Field & A. Sostek (Eds.), *Infants born at risk: Physiological, perceptual, and cognitive processes* (pp. 69–98). New York: Grune & Stratton.

Gardner, J. M., Karmel, B. Z., & Flory, M. J. (2003). Arousal modulation of neonatal visual attention: Implications for development. In S. Saroci (Ed.), *Perspectives on fundamental processes in intellectual functioning. Vol. 2: Visual information processing and individual differences* (pp. 125–154). Stamford, CT: Ablex, JAI (Elsevier).

Hüther, G., & Bonney, H. (2002). *Neues vom Zappelphilipp: ADS verstehen, vorbeugen und behandeln.* Düsseldorf, Germany: Walter Verlag.

Moll, G. H., & Rothenberger, A. (2001). Neurobiologische Grundlagen: Ein pathophysiologisches Erklärungsmodell der ADHD [Special issue: Unaufmerksam und hyperaktiv]. *Kinderärztliche Praxis: Soziale Pädiatrie und Jugendmedizin, 72,* 9–15.

Murray, L., & Carothers, A. D. (1990). The validation of the Edinburgh Postnatal Depression Scale on a community sample. *British Journal of Psychiatry, 157,* 288–290.

Papoušek, H. (1969). Individual variability in learned responses in human infants. In R. J. Robinson (Ed.), *Brain and early behavior* (pp. 251–262). New York: Academic Press.

Papoušek, H. (2003). Spiel in der Wiege der Menschheit. In M. Papoušek & A. von Gontard (Eds.), *Spiel und Kreativität in der frühen Kindheit* (pp. 17–55). Stuttgart, Germany: Pfeiffer bei Klett-Cotta.

Papoušek, H., & Papoušek, M. (1977). Das Spiel in der Frühentwicklung des Kindes. *Pädiatrische Praxis (Supplement), 18,* 17–32.

Papoušek, H., & Papoušek, M. (1979). The infant's fundamental adaptive response system in social interaction. In E. B. Thoman (Ed.), *Origins of the infant's social responsiveness* (pp. 175–208). Hillsdale, NJ: Erlbaum.

Papoušek, H., & Papoušek, M. (1984). Learning and cognition in the everyday life of human infants. In J. S. Rosenblatt, C. Beer, M.-C. Busnel, & P. J. B. Slater (Eds.), *Advances in the study of behavior* (Vol. 14, pp. 127–163). New York: Academic Press.

Papoušek, H., & Papoušek, M. (1987). Intuitive parenting: A dialectic counterpart to the infant's integrative competence. In J. D. Osofsky (Ed.), *Handbook of infant development* (2nd ed., pp. 669–720). New York: Wiley.

Papoušek, H., & Papoušek, M. (1999). Symbolbildung, Emotionsregulation und soziale Interaktion. In W. Friedlmeier & M. Holodynski (Eds.), *Emotionale Entwicklung. Funktion, Regulation und soziokultureller Kontext von Emotionen* (pp. 135–155). Heidelberg, Germany: Spektrum Akademischer Verlag.

Papoušek, H., Papoušek, M., & Bornstein, M. H. (2000). Spiel und biologische Anpassung. In S. Hoppe-Graff & R. Oerter (Eds.), *Spielen und Fernsehen. Über die Zusammenhänge von Spiel und Medien in der Welt des Kindes* (pp. 21–45). Weinheim, Germany: Juventa.

Papoušek, H., Papoušek, M., & Kestermann, G. (2000). Preverbal communication: Emergence of representative symbols. In N. Budwig, I. C. Uzgiris, & J. V. Wertsch (Eds.), *Communication: An arena of development. Advances in applied developmental psychology* (pp. 81–107). Stamford, CT: Ablex.

Papoušek, M. (1994). *Vom ersten Schrei zum ersten Wort. Anfänge der Sprachentwicklung in der vorsprachlichen Kommunikation.* Bern, Switzerland: Hans Huber.

Papoušek, M. (2003). Gefährdungen des Spiels in der frühen Kindheit: Klinische Beobachtungen, Entstehungsbedingungen und präventive Hilfen. In M. Papoušek & A. von Gontard (Eds.), *Spiel und Kreativität in der frühen Kindheit* (pp. 174–214). Stuttgart, Germany: Pfeiffer bei Klett-Cotta.

Papoušek, M., & von Gontard, A. (Eds.) (2003). *Spiel und Kreativität in der frühen Kindheit.* Stuttgart, Germany: Pfeiffer bei Klett-Cotta.

Rothenberger, A., & Hüther, G. (1997). Die Bedeutung von psychosozialem Stress im Kindesalter für die strukturelle und funktionelle Hirnreifung: Neurobiologische Grundlagen der Entwicklungspsychopathologie. *Praxis der Kinderpsychologie und Kinderpsychiatrie, 46,* 623–644.

Ruff, H. A., & Rothbart, M. K. (1996). *Attention in early development: Themes and variations.* New York: Oxford University Press.

Skrodzki, K. (2002). ADHD aus der Sicht des Kinder- und Jugendarztes. In H. von Voß (Ed.), *Unaufmerksam & hyperaktiv: Wissen und Praxis zur ADHD* (pp. 62–71). Mainz, Germany: Kirchheim.

Spitzer, M. (2002). *Lernen.* Heidelberg, Germany: Spektrum Akademischer Verlag.

Steinhausen, H.-C. (2000). *Psychische Störungen bei Kindern und Jugendlichen: Lehrbuch der Kinder- und Jugendpsychiatrie* (4th ed.). München, Germany: Urban & Fischer.

Watson, J. S. (1972). Smiling, cooing, and the "game." *Merrill-Palmer Quarterly, 15,* 323–340.

Wolff, P. H. (1987). *The development of behavioral states and the expression of emotions in early infancy: New proposals for investigation.* Chicago: University of Chicago Press.

Wolke, D., Rizzo, P., & Woods, S. (2002). Persistent infant crying and hyperactivity problems in middle childhood. *Pediatrics, 109,* 1054–1060.

Vygotsky, L. S. (1978). Mind in society: *The development of higher psychological processes.* Cambridge, MA: Harvard University Press.

ZERO TO THREE. (1994). *Diagnostic classification: 0-3. Diagnostic classification of mental health and developmental disorders of infancy and early childhood.* Arlington, VA: National Center for Clinical Infant Programs.

Contributing authors

Renate Barth, Diplom-Psychologin., Hoheluftchaussee 52, D-20253 Hamburg. E-mail: renatebarth@t-online.de

Dr. med. Caroline Benz-Castellano, Abteilung Wachstum und Entwicklung, Universitäts-Kinderklinik, Steinwiesstr. 75, CH-8032 Zürich. E-mail: Caroline.Benz@kispi.unizh.ch

Prof. Dr. phil. Günter Esser, Diplom-Psychologe, Professur Klinische Psychologie/Psychotherapie, Institut für Psychologie, Universität Potsdam, Postfach 60 15 53, D-14415 Potsdam. E-mail: gesser@rz.uni-potsdam.de

Dr. med. Tamara Jacubeit, Klinik für Kinder- und Jugendpsychiatrie, Psychotherapie und Psychosomatik, Holzfuhrstr. 25, D-58511 Lüdenscheid, E-mail: jacubeit@t-online.de

Prof. em. Dr. med. Remo H. Largo, Abteilung Wachstum und Entwicklung, Universitäts-Kinderklinik, Steinwiesstrasse 75, CH-8032 Zürich. Current address: Speerstr. 31, CH-8738 Uetliberg. E-mail: brlargo@bluewin.ch

Dr. phil. Manfred Laucht, Diplom-Psychologe, Zentralinstitut für Seelische Gesundheit, Klinik für Psychiatrie und Psychotherapie des Kindes- und Jugendalters, Postfach 122 120, D-68072 Mannheim. E-mail: laucht@zi-mannheim.de

Prof. em. Dr. med. Mechthild Papoušek, Institut für Soziale Pädiatrie und Jugendmedizin der Ludwig-Maximilians-Universität München, Heiglhofstr. 63, D-81377 München. Current address: Strassbergerstr. 43, D-80809 München. E-mail: Mechthild@Papousek.de

Prof. Dr. med. Franz Resch, Klinikum der Universität Heidelberg, Abteilung für Kinder- und Jugendpsychiatrie, Blumenstr. 8, D-69115 Heidelberg. E-mail: Franz.Resch@med.uni-heidelberg.de

Claudia Rupprecht, Diplom-Psychologin, Kinderzentrum München, Heiglhofstr. 63, D-81377 München.

Prof. Dr. rer. nat. Klaus Sarimski, Diplom-Psychologe, Pädagogische Hochschule, Keplerstraße 87, D-69120 Heidelberg. E-mail: sarimski@ph-heidelberg.de

Dr. phil. Michael Schieche, Diplom-Psychologe, Kinderzentrum München, Heiglhofstraße 63, D-81377 München. E-mail: michael.schieche@extern.lrz-muenchen.de

Prof. Dr. med. Dr. rer. nat. Martin H. Schmidt, Diplom-Psychologe, Zentralinstitut für Seelische Gesundheit, Klinik für Psychiatrie und Psychotherapie des Kindes- und Jugendalters, Postfach 122 120, D-68072 Mannheim. E-mail: schmidt@zi-mannheim.de

Dr. med. Nikolaus von Hofacker, Abteilung für Psychosomatik des Kindes- und Jugendalters, Städtisches Krankenhaus München-Harlaching, Sanatoriumsplatz 2, D-81545 München. E-mail: N.v.Hofacker@mnet-online.de

Ruth Wollwerth de Chuquisengo, Diplom-Psychologe, Kinderzentrum München, Heiglhofstr. 63, D-81377 München. E-mail: Ruth.Wollwerth@t-online.de

Dr. rer. nat. Harald Wurmser, Diplom-Psychologe, Institut für Soziale Pädiatrie und Jugend- medizin der Ludwig-Maximilians-Universität München, Heiglhofstraße 63, D-81377 München; Current address: Kinderklinik und Poliklinik der TU München, Kölner Platz 1, D-80804 München. E-mail: harald.wurmser@lrz.tu-muenchen.de